Social Change

Social Change

Third Edition

Jay Weinstein

ROWMAN & LITTLEFIELD PUBLISHERS, INC.
Lanham • Boulder • New York • Toronto • Plymouth, UK

Published by Rowman & Littlefield Publishers, Inc.
A wholly owned subsidiary of The Rowman & Littlefield Publishing Group, Inc.
4501 Forbes Boulevard, Suite 200, Lanham, Maryland 20706
http://www.rowmanlittlefield.com

Estover Road, Plymouth PL6 7PY, United Kingdom

British Library Cataloguing in Publication Information Available

Library of Congress Cataloging-in-Publication Data
Weinstein, Jay A., 1942-
    Social change / Jay Weinstein.
        p. cm.
        Prev. published under title: Social and cultural change.
        Includes bibliographical references and index.
        ISBN 978-1-4422-0299-3 (cloth : alk. paper) — ISBN 978-1-4422-0300-6 (pbk. : alk. paper) — ISBN 978-1-4422-0301-3 (electronic)
        1. Social change. 2. Progress. I. Weinstein, Jay A., 1942- Social and cultural change.
    II. Title.
    HM831.W46 2010
    303.4—dc22   2010008358

∞™ The paper used in this publication meets the minimum requirements of American National Standard for Information Sciences—Permanence of Paper for Printed Library Materials, ANSI/NISO Z39.48-1992.

Printed in the United States of America

Brief Contents

List of Boxes, Figures, and Tables   xiii
Preface   xv

PART I The Study of Change   1
1   The Social Scientific Perspective   3
2   Social and Cultural Evolution   31

PART II The Components of Change   55
3   Population Growth and Demographic Transition   57
4   The Heritage and Dynamics of Culture   84
5   Social Structures, Systems, and Processes   106

PART III The Engines of Change   133
6   Social Movements: Concepts and Principles   137
7   Movements and Revolutions in Context   159
8   The Process of Technological Innovation   194

PART IV Change at the Macrolevel   217
9   From *Gemeinschaft* to *Gesellschaft*: The Urbanization of the Human Population   219
10   A World Divided   247
11   The Market, Capitalism, and Socialism   275

PART V Planned Change: Making Tomorrow's Society   307

12 The Paradoxes of Development   309
13 Democratic Planning and Applied Sociology   331
14 The Political Economy of Globalization   346

Notes   367
References   385
Index   423
About the Author   431

Contents

List of Boxes, Figures, and Tables   xiii
Preface   xvii

PART I The Study of Change   **1**

CHAPTER 1 The Social Scientific Perspective   **3**

The Shape of Things to Come   3
The Science of Change Today   7
Critical Episodes: Scale and Intention   9
    Scale   9
    Intention and Order of Impact   10
    Evolutionary Impact   13
Stage-Setting Events: The Four Critical Episodes   14
    The Holocaust, 1939–1945   15
    The Rise of the Third World Nations, 1945–1975   17
    The U.S. Civil Rights Movement, 1954–1968   20
    The Fall of Soviet Communism, 1989–1991   23
    Oceania, 1984: A Fictional Account of a Changeless World   26
The Question of Progress   27
    "Progress" as a Value Judgment   28
    Progress for Whom?   28
Relevant Websites   29

CONTENTS

CHAPTER 2 Social and Cultural Evolution   31

Classic Evolutionism   32
    Organic Evolution and Ecological Systems   32
    Evolutionary Theory and Human Populations   33
"Fitness," Adaptation, and the Direction of Evolution   36
    Progressive Theory   37
    Cyclical Theory   37
    Regressive Theory   40
Progress, Complexity, and Race   41
    Race and Evolution   42
    From Many Evolutions to One   43
    Cyclical Theories   44
    Sorokin's Theory of Social and Cultural Dynamics   44
    Sorokin and His Critics   45
    Inevitability versus Tendency in Evolutionary Theory   46
    Creative Altruism and the "Third Way"   48
Summary   50
Relevant Websites   53

PART II The Components of Change   55

CHAPTER 3 Population Growth and Demographic Transition   57

Populations as Units of Observation   58
Population Size and Growth   59
Change in Size   60
    Birth   60
    Death   62
    Migration   65
    Changes in Rates of Natural Increase   65
The Malthusian "Laws"   67
Demographic Transition: The Roots of Global Inequality   69
    The Development of Mortality Control   69
    The Industrial Revolution and the European Transition   70
    Fertility Control: The Third Stage   71
    Demographic Transition in the Third World   75
Summary   82
Relevant Websites   82

CHAPTER 4 The Heritage and Dynamics of Culture   84

The Passing of Traditional Society   85
The Sacred and the Secular   87
    Religion as a Universal   88
    The Process of Secularization   92
    Reversals: Civil Religion and Neofundamentalism   94

CONTENTS

Language Change and Regulation   98
   Language and Evolution   99
   The Mechanics of Language Change   102
Summary   104
Relevant Websites   104

CHAPTER 5 Social Structures, Systems, and Processes   106

Changes in Relationships: From Primary to Secondary and Tertiary   107
   Primary Relationships: Family and Kin   108
   Secondary Relationships: Impersonal Ties   108
   Tertiary Relationships: Mediated Interaction   110
The Bureaucratization of Modern Society   111
   Group Membership: Definitions and Criteria   112
   Structural Variations in Bureaucracies   115
   Groups as Persons: The Political Dimension   121
Conclusion: The Invisible Hand in the Twenty-first Century   129
Summary   130
Relevant Websites   130

PART III The Engines of Change   133

CHAPTER 6 Social Movements: Concepts and Principles   137

Movements as Collective Behavior   138
   Movements as a Source of Change   139
   The Antisocial Element and Political Violence   143
Why Movements Occur   147
   Types and Degrees of Participation   148
   Leadership and Ideology   154
Summary   156
Relevant Websites   157

CHAPTER 7 Movements and Revolutions in Context   159

Movements, Autocracy, and Democracy   160
   Dissent in Democratic Societies   163
   Movements in Autocracies and Democracies: Summary 171
An Inventory of Some Major Movements: Past and Present   174
   Permanent Movements   174
   Semipermanent and New Movements   186
Afterword: The Anatomy of Revolution   188
Summary   191
Relevant Websites   192

CONTENTS

CHAPTER 8 The Process of Technological Innovation   **194**

Assessing Technology's Effects   197
Autonomous Technology   200
    Taking Control of Autonomous Technology   203
    Iatrogenesis, the Technology Delivery System, and the   206
       Participation of "Clients"
Cold Fusion and the R&D Society   212
Summary   214
Relevant Websites   215

PART IV Change at the Macrolevel   **217**

CHAPTER 9 From *Gemeinschaft* to *Gesellschaft*:   **219**
The Urbanization of the Human Population

The Invention of Cities   219
    Agricultural Revolution   220
    The Advantages of Centrality   222
    The Advantages of Surplus Labor   223
The Creation of the State   224
    Experiments in Democracy   228
    The Creation of the Economy   229
    Other Characteristics of Ancient Cities   231
World Cities and World Empires   234
    The Turco-Muslim and Chinese Empires   234
    The Collapse of Roman Europe   235
    The Age of Discovery in Iberia   236
    The Diffusion of Urban Society in Europe and Beyond   236
Science, Industry, and Urban Society   237
    Industrial Revolution in Europe   238
    Premature and Postindustrial Cities   239
Urban Explosion in the Third World   240
Conclusion: An Urban World in the Twenty-first Century   243
Summary   244
Relevant Websites   245

CHAPTER 10 A World Divided   **247**

Cultural Diversity: Normative and Value Differences   247
    Ethnic Subcultures and Diversity   248
    Cultural Relativism and Cultural Change   255
    The Norm of Reciprocity   257
International Stratification   260
    Complexity and Development   262
    The "Three Worlds" Concept   265

Dependency Theory 268
The Modern World System 269
Summary 272
Relevant Websites 273

CHAPTER 11 The Market, Capitalism, and Socialism 275

The Elements of Capitalist Economies 275
The Generation of Capital 276
The Market 276
Corporate Power 278
Firms and Multinational Corporations 279
Capitalists and Corporate Directorships 282
Capitalism in Transition 292
The Socialist Alternative 294
Socialism before Marx 294
Marxist Socialism 296
The Rise and Fall of Bolshevik Socialism 297
The Elements of (Actual) Socialist Economies 299
Capitalism and Socialism Today 302
Summary 303
Relevant Websites 304

PART V Planned Change: Making Tomorrow's Society 307

CHAPTER 12 The Paradoxes of Development 309

The Development Project 309
Ideals and Realities 311
Development and Evolution 314
The Costs of Development: Lessons Learned 316
The Demographic Component 321
Technology plus Altruism: Cutting the Gordian Knot 323
The Technological Fix: North-South Dimension and 323
Appropriate Technology
The Future of Altruism 324
Summary 328
Relevant Websites 330

CHAPTER 13 Democratic Planning and Applied Sociology 331

Planning Models 334
The Concept of Democratic Planning 337
Two Approaches to Democratic Planning 338
Democratic Planning and the Paradox of Control 343
Summary 344
Relevant Websites 344

CONTENTS

CHAPTER 14 The Political Economy of Globalization   **346**

    Globalization and Localism   348
        The Roots of the Global System   351
        The World System Today   352
    Information and Globalization   355
        Who Controls the System?   355
        Communication Technology and Cultural Lag   356
    Globalization: Geopolitical Dimensions   359
        World Government   362
        The Future of the World System   364
    Relevant Websites   366

Notes   367
References   385
Index   423
About the Author   431

Boxes, Figures, and Tables

Boxes

Box 1.1	Holocaust Denial	16
Box 1.2	*Brown versus Board of Education* Decision	21
Box 1.3	Timeline of the Fall of Communism in Eastern Europe, 1989	24
Box 2.1	Landmarks in Human Biological Evolution	34
Box 2.2	Dialectical and Linear Evolutionary Models	38
Box 2.3	The Golden Rule: A Cultural Universal	51
Box 3.1	United Nations and U.S. Refugee Protocols	66
Box 4.1	Tribal Religion in Australia	90
Box 5.1	Fictive Kinship	109
Box 5.2	The Power of Primary Relationships	110
Box 5.3	The Hawthorne Western Electric Study	117
Box 6.1	Mission Statement for ASA Section on Social Movements	139
Box 6.2	Narrative by American Playwright Arthur Miller	142
Box 6.3	Margaret Sanger: A "Great" Woman	152
Box 7.1	The Reichstag Fire	167
Box 7.2	The Lobbying Disclosure Act	170
Box 7.3	An Appeal from the Website of Burmese Dissident Aung San Suu Kyi	172
Box 8.1	U.S. Laws Mandating Social Impact Assessment, 1970–1986	205
Box 8.2	Matrix Relating Project Stage to Social Impact Assessment Variables	207
Box 9.1	Varna: A Model Stratification System in Early Civilizations	232
Box 9.2	Opposition to Caste	233
Box 10.1	Ethnic Conflict in China	249

Box 10.2   Gandhi and the Colonial Experience   253
Box 10.3   The Ravages of Destructive Entitlement   261
Box 10.4   United Nations Research Institute for Social Development   263
            (UNRISD)
Box 11.1   Deregulation Reconsidered   278
Box 11.2   The First Corporations   280
Box 11.3   Michigan's State Law Encouraging the Establishment   287
            of Employee-Owned Corporations
Box 12.1   USAID's History and Mission   310
Box 13.1   Association for Applied and Clinical Sociology   332
Box 14.1   China Postpones Internet Filter Software Plan   357
Box 14.2   Globalization and Development Variables for Selected Countries   359
Box 14.3   432 Planets   365

Figures

Figure 1.1   The McDonaldization of the World   5
Figure 1.2   Value of Online Media and Marketing Mergers and   6
              Acquisitions, 2004–2007
Figure 1.3   Order of Impact   12
Figure 3.1   Population Pyramids Depicting Three Types of Age   63
              Structures and Growth Potential
Figure 3.2   Malthusian Growth   68
Figure 3.3   Three Stages of Europe's Demographic Transition   72
Figure 3.4   Demographic Transition in Europe and the Third World   78
Figure 4.1   The Sacred Impulse Endures   89
Figure 4.2   Montreal   102
Figure 5.1   Tertiary Relations: Who Is Talking to Whom?   111
Figure 5.2   Dimensions of Group Membership   113
Figure 5.3   Direct and Representative Forms of Rule   125
Figure III.1 The Emancipation Proclamation   135
Figure 6.1   Factors that Influence Degree of Participation in a Movement   149
Figure 6.2   A General Model of Social Movement Growth   156
Figure 7.1   Tiananmen Square   161
Figure 7.2   Part of Martin Luther King's FBI File   165
Figure 7.3   Timeline of the Early Women's Rights Movement   176
              in the United States
Figure 7.4   Costa Rica Cloud Forest   186
Figure 8.1   University of Chicago   195
Figure 8.2   Hurricane Katrina, in the Air and on the Ground   199
Figure 8.3   The Technological Delivery System   210
Figure 9.1   Diagram of Central Place Theory   223
Figure 9.2   The Platonic Model of the State and Soul   227
Figure 10.1   The Development Continuum   266

Figure 10.2	The Three Worlds of Development	267
Figure 11.1	Reykjavik, the Capital of Iceland	290
Figure 11.2	Shanghai	298
Figure 11.3	China's Economic Growth	299
Figure 12.1	Small Plot in China	312
Figure 12.2	The Centre for Appropriate Rural Technology (CART)	324
Figure 13.1	Planning Models	336
Figure 13.2	Barack Obama as a Community Organizer	341
Figure 14.1	The Uros People	347
Figure 14.2	Localism or Globalization?	349
Figure 14.3	Gun over Golan	354

Tables

Table 1.1	Top 10 U.S. Media and Entertainment Corporations	7
Table 1.2	Online Media and Marketing Services: Top 10 Transactions January 2007 to July 2007	7
Table 1.3	The Original Members of the UN	18
Table 3.1	Comparative Age-Specific Fertility Rates	62
Table 3.2	Demographic Characteristics of the World's Twenty-five Most Populous Nations	76
Table 4.1	The World's Most Common Languages	99
Table 4.2	The 108 Families of the Languages of the World	101
Table 7.1A	Timeline of the U.S. Labor Movement, 1866–1905	179
Table 7.1B	Timeline of the U.S. Labor Movement, 1912–1947	180
Table 7.1C	Timeline of the U.S. Labor Movement, 1955–1999	180
Table 7.2	Annual Changes in U.S. Union Membership, 1970–2008	181
Table 7.3	Comparative Union Membership in Ten Industrialized Countries	182
Table 7.4	The Ten Least Democratic Countries in the World	185
Table 9.1	Percentage Urban, the World 1950–2050	220
Table 9.2	Traditional Forms of Patrimonial Systems	225
Table 9.3	World's Most Populous Urban Agglomerations: 2010	241
Table 9.4	The Most and Least Urbanized among Twenty-five Selected Nations	242
Table 10.1	Fifty Nations: UNRISD Index, World Type, and Development Variables	264
Table 11.1	The Thirty Largest U.S. Employee-Owned Companies	285
Table 11.2	The Twenty-five Largest Multinational Corporations	291
Table 11.3	The Twenty-five Largest U.S.-Based Multinational Corporations	292
Table 12.1	Development Aid Donors and Recipients	319
Table 12.2	Total External Debt, 1997 and 2002	321
Table 13.1	Features of Expert-Driven and Democratic Planning Approaches	339
Table 14.1	Globalization Indices	358
Table 14.2	Index of Globalization	360

Preface

I T SHOULD come as no surprise that the years between the publication of the first edition and the current third edition of this book, 1997 to 2010, have seen rapid and accelerating rates of change in human relations, from the interpersonal to the international level. The Internet and other pathways of electronic telecommunication continue to erode the traditional boundaries once separating people from one another. Globally, the seemingly unstoppable expansion of multinational organizations—corporations, agencies, and alliances—continue to standardize the way most of us behave, believe, consume, and even dream. Ours is an age in which the devastation of war and civil unrest in the Middle East, protests in Canada and Europe against corporate power, and the triumphs of Olympic competition in China can be observed in real time throughout the world.

Setting the Stage: A World United, A World Divided

During the early twenty-first century, humanity took a gigantic step toward creating a truly worldwide social system, thanks in large measure to innovations in transportation and communication technologies. This process, often referred to as globalization, is dramatically reflected in recent geopolitical events. For Americans and, in many ways, for people of all nations, the most traumatic of these events was the terrorist attack on New York City and Washington, D.C., on September 11, 2001. On that day, the people of the United States experienced a profound loss of life, of property, and—perhaps most enduring—of innocence. On that Tuesday morning in late summer, the apparently remote clashes between modernity and tradition, secularism and religious fundamentalism, and West versus East instantly became U.S. domestic concerns. Geographical distance could no longer insulate these competing worldviews and their champions from one another.

Just one decade earlier, the fall of Soviet Communism ended the half-century-long Cold War between competing visions of the ideal society. This largely unexpected event brought to an abrupt halt seventy years of experimentation with an alternative to capitalist democracy. In a manner parallel to the September 11 attack, a key cause of the collapse of the system was that the Soviet Union and the other Communist states of Central and Eastern Europe could no longer insulate themselves from the outside world. Through airports, seaports, radio broadcasts, TV satellites, telephones, and Internet connections, the capitalist culture and its "bourgeois" ways seeped in and insinuated themselves in the lives of ordinary citizens and their leaders. Ultimately, the governments of these states were not so much overthrown as they were cut adrift, isolated from and out of touch with those whom they supposedly represented.

International economic relations of the late twentieth century were transformed through the creation of several regional free trade agreements, including the still controversial North American Free Trade Agreement (NAFTA). These treaties were soon followed by approval of the General Agreement on Trade and Tariffs (GATT). This treaty establishes for the first time a truly universal framework of rules and procedures governing international trade. Because numerous technical and political issues remain unresolved, it has not been fully implemented, even after nearly two decades. Nevertheless, the GATT is envisioned as the cornerstone of a coordinated world economy.

The turn of the twenty-first century also brought the first small, but significant, steps in solving the sixty-year-long dispute over Palestinian sovereignty. This conflict, which originated with the ending of colonial rule in the region, has had a profound effect on international and interethnic relations. It often has preoccupied the United Nations, and it has frequently been linked to terrorist bombings, kidnapping, and hijacking. If and how this conflict is to be resolved is undoubtedly a major determinant of future geopolitical relations in the region and in the world. The granting of mutual recognition by the Palestinian authority and the government of Israel in 1994, as stipulated in the 1993 Oslo Accords, was a key event in many ways. It clearly represented a potential improvement in international (and interethnic) relations; and, as stressed by the principal author of the accords, sociologist Terje Rod Larsen, it also demonstrated how the insights of social science can be applied to achieve important practical ends. Yet, the Oslo Accords did not end all hostilities by any means; in fact, they led to increasing hostility by the enemies of the negotiation process.

Despite the many setbacks, however, a so-called road map to a two-state solution has been agreed upon in principle. The election in 2008 of a new administration in the United States—the major third party to the conflict—led to the appointment of former U.S. senator George Mitchell, the region's leading diplomatic expert, as special envoy. In the wake of these events, a policy shift toward active engagement in and support of the peace process appears likely. Thus, even amidst continuing violence and enmity, formal agreements and background events have now rendered only extremely difficult what was once thought to be absolutely impossible: peace in the Holy Land.

In North America and throughout the world, laws and customs that not long ago limited one's access to education, employment, and public facilities on the basis of ascribed statuses have been changed. Social relations everywhere are being transformed in response to movements promoting equality among ethnic groups and between women and men. These changes were profoundly affected by the election in November 2008 of Barack Obama, an African American, as the forty-fourth president of the United States.

For these and related reasons, concepts such as "exotic" and "outsider" are all but obsolete in this age of around-the-clock information services and satellite TV programming. With the appropriate connections, one can learn the intimate details of other people's lives in the most remote corners of our cities, nations, and world—people who would have been complete strangers if social relations were still dependent on face-to-face contact, as in previous generations.

As these events unfold, it becomes increasingly obvious that, along with news of international agreements, the acceptance of diversity, and the tearing down of walls, another clear message is racing around our information superhighways: the message of social conflict and intergroup tension. As Western Europe moved ever closer to becoming a megastate with a common monetary unit, a flag, an anthem, and visa-free borders, Eastern Europe continued to break up into ethnically distinct ministates on generally unfriendly terms with one another.

The United States, Canada, and Mexico have become a unitary trading bloc under NAFTA. Yet the internal forces of ethnic and class conflict, political separatism, and official corruption are seriously challenging the integrity of these nations. Although enormous strides have been made in formally recognizing and protecting basic human rights, interpersonal and intergroup relations at home and abroad are still often guided by informal, but deeply held, values and habits that deny the full humanity of one's neighbors and adversaries. People throughout the world are experiencing both more (and more intense) intergroup unity *and* more (and more intense) intergroup conflict.

For these and related reasons, social life has never been so complex, nor has it ever undergone such rapid, and rapidly accelerating, changes. These conditions are partly the result of our unprecedented capacity to control natural and human resources. Technological and sociological innovations since the 1960s have provided people with remarkable powers of cooperation. The activities of thousands, and even millions, of individuals are now routinely coordinated to achieve specific, predetermined goals in government, the private sector, and international diplomacy. These have made it possible to turn deserts into gardens, to wipe out traditional killer diseases such as smallpox and polio, and to reach the moon.

At the same time, such a high degree of control also carries the ever-present danger that things can become out of control in new and dangerous ways or fall under the control of the wrong people. Campaigns of ethnic cleansing, international organized crime cartels, family dissolution, nuclear reactor meltdowns, massive corporate fraud, government monitoring of our private affairs, and massive oil spills all are by-products of the same complexity and coordination that we point to with pride as evidence of progress.

This book is about these momentous and relatively recent changes in the human condition. It is premised on the understanding, shared widely among scholars in many fields, that people have never before so urgently needed the exceptional powers of cooperation they have developed. The kind of world that we leave to our children and grandchildren will be largely determined by how we use our new capacity to work together as individuals, groups, and nations.

These are times of great promise and of great danger. With the end of the Cold War, the threat of a worldwide nuclear holocaust has significantly receded. Yet thousands of armed warheads remain poised for firing in the arsenals of the United States and Russia. The technology to create weapons of ultimate destruction has now proliferated to remote and improbable regions: China, India, Pakistan, Iran, North Korea, Israel, and beyond. Political disputes left unresolved through two world wars and four decades of showdown and "brinkmanship" between Eastern and Western blocs continue to fester in Asia, Africa, and Latin America. The gap between the have's and the have-not's nations is widening, financial crisis resulting from corrupt practices in the U.S. housing market and on Wall Street in 2007–2008 instantaneously affected economies throughout the world. And social inequality is generally increasing within both the more and the less industrialized societies. In the United States, the only superpower remaining in the wake of the collapse of the USSR, more people are unemployed, homeless, and in prisons than at any time in recent history.

With these issues in view, this book brings the concepts and principles of social science to bear in an examination of (1) the major causes and conditions underlying our current situation and (2) the main choices and options we face as we strive to shape our individual and collective futures. The general perspective is sociological and, to a lesser extent, anthropological. But it also incorporates many ideas familiar to political scientists, economists, and geographers. The perspective directs our attention to collective phenomena such as values, norms, institutions, organizations, and populations. And, as the chapter titles indicate, our emphasis is on sociocultural dynamics: the fact that collective life, especially today, occurs in the context of ever-changing processes and systems.

As this perspective on change developed over the past two hundred years or so, researchers have crafted a distinctive way of analyzing the forces of globalization, ethnic conflict, social inequality, and related trends, one that differs from, yet complements, the approaches of journalists, historians, novelists, and other commentators. Three distinctive aspects of the perspective are featured in the following pages: (1) its scientific orientation, (2) its focus on cooperation and conflict, and (3) its superorganic character.

Whether applied by physicists or sociologists, the scientific method combines empirical research with theory building. Its ultimate goal is to explain observed events in a way that is faithful to the facts as we understand them, but always with reference to past experience, as embodied in laws and generalizations. Unlike journalism and other approaches, however, social science is not concerned with biographical details and personalities as such. Rather, it seeks regularities and patterns that extend beyond specific circumstances. In this way, it can account for what we observe and help to anticipate similar occurrences in the future.

With human relationships as their subject matter, however, social scientists have always found it especially difficult to develop unbiased and complete accounts of the phenomena they study. Although well aware of the need to avoid subjectivity and partisanship, they must nevertheless focus on the very issues that most people feel most strongly about and over which it seems natural to take sides: social inequality, autocratic rule, nationalism, religious movements, and the like. These methodological problems, too, are part of the story of social and cultural change.

In their concern with cooperation and conflict, social scientists seek to discover the conditions under which people work together toward common goals and the factors that lead them to act independently or at cross-purposes. History is viewed as alternating episodes of order and disorder, and society is characterized as a dialectical system, punctuated by rhythms of intergroup conflict and alliance, assimilation and differentiation.

A persistent theme has emerged and reemerged in the attempt to trace the causes and consequences of such processes, one that is especially relevant in today's problematic world. This is that the course of sociocultural change depends crucially on the intentional actions of people who mean to bring it about (or to prevent it). Unlike mechanical systems or organic evolution, society and culture develop in response to purposeful activity aimed at affecting their development. In this respect, the social scientific perspective stresses choice and decision making as the keys to the future. History does not *unfold*, nor does it simply *happen*: it is created by human beings, as they sit around conference tables and kitchen tables, deciding among the practical and moral alternatives that life presents them. Thus, sociocultural evolution is a superorganic process. It certainly includes physical and biological factors, but it is also directed in significant ways by goal-oriented actors. With the application of the very special superorganic item, technology, we can in fact override physical and biological influences or change their direction more or less at our discretion.

A Value Premise: Social Science for Democracy

Taken together, these three features—the combination of observation with theory, the focus on conflict and cooperation, and the recognition that change in human systems has an intentional, superorganic aspect—add up to a definite program, one that originated in late-eighteenth-century France, in the midst of democratic revolution. This is the program of social science *for democracy*. It is an orientation that sees research on social and cultural change not as an activity to be pursued merely as an end in itself to satisfy our curiosity or as a form of intellectual entertainment but rather as a contribution to the education of informed publics, groups of people with common interests who can exert influence on their representatives in government and industry. The program was developed particularly in the United States during the twentieth century by a distinguished line of scholars that includes John Dewey, Robert Ezra Park, W. E. B. Du Bois, Ralph Linton, Robert Lynd, C. Wright Mills, and Seymour Martin Lipset.

Democracy in this context refers to a system of self-rule in which members of society as a whole, not a small privileged elite, make the major decisions that will determine how and in what direction their institutions, customs, and basic beliefs will be altered (or preserved). In a narrow sense, democracy is a type of government that has several specific forms: direct, representative, parliamentary, and so on. More broadly, it is a method of collective management that applies to the workplace, the household, and other social relations beyond the voting booth and political parties.

By these standards, effective democratic participation can be achieved only to the extent that those responsible for the conduct of purposeful social and cultural change, the citizenry, are well informed about how the social world operates. In nondemocratic systems, from ancient patriarchies to contemporary autocracies, it is to the regime's advantage to keep a populace essentially ignorant of the details of group dynamics, stratification, and political influence. But when people are charged with their own destinies, such ignorance is intolerable. The knowledge that nonpartisan, scientific research can provide is, thus, viewed as a tool for democracy.

In Central and Eastern Europe, in the developing countries of the Third World, and in poor neighborhoods everywhere, people are currently engaged in massive and difficult struggles to establish self-rule in the wake of decades and centuries of one-party autocracy, imperialism, economic exploitation, and racism. For these reasons, social scientists have again placed a high priority on assessing democracy's prospects. Numerous books and articles address classic questions with renewed urgency: Are people meaningfully involved in the decisions that affect their lives? Are their options being limited or controlled by others with more power, wealth, and prestige? What are the consequences of elite rule in a world in which the privacy-invading technologies of George Orwell's *Nineteen Eighty-Four* seem primitive? Such questions indicate that democracy remains a crucial social ideal, especially today when our choices, and the extent to which they are truly ours, can be so consequential.

The large-scale social organizations that characterize modern life do not run themselves. Rather, those who participate most actively in their operation run them. Unfortunately, most people most of the time are prone not to participate to the maximum, and they are even less likely to seek greater control. The result, as Roberto Michels noted in the 1920s, is the ever-present threat of *oligarchy*—rule by the few. The antidote, if indeed there is one, is the creation of informed, active publics who understand the stakes involved in letting someone else make their decisions for them.

This book is written in the social-science-for-democracy spirit. My goal is to introduce you to a way of thinking and a body of literature that will help improve your powers as a citizen, so that you can pursue the choices you are (or should be) free to make more effectively. But being a citizen today, whether we like it or not, also means being involved in the lives of people in parts of the world that our parents may have never thought about and from segments of society with whom they might never have associated.

Now that Western civilization has entered its third millennium, there are approximately seven billion members of the species *Homo sapiens* on this planet. Less than one-third of them live in the industrialized nations of Western Europe and North America, but all have been deeply affected by the spread of modern, Western culture. This is the main fact of contemporary history: virtually anywhere one goes in the world today, Euro-American values, beliefs, and practices have made a lasting impact. If praise is to be given for the material progress and technological advance that distinguish our era, a large share of it is due to the West. If blame is to be placed for a century and more of war, depression, conquest, racism, imperialism, and dehumanization, the West is also the leading candidate.

Those who study social and cultural change today are deeply concerned about the costs and benefits of the spread of modernization. This book shares and reflects this concern. Whether one calls the current era "postmodern," "postindustrial," "postliterate," or "postacademic," there is a strong consensus among sociologists, anthropologists, and other scholars that these are indeed revolutionary times. In particular, many argue that the advantages of modern culture have diminished, whereas its liabilities have increased to such an extent that it is ripe for significant alterations. It may have been a progressive force in the past, but—the feeling is ominous—it is now becoming a largely reactionary influence.

Change is in the wind. The values of materialism, conquest, and egoism served to energize Western culture during its rise to industrial and political prominence. But today these values are undergoing a major reassessment, as the negative impacts of modernity are increasingly experienced in environmental degradation, financial crisis, civil and international conflict, and a growing sense of lost spirituality. As one would expect, some people welcome these changes, and others hope to resist them. But regardless of the final outcome, the next decades are likely to bring continued debate over the "decline of the West": is it real or just a fashionable slogan in intellectual circles, in the process of being recycled for the third time in the last hundred years? How did Europe come to exert such influence on social relations everywhere? What are the alternatives to a modern, Western, global culture?

In considering how social scientists answer these questions, this book explores the impact of recent, as well as longer-term, trends and transforming events on contemporary society. These include the dramatic shift from primary to secondary and tertiary relations, the rise of capitalism and the socialist alternative, the reinvention of democracy and the autocratic reaction, the Holocaust and its aftermath, the decolonization of the Third World, and civil rights movements in the United States and elsewhere.

Each of these trends and events has many important things to teach us, most of which can only be touched on in a brief survey such as this. However, one main lesson should be clear and obvious from the discussion that follows: we can no longer innocently treat some human beings as inherently inferior to others. Some individuals and groups may wish to continue structuring social relations, as in the past, on the assumption that certain groups are naturally meant to lead and others to follow; but there are simply too many dissident voices, historical precedents, and practical obstacles to allow such sentiments to prevail unchallenged.

Sociologists and historians have characterized the nineteenth century as the Age of Democratic Revolution. But, as we understand it today, the immediate impact of those revolutions was geographically limited and, in many cases, temporary. In addition, the prevailing concept of self-rule was restricted to the narrow political affairs of urban middle classes. With the benefit of more than a century of ferment and hindsight, it is obvious that our era will see democracy put to its greatest test, in a universal and complete sense.

I write this book in the hope that it encourages you to look more closely at the social relations in which you participate, through additional reading, further courses in social science, and your own research on change. The skills and knowledge you thus acquire will, I believe, help prepare you to take an active part in creating a world that truly reflects the human interest.

Organization of the Text

This book consists of fourteen chapters, divided into five parts. The parts are ordered cumulatively, with the earlier chapters focusing on concepts and principles and the later ones applying these in specific contexts. Each part is preceded by a brief introduction that ties together the main themes of the succeeding chapters. Within most of the chapters there is a chronological ordering, a look at societies of yesterday, today, and tomorrow. Most also have a comparative dimension, especially along First, Second, and Third World lines.

As the discussion proceeds, certain key trends and historical eras are examined and reexamined from different points of view. For example, several chapters mention the establishment of imperial and colonial ties between Europe and the rest of the world. Insights from Orwell's world of *Nineteen Eighty-Four* are also included in each part. And four critical episodes are used to illustrate or amplify points throughout the book.

Part I is about the social scientific approach to change: its origins, its main principles, and its distinctive perspective on contemporary events. Chapter 1 is a general introduction, and chapter 2 focuses on the master concept of evolution.

Part II analyzes change into its three main components, each corresponding to a chapter (3, 4, and 5, respectively): demography, culture, and social systems.

Part III (chapters 6 through 8) examines the "engines" of change, the activities that drive us from one era to the next: social movements, revolutions, and technological innovations.

Part IV consists of three chapters (9 through 11) on change at the macrolevel. These are the large-scale trends—urbanization, social conflict at the social and intersocietal levels, and market forces—that have made our world so complex and dynamic.

Part V (chapters 12, 13, and 14) looks ahead with a discussion of planned change: organized programs such as international development projects and broader movements such as the emergence of world government.

Each of the chapters has endnotes, and all but the first and last contain brief end-of-chapter summaries. An extensive reference list follows chapter 14, and the text is illustrated throughout with photos, figures, and tables.

Acknowledgments

I express my thanks to my students Maya Barak, Cathy Collins, Karen Schaumann, Ivy Forsythe-Brown, Jennifer Corwin, and Maria Marlowe for their assistance in preparing this book, and to Marcello Truzzi—who passed away during the preparation of the second edition—Fatos Tarifa, Joanna Scott, Liza Cerroni-Long, Raouf Hanna, Susan Rabinowitz, and Larry Reynolds for their comments on the previous two editions. A faculty research fellowship granted by the graduate school of Eastern Michigan University afforded me the opportunity to complete earlier drafts of this manuscript with a semester's leave from my teaching duties.

I am especially grateful for the suggestions of the editorial reviewers, whose well-considered comments made this a much more accurate and more interesting book: York Bradshaw, Indiana University; James Copp, Texas A&M; Richard Flacks, University of California, Santa Barbara; John Gagnon, State University of New York, Stony Brook; and Frank J. Weed, University of Texas, Arlington.

It has been a pleasure and a true learning experience to have worked with Rowman & Littlefield in bringing out the second and third editions. Dean Birkenkamp initiated the project that eventuated in the second edition shortly before leaving R&L. Alan McClare saw that edition through to production and was closely involved throughout the preparation of the third; I worked closely with him during production, and he exercised great care and concern to ensure that the technical aspects of the book would be as close to perfect as possible. It came as a shock and a very sad loss when I learned that Alan died suddenly in November 2009. He will be greatly missed.

No book of this scope could possibly be a solo effort, but I alone assume responsibility for all errors of commission and omission.

The Study of Change

PART I surveys the subject matter of social and cultural change, discussing the concepts, principles, leading authors, and illustrative cases familiar to contemporary sociologists, anthropologists, and other scholars in the field. Each of the two chapters that make up this part poses some broad, leading questions, such as "Why study change?" and "What is progress?" Each provides a few preliminary answers, but we return to these issues several times throughout the book.[1]

Chapter 1 is about the social scientific perspective: a way of looking at human relations that is grounded in theory and is applied to a broad range of contemporary events and issues. Chapter 2 continues along these lines, considering specifically how social scientists have grappled with the central but difficult concept of sociocultural evolution.

Those of you who have already taken an introductory course in sociology or anthropology will recall many of the concepts presented here: interaction, institutions, symbols, values, fertility control, and so on. You will also recognize the names of some of the classic authors whose works are cited, such as Adam Smith, Thomas Malthus, Karl Marx, Emile Durkheim, and Alfred L. Kroeber. In fact, you probably know a great deal about social and cultural change from other courses in social science, history, or humanities and from your own life experiences. In any case, you are aware that change, variability, and instability are very much part of social life, especially today. These first chapters are meant to reinforce and deepen your insights into our dynamic world.[2]

The Social Scientific Perspective

A GREAT SOCIOCULTURAL revolution is now sweeping our world. Centered in North America, Japan, and the urban, industrialized countries of Western Europe, it extends to the still largely rural, Third World nations of Asia, Africa, and Latin America and to the formerly Communist-dominated ("Second World") regions of Central and Eastern Europe. Rapid change, both peaceful and violent, is a fact of life that virtually everyone on Earth today has come to expect, if not unconditionally accept.

The Shape of Things to Come

This revolution is now boiling at or near the surface of contemporary social relations everywhere. With increasing regularity, it erupts into our daily affairs, taking on many different guises. In the United States, this revolution is evident in the conflict between the defenders and attackers of government regulation, in the debates about immigration—legal and illegal—about the country's participation in the United Nations, in the challenges to welfare programs for the poor, and in the post–September 11 concern about "homeland security." Here, and in other countries throughout the world, it has manifested itself in pro- and antiglobalization protests and movements for civil rights on behalf of formerly excluded ethnic minority groups, gays and lesbians, persons with disabilities, children, and senior citizens. It is also evident in our changing attitudes and behavior in the realm of gender. The realities that our parents and grandparents took for granted are now in such doubt that today we are even asking ourselves what it means to be a man or a woman.

Common to all of these debates, conflicts, challenges, and movements is the explicit recognition that something is wrong with society as we have known it. Those involved, regardless of their specific views on the various issues, acknowledge that serious short-comings and unwanted costs are now associated with the manner in which people have become accustomed to treating one another.

A historical juncture has been reached at which the old ways of managing human affairs, from the interpersonal to the international levels, are becoming less and less effective. Yet, despite the numerous possible options with which we have experimented or merely dreamed, no clear alternatives have emerged to guide us into a highly uncertain future. Just as modernity displaced feudalism as the dominant cultural form in Europe some 250 years ago, something is displacing modernity throughout the world today, although its precise dimensions remain largely unformed or unfathomed.

One evident feature of this revolution is its global character: in one way or another, it is affecting all of human society (see Sassen 1996, 1998). As sociologist Robert Schaeffer (2009) has noted in a recent survey of the phenomenon of globalization, "We live in a time of global change. But people experience change in different ways. Global change . . . affects some people more than others, and it can have different consequences—good and bad—for people in different settings" (xi).

Such widespread, and uneven, impact is now possible because of the expansive growth of bureaucratic organizations, especially multinational corporations, along with developments in electronic communication technologies. People living in large cities on every continent are now well connected through the automobile and other consumer items they make and buy, the fast food chains that are opening new branches near their homes or offices, and the kinds of music and TV programs they enjoy. With each passing day, people in the most remote hinterlands are being swept into this world system via roads and communication satellites. A trend, a movement, a style, or a new technology that originates in one place can easily find its way to the most far-off and unlikely adopters in practically no time at all.

This phenomenon is the subject of a highly influential study by George Ritzer (2008), professor of sociology at the University of Maryland. Entitled *The McDonaldization of Society*, the book and related works by Ritzer (1998, 2002) argue that the innovations in the mass production and marketing of hamburgers that made the McDonald's restaurant chain so successful have now become part of the emerging world culture. One can, Ritzer observes, find a McDonald's outlet virtually anywhere in the world, serving essentially the same main items (along with local specialties to maintain contact with "tradition"). Moreover, the characteristic methods of production and distribution introduced in the 1950s by McDonald's founder Ray Kroc are rapidly becoming part of the operating procedures in all industries, from machine tool production to gasoline service stations.[1]

It would be impossible to assess exactly what role electronic telecommunication has played in our global revolution, in part because its effects continue to reverberate and magnify as you read this. Some idea can be gained from considering the fact that an entire new social institution, the communication/information system, is now being formed. The tasks of creating, storing, and distributing information have become so important to modern society that they require their own unique niche in the social structure.

FIGURE 1.1 The McDonaldization of the World. With a degree of global reach unimaginable just a few years ago, consumer-oriented businesses like McDonald's have opened outlets throughout the world. This upscale McCafé might be located anywhere, but it happens to be on Nanjing Road, the main commercial area of Shanghai, China. Author photo.

Like other institutions, the communication/information system is a huge structure made up of large-scale social organizations, comparable in size and scope to entire economic or political systems. Best developed in the highly industrialized countries (but expanding everywhere), it consists of newly created bureaucracies, such as government ministries of communication and the vast system of technicians and managers who keep the Internet functioning. It also includes organizations that were formerly parts of other institutions: corporations, schools, government agencies, and even religious organizations such as missionary websites and TV networks.

Although it is still in its infancy, this institution's general character is evident in the new alliances being formed. These include the landmark agreement announced in January 2001 between America Online and Time (formerly Time-Life Publications)/Warner (formerly Warner Brothers Pictures). At $106 billion, it was the largest corporate merger in history, bringing together three Internet/information/entertainment giants.

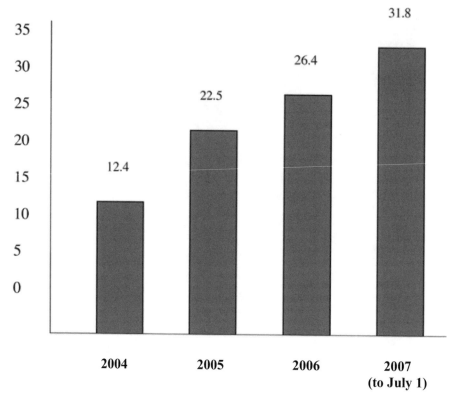

FIGURE 1.2 Value of Online Media and Marketing Mergers and Acquisitions, 2004–2007 (in $ billions). *Source*: Jordan Edmiston Group Inc. (JEGI) Database.

As indicated in table 1.1, Time Warner continues to top the list of U.S. media giants. Yet, it is the result of only one of dozens of such recent mergers and reorganizations that have linked industries ranging from computer hardware manufacturing to the marketing of entire TV networks, the publication of social science textbooks, and more (Shah 2009; Sterngold 1995; Sloan 1995). If we add to the list in table 1.1 the exclusively Internet and software companies Yahoo, Google, and Microsoft (with market values of $40.1 billion, $154.6 billion, and $306.8 billion, respectively), the magnitude of this institution becomes even more staggering (see Chon et al. 2003; *Mother Jones* 2007).

Electronic communication not only has contributed to the globalization of change but also has been a major force in accelerating the rate at which the old becomes obsolete and the newer replaces the new. In the 1960s, as the very earliest impacts of the microchip and related innovations were being felt, one student of cultural change remarked that "more than any other period in the history of [hu]mankind, ours is a time of change" (Stebbins 1965, 223). In 1990, these sentiments were expressed with renewed and even greater urgency by sociologist Anthony Giddens. Our age, he noted, is distinguished by its "sheer pace of change. . . . Traditional civilisations may have been considerably more dynamic than other premodern systems, but the rapidity of change in conditions of modernity is extreme" (Giddens 1990, 6). In fact, it sometimes seems

TABLE 1.1 Top 10 U.S. Media and Entertainment Corporations

Rank	Company	1000 Rank*	Revenues ($ millions)
1	Time Warner	48	44,788
2	Walt Disney	64	34,285
3	News Corp.	88	25,327
4	CBS	165	14,479
5	Viacom	218	11,467
6	Clear Channel Communication	330	7,099
7	Live Nation	557	3,692
8	Warner Music Group	572	3,516
9	E. W. Scrips	704	2,666
10	Regal Entertainment Group	721	2,598

* Ranking among the Fortune 500 listing of corporate revenues.
Source: "Fortune 500 2007," *Fortune*, April 30, 2007.

TABLE 1.2 Online Media and Marketing Services: Top 10 Transactions January 2007 to July 2007

Buyer	Seller	Price ($ millions)
Blackstone Group	Alliance Data Systems	7,687
Microsoft	aQuantive	5,732
Google	Double Click	3,100
Silver Lake and Value Act Capital	Acxiom Corp.	2,447
Hellman & Friedman	Catalina Marketing Corp.	1,700
Providence Equity Partners	Nextag	830
Venture Management et al.	Vertrue	800
General Atlantic	Network Solutions	800
Yahoo	Right Media	680
WPP	24/7 Real Media	549

Source: Jordan Edmiston Group Inc. (JEGI) Database

as if the world is changing too quickly, "starting very slowly but gaining impetus as it goes along, until today it accelerates at an almost frightening rate" (Blum 1963, 33).[2]

The Science of Change Today

Why? What has happened to make change the rule rather than the exception? How did this global revolution begin, and how might it end? What kind of future will emerge from all the apparent chaos?

This chapter provides some foundations for answering these challenging questions, beginning with a brief look at some of the major issues now of concern in the field of sociology and the related disciplines that study social change. With so many aspects of collective life accelerating, globalizing, or being reformed as a result of rapidly shifting ethnic and gender relations, social science, too, is undergoing a thorough reinvention (the earliest observations on this situation include Bauman 1989; Horowitz 1993; and Touraine 1989).

As is the case with people in all professions, social scientists have become increasingly aware that the knowledge and tools they have inherited from past generations are not entirely adequate to deal with today's realities. So much now happening is unprecedented, and, most seriously, so much of it was unanticipated by relevant experts, who, perhaps, should have seen what was coming.[3]

This round of intellectual self-examination is part of a broad-ranging cultural movement with roots in architecture, philosophy, and literature. Within the social sciences, two reinventions related to the movement have thus far proved to be especially relevant in gaining a more effective understanding of current conditions.

The first is a renewed interest in applying the analytical tools of sociology to historical material. This approach was developed extensively by social historians such as Fernand Braudel and Edward A. Wrigley and by historical sociologists, especially Immanuel Wallerstein, Stephen Sanderson, Charles Tilly, Theda Skocpol, Robert Wuthnow, and Daniel Chirot, all of whose works will be cited in this book. It seeks to trace the sources of today's social instability to transforming events of the past and to discover common patterns in history that would help explain contemporary political revolutions, religious movements, demographic transitions, and the like.[4]

The second is a reexamination of the concept of sociocultural evolution. This difficult and highly controversial concept was either openly employed or at least implied by nearly all of the classical theorists of change (Sanderson 1990; 2007, chap. 1 and afterword). Although contemporary social scientists are heirs to this tradition, and although evolutionary theory has shed significant light on the workings of society, we now know that the classic approaches were seriously flawed. In particular, the concept of sociocultural evolution, as traditionally applied, was intended to account for a vast range of changes in all regions of the world and throughout history (as well as prehistoric eras), many of which do not even remotely qualify as evolutionary. In addition, the traditional concept of evolution was far too deterministic because it denied the broad scope that choice and intention actually have in shaping human affairs. And, it was too often burdened with the theorists' ethnocentric biases to be of much use in scientific explanation. Classic social evolutionists typically assumed their culture was the most "highly" evolved. With these flaws in mind, how, one now wonders, can the undeniable advantages of an evolutionary perspective be preserved without giving in to the excesses of determinism and ethnocentrism?

The following section briefly considers these concerns. First we discuss the basis on which researchers decide what kinds of historical events and "episodes"—among all the possibilities—are viewed as especially significant in accounting for contemporary change. Anthony Giddens's (1981) definition of *episode* is used here: "Episodes refer to processes of social change which have a definite direction and form, analysed through comparative research, in which a major transition takes place in which one type of society is transformed into another" (82).

This overview is followed by a summary of four specific transforming episodes, profound social upheavals widely believed to have played an especially important role in setting the stage for the great drama now being played out on a global scale. These are (1) the Holocaust, (2) the rise of Third World nations, (3) the U.S. Civil Rights movement, and (4) the fall of Communism in Central and Eastern Europe. Subsequent chapters return to the four episodes at several points, and the discussion of evolution is continued at a more detailed level in chapter 2.

The final section of this chapter provides some concluding comments about the general direction in which humanity appears to be headed during the first decades of the West's third millennium.

Critical Episodes: Scale and Intention

In a strict sense, society and culture are always changing: friendships are formed and broken, families started and dissolved, and corporations merged and divested. In this respect, all social scientists must be concerned with dynamics, regardless of their area of specialization. Nevertheless, a certain kind of change has for several generations been viewed as unique and worthy of special attention. Thus, it has been treated as a separate topic under the specific label *social change*.

Two of the very earliest social scientists, Henri Saint-Simon and Herbert Spencer, drew attention to this distinction with their similar paired concepts of organic versus critical periods (Taylor and Saint-Simon 1975, 60) and industrial versus militant change (Spencer 1862, 1898).[5] Organic periods, years or decades of industrial change, are characterized by a relatively slow, orderly, and peaceful flow of events. The established order appears to be operating effectively, and disturbing influences from within or from other societies are insignificant. In contrast, critical periods are times of militant change during which relations, organizations, and institutions are being rapidly transformed, and the established order is under serious challenge from domestic sources and possibly from abroad. By these criteria, ours is surely one of the most critical periods in recent history.

In keeping with Spencer's and Saint-Simon's categories, contemporary social scientists emphasize the more militant types of change—not exclusively, of course, but as a major concern. This is clearly reflected in the kinds of events of special interest to historical sociologists today, including the four critical episodes.

Scale

The scale of change can vary from the small or microlevel to the large or macrolevel, depending on the number of individuals and relationships that are involved. As a result, there are two relatively distinct ways in which to understand how and why particular changes occur. Consider, for instance, an increase in the activities of a social protest movement such as the U.S. Civil Rights movement in the 1960s. At the microlevel, the focus is on individuals: their recruitment, leadership capabilities, and interests and motives for participating, remaining uninvolved, or even joining an opposition move-ment. At the macrolevel, emphasis is placed on the organizations associated with the movement (such as the Southern Christian Leadership Conference) and on the effects of international events and government policies on the movement's progress.

Of course, the two levels do not operate independently: the motives and interests of leaders undoubtedly affect the functioning of the organizations they lead, and vice versa. In fact, macrolevel change consists of several interconnected microlevel variations so that, in principle, explanations focusing on individuals and small groups should build up to explanations of interinstitutional and international relations. However, so many microlevel events are occurring so rapidly that such complete explanations are never possible in practice. Thus, the study of sociocultural dynamics has been, of neces-sity, somewhat compartmentalized.

In the discipline of sociology, in particular, the microlevel has been most thor-oughly explored within the subfields of symbolic interactionism and group dynam-ics, and the macrolevel is most often identified with "social change" and, within social change studies, with the specialization in political movements and revolutions. This macrolevel orientation also defines the kinds of changes researchers consider to be most important and how these episodes are tied to larger historical trends and institutional crises (Tilly 1984).

Intention and Order of Impact

Society and culture vary over time as the result of human actions. In some cases, this is the direct outcome of planning and purpose; in others, it is indirect, unanticipated, and unintended. Most often, however, the effects of our acts are a combination of intent and accident.

Intentional changes in laws, styles, or organizational structures come about because of concerted efforts on the part of people to bring them about (Sztompka 1991). Although these kinds of changes have always been possible, today they are the rule. The future course of events is now increasingly directed by the conscious actions of groups and organizations that are routinely and purposely engaged in promoting change. For-mal governments, economic systems, and other institutional structures are specifically charged with altering the way society is structured and functions, and they carry out this responsibility on a regular basis. At the same time, social movements, operating largely outside the formal system, are also vying for a greater say in determining how our social structures and values should be reorganized and reordered (chapters 6 and 7 feature the nature and impact of social movements).

In contrast, some trends just seem to take hold of their own accord, without any-one intending them: they emanate neither from conscious planning within established institutions nor from antiestablishment movements. The urbanization of human soci-ety illustrates this type of unintentional or nonpurposeful change.

At one time, not long before 1750, very few people anywhere in the world—less than 5 percent of the human population at the time—lived in cities. Today, in Europe, North America, and other places, more than three-quarters of the people live in metropolitan areas: in the cities, suburbs, and exurbs of urban societies. About one-half of the world's population—more than 3.5 billion people—are now urbanized (see Massey 2002; United Nations Population Division 2009). This shift came about as the result of myriad human migrations and other activities, many of them purposeful at the micro-level. But amidst all of these smaller purposes, nowhere was there a grand plan to create urban society as such. Rather, the many little acts and plans coalesced into a very large-scale, profound social and cultural change. Such instances illustrate well the observation of the legal historian Karl F. Savigny: "The outcome of the general will is no one's will in particular" (Savigny 1829, quoted in Schneider 1987, 185).

Purpose is often a matter of degree. At one extreme we find changes that are the direct result of explicit intentions. Technology is an especially important instance, as it is by definition knowledge with a purpose, or "know-how." Many inventions are purposeful in this sense, although, of course, not all inventions are successful. Television is by no means the invention of one person, but it was nevertheless the outcome of a conscious, largely planned collective project intended to discover how to transmit and receive visual images over distance. And that, indeed, was achieved. Yet, it is far from being its only effect (Bell 1989; Paik 1999; Singer and Singer 2005).

Television, like every other technological innovation, has had effects that extend beyond, sometimes far beyond, the achievement of its original, explicit objective. Television did not simply introduce the new cultural skill of sending pictures through the air. It has done, and continues to do, many other things. It made programs like *Sesame Street* possible. *Sesame Street*, in turn, changed the socialization experiences of North American children, and eventually children throughout the world (Waterman 1987, 164–66). And on it goes.

This characteristic of technology's effects is referred to as order of impact: first order, second order, and so on (Bauer 1966; Bauer, Rosenbloom, and Sharp 1969). Achievement of the explicit technical goal of research on a new technology, for example, the broadcasting of pictures, is a first-order impact, or a manifest function (Merton 1968, chap. 3). As effects reverberate through the social system, becoming more remote from the original intentions, the order increases. The creation of *Sesame Street* is one of TV's third-order impacts, and changes in socialization practices are fourth-order effects. As the order increases, the technological impact per se becomes progressively diluted because in proceeding from order to order through time, other factors enter the chain of causation (see figure 1.3).

The order-of-impact principle applies to other sources of purposeful change, such as government planning, social movements, and community organizing (Coria 2009; NEJAC 2006). Television did not, in itself, cause *Sesame Street* to be invented. Instead, a certain type of writing and acting also had to be developed. New theories of early childhood education required formulation. U.S. public television had to be established. And several other things had to occur (none of them pursued specifically with the goal of creating a certain type of children's program) before the TV–*Sesame Street* causal link was eventually forged.

This suggests a process in which the effects of one cause (e.g., a new technology, law, or organization) radiate outward through time. As they do, they join with other parts of

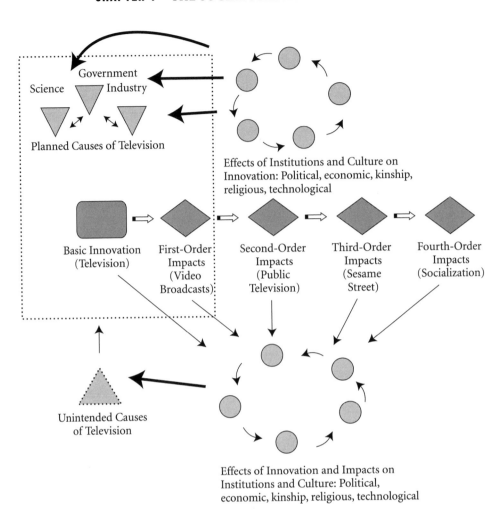

FIGURE 1.3 Order of Impact (Manifest Functions outlined).

the sociocultural system in which the cause was introduced, and thus create additional and increasingly remote effects. As the process continues, the number of unintended consequences, or latent functions and dysfunctions, of the initiating change multiplies. Participating individuals, such as inventors, legislators, consumers, and protesters, experience progressively less control over the ultimate outcomes of their actions, as the world they set out to change seems ever-more "autonomous" (van der Valk 1997; Winner 1977).

This image of radiating, higher-order impacts symbolizes how social scientists treat intention as relative. We know that people act collectively with purposes in mind and that bringing about social and cultural change is often one of their goals. Seeking change, they work in groups, make alliances, accumulate resources, and enter into communication networks. These social relations in which they participate very much affect the chances that their goals will actually be achieved. Yet, as plans are enacted, several other factors enter the situation to give rise to higher-order impacts.

Some of the factors are nonpurposeful, such as the size of the population in which the change is sought, the specific cultural values that prevail, and the characteristics of the organizations involved. But also included are the intentional acts of other actors: people who may be seeking different, even contradictory goals. These relations always complicate the path that joins intent with outcome. Depending on how others react and on the nonpurposeful influences, the potential results of intentional change, from the point of view of one who consciously seeks it, can thus range from direct success to partial realization and to dismal failure.

Actual outcomes depend on many things, some of which may be (at least temporarily) beyond our control. When we deal with complex, dynamic events and societies—especially over the course of decades—we find that there are highly elaborate causal chains linking intentional acts with their ultimate effects. In the case of transforming events such as the four critical episodes, this principle is realized in the form of historical ironies, simultaneous triumphs and setbacks, personal and interpersonal conflict, and a generally puzzling combination of progress and regress. No one would doubt, for instance, that a major outcome of the Nazi movement and the Holocaust was the humiliation of the German nation in the eyes of most of the world, including many German citizens. Yet, this was as far as possible from the goals of the perpetrators, who sought to establish a "thousand-year reign" of German nationalism over all of humanity.

Evolutionary Impact

The ideas of progress and regress and the possibility that change can lead to significant improvements and deterioration in social relations are closely tied to the concept of sociocultural evolution. This connection is discussed briefly here and again in chapter 2, of which it is the main topic. Because everything is always changing, it is never a simple matter to decide among those trends and variations that demand scientific attention and those that can be safely ignored. The possibility that some trends may be leading humanity in a specific direction (that we may wish to encourage or avoid) has guided researchers to focus on critical episodes, such as the Holocaust, and to be less concerned with (apparently) inconsequential changes, such as growth in the pizza delivery business.

Evolution is a leading concept in the history of social science, in part because it addresses the problems of survival, that is, why some populations and their sociocultural traits persist and grow over the generations whereas others decline and even become extinct. Contemporary researchers are keenly aware that there are both benefits and serious limitations in applying this (or any) type of organic metaphor to human relations, for sociocultural change is a superorganic process in which consciousness, intent, and meaning intervene between the organism and the environment in ways unknown among other species.[6]

One major advantage of the evolutionary perspective is that it underscores how a people's very existence may be at stake when its society and culture change. In fact, in the larger evolutionary scheme of things, our sociocultural systems, in themselves, can be viewed as general and often highly effective survival adaptations (Huxley 1953, chap. 6).

The human animal lacks the physical advantages of other species, such as running speed, powerful teeth and claws, the ability to endure long periods without food and water, the capacity of newborn individuals to fend for themselves, and the ability to fly. Instead, we have developed cooperative mechanisms and elaborate systems of symbols and tools, embodied in our sociocultural heritage, that compensate for these shortcomings. If somehow a human population suddenly lost its ability to cooperate and transmit cultural material within and between generations, one can imagine how impotent its members would be in coping with their potentially hostile environment, including other species and more advantaged humans. It certainly could not survive very long.

Some social and cultural changes have greater impact than others do on a population's capacity to adapt to its always-changing environment. For this reason, major discoveries, such as the development of electronic media, and massive movements, such as Third World nationalism, have received prime attention from theorists and researchers. Because these have clearly contributed to the ability of human populations to survive, they represent significant changes. Whether or not they should be properly termed "advances" is another matter, an issue that chapter 2 explores.

Stage-Setting Events: The Four Critical Episodes

Our special concern with macrolevel changes that (1) involve planning and purpose, (2) produce multiple higher-order impacts, and (3) appear to have significant evolutionary consequences leads us to take an especially careful look at certain kinds of transforming events. Included among these are four major episodes that, perhaps more than any other, made the first decade of the twenty-first century such a uniquely critical period.

These episodes involved millions and billions of people, hundreds of complex organizations, and they extended over thousands of miles of territory. In addition, all of them included a prominent component of intentional change: social movements and revolutions, legislation, and institutional planning. As a consequence, all were characterized by several second, third, and higher orders of impact. In each case, some goals were achieved with a high degree of accuracy, others met with less than desired optimal results, and, as often happens at this level of complexity, some outcomes even turned out to be the very opposite of what was intended by those who sought change. Such episodes are among the most consequential in altering individual lives, and they have had the greatest effects on the recent course of sociocultural evolution. Because of their extensive higher-order impacts, however, they are also the kinds of change that are the most challenging to explain in an adequate scientific manner.

The illustrative cases presented here are among the most frequently cited by contemporary social scientists (Gamson 1995). They are mentioned in all of the current introductory and social change texts, and they would surely be at or near the top of most researchers' lists of important, meaningful episodes in recent history.

Interestingly, many books in this area also discuss some events that did not happen—at least not exactly. These are the unvarying rhythms of life in George Orwell's antiutopian novel *Nineteen Eighty-Four*. Life in "Oceania" (Orwell's name for the imaginary country in which the novel's events take place) provides a useful comparison, for it is a fascinating and frightening portrayal of what the world would be like if there were no authentic social change.

The Holocaust, 1939–1945

Between 1939 and 1945, approximately twenty million civilians were killed by police and soldiers in more than twenty sovereign European nations, and millions more were driven from their homes and imprisoned.[7] These included members of several ethnic groups, members of Communist and other left-wing political organizations, and thousands of disabled people and gay men of various backgrounds (Freedman 1990; Plant 1986). The groups most affected were the Jewish communities of these nations, whose losses are estimated between 5.1 and 5.9 million (Anti-Defamation League 1993; Hilberg 1971, 1985). This episode is known as the *Holocaust*, from the Latin roots *holo*, meaning "all," and *caust*, "to burn." In Israel and in Jewish communities throughout the world, the Hebrew word that refers to a burnt offering, *Shoah*, is used. These terms vividly evoke an image of a great fire sweeping over the land, destroying everything.

The program was carried out under the strict control of the government of Germany, following the direct orders of its charismatic leader and chancellor, Adolf Hitler. The idea of such a program of mass destruction has ancient roots in Western civilization, but planning for its specific application began in 1923, when Hitler was serving a jail sentence in Munich for attempting to overthrow the government by force of arms. The plan was written down in a book, *Mein Kampf* ("my battle" or "my struggle"; Hitler [1925] 1948), which was to become a best seller in Germany and in Hitler's home country of Austria.

In terms of sheer numbers of people affected, the Holocaust was among the most monumental population control projects ever envisioned. The victims were selected according to criteria codified in laws and statutes. The best known of these are the so-called Nuremberg Laws of 1935. They were part of the official legal and political framework of Germany, Austria, Poland, and the other nations that came under Nazi domination during World War II. They refer to members of certain hereditary populations and political organizations as *entartete* ("degenerate") who are not entitled to civil rights, including, for some groups and under certain circumstances, the right to live (Dawidowicz 1975).

Much has been written during the past fifty years about this horrifying episode, although survivors tell us that nothing can describe or explain it effectively ("Fiftieth Anniversaries of 1995" 1995; Oliner 2000). There are now journals and professional organizations devoted to the subject, and Holocaust museums and memorials have been established in Israel, Central Europe, and the United States (Milton 1988). In fact, several books and articles have been written about the substantial interest that Holocaust study and commentary has engendered (see Alexander 2002; Levy and Sznaider 2006).

Box 1.1 HOLOCAUST DENIAL

Beginning in the early 1980s, a movement surfaced in the United States, France, and other nations that styled itself "Holocaust Revisionism" (Anti-Defamation League 1993). Its aim is to challenge the validity of the historical record that documents the major events surrounding the Holocaust and, in many instances, to challenge the very existence of the episode. As such, most scholars more properly refer to it as Holocaust *denial*. A leading spokesperson for the denial movement is David Irving. Irving has written extensively on the subject and has consistently claimed that no evidence exists to prove that millions of Jews died in Auschwitz and the other camps. As is true of other deniers, his position is that the accounts of the Holocaust were largely fabricated by Jews for monetary gain and in support of the State of Israel.

In the early 1990s, historian Deborah Lipstadt published an important book on the Holocaust denial movement (Lipstadt 1993). In it she argued that Irving is a fraud, a neo-Nazi, and an anti-Semite, whose "research" amounts to little more than pseudo-scholarship. Because of her pointed criticism of Irving and other leaders of the denial movement, Lipstadt achieved wide recognition and was in great demand as a lecturer and guest on talk shows.

In response to this notoriety, Irving filed a lawsuit in 2000 against Lipstadt and her publisher, Penguin Books, Ltd., claiming that he had been libeled. According to English law, the burden of proof is on the defendant in such a case, that is, Lipstadt and Penguin were forced to prove their case about Irving. Following a dramatic trial in London's High Court of Justice, Queen's Bench Division, on April 11, 2000, Presiding Justice Hon. Gray rendered the following judgment acquitting Lipstadt and the publisher:

> The charges which I have found to be substantially true include the charges that Irving has for his own ideological reasons persistently and deliberately misrepresented and manipulated historical evidence; that for the same reasons he has portrayed Hitler in an unwarrantedly favourable light, principally in relation to his attitude towards and responsibility for the treatment of the Jews; that he is an active Holocaust denier; that he is anti-Semitic and racist and that he associates with right wing extremists who promote neo-Nazism. In my judgment the charges against Irving which have been proved to be true are of sufficient gravity for it be clear that the failure to prove the truth of the matters set out in paragraph 13.165 above does not have any material effect on Irving's reputation. In the result therefore the defence of justification succeeds.

Source: Irving's website, www.fpp.co.uk/Letters/History/Don2511202.html; the Nizkor Project, www.nizkor.org/hweb/people/i/irving-david/judgment-00-00.html.

One of the most significant features of this enormous demographic change is that it was so purposeful: well organized and highly bureaucratized.[8] It occurred largely under the legitimate auspices of national authorities (Laqueur 1980; Wistrich 1985). It was institutionalized through a social movement, and it became official policy in several countries. At the same time, democratic institutions were systematically disassembled in Germany and in other Axis powers (Linz 1988). In place of a secular, democratic government, the regime was made sacred, worshiped as the true embodiment of a "superior race" (Cristi 2001).

This extraordinary authority was then used to destroy members of "lesser races": through invasion where the "inferiors" had a national territory and through internal "solutions" when the people had no homeland. The latter applied especially to political refugees, Jews, and the Sinti and Romani people ("Gypsies"; Lewy 2000; Ramati 1986). This was the most complete and most manifest application of a long-standing heritage of racism and anti-Semitism in Europe (Goldhagen 1996; Weinstein and Stehr 1999).

The legal and moral impact of the Holocaust has been enormous. The Nuremberg Tribunal, held in the fall of 1945, served to change the structure of international law (Taylor 1992; Woetzel 1962). The trial of Adolf Eichmann in Jerusalem occurred in 1961 (Arendt 1964). And numerous government and academic forums have been held to examine the events. In these contexts, questions have been raised concerning the limits of state power, human rights, complicity with immoral commands from social superiors, the meaning of evil, and countless other dilemmas that were revealed in their harshest light during World War II (Furet 1989; Levi 1988; Roth and Berenbaum 1989).[9]

The Rise of the Third World Nations, 1945–1975

In 1945, at the end of World War II, the United Nations (UN) was created (Glendon 2001; Schlesinger 2003). It was envisioned as the organizational framework for a new world government to replace the discredited League of Nations. At the time of its founding, fifty sovereign countries were members, nearly all of them located in Europe and the Americas (see table 1.3).

By 1975, at the thirtieth anniversary of the UN, there were over 150 member nations, most of them in Asia, Africa, and the Pacific region. One of these was the Jewish homeland of Israel, founded by UN mandate in 1947, in part as the result of a civil war in Palestine against the British administration and in part as a response to the Holocaust. The State of Israel was created in a territory that had been under British control since the World War I era and the collapse of the Ottoman Empire. In 1947–1948, the borders of the Palestinian Mandate territory and of Lebanon, Jordan, and Syria were redefined as constituents of Jewish, Christian, and Muslim holy lands. These boundaries have been under dispute since their creation.

India and Pakistan were also created in 1947–1948, two countries formed out of one to correspond to the homelands of ethnically homogenous populations (Inder Singh 1987; Khan 2007). These nations won their independence after a long anticolonial war against England, which had established sovereignty over parts of India some two hundred years earlier. The Indian independence struggle involved several leading

TABLE 1.3 The Original Members of the UN. As of 2009 there were 192 member nations of the UN, the majority of which are in the less industrialized countries of Asia and Africa. As this table shows, in 1945, of the fifty charter members, only thirteen are in Asia or Africa.

Country	Date (all 1945)	Country	Date (all 1945)
Argentina	24 October	Iraq	21 December
Australia	1 November	Lebanon	24 October
Belarus	24 October	Liberia	2 November
Belgium	27 December	Luxembourg	24 October
Bolivia	14 November	Mexico	7 November
Brazil	24 October	Netherlands	10 December
Canada	9 November	New Zealand	24 October
Chile	24 October	Nicaragua	24 October
China	24 October	Norway	27 November
Colombia	5 November	Panama	13 November
Costa Rica	2 November	Paraguay	24 October
Cuba	24 October	Peru	31 October
Denmark	24 October	Philippines	24 October
Dominican Republic	24 October	Poland	24 October
Ecuador	21 December	Russian Federation	24 October
Egypt	24 October	Saudi Arabia	24 October
El Salvador	24 October	South Africa	7 November
Ethiopia	13 November	Syrian Arab Republic	24 October
France	24 October	Turkey	24 October
Greece	25 October	Ukraine	24 October
Guatemala	21 November	UK	24 October
Haiti	24 October	USA	24 October
Honduras	17 December	Uruguay	18 December
India	30 October	Venezuela	15 November
Iran	24 October		

Source: Press Release: L/37/06, United Nations Information Services, Bangkok, July 3, 2006.

personalities of the day, prominent among whom was the charismatic leader Mohandas K. Gandhi.

The post–World War II anticolonial movement spread from the Middle East and India to other parts of the former British and other European empires. Region by region, the old colonial regimes disintegrated during the first thirty years of the UN (Chamberlain 1985; Wallerstein 1961, 1966). Throughout Africa and Asia, local leaders, who, like Gandhi, had received professional training in Europe or the United States, organized and eventually won the battles for independence.

These movements inspired political leaders and academics in Latin America, and beginning in the early 1970s, they declared themselves in league with the emerging nations. Even though these countries had been sovereign for a century or more, they were (and some still are) nearly as poor as the colonial areas of Asia and Africa. Thus, the struggle was defined as being against *neocolonialism*, a term coined by Ghana's independence leader, Kwame Nkrumah (1909–1972), to describe the implicit policies of political and economic domination pursued by European and North American governments (Nkrumah 1965).

In the late 1950s, a term was coined to describe these new nations plus Latin America: the *Third World* (Horowitz 1966; Worsley 1964). This designation distinguishes them from both the developed capitalist (First World) and the semideveloped socialist (Second World) countries of Europe and North America, and Japan. Through the efforts of India's first prime minister, J. N. Nehru, and the Yugoslav leader, Marshal Tito, the argument was put forth that the new nations should not be aligned with either of the two post–World War II power blocs, the United States and the Soviet Union. Thus, they were conceived as a "third" force in international relations, although many observers have concluded that nonalignment turned out to be largely a myth in a world divided by the Cold War.

The period during which the Third World was created included some of the boldest experiments in planned social change ever attempted, for these were also the three "decades of *development*" (Goulet 1977). It was an era of nation creation and building, and it was a time of large-scale attempts to improve significantly and rapidly the standard of living of some two billion people (which had increased to nearly five billion by the year 2010). The preceding centuries of colonial rule had been characterized by an asymmetry of power as well as the creation of vast disparities in wealth. This, it was hoped, would be rectified through massive investments, along with the creation of large-scale bureaucratic organizations to administer the investments in development projects, rural electrification, literacy programs, a Green Revolution (Karim 1986; Perkins 1997), and more.

Although Israel and India were among the first postwar new nations, they were not typical in having (to this day) civilian governments (Horowitz 1982; Horowitz et al. 1984). As the native people of the former colonial areas addressed the problems of independence and development, they established democratic constitutions, often modeled after that of the "First New Nation," the United States (Lipset 1963). Yet, in country after country, "emergencies" made it necessary to suspend the new constitutions, as military regimes came to the fore with their own, often autocratic solutions to the challenge of self-rule. At times, these were peaceful transitions, but typically they involved violent insurrection (Kposowa and Jenkins 1993; Skocpol 1994).

Another unexpected inheritance of the newly independent nations was internal ethnic conflict. Many of the Third World countries, including India, Pakistan, and Israel, are the creations of mapmakers. Natural territories of indigenous populations often have little to do with the boundaries that were drawn at UN headquarters or in postcolonial military negotiations. As a result, the original claims of indigenous people for independence from the European powers have more recently been echoed within the Third World. These have often been fostered by representatives of ethnic groups asserting their rights for independence from the new, local central authorities (Stephens 1993).

The struggles for democracy and against military rule, the ethnic conflict, and the development programs continue to this day (although center stage, in terms of the target for social reconstruction investment, must now be shared with the newly emerging Second World). Confrontations that have pitted Arabic and other Muslim nations (including Pakistan) against the United States and the West are significant by-products of the end of colonial rule. The momentum generated during the anticolonial struggles and the rush for development in the Third World by these and other events continue to have effects. Yet, it would be difficult to say with certainty whether or not the results correspond with what was desired by key actors. What is certain, however, is that James Joyce's prophecy that "the East will shake the West awake" has come true (see the detailed discussion of "the Easternization of the West" in Campbell 2007).

The fall of colonialism and the rise of the Third World have changed the terms of international relations and have redefined the quest for human rights and social and economic justice (Gastil 1986). Regardless of the specific impacts that lie ahead, the rise of the Third World represents the voice of the majority of humanity, demanding to be heard and to be treated as equals.[10]

The U.S. Civil Rights Movement, 1954–1968

On May 17, 1954, the U.S. Supreme Court handed down the landmark decision in the case of *Brown v. Board of Education of Topeka* (Cottrol, Diamond, and Ware 2003; Tushnet 1987).[11] This decision was the culmination of activity in the African American community and concern among academics and jurists in the decade following the return of the troops after World War II. African American leaders perceived the sharp contradiction between segregation and discrimination at home and in the armed services, on one hand, and, on the other, the ideals for which members of their ethnic group had just fought abroad (Powledge 1991).

Just prior to the end of the war, this "American Dilemma" was chronicled in an influential study, with that title, by the Swedish social scientist (and later Nobel laureate) Gunnar Myrdal (1944). Citing Myrdal's study, the *Brown* decision declared that officially sanctioned, state-authorized discrimination against "Negroes" was incompatible with the U.S. Constitution.

In one respect, this was simply the latest stage in a movement that had begun with the first slave revolt hundreds of years earlier (Bergman 1969; Lomax 1962; Moore 1981). But it was also a new beginning. It set a precedent of challenging the established, but morally wrong and now declared illegal, norms, values, and practices of intergroup relations in the country.

During the succeeding fifteen years, U.S. society and culture underwent a deep and lasting transformation (Morris 1984, 1999). In an atmosphere that was already politically charged as a result of the tragic and divisive war in Vietnam, the movement for equal treatment of African Americans expanded far beyond its previous scale. It spread from the southern states, where the 1955 arrest of Rosa Parks in Alabama set off the famous Montgomery bus boycott (Gibson-Robinson 1987), to Chicago and other northern cities. Participation rates in formal organizations increased, as did the number and size of informal demonstrations and organized protest marches (Branch 2006; Morris 1981, 1993).

Box 1.2 *BROWN VERSUS BOARD OF EDUCATION* DECISION

SUPREME COURT OF THE UNITED STATES
Brown v. Board of Education, 347 U.S. 483 (1954) (USSC+)
347 U.S. 483
Argued December 9, 1952
Reargued December 8, 1953
Decided May 17, 1954
APPEAL FROM THE UNITED STATES DISTRICT COURT
FOR THE DISTRICT OF KANSAS*

Syllabus

Segregation of white and Negro children in the public schools of a State solely on the basis of race, pursuant to state laws permitting or requiring such segregation, denies to Negro children the equal protection of the laws guaranteed by the Fourteenth Amendment—even though the physical facilities and other "tangible" factors of white and Negro schools may be equal.

(a) The history of the Fourteenth Amendment is inconclusive as to its intended effect on public education.

(b) The question presented in these cases must be determined not on the basis of conditions existing when the Fourteenth Amendment was adopted, but in the light of the full development of public education and its present place in American life throughout the Nation.

(c) Where a State has undertaken to provide an opportunity for an education in its public schools, such an opportunity is a right which must be made available to all on equal terms.

(d) Segregation of children in public schools solely on the basis of race deprives children of the minority group of equal educational opportunities, even though the physical facilities and other "tangible" factors may be equal.

(e) The "separate but equal" doctrine adopted in *Plessy v. Ferguson*, 163 U.S. 537, has no place in the field of public education.

(f) The cases are restored to the docket for further argument on specified questions relating to the forms of the decrees.

MR. CHIEF JUSTICE WARREN delivered the opinion of the Court.

We conclude that, in the field of public education, the doctrine of "separate but equal" has no place. Separate educational facilities are inherently unequal. Therefore, we hold

(Continued)

> ## Box 1.2 *BROWN VERSUS BOARD OF EDUCATION* DECISION (Continued)
>
> that the plaintiffs and others similarly situated for whom the actions have been brought are, by reason of the segregation complained of, deprived of the equal protection of the laws guaranteed by the Fourteenth Amendment. This disposition makes unnecessary any discussion whether such segregation also violates the Due Process Clause of the Fourteenth Amendment.
>
> *Source*: U.S. National Park Service, www.nps.gov/archive/brvb/pages/decision54.htm.

The African American churches played a historically central role in the movement. At the head of many of these marches was a Protestant minister from Atlanta who had studied the anticolonial strategies of Gandhi: Martin Luther King Jr. Another man inspired by the Third World independence movement was a Muslim minister from Michigan, Al Haj Malik al Shabbaz (Malcolm X), who served as spiritual leader and political spokesman for millions.

Violence and confrontation, often initiated by officially sanctioned attacks on participants, were very much part of the movement. But there were also comradeship and a spirit of liberation. As with the rise of the Third World, the ideals and the impact of the events continue to this day. The Civil Rights movement has contributed significantly to the culture and strategies of the movements for equal treatment of women and other minority groups, and to other challenges to existing U.S. (and world) standards of appropriate interpersonal relations.

In 1964, ten years after the *Brown* decision, Congress passed and President Lyndon Johnson signed the Civil Rights Act. It represented an answer, albeit not a complete answer, to the challenge of Reverends King and Shabbaz, other leaders, and the masses for whom they spoke. The movement continued to seek other legal, economic, and social reforms years after the act was signed. Increasingly, the issues of civil rights and protest against the Vietnam War were joined. Shabbaz and King began stressing the connection between the battlefronts in Southeast Asia and the confrontations on the streets in the United States, thus radicalizing their respective branches of the movement. And, like Gandhi before them, both were assassinated: Shabbaz on February 21, 1964, and King on April 4, 1968.

After 1969, in the wake of the bloodshed (recall that John F. Kennedy was assassinated in 1963 and Robert Kennedy in 1968), the movement shifted direction. New, younger leaders, such as Stokely Carmichael, Rap Brown, and Eldridge Cleaver, came to the fore, promoting programs of black community self-development, political power, and self-defense (Lockwood 1970). With increasingly militant responses from authorities, the hopeful insurgent spirit began to recede. It is not finished by any means, although unfortunately much of the literature on the effects of the *Brown* decision is about the limits of such change (e.g., Olzak, Shanahan, and West 1994). That key episode between the *Brown* decision and the death of the two leaders forms a boundary between that time and ours. The movement shook the United States and the rest of the world, and they continue to shake.

The Fall of Soviet Communism, 1989–1991

The reverberations of the U.S. Civil Rights movement contributed, in direct and indirect ways, to the collapse of the Berlin Wall on November 9, 1989 (Borrell 1989; Hamilton 1989).[12] The wall had come to symbolize the great divide between the First and Second Worlds at the end of World War II. Germany, and its wartime capital in particular, were split into two parts that corresponded to the conflicting claims of the Allies: the United States, England, and France on one side, and the Soviet Union on the other. The original dispute centered in large part on strategies for dealing with the new phenomenon of a pariah nation (Philipsen 1993).

The destruction of the wall by German citizens from both sides was a climactic (though not final) act in a social movement that had been sweeping Central and Eastern Europe since the Hungarian uprising in October 1956 (Adelman 1986; Opp and Gern 1993). It symbolized the end of a massive experiment in social planning and coordination, begun during World War I. It demonstrated that the Cold War and nuclear confrontation had come to an end and with it the serious risk of another kind of holocaust. And it symbolized the collapse of yet another empire, this one ruled from Moscow and encompassing Central and Eastern Europe.

There are many lessons yet to be learned about what went on in these largely closed countries between World War II and the late 1980s. We do know that they were autocratic to the core, that is, the political systems were designed primarily to maintain the power and privileges of the elite officeholders (Brzezinski 1989; Daswisha 1988). The systems were command states (Rose 1993), dependent on secret police forces, networks of agents provocateurs, and informers to maintain social control and ensure the stability of the regimes. The central governments had been largely absorbed by small groups of Communist Party elites who had a monopoly over the means of violence and control of an extensive penal system. Reflecting the height of cynicism, the rulers preached sacrifice and sharing, while they enriched themselves, families, and friends with stolen resources—all of this, it should be recalled, in the name of realizing Marx's classic utopian vision of a truly just society.

What is occurring now in the former Soviet republics and the old Warsaw Pact countries (plus the unique nonaligned former Communist country of Albania) could not have been conceived a few years ago. Indeed, on May 1, 1998, the unimaginable happened.

Following World War II, the United States and countries of Western Europe created the North Atlantic Treaty Organization (NATO) to combat the Warsaw Pact, as the two blocs faced off as the main Cold War alliances. In May 1998, NATO members voted unanimously to admit three of the former Warsaw Pact stalwarts, the Czech Republic, Hungary, and Poland.

The Bolshevist system seemed so durable (Kecskemeti 1991), and, with the help of Soviet nuclear technology, it appeared to pose a mortal threat to the very existence of humanity. As it has turned out, it had fatal flaws, of course. But was there anything good about it? Was the great Communist experiment the grotesque disaster that it now appears to have been, or are there things about it that should be preserved? Certainly there were, and still are, many people in these countries who sincerely believed in the

Box 1.3 TIMELINE OF THE FALL OF COMMUNISM IN EASTERN EUROPE, 1989

U.S. Department of State, Undersecretary for Public Diplomacy and Public Affairs

On the night of November 9, 1989, the Berlin Wall, the most potent symbol of the cold-war division of Europe, came down. Earlier that day, the Communist authorities of the German Democratic Republic had announced the removal of travel restrictions to democratic West Berlin. Thousands of East Germans streamed into the West, and in the course of the night, celebrants on both sides of the wall began to tear it down.

The collapse of the Berlin Wall was the culminating point of the revolutionary changes sweeping East Central Europe in 1989. Throughout the Soviet bloc, reformers assumed power and ended over 40 years of dictatorial Communist rule. The reform movement that ended communism in East Central Europe began in Poland. Solidarity, an anti-Communist trade union and social movement, had forced Poland's Communist government to recognize it in 1980 through a wave of strikes that gained international attention. In 1981, Poland's Communist authorities, under pressure from Moscow, declared martial law, arrested Solidarity's leaders, and banned the democratic trade union. The ban did not bring an end to Solidarity. The movement simply went underground, and the rebellious Poles organized their own civil society, separate from the Communist government and its edicts.

In 1985, the assumption of power in the Soviet Union by a reformer, Mikhail Gorbachev, paved the way for political and economic reforms in East Central Europe. Gorbachev abandoned the "Brezhnev Doctrine" the Soviet Union's policy of intervening with military force, if necessary, to preserve Communist rule in the region. Instead, he encouraged the local Communist leaders to seek new ways of gaining popular support for their rule. In Hungary, the Communist government initiated reforms in 1989 that led to the sanctioning of a multiparty system and competitive elections. In Poland, the Communists entered into round-table talks with a reinvigorated Solidarity. As a result, Poland held its first competitive elections since before World War II, and in 1989, Solidarity formed the first non-Communist government within the Soviet bloc since 1948. Inspired by their neighbors' reforms, East Germans took to the streets in the summer and fall of 1989 to call for reforms, including freedom to visit West Berlin and West Germany. Moscow's refusal to use military force to buoy the regime of East German leader Erich Honecker led to his replacement and the initiation of political reforms, leading up to the fateful decision to open the border crossings on the night of November 9, 1989.

In the wake of the collapse of the Berlin Wall, Czechs and Slovaks took to the streets to demand political reforms in Czechoslovakia. Leading the demonstrations in Prague was dissident playwright Vaclav Havel, co-founder of the reform group Charter 77. The Communist Party of Czechoslovakia quietly and peacefully transferred rule to Havel and the Czechoslovak reformers in what was later dubbed the "Velvet Revolution." In Romania, the Communist regime of hardliner Nicolae Ceausescu was overthrown by popular protest and force of arms in December 1989. Soon, the Communist parties of Bulgaria and Albania also ceded power.

The revolutions of 1989 marked the death knell of communism in Europe. As a result, not only was Germany reunified in 1990, but soon, revolution spread to the Soviet Union itself. After surviving a hard line coup attempt in 1991, Gorbachev was forced to cede power in Russia to Boris Yeltsin, who oversaw the dissolution of the Soviet Union.

The collapse of communism in East Central Europe and the Soviet Union marked the end of the cold war. The U.S. long-term policy of containing Soviet expansion while encouraging democratic reform in Central and Eastern Europe through scientific and cultural exchanges, information policy (e.g., Radio Free Europe and Radio Liberty), and the United States' own example, provided invaluable support to the peoples of East Central Europe in their struggle for freedom.

Source: U.S. Department of State, www.state.gov/r/pa/ho/time/rd/17672.htm

ideals of Karl Marx. And some believe(d) that the ruling party—and only party—was capable of implementing these ideals. As the system has unraveled, these and related political, economic, and social problems continue to surface (Rona-Tas 1994). Especially intense are the old ethnic rivalries that had been submerged or suppressed during Communist rule (Cviic 1991; Malis 1992).

For seventy years in the former USSR and forty years elsewhere in the region, ethnic identity was officially treated as a secondary or even lesser form of identification in relation to political definitions (whether or not one was a Communist). Indeed, from a Marxist-Leninist perspective, ethnic identity was an archaic form of social diversity that Communism would eliminate. Meanwhile, "back in the USSR" and elsewhere, implicit policies ensuring the domination of ethnic majorities, such as the Russians, were the rule.

With the fall of Soviet Communism, Third World–type claims of ethnic sovereignty have already created more than twenty new post–Cold War nations (Przewowski 1991). Civil war in Kosovo-Serbia and Macedonia, both parts of former Yugoslavia, concluded only at the very end of the twentieth century, and it continued well into the twenty-first century with the independence movement in Montenegro (a former Serbian republic) and in the Russian republic of Chechnya (see Codrescu 1991, 2000). Yet there is no turning back. Although a few people (openly) admit to wanting to restore the old system, it has essentially been delegitimated.

The end of Communist rule in Central and Eastern Europe represents a crushing defeat for autocracy. The command state, as a huge social change experiment to develop an alternative to capitalist democracy, was a major failure. Moreover, it is a path that seems unlikely to be pursued again in the near future. Whether it is simply a defeat for only one kind of autocracy, namely, the Communist kind, remains to be seen, for it is also possible that the conditions still exist that were so conducive to antidemocratic sentiment and behavior in 1917, 1933, and 1946 (Habermas and Michnik 1994; Michnik 2009). Thus, the end of autocracy, in this case, is not necessarily a prelude to democracy. That, too, remains to be worked out (Kolakowski 1990; Lipset 1994; Marsh 1991; Rose 1993; Szelenyi 1994).

Like the other three episodes, the fall of Communism is a complex matter. But it has clearly altered human relations throughout the world and for a very long time. The fact that it did so in a sudden, unexpected, and relatively peaceful way means that we still have much to understand about it. Few, however, would doubt that it represents a ray of light (though perhaps a thin one) where there had been decades of darkness.

Oceania, 1984: A Fictional Account of a Changeless World

Most of you have read or are familiar with the novel *Nineteen Eighty-Four* ([1949] 1984) by George Orwell, born Eric Blair (1903–1950). A brief review of the book is presented here, and at several other points the text turns to Orwell's powerful understanding of post–World War II Europe.

You will recall that the main character of the novel is someone we never actually meet. Indeed, Orwell gives us reason to believe that, like the Wizard of Oz, there may not be such a person beyond the huge images that are projected on the two-way television sets that are always turned on: this is Big Brother (affectionately referred to as "BB"). BB is the absolute ruler of an empire known as Oceania, a place in which the autocratic principles of Nazism and Communism have been realized in a perfect form. It is a world of state-authorized terror, secret police, and informers, in which social movements for political independence and civil rights are impossible—a world in which a revolution to topple "The Wall" can never occur. Oceania, Orwell warns prophetically, is a nightmare that could come true.

Orwell's book is an antiutopian account of change and stability. It was among the first of what is now a familiar kind of fantasy literature, although, as Orwell noted, it draws much from Yvgenii Zamiatin's *We* ([1924] 1993) and Jack London's ([1910] 1980) novel *The Iron Heel* (Orwell 1988, chap. 9). As a work of fiction, its style, method, and purpose differ from those of technical social science. But, as extremely well-written fiction, the book also contains much that aspiring researchers might wish to emulate.

Contemporary social scientists have frequently discussed Orwell and *Nineteen Eighty-Four* in this light (Aron 1967, 75; Calhoun, Light, and Keller 1994, 81, 574; Fromm 1961; Harper 1993, 202; Hyams 1973, 256–57; Robertson 1987, 98). The much-cited essay by Ralf Dahrendorf (1968) is especially relevant (see also Turner 1973; Weinstein 2001). Dahrendorf, in particular, focuses on the issue of "closure," the premise that society and culture in Orwell's fictional world cannot be affected by uncontrolled or external factors. He criticizes this assumption and applies the critique to the concepts of intention and purpose and to the major theories of change, Marxism and modernization theory.

According to Dahrendorf, in real human systems, goal-directed behavior and associated unintended consequences make Orwellian closure impossible. Similarly, the actual world system that has emerged since Orwell's death is far more open and has been so for a far longer time than *Nineteen Eighty-Four* would suggest.

Orwell's novel is a parable on democracy and autocracy. It was certainly intended as such, and for this reason Orwell and the book need to be placed in historical and political context. Most important, it was written immediately after the Holocaust and Nuremberg, in post–World War II London. English socialism ("INGSOC" in the book) was an important factor in the country and in Orwell's personal life. Communist regimes were being established throughout Central and Eastern Europe.

The text and context of *Nineteen Eighty-Four* relate closely to the four critical episodes discussed earlier in this chapter. There are numerous parallels between these real instances of change and Orwell's frozen portrayal of Oceania and its capital city Airstrip One. There is The Party, whose unchallenged leader is and always will be BB. We have its system of total control and the (ultimately futile) social movement to overthrow the system: The Brotherhood. Orwell also reminds us of the rule allowing only members of the Inner Party to turn *off* their television sets. Vividly portrayed are the state's use of terror and torture, the division of the world into three regional alliances, the fact that the enemy of BB (and object of the two-minute hate) is named Goldstein, and more.

Orwell was a keen observer of major social trends and a prolific writer of novels, short stories, and essays (see Orwell and Angus 1978). He chose to communicate some, but by no means all, of his most astute commentary in fictional form: In addition to *Nineteen Eighty-Four*, there is the closely related, brilliant parable *Animal Farm* (1946). He wrote much nonfiction as well, especially the highly sociological studies *The Road to Wigan Pier* (1958) and *Down and Out in Paris and London* ([1933] 1950). In so doing, he provided future researchers with a powerful source of insights and "thought experiments" that have enriched and extended the heritage of more conventional, scientific approaches.

The Question of Progress

The four critical episodes plus *Nineteen Eighty-Four*, individually and considered as a group, have much to tell us about where human society has been headed—recently and, on reflection, since the beginning of human existence. In particular, they vividly underscore the central, but ambiguous, concept of progress. When change is viewed over extended periods, over decades, generations, and centuries, can we discern an endpoint or, in Greek, a *telos* toward which we are bound? Can we say that, during a particular period for a specific group of people, things are improving? Or is it possible that social conditions generally deteriorate over time?

To take this line of questions to its extreme, can we understand the history and the prehistory of the largest of all groups, the human species, from this perspective? Is humanity as a whole progressing? Or is it regressing? Do contemporary society and culture provide people with a significantly better quality of life than that of our Stone Age ancestors or that of our grandparents? Or are we in some important ways worse off than in the past? As bold as such questions may appear, they actually reflect common and abiding concerns of scholars from a wide range of disciplines, nationalities, and eras.

"Progress" as a Value Judgment

Great care must be taken in defining words such as *improving* or *deteriorating* when we pose questions about social progress or its opposite. Social and cultural phenomena are highly complex, the more so when the size of groups is large and time spans for observing change are long, as in the four critical episodes. This makes it possible to select evidence, intentionally or unconsciously, in such a way that it will "prove" almost any point one wishes to make: that things are improving, that things are getting worse, or something in between. Indeed, political leaders, journalists, and other public figures do this as a matter of course.

Throughout, this book looks closely at the issue of progressive change and at the crucial value judgments that underlie our perceptions of progress. For example, as you are well aware, the number of personal computers in use in the United States has changed dramatically and in an ever-increasing fashion since the 1970s. This is evident, but is it good? Is it progress? The answers depend, of course, on one's values and interests.

Some see computerization as very positive, as another great step toward freeing people from drudgery and making it possible to perform previously unimaginable feats. Others see it as Big Brother's ultimate tool of oppression, a method for the powerful to intrude into the lives of ordinary people that is more effective than even Orwell could have imagined (Hourani 1987, 1994).

Progress for Whom?

Progress also depends on the institutional status of affected persons. Is a change, such as the recent replacement of automobile workers by computerized robots, bad? Does it reflect deterioration of conditions? The workers and their families probably would think so. But what about their employers, who might be quite pleased about the improvement in their cash flows? And how would the computer manufacturer, tax collector, or buyer of a new automobile evaluate such a decrease? In these cases, it appears that progress is in the eye of the status holder, depending on whether the status is worker, employer, tax collector, or consumer.

The four critical episodes all occurred during the past seventy years, during the lifetimes of ourselves, our parents, or our grandparents. They range from what most (but not all) people would agree is a clear case of progress, the U.S. Civil Rights movement, to a case widely (but, still, not universally—see box 1.1 above) viewed as a regression, the Holocaust. The other two events appear, on first examination, to be more ambiguous. If we think of all four together, remembering that the earlier ones did affect the later ones, it is difficult to come to a quick and definite conclusion about whether they indicate a generally progressive or regressive trend.

When one carefully analyzes the events, one sees deeply ingrained ambiguity, even in the seemingly clear-cut cases. In some of the higher ironies of history, the Holocaust included a kind of moral progress, the achievement of unprecedented levels of heroism and sacrifice by thousands of people (Gross 1994; Oliner and Oliner 1992; Rittner and Meyers 1986). The Civil Rights movement had its share of regressive outcomes, including the assassination of its leaders with at least some of the murderers never brought to justice. Can we say, definitively, that these, or the rise of the Third World nations, or the fall of Communism, were signs of definite progress (or regress)? For whom? Progress in what regard?

The point is that social and cultural change, at least of the magnitude we are considering, is typically characterized by both progress and deterioration, depending on one's value judgments. Change "takes" from the past and is painful to those who are attached to it; it "gives" to the future and is pleasurable to those lacking a positive stake in the past.

But, one might wonder, has there not been objective progress, sociocultural advancement, since World War II, since the mid-nineteenth century, or since Paleolithic times? For most social scientists, this question leads to an analysis of the concept of evolution, which chapter 2 explores.

Relevant Websites

At the end of each chapter is a list of website addresses (URLs) where you will find information, references, and other material related to the topics discussed in the text. Along with each address is a brief overview of what one can expect to find. As this edition went to press, the sites were all active and contained the specific features described. However, because of the dynamic nature of the Internet today, sites are quickly outdated, changed, relocated, or shut down. Because of this, you may find it difficult to locate some of the items listed in this and later chapters. We regret the inconvenience and recommend that you continue your explorations with the help of Google or another search engine. We can assure you that relevant sites, at times very many of them, can be found on virtually any topic discussed in this book.

http://gsociology.icaap.org/
The International Consortium for the Advancement of Academic Publication (ICAAP) maintains this site. It includes numerous links to resources on social and cultural change, especially—but not exclusively—in the discipline of sociology. It is listed at the websites of four American Sociological Association Sections, the British Sociological Association, the European Sociological Association, and the International Social Science Council.

www.mcdonaldization.com/
This site is a spin-off from George Ritzer's influential book, *The McDonaldization of Society*. It pursues many of the issues discussed in the book, includes an interactive posting, and has comments from several social researchers, including Ritzer.

www.southendpress.org/about/institute
Here is a social change advocacy site sponsored by South End Press. Students interested in activism to create progressive change in the United States and the world will find much of interest here.

www.nizkor.org/
www.fpp.co.uk/
These two websites contain material on the Holocaust and Holocaust denial. The first is the site of the Nizkor project, an organization dedicated to keeping an accurate record of the episode. The second is the official site of David Irving, leading Holocaust denier.

www.brownvboard.org/
This is the official website for information on the 1954 Supreme Court decision *Brown et al. v. Board of Education of Topeka et al.* The entire decision, transcripts of the trial, and background information can be found here.

www.iccnow.org/
Here one can find background on the International Criminal Court. The court itself maintains this site.

Social and Cultural Evolution

World history reveals social transformations and directional trends of sufficient generality such that typologies of social forms can be fruitfully constructed. These directional sequences of change constitute the bulk of what is known as social evolution.... However, social evolutionists show due respect for the unique and nonrecurrent in world history. The unique and nonrecurrent may [also] be legitimately called social evolution. (Sanderson 2007, 282)

The concept of evolution has had a unique and profound impact on the development of social science. For over one hundred years, it helped define the field's focus on historical events and trends that most directly affect survival and prosperity: agricultural revolution, industrialization, and urban growth. In fact,

the disciplines of sociology and anthropology were virtually born evolutionary, for most of the leading founders of these field[s] embraced evolutionism of one type or another, some of them strongly so. The person who is usually credited with being the "father" of sociology, Auguste Comte, had a thoroughly evolutionary conception of the development of modern industrial society, one based on a view of the expansion of the powers of the human mind. Emile Durkheim carried on some of Comte's basic evolutionary ideas.... Even markedly different thinkers like Karl Marx and Herbert Spencer were very much evolutionists. (Sanderson 2007, 1)

Beginning in the early 1900s, sociologists and anthropologists began to question the assumptions of the classical writers. Of special concern was the central thesis that human societies and cultures develop according to the same principles that apply to plant and animal species—varying over time as they struggle to adapt to their respective habitats. By the mid-1950s, the debate between evolutionists and their critics had led to a thorough reexamination of all social theory, reflecting how important the concept has been to our understanding of the human prospect (Cerroni-Long 1994; Flynn 1994; Sanderson 1990).

This chapter summarizes the classic position and various extensions, critiques, and revisions of it. Our aim is to assess the strengths and limitations of evolutionism today. To what extent does evolutionary theory help us understand the massive sociocultural transformations our species is now undergoing? Is humanity entering a new stage of a long-term evolutionary process? Is it a higher stage, and, if so, in what sense does it represent an advance over the past?

Classic Evolutionism

As noted, the concept of evolution was employed in the very first theories of social science in the late eighteenth and early nineteenth centuries by Adam Smith, Henri Saint-Simon, Auguste Comte, and especially Herbert Spencer. Charles Darwin was strongly influenced by Spencer's social scientific accounts, including the latter's notion of the survival of the fittest, acknowledging this in print (Darwin [1859] 2008; Spencer 1862; Turner 1993, 65n3). From this association, the ideology of social Darwinism, the literal application of certain biological principles to human relations, was developed.

The foundations of evolutionary thought extend back to ancient times, to the work of Aristotle, Plato, and even earlier philosophers, but by the mid-nineteenth century it was the idea whose time had come. During this period, it radically transformed natural science and the way we think about the world in general (Barzun 1981).

Organic Evolution and Ecological Systems

Evolution is a process involving the mutual and cumulative changes that occur as parts of a system interact with each other. Darwin's formulation focuses on variations in biological traits that eventuate in the creation of new species and the extinction of others. Over the course of time, organisms adapt with varying degrees of success to changes in their habitats, which include geophysical elements such as landforms, water resources, and climate, as well as other species. Those that do succeed can survive, breed, and thus continue the existence of their species; failure to keep up with environmental change leads to the end of reproduction and ultimately of the species itself.

Contemporary biologists now understand that new species most typically emerge when random genetic processes (mutations) create radically different organisms (mutants). The traits of the mutants vary so much from their parents' that it is impossible for them to produce viable, fertile offspring with normal members of their generation. If such mutants are able to survive and reproduce, a new species is created.

Some years after Darwin's death, the influential (and controversial) evolutionary biologist Ernst Haëckel coined the now-familiar term *ecological* to refer to this organism-environment system (Haëckel 1917). The word has the same Greek root, *oikos*, as in "economics," meaning "household." Haëckel used it to stress that nature is like a household: it has an orderly character, consisting of different "rooms" or niches, each of which is reserved for certain functions (as real households have rooms for sleeping, eating, and so on) that contribute to the maintenance of the whole. Each niche has a population of occupants that must adapt to the overall functioning of the ecosystem. Otherwise, better-adapted species with different traits will take their place.

As this pattern of niche occupants changes, the habitat is affected because of variations in the use of landforms and water resources and because of climatic effects (Huxley 1953). This continual alteration of organisms and environment as they adapt to one another creates a long-term process in which the surviving species of a given period are the ones best suited to the environment and the habitat is the one best adapted to its occupants. Thus, evolution reflects the "survival of the fittest."

The connection between the survival of populations, environmental change, and adaptation implies the principle of balance, or equilibrium. The various interrelationships among the parts of a system, along with the various impacts of the whole on each of its parts, make the system extremely interdependent. The slightest change in the activities of a niche occupant or in geophysical characteristics (such as the availability of water resources) could set off a long and cumulative chain of causes and effects, resulting in imbalance, or disequilibrium. The extinction of populations and species, as well as profound geophysical changes, can result from nearly any source. An especially graphic version of this process is the extinction and ecosystem degradation now occurring in the world's rain forest regions, which is mainly the effect of human activity.

Evolutionary Theory and Human Populations

The changing rain forest illustrates how people can dramatically affect the evolution of other species and their habitats. But human populations, too, have become extinct on many occasions or are in the process of becoming extinct today. Some have been the victims of natural disasters and loss of habitat, such as the population of Pompeii. Some have been victims of genocide, intended or otherwise, including several populations of native North American people. And others have blended or assimilated into larger populations under conditions of sociocultural diversity, such as the Normans and Saxons who, together with the native Celts, became the English.

We also know that there have been other species of *Homo* on Earth that are now extinct and that ours, *Homo sapiens*, evolved about 250,000 years ago. In this sense, human development is very much part of the evolutionary process.

Yet there is another way in which evolutionary principles might apply to human beings, that is, to long-range trends in *society and culture*. In fact, many social scientists have sought to describe and explain such processes using an evolutionary metaphor, as if they were biological evolution (Nisbet 1969). This is a very powerful association, for

Box 2.1 LANDMARKS IN HUMAN BIOLOGICAL EVOLUTION

Thousands of Years Ago

2,500: The genus *Homo* appears, evolving from *australopithecines* ancestors. The development of the *Homo* genus coincides with the appearance of tools in the fossil record.

1,800: The evolution of *Homo erectus*, in Africa. This species resembles modern humans and is thought to be an ancestor.

700: A common genetic ancestor of Neanderthals and humans is thought to have lived at this time.

355: *Homo heidelbergensis*, common ancestor of humans and Neanderthals, leaves footprints in a layer of volcanic ash in Italy. The species was similar to *Homo erectus* but had a larger braincase.

195: Omo I and Omo II, two fossil specimens discovered in Ethiopia, lived at this time. They are the earliest discovered fossil evidence for ancient *Homo sapiens*.

160: *Homo sapiens* living in Ethiopia near the Awash River are known to have practiced mortuary rituals.

150: The woman known as "Mitochondrial Eve" lived at this time, in East Africa. This fossil is the most recent common ancestor of human females.

70: The development of genes associated with speech. The development of "behavioral modernity," a set of behaviors and traits associated with modern humans. At around this time, the development of modern human culture began to accelerate rapidly.

60: The "Y Chromosomal Adam" lived in Africa. This fossil is the most recent common ancestor of human males.

50: Humans begin to migrate to South Asia.

40: Humans begin migrating to Europe and Australia.

25: The Neanderthals die out.

12: With the extinction of *Homo floresiensis*, *Homo sapiens* becomes the only living species of *Homo*.

The Roots of Human Civilization: Sociocultural Evolution of H. sapiens sapiens

10,000 BCE: Humans begin to develop farming in the "Fertile Crescent," a highly fertile crescent-shaped region in the Middle East that includes Ancient Egypt, Ancient Mesopotamia, and the Levant.

Source: Emma Lloyd, "A Human Evolution Timeline," Bright Hub Inc., July 2, 2009, www .brighthub.com/science/medical/articles/6040.aspx.

there are many interesting similarities between the evolution of species/habitats and the way in which aspects of human society and culture vary over time (see "Relevant Websites," chapter 1; see also Hawley 1968; Lenski and Lenski 1987; Parsons 1951, 1964; White 1949).

It is also important to remember that the evolution of species per se is an organic, not a superorganic, process. Mutation and other crucial biological principles, such as recombination, natural selection, and reproductive isolation, have no counterparts in the realm of sociocultural dynamics. They "cannot be compared; not in any way that has operational, as opposed to metaphorical, meaning for those whose primary concern is change in institutions, groups, traditions, and life styles" (Nisbet 1967, 234).

Organic evolution has produced *Homo sapiens*, a single, viable species that is currently growing in size (at near-record rates) and whose many still-surviving populations add up to a grand total of approximately 6.5 billion members, which is also an all-time high. In addition, we can be fairly sure that no new species of *Homo* has evolved lately (but see Teilhard de Chardin 1969). In this respect, human nature as a whole is the outcome of the same processes that have molded all members of the animal kingdom.

However, significant alterations have occurred time and again *within* specific human populations in specific habitats. This has happened in three main ways (as discussed in greater detail in chapter 3): through changes in the population's (1) size, (2) structure, and (3) geographical distribution. Some of these variations are strictly biological and are identical to those that occur in nonhuman populations, such as growth due to natural increase (variations in births and deaths). Others are partly biological and partly social, such as migration. Still others are strictly sociocultural: changes in norms governing the "proper" number of children per family or in technologies of sanitation.

As a human population adapts to its environment, a complex combination of all three types of factors determines how large it will be, its composition, and its territory. As these demographic features change, the groups, norms, and other social and cultural traits shared by members are altered. This, in turn, has a feedback effect on demographic process and on survival itself.

In brief, whereas all species experience changes in population size because birth, death, and migration rates vary over time, human beings can and do exercise significant, often purposeful, control over these variations. For this reason, it is a mistake to view social and cultural traits as if they independently and literally evolve. Rather, they change as populations change—in conjunction with organic processes. These transformations "do not represent the unfolding of predetermined or intrinsic tendencies. Instead they are the outcome of human responses to environmental and social changes, subject to the same laws of cause and effect as other scientific phenomena" (Sanderson 2007, 284).

Social and cultural traits give human populations very special, and in some ways advantageous, niches in their habitats. The fact that people possess and develop powerful technologies, including technologies of fertility and mortality control, provides them with the ability to alter significantly the conditions to which they must adapt. If, for instance, a nonhuman population is confronted with a habitat that has very low levels of water resources, it is faced with a certain range of prospects. It can either evolve the capacity to go without water, migrate, or die out. A human population confronted with a similar problem has the additional option of introducing water through irrigation or well-digging techniques.

In some instances, the extinction of human populations has resulted from sociocultural variations or from the failure to change in response to new environmental conditions. Peoples throughout history have become extinct because they did not develop adequate weapons in the face of conquest by well-armed members of an encroaching population. But traits, such as having obsolete weapons, can survive even when proved "unfit" in this way.

Superorganic change is different from organic evolution in part because, when a human population dies out, some of its culture may well be preserved. It can then be passed to other populations through diffusion or, in historical times, through written records. Such preserved cultural material includes knowledge and norms, even the unfit norms that contributed to the extinction of the population sharing them. One population's culture may even be revived, or at least partly so, by a succeeding (or conquering) population and transmitted to its later generations through enculturation. This occurred, for example, among the Bene Israel people of India, who had lost their ability to speak their traditional language of Hebrew and had to relearn it later from foreigners (Ausubel 1960, 221).

On the other hand, very "fit" social or cultural factors can be lost forever when a population that (uniquely) shares them becomes extinct without having transmitted them to another. You may recall from an introductory anthropology course that Ishi, the last member of the last existing Yahi population of California, died in 1916. At that moment, the Yana dialect of his childhood, which he did not use in his interactions with others, died as well (Kroeber 1961).[1] Thus, each time a human population becomes extinct, valuable, possibly survival-adapted cultural material might also disappear forever. Fortunately, there is a far smaller chance of this happening today than in the past, thanks in part to electronic media.

In any case, even though many human populations have become extinct and much cultural material has been lost, the species as a whole is surviving extremely well, at least by biological standards.

"Fitness," Adaptation, and the Direction of Evolution

The unique relationship that has been formed between human populations and their habitats is the result of the fact that people inherit traits in two distinct, although closely related, ways: biologically and culturally. Cultural heritage makes the growth and decline of human populations a far more complex matter than in other species, for the critical adaptation mechanisms and environmental changes that determine survival are, to an ever-increasing degree, under human control. Similarly, the persistence of social and cultural traits depends on conditions that might be unrelated to those that affect physical survival. Values, languages, artifacts, and customs have a life of their own that is relatively independent of the organisms that share them.

In view of these complicating factors, social researchers are especially concerned with two basic questions whose answers are taken for granted in organic theories:

1. Are the human populations that exist today better adapted than those that are extinct, and, if so, does this mean that the current social and cultural characteristics shared by members are also better adapted than in the past?
2. Are some existing peoples better adapted than others, and, if so, by what criteria: population size, growth rates, economic wealth? What are the traits that distinguish the fittest existing populations, and how do their societies and cultures differ from those of less fit populations?

In general, one can divide evolutionists into three main camps, or theoretical orientations, according to how they answer these questions: progressive, cyclical, and regressive (Lasch 1973, 1991).

Progressive Theory

Adam Smith, Auguste Comte, Herbert Spencer, Karl Marx, Emile Durkheim, Max Weber, and the majority of later theorists as well have generally agreed that (1) some existing populations and their social and cultural traits are better adapted than those of the past, and sociocultural evolution is essentially a process of improvement in adaptability, and (2) at the pinnacle of the evolutionary hierarchy are the peoples who share modern, Western culture. Although there have been significant disputes among those who accept these principles (especially along ideological lines), as a whole they make up the progressive mainstream of social evolutionists.

In his "Preface to *A Contribution to the Critique of the Political Economy*," Marx ([1859] 1969) argued that "in broad outlines Asiatic, ancient, Feudal, and modern bourgeois modes of production can be designated as *progressive* epochs in the economic formation of society" (504, my emphasis). For him and other radical and liberal theorists, populations that have reached the latest, most highly "bourgeois" stages are the fittest, and their survival proves it.

We should note here that the progress to which Marx was referring does not occur in an even, ever-increasing fashion. Rather, as the result of successive rises and overthrows of the modes of production, the overall drift of history is toward an increase in material culture. In any case, progressives, including Marxists, need not believe that everything is always getting "better."

Cyclical Theory

Among the major evolutionary models that diverge from this mainstream are the cyclical theories of Pitirim A. Sorokin (discussed later) and Vilfredo Pareto, the major figure in Italian social science at the turn of the twentieth century: "Pareto explicitly and emphatically rejected the theory of linear social evolution. . . . In its place he puts mainly a theory of cycles according to which social forms pass through a series of stages

Box 2.2 DIALECTICAL AND LINEAR EVOLUTIONARY MODELS

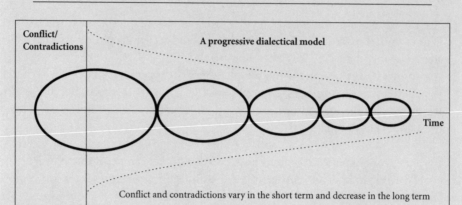

The **dialectic** is a mechanism that brings about change through the ironic success-leads-to-failure principle. Thus, in Karl Marx's **progressive** account (1867, 1: xxviii), Europe's feudal rulers contributed to their own downfall by inadvertently empowering their enemies, the bourgeoisie, over the course of centuries. At first, the Church and monarchy exploited this class for its commercial skills, which helped enrich their regimes. But in the process, the traders and financiers benefited from the patronage to the extent that they developed an ultimately decisive power base outside of the established system. By the end of the eighteenth century, they were able to overthrow the old regime thanks to its initial support.

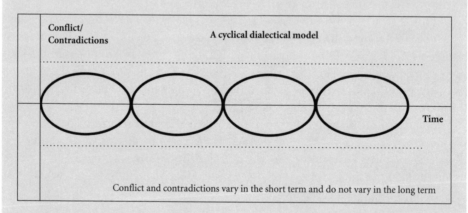

Cycles, on the other hand, are patterns that, according to Oswald Spengler, Vilfredo Pareto, and Pitirim Sorokin, are traced over longer or shorter periods of dialectical change, that is, all of these cyclical theories are also dialectical. The real difference between Marx's and, say, Pareto's account is that the former views the overall course of history as progressive, despite alternating periods of rise and decline, whereas the latter did not believe that things ever actually improve (or actually get worse, for that matter).

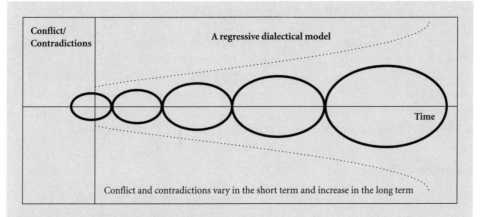

Plato and Sigmund Freud were dialecticians as well. But they saw the overall course of history as **regression**.

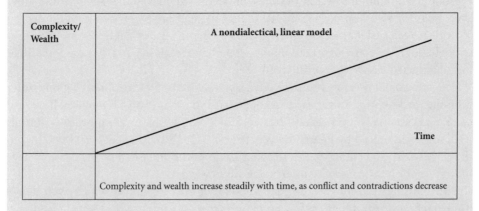

So-called **linear** models depict a course of evolution in which the rate of change is constant throughout the course of history. Usually associated with modernization theory, these are different from other types because they lack the characteristic stress on dialectic, conflict, and irony. However, modernization theorists, including functionalists such as Talcott Parsons (1951, 1964), recognize that events do accelerate and decelerate; and most agree that, in the very long term, the overall trend is acceleration (e.g., each successive age is shorter than the preceding one), not constancy as the shape of a line suggests. Thus, in comparison to other approaches, it is more accurate to think of modernization theory not as "linear" but rather as a nondialectical/progressive type (whereas the Marxist model is dialectical-progressive, Pareto's is dialectical-cyclical, and Freud's is dialectical-regressive). Sorokin is more difficult to classify, but overall his grand scheme is best viewed as cyclical to emphasize the recurring outcomes of the ideational-sensate dialectic.

which are *repeated again and again* in approximately the same order" (Parsons 1937, 178, my emphasis).

From this perspective, no era or culture can be designated as "higher" in any absolute sense. Processes akin to natural selection operate, through which some groups or ideas reign over others because they are more "fit," but only in the short run. Over longer periods, dominant groups become obsolete and fall victim to the very conditions that once worked to their advantage. As a result, we can expect to see periodic declines and falls, along with repetition of the same general styles and themes in different times and places.

Regressive Theory

Sigmund Freud, in his later sociological writings, departs even more sharply from the progressive position.[2] Viewing sociocultural evolution as an essentially regressive process, he argued that in the long run there has been significant deterioration in humanity's psychic conditions (for an extended discussion of this side of Freud, see Brown 1959). "If civilization is a necessary course of development from the family to humanity as a whole, then—as a result of inborn conflict arising from ambivalence, of the eternal struggle between the trends of love and death—there is inextricably bound up with it an increase in the sense of guilt, which will perhaps reach heights that the individual finds hard to tolerate" (Freud 1961, 80).

Freud was not the only observer of Western civilization to conclude that humanity is on the road to ruin. Conservative thinkers as far back as Plato have viewed historical change as essentially a process of deterioration. Numerous contemporary writers as well, some influenced by Freud and others not, from Oswald Spengler (see below) in the early twentieth century to Christopher Lasch in the latter half of the century, have taken exception to progressive interpretations of history.

Such disparity among leading theorists about the direction in which evolution is headed reflects the fact that, in the case of human beings, it is not clear how "advance" is to be measured. How do we judge that one culture is more highly evolved than another? What standard do we use to evaluate progress?

Spencer and other classic progressives used population size and growth rates, arguing that a large and robust population is healthiest and fittest. But, according to the development models used by most progressive theorists today, there is very little correlation between population size and advance. Moreover, the fastest growing populations now unexceptionably have the least developed economies. Marx pointed to the capacity of successive sociocultural systems (feudal, bourgeois, and so on) to generate surplus. But, as we are well aware, the societies with the greatest productive capacity also produce the most waste and do the greatest damage to the global ecosystem. Freud, writing during the early period of the Holocaust, stressed moral development, especially the burden of guilt and inner conflict different societies bear and express in destructive behavior. Yet the same civilization responsible for the Holocaust created in its aftermath the first viable framework for international representative government and the first-ever doctrine of universal human rights.

Progress, Complexity, and Race

Progressive evolutionism stresses that, as populations grow, they tend to undergo an increase in sociocultural complexity and structural differentiation and that this trend is tied to survival. Thus, the various "ages" through which *Homo sapiens* has passed since the extinction of other species of *Homo* represent increasing levels of complexity, progressive steps toward the creation of today's highly bureaucratic, diverse societies. The most recent, Historical Age, which began between five and ten thousand years ago, is marked by an evolutionary quantum leap in these factors made possible by agricultural revolution and the rise of impersonal, secondary relationships. According to this conception, just as plant and animal species have become more complex and habitats more differentiated during the course of the geological eons, human populations have followed the same pattern over the sociocultural ages. The ones that proved to be the "fittest" are today the most "highly" evolved. The still-surviving populations with simple, homogenous, and undifferentiated societies and cultures, the less "fit," occupy a "lower" position on the evolutionary scale.

It is this specific interpretation that leaves progressive evolutionism most open to criticism as a highly ethnocentric theory. Although this critique is most frequently leveled at Spencer's work, it applies just as readily to many of Spencer's contemporaries, as well as to more recent progressive theorists. It is unlikely that it is just a coincidence that the evolutionary perspective favored by social scientists who are members of the most complex, industrial societies happens to identify the most complex, industrial societies as the most "highly" evolved. And is it not arguments just like this, which views non-European people as "primitive," that have been used to justify conquest, colonialism, and imperialism?

One of the main flaws in this argument is that it assumes increasing complexity to be the *only* legitimate type of evolutionary advantage. "Increasing social complexity or differentiation is a basic evolutionary process. . . . But it is only one of numerous important evolutionary processes including 'dedifferentiation'" (Sanderson 2007, 86). With this in mind, one could just as easily view the societies or the sociocultural traits and institutions that have changed the *least* over the centuries and millennia as the ones best adapted to their environments. Thus, the most "primitive" people who have the least complex social systems—such as the Basarwa (Bushmen) of southern Africa—have proved by their survival that they are the "fittest."

A major discrepancy between the organic model and superorganic reality is apparent here. Darwin viewed the evolution of organisms as a very long-term process of increasing complexity, diversity, and differentiation over millions of years. Relying on the then-recent discoveries of the geologist Charles Lyell, he concluded that the earliest populated environments (about two billion years ago) had low levels of biological diversity and that the few relatively similar niches were occupied by simple, undifferentiated organisms. Over the very long course of geological time, the ecological systems became more complex, as did the new species that evolved to replace the older, less complex, and less well-adapted ones.

When he shipped out aboard the *Beagle*, Darwin took with him a copy of Lyell's first volume of the *Principles of Geology*. . . . Accepting Lyell's gradualist notion of geological change, Darwin began to look at the world around him, both animate and inanimate, in similar terms. Lyell and Darwin met soon after the return of the *Beagle* to England, and they soon became close friends, although Lyell would never fully accept Darwin's theory of evolution. (Treasures of the American Philosophical Society, www.amphilsoc.org/library/exhibits/treasures/darwin.htm)

At the dawn of the Paleolithic Age, our highly complex species appeared on the scene. So the entirety of the span of sociocultural evolution has occurred in a fraction of the time biologists allow for species to emerge, develop, and decline, and all of it with no substantial changes in the organism itself.

Race and Evolution

In order to account for this difference, the earliest theorists employed the concept of race, arguing that sociocultural evolution occurs at the level of organically distinct "subspecies," over centuries rather than eons. Many of the classic evolutionists believed that a close and natural connection exists between physical characteristics and sociocultural traits, observing that people who look alike also act and think in the same ways. Because nonhuman species struggle to dominate one another, they reasoned, biologically uniform groups of people must be involved in a similar process.

Influenced heavily by the classification scheme of Carolus Linneaus[3] and later by Robert Knox (1862) and Count Joseph Gobineau (Biddes 1970), this observation gave rise to the contemporary concept of "race." Linneaus, Knox, and Gobineau were largely responsible for the creation of the five familiar major categories: Caucasoid, Mongoloid, Amerind, Negroid, and Australoid (because of their origin in Asia, Amerinds are often classified as a branch of Mongoloid).

These categories correspond to the indigenous populations within the five general geographical areas that had very little or no contact with one another before the late fifteenth century: Europe, Asia, the Americas, Africa, and Polynesia. They have been further divided into subgroups and sometimes sub-subgroups, representing sets of populations within the larger areas that were relatively, but not absolutely, isolated from one another. For example, Alpine and Mediterranean were recognized as subraces of the larger Caucasoid group (one of the most widely used models was that summarized by anthropologist E. Adamson Hoebel [1966, 216–18]).

This categorization allowed the early evolutionists to conclude that the observed diversity of societies and cultures corresponded to the various racial categories and subcategories and that the former could be explained by the latter: a people's level of sociocultural evolution reflects the degree of evolutionary advance of their race.

With the benefit of research in genetics and related fields,[4] contemporary social scientists are now aware that so-called racial differences are highly relative (see Barkan 1992; Massin 1996; Weinstein and Stehr 1999). In fact, "Although the person on the street may still believe that races are biologically real, science has proven otherwise"

(Andreasen 1998, 200). The more isolated a population or subpopulation, the more likely it is to be endogamous, or "in-breeding." In such circumstances, a common gene pool is established over the course of generations, resulting in a high degree of physical similarity among members, along with considerable differences between them and members of other populations. The more inaccessible two populations are relative to each other, the less their members will share genetic material and associated physical characteristics.

"Races" and "subraces" are, thus, actually groupings of populations that have been in some contact with one another for a number of generations but have been inaccessible to outside populations.[5] Once new contacts are established, circumstances are right for previously distinct gene pools to become mixed. When this occurs, racial barriers disappear. This is because they never really existed in the first place but were instead a reflection of the absence of the opportunity to cross them. The more that two formerly separate populations interact (including those from different "racial" groupings) over the generations, the more likely it is that their members will come to resemble one another physically. It is important to stress that none of this applies to the organic evolution of species because under natural conditions it is impossible for two or more populations of different species to exchange genetic material.[6]

From Many Evolutions to One

The colonial era was crucial because, prior to it, geographically separate populations each pursued relatively independent courses of sociocultural change. There were many separate tracks of evolution occurring at the same time, depending on where a population was located. In some places (i.e., industrializing Europe), the process had reached the most "advanced" stage, while elsewhere (the yet-to-be-explored areas) circumstances had slowed or stopped the process at "lower" stages. The discovery of people who were physically very different from Europeans and whose sociocultural systems were apparently lower on the evolutionary scale gave major impetus to race science (and racism). As colonization extended farther and deeper into formerly unknown territories, the data to support the race/evolution connection—and "proof" that European society was more advanced—accumulated (see Lindqvist 1996). For world system theorists, however, "advance" in this context refers, in fact, not to race but rather to political-economic advantage in a global power relationship that began centuries ago.

The colonial experience served to connect humanity in a way that was unprecedented.[7] Since those times, people everywhere have increasingly become partners in a single, general evolutionary trend. Today, we are experiencing an especially critical, revolutionary period in this trend. Indeed, the main effects of globalization, including the conflict inherent in the inequalities between the more and less modernized peoples, probably lie in the future.

Whether or not we choose to label it "evolution," the kind of change witnessed today clearly is superorganic: its outcome is not determined by genetic factors, nor is it beyond the reach of planned institutional change, social movements, or higher-order impacts. The human population is rapidly becoming an interacting unit, aided significantly today by electronic media and the extensive networks of technology-mediated relationships they make possible. But this phenomenon is occurring in large measure because relevant groups and individuals mean for it to happen and are engaged in activities designed to bring it about. This, in turn, has helped motivate other groups and individuals to attempt to combat, reverse, or redirect the apparently inevitable march toward globalization.

Cyclical Theories

Progressive theorists, whether Marxists, modernizers, or another type, emphasize the cumulative, ultimately positive effects of growth, complexity, and the accumulation of wealth. In contrast, and often in conscious opposition to the progressive orientation, several social scientists have developed cyclical theories. In these, innovations are credited with leading temporarily to progress (according to specific measures such as wealth or control over natural forces) but not indefinitely. Rather, at some point, the process of innovation ceases being effective, a dialectic sets in, and new developments bring deterioration.[8] However, it is argued, things can deteriorate only so far before reaching a negative limit. At that point, innovations begin to bring progress once more. This continues for a while, until deterioration begins again. Different stages in the cycle differ in style and specifics, but over the long run there is neither cumulative advance nor deterioration. Rather, evolutionary processes ultimately return us to the same levels as in the past.

Various cyclical theories differ in detail, but all stress this quality of recurrence of traits as change is observed over longer periods (Sorokin 1947). Spengler's multivolume study of *The Decline of the West* (1926–1928) has been cited often for his argument that societies naturally go through successive cycles of growth, conservatism, and decadence and that Europe is in the final stage of its destined course. Pareto used a similar principle based on the writings of Machiavelli in a still-influential account of political change (Pareto [1901] 1968). Known as the theory of "the circulation of elites," it focuses on how ruling classes replace one another in an alternating manner.

Also included among cyclical theorists is one of the most prolific and most controversial sociologists of our time, Sorokin (Allen 1963; Johnston 1995, 1998; Matter 1974; Schneider 1964; Sorokin 1964). Through the course of many years of research, Sorokin developed a direct alternative to progressive evolutionary views. The main difference between Sorokin and his mainstream contemporaries was his assumption that neither capitalist industrialization nor socialism represented authentic "advances" in the human condition (Sorokin 1962). In fact, Sorokin's theory explains Marxism and modernization theory as two versions of materialism, themselves the product of a specific type of culture, valid only in relation to certain value judgments that are not universal.

Sorokin's Theory of Social and Cultural Dynamics

According to Sorokin, cultures evolve within fairly strict limits. At a given time, dominant beliefs and practices tend to reflect a general style or pattern, depending on the relative importance of ideals as opposed to the tangible evidence of the senses. Critical changes occur when one or another of these tendencies has reached its limits and the other begins to grow. Because even the most spiritual people need to eat, and even materialists have ideals, no "pure" cultural type is possible: all existing cultures contain a mixture of both elements. Thus, a point will always be reached at which a culture's dominant pattern is no longer effective and must temper or compromise with its opposite. This point of "saturation" marks the beginning of a new era, in which the former opposition takes over. During the course of decades, as cultures pass from one to another pattern, we note a rhythm of alternating domination and subordination between the nonmaterial and material worlds.

The cyclical quality of Sorokin's theory lies in the ordering of major periods. Complex contemporary cultures are in a highly materialistic, critical period, an era ripe for large-scale changes (Sorokin 1948, 1951). If the future follows past patterns, he argued, we are headed for a new age in which material culture will not be so highly valued and when we will not necessarily view the populations with the most conquest-oriented technologies as the most advanced. Although specific cultures clearly also vary in relation to other factors such as level of societal complexity, wealth, or population growth, the most consequential changes are not in these. Rather, the major stages are marked by the relative dominance of material culture in general, in comparison to values and other nonmaterial traits. Significantly, this can occur in cultures and civilizations at any level of industrial advance.

At one extreme, we find eras (such as the current one) in which material artifacts, their possession, and their development assume primary cultural priority. Material culture is the main concern in social relations from family ties to international affairs.

Things are considered the ultimate reality, and they dominate over ideas, which are viewed as derivative. Sorokin referred to these periods as highly *sensate*. At the other extreme are eras in which ideals and fundamental human values (truth, beauty, and justice) prevail as the ultimate reality and material things are viewed as secondary or derivative. These are referred to as highly *ideational* periods. Finally, between sensate and ideational eras, Sorokin discerned transitional periods that are characterized by a relative balance between the extreme types. These are referred to as *idealistic*.

Each of these stages is then subdivided into early, middle, and late eras. To underscore that he did not subscribe to the doctrine that things are meaningfully "better" today than in the past, Sorokin characterized the most recent period in European or U.S. history as a late or *cynical* sensate culture. Such a culture "encourages hypocritical conformity and facile adaptation in any way that will yield a 'payoff'" (Schneider 1975a, 83).

Sorokin and His Critics

As noted, Sorokin presently occupies an ambiguous place in the history of social science. He was involved in a political battle with some of his colleagues at Harvard University that eventuated in the temporary disbanding of the university's sociology department, the department that he had founded and chaired for some twenty years. In 1963, after being overlooked by the American Sociological Association's official nominating committee, he became the only person ever to be elected president of the organization as a write-in candidate (Johnston 1987). He had many admirers, but because his criticism of those with whom he disagreed was often less than diplomatic, he also had many foes.

The fact that political and personal conflicts have placed him outside the sociological mainstream is unfortunate because he was a brilliant man who had a great deal to say to people today. For reasons both legitimate and questionable, his work has been challenged on many fronts. Some critics have argued that the stages and cycles are merely the product of his imagination and of a highly selective interpretation of the data. Saturation and related mechanisms that Sorokin used to explain how one stage turns into another have been derided as mystical forces that have no basis in scientific fact.

His major theory of sociocultural change has been characterized as largely speculative, as pseudo-science, and as evaluative rather than descriptive. Some have argued that it is essentially a conservative (even religious) ideology based on an interest-serving use of evidence to prove that our age is hopelessly lost from a spiritual point of view. He was accused of using data and lengthy rational arguments to obscure reality rather than to clarify it, overwhelming his readers with clever intellectual tricks to prove a doubtful thesis by wearing them out with the sheer volume of information.

Sorokin was certainly one of the most productive (if not the most productive) writers of social science ever: He authored dozens of scholarly books and monographs along with hundreds of articles, as well as three autobiographies and several works of fiction. He was an active participant in the Russian Revolution on what turned out to be the wrong (Menshevik) side. He was imprisoned and exiled by the Bolsheviks but was personally pardoned by no less a figure than V. I. Lenin. In his adopted home in the United States, he was known as one of the most outspoken opponents of the excesses of our materialistic era. In fact, his major work, *Social and Cultural Dynamics* (1962), represents a mere fraction of his output, although nearly all of the criticism leveled against him focuses on it.

Sorokin believed he was sorely misunderstood by his critics. He felt they wrongly accused him of scholarly errors that he did not in fact commit, such as not being "empirical" enough, despite the fact that the main impression one gets from reading his *Dynamics* is that a large quantity of data was used to support the arguments. He was quite right in pointing out that the criticism was invariably based on a very selective reading of his vast works.

Inevitability versus Tendency in Evolutionary Theory

In fact, it is not difficult to read into Sorokin's stage theory the idea that people have no choice about where cultural change is headed. Thus, if our culture happens to be in a late sensate era, then the next step is certainly toward an idealistic transition and then early ideationalism. We cannot stay late sensate forever, we cannot go "back" to an early sensate age of discovery, and we cannot "leap ahead" to a late ideational golden age without passing through intervening stages in the cycle.

Sorokin and cyclical theory are not alone in this regard. Marxism, modernization theory, and the world system perspective have all been criticized because they suggest that certain outcomes of historical processes are inevitable (Horowitz 1980). For example, history is "on the side" of a transition from capitalism to socialism or all societies will *surely* become industrialized and urbanized.

The main problem with evolutionary theories, whether their focus is on repeating cycles as in Sorokin's case or the progressive stages of Marxism and modernization theory, is that they often appear not to account for intentional social change: legislation, institutional planning, technological innovation, and social movements. These kinds of activities are designed to bring about the changes we desire, not those that *must* occur according to evolutionary principles. Are such attempts to change the world on purpose all futile? Are the laws we pass, the movements we support or oppose, and the innovations that are created already determined in advance by cultural forces beyond our control? Are we, in short, destined to move to a certain kind of society and culture regardless of what we plan, seek to achieve, and do?

The notion of inevitable evolutionary stages and cultural cycles disregards the superorganic character of social life. It fails to account for the fact that people create their own laws that affect the production, distribution, and alteration of cultural items. People abide by their laws, more or less, and thus their beliefs and practices form patterns that are observed and incorporated into the theories of social scientists. But to believe that they are governed by the scientific laws thus created (as a falling object is "governed" by the laws of gravity) is to misunderstand why people act and change in patterned ways: because they want to achieve certain outcomes and to avoid others.

No doubt, the outcomes of our intentions often differ from and reverberate far beyond what we intend. But, through legislation, planning, and social movements, we can intend to modify the extent to which our cultures are sensate, our economies capitalistic, and our societies industrialized, and to some extent, we do get what we want. If the theories of cycles or stages were literally realized, then sociocultural change would be a closed, self-contained process. A particular population, such as that of the contemporary United States, would experience a certain transition to the next era, in sequence and regardless of what happens in other populations. The diffusion of ideas or artifacts into the culture from outside could have no significant evolutionary effect. No major war, certainly a nuclear war, could occur to upset the inevitable processes of accumulation, class struggle, or saturation.

Of course, we can never discount war, foreign influence, and other unanticipated possibilities. In fact, such "disturbances" have occurred routinely throughout the course of history. In this light, today's social change theorists are aware that we cannot literally project the patterns observed in the past into the future, as Sorokin (1964) himself acknowledged in defense of his particular theory. Yet historical trends do leave an indelible imprint on the course of later events. Sociocultural evolution does not proceed with certainty but is affected by what is probable and what is unlikely, by tendencies in human nature (see my comments on prophecy in chapter 1).

We choose, plan, legislate, and join movements, but these activities always occur within a particular sociocultural context. This includes the heritage of generations, the historical (and even prehistoric) accumulation of beliefs, practices, and artifacts. The weight of tradition is very heavy. The manner in which people set goals, make plans, and seek to change things is shaped by this context: the force of moral authority, the fear of negative sanctions, group loyalties, and all of the other social control mechanisms bring about high degrees of conformity to prevailing norms and values. This force extends even to the way we conceive of changing society.

Thus, in a sensate era, social movements are likely to occur in sensate style, even if their overt goal may be to restore idealism. The most radical antimodernist, anti-Western organizations, such as al Qaeda (the group responsible for the September 11 attack on the United States), get their messages to their followers with the help of the most modern Western technologies. According to Rohan Gunaratna (2002), "Al Qaeda is essentially a modern organisation, one that exploits up to date technology for its own ends, relying on satellite phones, laptop computers, encrypted communications websites for hiding messages, and the like" (11).

We surely have choices concerning how we will go about reforming or even revolutionizing our contemporary economic systems. But if these systems are at a highly advanced stage of capitalism, some alternatives are unthinkable, if not impossible, such as returning to a pastoral economy. Such tendencies make it possible to anticipate what courses of events are more likely, but they do not automatically determine what "must" happen next.

We refer to events as "likely to occur" because, although heavy, the weight of tradition is not irresistible. In any era, individual and collective ideas and practices can deviate from the mainstream by as much as 180 degrees, although such a turnaround is improbable. Antimodernist leaders might attempt to organize without telephones or cars (established counter-communities, such as the Old Order Amish people, continue to reject these innovations). However, cultural forces make "abnormal" change very difficult. Great imagination and creativity, or great despair, are required to make a true break with the momentum of tradition.

Creative Altruism and the "Third Way"

Sorokin personally believed in making such an imaginative break with the tendencies of one's own era. In his later years at Harvard University, he sought to create a social movement that would combat cynical sensate culture and its emphasis on domination, egoism, and self-gratification. "The practice of kindness and love is one of the best therapies for many mental disorders; for the elimination of sorrow, loneliness and unhappiness; for the mitigation of hatred and other antisocial tendencies; and, above all, for the ennoblement of human personality, for release in man of his creative forces, and for the attainment of union with God and peace with oneself, others, and the universe" (Sorokin 1948, 196).

In February 1949, Sorokin and his colleagues established the Harvard Research Center in Creative Altruism, with the support of philanthropist Eli Lilly and the Lilly Foundation (Johnston 1998, 2, 18–19; Matter 1974, xiii–xiv). The center's purpose was to promote planned cultural change, and under its auspices Sorokin wrote several books and articles on the subject (Sorokin 1950, 1954a, 1954b). In this work, he harked back to the democratic ideals of Saint-Simon and Comte (who introduced the terms *altruism* and *egoism* into social science)[9] and to Spencer's discovery of the superorganic realm.

Creative altruism is the conscious and purposeful insertion of the universal ideal of helping others, the Golden Rule, into planned change (see box 2.3). The strategy was developed on the basis of Sorokin's decades of unparalleled research and theorizing about the origins, problems, and prospects of our age, and it incorporates his distinctive terminology (*sensate*, *saturation*, and so on) along with his concern about the excesses of materialism, whether Marxist or bourgeois.

The specific idea of creative altruism clearly is the product of a somewhat marginal approach to the problems of sociocultural evolution. However, in its emphasis on prosocial behavior and spirituality and in its rejection of both traditional capitalistic and socialistic visions of the future, it is one among many attempts, past and present, to develop a "third way" to planned sociocultural change. Several more recent social scientists have come to similar conclusions as Sorokin's, although most are not cyclical theorists, nor do all necessarily use the term *altruism*.

Among those who continue to conduct groundbreaking research on altruism is Kristen Renwick Monroe (1996, 2001). Her work is of special interest because she has combined the study of altruism with the ongoing investigation of what was characterized in chapter 1 as the irony of moral progress during the Holocaust, that is, the selfless rescue of Jews and members of other persecuted groups during the Holocaust (Monroe, Barton, and Klingermann 1990; see also Fogelman 1994; Penner 1995). Others working in this field include the anthropologist Lionel Tiger, the influential planned change advocate Amitai Etzioni (1991), and—during an earlier generation—the founders of the democratic planning approach, Karl Mannheim (1950) and Philip Selznick (1949; their work is discussed in chapter 13 in this book).[10]

This movement is based on an explicit value judgment, that is, when we observe as scientists the awesome advantages that material prosperity—wealth, political power, and land—give to the few to exploit the many, we are right to object. For those who study social and cultural change, such inequities as slavery, caste, feudal bondage, and dictatorial government offend a universal sense of justice. As human beings, we are active participants in making social change, whether or not we wish to be, and our value commitments concerning justice and freedom ought to guide our actions as applied scientists. For Sorokin and others, this moral sense comes with the job of social scientist, and it should not be denied or denigrated as a compromise of scientific principles. As Comte argued some 150 years ago, one can and should be both scientific and concerned about the well-being of others (for a recent statement of these principles that is aimed at undergraduate sociology students, see Du Bois and Wright 2001).

Creative altruism rejects the hardheaded idea that inequity is somehow natural or inevitable, viewing it as merely part of the ideology of social Darwinism. Those who believe that somehow the price of progress is always domination of the many by the few are, of course, entitled to their opinion. But it is just that—an opinion—and it does not justify egoism. Selfishness is neither more nor less natural than altruism. Humans know and understand altruism, as do no other animals. This trait is part of our cultural heritage, not an evolutionary weakness as social Darwinism suggested.

Similarly, there are no laws of human nature that make it necessary for government to be run by an elite few who have special "racial" characteristics, or who are in possession of the true road map to the future. The Golden Rule, when applied to political relations, translates to equal rights for all members of society and an equal say in the decisions that affect their lives, that is, democracy. Many leaders, in Sorokin's time and ours, have argued that difficult circumstances "temporarily" require autocratic government. But this, too, is ideology, not evolutionary necessity. Autocracy is no more natural than democracy; rather, both are possibilities that are subject to a substantial degree of social engineering.

Those who seriously study social and cultural change have observed much injustice in the world and are intuitively offended by it. But, try as they have, no one has been able to prove either that such evils will always be with us or that they will "inevitably" be eliminated. Moral progress is possible, but there are no unconditional laws of history that will unerringly lead us to the downfall of unjust and exploitative social institutions. This view is contrary to the principles of Marxism-Leninism, which argue that The Party does have The Answer—and I think that Sorokin intended the contrast. We have made substantial strides since the days of slavery and feudalism against the persistent, patterned failure of people to live up to the Golden Rule. And we clearly have regressed at times, as well. But, above all, creative altruism stresses that the direction in which we will continue is not preordained. Rather, it is a matter of will and choice.

The scientific study of sociocultural evolution reveals that no doctrine, no party, and no system possess the exclusive secret of moral progress. Rather, moral progress depends on the outcome of collective, conscientious decision making, a reordering of our value priorities that today must involve each and every citizen of the world system.

All claims that a "solution" is the exclusive property of one party, group, or school of thought should be viewed as self-serving and ultimately egoistic.

One may, of course, agree or disagree with such proposals, for they are very much in the realm of values and policy, not fact. Yet they are strongly science based, and for this reason I believe they are worth your consideration. The concept of creative altruism (or whatever words one chooses to use) articulates well with the trends of democratization, globalization, and the information revolution that are now shaping the future, as later chapters illustrate. Moreover, at its 2009 meeting, more than forty years after the death of Sorokin, the American Sociological Association established a Section on Altruism and Social Solidarity (see Jeffries et al. 2007). In this respect, it may be the next concept whose time has come—again (see Hourani 1994; Payne 1995; Wuthnow 1995).

Summary

This chapter has focused on evolutionary theory, beginning with a summary of the principles of biological evolution. Because social and cultural change occurs within and between populations of organisms, biological evolution is an essential part of the

Box 2.3 THE GOLDEN RULE: A CULTURAL UNIVERSAL

All the great humanitarian religions are based on a principle similar to the Golden Rule. This is not a side issue but rather the heart of the major religions.

You shall love your neighbor as yourself.
Judaism and Christianity, the Bible, Leviticus 19:18, Matthew 22:36–40

According to the legendary Rabbi Hillel, the **Jewish** faith says, "What is hateful to you, do not do to your fellowman. This is the entire Law; all the rest is commentary."

Christians say, "Do unto others as you would have them do onto you."
Jesus said, "You shall love the Lord your God with all your heart, and with all your soul, and with all your mind. This is the great and first commandment. And a second is like it. You shall love your neighbor as yourself. On these two commandments depend all the law and the prophets."

Islam says, "No one of you is a believer until he desires for his brother that which he desires for himself."

Confucianism says the same thing: "Do not impose on others what you yourself do not desire."

To the **Hindu**, "This is the sum of duty; do naught onto others what you would not have them do unto you."

Buddhism says, "Hurt not others in ways that you yourself would find hurtful."

Taoism says, "Regard your neighbor's gain as your gain, and your neighbor's loss as your own loss."

A native **Yoruba** Proverb in Nigeria, Africa, says, "One going to take a pointed stick to pinch a baby bird should first try it on himself to feel how it hurts."

Even the **Wiccan** tradition of witchcraft says, "And it harm none, do what thou wilt."

Source: Compiled by William Du Bois.

human condition. Beyond this, however, many social scientists have viewed social and cultural change as if it were biological evolution, that is, they have mistakenly extended an organic metaphor to describe, as opposed to suggest, a superorganic process. The paleontologist George Gaylord Simpson has summarized this use of metaphor (or "analogy") and its shortcomings, noting that sociocultural evolution is itself a result of organic evolution, but it is something entirely different in kind.

> Although it is semantically correct and scientifically enlightening to call both "evolution," it is extremely important to recognize the difference in kind makes this in large part an analogy and not a straight equivalence. We may expect to find, and do find, that many general principles of evolution apply analogously to the two, but it is invalid and indeed dangerous to assume that equivalent evolutionary principles operate throughout the two and that principles discovered regarding one may forth with be applied to interpretation of the other. This fallacious sort of transfer is usually attempted from the field of biology to that of sociology. (Simpson 1951, 141)

The evolutionary approach has played a prominent role in sociology, anthropology, and other disciplines. It is most familiar as a progressive doctrine that stresses a long-term "advance" through cumulative growth and increasing complexity. It is integral to the two main schools of thought on long-term change, Marxism and modernization theory, but it also is incorporated in most alternative perspectives, such as the cyclical and the regressive models. Nevertheless, because sociocultural evolution essentially is a metaphor that does not exactly fit the reality to which it is applied, the approach leaves considerable scope for value judgments.

In particular, the principles of organic evolution have been used to give the appearance that a scientific basis exists for determining that some peoples are naturally superior or "more highly evolved" than others, whereas this is not the case. The best known of these polemical uses is social Darwinism (and its underlying principle of egoism), employed by Spencer and other evolutionists to this day. Critics of the controversial field of sociobiology claim that it has a similar, ideological bias (see Montagu 1980).

As a contrast to the evolutionary mainstream, the chapter also considered the work of Sorokin. Sorokin developed his comprehensive cyclical theory and the related idea of creative altruism in conscious opposition to Spencer's and other progressive models. This suggests that if we understand sociocultural evolution broadly enough, as a superorganic, partly intentional process in which there are no guarantees of progress or advance, the concept is worth saving. This is because, despite its limitations, evolutionary thought has revealed many truths about social and cultural change, including the very important historical correlation between industrial wealth, social complexity, and materialist values. It remains important because this correlation will almost certainly be the defining force in the creation of tomorrow's global society.

Relevant Websites

http://socio.ch/evo/index_evo.htm
This site has a wealth of information on social and cultural evolution, along with several links to bibliographical material, biographies, and online discussions on the subject.

www.montagu.org/home.htm
Home page of the Ashley Montagu Institute.

http://anthropology.si.edu/repatriation/projects/ishi.htm
This is the site dedicated to Ishi by the National Museum of Natural History, Smithsonian Institution.

http://library2.usask.ca/sorokin/correspondence/hrcca
This site is part of the University of Saskatchewan's Pitirim A. Sorokin Collection detailing the Harvard Research Center in Creative Altruism, as well as Sorokin's works and autobiography.

www.ushmm.org/
The site of the U.S. Holocaust Memorial Museum, Smithsonian Institution, contains a comprehensive link on race science.

www.anu.edu.au/polsci/marx/marx.html
www.emile-durkheim.com/
www.faculty.rsu.edu/~felwell/Theorists/Weber/Whome.htm
These three sites feature Marx, Durkheim, and Weber, respectively. The first is maintained by Australian National University and the second by the University of Illinois.

www.fordham.edu/halsall/mod/wallerstein.html
This comprehensive sourcebook on world system theory is posted at Fordham University.

www.altruisticlove.org/
This site, maintained by the Center for Altruistic Love at Humboldt State University, includes work by Professors Emeriti Pearl Oliner and Samuel Oliner.

PART

II

The Components of Change

IN THE PRECEDING two chapters, our emphasis was on the ways in which human societies are driven by highly complex forces. In general, these forces are far more subtle and elusive than those governing physical systems or even organic evolution. It was also stressed that today change is more common and more rapid than at any time in the past. This part, consisting of three chapters, examines some basic tools used by social scientists to help make sense of this unprecedented complexity and instability.

The chapters divide collective change into its three main components: (1) the demographic component, featuring population processes and transitions; (2) the cultural component, focusing on values, religion, and language; and (3) the social component, highlighting the shift from primary to secondary and tertiary relations. All three chapters also consider the work of some of the classic demographers, anthropologists, and sociologists, including Thomas Malthus, Karl Marx, Max Weber, Emile Durkheim, Alfred L. Kroeber, and Robert Redfield, not just as social scientists but also as students of change.

Chapter 3, on population, includes a discussion of Malthus's still-influential "laws" and a summary of one of the most consequential trends in contemporary history, the European demographic transition. This trend underlies many of the deepest inequalities between today's more and less developed areas of the world. Chapter 4 then considers some of the major principles of cultural change, including the sacred/secular dimension, the central paired concept of tradition and modernity, and the development and regulation of language. Chapter 5 completes the survey of the components of change with a look at how social relationships vary over time, particularly at the macrolevel. In the course of discussing population, culture, and society, one should remember that the three components are not separate in reality. Rather, they always change together, sometimes in harmony and sometimes in conflict, affecting one another in significant ways. The crucial interconnections among them are set aside temporarily here to emphasize the distinctive impacts of each. The following part, "The Engines of Change," concentrates specifically on how the three combine to shape our future worlds.

CHAPTER
3

Population Growth and Demographic Transition

THE DEMOGRAPHIC component of change consists of variations in the size, composition, and geographical distribution of aggregates of human beings, especially the kinds of aggregates referred to as "populations." The science of population is known as *demography*, from the Greek root *demos* meaning "the people" (similarly, *population* is from the Latin world *populus*, which also means "people"). This is the same root as in the word *democracy*, and there is a close connection between the two concepts, including the fact that effective democracy requires free access to accurate demographic information. The first section of this chapter introduces several demographic terms and principles, which are then used to examine (1) how populations change and (2) the principal causes and consequences of such changes.

In many respects, the demographic component is the most basic and least abstract of the three. Cultural and social changes include variations in relationships, institutions, values, styles, and other invisible entities. In contrast, demographers are concerned with concrete issues such as how many people live in a certain area, how many of them are young or old, whether their numbers have increased or decreased between two dates, and other more readily observable aspects of collective life. Demographic data are the starting point of social scientific research, that is, they refer to facts about actual human beings. Unlike psychology or history, however, the demographic focus is not on discrete individuals with unique personalities but rather on people as members of larger wholes: populations, subpopulations, cohorts (groups of individuals born at the same time), and other demographic aggregates.

Many demographic principles apply equally well to any species of animal. In this respect, they serve to remind us that ultimately social science is a branch of zoology and that people, like their anthropoid cousins, are conditioned to a considerable extent by their animal nature. Yet, among humans, the demographic imperatives are always combined with social and cultural factors, making us rather unusual anthropoids: "apes with angel glands," as the poet Leonard Cohen once put it.[1]

There are many ways in which the demographic component interacts with the process of globalization and affects current concerns about the process. Perhaps the most consequential among these are the magnitude and implications of the relative size and growth rates of the less industrialized, Third World nations. Following a survey of basic principles, we turn to these larger questions.

Populations as Units of Observation

A population (or "naturally occurring human population" in full) has three defining features that set it apart from other types of aggregates: (1) it is relatively endogamous, (2) it occupies a common territory, and (3) it is structured along biological, social, and cultural dimensions. Populations can be divided into subpopulations according to one or more of several criteria, including gender, region, social class, and age.

Much of the complexity in the study of social and cultural change stems from the great variety of possible subjects to research. This is even more evident when we consider how the organic and superorganic intermingle in human systems. Consequently, there are many potential units of observation whose variation can be studied, such as individuals, groups, "races," cultures, and societies. By beginning with the demographic component, however, we can greatly simplify this problem, for we see that, at root, *all collective changes occur within and between populations.*

Selecting the appropriate unit of observation is a necessary part of any scientific research. As Pitirim A. Sorokin (1947) noted, "Without the unit or the logical subject, no process, no dynamic state generally, is observable, thinkable, or describable . . . some unit, as a logical subject, change, or modification of which we assert, must be given" (53). In other words, choice of unit is important because it determines which variables and attributes are to be observed and measured. When social scientists use a population or another kind of aggregate as a unit of analysis, they are holding constant the fact that it is the population of interest and none other. They then observe changes in the variables that refer to it (rather than to individual persons, for example).

Some of these changes are strictly demographic and predominately biological, such as growth or decline in the size of a population, expansion or contraction in its geographical distribution, and shifts in the average age of its members. These processes are measured by variables such as number of individuals and rates of vital events, and they are common to all organisms.

But human populations also change with respect to the social relationships, groups, and institutions in which members participate. These are specifically superorganic changes, and they include such events as a shift in the occupational status of teachers. Note that an instance of superorganic change, such as upward mobility for teachers, is something that happens to a population, although it is experienced by individuals. That is, our unit of analysis remains the population, whether we are studying its birth rates or its occupational mobility rates.

Some changes that occur to populations are, strictly speaking, part of the culture(s) shared by members. A significant change that has been underway in Canada and Quebec for several years is illustrative: the change in laws regarding language. In a landmark series of legislative acts and judicial review that began in 1989, the province of Quebec has restricted the use of languages other than French on public signs and billboards. This is certainly a cultural shift. Yet, we stress, it is occurring in the lives of members of the populations of Quebec and Canada (of which the province remains a unique part).

I mentioned that by focusing on a population as our unit, we assume it to be constant. But even this is a relative matter, as its size and other demographic attributes also are varying over time. Quebec's population, in particular, in recent years has experienced an unprecedented decline in birth rates along with increasing rates of international immigration. These have clearly affected all aspects of the lives of its members, including their attitudes toward language.

A major advantage of studying populations as units is that they have a concrete, observable existence in time and space. Yet, like the less tangible social and cultural components, they are definitely collective phenomena. Thus, they help keep the social scientific perspective in focus and maintain a (logical) separation between the interpersonal and the biographical levels of change.

Many millions of individual lives were swept up into the four critical episodes introduced in chapter 1, yet each also was a massive aggregate event. The discussion of the Holocaust highlighted the changes that occurred during World War II in Jewish and other European populations and subpopulations. Some of these were strictly demographic, others social, and others cultural. The rise of the Third World nations consisted of a series of major demographic (as well as social and cultural) transformations in hundreds of local populations and subpopulations of Asia and Africa (and, in parallel ways, of Latin America as well). The U.S. Civil Rights movement (1954–1968) was a dynamic episode in the relations within and between ethnically distinct subpopulations of African and European Americans. And the fall of Communism happened to dozens of populations and subpopulations in Central and Eastern Europe and Northern Asia.[2]

Population Size and Growth

The one characteristic shared by all populations, cohorts, and other aggregates, and the most basic demographic variable, is size. It is measured simply as the number of individuals included, and it can range from two to millions or billions. With approximately 6.5 billion members, the current world population is the largest-ever aggregate of living human individuals. According to the assumptions of Nathan Keyfitz (1966), if we counted everyone who ever lived, we would have an aggregate of about seventy-two billion people. Thus, the human beings alive today represent approximately 9 percent of persons ever born.

The most basic type of demographic variation, therefore, is change in the size of an aggregate between two dates: we use the words *growth* for an increase and *decline* for a decrease. How and why changes occur in the size of a specific aggregate depends in large part on what kind it is. Naturally occurring populations, in particular, grow or decline in size as a result of four *vital characteristics*: birth, death, in-migration, and out-migration.

Change in Size

The size of any naturally occurring population changes because of the interaction among the four vital characteristics. This interaction is summarized in what is referred to as the fundamental equation of demography (Shryock and Siegel 1976, chap. 4):

$$G = (B - D) + (I - O)$$

where G is growth, B is births, D is deaths (also referred to as "mortality"), and I and O are in- and out-migrations, respectively.

Taken together, the first two terms constitute *natural increase* and the latter two make up *net migration*. We can also class birth and migration together as *incremental* factors (because they increment, or add to, the population size) and death and out-migration as *decremental* factors (because they diminish size). Growth or decline in the size of a population, then, depends on the balance between incremental and decremental factors or on the combined effect of natural increase and net migration.

Birth

Demographers use the terms *birth*, *fertility*, and *reproduction* to refer essentially to the same phenomenon viewed from different standpoints. For the child, the event is a birth, the mother experiences fertility, and the population reproduces itself. The most common measures of these are, respectively, crude birth rates (CBRs):

$$CBR = B/P \times 1,000$$

where B is the number of live births during a period (e.g., one year) and P is the total population size at midyear. For fertility, the most common measure is general fertility rates (GFRs):

$$GFR = B/F^* \times 1,000$$

where F^* is the number of fertile women at midyear (note that this measure controls for any distortions created by the sizes of the male subpopulation and nonfertile cohorts of women). For reproduction, it is the net reproduction rates (NRRs):

$$NRR = TFB/TF^*$$

where *TFB* is the total number of female children who are born and who survive their childbearing years, and *TF** is the total number of fertile women. An NRR of 1.0 indicates that a population is exactly reproducing itself with zero population growth (ZPG); a figure above 1.0 portends population growth, and a figure below 1.0 portends decline.

The GFR is a summary measure of all of a population's age-specific fertility rates (ASFRs) or

$$ASFR = Bi/Fi \times 1,000$$

where *Bi* is the number of births to women age *i*, and *Fi* is the total number of women who have reached age *i*.

With an estimated population size for the world in 2009 of 6,768,341,068 and an estimated 142,135,642 births for that year, the current CBR of the entire human population is approximately 21.0 per 1,000. It is about 17.4 in the United States, whose total population size (July 1, 2009) was equal to 306,808,280 with 4,295,316 births during that year. CBRs range widely among countries, depending in general on their level of socioeconomic development and age structure. Among the highest rates in the world is Afghanistan's with 47.0 per 1,000, and one of the lowest is Germany's, at 8.0. The GFR for the United States as of 2010 is about 66 per 1,000, and its NRR is just above 0.90, that is, the U.S. population is on trajectory toward ZPG. (All data are from U.S. Census estimates and can be found at the comprehensive U.S. Census website, www.census.gov/.)

The only cohort that can be affected by changes in birth rates, and always incrementally, is the youngest: age 0 to 1 (for one-year periods). Thus, if all else were equal, every birth would act to reduce the age of a population. The more births that occur, the younger the population becomes.

Fertility, on the other hand, is strongly age related. Because the fertility of women is what gets counted (in part because male fertility is more difficult to track), some cohorts experience no fertility at all: the youngest, conventionally defined as below age fourteen, and the oldest, conventionally defined as ages forty-five (or forty-nine) and above. Between these extremes, a cohort's fertility varies within a population in a fairly regular pattern, with very young and very old fertile cohorts having the lowest rates and fertility peaking during the early to middle part of the reproductive years. The details of this pattern differ from population to population, depending on factors such as average age at marriage and overall levels of fertility. For example, in the United States, the highest ASFRs are for ages twenty-five to twenty-nine, but they occur at younger ages in most Third World countries (see table 3.1).

The effect is that, all else being equal, a population with relatively large cohorts of fertile females grows at a faster rate than one with relatively many older women. Thus, age-gender structure and fertility exert a cumulative effect on one another over the course of generations: large cohorts of fertile women produce many children, which

TABLE 3.1 Comparative Age-Specific Fertility Rates (per 1,000 women at a given age)

Region	Age of mother						
	15–19	*20–24*	*25–29*	*30–34*	*35–39*	*40–44*	*45–49*
USA	57	113	113	85	36	7	0.3
Africa	136	267	272	219	149	79	27
Asia	45	186	183	108	56	22	7
Europe	27	98	102	62	23	5	0
Latin America	79	173	156	111	66	28	5

Source: United Nations Population Division, World Population Prospects: The 2006 Revision and World Urbanization Prospects: The 2007 Revision New York: Population Division of the Department of Economic and Social Affairs of the United Nations Secretariat, 2009; U.S. Census Bureau, International Data Base," December 2009, www.census.gov/ipc/www/idb.

lowers the age of the population. These growing, new cohorts then continue to add to population size as they reach fertile ages, and so on.

This effect can be discerned from the population pyramids in figure 3.1. It is evident that Mozambique's young cohorts will likely outproduce their parents when they reach ages fifteen and above simply because they are more numerous, even if the number of children born per woman continues to decline as it has during the past few years. Russia's young cohorts, in contrast, have fewer members than those of their parents' generation and are not expected to achieve even their parents' relatively low levels of fertility.

Death

The projected impact of birth on age structure was qualified with the phrase "all else being equal." This is because change in the size of populations and subpopulations does not depend solely on it. Even considering the effects of natural increase alone, that is, assuming a "closed" (to any increments or decrements due to migration) population, mortality plays a major role. It affects the size, always decrementally, of entire populations, of male and female subpopulations, and of each and every cohort. The basic measure of mortality is the crude death rate (CDR):

$$CDR = D/P \times 1,000$$

where D is the number of deaths that occur during a period in a population of size P. Like the GFR, the CDR is a summary measure of age-specific rates, so we also use age-specific death rates (ASDRs):

$$ASDR = Di/Ki \times 1,000$$

where Di is the number of deaths occurring to persons age i, and Ki is the total size of the i-year-old cohort.

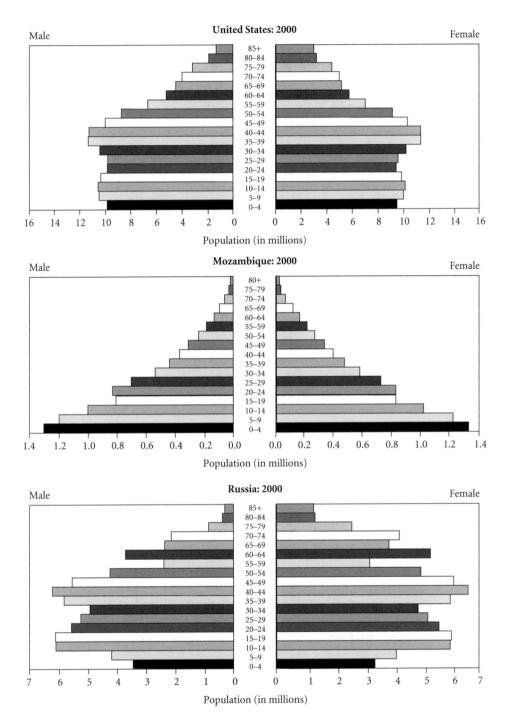

FIGURE 3.1 Population Pyramids Depicting Three Types of Age Structures and Growth Potential. *Source*: U.S. Bureau of the Census, International Data Base, www.census.gov/ipc/www/idb/country .php. Accessed March 17, 2010.

With approximately fifty-seven million deaths per year, the CDR for the world (2010 estimates) is 9.0 per 1,000. The U.S. rate is 8.0. The world's highest CDRs, of more than 30 per 1,000, occur in southern African nations, such as Mozambique and Botswana. The lowest rates, some less than 4.0 per 1,000, are found in the smaller countries of the Middle East that have very young populations, including Kuwait, Jordan, and the Palestinian Authority (West Bank).

Mortality has a significant association with age, so that CDRs are as much (if not more) affected by the age structure of a population than by its health conditions. Thus, age-specific rates portray more accurately the actual probabilities of death. The highest ASDRs occur at two points in a population's age structure: the youngest and the oldest cohorts. Especially important is the universally high level of infant mortality, the death rate of persons age 0 to 1. This is measured by the infant mortality rate (IMR):

$$IMR = Di/B \times 1,000$$

where $i = 0$ to 1 and B, as above, is the number of births.

From the beginning of human existence, and in the populations of all species, the young are the least likely to survive during a given period. Infant mortality is an especially sensitive indicator of standard of living, and it is the most significant part of general declines or increases in mortality. Infant mortality rates for the world as of the year 2010 ranged from over 180 deaths per 1,000 live births per year in Sierra Leone to 2.2 per 1,000 in Singapore. Canada's rate was 5.2, and the United States had a rate of 6.7, higher than thirty-six other countries, including Taiwan and Cyprus.

Because of its age-specific character, declining mortality typically affects a whole population in a way that might at first seem paradoxical. As its death rates go down, a population generally gets younger (Coale 1964). As fewer members of a population die (per capita), there is an increase in the size of elderly cohorts, so in this respect the population would appear to be aging. But this aging effect ordinarily is more than offset by an increase in the size of every cohort. As the population pyramids indicate, because the younger cohorts (especially infants) are usually larger than the older ones, general mortality decline brings a much more dramatic increase in the number of younger persons, thus lowering the average age.

The range of infant mortality levels that exists today reflects the latest stage in a long-term, worldwide decline. This is the case even in Sierra Leone, Mozambique, Afghanistan, and other places with high current rates. Some demographers estimate that, for most of human existence, IMRs were typically in the range of three hundred to five hundred. This means that, until recently (between fifty and two hundred years ago, depending on the country), a family could expect at least one child out of three to die before reaching one year of age. This decline in infant mortality marks one of the most significant demographic changes ever.

What is sometimes surprising is how recently the decline has occurred, in comparison to the one million years or so of human existence. Just a few generations ago, people would commonly report on the number of their children in terms such as "six, three living" or "two surviving" (something you can still hear in parts of the Third World).

Migration

Migration is closely associated with life cycle changes such as family formation and, more recently, going to college and retirement. Thus, it can substantially change the age structures of both sender and receiver populations. When the post–World War II suburban boom occurred in North America, for example, the population of the central cities began to age because of the out-migration of young couples and their children, while their parents and grandparents remained in the cities.

Similarly, populations that are receiving many recent migrants, whether international or interstate, or among rural, urban, and suburban areas, tend to be getting younger. Some of the most substantial second- and higher-order impacts of migration, such as changes in the labor force, are mediated by age structure changes (Massey, Goldring, and Durand 1994; Massey, Gross, and Shibuya 1994).

Migration is also selective with respect to gender. It tends to occur more frequently among men because of its association with job seeking or other "implementation strategies" (Berry 2008; De Jong et al. 1983) and because the labor force traditionally favors males. Frontier areas are well known for their high proportions of men and for the social problems associated with such conditions. This is clearly the case as well with the massive rural-to-urban migration streams now filling the large cities of the Third World (Weinstein 1991–1992). As the male household heads and older sons depart for the city in search of employment, the women remain in the village, still burdened with the traditional tasks of raising children, caring for the elderly, and tending to the fields and livestock. One researcher has summarized the situation succinctly in the title of her book on the urban trek in contemporary India, *Men to Bombay, Women at Home* (Dandekar 1986). The subject of migration's role in larger social trends and movements will be discussed shortly. First, though, let us briefly consider the structure of populations and how they vary over time.

Changes in Rates of Natural Increase

Changes in birth and death rates cause population growth to accelerate and decelerate. These changes have several possible, often multiple and/or cumulative, sources. In general, we can categorize these many causes into (1) those that are outside of human control and (2) those due to human control. The latter are usually, but not necessarily, intentional.

For most of human existence, both mortality and fertility were dictated by the first type of cause. If people were healthy and were not too seriously affected by natural disasters such as floods, epidemics, famines, and drought, they survived and had children (on epidemics, in particular, see Weinstein and Pillai 2001, 192–94). Otherwise they succumbed to these forces, the majority of them at young ages by today's standards. No population has ever achieved the absolute biological maximum number of children (referred to as *fecundity* and estimated to be approximately thirty throughout each woman's reproductive years, including possible multiple births). But birth rates were traditionally between two and three times higher than the current world CBR of approximately 21 per 1,000 population.

Box 3.1 UNITED NATIONS AND U.S. REFUGEE PROTOCOLS

An ever-growing number of migrants appeal to be admitted to a destination popu-
lation on the grounds that they are seeking refuge from political, racial, religious,
or social persecution. The rules that govern this phenomenon, issued by the United
Nations and the United States, are reproduced here.

United Nations High Commissioner for Refugees

Adopted at the 1951 United Nations Convention Relating to the Status of
Refugees
(A)ny person who, owing to a well-founded fear of being persecuted for reasons of
race, religion, nationality, membership of a particular social group or political opinion, is outside the country of his[/her] nationality and is unable, owing to such fear,
willing to avail him[/her]self to the protection of that country; or who not having a
nationality or being outside the country of his[/her] former habitual residence as a
result of such events, is unable or, owing to such fear, is unwilling to return to it.

U.S. Refugee Act of 1980

The Act adopts the definition of "refugee" contained in the 1951 UN Conven-
tion quoted above and its 1967 Protocol. Section 101(a)(42) of the U.S. Immi-
gration and Nationality Act (INA), as amended.
(A)ny person (A) who is outside any country of such person's nationality or, in the
case of a person having no nationality, is outside any country in which such person
last habitually resided, and who is unable or unwilling to return to, and is unable
or unwilling to avail himself or herself of the protection of, that country because
of persecution or a well-founded fear of persecution on account of race, religion,
nationality, membership in a particular social group, or political opinion, or (B) in
such circumstances as the President after appropriate consultation (as defined in
section 207 (e) of this Act) may specify, any person who is within the country of
such person's nationality or, in the case of a person having no nationality, within
the country in which such person is habitually residing, and who is persecuted or
who has a well-founded fear of persecution on account of race, religion, nationality,
membership in a particular social group, or political opinion.

The term "refugee" does not include any person who ordered, incited,
assisted, or otherwise participated in the persecution of any person on account
of race, religion, nationality, membership in a particular social group, or political
opinion. For purposes of determinations under this Act, a person who has been
forced to abort a pregnancy or to undergo involuntary sterilization, or who has
been persecuted for failure or refusal to undergo such a procedure or for other
resistance to a coercive population control program, shall be deemed to have been

persecuted on account of political opinion, and a person who has a well-founded fear that he or she will be forced to undergo such a procedure or be subject to persecution for such failure, refusal or resistance shall be deemed to have a well-founded fear of persecution on account of political opinion.

Source: United Nations High Commissioner for Refugees, http://www2.ohchr.org/english/law/refugees.htm; U.S. Department of Health and Human Services, Refugee Resettlement Office, www.acf.hhs.gov/programs/orr/policy/refact1.htm

Traditional death rates, too, were undoubtedly several times higher than the current world CDR of about 9 per 1,000. As a result, until recently, natural increase in human populations has been slow, punctuated by periods of population decline and driven by high levels of both births and deaths. If and when health failed (and, you will recall, it has always failed most often among the very young), people died. Thus, when conditions were good, populations grew; when they were bad, populations declined.

The Malthusian "Laws"

The preceding observation was formalized during the founding period of social science in England by Thomas R. Malthus. Trained as a minister and later (in 1805) selected as the world's first professor of political economy, Malthus engaged in a scholarly exchange lasting several years with the prominent writer and philosopher William Godwin (father of Mary Shelley, author of *Frankenstein*).

In contrast to Godwin's generally optimistic and rationalistic views, Malthus believed that the ancient pattern of alternating periods of slow growth and decline would inevitably continue into the indefinite future (Godwin [1820] 1964; Malthus [1798] 1960). He based his conclusion on what he assumed to be two natural laws. In fact, his word for them was *postulata*, a logical term even stronger than *laws* because it implies logically necessary truths: "First, that food is necessary for the existence of man. Second, that the passion between the sexes is necessary and will remain nearly in its present state. . . . Assuming, then, my postulata as granted, I say that the power of population is indefinitely greater than the power in the earth to produce subsistence for man" (Malthus [1798] 1960, 8–9).

From this, Malthus concluded that human populations always grow until they become too large for their requisite resource base. In contemporary terms, this condition is referred to as *surpassing the carrying capacity*: a situation in which the available food and other environmental resources no longer have the capacity to "carry" the population (Cohen 1995, 1997). At that point, a "check" occurs that results in increased mortality, and thus population decline. In Malthus's own words,

Population, when unchecked, increases in a geometrical ratio. Subsistence increases only in an arithmetical ratio. A slight acquaintance with numbers will show the immensity of the first power in comparison with the second. By that law of our nature that makes food necessary to the life of man, the effects of these two unequal powers must be kept equal. This implies a strong and constantly operating check on population from the difficulty of subsistence. This difficulty must fall somewhere and must necessarily be felt by a large portion of mankind. (Malthus [1798] 1960, 10)

The immediate causes of these checks to population growth are disasters: war, pestilence, and famine, which in turn bring "vice and misery." Decline continues, according to Malthus, until the balance between people and resources is restored. The population then begins to grow again, until the limit is reached and a new crisis ensues. Figure 3.2 shows this relationship between population increase and the growth of resources through several cycles, each of which ends with crisis as carrying capacity is exceeded.

It would be difficult to overestimate how influential this doctrine has been, both in scientific research and in the context of planned social change. Charles Darwin acknowledged his debt to Malthus for providing the demographic basis for the theory of evolution. As Darwin observed, Malthus's laws do appear to apply to populations of many nonhuman species (Darwin [1859] 2008, 40–51). In this respect, survival depends in principle on the precarious balance between reproduction and the ability of habitats to sustain the increase in the number of individuals born. In addition, Malthusian growth is a fairly accurate, though general, depiction of human demographic history up to the time of Godwin and Malthus in the late eighteenth century. The doctrine, revised as "neo-Malthusianism," continues to be applied as one of the principal theories that guide population policy formulation in Third World areas.

The simplicity and certitude of Malthus's laws clearly underlie the appeal of the doctrine to this day. But we might also ask whether Malthus would not have reconsid-

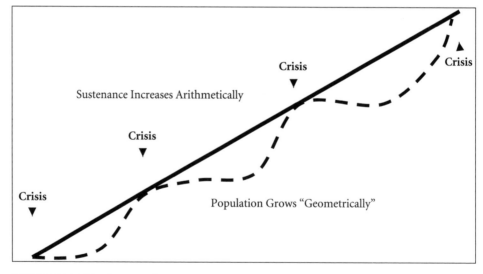

FIGURE 3.2 Malthusian Growth

ered his conclusion, even "assuming" his "postulata as granted," had he known of the events that were to occur in the decades following his death: rapid industrialization, urban growth, and the successes of the family-planning movement. This is because in the two centuries since Malthus's era, the populations and the resource bases of England and other parts of Europe have changed in ways that flatly contradict his predictions:

1. Since 1750, or even before, food production (of fruits, vegetables, meat, wheat, corn, and every other grain crop) has been increasing geometrically (i.e., exponentially).
2. After about 1850, the populations of England and many other countries began to exhibit only arithmetic increase. In fact, growth rates eventually declined to the point at which most European countries (including England) have fallen below ZPG.

In both instances, technological innovation has been the major cause of this reversal. In the case of food production, Malthusian laws have been challenged by new methods of breeding, growing, processing, and distributing food, methods based on scientific research more sophisticated and far more expensive than Malthus or his contemporaries could have possibly imagined—nor did Malthus foresee the substantial and widespread increase in the use of fertility control that began in England during his days at Cambridge. Since then, technological and value changes have created a new and fundamental separation between what he termed "the passions between the sexes" and reproduction: a true contraceptive revolution.

Demographic Transition: The Roots of Global Inequality

In the past two hundred years, Europe's populations clearly have experienced technological developments limiting the effects of natural growth and decline while expanding the scope of intentional demographic change. On these (and other) occasions, mortality and fertility have been subject to increasing human control and thereby have been altered through purposeful acts.

The resulting substantial and long-term shifts in the levels of vital events are referred to as *demographic transitions* because they necessarily involve significant changes in the rate at which a population grows (Beaver 1975; Menard and Moen 1987; Thompson 1929; Weinstein 1976, 1981). In such instances, and especially with the transition that began in Europe in the mid- to late eighteenth century, Malthusian laws (and other solely biological explanations of human population dynamics) fail to apply (recent general references on demographic transition include Bulatao and Casterline 2001; Jones 1997; Kalache 1997).

The Development of Mortality Control

Mortality control consists of human actions that intervene between the causes of death (disease and environmental hazards) and their impact on members of populations, especially the youngest members. Nutrition, sanitation, medical practices, and accident prevention are the major types of mortality control. Technologies to achieve these ends have been part of culture for a very long time, so that populations have rarely been entirely defenseless against the threat of high death rates. Nevertheless, until recent times, these technologies have remained at a relatively primitive level of development so that their effects have typically been marginal.

Thus, despite high levels of fertility, human populations have almost always grown very slowly. The most reliable estimates of the world's population as of ten thousand years ago provide a figure of approximately five million persons (Deevey 1960; Durand 1973; Weinstein 1976, chap. 3). This means that for *Homo sapiens'* first 240,000 years, when most populations were at the hunting-and-gathering stage, the rate of natural increase (RNI) for the species as a whole had an annual average of less than 1 person for every 250,000 in the population, or a tiny 0.0004 percent per year. Between twenty-five thousand and ten thousand years ago, in particular, the rate was about 0.003, 1 for every 33,000 (compare this with the rate in 2010 of 1.3 percent, or approximately 1 for 85). These averages include many periods during which Malthusian principles were fully operational and significant population declines occurred. (All rates reported are exponential averages.)

In the forty centuries between the late Bronze Age and the beginning of the Common Era, the world's average annual growth rate for the interval was between 0.018 and 0.028 percent, considering the lowest and highest estimates of the size of the human population for 1 CE of 133 million (Deevey 1960) and 300 million (Durand 1973). Between the fall of the Roman Empire and the Industrial Revolution in Europe, world population growth remained at or below the 0.1 percent level, with several eras of absolute decline: 1–600, 1200–1340, and 1600–1650 CE, in particular (Matras 1975, 21). In 1750, the world's population numbered about eight hundred million and had grown since 1 CE at an average annual rate of approximately 0.06 percent.

The Industrial Revolution and the European Transition

As the higher-order impacts of the Industrial Revolution spread throughout England, Scotland, and beyond, the effectiveness of mortality control, especially infant mortality control, increased enormously. For the first time in recorded history, technology, that is, applied knowledge designed to control nature, became the major cause of decline in a population's death rate.

By today's standards, these technological innovations were simple: draining swamps, improving nutrition through mechanization of food production, and boiling water. Yet they managed to help decrease intestinal parasites and malnutrition, the leading causes of infant death. In the one hundred years between 1750 and 1850, England's population grew at a rate of 1 percent per year, more than ten times the average of the preceding several centuries.

It may seem unnecessary to add that at the time people welcomed mortality control. Few people seriously resisted adopting these new technologies, for we naturally prefer life over death, whether it is one's own life, that of a spouse, or especially that of a newborn infant. An innovation that will improve the chances that one or all of these persons will live out the year is universally viewed as desirable.

In some circumstances, people did—and still do—believe that it is not right to intervene in natural processes such as life and death. But it has always been difficult for anyone to put that belief into practice when confronted with the real prospect of saving the life of one's baby. The results are evident in the rapid and widespread way in which mortality control is pursued wherever it is introduced. The reason for mentioning this is that the situation is quite different in the case of the acceptability of fertility control.

Outside Europe, in nineteenth-century Asia, Africa, and Latin America, high levels of mortality and slow, irregular population growth continued on their traditional course. In fact, significant increases in death rates occurred in the New World, as the war, pestilence, famine, vice, and misery associated with European conquest and colonization decimated local, indigenous populations (Petersen 1975, 380–86). At that point, population history bifurcated into two distinct tracks: one European and the other colonial.

Fertility Control: The Third Stage

The year 1750 marks the boundary between the first (slow-growth) and second (rapid-growth) stages of the European demographic transition, as shown in figure 3.3. From that point through the last one-half of the nineteenth century, mortality levels continued to decline in the wake of industrial growth. With most populations' fertility at or even above traditional levels, these declines translated into a then-unprecedented population explosion, with rates as high as 1.2 percent per year in the northwestern regions.

In comparison to the centuries and millennia of slow growth, the second stage of Europe's demographic transition was relatively short lived, lasting between 100 and 150 years. At about the time of Malthus's death in 1844, in England, parts of North America, and (possibly earlier) in France, another remarkable change was taking place. At that time, and in a manner entirely unaccounted for in Malthus's doctrine, fertility came under routine human control, and birth rates began to decline systematically. This marked the beginning of the third stage of the transition.

Fertility Control Technology Fertility control technology is classed into three types (Davis and Blake 1956). These are referred to as the three sets of *intermediate variables* because they intervene between the fecundity potential and the actual number of births achieved. The first set consists of *intercourse* variables, practices that affect the frequency with which women have intercourse and are thus "exposed" to the risk of conception. The most common intercourse-related practices are late marriage, the physical separation of spouses, and abstinence. The second consists of *conception* variables, practices designed to prevent conception when intercourse takes place. Such practices include coitus interruptus (withdrawal), sterilization through hysterectomy or tubal ligation for female partners and vasectomy for males, and rhythm techniques (i.e., the timing of intercourse to coincide with infertile days in the menstrual cycle). They also include the use of mechanical and physical contraceptives: intrauterine devices (IUDs), condoms,

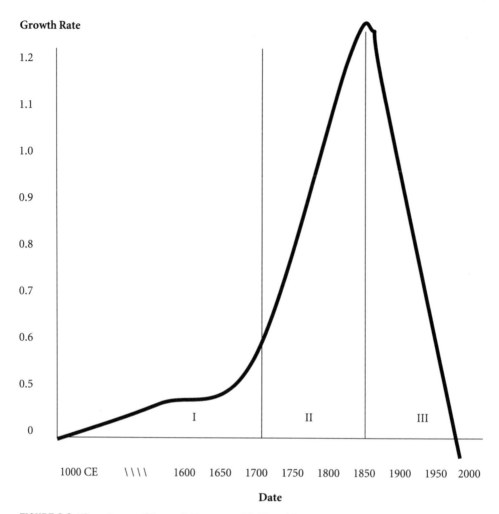

Growth Rate

FIGURE 3.3 Three Stages of Europe's Demographic Transition

spermicides, diaphragms, birth control pills, and steroid patches and injections. The third set consists of *gestation* variables, practices intended to prevent birth when conception has occurred, that is, voluntary abortion.

All three types of fertility control have been known and practiced to some extent since ancient times (Himes 1936). People have always been aware that they can limit the number of births, at least through the intercourse variables, by avoiding heterosexual contact. Contraceptive technologies, albeit crude by today's standards, have also been around for a long time. Before the dawn of civilization, animal herders discovered that stones and other small objects can serve as IUDs, and condoms made from animal bladders have been used for centuries. As is clear from the Old Testament, withdrawal was a well-understood form of birth control. The technologies of abortion, too, have been passed from generation to generation, often in association with the practices of midwifery and magic (Devereux 1955).

Despite the fact that fertility control technologies have been part of human culture for a very long time, they were rarely practiced until the middle of the nineteenth century and then only in a few European cities. The main exception is traditional intercourse variables, principally abstinence. Even in populations whose members purposely set out to have as many children as they possibly can (three of the most frequently cited are the Hutterites of North America, the Cocos-Keeling Islanders, and the Shipobo of Peru), occasional unplanned periods of abstinence cannot be avoided. Thus, even these populations achieve fertility levels well under 50 percent of potential fecundity. Yet, in comparison to the two types of intervening variables, the effects of abstinence are haphazard, and they are still compatible with very high levels of fertility.

The practices of contraception and abortion, although known, traditionally have been proscribed by law and custom. The overwhelming weight of social pressure, for most human populations and for most of the time that humans have existed, has been against such practices. They have not been considered socially acceptable and have been viewed as irrational.

This situation reflects the longtime domination of pronatalist values: a strong shared preference for many children. The most direct effect of this virtually universal trait has been a general avoidance of contraception and abortion (and, by and large, avoiding abstinence as well). Those in the past who did employ these practices did so as exceptions and often as social deviants. Archaeological research on ancient cultures routinely unearths fertility idols, but no *infertility* god has ever been found.

Because of the traditionally high rates of mortality, especially infant mortality, most demographers view the persistence of pronatalism as a sheer survival tactic, that is, if people were not strongly encouraged to have many children, the high rates of mortality would cause their populations to die out. Some have even suggested the evolutionary hypothesis that any antinatalist populations that may have existed are now of necessity extinct, so that the surviving ones are all pronatalist. We have seen a version of this in our time with the extinction of the United Society of Believers (Shaker people), who believed in absolute celibacy (Foster 1981; Stein 1992).

In any case, humans (1) are typically pronatalist and (2) typically have high levels of fertility. Of course, "typical" does not mean "always," and in about 1850, the atypical began to occur.

Third-Stage Fertility Decline When populations in Europe entered the third stage of demographic transition, traditional fertility control technologies became acceptable and their use came to be viewed as rational. These included late marriage, abstinence, withdrawal, and condoms, douching, and other contraceptive devices of the day.

These modest innovations indicate that the fertility declines that began around 1850 were not the result of a revolution in contraceptive technology. That came much later, after 1950 or so with the development of the Pill and, in the late 1970s, with subdermal steroids that are practically 100 percent effective. Rather, they were the immediate result of people abandoning pronatalist values and accepting existing practices formerly considered illegitimate.

Why, then, did these changes in values and practices occur at that time and in those places? The answer to this question takes us a long way toward understanding why, in general, fertility levels change in human populations. First, it is important that we know who actually first experienced these changes. Considerable research has shown that the acceptance and practice of birth control were originally, and still largely remain, strongest among the urban middle classes (Banks 1954, 1968; Wrigley 1969). Thus, in an important sense, widespread fertility decline is a higher-order impact of the growth and social dominance of this class and of the capitalist system on which it is based.

Moreover, in England at least, it occurred as part of a generational movement among members of the relatively new bourgeoisie, who, in the midst of unprecedented population growth and economic growth, had all experienced recent periods of economic crisis (Davis 1963), that is, they had experienced relative deprivation, an episode of loss following unprecedented prosperity (Easterlin 1968; Pampel 1993). These circumstances suggest that three main factors were working together to affect fertility control attitudes and practices:

1. The survival value of pronatalism was no longer relevant. This applied especially to the more prosperous members of populations well into the second-stage declines in infant mortality, such as the English urban middle class.
2. The role of children had shifted from producers to consumers of family resources. This was particularly relevant in families who had left the farm and who were now putting older children in school rather than into the workforce.
3. Large families were no longer providing support services for their members, such as health care, child care, shelter, emergency care, and support for the elderly. Instead, these services were increasingly being taken over by large-scale secondary organizations: schools, government programs, and private corporations (Weinstein 1978a). This was especially the pattern among urban dwellers who were educated to the ways of organized life and who had seen that their prosperity depends on minimizing the number of mouths that need to be fed.

These conditions, in combination with the acceptance of previously frowned-upon technologies of fertility limitation, converged on the new middle-class subpopulations of industrializing Europe: they brought about a major social movement promoting the conscious planning of small families. As early as 1822, the English demographer Francis Place had written a manifesto for the movement, providing it with "its first systematic theory and ethical rationale" (Petersen 1975, 516).[3]

Economic conditions supporting the family-planning movement were more or less established prior to 1800, but only after 1850 did the movement have the momentum to become institutionalized. In the subsequent one hundred years, England's CBR declined from nearly 60 to below 15 per 1,000, and, with the exception of a baby boom in the 1950s and early 1960s, it has continued on this course. By 2009, England's CBR had fallen to 12, with a NRR of 0.7 (well below the replacement level of 1.0).

Family-planning ideals and practices spread from parents to children and, via the movement, from English and other European urban, middle classes to other countries, other classes, and eventually even to rural areas. As is true of all such movements and diffusions of technology, this change met with varying degrees of resistance. Deeply entrenched values such as pronatalism do not simply disappear in the face of changed demographic and economic conditions, and organized support for high fertility remains to this day. Most of the world's major religions and nearly all of the local ones as well have retained their strong moral preference for unrestrained reproduction. In the United States, the Comstock Law, making it illegal to sell contraceptives, was not repealed until 1970 (Donaldson and Tsui 1990), although it had been routinely ignored in practice for decades.

Resistance to fertility control also occurs in populations and subpopulations that lack the economic, familial, or cultural supports for such a social movement. Industrialization, urban growth, and the rise of a middle class were and remain to this day necessary conditions for altering the survival value, economic role, and social support functions of offspring. Thus, at root, family planning is still a "bourgeois" concept. To the extent that populations are not bourgeois (the more rural, less industrial, and less middle-class majority of today's world), fertility levels remain relatively high.

In contrast, despite resistance from religion and other sources, family planning has prevailed in the industrialized world. The general population of every country in Western Europe and several in Eastern Europe long ago entered the third stage of demographic transition. The same is true in Canada, the United States, Japan, Australia, and New Zealand. More recently, smaller Asian countries such as Singapore and Taiwan, as well as Argentina and perhaps one or two other Latin American nations, have achieved low-fertility populations.

The pattern is clear: fertility decline, in historical perspective, is an unprecedented and dramatic demographic response to an equally dramatic revolution in the way people organize their lives. Demographic transition truly reflects social and cultural change. With the emergence of industrial society, low levels of fertility prevail for the first time in human existence in some populations. But what about the rest of the world?

Demographic Transition in the Third World

"The rest of the world" is, more or less, the Third World: all of the countries of Africa and most in Asia and Latin America. There, neither the causes nor the effects of the third stage have taken root (a few Second World countries in Central and Eastern Europe also have high fertility levels). Some fairly strong evidence now exists to indicate that the process has begun and that it is the result of a combination of two factors: (1) recently changing conditions such as industrial and urban growth, and (2) overt government policies in support of the family-planning movement. Nevertheless, fertility levels remain high: in some places, CBRs are at or above traditional levels of 50 per 1,000 (e.g., Uganda and Somalia—both with CBRs of 47.0 as of 2009). The highest-ever rates for the Third World as a whole (between 40 and 50 per 1,000) occurred as recently as 1980 (see table 3.2).

The sources of this difference between the industrialized countries and the rest of the world extend back to the 1750 period (and earlier), when demographic history separated

TABLE 3.2 Demographic Characteristics of the World's Twenty-five Most Populous Nations (base year 2009; rates per 1,000)

Country	Pop	CBR	CDR	NMR	GR	IMR	LExp
China	1,338,613	14.0	7.0	0	0.7	20.0	73
India	1,156,898	22.0	8.0	0	1.4	51.0	66
United States	307,212	14.0	8.0	4.0	1.0	6.0	78
Indonesia	240,272	19.0	6.0	-1.0	1.1	30.0	71
Brazil	198,739	18.0	6.0	0	1.2	23.0	72
Pakistan	174,579	26.0	7.0	-3.0	1.6	67.0	65
Bangladesh	156,051	25.0	10.0	-3.0	1.5	59.0	60
Nigeria	149,229	37.0	17.0	0	2.0	94.0	47
Russia	140,041	11.0	16.0	0	-0.5	11.0	66
Japan	127,079	8.0	10.0	0	-0.2	3.0	82
Mexico	111,212	20.0	5.0	-4.0	1.1	15.0	76
Philippines	97,977	26.0	5.0	-1	2.0	21.0	71
Vietnam	88,577	18.0	6.0	0	1.1	22.0	72
Ethiopia	85,237	44.0	12.0	0	3.2	81.0	55
Germany	82,330	8.0	11.0	2.0	-0.1	4.0	79
Egypt	78,867	25.0	5.0	0	2.0	27.0	72
Turkey	76,806	19.0	6.0	1.0	1.3	26.0	72
Congo (Kinshasa)	68,693	43.0	12.0	1.0	3.2	81.0	54
Iran	66,429	17.0	6.0	-3.0	0.9	36.0	71
Thailand	65,998	13.0	7.0	0	0.6	17.0	73
France	64,420	13.0	9.0	1.0	0.5	3.0	81
UK	61,113	11.0	10.0	2.0	0.3	5.0	79
Italy	58,126	8.0	11.0	2.0	0	6.0	80
South Korea	48,509	9.0	6.0	0	0.3	4.0	79
Ukraine	45,700	10.0	16.0	0	-0.6	9.0	68

Source: U.S. Census Bureau, "International Data Base," December 2009, www.census.gov/ipc/www/idb.

Key: Pop, total population size in millions; CBR, crude birth rate; CDR, crude death rate; NMR, net migration rate; GR, growth rate (in percent); IMR, infant mortality rate; LExp, average life expectancy in years.

into the two tracks mentioned. While European explorers and colonists were establishing settlements throughout Asia, Africa, and Latin America, the fruits of industrial revolution (and the consequent improvements in mortality control technologies, in particular) were largely confined to Europeans. In fact, since early in the Age of Exploration, around the year 1500, overseas Europeans purposely established a pattern of not using local resources to create indigenous industrial revolutions. Instead, these resources were sent back home, to be invested in Europe's economic growth.

Thus, while Europe entered the second stage of demographic transition, the rest of the world continued with traditionally high levels of mortality for a century and more. The only exceptions, North America, Australia, and New Zealand, are also exceptional in that the overseas Europeans there created their own national populations, which did experience transition at about the same time as did many countries in Europe. Not coincidentally, the European settlers did retain local resources to finance a domestic industrial revolution, after winning independence from the European colonial power that claimed them.

When the second stage of demographic transition did spread beyond Europe and European settlements, it arrived with momentous results. Beginning some time after 1850, then-current European mortality control technologies began to diffuse to local populations in the Third World. Their effects are shown in figure 3.4, where we see that the most dramatic impacts occurred after World War I and continue to this day. As of the year 2000, the average CDRs for the more developed and less developed countries were 10 and 9 per 1,000, respectively. This indicates that, because of the effects of age structure, Third World mortality levels are now in fact lower than those in Europe (compare this to the difference in birth rates of 11 and 27).

In approximately seventy-five years or less, Third World countries achieved mortality declines that had taken two hundred years in Europe. For example, according to the *Census of India* (1921 and 1971 enumerations), as late as 1920, the country's CBR was 48.1 and its CDR was 47.2. This is an RNI of just 0.09 percent per year. Fifty years later, by 1970, the CBR had declined to 41.2 and the CDR to 19.0. Thus, the RNI had increased from practically zero to more than 2.2 percent. This steep decline in mortality levels occurred because the death-reducing technologies that the Third World adopted were much more advanced than those available during the early days of the Industrial Revolution. Thus, the Third World has been able to not only take advantage of more sophisticated and effective methods of sanitation, accident prevention, and nutrition but also benefit from modern vaccines and antibiotics. In the course of institutionalizing effective death-control technologies there, the dreaded disease smallpox, which caused millions of deaths in Europe and North America even during the second stage of their demographic transitions, was eliminated: the virus itself has been nearly completely contained.

The concept used to describe this type of delayed, but more powerful, impact was introduced by the U.S. sociologist and economist Thorstein Veblen: *the penalty of leadership* (Veblen 1939). In the context of modern European history that was the focus of his research, he observed that, although England industrialized first, it paid the penalty of taking the lead when Germany quickly caught up in the later nineteenth century. The irony is that it did so by incorporating innovations that the English had developed over the several preceding decades.

Similarly, during the second stage of its demographic transition, Europe required a relatively long period to achieve low mortality levels, thus experiencing many deaths in the process. In contrast, Third World countries were "rewarded for being second" with a more rapid decrease in death rates (Schneider 1975a, 52–53). The number of lives that have been saved in the Third World is phenomenal, and, to repeat the apparently obvious, people have generally been very happy to be among the first generations whose babies will all (or nearly all) survive to adulthood.

The immediate demographic impact is equally great. During the past several decades, populations throughout the Third World have achieved their largest sizes ever

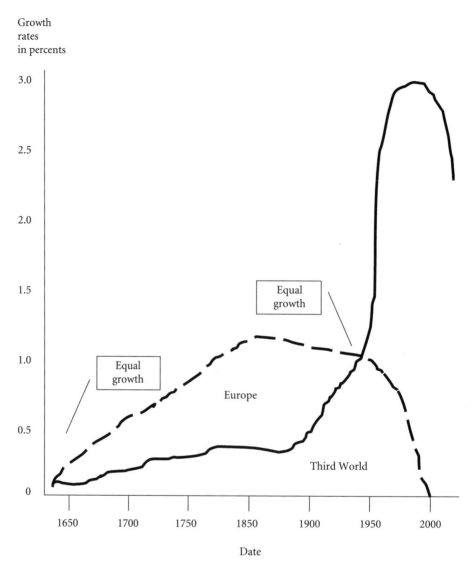

FIGURE 3.4 Demographic Transition in Europe and the Third World. Growth rates in the two regions were equal prior to 1650, and they were equal again three hundred years later in 1950.

and have been growing at unprecedented rates. The second stage of transition in Europe brought population explosions to the then-industrializing countries, but populations continue to explode far more rapidly in the Third World today. At the peak of growth in Asia and Africa during the late 1970s, annual rates of natural increase reached, and in some countries exceeded, the 3 percent level. This is nearly triple the highest rates achieved during Europe's explosion. One need not be a demographic determinist to appreciate the role of population growth in our current sociocultural revolution.

As is typical, by far the largest share of this increase is in the youngest cohorts (note Mozambique's population pyramid in figure 3.1). Every year, millions of children are born into, and in unprecedented proportions are living and growing up in, Third World populations, exerting unprecedented demands on food supplies, housing, schools, and nearly every other kind of resource.

Malthusian Responses to Third World Population Explosion

As with many "rewards" brought by large-scale change, the Third World baby boom has created significant challenges. From a Malthusian point of view, conditions are ripe for war, pestilence, famine, vice, and misery. As a consequence, Malthus's views have recently experienced a significant revival. His spirit lives in research on the current Third World population explosion and in the extensive programs of applied social change established in Third World countries, including widespread government-sponsored support of the family-planning movement.[4]

In studies of the extent to which Malthusian "checks" have taken effect in Third World countries, most researchers have concluded that this has not (yet) happened in any significant way. There is certainly plenty of war, famine, and the rest, but it is doubtful that such social problems are either (1) more serious than they were before the population explosion began, or (2) directly related to population growth per se as mortality decline continues largely unabated.

Malthusians do not accept such findings as conclusive, for their position assumes an inevitable linkage between growth, scarcity, and social disorder. Assuming the prophetic role, they warn that, even if the problems are not manifest now, they will occur unless something is done, and done quickly, to halt population growth. "If present growth trends in world population, industrialization, pollution, food production, and resource depletion continue unchallenged, the limits to growth on this planet will be reached some time within the next hundred years. The most probable result will be a rather sudden and uncontrollable decline in both population and industrial capacity" (Meadows et al. 1972, 29; for a contrasting position, see Cohen 1995; Simon 1981). From this point of view, the general answer to the question "what needs to be done?" is equally obvious. "We must rapidly bring the world population under control reducing the growth rate to zero or making it go negative" (Ehrlich 1968, 131).

How can or should this be achieved? That depends, of course, on what we think is happening now and what we believe will happen if we fail to act. But because Malthusians have a clear idea about both matters, for them the choices as to what action to take are limited to three basic positions: classic Malthusian, noninterventionist, and neo-Malthusian.

Malthus's own views on the subject varied during the course of his exchange with Godwin (as the former become more rationalistic and the latter more pessimistic). His major emphasis, however, was on a type of fertility control that he termed "moral restraint," which is essentially the same as the intercourse variables of late marriage and abstinence. This is the classic Malthusian solution to the problem of population explosion.

Another position, which is implied in Malthusian laws but generally not advocated by him, is to let nature take its course. If a population has become too large, then increasing death rates are the natural response. As tragic as it may be at the individual level, according to this position, high mortality is the adjustment mechanism that populations use to return to the proper size when growth has gone too far (Hardin 1980). So population explosions will, and should, take care of themselves.

This "benign neglect" approach is compatible with social Darwinism because it supports the idea that the fittest populations are the ones that can maintain a healthy growth rate and that population explosion and the subsequent checks are signs of mal-adaptation to the environment. In terms of the fitness of the species, then, population growth should be allowed to make its own natural adjustments.

The third position, neo-Malthusianism, is the most prominent version in population research and policy formation today (basic sources include Ehrlich 1968; Hardin 1973; Hardin and Baden 1977). The "neo" refers to the fact that this position supports the use of contraception- or even gestation-related technologies of fertility control. You might recall that Malthus himself was not in favor of condoms or other artificial means of birth control, though in his last writings he was beginning to acknowledge their potential value. As mentioned, Malthus's contemporary, Place, is usually credited with being the founder of the family-planning movement, and thus the first neo-Malthusian.

Contemporary neo-Malthusians have made substantial contributions to the academic discipline of demography. They have also substantially influenced the population policies of Third World governments, of the United Nations and other international bodies, and of nations involved in large-scale transfers of fertility control technologies to the Third World. The impact of neo-Malthusianism is especially evident in the work of the donor of practically all population aid in the world, the U.S. Agency for International Development (USAID; McKinlay and Mughan 1984, chap. 2; Weeks 1992, 443). Through the auspices of this agency, several billion dollars have been directed to Third World family-planning programs.

The results of these transfers have been mixed, and they are subject to widely differing interpretations. Fertility levels in most Third World countries have fallen to some extent since the 1970s. In some places, including Taiwan, Korea, and Singapore, it is clear that the third stage of transition has been reached and that family planning has played a decisive role. China, too, with the world's largest population, has achieved dramatic declines in fertility, especially during the 1980s, based on a strongly autocratic, neo-Malthusian approach (Ferraro 1995). In other places, such as India and Northern Africa, less spectacular declines have occurred, and in some places, such as sub-Saharan Africa and many Asian nations, the population explosion continues unabated.

In most instances, the actual effect of family planning is difficult to discern because its introduction has occurred along with so many other social, cultural, and demographic changes. Even when the appropriate correlation and time sequence exist, the increase in the number of people availing themselves of family-planning technology may be a spurious cause of observed fertility decline (Weinstein and Pillai 2001, 353–56).

Non-Malthusian Responses During the last three decades of the twentieth century, books and articles began to appear in which researchers and policy specialists took issue with the validity of the causal link between family planning and population growth. Criticism was also marshaled against the neo-Malthusian approach itself (e.g., Ahlberg 1998; Simon 1981, 1989; see also Mamdani 1972; Weinstein 1976). Serious questions were raised about the type and extent of social problems the Third World was actually experiencing, the role (if any) played by population growth as a cause, and the practicality and morality of promoting family-planning program in overwhelmingly pronatalist cultures (Hauerwas 1977; Warwick 1974, 1975; Warwick, Merrick, and Caplan 1977; Weinstein 1982, chap. 14). Several different scientific, political, and ethical issues were raised in a general line of non-Malthusian criticism. This line can be clearly traced back to Godwin, who first took issue with Malthus's natural law doctrine, and with his philosophy of human nature and grasp of the facts of population as well.

Since the early 1980s, non-Malthusian approaches have been well represented in both academic research and policy contexts. A leading non-Malthusian economist, Julian Simon, formulated the U.S. position at the 1984 International Conference on Population and Development (ICPD) II in Mexico City, which was a complete reversal from the strongly neo-Malthusian policy presented by the United States ten years earlier at Conference I in Bucharest. Conference III, in 1994 in Cairo, was characterized by less discussion of "laws" of population and more about the complex relationship between population and social organization, technology, values, and environment (Ashford 1995).

As a result of these challenges, research and policy formulation about the Third World population explosion have largely ceased treating demographic principles in isolation from these other factors. Population policy, as the plenary reports of ICPDs II and III explicitly state, is an integral part of *general* social policy. To underscore this shift, as an alternative to a fourth ICPD (which would have occurred in 2004), the United Nations Population Fund (UNFPA) designated July 11 as "World Population Day." In conjunction with this designation, an "ICPD Plan of Action" was published that emphatically views population issues in the context of social, cultural, and economic concerns (UNFPA 2004). The plan seeks to

- enact laws and policies to protect the rights of women and girls;
- ensure equal access to primary education for girls and boys;
- ensure universal access to reproductive health services as part of basic primary health care;
- empower women and girls socially and economically;
- prevent HIV infection; and
- end gender-based violence.

As has been stressed throughout this chapter, population dynamics constitute one essential, but never isolated, component of collective change. This has never been demonstrated more clearly than in the demographic transitions currently underway throughout the Third World.

Summary

This chapter has outlined the principles of population change. First, we defined populations as endogamous, territorial, and structured along biological and sociocultural dimensions. Next, the chapter examined the ways in which populations can change in size, composition, and geographical distribution. These concepts and principles were then employed in explaining population dynamics in relation to other types of social and cultural change.

Then followed an analysis of the three-stage European demographic transition, which highlighted several aspects of population change that are likely to affect the future course of world and regional population growth: the family-planning movement, Third World population explosion, and the debate among Malthusian and non-Malthusian commentators and policy specialists.

The following chapter focuses on the cultural component, reexamining many of these same concepts, principles, and illustrations (structural differentiation, urbanization, "race," and so on) from a different, but complementary, point of view. Because populations are the units of analysis, the next chapter and the remainder of the book expand on the demographic content. This will provide ample occasion to recall our general theme that sociocultural change always takes place within and between naturally occurring human populations.

Relevant Websites

www.census.gov/
This is the home page of the U.S. Census Bureau website. It provides easy access to a wealth of information about the United States and, with its International Data Base (IDB), most countries in the world.

www.cdc.gov/nchs/
The U.S. National Center for Health Statistics (NCHS), a Bureau of the Department of Health and Human Services, maintains this site. The focus of the numerous databases accessible here is on vital characteristics: birth, marriage, illness (morbidity), and death.

http://worldbank.org/
http://unstats.un.org/unsd/
www.undp.org/
These three sites provide information on international demographic trends. All three are from UN affiliate organizations. The first is the World Bank, the second is the UN Statistics Division, and the third is the United Nations Development Programme (UNDP).

http://adsri.anu.edu.au/
Australian National University (ANU) maintains several websites noted for their accuracy and for the numerous links they provide to related resources. This is ANU's Australian Demographic and Social Research Institute site.

http://www.nidi.knaw.nl/en
This is the site of the Interdisciplinary Demographic Institute (NIDI) in The Hague, Netherlands. This institute was founded in 1973 with the mission of conducting research and developing software in conjunction with its research projects.

www.prb.org/
www.prb.org/Educators/Resources/Glossary.aspx
The first site is the home page for the Population Reference Bureau (PRB), a private research organization in Washington, D.C. PRB has an online glossary of demographic terms at the second site.

www.popassoc.org/
www2.asanet.org/population
These are the URLs for the two leading professional associations of demographers in the United States. The first is the Population Association of America, and the second is the Population Section of the American Sociological Association.

www.state.gov/g/prm/
The U.S. Department of State's information on international migration is under the jurisdiction of the Immigration and Naturalization Service and can be found at this site.

CHAPTER
4

The Heritage and
Dynamics of Culture

Culture is a human invention that plays an essential role in a population's adaptation to its environment. It includes the most fundamental features of collective life: norms, values, and languages, as well as tools and other material objects. The units of culture, referred to as "traits," are combined and organized in virtually limitless ways to create larger structures: artifacts, complexes, and whole cultures. These are shared by members of populations and are passed between generations through *enculturation*. The related process, in which cultural traits are transmitted from members of one population to another, is referred to as *diffusion*, and the learning experience as *acculturation*.

It was once believed that people are the only animals that use tools and language and, therefore, possess culture. However, zoological research has cast considerable doubt on this view (see Bonner 1980; Bright 1994). "One vestige of human uniqueness still often cited by anthropologists is culture. However, this notion has been challenged in recent years with numerous demonstrations of 'culture' in other species, particularly primates" (Sapolsky 2006, 17). Nevertheless, it still is generally acknowledged that humans have developed such skills in an exceptional way. And although we do not know enough about nonhuman (especially cetacean) languages to compare directly with ours, it is clear that our type is unusual. For instance, we have written forms and an apparently higher degree of complexity.

So, if we are not the only animals to have culture (depending on how the term is defined), we do seem to use and depend on it in a special way. As the anthropologist Donald Brown (1991) noted,

Although humans are not unique in their possession of culture—patterns of think-ing and doing that are passed on within and between generations by learning—they certainly are unique in the extent to which their thought and action are shaped by such patterns. [People] are aware of this uniqueness and posit a difference between their way—culture—and the way of nature. (130)

Cultural change, in this sense, is a transformation in a population's "patterns of thinking and doing," especially the kind that renders the taken-for-granted world of one generation no longer compatible with the heritage of previous ones. The differ-ence between "culture" and "nature" to which Brown refers corresponds to the division between superorganic and organic processes, and it makes the evolution of human systems a (partly) conscious, purposeful undertaking. Cultural change is the outcome not only of "blind forces" of adaptation and survival but also of movements, inventions, and official actions undertaken with change in mind.

This chapter examines some of the ways in which (distinctively human) cultural traits and larger structures vary, the causes of such variations, and their effects. The discussion is divided into three main sections, each of which focuses on a specific, long-range cultural transformation: (1) the passing of traditional societies, (2) the process of secularization, and (3) the development and regulation of language. These are central topics in contemporary sociology, anthropology, and related fields, in part because they illustrate well the superorganic quality of sociocultural change. Most important, per-haps, they are also among the major causes of today's global revolution.

The Passing of Traditional Society

As intercultural contact on a worldwide basis became routine, especially during and after the era of European colonialism, non-European societies began to lose their distinct, local beliefs, values, and institutions. In the process, they have increasingly adopted European and, more recently, American ways, partly through coercion and partly voluntarily. Many social scientists believe that if this trend continues, we may soon find ourselves in a world in which there are no more living traditional societies.

Cultures differ in the extent to which they encourage or accommodate change. For most of human existence, nonmaterial culture especially changed at a slow pace. Values and value systems, languages, and other cultural forms tended to remain stable over decades, even centuries, and attempts to alter them ordinarily met with resistance or were not even considered. Such cultures are referred to as *traditional* to stress the fact that their beliefs and practices are based directly on past practices, or are "handed over" (*traditio*, in Latin), from previous generations.

According to Max Weber's theory of social action, tradition is one of three forms of cultural authority (Weber [1922] 1968, 212–54).[1] The three are alternative sources for determining what is and is not acceptable in a particular culture. The other two are *charisma*, the unique powers of an individual's personality, and *rational law*. The latter, rational-legal authority, is a highly impersonal form. Its definitions of right and wrong, and good and bad, do not depend solely on traditional sources such as kin and king. Rather, these are determined through formal public procedures, legislation, and judicial review. This form allows and encourages changing standards and is clearly the dominant one in modern societies everywhere.

Nevertheless, as Weber acknowledged, all cultures are traditional to one degree or another. Even people considered to be the least family oriented, such as contemporary European-background North Americans, still speak the language of their parents and share most of their core values. Moreover, every population must, over the course of many generations, go through periods during which tradition plays lesser or greater roles. Thus, like other terms in our vocabulary of change, "tradition" is relative; it depends on time, place, and the specific population of interest. No culture is entirely or unvaryingly traditional, and none is entirely tradition free.

The contemporary world is certainly dominated by what is modern, "up-to-date," in the United States. Yet a process of two-way diffusion continues and accelerates (Campbell 2007). Today, people everywhere are also influenced by styles from the Third World, Euroculture, Japan, and now even Russia. With a powerful boost from the media and multinational corporations, a single world culture has taken on a life of its own in fewer than three decades, and it increasingly is a global system rather than simply European or American. The old colonial-based, core-periphery distinctions may still hold, but diffusion is no longer necessarily bound by space or time. Styles that are prevalent in any part of the world today can be instantaneously demonstrated anywhere else, with the Internet, TV images, and advertising campaigns providing a potent impetus toward adoption.

Who at this point can say what local cultural styles are reflected in fast food, blue jeans, and rock 'n' roll? Technically, they have roots in U.S. youth culture of the past half century, but for the past several years, they have belonged to the world and have established their own "traditions" everywhere.

These diffusions have been part of one of most significant cultural changes in recorded history. To convey how fundamental the loss of diversity and the subsequent leveling have been, the sociologist Daniel Lerner coined the suggestive phrase "the passing of traditional society" (Lerner 1958, from which I borrowed the title of this section). Because of the close connection between traditional culture and kinship, this is another way to refer to the long-term, worldwide transition from primary to secondary and tertiary relationships (see chapter 5).

While the number and variety of local cultures are decreasing at the world level, the great acceleration in contacts between formerly distinct groups has contributed to an increase in the cultural diversity within populations. Millions of people who trace their origins to formerly colonial and other non-European areas now live and reproduce as members of ethnic subpopulations in every country of Europe (especially the former colonial powers), in North America, and elsewhere. In general, European languages, values, and material culture have tended to dominate wherever contact has occurred. But formerly exotic customs and practices have also been incorporated routinely into European culture, to an extent that few people realize until they stop and think about it.

Because many elements of tradition persevere even in the most nontraditional cultures, the past continues to be a major force in shaping the lives of people everywhere. Rather than the passing of tradition per se, therefore, it might be more accurate to speak of the passing of the era of relative isolation and independent cultural evolution. This development has been accompanied by the consequent loss of a large measure of human diversity between, but not necessarily within, communities.

Traditional cultures have yielded to a centuries-long assault in which local languages, customs, and beliefs have been challenged by the "latest" styles of industrializing Europe. Today, every population in the world has been affected by and has to some extent adopted modern ways, and the process has accelerated rapidly under the impetus of electronic communication technology and air and space travel. Yet no culture is entirely rational-legal, not even in Europe or North America. Some traditions simply persist, and some outmoded ones have a way of getting revived. Traditional authority, although subordinate to rational law virtually everywhere today, always will have a voice as long as there are families to "hand down" cultural traits.

Under such circumstances, we can expect local and global cultures of the future to continue to be transformed, but not with a sure and steady "passing" of tradition. Rather, it will be the result of interaction and conflict between rational-legal and traditional forces. One could also speculate that this interaction will be punctuated by periods of militant change as well, in which charismatic individuals challenge both tradition and the law.

It might seem quite accurate to speak of this process as *modernization*, but the term often conceals more than it reveals. Given what has actually happened to traditional society, within and outside of Europe, it may be more revealing to view it as rationalization, as rules and formal procedures replace personal authority everywhere. But regardless of the label we use, the important thing to remember is that it has never simply "taken over" without a struggle.

The following sections focus on how this dialectic of tradition and modernity are expressed in the dynamics of two central cultural institutions, religion and language.

The Sacred and the Secular

As a single world system emerges and takes shape via information superhighways and multinational organizations, the place of religion and religious ideals in humanity's future remains uncertain (Roof 1991). In social science terms, this reflects unsettled conflict between the sacred and secular aspects of contemporary culture. The search for the sources of this uncertainty, as well as speculation concerning how the conflict might be resolved, has led to a thorough reassessment of the role of religion in social change, and it has produced some of the most interesting studies and the liveliest academic debate in years.

The fact that the sacred-secular conflict is unsettled is interesting for two reasons, both of which are explored in this section. First, the tension between these two essential cultural realms underlies the current increase in the number, size, and intensity of certain social movements (and other types of intentional change), some striving to loosen or eliminate religion's hold on people's lives and others striving to increase it. Second, it was largely unexpected by social scientists of earlier generations, who were convinced that ours would be an entirely secularized world.

In some respects, a religion-free culture does appear to be inevitable. The long-term trends of demographic transition, industrialization, and urbanization experienced in Europe and North America were accompanied by a substantial, cumulative decline in the power of organized religions in political, economic, and other realms (Lidz 1979). You will recall from chapter 2 that Pitirim A. Sorokin (among many others) argued that our era is marked by an almost complete absence of moral and spiritual ideals in government, business, and everyday affairs. Thus, as the world's populations, economies, and geographies merge and converge on the Western model, secularization is bound to spread as well.

Nevertheless, religion always was, is, and remains a cultural universal. Its role has certainly changed since the time of the Protestant Reformation and the Industrial Revolution, in Europe and wherever European culture has had an impact. But it has not disappeared in any society to date. Even when rejected in its traditional forms, as it is among many groups today, it has a way of expressing itself in new institutional guises: as in the worship of the state, naturism-vegetarianism, cults of science, and other movements.

Moreover, religious revivals are sweeping the world, with missionary activity on the rise in several established denominations, Christian and non-Christian alike (Wuthnow 1983, 1992). Between the mid-1990s and the early years of the twenty-first century, national political leaders in the United States began to forge unprecedentedly strong links between government and organized religion (with resulting controversy over the meaning of the First Amendment to the U.S. Constitution; Lynch 2002; see also Doner 1998; Oldfield 1996). Religion has asserted itself in liberation movements in several Latin American countries (Candelaria 1990). And, as was brought home with tragic clarity to Americans on September 11, 2001, apocalyptic religion has once again become a key factor in world politics (Clarkson 1997; Esposito 2002). Several theocratic governments now reign in Central and Southern Asia—for example, Pakistan and Iran, and the ancient theocracy of Tibet remains at a political standoff with China, one of the world's most thoroughly antireligious regimes.

These trends indicate that, far from replacing or obliterating the sacred impulse in human culture, secularization can in fact stimulate religion as a powerful countervailing force. Reflecting on this dialectic, sociologist of religion Victor Lidz (1989) observed that "our understanding of secularization will probably be much affected by the experiences of non-Western societies over the next several decades" (737).

Religion as a Universal

Current interest in non-Western religious experiences is, itself, something of a revival (see figure 4.1). The social scientific study of religion was initiated in such societies some one hundred years ago when Emile Durkheim ([1912] 1965) conducted his pioneering research on the religion of the Aboriginal populations of Australia. Since that

FIGURE 4.1 The sacred impulse endures at the Angkor Wat city temple complex in Cambodia. Constructed in the early twelfth century by the Khmer King Suryavarman II, it was established as a Hindu temple dedicated to the God Vishnu. It continues to serve as a major religious site for Theravada Buddhists throughout the world. Photograph by Catherine Collins; used with permission.

time, social scientists have understood that all cultures contain beliefs, practices, and artifacts that create a divide between the sacred, or "holy," realm and the secular, "profane" world.

Durkheim's study was based on fieldwork conducted by anthropologists during a period when the Aboriginal people were just acquiring literacy. Theirs was viewed as an especially "primitive" culture, and Durkheim reasoned (in an evolutionary manner) that, by studying their religious beliefs and practices, we could understand all religion in its most elementary forms. He was also convinced that he was observing the twilight of traditional religion, and he wrote with a sense of urgency about preserving data on these "purer" elements before they disappeared beneath the secularizing influence of European culture.

Durkheim noted that three elements determine the way that Aboriginal, and therefore all, cultures define the sacred and secular dimensions:

1. Religion is an institution. It is a large-scale collective invention intended to help people solve problems in their relationships with each other and in adapting to their habitats. In traditional cultures, there is always considerable overlap between kinship and religion, as in the practices of ancestor worship and clan totems, whereas increasing social complexity leads to the growth of a separate, specialized set of specifically religious norms and organizations.
2. The problems addressed by religion deal with the unknown and possibly unknowable aspects of life: Who was I before I was born? Where will I go after death? How did the world begin? What lies beyond the stars?
3. It is a serious matter that some cultural items are included in the religious institution and others are excluded. There is always a boundary between the religious and nonreligious realms of life, even when religion and kinship intermingle as they do in traditional cultures.

In the Australian populations that Durkheim studied, the domains of religion and the ordinary world were thus strongly separated, yet intimately related. We now understand this basic tension to be a cultural universal: religion is a part of life everywhere, but it is a part that is set aside, and reserved, as "special" and "out of this world."

Box 4.1 TRIBAL RELIGION IN AUSTRALIA

Australian Aboriginal Shield (Darkur). North Queensland. Photographed by Gaius Cornelius at the Royal Albert Memorial Museum & Art Gallery, February 2006. Image in the public domain.

The people who crafted this shield were the subject of Durkheim's classic study of religion and culture, first published in 1900. Today, they maintain a website that includes a discussion of their religion.

The Dreaming

The Dreamtime has become a handy phrase used to describe what is in fact a sophisticated and interconnected mosaic of knowledge, beliefs and practises concerning the creativity of Ancestral Beings, and the continuity and values of Aboriginal life.

The vibrant ceremonial and religious life of Northern Territory people generated a spectacular array of art forms, including body painting and personal ornamentation, ground sculpture, bark painting, wood carving, and rock painting and engraving. Artistic creativity and innovation were informed by religious belief. Designs and motifs embodied multiple sets of meanings about group ownership of lands and relationships to particular Ancestral Beings. These expressions, along with the rich oral traditions, elaborate song and dance styles and personal performance of them, were all regarded as manifestations of the original ancestral creative power. Each generation accepted responsibility for passing on the economic, social and religious knowledge, beliefs and actions that ensured the reproduction of Aboriginal societies and cultures.

Before the dawn of the present age was "the Dreaming," or the Alchera of the Aranda, a time when the ancestors of the Aborigines wandered over a featureless land. These ancestors were unlike people of today; they possessed special powers and were so intimately associated with certain animals and plants that an ancestor of the kangaroo totem "may sometimes be spoken of either as a man-kangaroo or as a kangaroo-man." As the ancestors journeyed over the land, their actions gave it form, creating the natural features such as rivers and ranges. The land they shaped is today occupied by their descendants.

During their travels the dreamtime ancestors carried one or more sacred *tjurunga*, each "intimately associated with the idea of a spirit part of some individual." Many *tjurunga* were buried, each burial site marked by a natural object such as a rock or a tree.

Other places of significance are where ancestors entered the earth, at which time they died, but their spirits remained within the buried *tjurunga*. These places were also marked by natural objects.

There are thus at the present day, dotted about all over the Arrernte country, a very large number of places associated with these Alcheringa spirits, one group of whom will be Kangaroo, another Emu, another Hakea plant, and so on. When a woman conceives it simply means that one of these spirits has gone inside her, and knowing where she first became aware that she was pregnant, the child, when born, is regarded as the reincarnation of one of the spirit ancestors associated with that spot, and therefore it belongs to that particular totemic group.

Source: Geoff Moore, "Aboriginal Art Online," http://aboriginalart.com.au/.

Strong prohibitions exist in all cultures against violating the norms of separateness. If an artifact, such as a wine cup, is used for religious ceremonies, it is to be saved only for those occasions. Similarly, many everyday things (such as shoes, in the Muslim world) are not allowed in religious contexts. When the sacred and the secular are mixed in prohibited ways, there is a universal understanding that the former has been polluted, that it is "unclean." This applies to nonmaterial items as well as to objects: certain symbols, words, and norms are widely understood to be either religious or not, but rarely, if ever, both. Durkheim referred to this difference, in French, as *le sacre et le profane.*

The Old Testament makes this distinction in clear and direct terms. In the original Hebrew, the text reads, "Oolhavdeel bain ha'kodesh oovain hacol oovain hatamai oovain amador" ("And that ye may put difference between the holy and the common, and between the unclean and the clean" [Leviticus 10:10]).

The Process of Secularization

For many thousands of years, people generally viewed the sacred realm as dominant, and religious authorities such as priests and prophets occupied a special, elevated status; in Sorokin's terms, *ideational* values dominated. Even civil authority, when it emerged as a separate institution, depended formally on religious sanction, as in the doctrine of the divine right of kings. Ceremonies and social gatherings were required to have the blessings of religious officials: weddings, funerals, celebrations, and even athletic contests and other occasions that appear by contemporary standards to be purely secular (we still observe this today in invoking prayer prior to public events).

The Middle Ages are widely understood to have been an especially religiously oriented period in the West and beyond. Between the fall of Rome and the fifteenth century, all of the major religious cultures in Europe and the Middle East (Christianity, Islam, and Judaism) supported sacred societies. The Bible, Qu'ran, and Torah were accepted as the highest authority in the community, and secular affairs were to be guided and in every way bound by spiritual norms and ideals. In China, under the influence of Taoism, Buddhism, and especially Confucianism, a uniquely close and practical relationship was forged between the sacred and secular realms. Outside of the major empires and kingdoms, in parts of Asia, Africa, the New World, and the Pacific Islands with which contact had not yet occurred, traditional theocratic tribal cultures and civilizations were the rule.

Of course, there were exceptions. Clearly some amount (sometimes a considerable amount) of deviation occurred, at both individual and group levels. Instances of what various cultures considered sacrilege, paganism, and atheism, along with many movements to free one or another organization from sacred authority, can be found throughout recorded history. However, the principle of sacred over secular was rarely opposed.

Then, as the feudal era was drawing to a close in Europe, a widespread secularization movement began among the urban populations of several Christian empires. This movement had many profound consequences on the cultures involved, and because of the imperial systems that these cultures dominated, it eventually affected the world as a whole (Chadwick 1990; Fubini 2003; Swatos and Christiano 1999).

A central event was the disestablishment of the Roman Catholic Church, which culminated in the Protestant Reformation in Northern Europe beginning in the mid-1500s. Equally significant was the fall of the hereditary monarchies, which had operated under the official sanction of the pope. The successes of the mercantile and emerging capitalist economic systems provided a material challenge to the authority of established religions, as these proved to be more effective means of producing wealth than the land rents and tribute collection on which organized religion depended. Moreover, the secular economic systems required the practice of interest finance, which was considered usury and a sin in orthodox Roman Catholic and Muslim cultures.

These and related events of the era led to the rise of the specifically modern cultural pattern of individualism. With the fall of feudalism, a spiritual separation emerged between the individual person and larger collective wholes: family, estate, and congregation (Frankfurt Institute for Social Research 1972, chap. 3). In the process, the concept of individual rights and obligations, distinct from those based on hereditary group membership, was established. Protestantism promoted the doctrine that a valid, direct line of communication existed between the individual and God and that this direct access did not require mediation by a larger institution such as the medieval church. Representative political systems made the citizen sovereign over formerly higher, religiously sanctioned authority. And capitalism encouraged material success over otherworldly concerns about the sins of ill-gotten wealth. Taken together, these trends provided a significant force in pushing European culture toward the secular end of the sacred-secular continuum.

Between the 1600s and turn of the twentieth century, the institutions of secular government and economy developed in the capitals of Europe and spread throughout their colonial systems. Sacred authority was challenged virtually everywhere. But each culture touched by European secularization responded in a unique way, depending on the importance it attached to the sacred realm, the extent of domination by European culture in general, and other factors. To complicate matters, at the same time that Europe was diffusing its emerging secular principles to the colonized areas, it was also exporting its own sacred culture—itself in the process of secularizing—via missionaries.

These developments emphasize that the spread of European culture did not simply create secular societies throughout the world. In fact, Europe itself is far from entirely secularized to this day. However, postfeudal European culture did—and continues to—undermine sacred authority and to promote mundane principles of individualism, economic prosperity, and practicality wherever it has diffused. The result is that some measure of civil authority is exercised over religion in most places today. Yet everywhere a certain higher standing, at least symbolically, is provided for sacred beliefs and institutions.

When the leading theories of social and cultural change were being formulated in mid- to late-nineteenth-century Europe, secularization appeared to be an irresistible and universal force. As a result, there was near-unanimous agreement on this issue among scholars who otherwise represent very different political positions, disciplines, and cultural backgrounds. Karl Marx, Herbert Spencer, Weber, and Durkheim, for example, all considered secularization to be the wave of the future. They believed that the separation of sacred concerns from everyday life and the subordination of religious values and institutions to civil authority were inherent parts of modern institutions. In fact, one gets a strong sense from these earlier accounts that religion, on the one hand, and democracy, capitalism, and individualism, on the other, cannot coexist for long and that religion will inevitably yield to modernity.

> The three "classical" sociological theorists, Marx, Durkheim and Weber thought that the significance of religion would decrease in modern times. Each believed that religion is in a fundamental sense an illusion. The advocates of different faiths may be wholly persuaded of the validity of the beliefs they hold and the rituals in which they participate, yet the very diversity of religions and their obvious connections to different types of society, the three thinkers held, make these claims inherently implausible. (Giddens 1997, 536)

These are generally progressive theories in that they forecast increasing Westernization, with secularization a natural part of the same process. Marxism, as the most activist among these theories, specifically promotes the dominance of civil over sacred institutions, and the Marxist-Leninist version later developed during the Russian Revolution views secularization as the only legitimate path to evolutionary advance (that is, religion is considered to be an inherently reactionary institution). Modernization theory, which is more closely associated with politically liberal reform strategies, also prescribes secularization as a necessary condition for a viable capitalist economy and industrial growth. From this perspective, religious ideals and organizations cannot be permitted to interfere with the operation of markets and representative government.

Reversals: Civil Religion and Neofundamentalism

Several recent events and movements have helped to raise doubts about the inevitability of secularization and about its wisdom as a social policy as well. As sociologist Peter Berger (1969) summarized our new awareness of the power of religion, there is a "rumor of angels" abroad in contemporary society.

Two movements are of special interest, in part because they illustrate the nonlinear character of cultural change: that processes do not always exhibit steady, cumulative increase but often display instability and reversals. One of these is the rise of the seemingly contradictory institution of civil religion. The other is the reemergence of religious fundamentalism around the world. Neither of these could have been easily anticipated by the early social scientists, although one author, Alexis de Tocqueville ([1835] 1969), did observe the former in his studies of the United States. These movements reveal that religion has a far higher degree of resiliency, an ability to persist in the face of secularization, than was once imagined.

Civil Religion Civil religion is the collective valuation of political organizations, beliefs, and practices as sacred. The term, coined in the mid-1700s by the philosopher Jean Jacques Rousseau, refers to a creed involving "the sacred nature, the sacred ideals, the sacred character, and sacred meanings of [one's] country—its blessedness by God, and its special place and role in the world and in human history."[2] It is expressed, for example, when mistreatment of a national flag or other symbol is viewed as "desecration." In his studies of the United States, Robert Bellah (1992; Bellah and Hammond 1980) has revealed the many intricate, and often ironic, ways in which Americanism has become a creed that has replaced (or, more accurately, supplemented) traditional forms of religion. Thus, the common view of the United States as a highly secularized society misses how deeply religious it actually is, although these sentiments are not always expressed through traditional institutional channels.

Bellah and others (see also Hadaway, Marler, and Chaves 1993; Schneider [1975b] 1985, 294–99) have observed this phenomenon in other industrialized countries as well, suggesting that the worship of the state may be a peculiarly modern expression of the religious impulse (not just an American trait; see Rouner 1986). In fact, this practice is directly associated with the Holocaust. By elevating the Reich to the status of a sacred institution—and the party and führer as its guardians—Hitler turned his race war into a truly holy crusade (Winkler 1979; Wistrich 1985). Public ceremonies, the proliferation of state holidays, the symbolism of the swastika, and many other familiar artifacts of Nazi dramaturgy helped produce what can only be called religious fervor among the masses.[3] The Nazi experiment with civil religion was especially instructive not only because it gave sacred authority to otherwise thoroughly immoral acts but also because it brought about a landmark confrontation between civil authority and established, organized religion. Hitler was baptized in the Roman Catholic Church, but he did not attend mass and was frequently at odds with the Church hierarchy on both political and moral grounds. As part of his policy of total coordination (*Gleichschaltung*), he attempted to subordinate Germany's Catholic and Protestant congregations to party control and doctrine, that is, to "Nazify" them (Conway 1968; Delzell 1974; Morley 1980).

This turned out to be one of the least successful aspects of his program, and, as a result, the churches (priests, ministers, and parishioners alike) provided one of the few effective sources of resistance to the regime (Friedman 1978; Rittner and Meyers 1986). The many lives that were saved and the destruction that was prevented by these people and organizations testify to the fact that traditional religion can be a vital progressive force in contemporary society, even when pitted against a self-conscious project to replace it.[4]

With the defeat of Nazism, the modern world has recoiled to a considerable extent from such overt and destructive manifestations of civil religion. We are now fairly sensitive to the potential excesses involved in treating what is properly secular in our political institutions as if it was sacred, holding mass rallies to worship a political party, leader, or ideology. Yet these things do continue: in legislation on flag burning, public challenges to the "patriotism" of elected leaders, political party conventions, and many other forums (Bellah 1987). Moreover, they appear to be the natural result of the process of secularization: as traditional religious institutions and ideals are subordinated by the modern state and economy, the universal need for a sacred realm gets expressed in nontraditional forms, including extreme nationalism such as that under the Nazi regime.

Fundamentalism Religious fundamentalism is an alternate response to these same pressures. The term *fundamentalism* was first used in conjunction with a religious movement in the United States, inspired by the Great Awakening revivalism in western New York State of the mid-1800s.[5] Its current version emerged shortly after the end of World War II, and it has been rapidly accelerating as a worldwide movement since the 1970s (Kepel 1994). "Today it is used to describe Evangelical Christians, Iranian revolutionaries, ultra-orthodox Jews, militant Sikhs, and Buddhist resistance fighters, among others" (Beeman 2002, 129). It is motivated by the belief that all of our major social problems are the result of secularization.

Because modern political and economic institutions have subordinated traditional religion, supporters argue, people have lost their moral direction. Our beliefs and actions are no longer guided by God-given values, and as a result society is experiencing unprecedented levels of "vice and misery." The solution, according to fundamentalists, is to restore the rightful place of religion as the main and central social institution, and to reincorporate traditional—that is, fundamental—religious values in our lives.[6] The current rise of fundamentalism is a fairly recent phenomenon, but, of course, these are very old ideas whose diagnosis and therapy could apply to any era. As William Beeman (2002) notes in his informative chapter on the subject, "It is a common mistaken practice by laymen, including government officials and journalists, to view fundamentalist movements as localized, recent phenomena. This misperception always leads to shock and surprise when these movements emerge to challenge a dominant social order" (130).

In fact, the spread of secularism within and beyond Europe has met with similar resistance from several different sources over the centuries. Restoration movements occurred throughout the continent between 1700 and 1900, including counterreformations in Roman Catholic countries and the influential Chasidic movement in the Jewish communities of Poland and Lithuania (Buber 1960). In addition, in the more marginal populations of the European colonies, such as the hunting-and-gathering peoples of Central Africa and Amazonian America, traditional religion put up a relatively effective resistance to secular influences. In these few remaining isolated areas, tribal practices persist largely intact to this day. And three very old theocratic states, the Vatican, Tibet, and Bhutan, endured through the colonial era, although they recently have had to make accommodations with civil authorities. Thus, religion has never entirely "died out," as once expected.

Nevertheless, the main effect of European cultural influence abroad has been in the direction of secularization, or, at least, it has been widely perceived in this way. Thus, as Third World independence leaders began to challenge colonial rule, secularization, too, was attacked by some because of its association with cultural imperialism. In an effort to restore local, traditional religious values, fundamentalist factions formed within the broader, nationalist movements.

An important precedent was set in August 1947, when Pakistan was granted independence and Dominion status within the British Empire as a "Muslim homeland." Its constitution of 1956, which nullified the country's Dominion status and established the Islamic Republic of Pakistan, provided a framework for an entirely novel form of political system, a representative theocracy (Ishtiaq 1991).

From the perspective of religious authorities, Sharia law, derived from the Qu'ran, would be the basis on which Pakistan's civil and criminal law are established, with the Qu'ran having precedence in cases of conflict. Civil authority is viewed as the source of practical, day-to-day law and order, and the constitution prescribes a democratic, parliamentary form of government (Ashford 1967). But unlike other postcolonial representative systems, such as that of India (which formed a larger whole with Pakistan during British rule), Pakistan's constitution and, formally, its day-to-day application should be subject to the sanctions of a religious council (Dawood 1994).

Nevertheless, from its earliest days, the Islamic Republic of Pakistan has in practice been a largely secular nation, as the priority between civil and religious law remains unsettled to the present (an-Naim 2008). Complicating matters, the country has experienced several military coups and years of authoritarian military rule. This situation has preempted the claims of the supporters of both religious and secular interpretations of the constitution; and it has forestalled any possible settlement of the issue.[7]

The model of an Islamic state has been pursued in other parts of the Islamic world since 1948, in movements reacting to the perceived excesses of secularization and in organized attacks on European cultural imperialism. One of the most successful of these traces its origins to the anti-Western movement founded in 1875 by Jamal-al-Din (Asadabadi) Afghani. It eventuated in the Iranian Revolution of 1979, in which a new Islamic Republic was declared (Beeman 2002, 133–34; Moaddel 1993). Since that time, Egypt, Algeria, Israel, and several Balkan republics have been deeply affected by religious fundamentalist movements seeking to establish representative theocracy. And these are likely to continue for some time as the (previously unanticipated) counterpoint to secularization.

The revolution in Iran during the 1970s was overtly organized to combat Western imperialism. As in Pakistan, fundamentalist leaders were able to interpret this as a spiritual struggle against secular institutions and to prevail in forming the postrevolutionary state. In this respect, there are some interesting parallels, as well as contrasts, between Iran's experience and another revival of traditional religion, that is, in Central and Eastern Europe (especially, but not only, Poland) in the decades following World War II. There, too, Church authority challenged a secularized, foreign-dominated (i.e., Soviet-dominated) regime. In both instances, religious leaders were able to promote desecularization as a doctrine of political, as well as spiritual, liberation.

Perhaps the major difference between these two cases is that in Europe the Church did not exercise a monopoly over defining the situation and forming the new state. In Poland, in particular, organized labor played a major, independent role, although the Church and Solidarity supported one another in their struggles against the Communist regime. Thus, religion is now permitted and protected in Central and Eastern Europe (Bourdeaux 1995; Lewis 2000). But it has by no means replaced secular authority as it has in Iran. These post-Communist regimes are definitely not theocracies.

The recent Iranian and European revolutions, different as they are, share an important, common theme: the reassertion of traditional religious ideals as a form of social protest. In each, we find the argument that secularization has gone far enough and that the sacred dimension needs to be restored to its rightful place in human affairs.

Stated in this general way, the theme should be familiar to everyone in some form or another. Throughout the world, religious leaders and spokespersons have become prominent actors in major antiestablishment activities (Candelaria 1990). These are not just Muslim clerics fighting what they perceive to be Western immorality or Polish priests organizing against Communist autocracy but also leaders of the U.S. Civil Rights movement and of the opposing groups on the "religious right" (Wuthnow 1983). From all sides and for a wide variety of (sometimes seemingly contradictory) reasons, appeals can be heard to return to "the faith of our fathers," or some other faith, at the risk of suffering further consequences of excessive secularization (Wuthnow 1995). Thus, the term *fundamentalism*

> does seem to serve a useful purpose as a characterization of a repeatedly occurring and nearly universal human social phenomenon. The deeper comparative understanding of fundamentalism may forestall the frequent dismissive attitudes exhibited by groups sharing common beliefs toward each other. As Lionel Caplan, editor of a prominent collection of essays on the subject has noted: "an adequate understanding of fundamentalism requires us to acknowledge its potential in every movement or cause. . . . We are all of us, to some degree and in some senses, fundamentalists." (Beeman 2002, 130)

Fundamentalism, like civil religion, can be understood as a reaction to such excesses, a product of (1) the decline in the status of traditional religion and (2) the resiliency of the sacred impulse (Kepel 1994). The movement and the better world it promises satisfy an apparent need that Marx and many of his contemporaries felt could and would be eliminated under the appropriate political and economic circumstances. We are now aware that secularization does not necessarily replace religious thought and activity and that it can in fact stimulate them. So, as forces promoting both the sacred and the secular simultaneously diffuse to and within non-Western societies, religion's role will remain in dispute, a powerful source of conflict, perhaps, as Lidz (1989) suggests, for "the next several decades" (737).

Language Change and Regulation

Languages are among the most important systems of nonmaterial culture. In fact, some anthropologists have referred to culture as language (Hall 1966). This is a very popular and effective metaphor, for if we can understand how languages change, we will certainly know much about the dynamics of culture in general (this statement is a variation of the Whorf-Sapir hypothesis; see Whorf 1940; Sapir 1958). It also is important to remember that it is *just* a metaphor. In actual fact, cultures *contain* languages, along with numerous other items and wholes. There is not even a simple one-to-one correspondence. Many cultures have more than one language, and some share a common language with others. (As Winston Churchill said of the Americans and British, they are a single people divided by a common tongue.) See table 4.1 for a list of the world's most common languages.

Like other cultural items, living languages are always in the process of changing, although normally this is a gradual and largely imperceptible process, even between generations. Two main types of variation are (1) changes *in* a language, or variations over time in grammar, vocabulary, and other features, and (2) changes *of* language, as when a new one comes into being, a foreign one is newly adopted, or an old one dies out. At times, the two types of changes converge, as when the changes in a language become so great that the outcome is the change of a language, for example, the creation of a new one.

Language and Evolution

The study of language is an ancient pursuit and can be traced back to the works of Plato. It was of special interest during the era of social science's institutionalization in Europe during the mid- to late nineteenth century, when Weber, among others, was greatly influenced by the linguistic movement of the day. At that time, interest in the dynamics of language change was closely tied to evolutionary theory, and research was undertaken to discover a basic or original mother tongue from which all others were derived.

Based on the close connection between language and culture, this search for a single linguistic source was part of the quest for the original, pristine civilization: the sociological "missing link" between prehistoric times and the advanced European cultures of the

TABLE 4.1 The World's Most Common Languages

Rank	Language	Speakers (in millions)
1	Mandarin Chinese	1,075
2	Hindi/Urdu	575
3	English	514
4	Spanish	425
5	Russian	275
6	Arabic	256
7	Bengali	215
8	Portuguese	194
9	Malay/Indonesian	176
10	French	129
11	German	128
12	Japanese	126

Source: "Top Twelve Earth Languages by Number of Speakers," 1999, http://personal.bgsu.edu/~swellsj/languages.html.

era. The German word for this civilization is *Urvolk*, meaning the "original people" (associated with the ancient Babylonian city of Ur).

During the late nineteenth century, the very old cities of Mohenjo-Daro and Harappa were unearthed in the Indus River Valley of British India (today's Pakistan; Guha 2007; Possehl 1999). These and similar discoveries on the subcontinent inspired the founding of the field of Indology, which played a leading role in social scientific research at the end of the nineteenth century (Weber 1958). The language of the ancient North Indian civilizations was Sanskrit, which is still used in religious rituals today and is the source of Hindi, Gujarati, and dozens of other regional languages. It was thus concluded that the language from which Sanskrit is derived, so-called Indo-Aryan, was the original tongue, and that the Aryan people who inhabited Mohenjo-Daro were direct descendants of the *Urvolk* (Veblen [1913] 1969, [1915] 1969).[8]

Later research has shown that Indo-Aryan/Sanskrit was an important contributor to the European linguistic stream. In fact, more than 440 languages are classified under the related category "Indo-European." But it is not the root of every European language, let alone every language in the world (see table 4.2). Moreover, it is an amalgam of not one but several earlier languages. With the benefit of hindsight, we now realize that the search for an "original" language or culture is futile. Language, both spoken and written, like so many other major cultural products, was apparently invented several times and in several different places.

More recent studies of non-European tongues and of the effects of European culture contact on local languages have revealed that languages actually change in many different, often complex, ways.[9] Certainly, they do not simply evolve from "primitive" to "advanced" forms in a single pattern. Some languages are simpler than others because of the number of cases of nouns, some by virtue of the size of their alphabets, some by the number of irregular verbs, some because they are or are not tonal, and others by the size of their vocabulary.

In any case, there is no particular correlation between most of these measures and the degree of social complexity. For example, the languages of the tribal peoples of North America have far more noun cases than the two main European languages, English and French. Some European languages, such as Latin, are almost perfectly regular; others, such as English, are among the most irregular known. Such facts indicate that there is no basis for determining what a primitive or "basic" language might be like, let alone how one might evolve to become more "advanced."

The main exception to this lack of correlation is that the most complex, bureaucratic societies tend to have languages with the largest vocabularies (perhaps reflecting the broad range of possible experiences that its members can have). These also happen to be the societies with the greatest contact with other, distinct cultures. English, the language of global bureaucracy, leads the way today with over four hundred thousand words.

Many thousands of languages, living and extinct, have now been documented and studied, most of which are completely unrelated to Sanskrit (see www.ethnologue .com/). Each one developed in response to a multitude of partly unique demographic factors, such as different environments, population sizes and structures, and types of contact with other cultures. In addition, contemporary languages are typically subject

TABLE 4.2 The 108 Families of the Languages of the World (number of languages in parentheses)

Afro-Asiatic (372)	Geelvink Bay (33)	Oto-Manguean (172)
Alacalufan (2)	Guahiban (5)	Paezan (1)
Algic (40)	Gulf (4)	Panoan (30)
Altaic (65)	Harakmbet (2)	Peba-Yaguan (2)
Amto-Musan (2)	Hmong-Mien (32)	Penutian (33)
Andamanese (13)	Hokan (28)	Pidgin (17)
Arauan (8)	Huavean (4)	Quechuan (46)
Araucanian (2)	Indo-European (443)	Salishan (27)
Arawakan (60)	Iroquoian (10)	Salivan (2)
Artificial language (3)	Japanese (12)	Sepik-Ramu (104)
Arutani-Sape (2)	Jivaroan (4)	Sign language (2)
Australian (258)Austro-Asi-	Katukinan (3)	Sino-Tibetan (365)
atic (168)	Keres (2)	Siouan (17)
Austronesian (1262)	Khoisan (29)	Sko (7)
Aymaran (3)	Kiowa Tanoan (6)	South Caucasian (5)
Barbacoan (7)	Kwomtari-Baibai (6)	Subtiaba-Tlapanec (4)
Basque (3)	Language Isolate (30)	Tacanan (6)
Bayono-Awbono (2)	Left May (7)	Tai-Kadai (70)
Caddoan (5)	Lower Mamberamo (2)	Torricelli (48)
Cahuapanan (2)	Lule-Vilela (1)	Totonacan (11)
Cant (1)	Macro-Ge (32)	Trans-New Guinea (552)
Carib (29)	Maku (6)	Tucanoan (25)
Chapacura-Wanham (5)	Mascoian (5)	Tupi (70)
Chibchan (22)	Mataco-Guaicuru (11)	Unclassified (96)
Chimakuan (1)	Mayan (69)	Uralic (38)
Choco (10)	Misumalpan (4)	Uru-Chipaya (2)
Chon (2)	Mixed Language (8)	Uto-Aztecan (62)
Chukotko-Kamchatkan (5)	Mixe-Zoque (16)	Wakashan (5)
Chumash (7)	Mosetenan (1)	West Papuan (26)
Coahuiltecan (1)	Mura (1)	Witotoan (6)
Creole (81)	Muskogean (6)	Yanomam (4)
Deaf sign language (114)	Na-Dene (47)	Yenisei Ostyak (2)
Dravidian (75)	Nambiquaran (5)	Yukaghir (2)
East Bird's Head (3)	Niger-Congo (1489)	Yuki (2)
East Papuan (36)	Nilo-Saharan (199)	Zamucoan (2)
Eskimo-Aleut (11)	North Caucasian (34)	Zaparoan (7)

Note: English is one of 443 Indo-European languages. Note the inclusion of three "artificial" languages.

Source: Ethnologue, "Languages of the World," www.ethnologue.com/.

FIGURE 4.2 Montreal, the cultural and commercial capital of the Canadian province of Quebec, is subject to language legislation and planning. Here and throughout the province, this regulation affects the use of language in the schools, the courts, and in other official contexts. It also prohibits the display of commercial signage in which a language other than French predominates. Author photo.

to conscious regulation. Publishers of dictionaries and other reference works, government commissions, language academies, and educational institutions are routinely involved in legislating language form, content, and usage (Burchfield 1988; *Oxford English Dictionary* 1989). In all respects, language change is a model superorganic process.

The Mechanics of Language Change

In very small populations that share an exclusive language, there is little variation in how individuals use it. However, in larger populations with a single language, or in two or more distinct populations that speak the same language, diverse experiences and social contacts create subcultural differences that are reflected in dialects (see the classic discussion of American English and its dialects in Mencken 1921). In most U.S. cities, one can clearly distinguish between European American and other ethnic dialects, African and Hispanic American in particular: they are all versions of English, but they reflect and express the different experiences of the respective groups. In areas that contain several ethnic subpopulations or are in routine contact with foreign cultures, such as Louisiana and southern California, dialects may include elements from more than one language.

Under these circumstances, new languages can emerge in several ways. For example, local dialects can be combined and codified into a common new language that differs from its constituents to such an extent that users of each eventually cannot understand one another without translation. This occurred in the development of English, French, and several other European languages.

In contrast, older languages that are shared over a relatively large area can be transformed through local usage to create distinct but related variants. Latin, Sanskrit, and the South Indian language of Dravidian are ordinarily used today only in such geographically and nationally separated forms,[10] but the older versions are reserved by religious organizations for scholarly and ritual purposes (that is, they have become part of the sacred realm). So the original languages are not quite alive, nor are they extinct. Rather, they persist in a state of suspended animation, neither growing through the acquisition of new vocabularies or usages nor entirely forgotten. Until the founding of the State of Israel in 1948, the Hebrew language had these characteristics, only to be revived as an official language of a civil society.

Languages die altogether or become extinct when they are no longer used at all. Some have suffered this fate as the result of conquest and genocide, as the last members of the populations that share them pass away without progeny. This happened to numerous local languages of the colonized areas during the age of European imperial expansion, including several dozen in the Western Hemisphere (such as the Yana dialect of California discussed in chapter 2) and Africa. The process continues today among the rain forest people of the Amazon basin in South America. Some languages have died through assimilation of an ethnic subculture into a larger culture, as has occurred through the process of "Sanskritization" of local tribal peoples in India (Klass 1978; Singer 1968, 1972) and via urbanization in Africa. And some languages have reached the brink of death only to be resuscitated through the conscious efforts of preservationist movements. These include Gullah, the language of former slaves in coastal Carolina and Georgia, and Yiddish, the language of the Jews of Eastern Europe (see http://coastalguide.com/gullah; see also Benjamin 1994; Jones-Jackson 1976). The Yiddish revival—which is now occurring among non-Jewish populations of Central Europe—is especially well documented.

> In the 20th century alone, Yiddish, once a thriving language spoken by millions of Eastern European Jews, became something of an endangered tongue, its legacy maintained by scattered communities in North America and the Soviet Union. Now Yiddish is undergoing what many see as a revival. (Chan 2007)

"Acknowledging Yiddish's 'very long and often very fraught past,'" as Jeffrey Shandler, associate professor of Jewish studies at Rutgers University, has observed, "we often measure the state of a language and culture against the past, especially the period immediately before World War II, when Yiddish is the most widely spoken of any Jewish language in history and is the center of a vernacular culture of unprecedented scope in the Jewish experience" (Chan 2007).

The stock of living languages today represents the outcome of several interrelated processes: isolated development, conquest, genocide, assimilation, the creation of local variants, and the evolution of dialects into independent languages. Because of the intimate ties between culture and language, these closely parallel the sources of cultural survival and adaptation, in general. Overall, ours is an era of contraction in linguistic stock (and of cultures). Few natural languages are being created, and many continue to die out. Meanwhile, standardization is rapidly occurring under the impetus of worldwide electronic communication. The same words, phrases, and other elements are simultaneously entering local languages everywhere. Typically, these are English words or product names and slogans that are used on television (one French Academy member recently called it "linguistic pollution").

In fact, the English language itself is the most widely spoken second language in the world, and it continues to spread. In this respect, it is playing a role once envisioned for Esperanto, an invented, perfectly regular language based on Latin and its variants (Janton

1993).[11] Because of the extent and dominance of the British Empire up to the early 1900s, and the subsequent emergence of the United States as a world power, English is today the language of science, business, and, perhaps equally important, of CNN and MTV. Barring a serious reversal of these trends, it promises to be the de facto official tongue of the world system.

Summary

This exploration of the cultural component has ranged over a wide variety of topics. Beginning with a brief definition of culture, the chapter focused on three specific trends: the passing of traditional society, secularization, and language change and regulation. Despite the fact that it is long and at times complex, this chapter has touched on only a small fraction of the topics and issues of concern to contemporary students of culture change. The criterion used to select some things (and ignore others) is their relevance in explaining how and why the world is now changing so rapidly. Thus, I believe, secularization and the rest are likely to occupy center stage on the human scene in years to come. For the same reason, later chapters return to these trends, using this discussion as a guide and adding a few additional, necessary comments on the cultural component.

Relevant Websites

http://aboriginalart.com.au/
The Australian Aboriginal Art and Culture website. A wealth of art, music, poetry, and so on.

www.ethnologue.com/
This site contains an online catalog of languages of the world. It includes 6,800 main languages along with 41,000 alternate names and dialects and the Ethnologue language family index.

http://coastalguide.com/gullah
Here is a Gullah website with information about the language, culture, and music of the people descended from freed slaves along the coasts of South Carolina and Georgia.

www.esperantic.org/
For those who would like to learn Esperanto or learn about it, this is the site of the U.S. Esperantic Studies Foundation. Their postal address is 900 Northampton Street, NW, Washington, D.C., 20015-2951.

www.fnccec.com/index.html
For those who thought that the Government of Quebec is the only group in Canada interested in language rights, this is the Canadian aboriginal language rights site.

www.history.navy.mil/faqs/faq61-2.htm
www.history.navy.mil/faqs/faq61-4.htm
These are two sites dedicated to the code talkers, whose story was fictionalized in the movie *The Windtalkers*, maintained by the U.S. Navy. The first is a brief history of the Navajo Code Talkers. The second is the now declassified code talker's dictionary.

http://anthro.palomar.edu/culture
This site is entitled "Human Culture: An Introduction to the Characteristics of Culture and the Methods Used by Anthropologists to Study It." It is posted by Palomar College, California.

www.helsinki.fi/~tasalmin/nasia_index.html
A listing and discussion of extinct or nearly extinct languages of northeastern Asia. Posted by a language studies association in Finland.

Social Structures, Systems, and Processes

T HIS CHAPTER features the last of the three components of collective change, *social* dynamics. Setting aside specifically demographic and cultural processes and trends, the focus here is on the ways in which interpersonal relations have been altered over the course of the past several generations. As in previous chapters, the main concern is in understanding the sources of the vast, complex global society that is now emerging, a society that knows no international borders and in which space and time are no longer obstacles to communication.

At the most basic level, the social component consists of interactions: relatively brief episodes of joined, goal-directed behavior.[1] Beginning with the simplest type involving only two actors, the dyad, they are combined in various ways to form larger structures, up to and including whole societies and intersocietal systems (Kroeber and Parsons 1958). Sociologists usually distinguish between seven levels of scale, from the micro- to the macrolevel:

A. Microlevel
   1. Interactions are the basic units.
   2. Relationships are systems of interactions.
B. Micro- to mesolevels
   3. Groups are systems of relationships.
C. Mesolevel
   4. Organizations are systems of groups.
   5. Institutions are systems of organizations.

D. Macrolevel
   6. Societies are systems of institutions.
   7. Intersocietal systems include regional and world government, empires, and other very large structures. (Tilly 1984)

These levels are listed in ascending order of complexity, with the last five suggesting stages of evolutionary advance. That is, according to many evolutionists, the very earliest humans were able to sustain themselves only in small groups, but with time it became possible for the better-adapted populations to develop ever-larger, more complex structures (see Sanderson 2007, 235–46). Our current global revolution can thus be considered the latest stage in this millennia-long process. The most intense changes are now occurring at the last two levels, as humanity attempts to establish the ground rules for managing the current, explosive growth of large diverse societies and intersocietal systems.

The following sections take us through these levels with discussions of the social trends that have contributed most to the globalization process. First, the general theme of decline in primary relationships briefly mentioned in chapter 4, in connection with the passing of traditional society, is presented. Starting at the interpersonal level, the chapter moves to groups, to organizations, and then to institutional change. This discussion features the processes of institutionalization and the steady growth in the number, complexity, and degree of specialization of our social organizations and institutions. The chapter concludes at the societal and intersocietal levels with an analysis of bureaucratization, the long-term trend that has, perhaps more than any other, shaped contemporary social relations.

Changes in Relationships: From Primary to Secondary and Tertiary

Relationships are made up of interactions between occupants of complementary statuses, such as parent-child, teacher-student, and buyer-seller. Relationships have several attributes that can vary over time. These include the number of statuses and actors involved, the larger groups with which the statuses are associated (such as families, work groups, or athletic teams), whether they are ascribed or acquired, whether they are hierarchical, and whether the relationship is primary, secondary, or tertiary. For instance, in the case of a buyer-seller relationship, when a prospective buyer who formerly had a partner separates and proceeds to act alone, the relationship has changed because of a decrease in the number of statuses.

From time to time, the very norms that govern relationships are altered, not just the statuses or status occupants. This often has far-reaching consequences because in larger populations many millions of individuals may be involved. For example, in many societies, certain buyer-seller relations that once required a partnership have recently been altered by law. Now, one individual alone is allowed to make a sale or purchase, which obviously affects the way business is conducted in many situations. This did in fact occur with the recent changes in property law in the United States regarding the rights of married women. Until just a few years ago, the decisions of wives in real estate and other major transactions depended on the consent of their spouses. This is no longer the case, as women have been recognized (although still not completely) as legitimate contracting parties. Such a change clearly goes far beyond the bounds of any specific relationship or the experiences of any particular woman—or man.

The shift from primary to nonprimary relations is a similar type of normative change, perhaps the most important microsociological transformation that has ever occurred. It already was referred to in connection with the passing of tradition and as a leading theme in progressive evolutionary theories. The next section examines this shift as the underlying force in today's global revolution.

Primary Relationships: Family and Kin

Primary relationships depend on close personal ties, or intimacy. Participants are expected to care about the other as a whole person; they interact with respect to not just the status occupied but also all of the other's statuses. The interactions that make up primary relationships have an emotional character that includes both positive and negative feelings. Participants feel strongly about their and the other's role obligations. The term *primary* means (1) such relationships are the types that develop first in the lives of most people and (2) according to the values dominant in all cultures, they ought to be the most important in our lives. They were also the first type experienced by humanity and, until relatively recently, virtually the only type.

The defining primary relationship is that between parent and child. Other, non-familial ties, such as friendships, can be primary, but we think of them as family-like, and participants sometimes refer to one another as "sister," "brother," and so on. This practice of "fictive kinship" indicates that our earliest, and deepest, relationships serve as models for many others (Chatters, Taylor, and Jayakody 1994; see also Ibsen and Klobus 1972; see box 5.1).

As a primary relationship is established, its whole-person aspect and emotional intensity create a strong and long-lasting sense of mutual loyalty. This is the *primary bond*, and it may be obvious why it has been referred to as the "glue" that keeps society together. Such bonding provides a permanent basis for cooperation. In fact, because the primary bond is a human universal and is so closely tied to parent-child relationships, cooperation has been viewed as instinctual behavior (although the true boundaries between what is and what is not instinct in this case remain in dispute). Paradoxically, such intensity also means that the primary bond provides a permanent basis for social conflict, as most conflict (and violence) occurs between relatives and close associates (see box 5.2).

Secondary Relationships: Impersonal Ties

Secondary relationships are relatively impersonal. Participants are expected to be concerned only with the statuses of interest, not the whole person, as seen in the interactions between a military superior and a subordinate, which many sociologists view as

Box 5.1 FICTIVE KINSHIP

The social universe established by kinship cannot be defined solely in terms of biology and marriage alone. Indeed, kinship establishes the base, but not the totality, of what individuals think of as family. The roles that family plays in a society are not complete without the inclusion of fictive kin relationships. They are fictive in the sense that these ties have a basis different from bonds of blood and marriage, not in the sense that these relationships are any less important. In many societies, fictive ties are as important as or more important than comparable relationships created by blood, marriage, or adoption.

Briefly defined, fictive kinship involves the extension of kinship obligations and relationships to individuals specifically not otherwise included in the kinship universe. Godparenthood (or coparenthood), in its many manifestations, is the most commonly cited illustration, but there are numerous other examples. In many societies, people have "aunts" or "uncles" who are merely their parents' closest friends. Members of religious movements may refer to each other as "brother" or "sister" while observing the rules and prohibitions attached to those statuses. Crime networks and youth gangs employ kinship bonds and ideas of "blood brotherhood" as organizing principles. Nontraditional family forms such as gay and lesbian unions may be defined in traditional kinship terms.

Source: Richard A. Wagner, "Fictive Kinship," 1995, http://family.jrank.org/pages/630/Fictive-Kinship.html#ixzz0SbF6GEVm.

the model secondary relationship. Here, the soldier salutes the uniform, not the wearer, indicating that secondary relationships are depersonalized. So, whereas a mother should be concerned about her child's military career, to an officer, the welfare of the enlisted person's mother is irrelevant. At least, it is irrelevant to the officer as such. Of course, because we are more than the statuses we occupy, the officer *as fellow soldier* may well be genuinely concerned.

Secondary relationships tend to be emotionally neutral, and specific participants are relatively replaceable. For example, during a military operation any officer and enlisted person pair, such as a gun commander and gun loader, can be replaced by competent substitutes without substantially changing the relationship. In contrast, a mother-child relationship can no longer be sustained when one or the other participant is no longer available.

Because secondary relations lack the primary bond, they tend to be less permanent. When the specific task for which a relationship is formed is completed, it can dissolve with little emotional cost. In contrast, primary relations tend to be lifelong, and when they are severed, it is often with pain. In this and related ways, the world of secondary relationships in which most of us now live is a fleeting, affect-free, and cold world (Max Weber referred to it as *icy* cold).

Box 5.2 THE POWER OF PRIMARY RELATIONSHIPS

This is W. I. Thomas's classic discussion of the power of *primary relationships*. Thomas, Simmel, and Mead are recognized as the pioneers of microsociology.

The family is the smallest social unit and the primary defining agency. As soon as the child has free motion and begins to pull, tear, pry, meddle, and prowl, the parents begin to define the situation through speech and other signs and pressures: "Be quiet," "Sit up straight," "Blow your nose," "Wash your face," "Mind your mother," "Be kind to sister," etc. This is the real significance of Wordsworth's phrase, "Shades of the prison house begin to close upon the growing child." His wishes and activities begin to be inhibited, and gradually, by definitions within the family, by playmates, in the school, in the Sunday school, in the community, through reading, by formal instruction, by informal signs of approval and disapproval, the growing member learns the code of his society.

Source: W. I. Thomas, *The Unadjusted Girl* (Boston: Little, Brown, 1923, 45). Photo used by permission of the American Sociological Association.

Tertiary Relationships: Mediated Interaction

Both primary and secondary relationships require that actors have some direct experience of each other: "face-to-face" contact. In fact, primary relationships typically include prolonged periods of intense, direct interaction. Tertiary relationships, in contrast, are mediated: interactions occur, although participants are separated by space (Abu-Lughod 1966; Hintz and Couch 1978).

Tertiary interactions involve communication through media, "go-betweens" such as messengers, exchanges of letters, and a wide range of electronic media, including cell phones, TV, radio, fax, and e-mail, and social-networking sites such as Facebook and Twitter (see www.whatissocialnetworking.com/; Tilly and Wood 2009, 103–6; Wysocki 1996). Relationships formed in the course of such exchanges can be intimate or impersonal, and they can develop into secondary or even primary ties, as when pen pals meet and, in due course, get married.

Tertiary interactions often occur as part of primary and secondary relationships, with most occupations today requiring both face-to-face and mediated communication among coworkers, and most families staying "in touch" by phone. And it is possible for

FIGURE 5.1 Tertiary Relations: Who Is Talking to Whom? The two people shown here are friends and are participants in a primary relationship. As they experience a face-to-face encounter, they are also participating in tertiary relationships via their cell phones. Could they be talking to one another, thus combining these two levels simultaneously? Photo by Vojko Kalan. Image in the public domain.

a face-to-face relationship to become tertiary, as when old friends part forever but still remain in contact in other ways.

The Bureaucratization of Modern Society

Bureaucracy is the centerpiece of Weber's classic theory of social and cultural change (Weber [1922] 1968), and it is a crucial concept in contemporary studies of complex organizations. In fact, the general increase in the domination of complex secondary organizations that we have been discussing is often referred to generically as *bureaucratization*.

Bureaucracy literally means "rule by office," which emphasizes the fact that it is not rule by persons. It is based on an overarching value that secondary relationships are preferable to primary ones and that norms of membership, other norms and roles, and sanctions for conformity and deviancy should be based on certain acquired, not ascribed, statuses.

This value governs all formal relationships in a bureaucratic organization; no rule or role should apply to a particular individual. Rather, all should apply to any individual who possesses certain transferable skills. The emphasis on the rule of expertise, that experts and not persons have authority, has provided another colorful synonym to our sociological vocabulary: *meritocracy*.

There is a clear and direct contrast between bureaucratic forms of organizations and kinship structures. In the latter, primary relationships and ascribed statuses are everything. The significance of this contrast inspired Weber and many of his contemporaries to envision a great battle occurring in their societies between family and family values, on one side, and bureaucracy and bureaucratic values, on the other. It was viewed as a formative battle, and each theorist gave a special name to the two forces. For Ferdinand Tönnies ([1887] 1957), they were *Gemeinschaft* versus *Gesellschaft* (kinship community and complex organization); for Emile Durkheim ([1893] 1933), they were mechanical versus organic solidarity. Earlier, and in a more evolutionary vein, Herbert Spencer saw these as the lowest and highest levels of social complexity, respectively, according to his five-stage scheme.

Significantly, most of these theorists viewed bureaucracy as the inevitable winner of the battle. And many, including Weber, felt very sad about it, for bureaucratization seems to represent a loss of something authentically human. As Weber especially appreciated, bureaucracy is a powerful force. To the extent that it works, and it certainly does not always work perfectly, it is the most efficient form yet devised to create and maintain large-scale cooperative relationships. It can do virtually anything that people need or want to do— survive, prosper, do harm to (or benefit) the environment, undertake acts of altruism, or commit acts of genocide—more effectively than any other known system, certainly more so than the traditional *Gemeinschaft* ways. From this perspective, bureaucracy has replaced family because it performs so many traditional family functions better.

Today, we are more sensitive to the possibility of debureaucratization, difficult as it is, and to the reassertion of the importance of family values. But for most sociologists, the change is more or less permanent. Bureaucracy is here to stay. Although we occasionally are able to limit or prune it, most of us are aware that we would be considerably worse off without it. Even those who are engaged in debureaucratization and family value movements realize that they need bureaucracy to promote their causes. The problem for social scientists, and people in general, today is not that bureaucracy is an implacable and insidious foe of humanity. Rather, it is how to determine what kinds of goals we set and pursue with them: altruistic, genocidal, or other.

The following sections probe more deeply into the workings of bureaucracy with a look at three features that set them apart from other kinds of groups. First is the status of membership (these are largely voluntary organizations). Second is their internal structuring (they are highly complex and include both formal and informal systems of norms). Third is their capacity to have *persona* (they can act and speak as persons). In discussing the last of these, we also return to the three forms of authority introduced in chapter 4 in considering the crucial link between bureaucracy and democracy. Figure 5.2 illustrates the dimensions along which group membership varies.

Group Membership: Definitions and Criteria

To this point, I have generally reserved the word *member* to refer to one of several individuals in a population, subpopulation, or other physical aggregate to stress that people

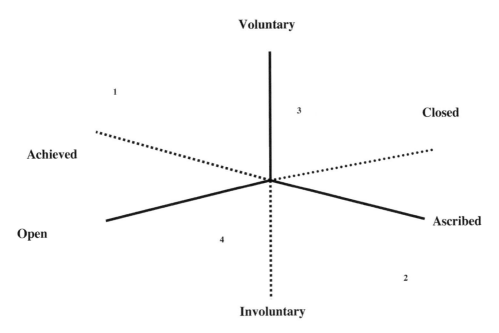

FIGURE 5.2 Dimensions of Group Membership

belong to populations but participate in social relationships. However, the term also applies to a particular social (not merely demographic) status, that is, whether a person is considered to be in or out of a group or organization. In this sense, membership depends on a shared definition: whether actors accept each other as members rather than on endogamy, territoriality, or objective structural characteristics, as in the case of populations and aggregates. Two individuals may reproduce and, with their children and their children's children, be members of a particular population. But it is by social definition that they are members of a religious organization.

Membership and Voluntary Associations A social member of a group is also a physical member of an aggregate, the one consisting of all of the social members. This distinction is important because the physical membership of a group may vary, as individuals change their social status from in to out or out to in, while the group itself endures. Groups, therefore, provide for continuity over time of statuses, roles, and relationships in relative independence of the demographic processes of birth, death, and migration.[2]

One of the most important aspects of secondary group membership is that it is more or less voluntary. "Research on voluntary associations has long observed that membership is a powerful force for individual and societal integration" (Glanville 2003, 1). Individuals are to varying degrees free to choose which groups they join and whom they accept as members. At the least voluntary extreme is the family, in which membership status ordinarily is ascribed (determined directly by biological factors), although adoption is a more voluntary means of joining. We would also not consider confinement to jail, prison, or another "total institution" (Goffman 1961) to be voluntary, although they are not directly based on ascribed statuses. At the most voluntary extreme, in contrast, are friendship groups such as pals who get together for after-school basketball.

Groups and organizations always have a mixture of voluntary and involuntary elements. In countries where the military draft is compulsory, "voluntary" membership in the army is virtually ascribed for members of the eligible gender(s) and cohorts. On the other hand, those who belong to a group of workers at an office, in their roles as workers, ordinarily become members of their own volition. Yet they are not entirely free in their choices: most people believe they must work (although there are other ways to survive), and maybe for some workers, their present job is the only one they could get.

Membership Criteria Individuals are permitted to join some groups and organizations but not others based, in part, on explicit criteria of membership, that is, whether the person qualifies to belong according to the group's norms. Thus, although membership in a military unit, group of office workers, or informal basketball team are all, to a degree, voluntary in comparison to membership in the family of one's parents, the first three depend nevertheless on a process in which candidates are evaluated and judged acceptable or unacceptable.

Membership criteria differ from group to group, and they can change over time within a particular group or organization. The differences depend on the relative importance of ascribed versus acquired statuses of candidates. The criteria used in the military include some ascribed statuses. To qualify, a candidate must be a certain age, be within a "normal" range of physical and mental characteristics, and be a resident (or, in some places, a citizen) of the nation. In the past, gender was also a primary consideration, as only men could serve. This has changed in North America and other places, although the specific unit within a larger military organization to which a new recruit is assigned still depends on this ascribed characteristic.

Some characteristics used as criteria for membership in a military unit clearly are ascribed, such as age, but others, such as weight, some disqualifying physical and mental conditions, and even height, are partly acquired. Typically, other partly acquired statuses, such as scores on intelligence tests and levels of academic achievement (e.g., a high school diploma), are counted as part of one's psychological qualifications. Residency and citizenship are also more subject to the control of individuals than their age or gender, although even gender can be medically changed.

In comparison to the military, membership in a group of office workers, in most complex societies today, depends little on ascribed characteristics. Gender, age, height, and weight are less relevant, whereas learning abilities, academic achievement, and the possession of specific skills are more important. Yet, nearly everywhere, membership in such groups also requires residency status (or a work permit for recent immigrants) and some minimal mental and physical capacities, which are partly ascribed.

Membership criteria are applied not only when an individual enters a group but also when a member exits. Again, we find a wide range of variation in terms of the degree to which members may leave on their own volition or cause another to leave involuntarily. In some groups and organizations (like the U.S. Congress), membership lasts only for a limited period that is understood at the time of entry, at which point it is not terminated but rather expires. In others, such as a group of office workers, members may leave freely and may be terminated if they are found to fall short of established standards of performance. In other groups, such as a military unit, leaving before the term of service has expired is a difficult, but not impossible, undertaking. In contrast to all of these, a member of an involuntary group continues to belong until death (or, as in the case of incarceration, until the term is fully served or commuted).

Open and Closed Groups The extent to which a group or larger structure is closed or open depends on membership criteria and how they are applied and enforced (Popper 1952). An open group has relatively loose criteria and depends less on ascribed and more on acquired (and more easily acquired) characteristics. A closed group has strict, ascribed, or difficult-to-acquire criteria for entry and exit. An involuntary group, thus, is also the most closed.

Over the course of human existence, societies have differed in the extent to which participation has been open or closed. But during most periods and in most places, group life has been dominated by involuntary membership and closure, although there have always been exceptions. Beginning at about the time of the Industrial Revolution in Europe, voluntary and open groups became more prominent. This change was ultimately incorporated into the laws of many societies, often as the result of social movements on behalf of excluded categories. In this way, certain traditional types of closure, based on physical characteristics, kinship, and gender, became prohibited. Today, in North America and elsewhere, closure based on ascribed statuses, as well as dismissal without due cause and due process, are subject to serious legal challenge. Membership has, in some respects, become a right.

The types of groups available to people determine their opportunities to enter into cooperative relationships. When social ties are confined only to ascribed statuses, the individual's capacities and entire world are limited. When people can freely enter and leave a wide range of groups that depend on other kinds of statuses beyond kinship, gender, and age, they can accomplish much.

In summary, voluntary associations played a very small part in people's lives until quite recently. This phenomenon contributed to the overall stability of traditional cultures and civilizations, reinforcing their slow pace of change. Today such organizations are essential to the functioning of society and are an additional source of its dynamism.

Structural Variations in Bureaucracies

In every organization, interactions and relationships become patterned over the course of time: the same words and language are used, certain activities become ritualized, and the behavior of members in their roles as members becomes predictable. Then, during critical periods, these regularities and patterns are altered, and organizational routine is disrupted. Two paired concepts have proved especially useful in understanding how this kind of social change occurs: *formal* versus *informal*, and *rigid* versus *flexible*.

From Informal to Formal Structures Secondary organizations have both a formal and an informal structure. The first consists of the regularities referred to in the official norms that are publicly understood to govern the group and that are usually committed to writing: the code of rules, constitution, or other specific regulations. The informal structure consists of the regularities in group behavior not referred to in the formal rules but agreed upon by members in their interpersonal relations.

All aspects of group life, including membership criteria, operate according to both formal and informal norms. Thus, a group might have no explicit prohibitions against individuals with particular ascribed statuses and still exclude or dismiss them by virtue of informal standards: a group of office workers may exclude women, despite the fact that it is not a formal rule, because there is informal agreement to that effect. When membership or dismissal decisions are legally challenged, it is often the informal structure whose effects are most difficult to discern.

Because both formal and informal structures are normative, acts in relation to both are subject to definition as conforming or deviant, and both are subject to appropriate sanctions: formal or informal. At times, informal norms contradict formal ones, in which case actors cannot possibly be entirely rule abiding but may choose only what type of deviant act they will perform. In a landmark study of the gypsum mining industry, sociologist Alvin Gouldner (1954) observed a range of accommodations between formal and informal norms within a single organization. These varied from (1) complete agreement between the two to (2) complete disregard of the formal norms by all concerned, whereby everyone was technically deviant.

The study was conducted at a time when it was acceptable to smoke on the job, but because of the nature of the work, there was a strict policy against it at this company. Gouldner found that, in some contexts, such as when the workers were actually digging in the mine, the formal norm was always obeyed; the workers accepted it and personally enforced it among themselves. He labeled this pattern "representative" bureaucracy to indicate that it was a matter of mutual agreement. On the other hand, in the office no one paid any attention to the rule or the prominently posted "No Smoking" sign. Workers and supervisors alike lit up whenever they chose, clearly following their own informal norms despite official policy. The only time they put out their cigarettes in the office was when the fire marshal came on an inspection visit. For obvious reasons, Gouldner called this pattern "mock bureaucracy."

An even more influential study of the interplay between formal and informal structures is the much-cited case of the workers at the Hawthorne Western Electric telephone assembly plant near Chicago (Roethlisberger and Dickinson 1939). A small group of new workers had written orders—a formal norm—to produce at the highest possible rate consistent with quality and safety. When researchers measured their output compared to an experimental standard, one based on controlled observations of similar groups, they found considerable deviancy. It was not simply a matter of some individuals performing below standard; all of them were performing well below the maximum. They seemed incapable of producing nearly as many phones per day as the experimental groups. In fact, because of how the assembly process was organized, this had to be the result of some type of cooperation (see box 5.3).

Box 5.3 THE HAWTHORNE WESTERN ELECTRIC STUDY

The "Hawthorne Effect"

What Mayo urged in broad outline has become part of the orthodoxy of modern management.

—Abraham Zaleznik, Professor of Leadership, Emeritus,
Harvard Business School, 1984

In 1966, Roethlisberger and William Dickson published *Counseling in an Organization*, which revisited lessons gained from the experiments. Roethlisberger described "the Hawthorne effect" as the phenomenon in which subjects in behavioral studies change their performance in response to being observed. Many critics have reexamined the studies from methodological and ideological perspectives; others find the overarching questions and theories of the time have new relevance in light of the current focus on collaborative management. The experiments

(Continued)

Box 5.3 THE HAWTHORNE WESTERN ELECTRIC STUDY (Continued)

remain a telling case study of researchers and subsequent scholars who interpret the data through the lens of their own times and particular biases.

"Instead of treating the workers as an appendage to 'the machine,'" Jeffrey Sonnenfeld notes in his detailed analysis of the studies, the Hawthorne experiments brought to light ideas concerning motivational influences, job satisfaction, resistance to change, group norms, worker participation, and effective leadership. These were groundbreaking concepts in the 1930s. From the leadership point of view today, organizations that do not pay sufficient attention to "people" and "cultural" variables are consistently less successful than those that do. From the leadership point of view today, organizations that do not pay sufficient attention to people and the deep sentiments and relationships connecting them are consistently less successful than those that do. "The change which you and your associates are working to effect will not be mechanical but humane."

Note: The results of the famous Western Electric Study led to the creation of the field of Human Relations in Industry. The Hawthorne Effect: performance improves because performance is being observed (with no other changes).

Source: Harvard Business School Baker Library historical collections, www.library.hbs.edu/hc/hawthorne/09.html#nine.

It appeared as if the Western Electric employees were conforming to a different norm, and, as it turned out, they were. It was a norm that had been established informally long before the study began by workers who had retired or moved on to other groups after they had handed it over to the current members. It reflected the workers' definition of quality, safety, and (something perhaps not considered in the formal rule) comfort. When members broke the informal rule, they were considered "rate busters" and received sanctions from their colleagues, including a "playful," but painful, punch to the arm.

Change in organizational structure or functioning usually follows when such contradictions between formal and informal norms become manifest. Rates of deviancy from either the formal or informal norms can vary (e.g., workers are encouraged to be more "cooperative"), or the formal rules can be purposely amended, with the intent of altering patterns of behavior more in the direction of the informal norms. The latter is called "formalization," and it is similar to the institutionalization of former deviant practices discussed. It did occur at the Western Electric plant when, as a result of the study, official work rates were lowered. This turned out to be a pioneering reform in the human relations in industry movement.

From Rigid to Flexible Bureaucracy As part of the long-term transition from less to more voluntary forms of association, groups and organizations have generally become less rigid. Bureaucratic codes of conduct and constitutions are now routinely subject to negotiation and change. Channels increasingly exist for informal norms to become formalized. Today's Western Electric workers stand a far better chance than their predecessors of having their work rate accepted as the standard instead of the bureaucratically "correct" but less human experimental norm.

The corporate world has signaled this shift by gradually abandoning the old, rigid concept of production—one product per stationary plant using one specialized workforce—in favor of "flexible integrated manufacturing." In this system, any group of workers in any factory can change any aspect of the production process, including the end product itself, in a matter of days (Flexible Automation and Integrated Manufacturing Conference [FAIMC] 1993). The new industrial rule is that rules can be amended. This is a significant shift, for it reflects the formal acceptance of change itself as a positive value in a characteristically highly conservative institution (Tavalage 1988).

Such flexibility is conspicuously absent in older types of bureaucracies, which have been called "structures of rules" because their operation is invested with unimpeachable rational-legal authority. Group activities are subordinated to the rules, and individual or informal interests are treated as irrelevant and dispensable. By narrowing the range of acceptable acts in these ways, such organizations are prone to a high degree of stability, which is reinforced by a rigid internal structure. Although these correspond to our popular stereotype of bureaucracy, they are in fact becoming less common by the day.

Because it is rule governed, bureaucracy is an ideal engine of peaceful change. As a structure of authority, it makes power relationships—that is, regularities in who can force whom to act in particular ways—that are legitimate and lawful. Because it operates according to rational-legal principles, it actively opposes both tradition, which resists change, and charisma, which promotes militant, disruptive social transformations.

By the same token, rule *governed*, in the old sense, can easily become rule *bound*. This is bureaucracy's major liability. Rules are the only source of a bureaucracy's authority, beyond any specific authority figures, so they can assume precedence over everything else. Organizations can grind on for reasons that are apparently beyond human comprehension or control. Bureaucracies are prone to a familiar kind of ritualism in which participants act rationally in obeying the rules, but, at the same time, the organization is involved in a totally senseless mission. Some organizations even appear not to need any goals at all; they just keep running because the rules say so. (Franz Kafka's novel *The Trial* [(1956) 1968] provides a chilling account of such pointless but persistent bureaucracies.)

As a general organizational trait, this excessive focus on the rules is known as *goal displacement*, and it is so common that many sociologists have viewed it as a necessary part of bureaucratization. Its discovery in the late nineteenth century and subsequent research on the phenomenon and its impacts constitute one of social science's major achievements, for the notion of goal displacement allows us to understand individual rationality as relative to specific sets of means and ends, rather than as an absolute.

In expressing this relativist position, Weber and the Hungarian-born sociologist Karl Mannheim referred to two modes of organizational activity. Mannheim's terms are *technical operations* and *substantive outcomes* (see Horowitz 1983, 45; Mills 1968), terms that correspond directly to what Weber called *Zweck* rationality and *Wert* rationality, respectively, in his theory of authority. This distinction explains how it can happen that people in bureaucratic contexts may act quite rationally at the technical level (*Zweck*) as they routinely, and correctly, connect means to ends, while the ends themselves may be quite irrational at the substantive level according to widely held standards (*Wert*).

Bureaucracy and the Banality of Evil   In this manner, even genocide can be made "rational" when it is performed in bureaucratic organizations in which participants are tied to functional routines (Horowitz 1980). This is what Hannah Arendt was pointing to when she coined the powerful concept of "banality of evil" in reference to those who carried out the Holocaust (Arendt 1964). The organizers of the death camps, including Supreme Commandant Adolf Eichmann whose trial Arendt studied, argued that they were guilty of no crimes because they were only following organizational rules and never personally killed anyone. They were thus truly banal, ordinary people caught up in extraordinary circumstances that they claimed were beyond their control. They had no choice, they argued, but to obey the law and their superiors.

As you may know, this defense was repudiated by the Nuremberg Tribunal of 1945 and again at Eichmann's trial and appeal in 1961–1962. The findings are now part of international law and signal a major—perhaps the most dramatic—example of the recent shift from rigid to flexible bureaucracy, for they redefine the force of norms in groups and organizations, not just in one society but for humanity in general. One recent landmark in this respect was the creation of the International Criminal Court (ICC) in 2002. This measure institutionalized the prosecution of cases of genocide and crimes against humanity that had previously occurred on an ad hoc basis (see chapter 1).

This redefinition covers three main issues:

1. Members of organizations are responsible for knowing what formal ends are being served by their acts. Thus, goal displacement can no longer be used as a moral or legal defense of the ultimate outcomes of one's acts. This means that Eichmann was responsible not merely for ensuring that the transportation of railway cargo to the east occurred in an orderly fashion but also for knowing that the cargo consisted of innocent civilians who were being transported to their certain deaths. He was declared guilty of mass murder because he was, in principle, the agent of the deaths of the civilians.
2. Members of organizations who are required to act in functionally rational ways to achieve formally irrational ends have the legal right and the moral duty to disobey orders. People in Eichmann's position today are expected to report order givers to their supervisors when they insist that formally irrational procedures be followed (the theme of the movie *A Few Good Men*). If necessary, one is encouraged to take it all the way to the "top," the ICC or World Court in Geneva, which have been charged with enforcing the new norms of bureaucracy.
3. Members of organizations, and members of societies in which the organizations operate, are responsible for knowing what the ultimate goals are and for amending them if they are irrational. Structures must not be so rigid that rules cannot be changed. In other words, organizations are subject to the will of the people, not the other way around.

These three points underlie a revolution in our understanding of the relationship between the individual and the group. Whereas in the past social values typically stressed the priority of the organization, we have learned how destructive the consequences of this can be under contemporary circumstances and with the aid of modern technologies of social control. As is to be expected, however, such a massive change has revealed a lag, for these principles express ideals, not realities. Such principles can be effective only if the right of people to participate in changing the structure and goals of organizations is guaranteed; they require institutionalization. But this means that society must be organized in a highly democratic fashion, more so than is the case anywhere today (although some societies are closer than are others). It also means that no group can be systematically excluded from organizational decision making in government, business, or other public contexts, and no one can be forced to obey duly constituted laws they believe to be immoral without due process. Lacking such extensive democratic rights and protections, the assertion of the sovereignty of individuals over groups is just an assertion, and it cannot by itself combat the bureaucratic tendencies toward goal displacement, substantive irrationality, and being rule bound.

Bureaucratic organizations are found in all contemporary societies, from the most democratic to the most autocratic. They have been part of ancient civilizations as well, including China, India, and Imperial Rome.[3] They can be, and have been, powerful forces in serving autocratic ends, especially when social values support the group at the expense of the individual and when structures are rigid and closed.[4] Nevertheless, since 1945 at least, we know that it is the rulers who are the enemies of democracy, not the organizations as such or their "inviolable" rules.

Bureaucracy was once believed to be naturally antagonistic to democratic procedures and participation, but we are now aware that this is not the case. Large-scale organizations can, and do, serve democratic purposes and democratic leaders. And with the Nuremberg and Eichmann protocols, the opportunity has been presented to make our bureaucratic world even more democratic. In fact, the prosecution of Nazi war criminals such as Eichmann, and more recently of the Serbian dictator, Slobodan Milosevic, were possible only because the justice system is so bureaucratized. Yet, this is such a new way of viewing organizational authority that our social structures have not yet caught up with our cultural ideals. The lag between principle and practice needs to be closed before we can be assured that bureaucracy will not be put to the service of more "final solutions."

Groups as Persons: The Political Dimension

Like individuals, groups are able to behave and "speak" as persons (to have a *persona*, in legal terms; Vincent 1989).[5] This can occur directly, as when office workers jointly write and publish a report. In such cases, cooperation is visible and manifest; an observer can see people joining their behavior for a common goal. Group action can also take place through indirect representation, as when a specific office worker delivers a report to a printer on behalf of the group. Groups speak as persons when they authorize one or more members to represent them in oral or written form. Thus, department heads in an office correspond with one another "in the name of" their constituents.

This quality reflects the most advanced level of collective action, whereby a group has achieved the capacity to act for itself. In contrast, some groups can function only in themselves, passively directed by nonmembers. Marx first highlighted the distinction in his analysis of the role of social classes during political revolutions (Engels [1871] 1969; Marx and Engels [1864] 1970, 63–79), although it applies equally well to a wide range of situations, including the routine operations of bureaucratic organizations.

You will recall from chapter 3 that a demographic aggregate is a physical collection of individuals who are alike with regard to common, objective characteristics, such as all women in the 20–25-year cohort in the population of the state of Michigan. Technically, such a collection is not a group at all; it is merely a category, until and unless its members participate in relationships and abide by common norms. At that point it becomes a group *in itself*, a characteristic that would describe the citizens of the town of Dearborn, Michigan, for example.

A group *for itself* is created when participants act and speak collectively and cooperatively as a person. For instance, the Dearborn School Board has achieved this status. Such groups not only exist passively but also are able to act according to what they perceive to be their common interests—what is "good" for the whole. In this light, a group's persona depends in part on its ability (1) to define what its interests are, collectively or by authority of specific individuals, and (2) to act authoritatively in pursuing them.

Marx was especially interested in the conditions necessary to cause a group in itself, such as factory workers, to become a group for itself: a working-class movement. The key turning point, according to Marxist theory, is when collective consciousness develops (Marx and Engels [1848] 1969, 126). Participants come to share a definition of themselves as members of a larger whole, to understand that this whole has its own interests beyond those of any particular member, and to understand that it has the ability to define and achieve common goals in collective action.

Marx's studies of the rise of the bourgeoisie in Europe focus on class consciousness. But the principles apply to not just classes but also any group or organization (see Chong and Rogers 2002). Families are the oldest and most basic type of a group for itself, in which collective consciousness is created and reinforced, largely automatically, through the primary bond (Engels [1884] 1969, 209–55). In populations whose level of social organization does not go beyond kinship relationships, group interests correspond closely with survival imperatives and environmental adaptations, that is, what is good for the aggregate is good for the group because the two closely coincide.

When secondary relationships emerge, however, collective consciousness and collective action become problematic. At that point, something other than the natural bond of kinship is required to bring about a shared definition of group interests. Marxist theory stresses two conditions: (1) common formative experiences that create an "existential bond" (for workers, this is the common experience of working together and being exploited by another [owning] class), and (2) leadership by individuals who can authoritatively define common interests and relate them to the bonding experience. Marx referred to this latter condition as "vanguardship," indicating not only leadership but also direction in the pursuit of progressive change. In his theory of working-class revolution, this vanguard role was, of course, to be played by the Communist Party (Marx and Engels [1848] 1969).

In seeking the reasons that groups in general achieve collective consciousness, contemporary sociologists retain the Marxist emphasis on these two formative conditions. Thus, to become a group *for* itself, a group *in* itself needs to undergo bonding. And it must develop an authority structure that is capable of turning the subjective experiences of members into an awareness of common interests and of instilling the shared belief that they can—and should—act on them (Tsoukalas 2007). With this accomplished, groups can participate as autonomous actors in cooperation or, as Marxists stress, in conflict with other groups (for Simmel [1955], cooperation and conflict were complementary aspects of group behavior). Lacking these, a group remains an object that can be manipulated according to the will of others who are pursuing their own interests.

Persona and the Forms of Authority The form of cultural authority that is prevalent significantly affects the kind of persona that a group or organization develops: tradition, charisma, or rational law. As noted, tradition is the ancient, original method of defining correct beliefs and practices. In the context of group leadership, it is closely tied to kinship and, later in history, to patrimonial rule. Rational-legal authority is a recent innovation, whose dominance can be traced to the fall of feudalism in Europe. Charisma, based on extraordinary personal characteristics, is the most dynamic of the three and has played a prominent role during critical periods throughout history.

Charisma gives some individuals the authority to control, represent, and define the interests of a group or organization because of their unique personalities, not because the normative frameworks of tradition or law authorize them. Charismatic leaders are uniquely capable of creating and directing a group for itself, of identifying themselves with the group's persona. "I am the Party; I am the Reich," railed Hitler, and "L'etat c'est moi"("I am the State"), declared seventeenth-century French king Louis XIV.

As such, charisma is unstable. It is effective in movements that seek to gain political control from outside the system, but a successful charismatic leader must eventually employ traditional or rational-legal means to maintain control. This is called the *routinization of charisma*, and it is a common feature of all social changes that are initiated by protest movements.

Gandhi and his associate Mohammed Ali Jinnah (leader of Pakistan's independence struggle) were charismatic individuals. This quality allowed them to direct and speak for millions of people, against tradition and against prevailing law, during the anticolonial movement in British India. But it was their organizations, the All-India Congress and the Muslim League, respectively, that turned their charisma into rational-legal authority. The organizations created, defined the interests of, and eventually ruled the new nations of India and Pakistan long after the deaths of the principals. Ironically, the Congress and Muslim League were effective because they operated according to the same routine and regulated principles that had brought success to the colonial authorities: they were good bureaucracies.

In our discussion of rational-legal authority in chapter 4, we saw that this form first appeared in Europe between the sixteenth and eighteenth centuries. It is the modern source of group persona, stipulating that the acts a group undertakes for itself, group interests, and the designation of those individuals who legitimately represent the group are all subject to the authority of formal laws, not patriarchs, kings, or charismatic leaders. This concept of group action fits perfectly with bureaucratization because the rise of bureaucratic society coincides (in theory and in history) with the institutionalization of rational-legal authority. In historical perspective, this was a fundamental innovation in the very long-term process of structural change.

We can divide this process into four stages, which also summarize several of the main characteristics of the bureaucratization process:

1. In the distant past, collective decisions were governed by general kinship norms. In little-tradition cultures, dominant family members were authorized to decide, speak for, and define the interests of the group.
2. Subsequently, great-tradition authority figures, such as hereditary rulers and religious leaders, came to play these roles in secondary groups and organizations. This is one of the conditions, along with the generation of an adequate economic surplus, that allowed for urban settlement. Secondary authority first began to replace primary relations in populations of the Middle East about ten thousand years ago, although kinship continued to dominate the day-to-day lives of most people. In these and other times and places, such as Central and South America about three thousand years ago, the transition was also connected with agricultural revolution.
3. For the past few centuries, especially since the beginning of the Industrial Revolution in Europe, to an unprecedented extent people have been able to create and sustain new groups and organizations, or to reform old ones, with rational-legal procedures. At this point, classic bureaucracy began to dominate over traditional organizational types.
4. Since the end of World War II, large-scale organizations have become more open, flexible, and (at least in principle) subject to the collective will of members.

When and where these stages have occurred successively, the latter three reflect cumulative increases in a population's capacity to exact cooperation from members. Each is also further removed from mechanical solidarity, from *Gemeinschaft* forms, and successively more impersonal, differentiated, and complex.

Traditional rule is characterized by social conditions that support nonrepresentative authority structures. People who are not in positions of authority are expected to obey unquestioningly their superiors. In this type of society, hereditary rulers (or conquerors) alone are entitled to speak for groups and to define group interests. As a political system, this is a *direct*, or *classic, autocracy*.

In such a system, rulers tend to define the good of the whole as coincident with their own welfare. However, a few traditional societies of this type have employed procedures of *direct* (or *classic*) *democracy*, in which group goals and interests are defined by members, independently of the interests of particular leaders. Here, all group members physically assemble and debate issues until a unanimous consensus is reached. The democracies of ancient Greece, with their restricted definition of membership, were modeled along these lines. Although these systems achieved some success, most proved to be unwieldy, often taking an inordinate amount of time to reach consensus on even the simplest matters. They also proved to be unstable under pressure from autocratic movements. They were necessarily small and closed, and they were extremely undemocratic in the contemporary sense, requiring economic and military support from a large, nonparticipating group of slaves, women, or others excluded from membership.

Rational-legal authority, in contrast to both types of traditional direct rule, is a representative system. It is an indirect method of impersonal governance in which collective action is determined by universally applicable laws and procedures, not by hereditary monarchs or assemblies of the select few. Groups are considered to be legitimately speaking and acting for themselves only when abiding by public, impersonal norms.

Since the late eighteenth century, two broad types of representative systems have been established: (1) those in which bureaucratic organizations are open, flexible, and defined as subject to the sovereignty of members are *indirect or representative democracies*, and (2) those in which organizations are closed, inflexible, and defined as sovereign over members are *representative autocracies* (also referred to as *dictatorships* and *totalitarian* regimes, although the three terms have slightly different meanings; see figure 5.3).

Democracy and Autocracy in Conflict In the wake of the Industrial Revolution in the eighteenth century, some societies undertook a wholesale, revolutionary shift from essentially traditional to essentially rational-legal organizing principles. This led to the

	Closed/Rigid Structure	Open/Flexible Structure
Direct Hereditary	**Classic Autocracy** Patriarchal and Patrimonial rule	**Classic Democracy** The Greek experiment, "Town Hall" democracy
Indirect Universalistic	**Modern Autocracy** Bolshevist and Fascist dictatorships	**Modern Democracy** Constitutional systems in North America and Europe

FIGURE 5.3 Direct and Representative Forms of Rule

founding of the first large-scale representative democracies, the earliest being in the United States (1776) and in France (1789).[6] The movement spread through the industrialized world until the early twentieth century, when it was countered with specifically antidemocratic revolutions. Where successful, these countermovements established the first representative autocracies: Soviet Bolshevism (1917–1924), Italian fascism (1924–1928), and German Nazism (1933–1939). This conflict between modern democratic and autocratic movements reached a historical climax in the Holocaust.

During the decades following World War I, bureaucratization had made it possible for governments to coordinate effectively the participation of huge populations (on the order of tens of millions of members). At the same time, the principal organizations—banks, armies, political parties, and government agencies—had achieved previously unprecedented levels of closure, rigidity, and sovereignty over participants. Together, these conditions set the scene for the rise of representative autocracy, modern totalitarianism, in industrializing Europe (Arendt 1958; Chirot 1994b).

Several partly unique factors conspired to push Russia, Italy, and Germany in this direction without affecting other European countries. After all, bureaucracy had made its mark throughout the Continent, and especially in England, which remained democratic through the entire period. How did England, France, and the United States avoid Communist and fascist revolutions?

Part of the answer is that the countries that did turn autocratic had all experienced a recent episode of "stage skipping" (Chirot 1989; Trotsky 1932, 1963; Veblen 1939). This occurs when a society moves from a traditional to a modern political system not through a general replacement of traditional culture but rather through the diffusion of selected items from a more modernized foreign culture, reaping the rewards of being second. This happened during the early twentieth century in Russia, Italy, and Germany. There, political leaders adopted bureaucratic organizational principles, largely from England and France, but they applied them in traditional, kinship-oriented cultural contexts (Dahrendorf 1967). In this way, the traditional traits of closure, rigidity, and group sovereignty were combined with impersonal norms of expertise and authority. The outcome was an effective system that served the interests of rulers, as the old regime had served princes and czars, based, however, on the rule of law rather than tradition.

The seeming contradiction between the rule of law and autocracy was resolved, in part, by the third form of authority, charisma. The antidemocratic movements were led by charismatic individuals—Lenin, Stalin, Mussolini, and Hitler—who, in collective behavior situations, had the authority to defy both law and traditional authority. The movements were then routinized in the form of charismatic *parties* that acted for, spoke on behalf of, and defined the interests of the people. Their authority, like the personal authority of their founders, came from the shared definition that the party is transcendent, that is, above the law. Because these systems were so closed, some of the parties were even authorized to define which subpopulations were and which were not "people."

This combination of closure and control was further reinforced by the application of relevant technological innovations. At the end of World War I, large-scale organizations in Europe and the United States had just begun to incorporate electronic communication technology—the radio, telephone, telegraph, movies, and phonograph— into their routine operations. In government, business, and the military, tertiary relations were increasingly integrated into routine bureaucratic activities: broadcasts of political speeches, telephone sales, and commercial radio. In the process, organizations gained unprecedented access to and control over members (Lowi 1981). When the autocratic regimes adopted these technologies, the individuals who controlled a few strategically placed organizations could literally direct how millions would act, which was truly totalitarianism.

With the aid of tertiary relations, contact between leaders and citizens of these regimes increasingly occurred without any face-to-face interaction. On occasion it was necessary to recharge charisma through personal appearances, but radio and film proved far more effective in the long run (Hull 1969; Leiser 1974). With relatively untried (and, by today's standards, primitive) telephone systems and two-way radio networks, Mussolini, Stalin, and Hitler found they were able to maintain instantaneous command over vast organizational networks. As much as we attribute the power of these regimes to the parties and personalities involved, such control would have been impossible without the new technologies.

George Orwell underscored this link between autocracy and communication technology in *Nineteen Eighty-Four*. Winston Smith, a worker at Minitrue (the "Ministry of Truth" in Newspeak), is one of the innumerable faceless persons in the government bureaucracy responsible for controlling the flow of information. Minitrue's output is determined not on the basis of maximizing access to the truth but rather by what are deemed to be the ruling interests of Big Brother ("BB") and The Party. Moreover, information must be collected with the same purpose in view: that which is useful to The Party is good for Oceania; otherwise, it does not exist.

No one has a right to conceal anything from Minitrue because all ideas that are harmful to the regime must be traced to their source, just as any ideas that will help the regime must be known and acted on. Telescreens also are receivers, and ordinary people cannot turn them off. An elaborate network of informers exists to detect instances of disloyal speech, writing, or "thoughtcrime." Minitrue, Winston eventually discovers, is not an information office but rather a social control agency, employing information for the sake of coordinating thought, speech, and behavior to serve the "proper" ends. The population, thus controlled, cooperates in serving Oceania and BB.

Of course, Orwell was not entirely making this up, for he had seen how autocracies (and democracies such as his own England) used information technologies in the prewar and World War II eras. Far from being fantasy, this part of *Nineteen Eighty-Four* is by today's standards an understatement, for Orwell did not foresee how soon Minitrue, modeled on wartime government bureaucracies, would be outdated, even primitive, in its technological sophistication and ability to persuade.

Democracy's Prospects in the Aftermath The recent turn toward more flexible bureaucracies is partly the result of the recognition among scholars and legal experts that technical efficiency is not sufficient to ensure (*Wert*) rationality. By the end of World

War II, it was abundantly clear that bureaucracies can be turned to any purpose one can imagine, sane or insane, and that they can even operate quite well with no purpose at all. The Nuremberg protocol established a formal standard to help deal with the moral and legal problems that this entails, and the standard was incorporated in the Charter of the United Nations. Thus, since 1945, it has been a matter of record that human life and human rights take precedence over any bureaucratic imperative.

A matter of record of this sort establishes official norms and values, but it does not alone cause people or groups to conform. The degree of conformity depends on associated sanctions, how they are applied, and actors' perceived costs and benefits in relation to competing values and norms. This is why autocratic regimes have continued to operate and to spread to areas where conquest and receptive conditions have made them possible (Linz 1988; Linz and Stepan 1978).

There are, however, consequential differences between the post–World War I and post–Cold War versions of representative autocracy. On the negative side, the technologies of mass control are much more advanced today. The potential now truly exists for an especially draconian government to spy constantly on all of its citizens and to liquidate (Orwell's term was "vaporize") any suspected enemy of the state at will and with no recourse. On the more hopeful side is our new understanding of national sovereignty. It is now understood that a set of basic human rights supersedes any government's official laws concerning treatment of its citizens, no matter how legitimate the laws may be by local standards. This awareness, alone, cannot eliminate autocracy, but it does make it very difficult for autocrats to operate in innocence. Rather, these days most claim they really are for democracy and human rights but are at least temporarily committed to an "innovative" way to achieve them (Sartori 1987, chap. 1).

Many currently functioning autocracies, including Libya, North Korea, Iran, and the Bosnian Serb "government," are clear outlaw regimes in the opinion of authoritative bodies such as the UN Commission on Human Rights and have been economically and diplomatically sanctioned accordingly. Some critics argue that these steps are still ineffective and largely symbolic, but they nevertheless reflect a new and fundamental premise of world culture: that people as people have the right to determine and pursue their own interests.

Prior to Nuremberg, no one was certain about the limits to which rational-legal authority, national laws, and bureaucratic regulations could be taken and still be considered inviolable, nor was there formal international consensus on the matter. The imprisonment and murder of members of *entartete* (degenerate) groups were perfectly legal acts in Nazi Germany between 1933 and 1945. But no decisive international action was taken to stop these acts until 1939, when the German army at last crossed undisputed foreign borders. In contrast, in July 1995 the International War Crimes Tribunal heard its first case in nearly fifty years. On the sixteenth of that month, the decision was announced that the political leader of Serbian Bosnia, Radovan Karadzic, and the general of its army, Ratko Mladic, had been found guilty of the crime of genocide (Nelan 1995). The acts cited had all occurred within the preceding several months. As it turned out, the orders of these two men were issued from the Serbian capital, Belgrade, by another indicted war criminal, Slobodan Milosevic.

Conclusion: The Invisible Hand in the Twenty-first Century

Because of the complexity and scale of contemporary societies, with their huge bureaucratic organizations and systems, change often appears to operate beyond the realm of human control. In pondering this situation, people are prone to believe that theirs is "a world they have not made." The truth behind such impressions is something of a paradox: most individuals have very little direct effect on the functioning of institutions and whole societies. But, at the same time, it is easier than ever for a few select people to control an entire corporation, political party, or nation.

Moreover, purposeful acts in larger structures are of necessity mediated many times over. At each step, higher-order impacts are affected by additional, cumulative causes beyond the originating acts. Thus, the chances that our personal goals will be exactly (or, in some cases, even remotely) achieved diminish as our organizations, institutions, and societies become more complex.

How, then, do these larger structures coordinate all the many individual interactions and relationships of which they are composed to function as they do? It was this very question that Adam Smith addressed at the birth of social science. His well-remembered answer is summarized in the phrase that is now virtually synonymous with classical theory of collective change: *the invisible hand*. This suggests that a powerful, unseen force gathers together the acts of many discrete individuals and groups for themselves (who are pursuing their own, self-interested goals) and turns them into a single, cooperating whole.

In a less mystical vein, Smith, Spencer, Durkheim, and others traced this force to the elaborate division-of-labor characteristic of contemporary societies, their organic solidarity. It is the norms and mediating structures, which are ultimately human creations, that behave as an invisible hand, coordinating individual acts in an apparently automatic way and in seeming independence of anyone's specific interests and intentions.

The invisible hand is a very effective metaphor, for it recognizes a complex process in which "emergent" (extra-individual) social outcomes are created. It thus remains an important symbol of the way in which larger structures operate. However, it is a metaphor that applies most faithfully to the kind of institutions and societies prevalent in Smith's day, when it was quite inconceivable for any individual or small group to coordinate the functioning of bureaucratic systems.

It is still beyond human capacities for anyone to exercise complete and perfect control over the thoughts and actions of millions or billions of others. Yet modern technology and autocratic government have made it possible for some people to achieve a degree of coordination that far surpasses anything Smith, Spencer, or Durkheim could have anticipated, even beyond what Orwell warned of in *Nineteen Eighty-Four*. At many points during the past half century, dictators and their parties have come very close to making the general will their own because of the advantages of organic solidarity in general and bureaucracy in particular.

We now know that large-scale coordination is not necessarily just the unintended consequence of discrete individual acts. In present-day economic institutions dominated by one or a few huge multinational corporations (hardly the microscopic firms envisioned by

Smith) and in totalitarian societies such as Nazi Germany (hardly the automatic division of labor envisioned by Durkheim), such coordination can closely coincide with the intentions of a few strategically placed individuals. This happens despite the fact that these practices are now viewed as deviant by international standards.

Summary

This exploration of macrolevel trends continues in part IV (chapters 9 through 11), which focuses on the development of representative government, urban growth, international stratification, the spread of capitalist economies, and how the "invisible hand" operates in guiding the apparently undirected processes that drive contemporary institutions and societies. Next, however, come some examples of deliberate change, collective undertakings that are specifically and consciously meant to transform society, culture, and population: social movements, political revolutions, and technological innovation. In these, the "hand" of collective outcomes is in its most *visible* state.

Relevant Websites

www.brocku.ca/MeadProject
This site is dedicated to the life and work of George Herbert Mead. Maintained at Brock University in Canada, it is the home page of the "Mead Project," which contains information and resources on the symbolic interactionist approach.

http://socio.ch/sim/bio.htm
Here is a biography of Georg Simmel, Europe's leading pioneer of microsociology.

www.humanities.mq.edu.au/Ockham/y64l09.html
Here is an online lecture on bureaucracy by John Kilcullen at Macquarie University in Australia. It contains several good references.

http://oasis.lib.harvard.edu/oasis/deliver/~bak00047
This site provides a brief summary of the Hawthorne Western Electric study, as well as a detailed listing of the Harvard Business School's complete archived collection of the study.

www.icc-cpi.int/Menus/ICC/Home
This is the official site of the International Criminal Court. Documents are in English and French.

http://untreaty.un.org/cod/icc/statute/romefra.htm
Here is the complete text of the Rome Statute of July 17, 1998, which established the International Criminal Court.

www.as.ua.edu/ant/Faculty/murphy/436/kinship.htm
Professor Michael Dean Murray of the University of Alabama Department of Anthropology has posted this glossary of kinship terms and concepts.

http://noosphere.princeton.edu/
Here is the home page for the Princeton University project on group and global
consciousness.

www.nizkor.org/hweb/people/e/eichmann-adolf/transcripts
The complete transcripts of the Eichmann trial have been posted at this site.

The Engines of Change

T HE FOLLOWING three chapters (6 through 8) explore the dynamics of social movements, political revolutions, and technological innovation. These differ from the kinds of activities featured so far in that they are meant to bring about significant changes in the ways society, culture, and population function. Whereas sociocultural processes generally operate to maintain order and preserve the status quo, movements and technological innovations are specifically designed to change the balance, in ways great and small.

Emile Durkheim was among the first to stress that, under ordinary circumstances, society and its institutions are conservative forces. They limit, constrain, control, and direct beliefs and practices in a way that ensures conformity and cooperation. In the process, the needs of the larger system are served; boundary maintenance, resource allocation, and the other functional requisites are satisfied, often at the expense of what might be considered personal freedom. Thus, even though we may disagree with the norms and values that prevail in society at large, there is always considerable pressure on us to suppress such objections, to behave as we are expected, and even to alter our feelings so that we accept the judgments of others as authoritative.

To emphasize this power of institutions, Durkheim coined the term *social fact*, reminding us that, although the elements of social structure may not be directly observable in the same sense as physical or biological objects, they nevertheless have concrete and consequential effects. In principle, we are always free to deviate, but we do so at the risk of being brought back into line through formal sanctions and the disapproval of significant others.

The ability of social facts to constrain and conserve is obviously a very important aspect of the human condition, but it is only part of the story. Deviant belief and behavior also are "normal" in that they occur in every society, past, present, and, it is safe to say, future. In this respect, people do not uniformly conform to each and every directive handed down to them from the past, from government, and from other established authorities. This is especially evident in large-scale, complex societies in which there is so much formal regulation that it is impossible for people not to break some rules some of the time. We are all at least a little bit deviant with reference to some standards (Henry 1990).

Of even greater significance, we now have organized means to change the rules of the game, so that what was once deviant, or even inconceivable, has become acceptable. These constitute the "engines" of change: programs, projects, and organizations that are consciously designed to alter social facts. In general, such activities are undertaken with the hope that some people's life chances and lifestyles will be improved in ways deemed impossible under the existing order. But they differ from individual acts of nonconformity in that their goal is to resolve perceived contradictions, lags, and injustices at the collective level, rather than to solve personal problems as such.[1] Because of the heavy weight of tradition, such attempts are bound to meet with a measure of resistance from established authorities. Thus, they are frequently surrounded by conflict and, especially in the case of movements and revolutions, even by violence. Change, in this respect, is rarely easy or smooth, for it inevitably challenges the vested interests of some groups. One major reason contemporary societies are exceptionally dynamic and prone to conflict is that movements and technological innovations are far more common than was the case for most of human existence. In fact, our age is distinctive in large part because these engines of change have themselves become increasingly regulated and institutionalized.

Procedures for reforming our laws are incorporated into modern constitutions. Social movements for gender equality, labor rights, and other causes have achieved a degree of permanence that matches the institutions they are designed to challenge. The twentieth century saw the creation of "permanent revolutions," a clear oxymoron to our ancestors. And the discovery and diffusion of new technologies have become highly programmed activities of multinational corporations, government agencies, and well-equipped and financed research and development labs. In these and other ways, organized deviance and dissidence are now as much a part of modern life as is organized conformity.

The chapters that follow look closely at these changes, their main causes, and their consequences. At several points, we will pause to reflect on how social protest has become highly routinized and how new inventions and discoveries are now planned years in advance. With all due respect for Durkheim's wisdom about the inertia of organized life, it is also true that the business of altering social life has for many people become just that: a business. And, as time passes, it appears to be an increasingly thriving one.

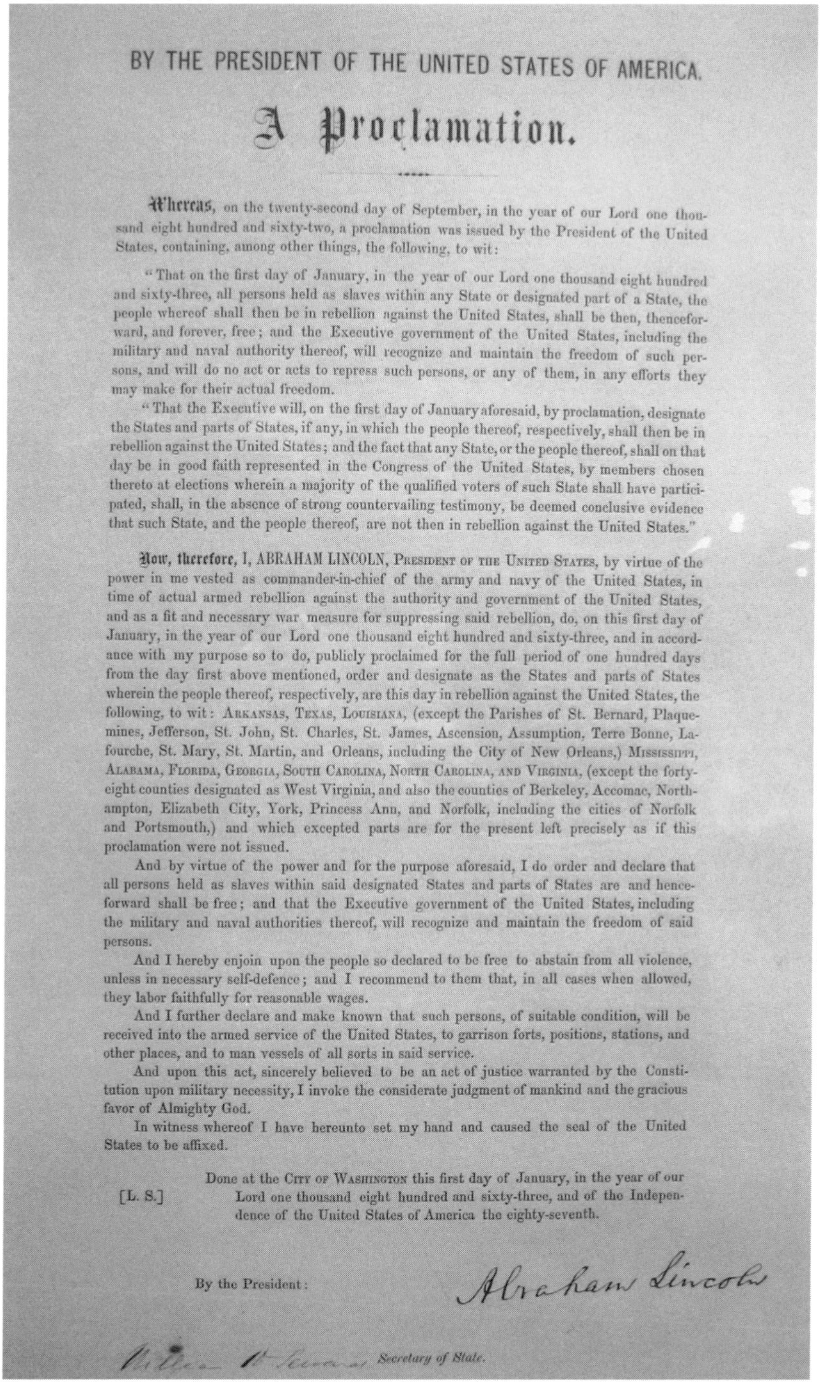

BY THE PRESIDENT OF THE UNITED STATES OF AMERICA.

A Proclamation.

Whereas, on the twenty-second day of September, in the year of our Lord one thousand eight hundred and sixty-two, a proclamation was issued by the President of the United States, containing, among other things, the following, to wit:

"That on the first day of January, in the year of our Lord one thousand eight hundred and sixty-three, all persons held as slaves within any State or designated part of a State, the people whereof shall then be in rebellion against the United States, shall be then, thenceforward, and forever, free; and the Executive government of the United States, including the military and naval authority thereof, will recognize and maintain the freedom of such persons, and will do no act or acts to repress such persons, or any of them, in any efforts they may make for their actual freedom.

"That the Executive will, on the first day of January aforesaid, by proclamation, designate the States and parts of States, if any, in which the people thereof, respectively, shall then be in rebellion against the United States; and the fact that any State, or the people thereof, shall on that day be in good faith represented in the Congress of the United States, by members chosen thereto at elections wherein a majority of the qualified voters of such State shall have participated, shall, in the absence of strong countervailing testimony, be deemed conclusive evidence that such State, and the people thereof, are not then in rebellion against the United States."

Now, therefore, I, ABRAHAM LINCOLN, PRESIDENT OF THE UNITED STATES, by virtue of the power in me vested as commander-in-chief of the army and navy of the United States, in time of actual armed rebellion against the authority and government of the United States, and as a fit and necessary war measure for suppressing said rebellion, do, on this first day of January, in the year of our Lord one thousand eight hundred and sixty-three, and in accordance with my purpose so to do, publicly proclaimed for the full period of one hundred days from the day first above mentioned, order and designate as the States and parts of States wherein the people thereof, respectively, are this day in rebellion against the United States, the following, to wit: ARKANSAS, TEXAS, LOUISIANA, (except the Parishes of St. Bernard, Plaquemines, Jefferson, St. John, St. Charles, St. James, Ascension, Assumption, Terre Bonne, Lafourche, St. Mary, St. Martin, and Orleans, including the City of New Orleans,) MISSISSIPPI, ALABAMA, FLORIDA, GEORGIA, SOUTH CAROLINA, NORTH CAROLINA, AND VIRGINIA, (except the forty-eight counties designated as West Virginia, and also the counties of Berkeley, Accomac, Northampton, Elizabeth City, York, Princess Ann, and Norfolk, including the cities of Norfolk and Portsmouth,) and which excepted parts are for the present left precisely as if this proclamation were not issued.

And by virtue of the power and for the purpose aforesaid, I do order and declare that all persons held as slaves within said designated States and parts of States are and henceforward shall be free; and that the Executive government of the United States, including the military and naval authorities thereof, will recognize and maintain the freedom of said persons.

And I hereby enjoin upon the people so declared to be free to abstain from all violence, unless in necessary self-defence; and I recommend to them that, in all cases when allowed, they labor faithfully for reasonable wages.

And I further declare and make known that such persons, of suitable condition, will be received into the armed service of the United States, to garrison forts, positions, stations, and other places, and to man vessels of all sorts in said service.

And upon this act, sincerely believed to be an act of justice warranted by the Constitution upon military necessity, I invoke the considerate judgment of mankind and the gracious favor of Almighty God.

In witness whereof I have hereunto set my hand and caused the seal of the United States to be affixed.

[L. S.] Done at the CITY OF WASHINGTON this first day of January, in the year of our Lord one thousand eight hundred and sixty-three, and of the Independence of the United States of America the eighty-seventh.

By the President: Abraham Lincoln

William H. Seward, Secretary of State.

FIGURE III.1 The Emancipation Proclamation was written in response to a long and bloody Abolitionist Movement. Its two parts, one signed in September 1862 and the other on New Years Day 1863, marked the beginning of a series of actions in which slavery was made illegal throughout the United States. Reproduction by George Chriss. Image in the public domain.

Social Movements:
Concepts and Principles

> Congress shall make no law . . . abridging the freedom of speech, or of the press, or of the people peaceably to assemble, and to petition the Government for a redress of grievances.
>
> —Constitution of the United States, Amendment 1, I

T HIS CHAPTER is about the social activities that occur outside of formal institutional channels: the things that do not, cannot, or will not be encompassed by a society's established norms and organizations. Referred to generally as collective behavior, they can take many different forms: crowds, rumor spreading, fad following, urban legends, strikes and mass demonstrations, public opinion formation, social movements, and revolutions (Brunvand 1999, 2001; Oberschall 1973; Smelser 1963, chap. 1).[1]

There are hundreds, perhaps thousands, of viable social movements in the world today, and one is bound to affect all citizens at some time in their lives (Etzioni 1991).[2] As they run their course, many will die out for lack of support, some will survive only as symbolic protests confined to the margins of political life, and some will be defeated by defenders of the status quo or by more effective countermovements. But others will have a lasting impact. Under these circumstances, we can be assured that tomorrow's society will be shaped by not only the elaborate institutionalized systems of coordination and control discussed in the preceding chapter but also the relatively spontaneous attacks on these systems from movements and related forms of collective behavior. And you will almost certainly be a participant.

Since the 1960s, in particular, social movements have been struggling for access to the centers of power and for direct political influence. Distrust in established elites, dissatisfaction with existing political institutions, and growing confidence in the capabilities of the increasingly educated citizenry have given rise to ever-newer waves of mobilization (Blühdorn 2009, 407).

The following discussion underscores these observations, providing a more complete picture of how societies are actually transformed (Chirot 1994a). With outbreaks of collective behavior always a distinct possibility, the path of sociocultural change rarely proceeds in a straight line. Rather, it is marked by twists and turns, as movements arise, institutions adjust, and movements respond: a continuing dialectic between the forces of establishment and dissidence.

Movements as Collective Behavior

Collective behavior was first analyzed in detail by the French psychologist Gustave Le Bon ([1895] 1960). The U.S. sociologist Herbert Blumer is widely recognized for developing the foundations for our current theories in the field (Blumer 1951, 1962). It is a type of interaction in which the process of coding, sending, receiving, and decoding symbols is compressed and formal role playing is relatively absent (McPhail 1989). It occurs in situations in which norms are unclear or ambiguous, and it is unpredictable in terms of prevailing rules. It can occasionally be a destructive force in relation to established institutions.

Relatively little rational deliberation takes place in collective behavior situations. Instead, participants become involved in circular reaction in which the strongly emotional words or actions of one actor are reflected in equally strong words or actions of a second through imitation, attack, or another seemingly automatic response. Because it is relatively spontaneous, collective behavior is an effective stimulator of change. With interpersonal responses so rapid and cumulative, it can produce immediate results in ways that symbolic interaction cannot.

This volatile, unstable character also makes collective behavior especially prone to getting out of hand. Compared to more structured contexts, it is likely to lead to deviancy and disorder, especially during critical periods of large-scale sociocultural change. In such situations, it generally accelerates the pace of events, which in turn sets the scene for additional outbreaks of collective behavior.

Because ambiguity is part of every social encounter, with norms always subject to varying interpretations, there is at least a bit of collective behavior in even the most structured situations. Similarly, much of the interaction that occurs in collective contexts, even riots, remains routine (McPhail 1991; McPhail and Tucker 1990). Like our established values and norms, collective behavior is part of our cultural heritage. People learn how to act in crowds, spread rumors, and relate to social movements from parents, teachers, and peers. With the help of TV and movies, we can vicariously experience protests and riots that occurred in the past or in remote parts of the world. Thus, even though collective behavior is relatively uncommon and unusual, it is nevertheless a normal aspect of social life.

Box 6.1 MISSION STATEMENT FOR ASA SECTION ON SOCIAL MOVEMENTS

ASA Section on Collective Behavior and Social Movements

The ASA Section on Collective Behavior and Social Movements (CBSM) was created in 1980 to foster the study of emergent and extrainstitutional social forms and behavior, particularly crowds and social movements. Our interests run from disasters and riots to rumors and panics; from popular culture to strikes, revivals and revolutions. With over 800 members, CBSM is one of the ASA's largest and most active Sections.

Brief Historical Overviews

- Animal Rights Movement
- Civil Rights Movement
- Children's Rights Movement
- Conservative Movement
- Disability Rights Movement
- Elders Rights Movement
- Environmental Movement
- GLBT Movement
- Human Rights Movement
- Labor Movement
- Peace Movement
- Progressive Movement
- Women's Movement

Note: The Section's mission statement and list of publications identifies movements as a form of collective behavior and identifies some of the many types of movements that are active today.

Source: Excerpt from the website of the American Sociological Association Section on Collective Behavior and Social Movements, www2.asanet.org/sectioncbsm.

Movements as a Source of Change

Like other forms of collective behavior, movements and political revolutions are relatively spontaneous and, to some extent, beyond the control of established authority. Subject to neither tradition nor rational law, all are conducive to charismatic leadership. And, like other forms of change, movements and revolutions occur in ambiguous circumstances, when important cultural lags and leads are manifest, just as rumors emerge in the absence of authentic information.

Movements differ from the other forms in part because of their scale: they are the largest, most organizationally complex, and most permanent. They can involve millions of participants and last for generations. And they can exact a very high degree of cooperation among otherwise unorganized aggregates of people, unified through their participation in the movement itself—not, it is to be stressed, through the usual economic, governmental, or other institutional systems.

At one stage or another in their life cycles, many movements develop within themselves formal organizations that claim to represent all or some participants. These can become very large, impersonal bureaucracies: counterinstitutions developed outside established structures. Yet one distinctive feature of a movement is that it is always more encompassing than any organization. Participants need not be (and most are not) official members of formal groups. Thus, one should not "confuse a movement's collective action with the organizations and networks that support the action, or . . . consider the organizations and networks to *constitute* the movement" (Tilly and Wood 2009, 6). For example, a crucial role in the U.S. Civil Rights movement was played by organizations such as the Southern Christian Leadership Conference (SCLC)—founded by Martin Luther King Jr.—and the National Association for the Advancement of Colored People (NAACP). But, as a whole, the movement has always included millions who were unaffiliated (Bracey 1971; Wood and Jackson 1982).

Movements are specifically goal-directed, purposeful activities in which people join and participate with the overt understanding that they are working with others to accomplish one or more explicit aims (Etzioni 1991). In the process, the movements experience successes and failures that affect their size and character through their life cycles. Some are very short lived because their goals are easily accomplished, leaving them no further purpose to continue, or because it becomes immediately apparent to potential participants that the goals are impossible, impractical, or undesirable. Others have lasted a very long time and ebb and flow with the decades and centuries. These include the international labor and U.S. Civil Rights movements and the very special case of the movement for gender equality.

Purpose, success, and failure also signal the possibility of unintended consequences and dialectical outcomes. In fact, surprises and unanticipated turns of event appear to be among the most predictable aspects of revolutionary movements (Coleman 1995; Dahrendorf and Soros 2000; Kiser 1995; Kuran 1995; Portes 1995; Wachter 2006). Because they occur outside of established channels, they must be somewhat innovative. New rules, beliefs, and practices are sought, or old ways are meant to be restored in new contexts. Participants often operate in uncharted waters, with little precedent to rely on in assessing what may or may not be realistic goals. All of this is reinforced by spontaneity, as movements can continue on in a given direction even when it becomes apparent that it is the wrong one.

As a result, movements and revolutions have a strong "runaway" potential, often resulting in outcomes that participants did not want or that do them great harm (Tilly 1995). These include the common backlash effect, in which the rise or growth of a movement causes an increase in organized activity against it, which can eventually bring about its downfall (Faludi 1991; Frank 2004, 5–8). This has occurred throughout the course of history in the form of counterrevolutions, reactions, and counterreformations. The anti-Communist movement in the United States during the decade or so following World War II was of this type (Kovel 1994).

The end of World War II was a high point in the history of the Communist movement. Russian troops had retaken most of Europe from Germany, the Red Army had liberated the death camps and was hailed by the survivors as saviors, and Communist regimes were newly installed in seven countries, plus the three Baltic states and a large portion of Germany. In the United States, as in the rest of the capitalist world, Communist and other left-wing ideals and organizations gained renewed appeal, particularly among intellectuals and organized workers.

This surge toward the left was a source of great concern among politicians, businesspeople, and the middle class. The two leaders of the Western world at the time, President Harry Truman and Prime Minister Winston Churchill, were avowed anti-Communists. In this atmosphere, momentum gathered throughout the nation to combat Communism's spread before it was "too late."

This perception was not entirely new. A similar bout of anti-Communism had broken out after the Bolshevik victory of 1917—nor was it entirely paranoid, for Stalin was then at the height of his powers. It was known that the USSR had developed an atomic bomb, and their first public tests in 1950 proved it. Moreover, wartime alliance between the United States and the Soviets had helped fortify the ties between party headquarters in the Kremlin and the tiny, but strategically important, U.S. Communist Party (CPUSA). Now that the United States and USSR were avowed enemies on opposite sides of what Churchill labeled the "iron curtain," the CPUSA symbolized the nation's point of greatest vulnerability to Soviet espionage.

Under the leadership of local officials, religious spokesmen, and high-ranking national figures, including the charismatic senator from Wisconsin, Joseph McCarthy, an all-out campaign was launched against the CPUSA. It was investigated for possible influence in the nation's labor unions (where it had made only limited headway in the past), entertainment industry, academe, and government, and eventually even the U.S. Army. All sorts of people were suspected of being Communists or of having "ties" to party members. Soon, other radical and liberal organizations came under scrutiny as Communist "fronts" (Schrecker 1998).

In 1951, both houses of Congress began lengthy and elaborate hearings to reveal the actual extent to which Communism had infiltrated into major U.S. institutions, the principal one in the Senate being chaired by McCarthy. A great dread pervaded the country that the Communists were taking over, the U.S. party was beginning to "run things" from behind the scenes, and the Russians were going to drop atomic bombs on us if we resisted their campaign to take over the world. People truly were swept up in the movement. The call to appear before McCarthy's subcommittee caused great fear among potential "suspects," to the point at which at least one man committed suicide when people close to him were subpoenaed.

By late 1952, it was evident to less passionate observers that some elements of the movement had turned entirely paranoid, and moderate voices began to prevail. McCarthy's theories were soon repudiated, and he was strongly sanctioned by his colleagues, just short of being dismissed from the Senate altogether. By the mid-1950s, the movement had receded substantially, though it was by no means dead (see chapter 7 for more on the McCarthy era). During those few turbulent years, however, Communism

Box 6.2 NARRATIVE BY AMERICAN PLAYWRIGHT ARTHUR MILLER

McCarthyism

Throughout the 1940s and 1950s America was overwhelmed with concerns about the threat of communism growing in Eastern Europe and China. Capitalizing on those concerns, a young Senator named Joseph McCarthy made a public accusation that more than two hundred "card-carrying" communists had infiltrated the United States government. Though eventually his accusations were proven to be untrue, and he was censured by the Senate for unbecoming conduct, his zealous campaigning ushered in one of the most repressive times in 20th-century American politics.

While the House Un-American Activities Committee had been formed in 1938 as an anti-Communist organ, McCarthy's accusations heightened the political tensions of the times. Known as McCarthyism, the paranoid hunt for infiltrators was notoriously difficult on writers and entertainers, many of whom were labeled communist sympathizers and were unable to continue working. Some had their passports taken away, while others were jailed for refusing to give the names of other communists. The trials, which were well publicized, could often destroy a career with a single unsubstantiated accusation. Among those well-known artists accused of communist sympathies or called before the committee were Dashiell Hammett, Waldo Salt, Lillian Hellman, Lena Horne, Paul Robeson, Elia Kazan, Arthur Miller, Aaron Copland, Leonard Bernstein, Charlie Chaplin and Group Theatre members Clifford Odets, Elia Kazan, and Stella Adler. In all, three hundred and twenty artists were blacklisted, and for many of them this meant the end of exceptional and promising careers.

During this time there were few in the press willing to stand up against McCarthy and the anti-Communist machine. Among those few were comedian Mort Sahl, and journalist Edward R. Murrow, whose strong criticisms of McCarthy are often cited as playing an important role in his eventual removal from power. By 1954, the fervor had died down and many actors and writers were able to return to work. Though relatively short, these proceedings remain one of the most shameful moments in modern U.S. history.

Note: This narrative by American playwright Arthur Miller is from the Public Broadcasting System series *American Masters*. It provides insight on the anti-Communist movement from the perspective of a leading intellectual who was targeted by McCarthy and his followers.

Source: Arthur Miller, "McCarthyism," PBS *American Masters*, August 23, 2006, www.pbs.org/wnet/americanmasters/episodes/arthur-miller/mccarthyism/484.

and many other, more popular left-wing movements did suffer serious setbacks. The anti-Communist backlash, responding to threats real and imagined from an expanding movement, brought results that certainly were not in the interests of what has become known as "McCarthyism." In fact, its limited success ultimately led to its failure.

The Antisocial Element and Political Violence

Movements often operate with the explicit aim of affecting the agendas of government, business, and other institutions, seeking to have their goals taken seriously and to change the rules of the system in their favor. Such reform-oriented movements tend to be short lived, particularly if they promote a single issue and are met with a receptive audience within the establishment (Derksen and Gartrell 1993).

As the goals of reform movements become more inclusive, they can expand their horizons to altering the structure of one or more institutions: to change not only the agenda and the rules of the game but also the prevailing methods of setting the agenda. In this way, reform movements turn their attention to what they perceive to be the root of the problem; they become *radicalized* (from the Latin word for *root*; see Schwartz 1976). Protestantism, for example, began as a reform movement among members of the established Roman Catholic Church. But it became so radically opposed to the existing system that it eventually sought to, and in many countries did, replace it altogether (Léonard 1968; Troeltsch 1958). Movements such as these typically meet with considerable resistance and opposition, especially as they become more radicalized. Their course is affected significantly by the way in which established authorities react to them, as the movement and the establishment engage in relationships of backlash, reciprocity, and revenge. In the presence of such conflict, and as compromise fails, violence becomes increasingly likely (see Della Porta 2006). Life is then dramatically changed for participants, opponents, and neutral parties alike. Society is profoundly transformed, although not necessarily in ways anyone actually intended.

The prospect that radical movements can turn violent is a major reason novelists, social scientists, and others have been fascinated with them, despite the fact that they are relatively rare occurrences. When movements do become bloody, they reveal an exceptionally plain view of the workings of power (McPhail 1994). Political power, the capacity to make others do your will, ultimately depends on violence or its threat. I use the word "ultimately" because under ordinary circumstances it is not necessary for the powerful to enforce their will so harshly. Rather, the rules of our institutions and actions of our leaders are authorized through traditional and rational-legal means to constrain the way in which we behave (as discussed in chapter 5). They are considered legitimate by society at large and do not need to be supported by violence when challenged. But as social movements become radicalized, they constitute a growing threat to powerful individuals and groups and to the very authority of the system. This is reinforced by the urging of charismatic movement leaders, who can credibly tell their followers to stop obeying the old rules. At that point, both sides must decide between conceding, compromising, or continuing the conflict on a violent plane.

Several different things can happen at that critical juncture. At one extreme, the establishment can choose never to concede or compromise with any movement and to kill anyone who even thinks about supporting one. Many Communist and fascist autocracies came close to realizing this ideal. Following their model, George Orwell made Oceania of *Nineteen Eighty-Four* movement proof.[3] On the other hand, the outcome can be peaceful. The establishment may be unable or unwilling to use the means of violence at its disposal. This was the case when Communism fell in Czechoslovakia in 1989–1990, in vivid contrast to the situations two decades earlier when the Prague rebellion of 1968 was crushed by Soviet troops (Talbot 1992; Wheaton 1992).

Social movements, even well-organized and highly radicalized ones, do not necessarily lead to violence in their conflict with the status quo. Yet, because of their antisocial character and the nature of power itself, conflict can and does happen (Reich 1995). Collective violence is not a simple thing: the conditions under which it occurs, who is likely to perform such acts, whether and in what manner it is reciprocated, and how it eventually ends all vary considerably from case to case (White 1993). What is constant is that leaders of the establishment and leaders of movements are well aware of its potential. This affects the way in which we relate to such movements and how we perceive them, and why we are all, perhaps, a bit in awe of them.

Although the issue has been debated for centuries, it still remains something of a puzzle that people become violent (Bradby 2000). *Webster's Third International* dictionary defines *violence* as "exertion of any physical force so as to injure or abuse." The "so as to" clause is very important because it indicates deliberate, premeditated action. So, accidental injury and abuse are not strictly speaking violent, whereas some very personal acts, including suicide, do qualify. In legal terms, violence requires at least momentary forethought.[4]

As in many other areas, Sigmund Freud established the contemporary scientific foundations for understanding this phenomenon, and psychopathological explanations dominate in the field to this day (Freud 1947; Martens 2001). From a Freudian perspective, the capacity of the human organism to exert physical force is associated with aggressive instincts lodged in the id. It is part of our animal nature whose potential exists prior to socialization, and it is closely tied to survival (Lorenz 1966).[5] But, as intentional behavior, violence is also something that is learned.

In order to behave violently, and not merely forcefully, children must be taught that certain acts will cause injury and abuse and also how specifically to perform them. Children have even been observed to rehearse it on toys or other objects, pets, and siblings. As with other aspects of socialization, the most effective way to learn how to be violent is to be the object of violence.

As individuals mature, they are taught to direct their aggressive instincts into socially approved channels. In particular, they learn under what circumstances violence is or is not appropriate, acceptable, or necessary according to the norms and values of their culture and subculture. The Jain culture has absolute standards on this matter, summarized by the term *ahimsa*: "no violence" (Martindale 1962, 196–98, 213–16). This standard was later incorporated as the central doctrine of the modern, nonviolent movement by Gandhi, who was educated by Jain priests (Roy 1984). In Hitler's

Germany, in contrast, it was every citizen's patriotic duty to see that the most extreme forms of violence were done to all who "deserved" it. In fact, as Christopher Browning (1992, 1993) describes it, ordinary people in Nazi Germany were resocialized to accept violence toward "degenerates" as a positive act.

All violent acts have a combination of expressive and instrumental elements (Balow 1978). Because they tap into such deeply biological aspects of the soul, they provide a real physical thrill, even to professional torturers and executioners who perform such acts routinely (Freud 1947). In this respect, violence can be highly expressive, habit forming, and contagious. Yet even the most crazed sadists or masochists act in the belief that there is a purpose to their behavior, and that the violence is serving a "higher" end.

Beginning with Georges Sorel's ([1905] 1950) classic studies of nineteenth-century political movements, social scientists have emphasized the difference between (1) the violent acts performed by individuals of their own volition, whether instrumental or expressive, and (2) those undertaken by organized groups. As Sorel pointed out, the second type, collective or political violence, cannot be understood in purely psychological terms, but of necessity also involves the cultural component (shared norms, values, and goals). Such violence occurs in many guises, ranging from riots to gang activity and international warfare.

> Political violence then is the use of physical force in order to damage a political adversary. If we leave aside state or state-sponsored violence, political violence comprises collective attacks within a political community against a political regime. In these situations, violence may emerge intentionally or unintentionally. . . . In general, political violence consists of those repertoires of collective action that involve great physical force and cause damage to an adversary in order to impose political aims. (Thomas 2001, 40)

The violence associated with social movements is highly instrumental and collective, and it can be initiated or perpetuated by either side: by movement participants, established authorities, or their representatives and surrogates. This aspect emphasizes that a common perception of protest movements as destructive is a partial truth. Both protestors and the establishment they oppose can become violent under conditions of overt conflict. Even nonviolent movements have been met with violent reactions from authorities, including several confrontations between British troops and Gandhi's followers during the Indian independence struggle and struggles between police and protestors during the U.S. Civil Rights movement.

Political movements and revolutions have been favorite subjects of students of social and cultural change for a very long time. The reasons may be obvious. A change in the way formal political authority is distributed and exercised, especially in which participants might injure or kill one another, tends to affect all cultural, social, and demographic trends in a special and direct way. Those who rule the state have the means—armies, police forces, and a virtual monopoly of weapons—to enforce their standards on the ruled, to make them behave and believe as the state deems appropriate in any aspect of their lives that it chooses to define within its domain.

Political movements and revolutions are distinct, well-tried forms of activity in contemporary nation-states (Tilly and Wood 2009). Moreover, by virtue of how our institutions operate today, a change in or of regimes almost automatically means a change in the rules governing markets—and in family, religion, and information-oriented realms of life as well. For these reasons, much of our theoretical understanding of movements is based on studies of political insurgency and revolutions. But this is bound to give a very partial picture, considering how consequential nonpolitical revolutions can be: the scientific, industrial, contraceptive, and information ones, to name a few.

Nevertheless, some theories tend to see all consequential social transformations as emanating from the state. Thus, it is argued, the only way that our norms, values, and institutions can really change is through fundamental political reforms and revolutions. Many social theorists, in their role as activists, have applied this insight through their own participation in movements, and most have gravitated naturally, so it would seem, to specifically political causes. By the late eighteenth century, this group had formed something of a new class of people, the *revolutionary intellectuals*, who sought to alter society as a whole by replacing the old political system with a new and better one (Benda 1955; Gouldner 1975–1976). Among its most influential members was Karl Marx. Although Marx was not the first theorist of change to organize a social movement designed to seize state power to create a better world (Plato is often accorded this honor), he certainly is the definitive role model for most who followed him.

Marxism and other such theories justify a political role for the intellectual. They are prone to reflect the theorist's appetite for power, and in fact many intellectuals have identified with Marx or Lenin. But why focus only on the state? Why not emphasize the importance of reform or revolution in the information institution, in the economy, or in religion? This would justify a different path to consequential change, and a different role for activist-theorists: as prophets, entrepreneurs, or even "priests," as the early French sociologists urged (see Pitirim A. Sorokin's critique of revolution in political and nonpolitical realms in Sorokin and Lunden 1959).

It is clear that no other institution can provide the effective positions of influence that the modern state has monopolized. Today, political decisions control economic trends, the flow of information, and even the family. This is true, but only partially so, especially in complex societies. Externally initiated changes in any institution, including the entertainment industry, can be as revolutionary as a change of regimes.[6] Moreover, nonpolitical reforms and revolutions can be the cause of political change just as readily as they are its effects.

Movements and revolutions are not necessarily political in the strict sense of the word. Other sources of protest have been studied and other kinds of movements have been endorsed by social scientists from the days of Henri Saint-Simon to Sorokin's era and the present (Useem 1975). The fall of Communism in Europe, in addition to all of the other ways in which it has shaken the world, has also called into question the mystique once associated with Marxist theories of revolution (Chirot 1991; Antohi and Tismaneanu 2000). Under these circumstances, it is now important to reconsider how things are and are not altered by movements aimed at seizing state power. This begins with a review of the principles underlying all movements, including, but by no means exclusively, political ones.

Why Movements Occur

This section discusses the major causes of social movements: why people support or oppose them, what roles participants play, why movements emerge under some circumstances and not others, and how they develop over the course of their life cycles. There are many different kinds of movements, but they are alike in being cooperative activities through which people pursue common goals. They differ from institutionalized procedures in that they begin outside of and in opposition to officially authorized, established channels, and they are only partly organized.

Every movement has its own natural history that includes a beginning, a middle, and an end. Their histories vary according to (1) the changes that occur in the relationship between the movement and the institutions and (2) the extent and quality of the movement's organized versus its nonorganized sectors (Koopmans 1993). They arise when people perceive that something is wrong with one or more aspects of their collective lives and that the established institutions are not effectively attending to the problems. Based on such perceptions, they then plan and carry out acts designed to rectify the situation (see Goodwin and Jasper 2009, part II).

Several different tactics and strategies are available to participants, including public demonstrations aimed at gaining attention and support for the cause, education programs to influence officials to reform the institutions, and violent revolutions to seize state power. Once underway, a movement is very much a process, so that its goals, tactics, strategies, leadership, degree of militancy, and several other features shift with ever-changing circumstances.

The fact that movements begin with perceptions gives them a strong subjective element. Perceptions can be mistaken, and they surely differ from person to person. What is an intolerable injustice to one can be perfectly acceptable to another. The reasons some people join movements and others do not must, therefore, lie in not only the actual circumstances to which they take exception but also their interpretations of the situation. To paraphrase Dickens in *A Tale of Two Cities*, even in the worst of times a few people will cling to the belief that all is well, and even in the best of times, many remain discontented. Moreover, in addition to the perception that something is wrong, participation must be motivated by the belief that the solution is not forthcoming from established authorities. This, too, is often a matter of interpretation, as people who agree that change is needed may still differ about whether a movement is the appropriate course or if reform can be accomplished from within the system.

People confronted by what they believe to be failing institutions have a range of responses from which to choose. All of these are "deviant" in comparison to the normal pursuit of established goals with established means, but only some eventuate in participation in movements (Gurr 1970; Merton 1968, 183–85). Why do participants not pursue criminal or other individual outlaw careers? Why do they seek activist solutions rather than the ritualism of obeying rules they do not believe in or the retreatist course of simply dropping out (mentally, at least)? Why are movement participants, in contrast to other antisocial individuals, inclined "to define private problems as public issues?"

Types and Degrees of Participation

Contemporary social scientists view the act of joining a movement as a rational response to a perceived problem (Opp 2001). This sensitizes us to the variety of ways in which people can participate. Some may make only a minor commitment, perhaps just a silent one of simply "being for" one cause or another. Others may devote their whole lives to a movement or to movements generally, in the case of some career activists (McCarthy and Zald 1973). Some lead, and others follow. To the extent that we calculate the costs and benefits of participation, we also obviously decide how much of ourselves we are willing to (or dare to) give and the extent to which we want to direct the movement's course.

Numerous studies have been conducted on the types and degrees of movement participation, with an emphasis on recruitment, leadership, and the conditions that make some people deeply committed. One typology, which applies to many forms of collective behavior, identifies four degrees of participation. These range from curious spectators lacking any real commitment to the insecure who simply belong, to the concerned rank and file, and all the way to the ego involved whose very identity is tied to the movement (Turner and Killian 1972). Nearly everyone in contemporary society plays one or more of these roles, often at the "concerned" end of the continuum. In the process, the crucial features of a movement (its size, frequency, and activity patterns) vary. How these vary depends on the number of people who at a given moment see an advantage in changing their level of involvement (or in becoming curious spectators in a cause that is new, at least to them).

Based on the studies of Amitai Etzioni, Mayer Zald, Louis Zurcher, and others (Etzioni 1991; McAdam and Paulsen 1993; McCarthy and Zald 1973; Snow, Zurcher, and Ekland-Olson 1980), sociologists concur that degree of involvement is largely determined by a combination of three factors (see figure 6.1):

1. Interpersonal influences,
2. Experience in (establishment) organizations, and
3. Biographical characteristics, such as age and occupation.

Of the three, the first is ordinarily the leading factor. People become more highly committed when their significant others, such as relatives, friends, professional associates, and neighbors, set the example. Alternatively, those who have little contact with movement activists are likely to remain neutral spectators (McAdam and Paulsen 1993). As in the corporations and government organizations of the establishment world, "who you know" also makes a critical difference in the way people relate to movements.

In addition, activists at all ranks, not only leaders, tend to have important organizational skills such as the ability to plan, communicate effectively, and cooperate with diverse groups. Apparently, these skills carry over from institutional routines to anti-institutional activities and are as essential to successful attacks on the status quo as they are to its defense. This is one reason the permanently unemployed, the *Lumpenproletariat* ("bums"), were not welcomed into the early Communist movement. Marx and Frederick Engels argued that they were not properly disciplined by industrial organization: "The lumpenproletariat, this scum of depraved elements from all classes, with headquarters in the big cities, is the worst of all possible allies. . . . Every leader of the workers who uses these scoundrels as guards or relies on them for support proves himself by this action alone a traitor to the movement" (Engels [1870] 1969, 163).

In contrast, people with the "right" personal contacts and organizational experiences are especially likely to make meaningful contributions to social movements. When large groups are in such a position and when pressures to participate are especially widespread, movement activity is prone to increase.

The third element is time and opportunity. People need to be not only convinced of the appropriateness and the efficacy of their participation but also in a position to commit themselves to what is ordinarily an unpaid occupation, although better-organized movements do provide a few participants with well-compensated careers. This fact serves to explain why students, intellectuals, religious officials, others with nonroutine jobs (Lipset, Trow, and Coleman 1956), and laid-off workers are often the most highly involved. The greater demands on the time and energy of people with more ordinary work schedules usually do not permit them to participate beyond the

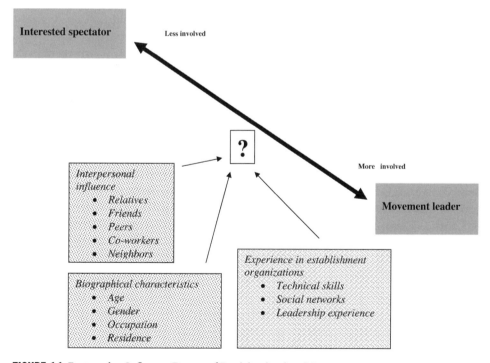

FIGURE 6.1 Factors that Influence Degree of Participation in a Movement

spectator end of the continuum. When we consider these factors together, it is apparent that people participate actively in social movements for much the same reasons they do anything else. It serves their interests, close associates influence them to do it, they have relevant experiences from other realms of their lives, and they are free to do so.

Because the boundaries between movement participation and other types of instrumental behavior are always shifting and are easily crossed at the spectator end of the continuum, it is pointless to search for a specifically movement-type personality (the "true-believer" syndrome, as Eric Hoffer [1951] called it). Any ordinary person can be attracted to antiestablishment activities if the circumstances are appropriate. Nevertheless, it is difficult not to believe that the pioneers and leaders of major social protest movements are extraordinary individuals. In opposing the established order, they exhibit a level of courage (or foolhardiness) of which most of us are not capable.

These are likely to be unusual individuals in any case because they often come from high-ranking families. According to the "blocked mobility thesis" (Ehrenreich 1990; Gouldner 1975–1976; Mizruchi 1983), committed movement participants are ordinarily successful people, but their successes are only partial. At some point in their lives, their desired course of upward social mobility is obstructed: a promotion does not come, a job is lost, or they are defeated in some competitive realm by an adversary (see also Perelman 1987). This encourages them to seek their goals through extra-institutional channels. Thus, they become more ego involved. With the time and skills, they can have considerable impact. For these people, the movement provides a new opportunity to be winners, by changing the rules of the game.

Political movement leaders, especially radicals, may well be special kinds of people, and the fact that their lives are often marked by conflict does make them extraordinary. But, in these respects, establishment political leaders are equally unusual. Anyone who works near the centers of state power—from without or within—is never more than an instant removed from violence. In confrontations between movements and authorities, the potential for the manifest use of violence is increased. And, after all, when people pound uninvited on the doors of government, they are challenging those who control most of society's technologies of death.

In a broader perspective, most movements are not of this kind, and most movement leaders are hardly so daring. Rather, they are more often people like your neighbors, who get sufficiently disturbed by plans to put a gas station on the corner that they begin a petition drive. Or they are like the "radical" doctors who first put pressure on the American Medical Association to classify tobacco as a dangerous substance, despite the fact that many leading members smoked (Breo 1993; Gloede 1985). These people lead movements because they assume leadership roles in the course of their normal activities and, under specific conditions (e.g., a request for rezoning is announced or a new study is published linking tobacco with disease), find themselves in opposition to some established norms, beliefs, or practices. The prospects that they will be highly involved as leaders as opposed to, say, honorary presidents or simply endorsers depends on their personal contacts, organizational backgrounds, and availability.

Political and other protest movements typically have a charismatic aura, which adds to the impression of leaders as highly unusual people. They must have the very rare capacity to make others defy existing law and tradition and follow them, to instruct that "it has been said unto you, but I say unto you." Their physical appearance, words, and deeds, and the legends that surround them, must grant them authority in the eyes of others, not just on a different basis from custom, but despite it.

Radical movements can have profound consequences in the lives of all concerned. Because of this, and because of the charismatic nature of movements in general and radical leadership in particular, it is easy to understand why it sometimes seems as if history is essentially created by the acts of extraordinary people—that is, every once in a while, highly charismatic members of elite social groups (priests and ministers, professors, and aristocrats) experience blocked mobility, organize movements, and change the world. In support of this view, we often draw on examples such as *Prince* Siddhartha Gautama Buddha, *Father* Martin Luther, the *wealthy landowner and lawyer* Thomas Jefferson, and Karl Marx, *Ph.D*. It is thus known as the "Great Man" thesis.

Of course, one need not be a man to be a charismatic movement leader. Joan of Arc, Susan B. Anthony, Rosa Luxemburg, Mother (Mary Harris) Jones, Margaret Sanger (see box 6.3), Rosa Parks, Rachel Carson, and Nobel Laureate Mother Teresa are just a few of the better known "Great Women" of history (Zuckerman 1991). Since the summer of 1995, the attention of human rights activists has been turned to Myanmar (Burma). There, Nobel Peace Prize Laureate Aung San Suu Kyi (see box 7.3 in chapter 7) has been involved in a decades-long struggle with the military regime, including years in prison and house arrest, for her "crime" of criticizing the government, one of Asia's most closed, autocratic regimes (Erlich 1995; Htwe 2009). These are exceptional individuals to be sure. Women have rarely been welcome in leadership positions in any context, and this seems to be one tradition that even the most radical antiestablishment movements have maintained.

Regardless of their gender, it would be difficult to imagine what the world would be like if it were not for these kinds of people. Don Martindale, one of the most learned of the Great Man theorists, put the case directly in his survey of radical movements in China, India, the ancient Middle East, Greece, and Western Europe: "Only the individual creates or destroys social forms. When communities arise and are destroyed, certain persons play a central role in the process. These include the intellectuals of the community. It is their task to provide the ideas and institutions which modify primary institutions sufficiently to make total ways of life possible" (Martindale 1962, ix). Thus, without Gandhi's inspiration, there would have been no nonviolent U.S. Civil Rights movement; without Susan B. Anthony's perseverance, women would still not have the right to vote. Or is this really the case?

Sociologists of change have a habit, which goes back to the work of William F. Ogburn (1922), of minimizing the role of specific individuals as innovators. Ogburn was especially concerned with inventors of new technologies, showing that many key discoveries were made independently by several people at about the same time in similar, but unrelated, circumstances. These include the heliocentric model of the solar system, calculus, the telephone, the automobile, telegraphy, and numerous other discoveries that we usually attribute to a single pioneer such as Copernicus, Newton, or Alexander Graham Bell.

Box 6.3 MARGARET SANGER: A "GREAT" WOMAN

In 1872, Anthony Comstock, an American moralist and a reformer, led a movement to have the U.S. Congress enact a bill that prohibited the mailing of "obscene" material. The term was broadly defined to include literature that provided information on the prevention of conception. Violation of the law resulted in five years' imprisonment and a fine of five thousand dollars. Over the years, this law was ignored far more often than it was obeyed. But it did serve to keep communication about fertility control and sales of contraceptive devices such as condoms (which had to be advertised as "for the prevention of disease only") clandestine until 1970, when it was finally repealed. The major effect of the Comstock Law and the cultural milieu it represented was to make it difficult for the family-planning movement to be considered a morally and legally acceptable cause.

Margaret Sanger. Photo by Underwood and Underwood, 1922. Library of Congress Prints and Photographs division, reproduction number LC-USZ62-29808.

Thus, it took militant social reformers like Margaret Sanger to bring the issue to the attention of the public and, ultimately, to help give it legitimacy.

Sanger, one of the best-known social activists in the United States, had a profound impact on her country's family-planning movement. She was born in 1893 in Corning, New York, and trained as a nurse in a White Plains hospital. During her professional career, she observed that most of her patients desperately wanted information about birth control but did not have access to it for various reasons. Subsequently, she abandoned nursing and devoted her life to the dissemination of knowledge about family planning. In 1914, she was arrested under the Comstock Law for circulating the magazine *The Women's Rebel*, which contained information on contraceptive techniques. When, in 1916, the case against her was dismissed, she immediately established the United States' first birth control clinic, in Brooklyn. This was seen as a public nuisance and led to her arrest and thirty days' imprisonment in the Queen's County penitentiary. Undeterred, she continued her political campaign that included making it legal for physicians to provide birth control information to women, as well as founding the still-powerful Planned Parenthood Association of America.

The impact of Margaret Sanger's work was both widespread and long lasting. For example, in England, Marie Stopes followed Sanger's example by opening a birth control clinic specifically aimed at serving poor women and catering to their needs for birth control information and technology. Based on Sanger's activities and arguments, during the early 1930s in the United States, the American Medical Association began to officially support family-planning services as an essential component of medical services. And further substantial policy strides were achieved after World War II.

Source: Jay Weinstein and Vijayan K. Pillai, *Demography: The Science of Population* (Boston: Allyn & Bacon, 2001), 428–29.

This view also accords with what we know of the basic inventions of prehistory: fire building, the plow, and cities. The great mysteries are not solved just once, but their depths are sounded again and again, to paraphrase David Livingstone, antislavery activist and rediscoverer of the source of the Nile. Innovations (and other discoveries) occur when they are ready to, so to speak, and innovators show up to play their necessary role. This same principle applies to radical movement leaders.

Based on this understanding of the role of "great" individuals, had Gandhi or Anthony never been born, another man or woman would have taken their place, for the circumstances were conducive to forming the movements that made them famous. The time, the place, the state of established society, and other factors were right to give any number of qualified potential leaders the inspiration and dedication necessary to promote their cause. This, of course, puts the matter in a much more sociocultural light. It does not deny the greatness or the charismatic qualities of such individuals, but it places the emphasis on the collective nature of their work. Like other innovators, they are, indeed, conspirators who have made history, but it is largely because history has "conspired" to make them so.

Charisma is a property of leadership, and only in context does it apply to specific people. All of us have the potential to be persuasive, greatly admired, or deeply hated, as is a charismatic leader. But very few get the opportunity to develop and apply these skills as a career. The mantle of leadership can bring out the charismatic side in even the most routine personalities. The charismatic quality of movement leadership can be passed on from teacher to student, parent to child, and husband to wife. It can even be transferred from a person to a party, as occurred in 1922 when Lenin died and Leninism was born.

Charisma is never realized in a pure, unadulterated form. All charismatic movement leaders depend to some extent on legal standing (such as the presidency of a movement-related organization), official titles, and appeals to tradition in order to maintain their credibility with those whom they lead. And all traditional and representative authorities must have at least a limited ability to rule by personal influence alone, as even the most detailed legal codes are subject to individual interpretation when applied in real situations.

Charisma is not the exclusive possession of movement activists, although movements are uniquely charismatic formations. Many of our most successful politicians, business executives, and other establishment leaders have a charm and persuasiveness that transcend the more mundane bases of authority (John F. Kennedy is usually remembered as a charismatic president, and George Patton as a charismatic soldier). Like those who head radical movements, these are people well disposed to persuade, organize, and support others. The main difference between them and leaders of social protest is that their biographies did not happen to cross the trajectory of a relevant protest movement at the appropriate point.

Some movements have changed the very nature of social life, and Great Men and Women have led many of these. But it would be wrong to conclude that contemporary society is, therefore, the product of their genius and that things will change again in significant ways only when the next Joan of Arc or Copernicus comes along. This is because one can never prove or disprove that events would have been different were it not for person X. (Such a statement, called a *counterfactual*, is a form of circular argument; it is always true by the rules of logic alone.)

The human world is constantly changing, now at ever-increasing rates. Movements are readily available as alternative means to upward mobility and other rational payoffs. As long as there are leaders in any realm, there will be plenty of qualified recruits for movement leadership. No doubt, some of them will be, or will become, sufficiently charismatic to leave their mark. It is also likely that some will fail. These things are fairly certain. What remains to be determined, and is one of the puzzles that makes life interesting, is the matter of when and how these Great People will be joined with their great opportunities.

Leadership and Ideology

The observation by Martindale just quoted (Martindale 1962, ix) mentions the crucial part that intellectuals play in movements. An intellectual is an expert at using symbols, a commentator on contemporary experience (de Huszar 1960; Mannheim 1968). It is a very old status, traditionally part time or closely tied to religion (as with prophecy), but it came to prominence as a secular career during the Enlightenment. Contemporary intellectual occupations include journalism and several of the arts. Within this broad framework, intellectuals pursue various specific activities: studying, writing, public speaking, editing, publishing, lecturing, and administering. More people are involved in such full-time, remunerated employment today than ever before, while most educated (including self-educated) people are part-time amateurs at it. These occupations are in the midst of fundamental redefinition today because of their association with the relatively new and still-forming information communication system.

Intellectuals perform a function that is especially necessary in large-scale, impersonal societies; that is, they help interpret often-remote and apparently unconnected events in a way that makes them meaningful to their audiences (Weinstein 1987). By virtue of their training, tradition, and (for some) charisma, they are granted the authority to observe and interpret aspects of reality for laypeople who lack the expertise or the opportunities to do so for themselves.

Intellectuals are uniquely attracted to movements, especially to positions of leadership. People in every walk of life may experience increasing commitment in relation to one cause or another, but intellectuals are especially available for such service. Many have occupations that are full time, but few are of the nine-to-five variety. In addition, professional intellectuals are often cultural elites who commit to a movement as actual or aspiring leaders, especially if blocked mobility is a factor. Although not all movement leaders are recruited from the ranks of professional intellectuals, all must play the intellectual role regardless of their personal backgrounds. So it helps to have a head start with experience in organizational skills, especially the art of manipulating symbols. Movement intellectuals have great potential power because they help shape perceptions.

As it is the intellectuals' job, in general, to interpret events for an audience, in a movement they lead the way in defining situations as real. They can persuade others that a problem exists, that its source lies in the failure of established norms or structures, and that another solution, the movement's cause, is available. Since the time of the French Revolution, these kinds of persuasive interpretations have been referred to as *ideologies* and those who specialize in creating and communicating them as *ideologues*. Professional intellectuals are well qualified for this task.[7]

An ideology is a distorted account that serves the interests of some group for itself. It distorts not by telling untruths but rather through its focus on only the facts that support its case. Karl Mannheim (1968), the first to develop a systematic theory of ideology, distinguished between *ruling ideologies* and *utopias* (see chapter 12 for more on the concept of utopia). This distinction emphasizes how some accounts justify the past or present, whereas others (the latter) are oriented toward a promised future. Both are kinds of ideologies in that they have the same structure and function (Frankfurt Institute for Social Research 1972, chap. 6). The former, however, are associated with groups that hold power or ultraconservative groups that seek to recapture it; the latter characterize protest movements, especially left-wing political causes.

Ideologies (and utopias) have two parts or phases, the *report* and the *command* phases (Gouldner 1975–1976). The first part is descriptive, a report on the health or proper functioning of some established practice or institution. In ruling ideologies, evidence is selected to show that all is well and that the established ways are intact and effective. Movement utopias, in contrast, seek to prove that something is wrong and that the fault is with the system. The command phase is prescriptive; it is a therapy that tells people what to do to make things better. In ruling ideologies, this is a directive to behave in such a way that the status quo is maintained; in movements, it is a command to change things in a particular direction. Ideologies and utopias differ from ordinary myths and fictions in their degree of elaboration: they are relatively long, involved accounts that seem to explain everything. They are the products of conscious, collective, and partisan efforts often extending over generations. Some tell a convincing tale that, nevertheless, is crafted to benefit a movement, party, or regime.[8]

A movement leader as ideologue performs the definitive task of "fanning the flames of discontent" (Industrial Workers of the World [IWW] 1984). This reinforces and is reinforced by the charismatic nature of the situation and role. Ordinarily law-abiding people defy authority only when they are convinced it will serve their interests to do so; an effective leader is one who has the power to convince. Ideology serves in this task by giving reasons to rational individuals that they should act and not remain merely interested bystanders. When conveyed by a charismatic leader, the command or therapy seems especially urgent and appropriate.

Summary

Taken together, these observations provide a highly relativistic picture of the causes of social movements. Figure 6.3 summarizes the major contributing factors discussed

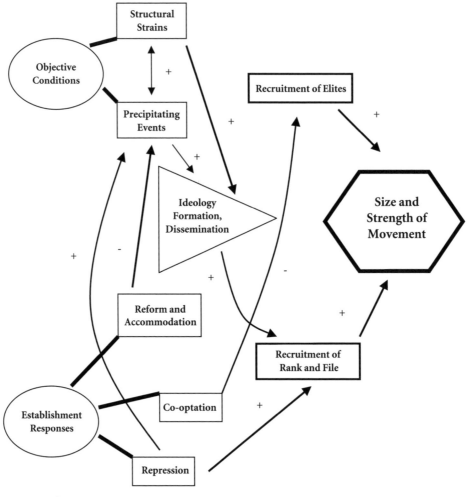

FIGURE 6.2 A General Model of Social Movement Growth

in this chapter. First and foremost, movements are (today in any case) always on the verge of occurring: Where you find modern institutions, you find the potential for protest. Movements rise and fall as prospective participants become more or less committed, in accord with what they deem to be the least costly and most beneficial course of action.

Their deliberations are shaped by existing and evolving ideologies, as articulated and communicated by leaders in their roles as ideologues. Contradictions and lags occur with the normal operation of any system, but it is largely up to movement intellectuals to define these as precipitating events. Actual discomfort or suffering aids in recruitment efforts, and relative deprivation, is especially effective in this regard. Still, people must come to believe that their problems lie with the established order itself; otherwise, they will respond in some nonactivist manner: innovation, retreatism, or ritualism. It is the ideologue's job to make this connection. Meanwhile, the establishment has the opposite task, always with an interest in avoiding serious crises and managing precipitating events so they do not accumulate.

Some movements fizzle out in a very short time. Others have been around for centuries and have won major victories. Some have changed things in minor ways, such as zoning ordinances in an urban neighborhood. Others, such as the movement that overthrew feudalism in Europe, have changed the world.

Movements have revealed widely perceived injustices in the way our institutions operate. But they also have been the source of equally serious injustices, including leading loyal followers to their doom. Movements can occur because conditions clearly warrant them, and they can erupt for no apparent objective reason. Finally, some conditions in our societies and in the world today appear to be crying for a movement to rectify them but have failed to capture sufficient attention or inspiration (thus far).

This discussion continues in chapter 7 with a look at movements and revolutions in different types of societies and at some formative movements of the past, present, and likely future.

Relevant Websites

www.nyu.edu/projects/sanger
New York University maintains this site on the life and work of Margaret Sanger. Much of Sanger's work in promoting the family-planning movement took place in New York, and it was in that city where she founded her first clinic.

www.plannedparenthood.org/about-us/who-we-are/history-and-successes.htm#
Sanger
www.time.com/time/magazine/article/0,9171,988152,00.html
The first of these two sites on Sanger is maintained by Planned Parenthood, the organization she founded. The second site features her profile as one of the "100 Leaders of the Twentieth Century."

www.sociosite.net/
www.wsu.edu:8001/~amerstu/smc/smchomefr.html
These two sites focus on social movements. The first is a link on the comprehensive Sociosite network. The second is an excellent master site from Washington State University with a glossary, discussion of types of movements, and so on.

www.trinity.edu/~mkearl/socpsy-8.html
Trinity University in San Antonio, Texas, maintains this site on social psychology and the sociology of collective behavior. It includes data, illustrations, and a history of the field.

www.asanet.org/section/cbsm.cfm
Here is the main page for the Collective Behavior and Social Movements Section of the American Sociological Association.

www.mkgandhi.org/
One of numerous Internet sites on Gandhi, this is maintained by the Mohandas K. Gandhi Foundation.

Movements and Revolutions in Context

ACCORDING TO the principles outlined in chapter 6, well-organized forms of collective behavior such as social movements cannot be properly understood unless we have a very good idea about the types of societies in which they occur, their scope, and their goals. Our examination of movements continues in this chapter with a closer look at these contextual factors. Following a brief introduction, the discussion is divided into three main sections. First is a comparison of movements in autocratic and democratic systems. Here we focus on the fact that in the former dissent is viewed as intolerable, whereas in the latter it is protected activity. Next a range of specific movements is considered, including some that have existed for a very long time and that are likely to affect social relations throughout the world for many years to come. The chapter concludes with an afterword on political revolutions, a very special and perplexing topic among those who study sociocultural dynamics today.

Movements are intended to bring about change from outside normal institutional channels, but they are conceived, promoted, managed, and altered through the course of their life cycles in direct, often intense, and conflict-filled relations with existing institutions and their authorized officials. Participants and leaders are recruited from the same general population that provides personnel for business, government, education, and religious organizations. Their ideologies, basic goals, strategies, and tactics are transmitted from individual to individual in the same manner as other cultural beliefs and practices: through primary enculturation, peer socialization, books and electronic media, and diffusion from external populations. And their successes and failures are always partly the result of the quality and strength of the reactions of authorities as they attempt to manage dissent in the interests of stability. When successful, movements and their organizations may themselves become part of the (newly reformed) establishment.

Organized protest is to be expected where lags and contradictions are especially manifest, precipitating events are frequent, movement ideologues are effective in tying specific injustices to systemic failures, and authorities are inept in their responses to the structural contradictions (and to the movement itself). Lacking one or more of these conditions, participation rates are likely to be low, as are levels of commitment and the ability of leaders to recruit and mobilize others to confront the status quo.

In the case of political movements and revolutions, the effect of general social conditions on the loyalty of intellectuals, the police, and the military is especially critical in determining the prospects for victory (Skocpol 1994). When large numbers of intellectuals are disaffected, and are thus no longer available to produce and disseminate establishment ideology (and criticize movement utopias), state authorities are especially inclined to resort to violence as a management strategy (Tilly 1989). When police and military officials, especially high-ranking officers (e.g., colonels suffering blocked mobility), become disloyal, the regime has little or no recourse but to concede defeat to the movement. At that point, the balance of power has shifted with the affiliation of those who possess the means to enforce it (Horowitz 1982; Horowitz, Welch, and Norton 1984; Moore 1979; Skocpol 1976, 1979).

Movements, Autocracy, and Democracy

The characteristics and prospects of movements, whether political, religious, or cultural, are as varied as the social contexts in which they have occurred (Alemán 2004). It is important that we do not lose sight of this diversity because of scholarly concern with the much more narrow issue of why some major political revolutions have succeeded (see Tilly and Wood 2009). Nevertheless, politics does have an impact on every type of movement, large or small, in two major ways.

First, all institutions (not only the state) must respond to the functional requisites of boundary maintenance, and each must manage internal conflict and cooperation. To accomplish these, each develops its own micropolitical system. Religions, families, corporations, and information-related organizations all have internal power structures, "constitutions," and systems of rules and social controls. Thus, movement activities are in principle political acts because they represent challenges to these microsystems.

Leadership, even in a purely expressive movement such as religious fundamentalism, clearly is a political status (Wuthnow 1983). This is why successful professional activists can organize on behalf of several different types of causes over the course of their careers (Zald and McCarthy 1979): they understand authority and know how to use it and how to coordinate the acts of others. Movements have a political dimension because they are (partly) organized and because they engage in power struggles with established institutions.

A second way in which politics affects even nonpolitical movements is that, to some degree, all fall under the scrutiny and control of the state: more so in closed, rigid

FIGURE 7.1 Tiananmen Square looking toward the Forbidden City. This photograph shows tourists visiting Tiananmen Square in central Beijing, China, in July 2004. Fifteen years earlier, in the summer of 1989, the square was occupied by thousands of students demanding democratic reforms from the Communist government. In a bloody episode, well remembered throughout China and the world, Red Army troops stormed the square with tanks and automatic rifles, killing or injuring uncounted hundreds of protestors. Although far more subdued and largely hidden from the authorities, China's prodemocratic movement continues to the present. Author photo.

systems and less so where there is openness and flexibility. Thus, the quality, type, and prospects of organized protest vary significantly according to whether the established government is direct or representative, dictatorial or democratic. For example, after World War II, movements aimed at securing greater civil rights for ethnic minorities intensified in both the United States and the Soviet Union (among Muslims and Jews in particular in the latter; see Bourdeaux 1984; International Conference on Collective Phenomena [ICCP] 1985). Although there was much in common in these two sets of movements, their shorter-range goals and strategies were not at all similar.

In the United States, the movement sought to change the laws of the land, but in the Soviet Union the main goal for most participants was emigration or, as in Chechnya, political independence. These movements had considerably different impacts, recruited very different kinds of people, and were met with different responses from established authorities. The federal government in the United States embraced the cause by 1964, whereas the authorities in the USSR continued to oppose it fiercely, reflecting the authentic contrast between democratic and autocratic approaches to dissent (Hughes and Sasse 2002).

Although most comparative research has been concerned with movements in contemporary industrialized and industrializing societies, one older type has received considerable attention from historians, anthropologists, and sociologists. These are uprisings and rebellions of oppressed masses against feudal and colonial authorities. Official records indicate that such uprisings constituted a serious drain on state resources, as money and personnel were required to manage dissent and maintain civil order. And they had more serious consequences as well.

The historian Ranajit Guha (2009) has aptly titled this line of research "subaltern" studies, to emphasize that such protest was organized by groups formally defined by the established institutions as social and legal inferiors (Guha and Spivak 1988). In fact, given the patrimonial nature of the systems, the role of the masses was very much like that of children in a traditional family: in society but not (yet) of it. Their protest causes generally focused on being treated more like the "adults" and to be accorded the same rights as their "superiors." Obviously, to become committed to such causes requires considerable courage.

These dramatic movements were especially relevant because from them emerged the revolutions that overthrew feudalism and colonial rule. Included is the well-documented "native resistance" in British India. There and elsewhere, subaltern movements were necessarily radical because their goals were in principle contrary to the established order (see Ludden 2001). Authorities viewed such uprisings as serious threats to the status quo, with good reason.

Feudalism and imperialism are, each in its own way, structurally conducive to such protest because of the glaring inequalities between rulers and ruled. The deprivation of local peoples under imperialist regimes was plainly visible in the contrast between their life chances and those of the elite (Schmookler 1995). Nevertheless, such regimes were generally able to maintain the legitimacy of the rigid stratification systems and, of crucial importance, to retain the loyalty of intellectuals such as religious leaders and members of educated classes. This phenomenon minimized the chances that the usual bouts of taxation and tribute (as well as war, pestilence, famine, vice, and misery) would be turned into precipitating events. Thus, even after generations of the most gross and obvious deprivation imaginable, subaltern movements had difficulty in recruiting the intellectual leadership necessary to overthrow the regime.

But this was not always the case. On several occasions, elites in feudal societies have "gone over" to the masses to become ideologues and movement leaders. This practice is known in Russian as *narodism*, "fraternization with the common people or peasants," and the practitioners as *narodniks*.[1] With the help of such people, objective conditions have been turned into opportunities to fan the flames of discontent, and masses have been mobilized to confront authorities. Such movements defeated feudalism in Russia and elsewhere in Eastern Europe. Similarly, in India and throughout the European colonial empires, educated native people such as Gandhi and sympathetic colonial authorities (e.g., Eric Blair, alias George Orwell; see Orwell 1935) have attempted to turn the suffering of the masses into rebellion in much the same kind of Third World narodism.

Cumulatively, subaltern movements have often led to fundamental political, economic, and cultural revolutions. But their specific outcomes are often better described by phrases such as *put down* and *crushed*. They have generally lacked a well-organized military, including capable officers willing and able to refuse to defend the establishment or even to go over to the masses themselves. Typically, poorly equipped peasant soldiers have found themselves impotent in violent confrontations with the king's forces or the colonial brigade.

An especially tragic example, and one of the most destructive cases of genocide in recorded history, occurred in China during the Yuan Dynasty between 1311 and 1340 CE (Beck 2007; Mu 1982, 91). Over this thirty-year period, the armies of the Mongol emperor killed uncounted millions of peasants in response to a tax revolt.[2] But perhaps the greatest-ever acts of collective violence were performed, more deliberately and methodically, during the era of European colonialism in Asia and Africa (as Fanon 1963 argues; see also Katz 1994, 87–90). Over the course of centuries, hundreds of millions of native people were socialized through torture, enslavement, and deprivation to accept their inferior status as natural because they were "lesser beings" (Lindqvist 1996).

The characteristic brutality of establishment responses to subaltern movements is a direct reflection of a closed and inflexible state. The only contemporary cases of such complete suppression in reaction to social protest come from twentieth-century totalitarian regimes, such as Stalin's USSR, Hitler's Germany, and Saddam Hussein's Iraq. This comparison highlights a pattern: autocracies are in principle especially prone to few, infrequent, but radical, outbreaks of movement activity.

Dissent in Democratic Societies

Contemporary representative democracy emerged as the outcome of successful revolutionary movements in the United States, France, and other European nations beginning in the late eighteenth century. The system was consciously crafted to limit the arbitrary power of established authority, and it provided explicit common civil rights and a legitimate method for the redress of grievances for all citizens. Technically, the rulers of these democracies (who are also the ruled) can grant authority but not sovereignty to their representatives: no one, including the president or prime minister, is above the law. Thus, the very process of political participation is a kind of institutionalized movement.

With the open-party system as it has developed through the years, the boundaries between the inside and the outside of official structures have become intentionally blurred. These formative conditions make democratic societies uniquely permissive and accommodating to organized attempts to change prevailing norms, values, and practices. As a result, movements are common, usually narrow and issue specific, and rarely radical or violence prone.

During 230 years of representative democracy, the system has proved to be extremely ingenious in directing dissent into peaceful and resolvable channels. In every generation, the flexibility and openness of the system have been tested, with the cumulative effect that more individuals are included and a wider range of "acceptable" behavior is permitted than ever before. The United States, in particular, has long been known as a country that tolerates nonconformity, both religious and secular. In part because the United States lacks a feudal tradition, individualism is encouraged over group loyalty. Citizens are thus faced with a rather unusual paradox: they have ample opportunity but comparatively little reason to protest against the status quo.

Constitutional protections of free speech and the right to assemble and petition authorities reflect the strong hand of movement-oriented ideologues in formulating the democratic rules of the game. This has given unprecedented latitude for intellectuals in democracies to express dissenting views without being considered antisocial, and some are paid well for doing it. In comparison to their counterparts in other types of systems, educated elites in democratic societies who take issue with the establishment generally play the role of loyal opposition and gadflies, rather than organizers of mass protest.

Contemporary democracies are structurally conducive to movements. They tend to be complex systems in which centralized coordination is discouraged. This characteristic allows lags, leads, and substantial gaps between ideals and reality to emerge fairly regularly. This aspect is reinforced by systems of representation that have become highly mediated, with layers of individuals and organizations intervening between citizens as rulers and citizens as subjects. Political parties in particular, many of which began as social movements, embody a contradiction between individual sovereignty and group power. And although all people are technically entitled to legal appeals when they believe they have suffered as a result of the normal functioning of the institutions, not everyone actually gets her or his day in court. The process is long, complex, and expensive.

Repression in Democracies   Democracies have experienced their greatest challenges when precipitating conditions became serious and relative deprivation widespread, particularly during eras of economic depression. At such times, ordinarily loyal intellectuals and politicians have turned restive. They have created movement organizations and have recruited committed followers. Under these conditions, large masses capable of direct, radical confrontation with the democratic establishment have been mobilized: in the labor movement, in civil rights demonstrations, in the movement for gender equality, and on behalf of other causes.

Perhaps the most striking contrast between democracies and autocracies is in how the respective types of regimes have responded at such critical moments. Autocracies are not alone in their concern with state security. Even the most democratic systems have a stake in self-preservation, and all define a class of activity as "treason"—so antisocial that it is contrary to the legitimate interests of the government. In the face of such threats, democratic states are authorized to apply social controls, including the official use of violence.

However, in democracies, state authority in controlling movements is conditional in two ways. First, because protest is protected behavior, dissidence in itself cannot be construed as wrong or treasonous. Instead, authorities have the right only to limit, prosecute, and punish criminal or civil breaches that might occur in the course of dissident activity. Second, social control and official violence can be applied only through due process. All acts of authorities in a democracy are subject to the will of the citizen-rulers, even when they are acting to protect the order. Thus, even if participants do something illegal, the movement may not be simply "crushed" because participants are first and foremost citizens with rights. This, at least, is the theory of democracy.

The historical record, in contrast, indicates that democratically elected governments sometimes do establish networks of informers and spy on movements, especially those that authorities define as actually or potentially violent (O'Reilly 1983, 1994). Many Americans were surprised, and some were outraged, by the revelations in the late 1990s that Martin Luther King Jr. had been under constant surveillance by the FBI (see figure 7.2) during his years as leader of the Civil Rights movement (McKnight 1998). Moreover, a movement's manifest or potential violence or threats to property have often been cited to justify extraordinary use of official violence, mass arrests, and other acts that tend to immobilize external threats. At such intense moments (recall that movements are a

Martin Luther King, Jr.

Main File

100-106670

I. INTRODUCTION

A. The Mission Of The Task Force

1. The Problem

On November 1, 1975, William C. Sullivan, former Assistant Director, Domestic Intelligence Division, Federal Bureau of Investigation, testified before the Senate Select Committee to Study Governmental Operations with Respect to Intelligence Activities. He related that from late 1963 and continuing until the assassination of Dr. Martin Luther King, Jr., King was the target of an intensive campaign by the F.B.I. to neutralize him as an effective civil rights leader. Sullivan stated that in the war against King "No holds were barred." (Senate Report No. 94-755, Final Report of the Select Committee to Study Governmental Operations with Respect to Intelligence Activities, Book II, p. 11). This and other testimony describing this F.B.I. counterintelligence campaign against King reached the public through the news media. As a consequence there was a regeneration of the widespread speculation on the possibility that the Bureau may have had some responsibility in Dr. King's death and may not have done an impartial and thorough investigation of the assassination.

FIGURE 7.2 Part of Martin Luther King's FBI file describing the campaign to "neutralize him as a civil rights leader"

form of collective behavior into which authorities are also swept up), officials have been known to break the law, thus in a sense making the state itself a criminal (Barak 1991).

The fact that democratic regimes apply social controls based on a "perceived" potential for violence introduces a highly arbitrary element in the way in which they respond to radical movements. In particular, it allows the threat of violence from a movement to be used as a damaging pretext for those who are, in fact, politically opposed to its goals or strategies. By the democratic rules of the game, this is a serious abuse of power (Carrow 2002).

Democratic authorities have also acted as agents provocateurs in leading movement participants to violent or other illegal acts. In such cases, they have violated the principles of due process. At other times, officials have failed to prosecute illegal movement-related activities and have encouraged reactionary countermovements because they happened to believe in their cause. In parts of the United States, for instance, there was for many years an "understanding" between local law enforcement and the Ku Klux Klan about the harassment of African Americans and Jews (Nelson 1993).

In some cases, these breaches by authorities have been inspired by a "red squad" mentality, the anti-Communist ideology that extraordinary security is necessary because the threat of Communist insurrection is so serious (Kovel 1994).[3] This places a political strategy above the law, contradicting democratic principles, regardless of how necessary some may feel the strategy is (see box 7.1). In brief, democracies do not always live up to their lofty ideals in responding with due process to radical social protest.[4] Many lessons have been learned over the years about the dangers of official criminality and violence in democratic countries, from the labor, civil rights, and antiwar movements especially. One would hope they have served to bridge this gap to some extent.

For the generation that grew up in the 1950s, the rise and fall of Senator Joseph McCarthy was a critical and delegitimating episode (Buckingham 1988). During a highly formative period in their lives, Americans learned that officials would and could lie, break the law, and condone illegal activity. People saw their representatives stereotype social movements and organizations as "subversive," provoke law-abiding citizens, and destroy the lives of important intellectuals if they believed their cause just and the enemy sufficiently threatening. Then the nation saw the whole business repudiated.

Later, during the Civil Rights and anti–Vietnam War movements of the 1960s, undemocratic responses by authorities to violence and criminality (real and alleged) again occurred and eventually were revealed and criticized. The issue emerged once again in the mid-1990s in investigations of activities of U.S. federal agents in Idaho and Texas (Hamm 1997). And in the outrage following the attacks of September 11, 2001, laws were passed, such as the USA PATRIOT Act, that according to civil libertarians represented a serious blow to the freedoms of speech and assembly and to the rights to due process (Omara-Otunnu 2004; see also http://personalinfomediary.com/USAPATRIOTACT_Text.htm; and http://www.aclu.org/national-security/aclu-files-first-ever-challenge-usa-patriot-act-citing-radical-expansion-fbi-power). Yet, as serious as these abuses may have been (much remains unknown, especially in the more recent incidents), the fact that they have been exposed and publicly debated leads one to be optimistic about democracy's powers of self-renewal.

Box 7.1 THE REICHSTAG FIRE

On the night of February 27, 1933, Hitler's Prussian Interior Minister Hermann Goering carried out a plot in which storm troopers prepared a huge bonfire under the Reichstag and, it is suspected, with the help of a hireling with a Communist background, torched the building. Although, to this day, it has never been clearly established who was responsible, Hitler immediately took the initiative and blamed the Communists. The Reichstag fire was the pretext for issuing this decree, which suspended the civil rights of German citizens. The fire became a powerful campaign symbol, serving as a warning of an impending revolution that would allegedly bring destruction and death at the hands of Bolsheviks, internationalists, and Jews. Hitler was portrayed as the one last hope to prevent the certain doom the fire foreshadowed.

Decree of the Reich President for the Protection of the People and State (The Reichstag Fire Decree)
February 28, 1933

On the basis of Article 48 paragraph 2 of the Constitution of the German Reich, the following is ordered in defense against Communist acts of violence that endanger the state:

§ 1. Articles 114, 115, 117, 118, 123, 124 and 153 of the Constitution of the German Reich are suspended until further notice. The following are therefore permitted: limits on personal freedom, freedom of opinion, including the freedom of the press, the freedom to organize and assemble, the privacy of postal, telegraphic and telephonic communications, and warrants for house searches, orders for confiscations of property as well as restrictions on property beyond the legal limits otherwise prescribed.

§ 2. If any state fails to take the necessary measures to restore public safety and order, the Reich government may temporarily exercise the powers of the highest state authorities.

§ 3. State and local authorities must obey regulations issued by the Reich government based on § 2. . . .

§ 5 The following crimes currently punished by life imprisonment are now to be punished by death: high treason, poisoning, arson, causing explosions, causing floods, damaging railways.

Source: Daniel E. Rogers, "The Nazi Takeover: The Reichstag Fire Decree," University of South Alabama Department of History, October 13, 2009, www.southalabama.edu/history/faculty/rogers/348/reichstagfiredecree.html.

The Erosion of Representation and Movement Responses   Some democracies have been overthrown by radical movements that subsequently established autocratic regimes. The case of Weimar Germany was an especially important instance because it served as a prelude to the Holocaust (Shirer 1978, chap. 1). Antidemocratic takeovers also occurred in post–World War I Italy, Spain, Portugal, and Russia, and during the 1970s and 1980s in several Third World countries (Linz 1988). Obviously, democracy is not "revolution proof" (Lipset 1994).

When democratic governments have fallen, it has been to minority parties that can exploit (or, a common tactic, create) parliamentary crisis when the system proves incapable of functioning according to its own rules. This process has invariably been aided by precipitating events and disaffected ideologues capable of turning objective conditions to the regime's disadvantage. The newly captured state is then used to declare an emergency rule situation (with or without violent confrontations), whereby the revolutionary party is granted authority to form the government. It then systematically disassembles democratic mechanisms because its goals are "more urgent" than self-rule.

Capitalist democracies throughout the world experienced severe crises after World War I that climaxed in the crash of 1929. Internal movements and military conquest marked the subsequent decade, with all of continental Europe under one or another form of autocracy at the beginning of World War II. During the 1930s, the U.S. democratic system experienced its greatest challenge since the Civil War. Then and since, antidemocratic movements have posed unique dilemmas, for they, too, must be protected, even though their goals are subversive. In England and North America, however, democracy remained intact. Although radical political movements experienced their greatest successes to that date in recruitment, mobilization, and generating commitment, none was able to mount a successful attack on the system.

Some commentators have invoked the Great Men thesis to account for how the United States and the United Kingdom resisted the trend of the times toward autocracy: remarkable charismatic leaders, Roosevelt and Churchill, pulled them through depression, war, and the threat of internal subversion. But it is also true that these countries had geographical advantages that kept a continental movement at bay. Moreover, they were the wealthiest democracies and relatively resistant to precipitating events and agitation. Most important, their leaders, charismatic as they may have been, had been democratically elected by a still-loyal citizenry. They were authorized by their constituents to bring about fundamental reforms from within (as opposed to merely putting down the opposition). The system continued to redress grievances of the electorate, thus denying potential radical opposition parties the opportunity to develop a base of support. For the most part, dissident intellectuals were co-opted into serving the establishment, not arrested (Mizruchi 1983, appendix).

The rights to organize and grieve are essential. As Jefferson and the other founders wisely appreciated, tolerance is democracy's most effective response to protest. The democratic faith is that if the people are freely allowed to express their will, they will remain collectively loyal to their regime (and it *is* theirs under such circumstances). But, for better or worse, the minority will therefore always be permitted and, in some ways, encouraged to be disloyal in word, deed, and movement. More important than where one stands on particular partisan issues is that the system, including the internal resistance it protects, be continually probed, tested, and challenged rather than allowed to atrophy, as it has in many democracies prior to autocratic takeovers.

This restates an observation that has been made many times since Tocqueville's visit to the United States (Tocqueville [1835] 1969) and the later sociological writings of Roberto Michels (1959). The effectiveness of democratic systems depends crucially on participation. If the people en masse do not use the system to protect their collective interests, it will be used by oligarchs to benefit themselves. This is especially relevant today because well-financed parties and organized interest groups in democratic systems have come to play, or at least threaten to play, the role of oligarchs. This type of rule, referred to as a *plutocracy*, is a source of serious concern among many Americans, both within and outside formal government circles (Krugman 2002). "A plutocracy is defined as 'government by the wealthy.' The critical question that should concern us is whether the United States is already a plutocracy and what can be done to limit its power" (Kurtz 2000).

It is a fact that the agendas and decisions of democratically chosen representatives are inordinately influenced today by a few wealthy, powerful, and vocal groups, although it is less clear whether things really changed very much in this regard during the twentieth century. Some officials undoubtedly prefer this situation, and it may even be what the electorate wants. What is more likely, though, is that the electorate does not fully comprehend the extent to which our systems are biased toward elites because no one has the definitive answer to the "simple" question posed by C. Wright Mills (1956): "Who rules America?" Nor are we clear about the way such a bias affects our lives.

Today, most consequential political decisions in democracies such as the United States are no longer made through the inclusive, formal channels designed to translate the will of the electorate into policy. Rather, large corporations, professional lobbyists, and a variety of influence peddlers now determine legislative agendas, voting patterns on key bills, executive decisions, and court dockets. Because the system has become too large and complex to accommodate the simple principles of representation incorporated in our constitutions, organized interests have filled the vacuum as mediators between citizens and their representatives. As a result, a great deal of money has been spent (some of it illegally), and much time and energy have been devoted by organized interest groups to ensure that democratic government does *not* express the will of the majority (McChesney 2003). Rather, it is to their advantage that the system works instead to benefit those who believe they have the biggest stake in the decisions that are made. This situation, characterized by the ambiguities and incomplete information that accompany all forms of collective behavior, has given rise to several reform movements.

One, identified with democratic planning, has been of special interest to social scientists in part because of its roots in the Progressive Era's U.S. League for Industrial Democracy. Its diagnosis stresses that democracy today does not go far enough. The proposed command or therapy of this movement is "participatory democracy," the extension of democratic principles to the governing of industry and other institutional realms (see chapter 14; see also Cohen and Hale 1967). If organizations are going to be major players in representative government, it is argued, then they must also incorporate democratic rights and protections. A truly democratic *society* is necessary, not just a democratic government in an otherwise elitist system.

Other critics have proposed a more control-oriented solution to limit constitutionally outside influences, criminalizing some lobbying activities that are now protected. Still others see the decline in authentic representation as an opportunity for serious, even radical, reforms: term limits, the prohibition of fund-raising,[5] and even a restructuring of the two-party system itself. As a result of such efforts, and in one of the most interesting paradoxes of modern society, antilobbying movements themselves have become lobbyists.

This is but one example of an important, general trend. Because of the power of lobbying, people committed to social movements have recently created organized pressure groups with the aim of using the system to their advantage. Every cause seems to have a movement, and every movement seems to have at least one website and an 800 number. People interested in all sorts of protest causes can now easily reach a representative of a relevant organization with special access to legislators and other government officials, who is in the full-time business of attempting to make government work in the interests of the movement.

Box 7.2 THE LOBBYING DISCLOSURE ACT

Lobbying Disclosure Act of 1995–Current through October 1, 2007

[As Amended Through P.L. 110–81, Enacted September 14, 2007]
AN ACT To provide for the disclosure of lobbying activities to influence the Federal Government, and for other purposes.

Note: This compilation includes language from Public Law 104–65, as well as amending language from Public Laws 105–66 and 110–81. These materials are not official evidence of the laws set forth herein. Sections 112 and 204 of title 1 of the United States Code establish the rules governing which text serves as legal evidence of the laws of the United States.

For changes, after the closing date of this publication, to provisions of law in this publication, see the United States Code Classification Tables published by the Office of the Law Revision Counsel of the House of Representatives at http://uscode.house.gov/classification/ tables.shtml.

Be it enacted by the Senate and House of Representatives of the United States of America in Congress assembled,

SECTION 1. [2 U.S.C. 1601 note] SHORT TITLE.
This Act may be cited as the "Lobbying Disclosure Act of 1995."

In such a world, political participation means getting involved with networks and associations that may seem only remotely political. Yet they are likely to have an office in the capital. Today, these even include associations whose aim is to limit their own influence.

Movements in Autocracies and Democracies: Summary

There are many types of social movements. These vary according to the issue(s) on which they focus, the extent to which they are expressive or instrumental, the radicalness of their proposed reforms, and, as emphasized in this section, the kinds of societies in which they occur. They are made up of all sorts of people, from "true believers" to average citizens to charismatic "great" men and women. Their size and the degree of commitment of participants differ from place to place and change with the passage of time. Autocratic rulers have tried to eliminate them, and on some occasions have nearly, but never entirely, succeeded; democratic systems need them at the risk of becoming undemocratic.

The differences between movements, on one hand, and planned change from within, on the other, are often subtle and elusive. They all but dissolve when dissenting

SEC. 2. [2 U.S.C. 1601] FINDINGS.
The Congress finds that—
(1) responsible representative Government requires public awareness of the efforts of paid lobbyists to influence the public decisionmaking process in both the legislative and executive branches of the Federal Government; (2) existing lobbying disclosure statutes have been ineffective because of unclear statutory language, weak administrative and enforcement provisions, and an absence of clear guidance as to who is required to register and what they are required to disclose; and (3) the effective public disclosure of the identity and extent of the efforts of paid lobbyists to influence Federal officials in the conduct of Government actions will increase public confidence in the integrity of Government.

SEC. 3. [2 U.S.C. 1602] DEFINITIONS. As used in this Act:
(1) AGENCY.—The term "agency" has the meaning given that term in section 551(1) of title 5, United States Code.
(2) CLIENT.—The term "client" means any person or entity that employs or retains another person for financial or other compensation to conduct lobbying activities on behalf of that person or entity. A person or entity whose employees act as lobbyists on its own behalf is both a client and an employer of such employees. In the case of a coalition or association that employs or retains other persons to conduct lobbying activities,

Note: The law, passed in 1995 and amended in 2007, intended to limit the power of lobbyists.

Source: U. S. Senate, www.senate.gov/legislative/Lobbying/Lobby_Disclosure_Act/compilation.pdf.

ideals become established norms, revolutions become institutionalized, and authorities, including high-ranking military officers, take up the cause of protest. Many movements today are as highly organized and well financed as some institutionalized activities. They have become common, rational alternatives to achieve personal and collective goals. They have apparently always accompanied organized social life and are thus a natural part of our cultural heritage. However, never before have they played such a major role in the affairs of ordinary people.

It is virtually certain that today's movements will shape tomorrow's societies as much as, if not more than, our governments and other established institutions. As mentioned in chapter 6, it is also a safe guess that you personally will soon participate in one movement or more of consequence, if you have not already done so. For this reason, the study of movements, and especially their connection with democratic participation, is more than merely academic. It is also an important aspect of citizenship training.

Box 7.3 AN APPEAL FROM THE WEBSITE OF BURMESE DISSIDENT AUNG SAN SUU KYI

Last month two famous defendants—one adored, the other despised—appeared in courts nearly 10,000 km apart. Charles Taylor, the former President of Liberia, is being tried by a special tribunal in The Hague for murder, rape, torture and other war crimes allegedly committed during the decade-long conflict in neighboring Sierra Leone. Taylor—known as "Pappy" to child soldiers who, say prosecutors, were abducted, drugged and dispatched to commit atrocities on his orders—used his first appearance on the stand on July 14 to dismiss the charges as "disinformation, misinformation, lies, rumors." Meanwhile, and much more convincingly, Aung San Suu Kyi was protesting her innocence before a court in Rangoon. The Burmese democracy icon faces up to five years in prison for violating the terms of her house arrest after an American man swam to her lakeside home in Rangoon. The charges are farcical, the verdict a foregone conclusion: Suu Kyi is expected to be declared guilty on Aug. 11. But some in Burma's embattled democracy movement will turn to The Hague for solace. Taylor is the first African head of state to face an international war-crimes tribunal. Could Senior General Than Shwe, leader of the Burmese junta, be the first Asian?

This is not as far-fetched as it might initially seem. A compelling case for investigating war crimes in Burma is made in a May 2009 report by the International Human Rights Clinic at Harvard Law School. Called "Crimes in Burma," its authors are heavy hitters: they include one former judge and two former prosecutors from the International Criminal Tribunal for the former Yugoslavia, including the British lead attorney in the case against Slobodan Milosevic.

Central business district in Yangon (Rangoon) capital of Myanmar (Burma). This country is ruled by one of the world's most closed and dictatorial military regimes. Photo by Catherine Collins; used with permission.

Referring only to U.N. documents, the report lays out the "systematic and widespread" atrocities committed in Burma in recent years: killings, torture, rape, "epidemic levels" of forced labor, a million people homeless, the recruitment of tens of thousands of child soldiers, and—here they draw comparisons with Darfur—the displacement or destruction of more than 3,000 ethnic-nationality villages. These abuses were usually committed during armed conflict, which "strongly suggests" they are war crimes and crimes against humanity, says the report.

A precedent for acting on such abuses has been set by the former Yugoslavia, Rwanda and Darfur, the authors continue. They assert that with such overwhelming evidence from its own documents, the U.N. Security Council should establish a commission to investigate war crimes in Burma, then create a special tribunal to try those responsible for them. "The [U.N. Security] Council is the only body that can take the action necessary to respond adequately to the crisis in Burma," conclude the authors, before warning of "the painful consequences of inaction."

Source: Andrew Marshall, "Putting Myanmar's Junta on Trial," Daw Aung San Suu Kyi's Pages, August 7, 2009, http://dassk.org/index.php?PHPSESSID=169efda7738669dd9900b1a3decab033 &/topic,11111484.0.html.

An Inventory of Some Major Movements: Past and Present

In our introduction to the four critical episodes in chapter 1, it was noted that they are widely acknowledged to be among the "movements that have shaped our times." Nevertheless, they still fall far short of encompassing the entire spectrum of social protest. For this reason, the episodes need to be viewed in relation to other formative movements. With this in mind, here we identify several that have been especially consequential in the recent and not-so-recent past.

Permanent Movements

Some social movements have been around for a very long time. Three of them, in particular, appear to be as old as the institutionalized beliefs and practices they oppose: gender equality, labor, and democratic rights. I have termed these movements *permanent* to emphasize the fact that each generation does not newly discover the practice of organized dissent, nor does every era reveal for the first time certain serious social injustices and contradictions. Rather, there is always a residue of the unresolved social problems of the past and of the collective protest against them. The three causes are generally understood to be progressive. But my choices are not meant to deny that some movements on the right of the ideological spectrum, including fascism, have demonstrated the same long-lived and recurring character (Bell 1963; Laqueur and Mosse 1978; Wuthnow 1983).

Movements as enduring as these evidently speak to very general and deep-seated contradictions. They have gone through many stages in their respective life cycles, from quiescent to highly active. And they are so encompassing that they have developed within them branches and submovements, ranging from mildly reformist to radical/revolutionary and from specifically instrumental to highly symbolic. They have their distinctive histories, some of which have been recorded by official movement scribes. They have heroes and villains and their own legends and subcultures. Many millions of individuals throughout the world have identified, in one way or another, with these causes.

Gender Equality The movement for gender equality has the most ancient roots of the three and is, by far, the most encompassing in the number of people whose interests it presumes to represent (Beard 1993; Garland 1986; Tuttle 1986, 197, 365). Gender stratification, along with slavery, is the oldest form of social inequality. Indeed, most social historians agree that the two forms of subjugation have common origins, as evidenced by the widespread legal fiction that a woman is the "property" of her father or husband. Inequality between men and women is nearly a cultural universal, and it almost always favors men. It can be traced to a basic type of social differentiation, the division of labor along gender lines. This separates women and men into two classes, childbearers or caretakers and other occupations, respectively. There is considerable variation in how different societies define caretaking, associated domestic activities, and "other" jobs. Yet everywhere the biological fact of childbearing is associated with the cultural definition of "man's" versus "woman's" work (Kabagarama 1993, chap. 1).

Differentiation becomes stratification when the two types of work are evaluated and rewarded unequally, which has been the case for a very long time (Wright and Jacobs 1994). In this manner, childbearers are defined and treated as social inferiors. This situation is ordinarily justified with a ruling ideology to the effect that men are naturally superior because, on the average, they are physically larger and stronger. Some individual women (and perhaps even a few men) have always questioned the fact that men (as a class) are freer and better treated, but the potential for massive organized movements has been traditionally severely restricted by dominant pronatalist values and practices. Until the agricultural revolution, the lives of both men and women were tied to survival at the margins of subsistence. For women, this meant becoming pregnant at every opportunity because offspring were valuable production inputs and rates of infant survival were low.

Under conditions of near-universal poverty, the division of labor between genders was practically a necessity of life. Thus, all societies have been structurally conducive to the movement for gender equality, but until recently few have provided the opportunity for people to organize and to turn otherwise normal relations between men and women into precipitating events. Movements aimed at redressing gender inequality occurred very early in written history and have recurred in every era to the present (Rendell 1984). With the overthrow of feudalism in eighteenth-century Europe, the division of labor and social inequality, in general, was profoundly transformed, and the women's cause was joined with the political revolutions in bringing these changes about, especially in France (Hafter 1995). Nevertheless, the early representative democracies continued to incorporate feudal norms of gender relations, most blatantly in excluding women from participating as rulers (that is, voters) or representatives (Orloff 1993).

In addition, with urbanization and industrial growth, the economic status of women actually declined in these countries. The establishment of the "breadwinner system," in which the workplace and homestead became two distinct realms, severely restricted the opportunities for productive labor and a measure of economic autonomy that had been available to women on the farm (Davis 1984). These circumstances did, at last, provide the structural conduciveness and relative deprivation that sparked a critical period in the life of the movement.

Beginning in the mid-nineteenth century, antiestablishment protest on two crucial fronts, family planning (under the leadership of Margaret Sanger in the United States) and women's suffrage, struggled with eventual success to advance the cause of gender equality (Bausum 2004; Ward et al. 1999). As a result, the biological and legal bases for the treatment of women as inferiors were, for the first time in human existence, significantly challenged. The boundaries between woman's and man's work began to dissolve, and, by the early twentieth century, women in many countries were, in principle, entitled to the same rights and protections as men (see figure 7.3). These trends were reinforced during the Great Depression and World War II periods, as increasing numbers of women joined the labor force and, during the war especially, were required to assume traditional male roles.

Since World War II, the quest for gender equality has extended far beyond the rights to vote and work, to a critical reexamination of and challenge to some of our

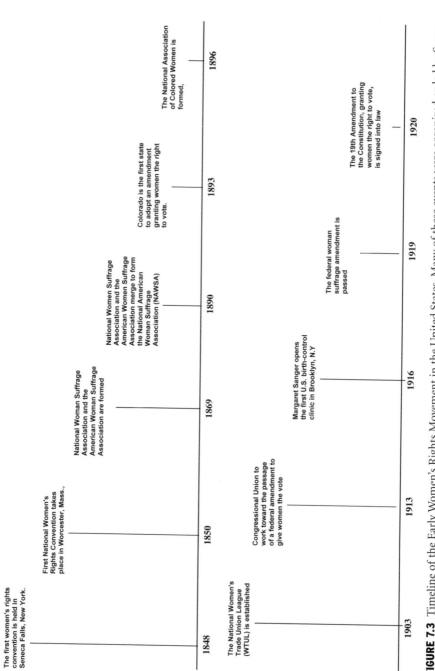

FIGURE 7.3 Timeline of the Early Women's Rights Movement in the United States. Many of these events were organized or led by Susan B. Anthony, Elizabeth Cady Stanton, Lucy Stone, and Margaret Sanger. *Sources:* http://womenshistory.about.com/od/suffrageoverview/a/timeline.htm; www.infoplease.com/spot/womenstimeline1.html.

deepest values, most enduring norms, and longest established practices. During the critical era of the U.S. Civil Rights movement, it became clear that the movement for the liberation of women, as it was then called, had profoundly revolutionary goals. Up to that moment in human experience, a great deal of social life had been premised on the assumption that women are necessarily less free than men, just as slavery was once based on a similar distinction between whites and blacks (for more on this connection, see Tuttle 1986, 12–13).

A society that has eliminated the necessity for a gender-specific division of labor (which the revolution in the technologies of reproduction has in fact accomplished) is no longer "required" to discriminate against women. This has introduced a very different basis for human relationships from anything we have known before. Of course, even in North America and Western Europe, where the movement is most active and influential, social life has hardly become perfectly egalitarian. To put it briefly, important movement goals still remain unattained: women are still paid less and command less respect in the United States and most other nations. However, we are probably much closer to equality than knowledgeable activists of even a few years ago could have imagined. Consider, for example, just how quickly our very language has changed. We are increasingly conscious of ourselves, perhaps for the first time ever, not as *mankind* but as *people*.

The movement continues to grow and, of special significance, to expand internationally (Basu and McGrory 1995; Bulbeck 1998). It is thus likely to have a long and complex life ahead, for most of the women in the world remain in childbearing roles, are tied to household activities, and are politically disenfranchised (Mohanty and Russo 1991). Moreover, resistance to equality for women exists everywhere. In some places, reactionary countermovements, some in the name of religious fundamentalism, have sought to restore traditional forms of male domination (Faludi 1991; Goodman 1993). In China and in other rural countries, women have exchanged their traditional role of childbearer for that of menial laborer (Ferraro 1995).

> Women are key to the development challenge. Throughout the developing world, women are at a disadvantage at the household, community, and societal levels. Within the household, women have less access to and control over resources and limited influence over household decisions. Beyond the household, women have limited access to communal resources, are under-represented in public decision-making bodies; have limited bargaining power in markets (such as the labor market), and often lack opportunities to improve their socioeconomic position. Therefore, efforts to reduce gender inequality are required on multiple fronts. (Bryan and Varat 2007, 1; Harcourt 2009)

These are true and serious countertrends, and they clearly stand as major obstacles in the movement's path. Nevertheless, the days when this is solely a man's world are just as clearly numbered.

Labor: The U.S. Experience in International Perspective The international labor movement is the prototype of organized, antiestablishment activity in pursuit of the two core ideals of freedom and equality (Brody 1993). In its current form, it dates back to the early nineteenth century when the industrial working classes began to fill the cities of Europe and North America. Since that time, it has diffused throughout the world.[6] Unions, federations of unions, and labor parties have been the principal movement organizations, although other groups and individuals, especially intellectuals, have played crucial roles (Western 1993).

From an international perspective, the movement was shaped, if not driven, from its inception by the "specter of Communism." In the United States, in particular, serious internal struggles were waged between Marxist revolutionary and non-Marxist (often anti-Communist) reform factions through the beginning of the twentieth century. Karl Marx himself was personally involved in the U.S. movement during the Civil War, in connection with the specifically ethnic German Workingman's Association. Overall, however, the impacts of Marx and Communist ideals were as opposition, "foreign" forces (see chapter 11 for more on Marx's influence in the capitalist countries of Europe).

Far from being Marxist, the major founding U.S. organization was the reform-oriented American Federation of Labor (AFL), begun by the New York tobacco workers' organizer Samuel Gompers in 1886. The AFL was not the sole representative of organized labor during this founding period, for it was challenged on the left by a powerful socialist coalition led by the Midwest railway workers' organizer and presidential candidate Eugene V. Debs (Ginger 1949; Young and Ruas 1999). Debs, in turn, had radical competition from the International Workers of the World (IWW) and the charismatic lumber worker from the West Coast, Big Bill Haywood (Carlson 1983).

The IWW, or "Wobblies," had an openly revolutionary ideology and program to which many Marxists contributed. But it was also distinctively American in its goals of "One Big Union" and "not higher wages, abolition of the wage system" (Dubofsky 1969). It had a homegrown, mass appeal that orthodox Marxism was never able to generate, and thus it might have led the U.S. version of a workers' revolt when this proved an impossibility for the U.S. Communist Party (CPUSA). At the beginning of World War I, with the IWW representing an authentic radical alternative, the course that the movement would take, left or right, remained in doubt.

With the Bolshevik victory in Russia in 1917, the radical wing of U.S. organized labor became extremely fractionalized, and establishment responses to alleged Bolshevist violence at home became repressive. As a result, Gompers and the AFL had no effective socialist competition for many years.

The Socialist Party of the United States never again achieved the broad coalition and following it had generated under Debs, although his successor, Norman Thomas, ran several "educational campaigns" during the succeeding decades. The Wobblies were all but destroyed by red squads, although, according to the organization's semiofficial historian, Utah Phillips, the spirit of the legendary organizer Joe Hill is still as "alive as you and me" (Industrial Workers of the World [IWW] 1984).

Major challenges to the strongly reformist and generally highly effective orientation of the movement have been mounted on a few occasions since that time, with varying degrees of success. But it is significant that the Communist Party directed none, nor did

TABLE 7.1A Timeline of the U.S. Labor Movement, 1866–1905

1866	National Labor Union founded
1869	Noble and Holy Order: Knights of Labor and Colored National Labor Union formed
1877	National uprising of railroad workers; Ten Irish coal miners ("Molly Maguires") hanged in Pennsylvania; nine more subsequently hanged
1881	Federation of Organized Trades and Labor Unions formed
1882	First Labor Day parade in New York City
1885	Successful strike by Knights of Labor on the Southwest (or Gould) System: the Missouri Pacific; Missouri, Kansas and Texas; and the Wabash
1886	American Federation of Labor founded
1887	Seven "anarchists" charged with the bombing in Chicago's Haymarket Square and sentenced to death
1890	Carpenters President P. J. McGuire and the union strike and win the eight-hour day for some 28,000 members
1894	Boycott of Pullman sleeping cars leads to general strike on railroads
1898	Erdman Act prohibits discrimination against railroad workers because of union membership and provides for mediation of railway labor disputes
1905	Industrial Workers of the World founded

Source: Green, College of Law University of Missouri, Kansas City, www.law.umkc.edu/faculty/projects/ftrials/haymarket/TIMELI.htm.

any have serious revolutionary aspirations. During the Depression, a secessionist movement within the AFL, led by mine workers' organizer John L. Lewis, formed a separate and more radical federation, the Congress of Industrial Organizations (CIO). Today, the AFL and CIO are reunited (AFL-CIO) and until 1995 claimed the vast majority of U.S. locals and members.

During the 1950s, several local unions associated with the automobile industry and transportation split with the national federation over key internal issues, including how to respond to the then-current anti-Communist insurgency (Zetka 1995). In seeking independence, the International Brotherhood of Teamsters, under the leadership of James Hoffa Sr., subsequently established a separate organization that was for many years the largest independent labor association in the country.

A recent challenge to what was for many years a virtual AFL monopsony (the labor equivalent to a monopoly) in several industries was launched in July 1995 (Kilborn 1995). Three unions, claiming a total membership of over eleven million, announced they would merge to form the country's largest-ever federation (surpassing the Teamsters by several million). The partners in this alliance are the old stalwarts of "Rust Belt" heavy manufacturing: the United Auto Workers, the United Steelworkers, and the International Association of Machinists, each of which had lost thousands of members in the past decades' shift to a postindustrial economy.

The labor movement in the United States, unlike its counterparts elsewhere (including in Canada), has generally not only avoided association with Communists but also rejected the option of forming a labor party (for a comparison with England, see Weakliem 1993). Rather, it has used interest group politics, urban machines, and

TABLE 7.1B Timeline of the U.S. Labor Movement, 1912–1947

1912	Bread and Roses strike begun by immigrant women in Lawrence, Mass., ended with 23,000 men and women and children on strike and with as many as 20,000 on the picket line; bill creating Department of Labor passes at the end of congressional session
1913	Woodrow Wilson takes office as president and appoints the first secretary of labor; William B. Wilson elected President of the United Mine Workers
1914	Ludlow Massacre of 13 women and children and seven men in Colorado coal miners' strike
1915	Joe Hill, organizer of Industrial Workers of the World, executed in Utah
1918	Leadership of Industrial Workers of the World sentenced to federal prison on charges of disloyalty to the United States
1924	Samuel Gompers dies; William Green becomes new AFL president
1925	A. Philip Randolph helps create the Brotherhood of Sleeping Car Porters
1932	Norris-LaGuardia Act prohibits federal injunctions in most labor disputes
1935	National Labor Relations Act and Social Security Act passed; Committee for Industrial Organization (CIO) formed within AFL
1936	AFL and CIO create labor's Non-Partisan League and help President Roosevelt win reelection to a second term
1937	Auto workers win sit-down strike against General Motors in Flint, Mich.; Brotherhood of Sleeping Car Porters wins contract with Pullman Co.
1938	Fair Labor Standards Act establishes first minimum wage and 40-hour week; Congress of Industrial Organizations forms as an independent federation
1946	Largest strike wave in U.S. history
1947	Taft-Hartley Act restricts union members' activities

Source: See table 7.3A.

TABLE 7.1C Timeline of the U.S. Labor Movement, 1955–1999

1955	AFL and CIO merge; George Meany becomes president
1957	AFL-CIO expels two affiliates for corruption
1962	President John Kennedy's order gives federal workers the right to bargain
1963	March on Washington for jobs and justice; Equal Pay Act bans wage discrimination based on gender
1965	AFL-CIO forms A. Philip Randolph Institute; César Chávez forms AFL-CIO United Farm Workers Organizing Committee
1970	Occupational Safety and Health Act passed
1972	Coalition of Black Trade Unionists formed
1974	Coalition of Labor Union Women founded
1979	Lane Kirkland elected president of AFL-CIO
1981	President Reagan breaks air traffic controllers' strike; AFL-CIO rallies 400,000 in Washington on Solidarity Day
1997	AFL-CIO defeats legislation giving the president the ability to "Fast Track" trade legislation without assured protection of workers' rights and the environment
1999	5,000 North Carolina textile workers gain a union after a 25-year struggle; 65,000 Puerto Rico public-sector workers join unions; Broad Campaign for Global Fairness pushes for economic and social justice worldwide; union movement organizes biggest program of grassroots electoral politics ever

Source: See table 7.3A.

considerable lobbying power in the Democratic Party to work essentially within the system.

As individuals, U.S. workers have fared extremely well in comparison to their comrades in other countries, despite the fact that at no time has anything close to a majority of the U.S. workforce belonged to unions (see table 7.2). The movement is largely responsible for establishing significant reforms in humanizing working conditions, establishing a minimum wage, securing the right to strike and to bargain collectively, and promoting antitrust legislation. Sociologists and others who have studied the movement generally agree that these benefits of working from within have been offset, at least in part, by the relatively low level of social welfare to which Americans are entitled. Citizens of countries with effective labor parties, in contrast, take such benefits for granted: housing subsidies, child allowances, and medical care (Lipset 1971, 1990).

Among the many factors, internal and external, that have shaped the labor movement during the past one and a half centuries in the United States and throughout

TABLE 7.2 Annual Changes in U.S. Union Membership, 1970–2008

Year	Number in thousands	Percentage of labor force
1970	18,088	23.5
1980	17,717	19.5
1990	16,739	15.5
1991	16,568	15.5
1992	16,390	15.1
1993	16,598	15.1
1994	16,740	14.9
1995	16,359	14.3
1996	16,269	14.0
1997	16,109	13.6
1998	16,211	13.4
1999	16,476	13.4
2000	16,258	12.8
2001	16,289	12.8
2002	15,979	12.6
2003	15,776	12.4
2004	15,472	12.5
2005	15,685	12.5
2006	15,359	12.0
2007	15,670	12.1
2008	16,098	12.4

Note: During the past forty years, the highest number of unionized U.S. workers, more than eighteen million, and the highest percentage of the workforce belonging to unions, nearly 24 percent, occurred in 1950. From that point until 2007 there was a steady decline in numbers and percentages. In 2008, the first significant increases occurred.

Source: Jelle Visser, "Union Membership Statistics in 24 Countries," *Monthly Labor Review* 129 (1) (January 2006): 45; U.S. Department of Labor, Bureau of Labor Statistics, "Union Affiliation Data from the Current Population Survey" (series numbers LUU0204466800 and LUU0204899600, 2008).

TABLE 7.3 Comparative Union Membership in Ten Industrialized Countries (in percents)

Year	USA	CANADA	JAPAN	EUROPEAN UNION	UK
1970	23.5	31.6	35.1	37.8	44.8
1980	19.5	34.7	31.1	39.7	50.7
2003	12.4	28.4	19.7	—	29.3
Percentage change between					
1970–1980	−2.5	3.3	−4.0	1.9	5.9
1980–1990	−4.0	−1.8	−5.8	−6.7	−11.4
1990–2003	−3.1	−4.7	−5.6	−6.7	−10.0
1970–2003	−11.1	−6.5	−15.4	−11.5	−15.5

Year	SWEDEN	NETHERLANDS	SPAIN	AUSTRIA	CZECH REP.
1970	67.7	36.5	—	62.8	—
1980	78.0	34.8	2.9	56.7	—
2003	78.5	22.3	16.3	—	—
Percentage change between					
1970–1980	10.3	–	12.0	2.2	6.0
1980–1990	2.8	−10.4	−0.3	−9.8	—
1990–2003	−2.8	−2.0	3.7	−11.5	−21.2
1970–2003	10.3	−14.2	3.4	−27.3	—

Note: Of the nations included in this table, the United States has consistently had the smallest percentage of its labor force belonging to unions. Only Sweden and Spain experienced an increase between 1970 and 2003. With a net loss of 11.1 percent, the United States experienced a relatively small decline.

Source: Jelle Visser, "Union Membership Statistics in 24 Countries," *Monthly Labor Review* 129 (1) (January 2006): 45.

the world, none may prove to be as consequential as the two challenges that leaders and the rank and file face today. One is the issue of how to adapt to the repudiation of Bolshevism, an event that has saddened some activists but has come as a relief to many millions more. The other is the question of organizing and promoting the interests of a labor force that is no longer dominated by industrial occupations.

In the first case, much work lies ahead in sorting out fact from fiction in the Marxist (and Marxist-Leninist and Marxist-Leninist-Stalinist) conception of workers and their "historical mission." What, now, are the relative advantages of revolutionary strategies for organized labor? How much did anti-Soviet feelings and the Cold War, two nonfactors today, distort the movement's vision and programs?

In the second case, the shift from blue-collar to white-collar society has placed the majority of workers in public sector jobs, service occupations, and various semiskilled positions in the information industry (Alfino, Caputo, and Wynyard 1998; Ritzer 2002; Western 1994). Government workers of the American Federation of State, County, and

Municipal Employees (AFSCME) form a major segment of the now-diminished AFL-CIO, and the largest single union in the United States is currently the American Federation of Teachers (AFT), almost all of whose members also work for local governments. Most of these jobs are not encompassed by the traditional definition of the working class, and most of the industries were, at least until recently, not unionized (because many did not exist during the movement's most active periods). The recent small but significant increases in the size of the organized workforce reflect a trend toward greater degrees of union activity among service and government employees.

> The percentage of American workers belonging to a union jumped in 2008, the first statistically significant increase in the 25 years that the figure has been reported, reversing a long decline in union membership. . . . [But] the rates of unionization between the private and public sector are starkly different. According to the new federal information, 7.6 percent of private-sector employees belong to a union, while about 37 percent of government employees do. Roughly 275,000 of the union-member surge—about two-thirds last year's gain—came from the public sector, according to the new federal statistics. Union gains in the private sector, by contrast, were meager. (Whoriskey 2009)

Thus, today's employees are, in some respects, in a position similar to that of the industrial workforce prior to the Gompers-Debs-Haywood era. They are poorly paid, lack medical coverage and other benefits, and are barely conscious of themselves as a group with common interests. As they now appear to be increasing their involvement in the labor movement, it will be most interesting to see how the movement responds to this change: from the lunchbucket-wielding, proletarian image to the uniformed, part-time McDonald's server concept of the working class.

Democracy: The Perennial Struggle The quest for democratic rights began in ancient Greece and probably earlier.[7] It was motivated by the audacious idea that large groups of people could and should govern themselves without the assistance of hereditary rulers who stood above the law. The movement was first institutionalized in its direct, classic form more than two thousand years ago. But at that time, and wherever it has become established (which is nearly always after a successful antiautocratic revolution), it has proved to be incomplete (Ober 1998).

The simply stated ideal of self-rule is extremely difficult to achieve. As we have learned over the years, it requires a very refined concept of rights, protections, and due process. It is effective only when there is a high degree of commitment and participation by citizens, and it must be fueled by large (and ever-growing) quantities of information freely flowing among all levels of society.

Beginning with the first Greek experiments—which lasted only about one hundred years—the principal obstacle to achieving "pure" democracy has been closure: the definition of some members of a population as nonmembers of civil society, such as slaves, women, and specific ethnic groups. Under such conditions, the system is glaringly contradictory, and it invites antiestablishment protest. As Marx observed of capitalism, democracy, too, bears the seeds of its own destruction. Through the centuries, it has thus been both a form of government and a social movement. In autocracies, it is a movement that poses an inherently radical threat to the status quo. In democratic states, it takes the form of political fundamentalism or puritanism.

In these various contexts, the democratic movement has succeeded in achieving our current, formally open societies. In the process, we have shown that the Greek concern with keeping the polis small does not apply to representative systems, as some of the largest populations in the world are self-governed (although the very largest, China, and the former third largest, the USSR, are or were not).

The movement is currently experiencing a resurgence of monumental proportions (and importance) in the former Communist countries of Central and Eastern Europe, and throughout Latin America. Despite the bloody suppression of the Tiananmen protestors in 1989, it remains the major antiestablishment force in China (Ching and Guobin 2007; Zhou 1993), to a significant extent with the help of the Internet (Guobin 2009). With the outbreak of widespread demonstrations in 2009, for which a contested election was a precipitating event, a prodemocracy movement manifested itself in Iran. Many observers were surprised to learn that such a high degree of dissidence exists within the civil society of this closed, theocratic state.

> Following up from . . . Iran's Presidential election, Tehran and other cities have seen the largest street protests and rioting since the 1979 Iranian Revolution. Supporters of reform candidate Mir Hossein Mousavi, upset at their announced loss and suspicions of voter fraud, took to the streets both peacefully and, in some cases, violently to vent their frustrations. Iranian security forces and hardline volunteer militia members responded with force and arrests, attempting to stamp out the protests—meanwhile, thousands of Iranians who were happy with the election outcome staged their own victory demonstrations. Mousavi himself has been encouraging peaceful demonstrations, and called for calm at a large demonstration today (held in defiance of an official ban). (*Boston Globe* 2009)

Structural conditions are conducive to democratic movements in democratic countries as well. In these cases, the United States and Western Europe in particular, the main concern is the growing lag between government and governance, as interest group politics has increasingly pushed the crucial activities of agenda setting and decision making beyond formal representative channels.

> Liberal democracy is recognized and valued as a norm for political systems. Yet the promises implicit in the ideal of democracy often remain unfulfilled. While in the formerly communist countries of Eastern Europe a stable democratic culture is only gradually evolving, the ever-increasing extent to which the life of European citizens is determined by actors and developments at the transnational or even global level draws attention to the fact that, beyond the nation state, satisfactory structures of democratic governance have not yet been established. Perceived

democratic deficits, i.e., the discrepancy between normative ideals of democratic self-determination and the factually experienced lack of control over key conditions shaping everyday life, are a continuous source of political mobilization at the grass roots. (Blühdorn 2009, 407)

In addition to these relatively localized movements, and in view of the impacts of rapid globalization, a strong impetus now exists for establishing a world-level democratic system. The leading movement organization in this field is the World Social Forums (WSF). The group was founded in 2001 in Porto Alegre, Brazil, in response to the World Economic Forums sponsored by the G-8 group of the largest industrialized nations. Based on the perception that the G-8 vision of the global system is essentially oligarchic, the WSF established as the first principle of its charter a commitment to "interlinking for effective action, by groups and movements of civil society that are opposed to neoliberalism and to domination of the world by capital and any form of imperialism" (Boyer 2008, 141).

Such developments lead us to wonder once again about the emerging world government. Will it continue on its sometimes shaky, democratic trajectory? Or will the forces of autocracy, elitism, and the seemingly implacable powers of multinational corporations prevail? Much remains uncertain, but we do know that the struggle for self-rule in its most basic sense will be with us for the next several generations. The outcome will depend, in large measure, on the success of organized prodemocratic protest and the work of its main agencies, including Amnesty International, the American Civil Liberties Union (ACLU), and, of special importance, the UN Commission on Human Rights (see chapter 10).[8]

TABLE 7.4 The Ten Least Democratic Countries in the World

Country	Dictator	In power since
Sudan	Omar al-Bashir	1989
North Korea	Kim Jong-il	1994
Burma (Myanmar)	Than Shwe	1992
Zimbabwe	Robert Mugabe	1980
Uzbekistan	Islam Karimov	1990
China	Hu Jintao	2002
Saudi Arabia	King Abdullah	1995
Turkmenistan	Saparmurat Niyazov	1990
Iran	Seyed Ali Khamane'I	1989
Equatorial Guinea	Teodoro Obiang Nguema	1979

Note: A "dictator" is a head of state who exercises arbitrary authority over the lives of his citizens and who cannot be removed from power through legal means. The worst commit terrible human rights abuses. This present list draws in part on reports by global human rights organizations, including Human Rights Watch, Freedom House, Reporters without Borders, and Amnesty International.

Source: David Wallechinsky, "*Parade*'s Annual List of the World's Ten Worst Dictators," January 2, 2006, www.parade.com/articles/editions/2006/edition_01-22-2006/Dictators.

Semipermanent and New Movements

Each of these three permanent movements has gone through many changes over the decades and centuries, and each is now made up of local branches, factions, and sub- and countermovements. Nevertheless, even taken together, they encompass only a tiny fraction of the organized protest activity that is now occurring.

The Varieties of Protest Today The realm of social dissidence now also includes religious fundamentalism, family planning, ecological concerns (Taylor 1995), and nationalism and racism, including an upsurge in neofascism in several countries (Anti-Defamation League [ADL] 1993). In addition, there are peace, antinuclear, and messianic movements in most of the world's major religions; other groups are awaiting the end of the world; and some have members who believe that humans have been contacted by beings from other planets.

All of these have followers, numbering in the hundreds of millions in the cases of religious fundamentalism and nationalism. As the years pass, they, too, will affect the way our institutions function. Many will undoubtedly achieve success and inspire reaction in the form of new norms, values, and practices. These movements will also have an impact on the more general gender equality, labor, and democratic causes, as all compete for the attention, money, and time and energy of potential participants the world over.

When stressing that the future is being planned in advance to a greater extent than ever before, one therefore needs to remember that the planning is occurring at several

FIGURE 7.4 Costa Rica Cloud Forest. The government of Costa Rica has been recognized by the environmental movement for its efforts to preserve its ecosystem, including the cloud forest pictured here. In a relatively short time, environmentalism has grown from a concern of a small group of scientists and activists to a cause embraced by governments throughout the world. Author photo.

different sites and that not all of it is official. The "outcome of the general will" cannot possibly be anyone's "will in particular" under such conditions.

Creative Altruism In the very long view, perhaps the most basic movement among all that have been mentioned in this book is creative altruism. It is an old idea, part of Henri Saint-Simon's and I. Auguste Comte's founding ideals for their "science of society" and revived in Pitirim A. Sorokin's critique of late sensate culture (Johnston 1995; Matter 1974; Sorokin 1954a). This movement attacks contemporary civilization at its core in opposing the values of egoism and materialism, tendencies that many theorists have viewed as parts of human nature.

Sorokin traces the roots of creative altruism to such ancient thought systems as Buddhism and to the pacifist, communal utopias of Gandhi (Sorokin 1948). It has also surfaced in the counterculture movement of the 1960s (Roszak 1969) and in similar outbreaks of antibourgeois youthful rebellion before (Schneider 1975a, chap. 4) and since (Roszak 1994). It is still relatively small and unorganized, and it remains somewhat on the fringes of contemporary protest ideology, although several foundations and academic organizations now regularly pursue research and outreach programs on the subject.[9]

In addition to the revival of scholarly interest in altruism, several other efforts to further the promotion of creative altruism have recently emerged. Of most immediate interest is the creation of a new American Sociological Association (ASA) Section information on Altruism and Social Solidarity. This Section, organized by Vincent Jeffries, Samuel Oliner, Edward Tiryakian, Lawrence Nichols, Barry Johnston, and other Sorokin scholars, held its first formal session at the 2009 ASA Meeting (see Jeffries et al. 2007).

Because its command or therapy stresses education and moral reawakening (Sorokin 1954b), it is more akin to religious revival than to political revolution. This aspect has made it less appealing to contemporary activist intellectuals, most of whom share the secularism of Marx, Max Weber, and the other classic theorists.

According to the doctrine of creative altruism, most of the major problems now facing humanity stem from our current obsession with self-gratification. These range from autocracies that place the interests of the party before everything else, to democracies distorted by corruption and nationalistic and racist regimes that defy world government. Our ruling ideologies and norms, especially in economic and political relations, encourage behavior that maximizes personal gain in material things at the expense of other people. Under these conditions, the level of cooperation required to carry out the major tasks of social reconstruction, so that we can sustain one world at peace, cannot be achieved (Wuthnow 1995).

As individuals, groups, organizations, institutions, and nations, we are all inclined to exploit rather than to repair the liabilities of others, liabilities such as being less powerful, less knowledgeable, or in greater material need. But the world system is so interdependent today that the weaknesses of some are bound to weaken all eventually, sooner rather than later as the process of globalization accelerates. On this basis, it is argued, altruistic principles such as the golden rule, love of kind, and humanist idealism need to be reincorporated into our daily lives and sociocultural structures. This,

Sorokin and other proponents believe, will greatly assist our species in achieving the potential that 250 millennia of evolution, devolution, and revolution have provided.

Afterword: The Anatomy of Revolution

ORGANIZER: Come The Revolution we will all eat caviar.
RECRUIT: But I don't like caviar.
ORGANIZER: Come The Revolution you will like caviar.
—A joke from the underground

From the days of Rousseau and Hegel, and with urgency since the Marxist "watershed" of the 1848 era (Zeitlin 1968), social philosophers and scientists have reserved a special place in their accounts of change for political revolutions (Goldstone 1989). A specific sociology of revolutions was first outlined by Sorokin (1925), and most of the major theorists since that time have attempted to understand how and why they occur (see especially Eisenstadt 1978; Skocpol 1994; Tilly 1989).

There is considerable dispute surrounding these questions, much of it based on semantic issues, that is, explanations of revolutions often stand or fall on what does and does not count as an "authentic" one. Here the dictionary is of little use because the original meaning of the term is the one that still applies to planetary motion: something that "comes around again." This meaning indicates that the earliest commentators viewed momentous changes of the existing order as a return to an earlier era, in accord with a cyclical theory of history. But in France (1789–1815) and Russia (1905–1917), the transition was marked by a new and unprecedented regime, rather than a return to a golden age. In this regard, the "revolutionary" character of such changes lies in (1) their scope and (2) the rapidity with which they happen. Thus, as Sorokin (1925) first pointed out, revolutions can take place in any realm, provided that entire institutions (not just smaller groups and isolated beliefs and practices) are significantly and quickly transformed.

To refer to agricultural, industrial, and computer revolutions is not to speak metaphorically. Rather, these are as authentic as political revolutions and can change people's lives as fundamentally, if not more so. Social scientists and historians often point out that "a sudden overthrow of the state in and of itself is not necessarily a revolution if it only means that one political elite has replaced another with no popular base or broader implications for social transformation" (Harper 1993, 185). They distinguish between "authentic" cases and coups d'état, palace uprisings, and other less consequential forms of regime change.

This distinction also acknowledges that many radical political movements wrongly style themselves as revolutionary. Such deception can be a strategy to elicit support from masses who desire fundamental changes, not just a new set of political leaders. Or it can be used to take symbolic advantage of identifying with "The Revolution" (the one that, according to Marxists, will bring about world Communism). It can also justify massive criminality by declaring the old order and its laws invalid.

On these grounds, some commentators would also prefer to discount the fascist takeovers in post–World War I Europe as revolutions, although the movement's leaders claimed the title (in fact, Mussolini styled his a "permanent" revolution). From this perspective, changes need be not only rapid and fundamental but also progressive to qualify as authentically revolutionary.

Some researchers have argued that the events that occurred in North America in the 1776–1789 period did not constitute a revolution either because the English language and many British customs were maintained (Goldstone 1986; Harper 1993, 196; cf. Lipset 1990). This is a rather curious argument. On the continent at the time, there were in fact two major political reform movements: the Whigs and the Tories. Both sought fundamental changes in the status quo, but the former styled itself as revolutionary and struggled to overthrow monarchical rule, whereas the latter sought to create a continental confederation under the king.

The outcome has provided us with one of the most effective comparative cases in social science because both sides got their way. Two new nation-states, made up of people with the same ethnic heritages and living closely together, were created after 1789. Their differences, which are sometimes subtle but extremely important from a sociological perspective, can be traced precisely to the fact that one, the United States, was created in the aftermath of a revolution and the other, Canada, remained a dominion of the Empire for nearly two centuries, although from 1789 on, its social and cultural development diverged sharply from that of the motherland (Lipset 1990, chap. 1).

Indeed, if the overthrow of a regime and other consequential changes do not qualify as a revolution because the language and customs of the old order (such as drinking tea at dusk) are retained, then the French, Russian, and Chinese revolutions were not "the real thing" either. Indeed, with the benefit of information still being revealed about the Bolshevik regime, it appears that the enthusiasm over Lenin's defeat of autocracy was grossly overstated. Was there, in fact, a revolution in Russia, or was it just another grand coup that delivered the same czarist wine in new Communist bottles? Such questions are endless, and in principle irresolvable, because they ultimately depend on a value judgment concerning how "basic" and how "permanent" a regime change must be to qualify. As a result, some authors, Humpty-Dumpty style, use the powerfully evocative term to mean whatever they choose.

The title of this section is taken from a classic study first published several decades ago by historian Crane Brinton (1938). In it, he focused on the most dramatic, and typically violent, upheavals of collective behavior that eventuate in the toppling of regimes. He showed that even these episodes operate according to a set of common, rational principles and have a characteristic life cycle. Many of Brinton's examples were drawn from France in the 1789–1815 era, which he and most other scholars view as a prototype. But it is essentially a comparative study meant to establish a general theory of revolutions.

Sociologists and historians have since adapted and made several contributions to this theory, both by applying new methods to collect and analyze relevant data and by incorporating general insights on collective behavior and movements into research in this specific realm. Much of this research is guided by the question "What conditions are necessary and sufficient for a successful political revolution?" Our discussion in this and the preceding chapter has summarized the findings of this work to the present. Clearly, as Skocpol (1979) notes, factors such as regime legitimacy, the role of intellectuals, and precipitating events are decisive.

There is, however, another very innovative work in this area that we have not yet mentioned. This is an anthology assembled by the sociologists Philip B. Springer and Marcello Truzzi with the self-explanatory title *Revolutionaries on Revolution* (1973). Its list of authors is impressive. It includes Marx, Karl Katusky, Leon Trotsky, Haywood, Rosa Luxemburg, Peter Kropotkin, Che Guevara, Vo Nguyen Giap (who engineered the Communist victory in Vietnam), Stalin, Mother Jones, Debs, Fidel Castro, Mao Zedong, Mussolini, Hitler, Anwar El Sadat, and, of course, Lenin. These highly knowledgeable people discuss, in their own words, such key topics as revolutionary discipline, gradualist versus radical tactics, strike strategies, anarchism, guerrilla warfare, relations between intellectuals and the rank and file, propaganda, the role of organizations, and internal security.

What is most interesting about this collection is the degree of detailed knowledge possessed by the contributors about society, its weaknesses, and human nature. These are clearly scholars of insurrection whose acts are rational, calculated, and one might even say "cold-blooded"—a far cry from the hysterical true-believer image purveyed by some early collective behaviorists. It is also obvious from works such as these that the revolutionary occupation has its own traditions, styles, schools of thought, and specific skills, and in surprising ways is as instrumental as any other, more common, job—but such an exciting job! According to these participants and to the social scientists who seek to understand their motives, political revolutions are won by movements with central coordinating organizations, led by dedicated people who are strongly committed to their cause. They work with persistence and patience, exploiting structural contradictions and precipitating events to discredit the regime. Always mobilizing, revolutionary movements seek to increase the degree of commitment among followers, win over establishment ideologues, and, eventually, convert the police and army. Far from being spontaneous outbursts, revolutions succeed when they are better organized than the regime they seek to topple.

Recognizing intimately that revolutions seek power and that power is based on violence, revolutionaries unequivocally define the regime as a military enemy. This entails the need for specific strategies of security and the use of physical force. Thus, all successful revolutionary movements are ultimately a form of guerrilla warfare, in symbol or in fact. "Is the enemy strong? One avoids him. Is he weak? One attacks him," as General Vo Nguyen Giap concisely put it (quoted in Springer and Truzzi 1973, 83). This, in a very blunt sense, is the "secret" of successful revolutions.

As the exploration of the causes and consequences of large-scale social and cultural change continues, the subsequent chapters examine political revolutions at several points. At the same time, one must bear in mind that not all social movements are directly aimed at seizing state power and that most are not especially radical. Moreover, not all overthrows of existing regimes are revolutionary, nor are all revolutions specifically political.

Overtly revolutionary political movements can fail to deliver on their promises to create a better society, and in many instances they have proved especially vulnerable to rigidity, closure, and autocratic rule when they become institutionalized. Although ideologues may be convinced otherwise (that comes with the job), political revolutions are not panaceas for solving all social problems. They are tricky, dangerous undertakings that have often inspired reaction. The theories of social scientists and the accounts of movement intellectuals alike underscore this highly volatile strain in the anatomy of revolutions.

Summary

Social movements all share certain features with other, less organized forms of collective behavior. Their occurrence signals the presence of lags and discontinuity in the way norms, values, and social structures fit with one another. They grow or diminish in size according to their own inner logic, relatively independent of the general course of larger social, cultural, and demographic processes. And they are typically viewed by established authorities as problematic, requiring some sort of response or counteraction. These factors cause dynamic movements that are uniquely powerful engines of change.

Nevertheless, because they are always goal oriented and usually managed and directed by self-conscious leaders, movements are decisively shaped by the sociohistorical contexts from which they emerge. The preceding discussion illustrated this context-bound aspect of movements, focusing on protests designed to bring about significant reforms and major transformations in the functioning of institutions (especially, but not exclusively, political institutions). Our survey revealed a considerable range of sizes, philosophies, tactics, and outcomes associated with such movements. These range from traditional cultures in which social protest is virtually unknown to the typically violent and usually swiftly repressed insurrections of feudal peasants and colonized peoples. They include the modern autocracies of the Soviet Union and Nazi Germany in which any type of movement was viewed as a potential threat to the state, as well as contemporary democracies in which protest is viewed as a basic human right (although a right that is on occasion observed in the breach).

Comparative research on these various movement-context associations suggests that, whereas social life is always conducive to one or another type of organized dissidence, the prospects that major changes will actually result from antiestablishment protest depend upon the kind of establishment that prevails. Even such matters as the amount of blood that may be shed and the number of movement intellectuals who might be co-opted by the authorities are determined by contextual factors such as societal complexity and the degree of closure or rigidity of groups.

This variability is especially evident in the cases of permanent movements, such as those promoting gender equality and workers' rights. Because such causes have long histories, extending back decades and even centuries, and because they transcend national and ethnic boundaries, their ebbs and flows can be discerned in a wide range of contexts. They reveal how intimately cultures and countercultures relate to one another, despite the fact that, by definition, they are in opposition. It is therefore noteworthy that the permanent movements featured here are today experiencing extremely critical periods of change, not just in one country but throughout the world. It is also of considerable interest, in view of Sorokin's theory of sociocultural dynamics, that a very old (but, in our materialistic culture, rather unusual) movement that speaks to the need for a universal ethic of altruism—"creative altruism," as Sorokin labeled it—has begun to stir at the margins of our religious and secular institutions and in the established social sciences as well.

These developments are responses to globalization and the associated revolutionary changes currently transforming social life everywhere. In the broadest sense, crises associated with gender relations, labor relations, democratic participation, and so on now form the context for future change, the "backdrop" against which the trends of the next millennium will be played out. Militant change has become normalized. Nothing, it seems, is now beyond question, challenge, or protest. In such a world, it is inevitable that ordinary people will be swept into the fray. Under the circumstances, contemporary sociologists, and others who study social and cultural change, have pursued with renewed interest some fairly classical questions about the phenomena of revolutions: What are they? What forms can they take? Why do some succeed and others fail? And, after all, what does revolutionary "success" mean?

With such issues in mind, the chapter concluded with a distinction between specifically political revolutions and other types of movements, including a view of the former from the "inside." As those who know remind us, the political-revolutionary route to change is a treacherous one, although it may prove to be the only correct route.

In chapter 8, our attention turns to another sort of engine of change, technological innovation. On first consideration, innovations appear to be very different from movements and revolutions. They seem to represent a more peaceful, controlled, and beneficial approach to change, far removed from the politics and emotional intensity of protest. Yet one need not be an expert in the field of social impact analysis to realize that technology does not always produce positive results. Even without including the specific tools of warfare and mass destruction, far more lives are taken every year by unintended side effects of technology than by even the bloodiest bouts of political insurgency. As noted in chapter 8, this and related social and political aspects cause the innovation process to resemble social movements in many, often surprising, ways, including several parallels between inventors and movement intellectuals.

Relevant Websites

www.lib.virginia.edu/area-studies/subaltern/ssmap.htm
The *Journal of Subaltern Studies* at the University of Virginia maintains this site. Included here are numerous references, links, and online articles discussing anticolonial and antifeudal movements throughout history.

www.russianarchives.com/index.html
This is the URL for the Russian Archives Online Russian History project.

http://personalinfomediary.com/USAPATRIOTACT_Text.htm
This site contains the full text of the USA PATRIOT Act, passed overwhelmingly by both houses of Congress in the wake of the September 11 attack on New York and Washington, D.C.

http://action.aclu.org/reformthepatriotact/
The ACLU maintains this site on the USA PATRIOT Act. Several informative links to documents, legal arguments, and opinions of interested laypersons are provided.

www.trussel.com/hf/stalin.htm
This amazing document is the complete text of Soviet premier Nikita Khrushchev's denunciation of Stalin. It was originally delivered on February 24–25, 1956, at the Twentieth Communist Party Congress.

www.writing.upenn.edu/~afilreis/Holocaust/gill-white-rose.html
Here are excerpts on the White Rose, the small but significant student movement in Nazi Germany that dared to defy Hitler's rule. The site is maintained at Pennsylvania State University.

www.picturehistory.com/find/p/4419/mcms.html
You might have seen some photographs of women doing "men's work" during World War II. Here is a site with many such pictures.

www.secularhumanism.org/
This is the home page of the Secular Humanism Association, an antilobbying lobby organization.

The Process of Technological Innovation

Technology is neither positive nor negative, nor is it neutral.

—Melvin Kranzberg (quoted in Simon 2009)

Since the days of Herbert Spencer in the mid-nineteenth century, social scientists have considered the adaptations that populations make to their habitats to be a prime cause of collective change. In this light, cultural practices and social structures are viewed as inventions designed to contribute to survival and prosperity in the face of environmental challenges. The subject of this chapter is the cultural complex that figures most prominently in this process, technology: the stock of "know-how" developed or borrowed by a population to extend its members' capacity to overcome natural physical and biological limitations.

Technology is a distinctly, if not exclusively, human possession, and it has provided us with a powerful advantage over other animals. Its quality and level of sophistication are often deciding factors in competition between groups over scarce resources and over each other's domains. Thus, it has played a critical role in evolutionary processes, both actual and metaphorical. It has allowed humanity to destroy entire species, and it has brought us to the brink of creating new ones and resurrecting the extinct or nearly extinct. It has given us the ability to kill in a virtual instant all the inhabitants of this planet, and it has provided us with the potential to inhabit other worlds. For better and worse, as our technologies develop, so shall we all.

William F. Ogburn is recognized as the first sociologist to explore systematically the ways in which tools, machinery, and other inventions cause sociocultural change. By the World War I era, when Ogburn was a young professor, it was evident that the usual objects of social research—bureaucracies, constitutions, and languages—had done much to transform life in the United States and elsewhere. Yet it was clear that innovations in material technologies such as cars and telephones were equally responsible. With this in view, Ogburn and his Chicago School colleagues undertook to explain how our inventions impact our societies, a highly ambitious and difficult project, as it has turned out:

> That technology is considered a source of social change is indicated by various expressions often heard. Gunpowder destroyed feudalism. Railroads created cities. The steam engine increased divorce. The automobile is moving the department store and supermarket to the suburbs. The airplane reranked the great military powers . . . [but] to explain how inventions cause social change is not a simple task. (Ogburn 1957, 12)

One place to begin, Ogburn suggested, was to consider what gunpowder, railroads, steam engines, automobiles, and airplanes have in common—that is, they extend the

FIGURE 8.1 The University of Chicago, home of the first Department of Sociology in the United States. William Ogburn, an early member of the "Chicago School," pioneered in viewing technological innovation as a cause and an effect of sociocultural change. Photo by Jevnin, used under a Creative Commons license 2.0; posted October 28, 2005, at http://commons .wikimedia.org/wiki/ File:University_of_ Chicago_USA3.jpg.

power of the five human senses and help us overcome our biological limitations. Once we have a better idea about that, it will be easier to understand what can happen when a culture experiences the invention or diffusion of such items. Technological innovations have transformed social life in many ways throughout the course of human existence. The earliest social scientists assumed this as a basic factor in their accounts of progressively higher evolutionary stages, each of which is ushered in by a major material discovery: fire, stone tools, the plow, and the steam engine. Those who speak of our current era as the "Information Age" have this same association in mind.

In chapter 2 and at other points, several pertinent limitations in the evolutionary metaphor were noted, including the judgment that a population's level of advance should be measured in terms of how effectively its members can conquer nature and other populations. Pitirim A. Sorokin's cyclical theory was presented as an alternative to this view, indicating that advance is always relative to the dominant cultural pattern of an era— ideational, idealistic, and sensate—and that conquest has positive associations only in the last instance.

In this account, the fates of specific populations rise and decline as social and environmental circumstances dictate, whereas technological development generally follows according to the values of those in a position to innovate. Technologies capable of destroying extensive forests, shorelines, and wetlands to make way for mills and factories were invented long before the means to save them were understood. But such vast lags did not in themselves *cause* Western civilization to become conquest oriented. Rather, the order of discovery represents preexisting cultural priorities: industrial growth before environmental conservation.

More recently, critics of Western development models have joined in the suggestion that we have erred in equating progress with technological prowess. They do not deny that technology has been and will always be a consequential force in society, but they remind us that innovations can have no effects in and of themselves. "New technology comes into an already existing social and technological framework. . . . What we really mean by 'the social consequences of technology' is 'the social consequences of technology that people have chosen to use in particular ways'" (Schneider 1975a, 50n).

This chapter examines the complex relationship between technological innovation and sociocultural conditions. The discussion is divided into three main sections. First is an overview of the field of technology assessment. Here, we focus on the emergence of what has been called the "R&D (research and development) society." Following this is a discussion of the "autonomous technology" thesis. This is the classic theme in literature and technology studies that humanity has—in the manner of Frankenstein's monster—lost control of the technologies it has created. The chapter concludes with an inventory of some of the policies and programs intended to (re-)gain control of the innovation process.

When we consider the substantial resources now dedicated to the technology/society interface and the many ways in which it has affected contemporary life, it is evident that the late-eighteenth-century ideals of minimal control and "invisible hands" no longer have any basis in reality. For better or worse, technology has served to undercut natural forces and historical drift and to place the responsibility for sociocultural change squarely in human hands (Fromm 1968).

Assessing Technology's Effects

Since the mid-1970s, much relevant research on technology and society has been conducted outside the traditional fields of anthropology and sociology in new interdisciplinary specialties such as science, technology, and society studies (STSS; see Hackett et al. 2007; see also Cohen 1994; Jasanoff 1995; Spiegel-Rosing and Price 1977);[1] social impact analysis or assessment (International Association for Impact Assessment [IAIA] 2009; Glickfeld, Whitney, and Grigsby 1978);[2] and technology assessment (Porter et al. 1980). This work has revealed that the sociocultural contexts into which innovations enter and the choices concerning how they are to be used are indeed decisive in determining how people will be affected: whether or not they will benefit, what aspects of their lives need to be changed to accommodate the new technologies, and whether they will consequently become freer or subject to greater manipulation by authorities (Drucker 1986).

The experiences of the Green Revolution that began in the 1960s provide a landmark in this field of research (Karim 1986). During the course of this program, new fertilization and irrigation techniques that proved to be effective in raising productivity on farms in the United States met with success in many Third World regions to which they were transferred. The agricultural scientist most responsible for the Green Revolution innovations was Norman Bourlag (who died at age ninety-five in 2009). "Dr. Borlaug's advances in plant breeding led to spectacular success in increasing food production in Latin America and Asia and brought him international acclaim. In 1970, he was awarded the Nobel Peace Prize. . . . He was widely described as the father of the broad agricultural movement called the Green Revolution" (Jonas and Wheaton 2009, A1).

Yet, "the Green Revolution eventually came under attack from environmental and social critics who said it had created more difficulties than it had solved" (Jonas and Wheaton 2009, A1). Despite their positive results in some areas, these same innovations failed miserably in others. In fact, they worsened the plight of many poor farmers. The original assumption, that the innovations would "automatically" increase output, turned out to be naive and overly simplistic. What was learned is that if farms resemble their counterparts in the United States—large, owner operated, and mechanized—the technology works. But if they are very small and owned by absentee landlords, the innovations can become so costly that overall productivity is actually lowered.

For uncounted generations, Third World farms have depended on cow dung and river water for fertilization and irrigation and have thus been able to benefit from nature for free, albeit meager, supplies of energy. Farmers have eked out a living, with perhaps a small share of any surplus left for themselves to be marketed in a good year, after most of it goes to the landowner. When presented with modern technologies, however, these people suddenly found themselves in greater debt than ever to others, landlords and pawnbrokers, who, in accord with traditional values, were not especially concerned with productivity (Nair 1969). Because such debt is ordinarily discharged through bondage, a form of indentured servitude, the owner has a vested interest in keeping the operation small and dependent on free human labor.

The basic lesson in such experiences is that all innovations are culturally specific. Their effectiveness depends on prevailing values and relationships, such as who owns

197

the farm, as much as on purely technical considerations, such as the exact nitrogen content of a new fertilizer (Ghai and Radwan 1983, 17–27). As a result of these discoveries, we are now aware that the higher-order impacts of a technology vary according to which groups and individuals are most affected and whether the effects are judged to be harmful or beneficial.

Since the mid-1980s, a great deal of concern has been expressed about technological disasters such as the gas leak at the Bhopal, India, Union Carbide plant in 1984; the Chernobyl meltdown of 1986 in Ukraine; the Exxon *Valdez* tanker accident in Alaska in 1989; and the Houston oil terminal flood in 1994.[3] On January 1, 2000, in Baia Mare, Romania, a tailings dam at a gold mine ruptured and for four consecutive days released water contaminated with cyanide into a tributary of the Danube River. The cyanide reached levels of over seven hundred times normal concentrations and killed all living species in its path (UN Environment Programme, www.uneptie .org/scp/sp/disaster/index.htm).

The destruction of the U.S. Gulf Coast in October 2005 that resulted from Hurricane Katrina was viewed by many as a "natural disaster." Yet, most of the nearly two thousand people who lost their lives—and a large portion of the property damage as well—were victims of drowning and toxic contamination brought on by the floods that occurred after the levees failed. Subsequent investigations revealed that the failure was an unanticipated consequence of a technology upon which millions of people had depended for decades (U.S. Congress 2006).

This combination of natural and technological factors associated with Katrina gave rise to a new term in the vocabulary of the social study of technology: "natech disaster." Research conducted in the wake of Katrina has shown that numerous past instances of loss of life and property that were originally classified as the effect of natural causes were in fact natech, that is, they were equally the result of higher-order technological outcomes. J. Steven Picou, one of the sociologists to first use the term "natech," has discussed this type of disaster and its impact on people's lives.

> First and foremost, natech disasters are systemic events that chronically permeate and contaminate both the ecological and social environments. These consequences are generated through the synergistic interaction of natural forces with engineering, production and technological systems of industry and government. Natech disasters may take many forms and their actual ecological, social, medical and psychological consequences are not immediately identifiable. In fact, the impacts of natech disasters, similar to technological disasters, are often masked by latent health risks due to toxic exposure and slowly evolving patterns of collective stress, anger, anxiety and depression. (Picou 2009, 41)

These clearly unintended, but nevertheless recurrent, kinds of impacts are especially tragic today because of the size of the human settlements in the danger zone and the scale at which the technologies operate (billions of cubic feet of toxic gas, tons of radioactive fuel, and millions of barrels of petroleum). Reports of the carnage match the worst wartime accounts of lost battles. Some of our technologies are so huge and

FIGURE 8.2 Hurricane Katrina, in the Air and on the Ground. The storm made landfall near New Orleans, Louisiana, on August 28, 2005. The death and destruction caused by Katrina were the result of a combination of natural and technological factors. This led to its designation as a "Natech Disaster." NOAA satellite images of Hurricane Katrina taken from Wednesday, August 24, 2005, to Tuesday, August 30, 2005. These images were taken by NOAA's Geostationary Operational Environmental Satellite (GOES). Images in the public domain. Stock photo of Katrina on the ground provided by www.aradise.com/.

powerful that they could have final and devastating higher-order impacts on the planet and all of its inhabitants. So we have the "nuclear winter" and "ultraviolet summer" scenarios, forecasts of dead oceans, acid rains, and Malthusian catastrophes: all problems created by technological "solutions."

The element of irony is especially apparent in the last mentioned scenario, demographic collapse, for the exceptionally high rates of population growth in today's Third World, which (according to Malthusians) are rapidly pressing against the limits of environmental carrying capacities, are second-order impacts of innovations even more popular than the transistor radio: the technologies of infant mortality control. If these were somehow to be withdrawn—no more polio vaccines at age six months, for example— the population problem would solve itself. But who in their right mind would be the first to give them up? As Nobel Laureate Gunnar Myrdal (1970) expressed it, "Complacency about or even tolerance of a high level of mortality because it slows down population growth is simply not permissible" (152).

In a similar vein, the seas would be much cleaner if we would just stop using oil, and there would be no more acid rain if we completely deindustrialized. Rather than taking such drastic steps, however, most people have passively agreed to accept the bad along with the good. Disasters are counted as unfortunate, and, with the help of social and environmental impact analysts, future recurrences are mitigated through techno-logical improvements and reforms in regulations governing safety and use. Meanwhile, the technologies continue to be developed, diffused, and adopted.

Why? Obviously, we still use technologies because some people continue to ben-efit from the production of lethal gas in urban areas, storing petroleum at the mouths of volatile rivers, and so on. This includes people from all walks of life: owners who profit, governments that receive tax revenues, and workers who can earn money that would otherwise be unavailable—as long as they are willing to take the necessary risks.

In an address delivered at Santa Clara University on "The Unanticipated Conse-quences of Technology," Tim Healy (2008) summarized these issues.

[Because the] problem of unanticipated consequences . . . is so common to all of what we do in life, it should not come as a surprise that the study has led to some very general results or positions which we might apply to all of our lives. We close here with a brief list of some of these results.

- Life is very complex, more so than we admit.
- All of our actions have unanticipated consequences.
- We bear a moral obligation to take our positions tentatively, with humility in the light of our ignorance.
- Short-term and long-term values are often different, often contradictory.
- Uncertainty can be reduced but there is always a cost.
- It is desirable to reduce uncertainty—but not to eliminate it.

In the end we are left with a dilemma—which is hardly surprising. We act with uncertainty about the consequences of our acts, and yet we have to act, for even to do nothing is to act, and there will be consequences. Change is an inherent part of life. Part of that change is natural, part is within our control. We have a right to act, but we also have an obligation to accept some level of responsibility for the unanticipated consequences of our actions. That level of responsibility is as hard to define as the unanticipated consequences themselves, but it is there nonetheless.

Autonomous Technology

The "social shocks" (Lawless 1977) caused by recent industrial accidents have stimulated a traditional fear in Western culture, one that goes back to the ancient Greek myth of

Prometheus and was later expressed in Mary Shelley's classic novel *Frankenstein* (Landes 1969). These stories are prophecies of doom that stress a tragic frailty, and vanity, in our technological aspirations: some secrets of nature are not meant to be possessed by human beings. If they happen to be stolen from the gods (as the Prometheus myth puts it), the inventions that follow will eventually come to dominate the culprits and ultimately destroy them. This is obviously a powerful sentiment, and so widespread that people not familiar with specific accounts of accidents such as Chernobyl are nevertheless well acquainted with their moral lessons: if we tamper too much with technology, we will be very sorry. Reports of massive radiation leaks and chemical spills remind us of Victor Frankenstein's outburst: "I have created a monster!"

Philosophers and social scientists throughout the world continue to debate whether or not technology has taken over and turned on its creator in this way (see Postman 1993; and, specifically with reference to cloning, van der Valk 1997). The urban planner Lewis Mumford (1963, 1967), the political scientist Don K. Price (1965), and particularly the French philosopher Jacques Ellul (1964) were influential in fueling the discussion after World War II. By the mid-1990s, the issue had become part of the lore in technology assessment and the other disciplines that study the impact of innovations (Roszak 1994; see also Weinstein 1982, chap. 8).

Ellul's name is widely recognized in this debate for his view that, as industrial society has evolved, the social and political lives of its members have been dominated increasingly by the need to service and sustain a prime technological project, one that is ultimately self-destructive. This is the project of replacing human labor by machines in work, leisure, and all cultural pursuits. In the process, Ellul argued, creativity and self-determination have virtually disappeared. Autonomous humanity has been replaced by "autonomous technology" (Ravetz 1978; van der Valk 1997; Winner 1977).

This is a very broad and sweeping indictment, and it would be difficult, if not impossible, to prove it definitely. It does, however, suggest that the higher-order impacts of modern technologies include strains and stresses that, although less obvious than industrial explosions, may in the end prove to be far more consequential. Five specific impacts have been of special concern to proponents of the autonomous technology thesis:

1. *The technological imperative.* Innovations designed to solve specific problems create needs that, themselves, can only be satisfied with further innovations. Computers need software, cars need fuel, and so on. Thus, the decision to innovate in one area reverberates to others. To invest in a new technology requires a commitment to invest in whatever it takes to keep it running, in good repair, and constantly updated. Once people find themselves on the slippery slope of development, they require a regular "technological fix." Much as drug addicts become slaves to their habit, society surrenders control of its future to the dictatorship of the machine.

2. *Reverse adaptation.* New technologies require new technical skills so they may be effectively operated, maintained, and developed. This gives prestige and increasing authority to those with technical expertise, and it places a premium on specialized training in electronics, nuclear engineering, genetic sciences, and other advanced fields (Knoke and Kalleberg 1994). As a result, a new elite has emerged, which Price

(1965) has called "the industrial estate." These people are uniquely equipped to affect R&D agenda setting because they have access to knowledge and procedures incomprehensible to the average citizen. By virtue of their deep, but narrow, educational backgrounds and professional interests, however, they tend to view problems in functionally rationalist terms. They are masters of technique, "technical virtuosos," but have no special talents in deciding how the techniques should be applied. Such technical virtuosity has become valued as an end in itself, displacing substantive goals such as improvement in the human condition. Discoveries are pursued because of their logical necessity, not necessarily because they will result in something worthwhile. Today's engineers assume the role of social prophets and, like the Henry Fords and Charles Lindberghs of an earlier era, are granted authority to comment on and influence aspects of modern society that are beyond their true qualifications.

3. *Environmental degradation.* Many of the higher-order impacts of innovations in industry are not immediately discernible but instead accumulate over the years until they make their presence felt as natech disasters such as polluted air, land, and water, and despoiled ecosystems. The Love Canal incident near Niagara Falls, New York, resulted from the revelation in 1981 by government scientists that the local groundwater in an exclusive residential suburb had become carcinogenic through decades of dumping by chemical plants (House Committee on Energy and Commerce 1983). A similar situation occurred a few years later in suburban Detroit, where a massive public-private partnership was formed to restore several square miles of riverfront property poisoned in the course of producing cars (Hill and Indegaard 1988). These are not industrial disasters in the usual sense. Rather, they represent discoveries of past neglect or ignorance of a crucial natural principle. If a technology is potent enough to alter, to our specifications, controlled physical, chemical, or organic processes in the lab or factory, its effects can easily spill over to where they were never meant to be felt and largely beyond our control. Observers have wondered how many more "surprises" such as Love Canal, holes in the Earth's ozone layer, or Hurricane Katrina lie ahead as our techniques improve for unearthing evidence of cumulative environmental degradation.

4. *Insecurity.* To the extent that technology is now our master, the future has become increasingly uncertain. Since the earliest studies of the impacts of automation (Ogburn 1934; Pollack 1957), social scientists have been aware of the stresses to which industrial workers are prone as they look ahead with trepidation to the next innovation that will replace them. In a world where technological advance appears to have a higher priority than the security of the individual, everyone is in potential danger of becoming obsolete.[4] Thus, we continually seek new information, willingly provided by industries whose sole business it is to produce it. We need perpetual upgrades of the items and equipment on which our work and leisure depend, and we anxiously seek news about possible breakthroughs that might provide advantages to competitors at home and abroad. Technological society is filled with nervous people, worried over the prospect that they will be bypassed by progress (Glassner 1999). Those who promote stress management and other coping methods rush to serve an ever-expanding market for their wares (Kaminer 1992).

5. *Centralization of control.* Innovations in telecommunications, combined with techniques of minority rule such as mass propaganda, have made it possible for a few strategically placed individuals to profoundly affect the fates of millions. In this respect, technological advance has helped erode independent initiative: families, neighborhoods, and local communities are no longer sovereign, capable of pursuing their own interests as they determine. Instead, all of our activities, even our thoughts and ideals, are increasingly subject to coordination by higher authorities in keeping with the technological imperative. You may not want an Internet connection in your home, perhaps on the grounds that it is just another way for strangers to impose on your privacy. But the chances are good that you will get one soon, or you already have one, if you can afford it (or even if you cannot). Such decisions are no longer really up to the individual in the traditional sense. Rather, they are made "for" us by virtue of the way government and business operate. By the same principles, the process does not end with giving in to the technological imperative. With an Internet connection, you have yet another link with the global networks and their additional and unending demands to respond to ever-more remote events.

All of these impacts have occurred in recent years as the result of the diffusion of industrial, electronic, and a broad range of other innovations, and people in all modern and modernizing societies have experienced them. These current realities, and the long tradition of mistrust of technology represented by the Prometheus myth, have given proponents of the autonomous technology thesis a very important say in the study of higher-order impacts. Nevertheless, the thesis has also been criticized from a variety of disciplinary and ideological viewpoints. As critics have noted, the main limitation of the thesis is not that it is false but rather that it is only a partial truth.

Taking Control of Autonomous Technology

For each of the five types of negative impacts listed, evidence can be produced to show that innovations can also have the opposite effects, as well as many less drastic outcomes that lie between the extremes. Chapters 13 and 14 briefly consider the issue of centralization. There it is argued that, in itself, central planning is not an evil. Indeed, it has enormous advantages in coordinating collective efforts, especially when a large number of people need to be mobilized to face an emergency. The problem lies in the fact that, under Bolshevist and other autocratic systems, the planners become insulated from the people on whose behalf they are presumably working. They and they alone can determine what constitutes an authentic emergency. Truly democratic planning, on the other hand, is as centralized or as decentralized as the well-informed citizenry deems appropriate.

The same technologies that give power to influential minorities have also provided the majority with independent access to vast resources. Big Brother may be watching us, but through the very real power of the media, we are also able to watch him. The extent to which this potential for "centralized decentralization" will actually be realized depends on social and political participation, not on the autonomy of the technologies themselves.

It is true that our R&D industries have promoted technical virtuosity, that their products may right now be destroying the very ground on which we walk, and that we all, students and teachers, children and parents, are anxious about what technology will do to us next. But countless positive impacts of innovation have also been recorded. Modern people have the healthiest children, the longest average life expectancies, the highest literacy rates, and the greatest abundance of food and material wealth ever achieved. It is hardly an accident that they also possess the most potent technologies and have used them for both good and bad purposes.

The rapid and widespread diffusion of modern innovations, especially to the Third World, has been responsible for great damage, but it is also the source of knowledge that has allowed us to minimize costs and maximize benefits more effectively than ever. A key example of these lessons learned is the appropriate technology (AT) movement, which began in the early 1970s (Jéquier 1979, 1981). This approach to technological innovation is critical of the typical negative impacts created in rural Third World nations by high-tech approaches imported from highly industrialized societies. As an alternative, it emphasizes the value of indigenous, low-energy, and small-scale solutions to problems of food production, housing, manufacturing, and the like. "Appropriate technology is here characterized as having one or more of the following features: low investment cost per workplace; low capital investment per unit of output; organizational simplicity; small-scale operations; high adaptability to particular social or cultural environments; sparing use of natural resources; and, very low cost of final product" (Jéquier 1979, abstract).

Technological shocks, for all the harm they have caused, have also inspired the new fields of AT, technology assessment, technology policy studies, and social impact analysis that are meant to set things right. This commitment is clearly expressed in the mission statement of the International Association for Impact Assessment (IAIA; whose website is at www.iaia.org/):

> Impact assessment, simply stated, is the identification of future consequences of a current or proposed action. IAIA, simply stated, is the international association for people involved in impact assessment. Since 1980, IAIA has been bringing together researchers, practitioners and users of the various types of impact assessment from around the world. It includes social, environmental, economic, health, and all other types of impact assessment. One unique feature of IAIA is our mix of professions. This gives outstanding opportunities for interchanges, which are encouraged in various ways. Our members are university teachers and researchers, national and local government officials, corporate planners and managers, NGOs and public interest advocates, private consultants, policy analysts, and students. They cover the social and some natural sciences. (IAIA 2009, 2)

The discovery that technology has negative higher-order impacts is no longer a secret. In fact, it has been institutionalized in organizations whose mission it is to determine the likely unintended effects of innovation, including the International Labor Organization and, in the United States, the General Services Administration (GSA), the National Oceanic and Atmospheric Administration (NOAA), and the congressional

Office of Technology Assessment (OTA).[5] In the United States and several other countries, federal law now mandates social and environmental impact statements for any major field trial of a new technology, including estimates of the prospects of cumulative environmental degradation (see boxes 8.1 and 8.2).

These reforms may, in the end, be the most consequential of technology's higher-order impacts, for they represent an awareness that the innovation process can get out of control, that it has done so in the past, and that there are specific critical areas in

Box 8.1 U.S. LAWS MANDATING SOCIAL IMPACT ASSESSMENT, 1970-1986

Date	Law	Provisions
1970	National Environmental Policy Act of 1969	Calls for the integrated use of the social sciences in assessing impacts "on the human environment." Also requires the identification of methods and procedures . . . which ensure that presently unquantified environmental amenities and values be given appropriate consideration.
1976	Magnuson Fishery Conservation and Management Act, as amended (16 U.S.C.A. 1801, es seg.)	Where a "system for limiting access to the fishery in order to achieve optimum yield" is deemed necessary, the act requires the Secretary of Commerce and the regional Fishery Management Councils to consider in depth the economic and social impacts of the system.
1978	U.S. Council on Environmental Quality 1978 (40 CFR 1500-1508). Regulations for implementing the procedural provision of the National Environmental Policy Act.	"'Human environment' shall be interpreted comprehensively to include the natural and physical environment and the relationship of people with that environment."
1978	Outer Continental Shelf Lands Act, as amended (43 U.S.C.A. 1331 es seg.)	"The term 'human environment' means the physical, social, and economic components, conditions and factors which interactively determine the state, condition, and quality of living conditions, employment, and health of those affected directly or indirectly" by the resource development activities in question.

(Continued)

Box 8.1 U.S. LAWS MANDATING SOCIAL IMPACT ASSESSMENT, 1970-1986 (Continued)

Date	Law	Provisions
1980	Comprehensive Environmental Response, Compensation and Liability Act (26 and 43 U.S.C.A. es seg.)	Calls for working with affected publics through community relations programs and assessing community and state acceptance of Superfund plans and affecting local populations.
1982	Nuclear Waste Policy Act	Calls for the preparation of an EIS, specific demographic limitations on siting the nuclear repository; inclusion of affected Indian Tribes in the siting process and impact assistance.
1986	Superfund Amendments and Reauthorization Act	Work with an affected public through community relations programs and assessing the acceptance of plans by local communities.
1986	Council of Environmental Quality (40 CFR 1500-1508) reissue of regulations implementing the procedural provisions of the National Environmental Policy Act	The treatment of incomplete or unavailable information is clarified.

Source: U.S. National Oceanic and Atmospheric Administration (NOAA), "Guidelines and Principles for Social Impact Assessment," May 1994, www.nmfs.noaa.gov/sfa/social_impact_guide.htm.

which we must be especially alert. With this knowledge, we can remain sensitive to technology's runaway potential, but unlike Victor Frankenstein, we need not run away from it any longer. The institutionalization of technology assessment and social impact analysis in the innovation process marks a symbolic return of control over controlling technologies back into human hands. Of course, as people familiar with these fields know, officials may choose to ignore assessments of probable future impacts that they do not like. And that, as is true of much else associated with technology's effects, is today a political, not a scientific, issue.

Iatrogenesis, the Technology Delivery System, and the Participation of "Clients"

One of the most important new directions in the study of technological impact has come from the field of social problems. In this work, attention is focused on the

Box 8.2 MATRIX RELATING PROJECT STAGE TO SOCIAL IMPACT ASSESSMENT VARIABLES

SIA Variable	Specific indicators
Population Characteristics	Population change Ethnic and racial distribution Relocated populations Influx or outflows of temporary workers Seasonal residents
Community and Institutional Structures	Voluntary associations Interest group activity Size and structure of local government Historical experience with change Employment/income characteristics Employment equity of minority groups Local/regional/national linkages Industrial/commercial diversity Presence of planning and zoning activity
Political and Social Resources	Distribution of power and authority Identifications of stakeholders Interested and affected publics Leadership capability and characteristics
Individual and Family Changes	Perceptions of risk, health, and safety Displacement/relocation concerns Trust in political and social institutions Residential stability Density of acquaintanceship Attitudes toward policy/project Family and friendship networks Concerns about social well-being
Community Resources	Change in community infrastructure Native American tribes Land use patterns Effects on cultural, historical, and archaeological resources

(Continued)

Box 8.2 MATRIX RELATING PROJECT STAGE TO SOCIAL IMPACT ASSESSMENT VARIABLES (Continued)

Social Impact Assessment Variables, by Project/Policy Setting (type) and Stage

Project/Policy Settings (type)	Project/Policy Stage			
	Planning/Policy Development	Construction/ Implementation	Operation/ Maintenance	Decommission/ Abandonment
Hazardous Waste Site	Perceptions of risk, health and safety	Influx of temporary workers	Trust in political and social institutions	Alteration in size of local government
Industrial Plant	Formation of attitudes toward the project	Change in community infrastructure	Change in employment/ income characteristics	Change in employment equity of minority groups
Forest Service to Park Service Management	Interested and affected publics	Trust in political and social institutions	Influx of recreation users	Distribution of power/authority

Source: U.S. National Oceanic and Atmospheric Administration (NOAA), "Guidelines and Principles for Social Impact Assessment," May 1994, www.nmfs.noaa.gov/sfa/social_impact_guide.htm.

phenomenon of *iatrogenesis*. This medical term, first introduced to social scientists by Ivan Illich (1974) and Louis Schneider (1975a, [1975b] 1985) literally means "physician induced." It refers to side effects that occur in the course of therapy, as a result of the use of examining or surgical instruments, medication, or the very presence of the physician. In its original meaning it is a neutral concept that could apply to harmful, beneficial, or inconsequential outcomes, provided they differ from the explicit goal of the treatment. In medical texts, however, it is nearly always discussed in terms of negative effects, most often illustrated by cases of inadvertent drug reactions.

Illich, Schneider, and others have extended this medical insight to the general study of social problems by noting the similarity between physicians, on one hand, and pathologists of any discipline, such as youth counselors or corrections officials, on the other (Machalek 1979; Schneider 1975a, [1975b] 1985; Weinstein 1982, 1991).[6] In each case, a relationship is established between an expert and a client in which the former is expected and authorized to diagnose a problem and prescribe a remedy (Parsons 1975). The client is, accordingly, expected to accept the expert's authority and to submit to whatever treatment is deemed necessary. In the process, the client grants liberties to the expert that would ordinarily not be extended to anyone else. By submitting to the will of a pathologist, clients forfeit some of their freedom because they deem the cure to be more important.

> Widely recognized as a phenomenon, the debate is over its extent. The term [iatrogenesis] was introduced into social science by Ivan Illich as part of his more general attack on industrial society and in particular its technological and bureaucratic institutions, for limiting freedom and justice and for corrupting and incapacitating individuals. . . . [These] arguments may be placed in the context of wider debates about the excessive professionalizing and bureaucratization of modern life. Other sociologists (such as Jack Douglas) have suggested that medicine is not the only sphere in which the activities of the professionals may have unintended consequences: attempts at intervention in other social problems sometimes seem merely to exacerbate the original difficulties. This is also part of the labeling theory of deviance. (Marshall 1998)

For obvious reasons, this model is known as the "clinical model" for responding to social problems. Individuals who are victimized by others, like people suffering from an illness, consult an expert in the hope of getting relief. They assume a subordinate role in the relationship, and they presume the professional's knowledge is more valid than their own. These factors render clients especially vulnerable to the will of experts, which makes it possible for the cure to be undertaken (the therapy will not work if clients resist). At the same time, they are also susceptible to the effects of mistaken diagnoses and faulty treatment, "the slip of the knife," in medical terms. This suggests that, in the extreme, "societies weaken the will of their members, by paralysing 'healthy responses to suffering, impairment and death.' Here, the whole culture becomes 'overmedicalized,' with doctors assuming the role of priest, and political and social problems entering the medical domain" (Marshall 1998).

Such unintended outcomes cannot occur unless clients submit willingly or under coercion to having their privacy invaded. But, then, effective therapy cannot occur either. The knife cannot slip if we prohibit its use, nor can it relieve our suffering.

The model also describes the way in which sponsors of technological innovations relate to their clients: governments, corporations, and the general public. The comparison is not entirely metaphorical, as medicine itself is a technological discipline. Rather than working in a literal clinical setting, however, engineers participate in a "technological delivery system" (TDS; Porter et al. 1980; Wenk and Kuehn 1977). This system has been established to link R&D labs with field experimenters and end users, very much in accord with the practices pioneered during the Great Depression by the agricultural experiment stations.

At one end of the TDS are the experts (engineers and planners) who, at the request of clients, diagnose the source of an identified problem and recommend a (technological) therapy. At the other end are the proposed adopters whose cooperation is required if the solution is to be effective. Mediating between these are the various communication channels, peer networks, and marketing procedures that ensure the smooth flow of information and feedback necessary to keep the system responsive.

In this manner, the TDS is specifically designed to ensure that users and other affected groups understand and comply with the directives of the engineer (see figure 8.3). As in the medical pathologist's clinic, the prevailing assumption is that the expert knows what is good for the client and has the authority to issue prescriptions. The client is expected to acknowledge this, at the risk of being suspected of bad faith. Laypersons are thus appropriately vulnerable both to the treatment and to whatever side effects and errors that may result. The new role of the technology assessor in the TDS is to see to it that harmful higher-order impacts are minimized.

The 1980s and 1990s saw a dramatic upsurge of lawsuits in the United States against physicians and other professionals over iatrogenic symptoms. It was a true "malpractice crisis," as one professor of medicine called it (Myers 1987). Since then, the effects have

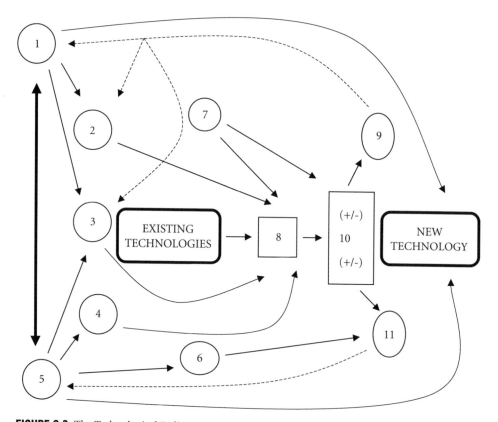

FIGURE 8.3 The Technological Delivery System

Key: 1. Government funding; 2. University research; 3. "Think tank" research; 4. Corporate R&D; 5. Revenue financing; 6. Marketing; 7. Government regulation; 8. Prototype technologies; 9. Impacts; 10. Technology assessment; 11. Market factors.

Sources: Adapted from Drucker (1986); Porter et al. (1980); and Wenk and Kuehn (1977).

reverberated to technology assessment and other fields that monitor innovation. Motivated partly by the desire to protect their professional interests and partly in appreciation of the power and complexity of modern technologies of therapy, practitioners have undertaken to reform the classical clinical model (Mechanic 1985). In place of the traditional top-down approach, they have moved steadily toward a collaborative mode, in which the client's advice is genuinely valued. The expert is now encouraged to discuss iatrogenic issues explicitly, warning that technical know-how is never perfect.

Treatment, thus, increasingly resembles a cost-benefit analysis, in which it is assumed that the client is entitled to full disclosure, including disclosure concerning the limits of the professional's expertise. These reforms acknowledge and accept the dangers inherent in the vulnerability of laypersons and the inevitability of iatrogenesis, and they seek to protect all interested parties. They are not meant to create a foolproof system. That cannot happen as long as we continue to take an active hand in our own fates, to seek cures and solve problems rather than accept misfortune or discomfort passively. We will always need to forfeit some autonomy to experts who can do us great good or great harm. The reforms have, however, introduced the ethical principle of informed consent into the technological innovation process, which has already helped to open communication and to encourage the active participation of clients in the enterprise.

The older, dependent role of the client had its advantages. It made the expert's job relatively easy. But its disadvantages have become increasingly evident, in malpractice litigation and other contexts. Physicians, dentists, psychologists, counselors, and now engineers increasingly support greater responsibility on the part of clients, who agree to undertake a prescribed course of treatment with a clear understanding of their options and possible consequences. As intended, this also protects the expert, who is less likely to be blamed if problems arise, especially if, as is now customary, clients willingly sign a statement to that effect.

Through the efforts of technology assessors, these reforms are currently being incorporated into the innovation diffusion process. End users and target populations are no longer exclusively viewed as objects to be manipulated (for "their own good") by omniscient professionals, propagandists, and consent managers. Instead, public hearings for major innovations have been written into national and local law throughout the world (see boxes 8.1 and 8.2). Reports on potential iatrogenic outcomes are prepared by impact analysts and made freely available to adopters and the general public.

Whether inspired by fear of engineering malpractice (a growing field of law), memories of the horrors of Bhopal and Chernobyl, or a genuine interest in democratic planning, the industrial estate has begun to promote an authentic two-way information flow in the TDS. In this shift, the basic wisdom of the extension service programs has been rediscovered. Technologies that truly work must be the product of cooperation and mutual respect between expert and client.

With a strong assist from technology, modern society has taken the art of meddling in its own course of evolution to unprecedented heights. Very little merely "happens" in human affairs anymore. Rather, changes are engineered, at massive scales and often at cross-purposes. This phenomenon is evident in our individual trials and tribulations such as job transfers or tax hikes, and it applies as well to critical episodes such as the Holocaust and the fall of Communism.

We can be pretty certain that the values, activities, and experiences of our children and their children will differ from our own even more than we have strayed from the ways of our immediate ancestors. And we can be equally sure that the changes will result from conscious decision making, planning at local and global levels, and the invention and diffusion of new technologies, much of it *meant* to make things different. What remains very much in doubt is the extent to which ordinary members of subsequent generations will be able to realize their express interests in the changes that do occur. Planning goes on, but so do unintended outcomes.

Recent concerns about iatrogenesis and malpractice suggest that side effects are the price we pay for therapy. But democratic principles governing the relationship between experts and laypersons can help anticipate and mitigate the most serious consequences. The essential thing is that, provided they are willing to share responsibility for the results, ordinary people do have new opportunities to take an active part in decisions that were once the exclusive domain of those in formal authority.

Cold Fusion and the R&D Society

The alleged discovery of "cold" fusion (CF) in 1990 provides an especially dramatic and ongoing illustration of the social dimensions of technological innovation (Ricci, DeMarco, and Sindoni 1990; Voss 1999). In the spring of that year, professors B. Stanley Pons and Martin Fleischmann at the University of Utah announced they had made the long-heralded breakthrough in nuclear engineering: the production of a fusion reaction at normal temperatures (National Cold Fusion Institute 1990).

This might well have been a momentous discovery because the only other way we know how to create fusion requires extremely high temperatures (e.g., those achieved by a fission reaction, that is, an atom bomb). The latter, "hot fusion," process is considered most promising by government and industry, but it is difficult to achieve, and, of primary importance, it is inefficient. A kilowatt-hour of electricity generated in such a way now costs far more than one produced with coal, oil, or fission alone. The Pons-Fleischmann discovery promised virtually free energy, if it is authentic.

Scientists and engineers the world over remain very much at odds over this issue (Taubes 1993). Following the initial announcement, a series of controversies arose over the researchers' methods, the accuracy of their observations, and their understanding of scientific principles. Most, but not all, physicists continue to believe that cold fusion is impossible. On that basis, earlier promises of large-scale state and federal funding were quickly withdrawn.

In 1993, Pons and Fleischmann quit their university jobs to begin working for a foundation sponsored by the owner of the Honda Automobile Corporation, who does believe in cold fusion. Meanwhile, the research and controversy continue within the established scientific community. According to the August 2009 issue of the *Cold Fusion Times* (2009), the study of CF "is the scientific heresy that just won't go away." In March

2009, the online physics journal *The New Scientist* reported on a presentation from the recent meeting of the American Chemical Society.

> Twenty years to the day that two electrochemists ignited controversy by announcing signs of cold fusion at an infamous press conference in Utah, a separate team has made a similar claim in the same US state. But this time, the evidence is being taken more seriously. . . . Now Pamela Mosier-Boss and colleagues at Space and Naval Warfare Systems Command (SPAWAR) in San Diego, California, are claiming to have made a "significant" discovery—clear evidence of the products of cold fusion. On 23 March, the team presented its work at the American Chemical Society's spring conference in Salt Lake City, Utah, a few months after the study was published in a peer-reviewed journal (*Naturwisse*). . . . Johan Frenje at the Massachusetts Institute of Technology, an expert at interpreting CR-39 tracks produced in conventional high-temperature fusion reactions, says the team's interpretation of what produced the tracks is valid. "I must say that the data and their analysis seem to suggest that energetic neutrons have been produced," he says, although he would like to see the results confirmed quantitatively. (Barras 2009)

Considering the fact that the potential for cold fusion "won't go away," it is likely that the future of nuclear engineering will, in large measure, be determined by this competition among governments and multinational corporations, as well as among scientific establishment and dissidents. If Pons and Fleischmann are right, then that future belongs to Honda. Armed with research technologies that can change the way we apply the laws of physics, it is these groups and individuals, not simply the structure of atomic nuclei, who will decide if and how fission will be a part of our children's and grandchildren's lives, if they really will live in an age of unlimited energy.

The cold fusion controversy highlights several features of the technological innovation process in modern societies. It is expensive, highly bureaucratized, dependent on the support of large organizations, and subject to decisions by learned councils that can be influenced by lobbying pressures and personal interests. Inventions issue forth from laboratories and think tanks at record-setting rates, often in response to real societal needs, but also to satisfy demands that were originally created by sponsors. Yet, there is no absolute guarantee that the time and other resources invested in the process will pay off in authentic discoveries—or at least discoveries that are accepted as authentic by relevant peers. In nuclear engineering, genetic research, microelectronics, and dozens of other fields, breakthrough discoveries are now being sought, next year's innovations planned, and cost-benefit analyses of field trials calculated.[7] And all of this requires expert teams of researchers, managers, proposal writers, corporate financiers, lobbyists, and public relations specialists.

Far from being a mysterious or random process, the act of creating new ways to solve the problems imposed by our biologies and environments (including the biological and environmental impacts of older technologies) is today an industrial enterprise, one often strongly supported or controlled by government. It depends less and less on the work of individual geniuses and great inventors and increasingly on coordinated group projects (Zuckerman 1977). Because R&D is so internationalized, the older distinction between imported and indigenous invention, which was always somewhat arbitrary, has been all but obliterated; at the same time, the global information highway has made the instantaneous spread of new knowledge a reality.

The discoveries that do manage to survive the checks and balances of this elaborate, global R&D system (perhaps something as radical as cold fusion among them) will be tomorrow's technologies. But, of course, many breakthroughs will not occur because they are not high on the civilian or military research agendas, or because they lack the proper material and political support (Studer and Chubin 1980). The problems that we may fail to solve, such as feeding the world's hungry, ending ethnic intolerance, and reversing the geometric growth in our prison populations, are not necessarily unimportant—nor are they all insoluble. This is something we will never know until the level of resources that went into the military application of fusion is dedicated to its peaceful use, to combating famine, or to other worthy goals.

Every day, corporate and political leaders, research directors, and peer review panels collectively determine what discoveries are to be pursued and how they will be used (Gibbons 1994; Hippel 1998). This is why social scientists have been concerned since well before the R&D society was fully developed that expert decision makers remain responsive to the will of the electorate and that their choices be made in the best interests of the citizenry at large. Lacking such protections, it is very difficult to avoid the drift toward *technocracy*, a form of autocracy that some pessimistic observers fear will be common in the twenty-first century.

Summary

Millions of people who grew up in the era between World Wars I and II were greatly entertained and enchanted by a series of novels written under the pen name of Victor Appleton (originally, Howard Garris) featuring the young hero Tom Swift. In each book, Tom and his friends would be faced with a serious problem or mystery whose solution was beyond the capacities of relevant adults. Always able to grasp the essence of the problem, Tom would invent a gizmo made of simple objects, such as flashlight batteries and old bed springs that would trap a dangerous thief or lead the way to a lost treasure. In the end, Tom's ingenuity would save the day, and he would be properly rewarded for his efforts as he gloried in his ability to show up the uncreative older folks. The message was clear: a clever boy could invent his way out of any problem.

As discussed in this chapter, the realities of technological innovation today have turned the Tom Swift model into a myth. As it has evolved during the twentieth century, the innovation process has become a highly complex, well-organized, and expensive undertaking. It is the work of groups, teams, laboratories, and universities, not freelancing creative youngsters. Its products, including the gizmos of nuclear and human engineering, do not always and inevitably solve problems, and may, in fact, make things worse. Today's Tom Swift would need a Ph.D. before he would be taken seriously by his elders, and a generous government research grant would contribute much to his credibility. Before he and his friends could chide the "old folks" for their timidity about considering bold breakthroughs, they would be wise to incorporate, buy some liability insurance, and hire an attorney (or find an imaginative corporate patron). Even then, they would need to concern themselves with the subtleties of adoption and adaptation, with the clear understanding that success in this realm depends as much on the appropriate political connections as it does on the laws of physics.

In the context of rapid globalization, sociocultural change will continue to be propelled by technology in unprecedented ways and at a hitherto unattained speed. Unfortunately, the choices we make about the kinds of technologies to promote and the actual results they will have—that is, whether they will save the day (when, most observers agree, the day needs some serious "saving")—depend on far more than the simple good will of a bright, inventive kid. Where we travel on our information superhighway and what we will do when we get there is still very much a matter of human control and volition. But, as is true of everything else about our dynamic world, it is a journey bound to be riddled with complexity, contradiction, and uncertainty. There may no longer be any sure and "Swift" solutions to our technological problems.

Relevant Websites

http://web.mit.edu/sts
www.stanford.edu/group/STS
Several universities throughout the world offer programs in STSS. These sites are maintained by two of the leading programs in the United States: those of Massachusetts Institute of Technology and Stanford University, respectively.

www.nmfs.noaa.gov/sfa/social_impact_guide.htm
These are the guidelines for social impact assessment (SIA) issued by the U.S. National Oceanic and Atmospheric Administration (NOAA).

www.rogerclarke.com/SOS/InnDiffISW.html
Australian National University (ANU) has an especially useful set of sites on a wide range of subjects. This is an ANU master site on innovation diffusion.

www.iatrogenic.org/index.html
This is the home page of the American Iatrogenic Association.

www.tomswift.info/homepage/oldindex.html
www.tomswift.info/homepage/
The home pages for Tom Swift Sr. and Tom Swift Jr. respectively. Actually, there are four generations of Tom Swifts, by various authors—all writing as "Victor Appleton."

www.uneptie.org/scp/sp/disaster/index.htm
This is the UN Environment Programme's chronology of recent technological disasters. Ample support is provided for those who accept the Frankenstein scenario.

www.ncat.org/
www.i4at.org/
Two leading organizations that promote appropriate technology: the National Center for Appropriate Technology and the Global Village Institute for Appropriate Technology, respectively. Note the use of Marshall McLuhan's concept of a global village.

PART

IV

Change at the Macrolevel

THE THREE chapters in this part discuss the long-range trends that have made contemporary social life so dynamic, highly organized, conflict prone, and globalized. In each, the concepts and principles introduced in our discussions of the components and engines of change are applied to a specific set of historical developments that extend from the dawn of civilization to the present. Along the way, the chapters consider the origins of the institutions and larger structures that have become a permanent part of the human condition: the first cities, the beginnings of social stratification, the earliest states and economies, and the world system itself.

Chapter 9 begins with an overview of the momentous shift from societies dominated by primary relationships to those in which secondary and tertiary relationships, bureaucracies, and metropolises have taken over. These trends have undermined the family and traditional authority, and they have made people from very different backgrounds alike in important ways.

Chapter 10 provides a counterpoint to this process of "cultural leveling" with a look at the things that divide people from one another: cultural diversity, social inequality, and nationalism. Here, one is reminded of the ambiguous, dialectical nature of social dynamics. Humanity is undoubtedly at a critical point in its long-term trek toward a single world culture, but we are just as surely undergoing a dramatic episode of what the anthropologist Gregory Bateson (1939) termed "schismogenesis": the system is tearing itself apart. For the past several decades, the pressures toward globalization have been matched and in some cases countered by the forces of parochialism, political separatism, and ethnic divisiveness. The result is a curious combination of the universal and particular in the human condition today. We are certainly becoming one world, but it is a world divided.

Chapter 11 explores the origin and growth of capitalism and the socialist alternative that it spawned. The economic system is the principal modern institution that is separate from and increasingly in opposition to kinship and tradition. This institution is so central and commonplace in contemporary society that we hardly think about it as a human invention. Yet, it is actually a relatively new arrival on the scene. In fact, we have not yet fully adjusted to it after many thousands of years without it. As it has grown and diffused over the centuries, it has dramatically altered the status of our species in the natural order. Beginning as a few scattered, tiny nomadic bands struggling to survive at the margins of subsistence, we are rapidly approaching a single global village, numbering in the billions and possessing the capacity to discover and settle new worlds—or to obliterate this one.

Looking ahead in this new millennium, we can be all but certain that urbanization, nationalism, and capitalism will continue to be major concerns. If the past is any guide, then these will prove to be indispensable to our survival and prosperity. Unfortunately, they are also likely to be frustrating obstacles in our attempts to realize our individual and collective dreams.

9

From *Gemeinschaft* to *Gesellschaft*: The Urbanization of the Human Population

O ne of the most obvious characteristics of today's very complex societies is their high level of urbanization.[1] This is the outcome of the close historical connection that has existed over the past several millennia between the growth of cities, on one hand, and institutional specialization, on the other. Cities tend to dominate social relations wherever they are established, even in predominantly rural populations. As world-level society has emerged, the number of cities and their size and scope of influence have continued to grow at an ever-accelerating rate.[2]

This chapter focuses on urban growth as a source of increasing societal complexity and as a major factor in the creation of the modern world system. These links demonstrate vividly that social life, at local and global levels, has been affected by cities more profoundly than it has by virtually any other human invention. It also points to the fact that the world of tomorrow will surely be an urban one (see table 9.1).

The Invention of Cities

For almost the entirety of human existence, populations were either nomadic or gathered in small settlements where inhabitants were engaged in primary production: the extraction of food and other resources directly from nature. These communities differed from one another over the centuries in size and permanency (as summarized

TABLE 9.1 Percentage Urban, the World 1950–2050

Year	Percentage urban	Year	Percentage urban
1950	29.1	2005	48.6
1955	30.9	2007	50.0
1960	32.9	2010	50.6
1965	34.7	2015	52.7
1970	36.0	2020	54.9
1975	37.3	2025	57.2
1980	39.1	2030	59.7
1985	40.9	2035	62.2
1990	43.0	2040	64.7
1995	44.7	2045	67.2
2000	46.6	2050	69.6

Note: Note the entry for 2007 when the 50 percent level was reached.

Source: United Nations Population Division, *World Population Prospects: The 2006 Revision and World Urbanization Prospects: The 2007 Revision* (New York: Population Division of the Department of Economic and Social Affairs of the United Nations Secretariat, 2009), http://esa.un.org/unup.

in Herbert Spencer's classification scheme shown in chapter 2). Yet, all were largely kinship based (*Gemeinschaft*), and their economies rarely provided more than bare subsistence for members.

When, as in the pastoral and horticultural stages, some measure of control and regularity could be exercised in food production, small surpluses were generated and hereditary rulers emerged. Nevertheless, the uncertainties of climate and other natural conditions kept these populations very close to the brink of survival, and settlements never developed beyond the size and structural complexity of a large village.

Agricultural Revolution

Beginning as early as ten thousand years ago in the Middle East, some populations discovered and applied the principles of irrigation systems, plows, and other relatively complex tools for planting and harvesting food crops and more advanced methods for breeding animals. Together, these technological innovations brought about what is now referred to as the agricultural revolution (Childe 1950; Cohen 1978; Weber 1976).

I indicate that "some" populations were involved because, at the time, the discoveries occurred only in selected places. Although these innovations were diffused to a limited extent, physical inaccessibility made for considerable variations in technological development between peoples who lived in what we would view today as relatively close proximity.

The new technologies freed production from the constraints of environment to such an extent that enough food and other resources could be systematically generated to provide for the needs of members and for a reliable and sustainable surplus. This permitted some individuals to be spared from providing basic necessities and to be supported by alternative forms of work (while others could be relegated to slavery, a common practice of the era). Thus, a division of labor became possible between subsistence and nonsubsistence occupations.

The new economy allowed, and indeed required, the farmer to produce every year more food than was needed to keep him and his family alive. In other words, it made possible the regular production of social surplus. Owing to the low efficiency of Neolithic technique, the surplus produced was insignificant at first, but it could be increased until it demanded a reorganization of society (Childe 1950, 5).

At about the same time, members of these early agricultural populations began to form and participate in secondary relationships to a then-unprecedented degree. Statuses were created that were based not on gender, kinship, or age, but rather on occupational specializations and other, nonfamilial criteria. As a result, relatively extensive and permanent social networks were established beyond kinship relations and hereditary ruling classes.

This Neolithic to Bronze Age transition, from nearly exclusively primary relationships to a combination of primary and secondary relationships, represented a major increase in social complexity. It made possible the separation of work and family (Sutton et al. 1994). No longer were people necessarily bound to support their immediate relatives through primary production. Instead, household members could perform other roles and support themselves and families with a portion of the surplus. Such arrangements were almost surely well known long before the late Neolithic era, but only later did it become possible to implement them in a regular and relatively widespread manner. I say "relatively" because primary relations were still, and have remained until just a century or so ago, the rule for most people everywhere.

The combination of a reliable economic surplus and regularized secondary relationships made it possible for the affected populations to create a new form of settlement: the city. Such settlements were not, and probably could not have been, sustained during the previous quarter million years in which *Homo sapiens* existed. Typically located in river valleys, they relied on an agricultural economic base.[3]

Archaeological research has shown that the present-day Palestinian city of Jericho, on the Dead Sea rift near the West Bank of the Jordan River, had been established by as early as 7000 BCE, making it the first verified urban settlement (Tushingham 1953). Later ancient cities of the Mideast, founded around 4000 BCE, included Ur, Sumer, Babylon, and Thebes (Kramer 1963); and around 2600 BCE, farther east in the Indus Valley of present-day Pakistan, the settlements of Mohenjo-Daro and Harappa were built. Since that time, these have been recognized as the cradles of civilization ("civilization" literally means "city culture").

Much the same sequence occurred in the Far East. "By 5000 BCE agricultural communities had spread through much of what is now called China, and there were agricultural villages from the Wei River Valley eastward, parallel with the great Yellow River" (Petersen 1975, 371). Although no direct evidence of urban settlement can be traced to that era, cities definitely existed by the beginning of "the first dynasty of which there is historical evidence [the Shang], who are thought to have begun their rule around 1750 BCE" (Chang 1986).[4]

By today's standards, these cities were small, with population sizes in the range of three to seven thousand. Their defining characteristic was thus a socioeconomic, not a demographic, one. A substantial proportion of their residents, sometimes most but rarely the entire population, was supported by nonprimary-sector economic activity (Petersen 1975, 401–10), still an essential aspect of urban life. Households remained the basic economic units, but they no longer directly depended on the immediate habitat for their sustenance. This phenomenon allowed the cities to achieve relatively high levels of population density, because the household-to-land ratio was not a limiting factor.

At this juncture, human settlements began to develop neighborhoods. These were the first internal structures, in which subareas or zones of distinct land uses (residential, commercial, and religious) formed a spatial division of labor that reflected urban social organization (Pirenne 1939; Sjoberg 1960). Perhaps the most significant effect of urban settlement was that it expanded the scope of social cooperation—and conflict. It greatly improved the ability of residents to coordinate their activities in adapting to the geophysical and human environment, which, in turn, accelerated the pace of both militant and industrial forms of change. Two main features of cities made this possible: (1) their centrality and (2) the availability of residents for nonsubsistence labor.

The Advantages of Centrality

Spatial location of the early cities was translated into social control, in accord with the geographic principle first developed by Walter Christaller (1972), central place theory.[5] This theory is based on the observation that a central location is the most efficient in terms of maximizing access to territory at any given distance: one kilometer, two kilometers, and so on. If the territory is populated, then centrality provides maximum access to its human inhabitants and whatever resources they produce. In this way, the residents of the early cities could coordinate the activities of many more nonresidents far more efficiently than was possible when settlements were small, relatively isolated, and dispersed.

Inhabitants of different areas remote from the city could now establish social and economic ties with one another, but not directly. Rather, these relationships were mediated by the city, through face-to-face relations among nonrelatives and tertiary contacts. In the latter case, indirect communication was facilitated by another "minor" invention of this remarkable era, writing. It became possible for settlements upriver to form relationships with those downriver and on either bank, that is, as long as they passed through the city. Thus, the cities provided a mechanism for increasing the level of social integration of populations that had previously developed only loose ties among essentially independent kinship units (extended families and clans).

Under these conditions, a new, complex, and powerful form of sociospatial structure was created: the city-hinterland, or core-periphery, relationship. This is a system of geographical stratification in which the coordination of social activity is achieved (1) at a large scale, involving more individuals than is possible with other structures, and (2) through relations of territorial dominance and subordination: the core rules the

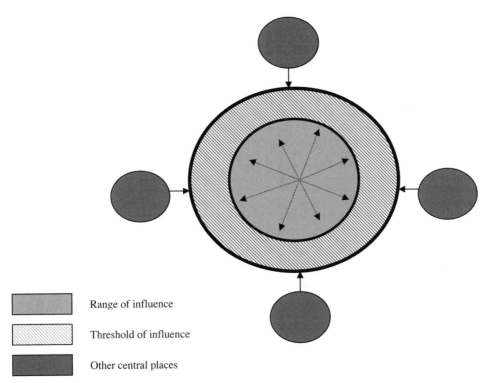

Range of influence

Threshold of influence

Other central places

FIGURE 9.1 Diagram of Central Place Theory. The influence of a central place extends in all directions and dominates the territory that is encompassed. The influence diminishes to a low threshold as the range approaches that of other central places.

periphery. With increased efficiency and extent of control, the system provided cities with new and more effective methods of domination.

As cities grew in numbers and size, the advantages of centrality created ever-more powerful core-periphery relations throughout the world, and the scope of control of urban settlements grew to enormous proportions. At its peak, Rome, with perhaps eighty thousand inhabitants, ruled an area of millions of square miles and the millions of people who occupied this territory. And, by the eighteenth century CE, a few cities in Europe—principally London—were capable of creating a core-periphery system that was truly worldwide in scope (as noted in our discussion of world system theory in chapter 2).

The Advantages of Surplus Labor

With the growth of secondary and tertiary relationships and the production of a reliable economic surplus, recognizable occupational specializations began to develop.[6] With large amounts of labor time available for nonsubsistence activity, other functions could be performed more effectively than with the system of kinship-based production. Like centrality, the availability of surplus labor caused, and was in turn

reinforced by, increases in social complexity and in the population's capacity to cooperate. Consequently, distinct occupational classes formed along the lines of (1) division of labor and (2) social hierarchy. The classes included hereditary rulers, military
personnel, craftspersons and manufacturers, priests and scribes, and traders, especially dealers in agricultural produce and keepers of (another invention of the times)
granaries.

At this point, it is believed, the division of labor between men and women became a
relationship of formal dominance, at least in the populations that were undergoing this
change. Thus, women's work came to be defined as domestic work, in part because it
had traditionally been associated with bearing children, and domestic work was defined
as less valued. In this respect, as most contemporary sociologists agree, urbanization
in itself has generally led to a decline in the status of women (Becker 1985; Davis 1984;
Weeks 1992, 300).

In terms of social differentiation, cities provided an environment that supports the
shifting of functions from the family to specialized groups and organizations. It is, therefore, quite accurate to speak of an urban *society*, or a distinctively urban *social structure*.
So, beyond a fairly low level, social complexity cannot be sustained without urban settlement. Cities are not only "carriers" of *Gesellschaft* culture but also its cause. It is significant
that urban social structure also includes nonurban dwellers, peripheral populations, and
agricultural occupations. Although not part of city life, as such, the inhabitants of the
hinterland and their activities were now defined and controlled by it.

The Creation of the State

In the early, great-tradition cities, we find the first clearly separate political institution,
the state. In fact, these cities and their hinterlands were states unto themselves: city-
states or polis in Greek (Burckhardt and Murray 1998).

> One of the hallmarks of Greek civilization was the polis, or city-state. The city-
> states were small, independent communities that were male-dominated and bound
> together by race. What this means is that membership in the polis was hereditary
> and could not be passed on to someone outside the citizen family. The citizens
> of any given polis were an elite group of people—slaves, peasants, women and
> resident aliens were not part of the body of citizens. Originally the polis referred
> to a defensible area to which farmers of a particular area could retreat in the event
> of an attack. The Acropolis in Athens is one such example. Over time, towns grew
> around these defensible areas. (Kreis 2000)

The number of city-states increased, and their influence spread between the agricultural revolution and the beginning of the Common Era. During this period, larger
regions, including those that make up some of today's nation-states, India, China, Iraq,
Israel, Jordan, and Pakistan, came to be dominated by systems of city-states.

The state emerged as patriarchs and warlords established legal codes, groups, and organizations to mediate between them and the larger populations in the city and hinterlands. In general, these groups were closed and rigid, and the power of the ruler was absolute. As in the earlier kinship-based systems of social control, no method of succession beyond inheritance or forcible removal was available. In this respect, the unchallenged powers of the patriarch (or, occasionally, the matriarch) over offspring and other kin was simply extended to nonrelatives. Family rule was transformed into classic autocracy, also referred to as *patrimonial* authority—that is, an extended form of patriarchy.

> A "patrimonial system" is defined as any form of political domination or authority based on personal and bureaucratic power exerted by a royal household. Patrimonialism is a relatively broad term, not referring to any particular type of political system. The crucial elements are that:
>
> 1. Power is formally arbitrary.
> 2. Administration is under direct control of the ruler. This means it involves the employment of retainers or slaves, mercenaries and conscripts, who themselves possess no independent basis of power, that is, are not members of traditional landed aristocracy. (Stavis 1999)

As in all states since that time, the force of law was ultimately supported by violence and its threat (Tilly 1990). To maintain such control, an independent military became one of the major organizational supports of the ruling classes. But, as in all systems undergoing the transition from militant to industrial change, raw power soon became authorized. With few exceptions, this was accomplished through traditional means of tracing lines of descent from one legitimate ruler to the next.

TABLE 9.2 Traditional Forms of Patrimonial Systems

Ruling system	Type of rule
chiefdom	one leader
gerontocracy	rule by a group of elders
patriarchalism	authority is exercised by a particular individual who is designated by a definite rule of inheritance—exercise of power is a private prerogative—no real administrative staff
patrimonialism	involves personal administrative staff, some constraints by tradition
sultanism	absolute authority is maximized, for self-interest; use of force to remove all constraints

Source: Adapted from Ben Stavis, home page, course material (Temple University Political Science Department, Philadelphia, September 1999), http://astro.temple.edu/~bstavis/courses/442patrimonial-system.htm.

The early cities introduced a fourfold stratification system that had not appeared, nor was it even relevant, in pastoral and other types of societies.

- At the top was a small, closed elite, which in practice was ordinarily a ruling family.
- The second stratum consisted of a larger group of military personnel, whose role was to protect the rulers and maintain their established order.
- Next came a much larger aggregate of ordinary citizens, or commoners.
- Finally, at the very bottom, were the nonpersons: noncitizens, captives, slaves, and others who did not fit into the other three strata.

This lowest stratum varied in size, but in many populations (Babylon prior to 600 BCE, for example), it was by far the largest, an indication of how dependent these early states were on human labor power.

In his classic dialogue on *The Republic*, Plato has Socrates argue that this stratification system represented an eternal form of social organization, equating it with the structure of the human soul. The rulers were the "kings," who, Plato believed, ought to be philosophers, like himself: thus, *philosopher* kings. Their role was parallel to that of the mind or higher intellect, and they were symbolized by the precious metal gold. The military were the "guardians," whose role was parallel to the emotions, and their symbolic metal was silver. The "commoners" were parallel to basic drives, and their symbolic metal was iron. All of them were, then, supported by a base of nonpersons.

When, Plato argued, this structure was intact, order and harmony prevailed, just as in the orderly soul the mind rules the emotions and the emotions control the drives (see figure 9.2). Disharmony and chaos therefore characterized any different ordering. This classic argument not only summarized and formalized the prevailing stratification system of the age but also served as a model of the ideal society for centuries.

The state structure and its military, in combination with the advantages of centrality and surplus labor, provided the city-state (e.g., Plato's Athens) with a new and highly effective means for establishing contact with previously isolated populations. The polis could support expeditions into new territory, diffusing its culture and society outward from the core, as well as diffusing exotic sociocultural traits from the periphery inward. With such territorial expansion came conquest and colonization, which in turn provided additional resources, including booty, to fuel urban population growth and the establishment of satellite cities and colonial regimes in the hinterlands. City rulers became conquerors.

The settlement of new territories also allowed for intermarriage and the blending of gene pools. Formerly isolated, smaller populations became subunits of larger, ethnically diverse populations under a single state. When city-states conquered other city-states, regional empires were formed and conquerors became emperors (Doyle 1986). At each step, we see the close and familiar relationship between increases in (1) size, (2) complexity, and (3) the capacity to dominate. All of these were now possible to a degree far beyond the scope of patriarchy and other preurban forms of social control.

THE STATE/SOCIETY   **THE SOUL/INDIVIDUAL**

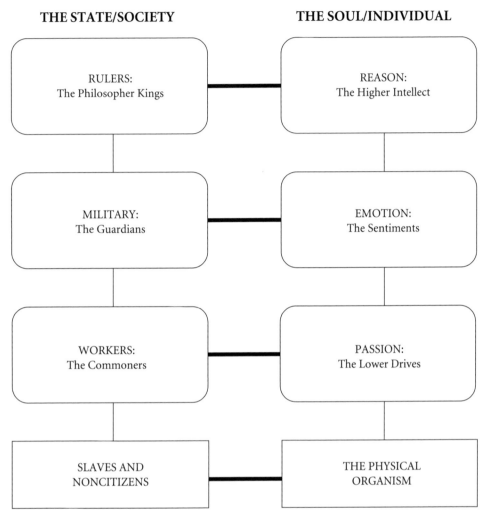

FIGURE 9.2 The Platonic Model of the State and Soul: The Classic Concept of Stratification (adapted from Plato's *Republic*).

The development and expansion of these early empires had a significant effect on intersocietal relations. Looking at historical documents chronicling the rise and fall of the ancient empires, one sees some populations surviving, prospering, and conquering, and others being conquered, being absorbed, or becoming extinct. In this struggle for survival, the fittest populations usually (but not always) were those with the largest and best-organized city-states. In this respect, complexity appears to be an adaptive advantage, and it is such observations that are often presented in support of classic evolutionary theories.

On the other hand, we now know that the city-states paid a price for their advantage of centrality and control, for they were especially vulnerable to attack and conquest by small but determined bands of invaders. Thus, populations with relatively simple societies occasionally did conquer powerful empires by striking directly at the point of coordination. To paraphrase the historian Edward Gibbon ([1776] 1921), the same roads that the early city-states used in their marches outward to conquer vast territories were used by their enemies, marching in the opposite direction, to conquer them (see also Schneider 1975a; Sorokin 1962). And, as Gibbon first pointed out, the new conquerors were not necessarily more "advanced," socially, culturally, or physically, than the urban emperors whom they defeated. In fact, they were often "barbarians."

In addition, many populations became urbanized in the process of expansion and conquest without ever undergoing an indigenous agricultural revolution. Rather, they benefited from the penalty of leadership by borrowing an innovation without having to pay for its development. Such facts indicate the limits of the evolutionary metaphor in understanding why some populations of the ancient Middle East survived and others did not—that is, size, complexity, and domination were very closely, but not necessarily, connected to the social, cultural, and demographic changes that took place in association with the rise of cities.

Experiments in Democracy

In some of the city-states of the ancient Greek Empire, in about 500 BCE, a nonhereditary form of authority was attempted (Ostwald 1986). It apparently had its origins in councils of elders and other tribal-level ruling associations. It was also based, in part, on principles of ethical monotheism practiced by the Hebrews living among the Greeks. According to this creed, all members of a population, including kings, were understood to be subject to the same higher (for the Hebrews, divine) source of authority. The Greeks called the new system *demokratia*, "rule by the population."

In the wake of social movements, hereditary kings were replaced by governing councils consisting of all declared eligible (Ober 1998). In practice, this encompassed only male residents, usually those who owned land or other property and were not themselves property (slaves). The membership base in these early democracies was quite limited and exclusive. They were closed groups. However, the degree of participation among the select citizens was extremely high. All decisions were made in face-to-face associations, huge assemblies, or *poli* (literally, "everybody"), and all decisions had to be based on unanimity. Even the individual leaders had to be elected by consensus. In some instances, the aversion to hereditary rule was taken to its extreme, with leaders selected through drawing lots (Sartori 1987, 115–16, 280–83).

For about two hundred years, several classic democracies survived, and many prospered. Industrial change predominated, and cultural production flourished. Athens became a major democratic city-state (its main adversary, Sparta, retained its monarchy) as well as a major center for the development of architecture, art, poetry, and philosophy.[7]

It influenced and attracted migrants from a vast hinterland, encompassing the Aegean, the Eastern Mediterranean, and Northern Africa. Among these immigrants were the appropriately named Democritus and the father of philosophy, Socrates. The discipline of philosophy, like so many intellectual breakthroughs we now count as part of Western civilization, was thus the product of cosmopolitan urban life and democratic revolution.

By the time that Socrates' leading disciple, Plato, assumed leadership in philosophical circles, monarchy had been restored in Athens and most other city-states. The democratic experiment was over, at least for a time. In reflecting on their immediate past, the classic philosophers considered the experiment a failure. Aristotle, in particular, viewed it as a "degenerate" form of rule. Like Plato, he believed that the value of the state derives from the quality of its rulers, not the method used to choose them.

Because classic democracy required the equal participation of all citizens, whether or not they were talented, wise, or capable, it often ended up producing a lowest-common-denominator effect. Democratic government was the result of compromises that included accommodations to inferior principles. At its worst, and Plato and Aristotle both believed that the worst had been achieved prior to the restoration of the monarchy, direct democracy deteriorated into "mob rule."

Despite these assessments, democratic values became a part of the heritage of ancient Greece that has long outlived its population. As Rome assumed Athens's role as the ancient world's dominant city-state, the successes (and the failures) of the democratic experiment were remembered. Thus, the Roman State, during its republican and imperial eras, was a mixed system. Essentially, it continued the practice of hereditary kings and imperial warlords (called *caesar* or, later in Russian, *czar*). But their rule was always mitigated, and to some extent directed, by the decisions of closed, direct democratic assemblies, including the assembly of elders or seniors that has endured to this day under its Latin name of *senate*.

With the fall of Rome in 455 CE, the senate and similar democratic institutions receded from practice but not from historical memory. In the thirteenth century, this memory was restored in a formal statement that guaranteed participatory rights for a (still-closed) group of nonrulers, the Magna Carta (Schneider 1975a, 44–45). In this way, the continuity of the idea of democracy was maintained and made permanent, while autocracy remained the principal form of state authority.

The Creation of the Economy

As the invention of cities led to the shift of social control functions from the family to the state, it also provided the conditions for a distinct system of extracting and using environmental resources. The foundation for a relatively independent economic system was the division between activities associated with the production of food and raw materials for clothing and shelter, on one hand, and what we now term secondary and tertiary sector activities (manufacture and trade, respectively) on the other. Prior to the agricultural revolution, all of these had been performed in kinship contexts. The generation of surplus made it possible for city dwellers to be sustained by the latter two activities alone.

The fact that a small, but important, segment of the Bronze Age population was no longer involved in direct (i.e., primary-sector) production meant that a method had to be established to feed them. The solution was a system of formalized exchange.

Agrarian and other nonagricultural societies had little need for anything more complex than simple barter, while kinship-based societies in which there was no surplus had little or nothing to exchange. In the cities, however, it became necessary to translate a person's labor time into commodities. Moreover, direct interpersonal relations were not adequate to conduct all of the transactions necessary. For example, a tailor could not depend on face-to-face interactions with a grower of wheat in order to exchange clothing for food. Rather, mediating structures and norms had to be established.

These conditions brought about a number of innovations that continue to be associated with urban society, most of them Greek innovations: money, markets, credit, and wages (Simmel 1978). However, the early urban economies retained several critical features of the kinship systems on which they were based. In the case of these exchange mechanisms, economic activity was not by any means free from the control of the ruling classes. Whenever scarcity or desire dictated, those in authority could dispose of a household's labor time and the agricultural commodities it produced. One method created to achieve this type of control was the exacting of tribute and taxes. In a practice that became institutionalized over the generations, rulers would require citizens and others in their domains to provide to the state labor time (in French, *corvee*), commodities, or money. This supported the ruling classes and freed them from all productive activity, it helped to underwrite missions of exploration and conquest, and it enriched the recipients.

As taxation and tribute systems became more common, the first censuses were conducted (Petersen 1975, 395–96; Weinstein and Pillai 2001, 25–26). In fact, the word *census* comes from a Sanskrit word meaning to assess or tax. These were crude and inaccurate by today's standards, and they often required the members of the population to report to the census taker, rather than the other way around. This system is described in the Old Testament (Numbers 1:1–4) and in the New Testament account of the birth of Christ: "And all went to be taxed, every one into his own city" (Luke 2:1–5). Nevertheless, they were essential for the financing of the early states and for estimating the potential size of their military forces. Practices such as tribute, taxation, and census taking are very much part of contemporary society. This is our inheritance from the ancient civilizations. But they now happen in far more complex and indirect ways because the scale of cities and their sphere of influence have increased by magnitudes.

Property and Inherited Status   The growth of surplus resources made it possible for substantial quantities of nonperishables—precious metals and jewels, tools, clothing, household goods, and land—to be passed on to future generations. Because urban populations were composed of unrelated households, and because most households in the hinterlands were rural and relatively isolated, inheritance began within distinct kinship lines. Among the most significant, but least visible, of these inheritances were occupational specializations. As with other aspects of these earliest economies, the "occupational specialization characteristic of town life was often incomplete, related to a continuing osmosis between rural and urban worlds" (Petersen 1975, 402). Inheritance also maintained the division of labor between genders, as fathers passed nonhousehold occupations to sons, and mothers passed household skills to daughters. This inherited division of labor was more or less rigid and closed, depending on other social and cultural factors. In some populations, especially those in the Indus Valley, it reached a highly perfected form (Weber 1958). There, occupational status was strictly hereditary.

This system was supported by strong religious norms that defined occupations, just as these cultures distinguished between all sacred and secular items, in terms of how ritually clean or polluted they were (see chapter 4). The offspring of marriages between members of discrepant families had no identity, and the parents suffered ostracism and other sanctions. Occupational strata were strictly closed, and the only form of social mobility possible was that which might occur after death.

This provision was taken very seriously at the time (and it still is by many people). An elaborate doctrine of reincarnation was developed or revealed to account for social mobility. According to the creed, people's status in the next life will be determined by how they perform the occupational and related social roles assigned at their present birth. The norms of endogamy and duty were rarely broken (Smith 1994).

In this way, the division of labor along kinship lines coincided with a system of ritual stratification, with the cleanest occupations at the top and the most polluted at the bottom. In Sanskrit, these norms and structures are known collectively as the *Varna* system (see box 9.1). Because social and economic stratification was tied to genetic inheritance through strict endogamy, members of the same strata had similar physical appearances and differed in appearance from members of other Varnas. These physical differences lie behind the English name for this system, *caste*, meaning "color."

Varna and other castelike systems of inherited occupational status endured for centuries. In fact, vestiges of caste can be found in even the most complex contemporary societies. And it is still a dominant, but no longer exclusive, form of stratification in India today. It was not, however, unchallenged. The system was part of the taken-for-granted world in the ancient civilizations, and it obviously served effectively in the performance of necessary urban and agricultural economic functions. However, not everyone accepted it as necessary and natural. Some were distressed by the fact that most people were fated to live miserable lives under the total control of priests, rulers, and the wealthy with no improvement in their material or spiritual status in sight while on this Earth. In one well-remembered case, rejection of the caste system inspired a major social movement.

In the sixth century BCE, a young Kshatryia (a prince) from the Eastern part of the Indus Empire was born in the city of Lumbini (now in Nepal). He developed an anti-caste doctrine that changed the world. His name was Siddhartha, later called Gautama Buddha: the enlightened one (see box 9.2; Martindale 1962,198–200).

Other Characteristics of Ancient Cities

Research on these ancient cities has revealed four additional characteristics that contrast in important ways with modern urban settlements:

1. As noted, the cities were generally very small by contemporary standards, with population sizes of five thousand or less quite common.

Box 9.1 VARNA: A MODEL STRATIFICATION SYSTEM IN EARLY CIVILIZATIONS

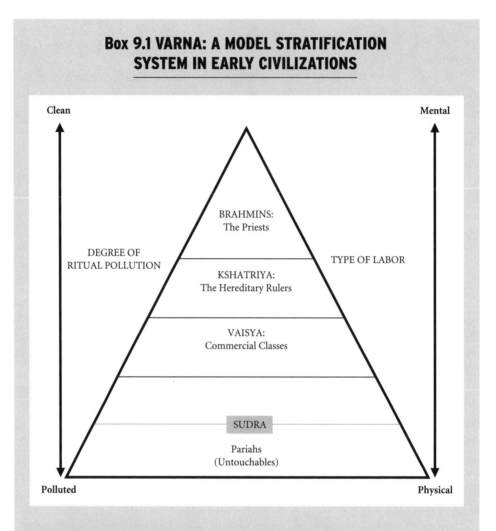

A form of stratification, the *Varna*—or "caste"—system, was practiced in ancient South Asia. It had four basic strata and many substrata, as shown above. It is difficult to determine exactly when the Varna system was created, except that it followed the establishment of the Indus Valley civilizations about four thousand years ago. The similarities between it and Plato's ideal society are hardly coincidental, which suggests that it was not confined to just one area. It obviously had its roots in agrarian society, but it is a specific product of an urban culture and occupational specialization.

Box 9.2 OPPOSITION TO CASTE

Millions of people throughout Asia and other parts of the world worship the Buddha, more than two millennia after his death, for his compassion and wisdom. Photo by Catherine Collins; used with permission.

Buddha's doctrine argues against the privileges of ascribed status, viewing every individual, Brahmins and Kshatriyas included, as subject to the same universal set of moral precepts. It also argues against the Brahmanic code, in which priests define reality for everyone else. In this respect, it is very similar to the ethical monotheism that had been codified in the city-states to the west. For its time it was, and perhaps for our time it still is, a revolutionary doctrine. As Buddha traveled and taught his views, the movement became an established religion in competition with the faith of the Brahmins. "Neglect of the masses [by the Brahmins] hastened the spread of Buddhism" (Innes 1971, 18). The case of Buddha indicates that, even as the ancient civilizations established a centuries-long legacy of caste-based rigidity and social inequality, they provided the earliest challenges to the system as well. This is relevant today because the larger tradition, which includes the mistaken view that some people are naturally superior to others, also contains the earliest recognition of what is now an established scientific truth: superiority and inferiority are socially created and are sustained by sociocultural (not biological) inheritance. As Buddha first taught, the view that inequality is "natural" is itself a social construction usually formulated by members of the "most superior" strata.

2. Not only were there very few large cities but also, in general, they were home to only a tiny proportion of regional populations: no more than 5 percent or so, whereas the other 95 percent remained tied to the land.

3. The culture of the cities closely reflected, and generalized, the culture of their hinterland populations. They were locally oriented as opposed to being cosmopolitan, as we understand the term today.

Urban settlement emerged on more than one occasion, in different parts of the world, and in some cases they were clearly independent inventions not influenced by diffusions from other populations. Although most research on the ancient cities focuses on the Mideast, India, and the Mediterranean, recent discoveries have shown conclusively that the same general pattern of agricultural revolution, population growth, and social differentiation occurred in several other places, though at somewhat later dates.

Indochina and other parts of East Asia had cities well before 1 CE, and at about that time extensive city-state empires were established in the New World. These include those of the Mayas, Aztecs, Incas, and several earlier populations from whom their members were descended (Adams 1997).

Less well known, but equally fascinating, are the ancient city-states of Africa (outside of Egypt). These include those of the Kush Empire, founded in about the seventh century BCE and the later settlements of Kumbi Saleh, Audoghast, Jangaba, and Birini Gazargamo, established by the ancient Ghana, Mali, and Kanem people (Shinnie 1965). As in other parts of the world, these were located in river valleys and functioned in generalizing local cultures into great traditions.

World Cities and World Empires

Between the first and fourth centuries CE, Rome became the center of the most extensive communication network that had ever existed. From this center, social and cultural traits were diffused outward to the British Isles to the north and west, to Saharan Africa to the south, and Central Asia to the east. The new monotheistic faith of Christianity, as well as technological innovations and political and economic institutions, emanated from the city to the hinterlands, bringing formerly inaccessible areas into a single intercontinental system. During this same era, however, the territory of the city-state of Rome itself contracted, and the capital's population size decreased by 50 percent, to less than two hundred thousand (Petersen 1975, 409).

The Turco-Muslim and Chinese Empires

With the fall of Rome and the breakup of its empire into local kingdoms, the center of urban culture shifted southward to present-day Bulgaria and Turkey: the Black Sea coast and to the city of Constantinople (Istanbul). From there, a new far-flung imperial system was created, which served to diffuse writing in the Greek and Arabic languages, the eastern rite of Christianity, and especially the newest monotheistic faith, Islam.

For the ensuing eight hundred years or so, the Turco-Muslim Empire expanded:[8] westward, reaching as far as the Iberian peninsula by the eighth century; eastward to India by the twelfth century, and northward to the borders of Russia by the thirteenth. Old city-states of the Mideast, such as the Prophet Mohammed's home of Medina, Jerusalem, or Al Kuds, its Arabic name, and Jericho were conquered by the Turks (Jerusalem/Al Kuds in 638 CE and Babylonia in 642), and new ones were established.

Civilization flourished during centuries of Turkish and Muslim rule. The cultures of the empire were strongly influenced by Aristotelian and, later, Islamic philosophies. Many of the innovations that were to become part of Europe's scientific revolution were either anticipated or developed independently during this era. Among these were the first attempts to render a scientific account of social and cultural change, as summarized in the works of Ibn Khaldun of Tunis (1958, 1987; Baali 1988).

Meanwhile, to the north in the Chinese coastal cities, especially Peking (Beijing), another continental empire was being established (Frank 1998; Martindale 1962, 109). There, the familiar pattern was repeated: Agricultural revolution led to the creation of city-states and, eventually, imperial centers. Writing, which was invented in China around 2000 BCE, developed under the administration of small and specialized classes of scribes and hereditary emperor-kings. As in other parts of the world, these groups gained access to the labor power of large classes of commoners and nonpersons, all of whom were organized in a castelike stratification system.

With the help of roads and irrigation systems, the control of the imperial court expanded outward from Beijing and provincial capitals. In 221 BCE, the Ch'in Empire gave China its first unified government. As early as this period, the country "covered most of the same area as it does today. Its historical development was characterized essentially by integration of an already common culture, rather than by external conquests of alien ethnic communities" (Mu 1982, 2). The empire endured for twenty-one centuries and five dynasties, three of which, encompassing some twelve hundred years, followed the fall of Rome.

Thus, the world's most massive national population (to this day), 90 percent of which was engaged in agriculture or other rural occupations, was organized into a single system by a few thousand literate people living in Beijing's walled Forbidden City on Tiananmen Square. Of all the early city-state systems of the ancient world, "the most successful one by far in terms of political continuity, size of population under governmental control, and administrative sophistication was that of China" (Totten 1982, xi).

The Collapse of Roman Europe

As the Turco-Muslim and Chinese empires expanded, Europe deurbanized. In the territories that had been under Roman jurisdiction, the trend toward increasing social complexity was halted and, in some cases, reversed. Thus, between the seventh and fifteenth centuries, social change in Europe was centered in the countryside and focused on the rationalization of agriculture. The older, castelike, urban occupational groupings developed into specialized associations, generically referred to by their Middle English name *guilds* (meaning "payers of tribute"). The system came to be known as *feudalism*, from the same root as in the word *fee*, indicating its basis in heritable rights to property. The three groupings, Church authorities, ruling families, and everyone else who paid tribute to them (in town and country), made up the first, second, and third estates, respectively.

During the entire period, no urban settlement in Europe achieved a population size even a fraction of that of imperial Rome. The feudal system proved to be highly effective in accumulating and centralizing wealth. Technological improvements in the plow, irrigation, and breeding, along with better roads and animal-powered vehicles, made it possible to maintain unprecedentedly high levels of productivity, despite numerous bouts of war, pestilence, famine, vice, and misery. The result was, in effect, a second agricultural revolution. The surplus created was directed to the cities, creating new opportunities for those pursuing nonagricultural occupations. Money began to flow more freely, as it came to replace land as the sole criterion of wealth. As the preceding figures indicate, toward the end of the fourteenth century, the medieval city-states experienced a period of relatively rapid growth, especially on the Italian peninsula.

Renaissance and Reurbanization By the beginning of the fifteenth century, the reemergence of urban society had brought about a new era of cultural production. It was, in many ways, similar to what had occurred in the city-states of the ancient world, and thus it was termed *Renaissance* ("rebirth"). The cultural innovations that had been developed in the Turco-Muslim Empire were diffused into European society, and ancient doctrines that had not been preserved in Christian Europe were reintroduced.

Some of the most significant technological advances of the Renaissance were in shipbuilding and navigation. These further contributed to the growth in the number and sizes of the cities of Europe. Both the Bronze Age and the Renaissance periods of urban growth were characterized by cumulative and cyclical increases in population density and social complexity. In the latter case, however, there was also an enormous upward shift in scale. Prior to 1 CE, vast territories were dominated by a single, large city, with Rome achieving the ultimate in both categories. By the fifteenth century, however, it had become possible for several city-states to emerge in relative proximity to one another and to intensively exploit less-extended hinterlands.

The Age of Discovery in Iberia

By the late fifteenth century, the center of European urban culture had shifted from Italy to the Iberian Peninsula. There were new technologies and old social customs, complex populations forming out of ethnically diverse subpopulations, and urban growth in a land-based social system. In addition, there occurred a series of refinements in urban economics: paper money, credit systems, banking, and finance. These and related changes allowed explorers like Vasco daGama, Fernando Magellan, and Christopher Columbus to take to the high seas.

The Diffusion of Urban Society in Europe and Beyond

In the ensuing decades, old ports were reached and new lands, new continents, and new worlds were discovered. Fleets were soon being launched from city-states in Holland

and other parts of Europe. With each successful expedition, and most early ones were *not* successful, resources flowed back to the city-states, to the financiers, and to the ruling families. The cities were enriched, as the new resources were invested in additional exploratory, and military, expeditions. An unprecedented level and wholly novel type of wealth was created, based not on the ability of a population to extract resources from limited, local environments but rather on systematically gathering it from outside the physical hinterlands of the city-state, beyond even the continental hinterlands of previous empires.

These economic changes had effects in both the city and the countryside. In the city, the organizations that made up the new economic institution grew, while they and their members prospered. In the countryside, resources were invested in improving production and in basic death-control technologies such as sanitation, nutrition, and protection against natural disasters. These raised levels of infant survival and, thus, spurred population growth. In these human labor-dependent agricultural economies, growing populations and improved technologies led to ever-higher levels of productivity. Finally, the loop was closed, as higher productivity meant increasing surpluses to be transferred to the urban economy. As a result, between 1500 and 1700, five major intercontinental empires were created. Supported by surplus generated in the colonies of Asia, Africa, and the Americas, urban populations exploded throughout Europe, as the proportion of Europe's population living in cities doubled. At the same time, European cities were created and grew at colonial ports abroad: Boston, Rio de Janeiro, Bombay, and Montreal. Collectively, these colonial systems and their city nodes constituted the first true world system, ruled by Europe with guns and sails.

With this shift, local traditions met with competition from others sources of cultural authority. In the emerging world colonial centers, rational law, urban authority in its postmedieval, modern form, for the first time seriously opposed the rule of custom. In the realm of knowledge and learning, philosophical and scientific research expanded and became institutionalized. While still essentially amateurs by contemporary standards (Ben-David 1971),[9] philosophers and scientists were able to demand an ever-increasing share of the economic surplus for investing in specialized research-teaching occupations. The universities, which had previously been dedicated exclusively to religious studies, provided the organizational framework for this new work. And it was there, in the middle of the seventeenth century, that the scientific revolution began (Merton 1970).

Science, Industry, and Urban Society

In the early 1700s, after several centuries of slow urban growth, a period of unprecedented rapid acceleration occurred in Europe. Newton's discoveries and the scientific revolution they inspired spread from London to other parts of Europe. Almost immediately, projects were undertaken to turn these discoveries into innovations to improve the technologies of sailing, navigation, warfare, manufacture, and agricultural production. This spirit of innovation served as the basis for [many] philosophical and technological enterprises. . . . Gifted and creative individuals now had a much greater range of opportunities to exercise their creativity than ever before. It was possible to discuss matters of politics, economy, and philosophy without fear of violent conflict, and there was fair scope for actually influencing policy. . . . Experimentation with steam engines, textile machinery, and other technological schemes began and were spurred on. (Ben-David 1971, 79)

Industrial Revolution in Europe

The experimentation with steam engines, a little toy developed in about 1740, was crucial. The principle is so simple that, with the benefit of hindsight, one wonders how it took so long to get around to it. Boiling water creates steam, which, as Newton had observed, generates force. If, instead of dissipating upward, the flow of steam from a boiling vessel can be directed to a specific target, then the force can be used to move the target. If the target is, say, a wheel, such as that which is turned in milling grain with an animal or person providing the motion, the force can be used to replace the animal or person. This idea, of replacing human and animal labor power with a mechanical device, was hardly new. But prior to the invention of the steam engine, no one really understood its full implications. It did not take long for the inventors to catch on. Within a few years, bigger and bigger steam generators were being harnessed to bigger and bigger mill wheels and to anything else they seemed to fit. "During the 80 years or so following 1760, England's economy and social structure underwent a complete transformation, commonly known as the industrial revolution" (Petersen 1975, 462).

The steam engine literally revolutionized English society and eventually the collective fate of the entire human species. In relation to cities and urban life, it brought about another wholesale, upward shift in scale and complexity:

> The groundwork was being laid in Europe (and particularly in England) for rapid urbanization. Technological advances and social organizational changes occurred along a number of fronts which eventually gave rise to the development of commercial agriculture and improved transportation and communications. With the coming of the Industrial Revolution the great period of city building got underway in earnest. (Frisbie 1977, 44)

With steam power, productivity increased to a previously unimaginable level. Thus, with adequate machinery, agricultural workers could each support themselves and their own households, and generate enough surplus to sustain one or more entire additional households, in the time once required to eke out a fraction of a single individual's needs. The majority of a regional population, even a substantial majority, could now be city dwellers. At the extreme, with sufficient trade, an entire population could now be sustained in cities with no domestic agricultural production at all.

Since the Industrial Revolution, this is exactly what has happened. In 1650, less than 2 percent of Europe's population was living in cities with twenty or more residents. The populations of London and Paris were well below one hundred (still only 20 percent of the size of Rome in 1 CE). But by 1800, England was 10 percent urbanized, and London (and Peking) had reached the one million mark. By 1900, one-half of England's population was living in cities. Today, 75 to 95 percent of the populations of larger industrial countries are urbanized (living in central cities or in the rapidly growing suburbs), and contemporary city-states, such as Singapore and Hong Kong, are 100 percent urban.[10]

At some symbolic moment in 2007, the entire world's population surpassed the 50 percent urban mark. And even though rates of urban growth have slowed in the highly urbanized countries, because they have achieved the saturation point, in the Third World urban growth is occurring and accelerating faster than has ever been experienced anywhere.

Premature and Postindustrial Cities

By the end of World War II, the trend of increasing social complexity that began with the invention of cities had reached a new stage. The world remained divided between the industrialized, urban societies of Europe and overseas European populations, on one hand, and the still predominantly agricultural populations of the colonized areas, on the other. Everywhere, however, gigantic European metropolises dominated political and economic life as well as cultural production and distribution. At the original colonial ports in Asia, Africa, and Latin America, cities such as Calcutta, Rio, and Nairobi had achieved population sizes in the millions, as large as or larger than Paris, London, and other European capitals.

The apparent anomaly of large Third World cities surrounded by populations still 70 to 90 percent rural was given the revealing label of "premature metropolis" by the Indian geographer Nirimal K. Bose. This is meant to indicate that these cities are the product of the same Industrial Revolution that brought about the urbanization of Europe. But, from the point of view of the local populations, it was not an indigenous revolution. The dual character of Third World society first described by Gunnar Myrdal, in which modern institutions and traditional values commingle, is thus reflected in geographical form as cities "out of phase" (Bose 1965, 251).

The colonial empires were established at these ports beginning in the late fifteenth century. The world system of the early twentieth century depended on the premature metropolises that had grown up around them to maintain the connections between Third World hinterlands and the core. By the dawn of World War II, the system had assumed a definite shape, with three interconnected features reflecting its colonial roots:

1. a long-standing system of mediated relationships involving the exchange of raw materials and commodities, the diffusion of cultural material, and the movement of human beings;
2. the domination of European economic organizations and culture, as reflected in the inordinate advantages that accrued to those with access to English and other European languages, and to sterling, dollars, and other foreign currency; and
3. formal political control of the premature metropolises and their hinterlands by European governments.

These conditions revealed the kinds of lags and contradictions that make for large-scale change, including political revolution. Immediately following World War II, Gandhi and other Third World intellectuals resumed their earlier work in organizing social movements to promote this revolution, eventually bringing an end to condition number 3. Nevertheless, the first two persist, and their impact increases daily as the metropolises grow to unprecedented proportions.

With political independence, the premature metropolises and their resident and hinterland populations have entered the world system with exceedingly complex, but not necessarily well-adapted, social structures. They contain both the "imported" complexities associated with industrialization in the modern sector and the additional complicating factor of nonindustrial forms of association (family, clan, and caste) still prevalent in the lives of the still-traditional majority. At the same time, entire national populations in core areas have been encompassed by urban-industrial society (see table 9.3).

By the 1970s, technological innovation and the world division of labor had allowed for the transcendence of central place theory. At that point, the proportion of the population engaged in manufacturing in the United States and several European countries fell below the 50 percent threshold. "White-collar society" was born. Moreover, the largest share of the populations was no longer residing in the politically incorporated cities. Instead, with the development of communication and transportation technologies and the shift from industrial to service occupations, the former advantages of the center gave way to the lifestyle opportunities of the suburbs. In most metropolitan areas of the United States and other industrialized countries, the suburbs now dominate the core. Not only has the majority of urban residents migrated from the center but so have the businesses, factories, and cultural facilities. With innovations in electronic communication, home offices, and the like, there is less and less of an advantage to being "in the middle of things."

Thus, in the twenty-first century, being some*where* matters relatively little. Thus, another period of deurbanization in the West began and continues to this day. This time, however, it is not associated with the simplification of social relations but rather with the achievement of such a large scale that cities proper have become smaller components of greater, continental, and intercontinental urban wholes.

Urban Explosion in the Third World

As urbanization has virtually reached its saturation point in the industrialized countries, the cities of the Third World are exploding. By the late 1990s, 43 percent of the human population lived in cities, with an overall rate of urban growth of about 2 percent per year. In North America, Europe, and Japan, an average of 77 percent of the population was urbanized, compared with 35 percent in Asia and Africa (Population Reference Bureau [PRB] 1995; see table 9.4). Central cities in the industrialized countries are hardly growing at all, and in the United States most have lost substantial portions of their populations to the suburbs since the 1960s. Rates of urban growth in the First and Second Worlds basically match general population growth, from just under 1 percent per year to less than zero population growth in most of Europe. In contrast,

TABLE 9.3 World's Most Populous Urban Agglomerations: 2010

Rank	City	Est. Population (in millions)
1	Tokyo, Japan	36,094
2	Mumbai, India	26,385
3	Delhi, India	22,498
4	Sao Paulo, Brazil	21,428
5	Dacca, Bangladesh	22,015
6	Mexico City, Mexico	21,009
7	New York, USA	20,628
8	Calcutta, India	20,560
9	Shanghai, China	19,412
10	Karachi, Pakistan	19,095
11	Cairo, Egypt	15,561
12	Manila, Philippines	14,808
13	Beijing, China	14,545
14	Buenos Aires, Argentina	13,768
15	Rio de Janeiro, Brazil	13,413
16	Los Angeles, USA	13,672
17	Jakarta, Indonesia	12,363
18	Guangdong, China	11,835
19	Osaka, Japan	11,368
20	Lagos, Nigeria	10,572
21	Moscow, Russia	10,526
22	Istanbul, Turkey	10,530
23	Shenzhen, China	10,196
24	Paris, France	9,958
25	Chicago, USA	9,932
26	Seoul, South Korea	9,738
27	Wuhan, China	9,339
28	London, Great Britain	8,607
29	Lima, Peru	8,375
30	Tehran, Iran	8,221

Source: United Nations Population Division, *World Population Prospects: The 2006 Revision* and *World Urbanization Prospects: The 2007 Revision* (New York: Population Division of the Department of Economic and Social Affairs of the United Nations Secretariat, 2009), http://esa.un.org/unup.

cities and urban areas in Third World countries such as India are growing at or above 3 percent per year, more than three times more rapidly (Weinstein 1991–1992).

Of the roughly four billion people in the world today who remain rural, over three-fourths, that is, three billion individuals, live in the villages of the Third World. Every year, approximately ninety million of them, nearly 250 per day, migrate to their already-crowded premature metropolises. There, most live in squalor, crowded into shanty-towns without sanitation or utilities. Supporting their large families, now swelled as the result of infant mortality declines, with the crumbs and scraps of the formal urban

TABLE 9.4 The Most and Least Urbanized among Twenty-five Selected Nations

	Country	Percentage urban	Rank in world
MORE DEVELOPED	Belgium	97	3
	Uruguay	94	4
	Argentina	91	7
	Japan	86	12
	Brazil	84	13
	Australia	83	14
	United Kingdom	80	17
	USA	79	18
	France	77	19
	Denmark	72	24
	Bulgaria	71	25
	Italy	68	27
LESS DEVELOPED	China	46	48
	Indonesia	43	50
	Myanmar	31	62
	India	29	64
	Viet Nam	28	65
	Bangladesh	25	68
	Afghanistan	22	70
	Kenya	19	72
	Nepal	17	74
	Ethiopia	16	75
	Cambodia	15	76
	Sri Lanka	15	76
	Uganda	13	78

Source: Population Reference Bureau (PRB), *World Population Data Sheet* (Washington, DC: Author, 1995).

economy, they have made Mexico City, Calcutta, Shanghai, and Bombay the world's most populous cities, now surpassing the size and explosive growth once identified with London, New York, and Paris.

As bad as these conditions are, rural life for most Third World people is, or is perceived as, much worse. They see the city as a land of opportunity, where there are jobs, money, or at least a bit of food to be begged or stolen, or some garbage to be scavenged. In the countryside, there is nothing, or so it is believed. Part of this perception is true: a person or family can survive on only their wits more easily in the city than on a barren, overworked plot of land miles from the nearest telephone. But life in Third World slums is brutal, as illustrated by a story that appeared in the Indian newspapers about the plight of a man in Bombay. It was a story I had heard many times before in my studies in other cities in India.

Ram came to Bombay from a village that was several hours by rail, and several rupees' train fare, south of the city. He had heard from a friend of a cousin that there were jobs available packing vegetables in central Bombay, and he was given the name and address of a contact. When he arrived, he found that hundreds of men were already lined up for what turned out to be a "possible" position; they would learn "later" whether it would actually open. Discouraged, he wandered off. When night came, he went back to the packing plant and tried to sleep on the sidewalk. Before long, however, a man was shaking him and demanding twenty-five rupees' rent for the space he was occupying.

During the next few weeks, Ram drifted, picking up loose change, trash, anything. He worked out a sleeping arrangement with a man from a neighboring village for ten rupees per night, on credit. By the end of the first month, he had secured several day assignments at the plant and had actually saved two hundred rupees, despite the fact that he was robbed twice. But he'd had it with Bombay. With his savings, he bought a new shirt and a ticket back home, to give life in the country another try.

When Ram arrived in his village, in his clean new shirt and obviously now gainfully employed in the packing industry, the town celebrated. In their eyes, he had made it, a successful urbanite after only one month. His family quickly arranged for a bride for him, and they were married soon afterward. As a wedding present, his family and friends bought them *two* tickets back to Bombay and a photograph of the bride and groom to put up in their new "house." And to Bombay they returned, Ram unable to explain how it really was.

Meanwhile, back in the countryside, in India and throughout the Third World, there remains a reservoir of potential migrants that is itself growing at rates at or above 2 percent annually (more than twice as fast as the U.S. population), an additional 110 future urban dwellers per day. Where will they go? How can they be accommodated when urban systems have already broken down as result of overpopulation? What about war, pestilence, famine, vice, and misery?

Managing the forces of hyperurbanization in the Third World will require some monumental solutions to match the unprecedented scale of the problem. In fact, it may turn out to be the leading item on the international agenda before too long. The pushes of urban life in a Third World *barrio*[11] and the pulls of material wealth and democratic rights in the industrialized countries are irresistible for most residents—with many, many more to come. Immigration of Third World people (legal, illegal, and refugee) is already a priority issue in the developed nations and, by all indications, it has barely begun.

Urban growth in the Third World cannot help but change society forever, in those countries and in ours. It brings opportunities, but it also brings poverty and social inequality. Great effort, ingenuity, and cooperation will be needed to maximize the opportunities and minimize the costs. Fortunately, we have never been better equipped, technologically and sociologically, to undertake such a project.

Conclusion: An Urban World in the Twenty-first Century

When the third millennium of the Common Era arrived, our world was vastly different from that of the ancient civilizations of the third millennium BCE. No significant social and cultural change can now occur anywhere without its effects being felt everywhere.

No major technological innovation will ever be "lost" because the local population in which it occurred became extinct. Urban social structure, with its several distinct institutions made up of large, complex, bureaucratic organizations, is now part of the lives of all 6.5 billion human inhabitants of Earth, regardless of where they make their homes. In all of these respects, we have achieved an ultimate in the millennia-long trend of increasing social complexity.

At the same time, there has never been a greater gap in the absolute levels of wealth possessed by the rich and the poor of the world. Never before has it been possible for the lives of so many to be unjustly dominated by so few through strategically placed positions of control in worldwide economic, political, and communication networks. When one asks, therefore, about what kind of world this is and about what lies ahead, it is essential to begin with an understanding of political and economic relations in the global system. This is because social and cultural change, from this point on, will be driven by—and will, of course, rebound back on—the development of these highly internationalized institutions.

The Industrial Revolution and its 250-year aftermath have established the building blocks out of which the new, global society will be shaped: economically, politically, and in many other respects. But what we often fail to remember, perhaps because it is so obvious, is that industrialization and urban growth have also given unprecedented scope to planned, intentional change. They have provided people with the power to shape their futures, to arrange these building blocks according to design and fore-thought in a way far beyond the scope of preindustrial humanity.

This is certainly not to say that the outcomes of our intention and planning are always as we hope and anticipate, nor that we are free of environmental limitations, as some idealists of the romantic era imagined. To the contrary, the unintended con-sequences of our technological, political, and economic innovations loom large. And we are beginning to understand what a dangerous oversight it has been to suppose that industrial progress allows us to "conquer" nature. Nevertheless, urbanization has ensured that tomorrow's world will be the product of unprecedented, global-level ratio-nal coordination (imperfect as it may be). Can it be directed to solving our unprec-edented, global-level social problems?

Summary

This chapter, the first of three on macrolevel change, has explored the fundamental and enormously consequential shift from *Gemeinschaft* to *Gesellschaft* forms of social orga-nization. Our species, which began its existence in Africa as small bands of hunters not much different from chimpanzees and other anthropoids, has now occupied all parts of the planet. Few of us actually hunt for our food, and our bands have become complex societies, nation-states, and international systems of communication and exchange. In the process, we have invented the distinctively human form of settlement we call "cit-ies," and over the course of centuries we have moved to these cities at ever-accelerating rates. Most significantly, the highest rates of urban growth today are occurring in the world's largest, most rapidly breeding, and poorest populations.

As our review of historical and comparative research indicates, the shift from the countryside to the city has meant far more than a change of residence. With it come new institutions separated from and, in many respects antagonistic to, the traditional family: new occupational statuses far removed from direct production or trade, new kinds of cosmopolitan ("heterogenetic") cultures, and new forms of social inequality. From a strictly demographic perspective, the human population is approximately one-half urbanized, but the reach of urban culture and political control extends to the farthest hinterlands. Because most people, regardless of where they make their home, are deeply affected by events that emanate from urban nodes of the world system, contemporary society is essentially urban society.

For people who live in the central cities and booming suburbs of the industrialized countries, this urban society is familiar and, if not always friendly, is nevertheless the context in which they seek their security and pursue their fortunes. However, for Ram in Bombay and the approximately two billion other Third World ruralites now contemplating or undertaking (willingly or not) a move to the metropolis, the terrain is far less familiar and the prospects anything but secure. As the urbanization of humanity continues, the attention of scholars and policy makers in government, business, and other realms will increasingly be turned to Ram and his peers because it is they who will demand the lion's share of already-scarce resources. Although it does not seem possible to meet these demands at this moment, it is also true that never before has such a huge pool of potential human talent been provided with the advantages that are known to accrue for those who can master the urban way of life. In this instance, if the past association between urbanization and technological revolution remains a valid precedent, we may find that hyperurbanization is one demographic problem that bears the seeds of its own solution.

Relevant Websites

www.historyguide.org/ancient/lecture6b.html
The History Guide has posted this interesting online history of Greek democracy.

www.fsmitha.com/
This is an account of the rise of ancient Chinese civilization.

www.demographia.com/db-world-metro2000.htm
This is one of the sites maintained by the private organization Demographia. It is a great source for urbanization information and other population links by subject.

www.prb.org/Educators/TeachersGuides/HumanPopulation/Urbanization.aspx
Here is the PRB link to world urbanization information.

www.aboutbuddha.org/
This is a Buddhist website that expands on the comments in box 9.2. It includes biographical and historical information and several links to the abundant Internet resources on Buddha and Buddhism.

www.brynmawr.edu/Acads/history/powell/312/description.html
www.uoguelph.ca/history/urban/citybibIV.html
These two sites focus on medieval cities. The first is an online course from Bryn Mawr College. The second contains an extensive bibliography.

A World Divided

U RBAN GROWTH and the spread of *Gesellschaft* forms of organization
have contributed significantly to the creation of a single, world-level society. But globalization has not been a steady, unimpeded process. Today's
world is as much characterized by division and difference as it is by unity. As humanity gropes its way toward becoming a group for itself, it is likely to continue to meet
with considerable resistance along the way from the divisive counterforces of material
inequality, ethnicity, and neocolonialism.

This chapter examines these sources of contemporary social conflict. The first section discusses cultural diversity—group-based differences in values and norms. Here
the revealing social psychological concept of "destructive entitlement" is used to explain
aspects of contemporary ethnic and religious violence. Next, the main features of the
international stratification system are outlined. Enormous disparities in wealth and
other resources divide our world of nations today. To a great extent, this is the legacy of
centuries of colonialism, and it has been a source of open conflict since the Third World
independence movement took off in the late 1940s. The chapter concludes with a look
at world system theory and the roots of cultural leveling.

When one considers how common such factors are today, it is clear that despite
the irresistible pull of economics, technology, and new standards of universal human
rights, the ideal of one world at peace is still a long way from being realized.

Cultural Diversity: Normative and Value Differences

Cultural diversity arises from differences in normative systems. These consist of the
rules and principles that define acceptable belief and practice. The most general and
abstract parts of these systems are values, our broad standards of goodness, truth, and

beauty. Norms are specific rules that express prevailing values, ranging from table manners to criminal and religious codes. Every culture and subculture, from the simplest to the most complex, has normative systems, and all are distinctive to one degree or another. Ethnic, national, religious, regional, and other forms of diversity are based largely on these distinctions (Parekh 2000). They can be a source of fascination and admiration, as people of different backgrounds learn to understand and appreciate the variety of human experience. They can also be tremendous irritants that inflame hatred and violence (Yinger 1994).

Ethnic Subcultures and Diversity

Until a fairly late date in human existence, perhaps some ten thousand years ago, ethnic subcultural formation was rare, probably occurring only as the result of conquest. Under such circumstances, cultural diversity was automatically associated with political domination, with one ethnic subpopulation establishing physical rule over another, often as master and slave. With the territorial expansion of the ancient empires in the Middle East, ethnic diversity, as it is understood today, became more common. Conquest and slavery continued to be practiced, but contact between the colonizers and local populations led to other forms of accommodation as well, although they were still generally hierarchical: provincial versus metropolitan, citizen versus foreigner, and so forth (Smith 1987).

Even during the golden eras of the ancient empires, such as Rome in 1 CE and China and the Muslim empires in the subsequent several centuries, the overwhelming majority of people continued to live in small, relatively isolated, and ethnically homogenous rural populations. In fact, the Chinese Empire, which by most standards was the most successful among the ancient civilizations, was—and still is—quite ethnically homogenous. Most people shared, and still share, the Han culture, with relatively minor regional differences and just a few smaller minority populations (e.g., Mongolian and Tibetan) at the peripheries of the empire.

Up to the end of the Middle Ages, cultural diversity was an exclusive feature of life in the city. Although these older cities and their cultures were politically dominant, as we noted in the preceding chapter, they encompassed only a tiny proportion of all social relationships in which members of a population were involved. Most people were not directly affected by members of ethnic groups outside their own. However, with European exploration, large and culturally diverse populations became increasingly common, particularly because of the unprecedented urban growth that occurred in the wake of colonization.

The ancient empires provided new opportunities for heterogeneous larger populations to be formed, but the rise and expansion of the European world system introduced an entirely new scale of ethnic diversity into social relations. As with many other trends of this type, this new scale did not replace the older means of subcultural formation such as slavery and conquest. Rather, it added a dimension to these older systems.

Several interrelated processes have gone into the creation of today's national aggregate populations, many, but certainly not all, of which are highly ethnically diverse compared to past standards.[1] In general, the existence of ethnic subcultures in modern nation-states reflects a history of regular and sustained contact with foreigners. The more contact experienced, especially during the era of European exploration, the greater the degree of diversity, all else being equal. Japan and China, two very large national populations with several very small ethnic subpopulations, were isolated from the impacts of the European expansion.[2] In contrast, India and the United States, both with highly diverse national populations, were the products of colonial expansion.

One of the major factors that brought about the cultural diversity that now characterizes the United States and other countries is the international division of labor, established by the European colonial powers. The earliest migrations of Europeans into the New World introduced the first form of diversity, as the native people came to occupy the lowest strata of the colonial order. Prior to that time, the indigenous populations were relatively small, isolated, and culturally distinct, although several major, multieth-

Box 10.1 ETHNIC CONFLICT IN CHINA

Kashi (Kashgar) cultural and religious center of the Chinese province of Xinxiang, home to the Uyghur people and the site of ethnic protests in 2009. Photo by Colegota, used under a Creative Commons License Deed, Attribution-Share Alike 2.5 Spain; http://commons.wikimedia.org/wiki/File:Kashgar-minarete-d01.jpg

China was and remains a relatively ethnically homogenous population. However, the small, minority (non-Han) segment includes over fifty ethnic groups. In 2009, the world's attention was focused on one of these groups, the Muslim Uyghur, most of whom live in the northwestern province of Xinjiang. In July of that year, two Uyghur workers died in a factory in southern China. This led to several days of street protests involving clashes between the police and protestors and members of the Han and Uyghur communities.

Source: News Asia Pacific, "Uighur Exiles Deny China Riot Claim," Aljazeera.net, July 6, 2009, http://english.aljazeera.net/

nic, indigenous empires existed at the time of European conquest (see the discussion of the rise of empires in chapter 9).

With colonial rule, these several cultures were brought under a single system, in part through a series of individual treaties and charters established between the European rulers and local leaders. In the Americas, especially, these contacts were often genocidal, with dozens of populations decimated and others greatly reduced in numbers. As migration from Europe continued, the native populations in these areas became very small and poor, powerless minorities.

In Central and South America, a relatively substantial amount of exogamy between Europeans and local people occurred during the colonial era. Thus, current populations represent a greater blending of European and non-European gene pools than in the United States and Canada. In many places in Central America, from Mexico south to Brazil and Argentina, native beliefs, practices, and artifacts have become integrated into the dominant European culture. Nevertheless, the incorporation of native cultures as subcultures of larger populations is not a significant source of ethnic diversity, even in the more mixed populations of Guatemala and El Salvador.

This is in contrast to the situation in Africa, India, and other parts of Asia where European explorers encountered larger native populations, often with their own long histories of imperial expansion. Genocide did occur, especially in confrontations between Europeans and smaller isolated tribal groups in these regions. But a more peaceful form of colonial administration was also extended over vast territories that had never been treated as units prior to that time. These areas contained tens of millions of indigenous people traditionally organized into dozens and hundreds of distinct local cultures (Levinson 1998). This resulted in the creation of a two-tiered system of ethnic stratification, similar to that in the New World, with the Europeans on top and the "natives" on the bottom (Sartre 1963).

In Africa and Asia, these indigenous strata were actually highly diverse, for several formerly isolated peoples were included in the new, single colonial administrative units. Because of the large size of these indigenous populations and because Europeans migrated to Africa and Asia less frequently than to the New World, the newly created, ethnically diverse societies were characterized by *minority rule*. A few Europeans culturally and politically dominated large masses of local people, whose various cultures became subcultures of the larger unit. With political independence following World War II, most of the former administrative units became new, ethnically diverse nations. The first multiethnic elections in South Africa, in April 1994, marked the elimination of one of the last political vestiges of colonial stratification on the African continent (Lewis 1994).

Another type of migration that affected the ethnic mix we find in many national populations today was the colonial system of labor importation and exportation. This occurred throughout the world: not only did Europeans travel to newly discovered and colonized areas of Asia, Africa, the Pacific Islands, and the New World, but they also shipped large numbers of laborers around the peripheries of their empires. The impact of this is clear when we recall that the colonial empires were in the business of extracting resources from the non-European peripheries for export to the European capitals and commercial centers. From there, these resources fueled the Industrial Revolution and further imperial expansion through the middle of the twentieth century and, in a new form, to this day. Human laborers, including the "black gold" of the slave trade, were thus treated as any other commodity: an input in the extractive system. Typically, this movement was not the exchange of free laborers as we understand the term today. Rather, some form of compulsion or involuntary service was associated with it: this included indentured servitude, prison labor, and servitude through fraudulent contract (such as kidnapping). The most notorious form of this labor marketing was the slave trade.

Over the course of more than three hundred years, between 1503 and 1835, millions of native African people were brought to the New World to work, usually on European plantations. There were some attempts to enslave Native Americans, but it proved difficult because they had indigenous roots and could easily escape or engage in warfare rather than submit to bondage. The importation of Africans was far more effective because these individuals had been entirely separated from their social and cultural supports. They were not allowed to speak their tribal languages, and worse, due to being treated as animals, they were "broken" of their drive to be free. Even then, the system was not entirely effective, as slave owners lived in constant fear of (often-violent) rebellions and runaways (da Costa 1994; Rucker 2001; Schuler 1970).

The African diaspora provided an additional, socially inferior stratum to the emerging, culturally diverse, overseas European populations. With emancipation in the mid- to late nineteenth century—1865 in the United States, earlier in Central and South America—this experience left its mark on intergroup relations in the form of low-status ethnic subpopulations. As was the case with integration of the indigenous cultures, however, substantial differences existed between regions of the New World in how African slaves and former slaves were treated (Elkins 1959).

Although slavery was technically legal in Canada until the early 1800s, its practice was very rare (Whitfield 2007). In fact, the country served as a refuge for runaways between 1776 and the end of the U.S. Civil War (Alexander and Glaze 1996). Today, its small African-background subpopulation can trace its ancestry to a double migration: from Africa to a New World region where there was slavery, and from there into Canada. Most of these people or their ancestors came from the Caribbean islands. Although they still rank below European-background Canadians in many respects, African Canadians generally have a higher status than their counterparts elsewhere in the Western Hemisphere (Hiller 2000).

Cuba, Jamaica, Haiti, other Caribbean island nations, and Brazil had slave systems comparable to that of the southern United States. Each differed, however, in its severity and subsequent integration of the ex-slave population (Stinchcombe 1994). To some extent, these differences were associated with the culture of the colonial power administering each area: English or Dutch Protestant versus Portuguese, Spanish, or French Catholic.

In 1793, after an intense three-year rebellion inspired by the French Revolution, slavery was abolished in the French-ruled portion of Hispaniola. On January 1, 1804, after a decade of civil insurrection, the former slaves declared independence as Haiti.

Thus, they became the second new nation, and the first modern republic led by non-Europeans (Montas 1975, 19–22).

The new nation of Brazil was formed some years later not by slaves but rather by the Portuguese colonists. There, the African slaves and their descendants retained a socially inferior status, but in some respects it has been relatively higher than that accorded former slaves in the United States. One reason for this difference is that exogamy was more common, so that the general population and culture are less segregated into distinct subunits (although one's skin color remains a very important mark of social status in contemporary Brazil; Telles 1994). Another reason is that in Roman Catholic Brazil, and to some extent in the other Catholic New World settlements, slaves were recognized as having eternal souls and their marriages and offspring were considered sanctified as those of free people. Both of these humanizing assumptions were denied in Protestant North America.

In addition to slavery, the less severe but equally involuntary system of indenturing contributed to colonial subculture formation. This system, in which people worked to repay a specific debt, brought laborers from the Indian subcontinent to other parts of Asia, such as Malaysia, and to Fiji; Africa, including South Africa and Uganda; and the New World, especially the Caribbean and Guyana.

These people entered the host populations at various positions, depending on the type of labor performed and other colonial policies (Warner and Swezey 1994). In the Caribbean and in Southeast Asia, groups from India came as plantation laborers and occupied the lowest statuses, even lower than free Africans in Caribbean populations such as Trinidad. In Africa, they tended to perform managerial and commercial functions, occupying social positions below the Europeans but above those of the indigenous people who did most of the manual work.

Division-of-labor distinctions were even created between specific East Indian subpopulations shipped abroad. People from the southern parts of the subcontinent generally did manual labor in the overseas colonial areas, so that even today, we find people with Dravidian cultural heritages wherever plantation work was done by imported Indians (Wiebe 1976). People from Gujarat and the Sind (now part of Pakistan) fulfilled the needs for commercial skills. Groups from the Punjab (now an area divided between India and Pakistan) served as police and military troops.

In every instance, colonial rule created a complex ethnic structure that generally consisted of (1) one or more dominant European cultures, often of a numerical minority, as in South Africa, (2) various lower strata of indigenous populations, and (3) imported former-slave, indentured, and other laborers (Kale 1998).

This legacy was to shape contemporary events in many significant ways. It was through this system that a young civil servant from Gujarat, Mohandas K. Gandhi, was sent in the 1920s by the British rulers to South Africa (Huttenbach 1971; Roniger 1925). There, he saw the system of stratified subcultures in full operation as *apartheid* (Afrikaans for "separate," or "apartness").

The European rulers, who made up about 10 percent of the population, were themselves stratified into two groups: the dominant English and the defeated Dutch-ancestry Afrikaners. They retained for themselves exclusive rights to own land, to obtain a formal

Box 10.2 GANDHI AND THE COLONIAL EXPERIENCE

Mohandas K. Gandhi in South Africa in 1900. Gandhi (center), a young lawyer, went to South Africa to help gain civil rights for Indian background South Africans (classified as "colored" in the apartheid system). This was the beginning of his lifelong struggle for social justice. Image in the public domain, photographer unknown. http://web.mahatma.org .in/pictures/images/piccat0007/sa_1024_0015.jpg.

Gandhi's observations on life and truth:

- Be the change you want to see in the world.
- The weak can never forgive. Forgiveness is the attribute of the strong.
- The best way to find yourself is to lose yourself in the service of others.
- Nearly everything you do is of no importance, but it is important that you do it.
- You may never know what results come of your action, but if you do nothing there will be no result.
- Whenever you have truth it must be given with love, or the message and the messenger will be rejected.
- Men often become what they believe themselves to be. If I believe I cannot do something, it makes me incapable of doing it. But when I believe I can, then I acquire the ability to do it even if I didn't have it in the beginning.
- When I despair, I remember that all through history the way of truth and love has always won. There have been tyrants and murderers and for a time they seem invincible, but in the end, they always fall—think of it, always.

education, and to participate in political affairs. Their European languages were elevated to official status. Below them were the Indian "coloureds," the imported Indian commercial groups, who, Gandhi discovered, had no independent rights under European law, a situation even worse than that at home. And below the Indians were the "mixed-races coloured" and native "blacks," the numerical majority but in fact serving the Europeans in a virtual system of bondage.

Gandhi reacted with outrage to the injustices of this form of stratified ethnic diversity. His response, delayed by an antifascist alliance with the British during World War II, became a major cause of the fall of the empire after the war. Indeed, Gandhi's reaction to the situation of "imported" Indians in South Africa was in large part responsible for the fall of the imperial system itself—and the rise of the Third World nations. And, as we know, Gandhi's legacy also had a powerful effect on the U.S. Civil Rights movement (Ericson 1969).

In the one hundred years between emancipation and the signing of the Civil Rights Act of 1964, the United States became a world political power and the wealthiest nation on Earth, then or ever. During this period, particularly between the Civil War and 1900, millions of migrants arrived from Europe, thus greatly increasing the ethnic diversity of the nation. Typically, each wave of new migrants entered the social structure below the older, better-established European groups but above the Native and African American strata.

As the industrial-agricultural economy grew and the population expanded across the continent, the migrants and their children learned English and the ways of the majority. With education came upward social mobility, a Western form of Sanskritization (Singer 1968, 1972). Thus, the system proved to be inegalitarian, but just, for there was a measure of "equality of opportunity," among the Europeans in any case (Harrington 1963; Weinstein 1978b). Most groups did, in one or two generations, achieve considerable success compared to the conditions in Europe from which they had fled (Handlin 1953a, 1953b).

But the colonial era and the slave trade had left their mark. The new immigrant groups began at the bottom of the social hierarchies in the United States, but at least they had access to these hierarchies. In contrast were the Native Americans and African-background people, along with the Spanish-speaking ethnic subcultures from the Southwest, who did not enter the United States through the "normal" migration route either. They continued to occupy the lowest statuses, with little or no access to the mobility available to European migrants.

In effect, these ethnic groups occupied lower caste positions in a class system, shut off from opportunities by formal and informal, and legal and illegal, discriminatory practices in education, employment, banking, housing, and access to public facilities and services. As a result, even though the United States was a land of opportunity for most Europeans, it was a land of contradictions and unfulfilled promises for the "other Americans," as the sociologist Michael Harrington (1963) has called them.

In his influential study first published in 1944, Gunnar Myrdal (1944) summarized these contradictions as "An American Dilemma." On one hand, the Constitution, other founding documents, and the general experience of the European immigrants supported the American creed that all people are created equal. On the other hand, the experience of the non-European minorities, especially the 15 percent of the U.S. population of African heritage, proved the American reality that some people were viewed and treated as inferiors.

As is generally true of contradictions of this type, recognition is the first, although never sufficient, step to resolution. Myrdal's research and other social scientific findings and opinions inspired the unraveling of the system of legal discrimination, targeting first and foremost the educational institution that had been an effective means to mobility for the European groups. In 1954, the "American Dilemma" argument was applied in the landmark *Brown v. Board of Education* decision that desegregated schools (see chapter 1).[3] During the ensuing decade, a movement erupted that was to change the very meaning of ethnic diversity in the United States and in the world. A major source of inspiration for this movement was the words and deeds of Gandhi (King 1999). Thus, through the work of Martin Luther King Jr. and his associates, Gandhi continued to struggle against the colonial legacy of "racial" stratification years after his death. "King came to realize that Gandhi was the first person in history to re-invent the Christian ethic of love as 'a potent instrument for social and collective transformation.' It was a short journey thereafter to unreserved acceptance of the Gandhian technique of nonviolence as the only viable means to overcome the problems faced by his people" (D'Souza 2003).

Cultural Relativism and Cultural Change

Cultural responses to the challenges of ethnic diversity have varied over time and from place to place. Prior to the European Age of Exploration, even the greatest scholars did not have the means to appreciate how much people can differ in what they understand to be beautiful, good, or true. They believed there were only a few authentic value systems in human experience and that these could be easily ranked in a universal hierarchy.

As a result, investigations in aesthetics, ethics, and epistemology tended to focus on discovering what are the best, most basic, or most natural values in human experience. Often these were self-serving accounts, in which investigators "discovered" that the values of their own culture were superior. At other times, especially with increasing contact and cultural diversification, such accounts were critical of the status quo; prevailing standards were questioned in favor of those in "better" times and places.

The European colonial experience engendered a tremendous increase in intercultural contact. The diversity that was subsequently revealed made the traditional search to determine the best or right value system obsolete. The new approach, which had been foreshadowed in the writings of Machiavelli and Ibn Khaldun, was to assume that there might be no absolute values. In light of the discoveries during the colonial era, this idea entered into the formal study of social and cultural change in late-nineteenth century Europe. With the establishment of the modern social sciences at that time, it was incorporated as the doctrine now known as *cultural relativism* (Herskovits 1972): "the recognition that one culture cannot be arbitrarily judged by the standards of another" (Robertson 1987, 593).

Based on this scientific position, there are many equally valid aesthetic, ethical, and epistemological systems. This perspective is opposed to *ethnocentrism*, the belief that one set of standards is superior to another and that the values of a particular culture (usually one's own) are defined as central. For a cultural relativist, ethnocentrism can be understood and accepted as part of human experience. It was, under the conditions in which people have traditionally lived, an apparently effective and normal survival adaptation. But it is, nevertheless, a scientifically unfounded belief. The "superiority" of some value systems is often a reflection of the fact that might has made right—that is, one culture is viewed as better than another because its bearers are politically dominant and can enforce their values on those whom they rule.

So, for example, musical tastes, standards of appropriate interpersonal conduct, food preferences, and countless other items differ between the subcultures of African-background working-class Americans and European-background members of the middle class. There is, in brief, authentic cultural diversity between these groups, as there is between any groups that differ substantially in ethnicity, class, or both. But the subculture of the European-background middle class is also dominant, although it is now waning. And it has been viewed by some as "better" or "more advanced." For example, some people believe that classical symphonies are a "higher" art form than hip-hop or that Continental French cuisine is inherently superior to the indigenous cooking of rural southern Louisiana. To a cultural relativist, however, the idea that one is "better," "higher," and so on is a belief and not a fact: it can never be proved true (or false, for that matter). The dominance we observe is a fact, but it is a social fact based on the unequal and historically dominance-centered relationships among the groups (Donnelly 1984).

Since the 1940s, the "secret" of cultural relativism has, in many parts of the world, diffused from the specialized academic culture of social science to the general public. Books have been written, courses have been taught, new disciplines have been created, and local, national, and international agencies and private organizations have been formed to discuss and promote the ideals of cultural tolerance. Indeed, we may be so familiar with the movements for the acceptance and appreciation of cultural diversity and for the promotion of more peaceful intercultural communication that we lose sight of the fact that these are relatively recent phenomena. In the past, ethnic and socioeconomic diversity were either so rare that they did not require this kind of management or "explained" as the result of differences in the quality of the "races" involved.

The doctrine of cultural relativism has not been accepted by everyone, in part because people find it difficult to believe that their ways and the ways of their parents and grandparents are not the best (since they are best for them). Another reason for the resistance is that, to some people, the doctrine seems to suggest that any code of interpersonal conduct is as good as any other, as long as it is part of the living culture of a population or subpopulation. So, for instance, if slavery or genocide are viewed positively or encouraged by a large and dominant group, and even promoted by the official laws of a nation, they should be accepted as valid because they are a legitimate part of a people's value system (see Spiro 1986).

Both of these concerns are taken seriously by social scientists, and neither has an easy solution. What we can say is that, for the first time in human experience, a forum for working out such contradictions now exists, as a truly world-level society is being created. Indeed, in the several agencies of the United Nations, in nongovernmental human rights organizations such as Worldwatch and Amnesty International, and in some multinational corporations, such as General Motors and Mazda, such work goes on daily. In fact, since the end of World War II, people throughout the world have been busy in attempting to reconcile (1) the rights and realities of local cultural diversity with (2) the need to authorize some common values on which humanity as a whole takes an official stand, such as against slavery, genocide, and other abuses (Carey 1970; Green 1958; Human Rights Watch 1995).

The key to solving this dilemma lies in the fact that, although there may be no cultural absolutes, some universal *standards* do exist. Lodged deep in the heritage of every existing culture are values that resemble our Golden Rule (see chapter 2). As the philosopher Immanuel Kant put it, "I am never to act otherwise than so that I could also will that my maxim should become a universal law" (Kant 1961, 580).[4] All cultures promote such an attitude and encourage hospitality and the humane treatment of strangers. Everyone learns these values, but unfortunately they are often compromised by what are held to be higher priorities or more urgent needs (Freud 1961, 56).

As humanity becomes one, cultural relativism is likely to become increasingly institutionalized as a part of value systems throughout the world. This phenomenon is already occurring but not without considerable struggle and conflict. Even though the doctrine provides for the most humane approach yet discovered to help deal with cultural diversity, it is paradoxically also contrary to some of our most basic beliefs as they have evolved over the centuries and millennia. Until very recently, ethnocentrism has been a normal and effective response to survival threats, and it is not about to disappear without considerable conflict.

The Norm of Reciprocity

Some cultural norms are very deep seated and resistant to change even in the face of large-scale value and social transformations. Among these, one has received special attention from social scientists, in part because it, too, is a cultural universal. This is the *norm of reciprocity*, a concept first introduced into sociology by Alvin Gouldner (1960).

Reciprocity is an essential feature of all systems, natural and artificial. The word literally means "returning forward" and implies a process of action, then reaction. The term stresses the whole cycle that the two actions make up; we say that each is the "reciprocal" of the other. The close synonym *complement*, or that which completes, underscores this part-whole relationship. This also is similar to the mathematical definition of "reciprocal": that $1/x$ is the (multiplicative) reciprocal of x, and vice versa. Note that $1/x$ multiplied by x equals 1 (the whole), regardless of the value of x.

In human culture, reciprocity provides a crucial dynamic element to social relationships and larger systems. It is part of the most informal interpersonal encounters, it is assumed in social roles, it is implied in a culture's folkways, and it is written into its *mores*. It is based on the understanding that social life consists of episodes that are not whole, not complete, unless an action is answered with a reaction. Like other norms, reciprocity is learned through enculturation and in interactions. It is, however, a very general norm; one might even call it a "master principle" of social life, as it underlies a wide range of more specific norms.

Reciprocity and Justice   In its most general form, the norm of reciprocity prescribes that the actions of another person that affect oneself require a response. If one does not respond, or responds inappropriately, the episode is not completed and the norm is breached. Reciprocity is associated with justice in the realm of ethics. An act is understood to be just when it is the correct reciprocal response to a prior act, and unjust otherwise (Rawls 1971). Because every response may be viewed by the other as an action that requires further response, reciprocity has a self-sustaining quality: it helps to make relationships endure.

Gouldner argued that the moral norm of reciprocity constitutes an important "causal force" in social life. The reciprocity norm dictates that ego should not end up gaining at the expense of the other's beneficial acts toward him or her. In contrast to equity theory, which suggests that people will react equally negatively to under- and overbenefiting, the reciprocity norm suggests that people will, above all, attempt to avoid *overbenefiting* from their socially supportive interactions (Uehara 1995, 483).

Acts of reciprocity, like many other aspects of our social life, are highly ritualized, that is, we often reciprocate in unconscious and automatic ways that have become habit through repetition. English speakers all know that the appropriate response to "Thank you" is "You're welcome." They don't even think about it in ordinary circumstances. It just happens, and, when it does, both actors accept closure to the exchange. But consider what occurs when you thank another person (as a reciprocal act in response to their doing something for you) and they do not reciprocate. It is, at least, uncomfortable. Or suppose that the other deviates from the norm even more by responding, "Thanks is not enough." We would certainly suspect that something is wrong and that the exchange is not yet complete (or, ethically speaking, justice is not yet achieved).

The same principles apply to less ritualized types of reciprocity. These range from economic exchanges between a buyer and a seller to interinstitutional and intersocietal systems. At every level, social relationships are guided by the shared understanding that actions call for appropriate reactions, and that inappropriate reactions require management. In a simple economic exchange, for example, when something of value is transmitted from one actor to the other, both actors expect that another thing of value will be returned: another object, a service (labor time), money, credit, and so on. Lacking such reciprocity, or when there is a dispute over the relative value of the things exchanged (the price is considered unjust by one of the participants), the transaction is not considered whole (Uehara 1995).

In such a situation, the actors are faced with a set of choices, each of which reveals something about how reciprocity works. They may continue to interact cooperatively, seeking to resolve the contradiction between expectation and outcome. They may simply terminate the relationship, perhaps to find another potential buyer or seller. Or they may react in conflict, perhaps vowing to "get even" (that is, restore justice) in due course. In larger structures, the norm and its principles of operation occur in not only economic exchanges but also familial, political, moral, and religious contexts. In such cases, the norm applies to not only individuals but also groups and even entire organizations.

The ancient Babylonian code of "an eye for an eye, a tooth for a tooth," which was later incorporated into the major monotheistic religions of Judaism, Christianity, and Islam, is based on a simple equality principle of reciprocity. Similarly, the elaborate *Kanun* of the Northern Albanian people, known as "The Code of the Mountains," is a detailed and explicit account of each and every pair of reciprocal responses likely to be encountered in the lives of the largely agricultural people for whom it was developed (Fox 1990). "Kanun is a custom, the laws of which are meant to govern the slightest human action. The cornerstone of Kanun is the *Besa* or word of honour. Honour has an extreme importance in Albania."[5] The *Kanun* specifies the appropriate manner in which breaches are to be rectified: what actors or outside authorities should and should not do when acts are not reciprocated in the prescribed ways. Thus, sanctions are viewed as part of the reciprocity relationship (Tarifa 2008).

These ancient codes and canons are inadequate to encompass all contingencies of social life in complex, industrial societies. However, their underlying concepts, and particularly the assumption that exchanges must be completed for the sake of justice, remain operative even in more modern constitutions and normative systems (Moore 1979). The norm of reciprocity can contribute to both stability and change. When its application in specific social situations is understood and accepted by all actors concerned, it enables them to attain a very high degree of cooperation practically automatically. When actors are not in agreement about the appropriate way to respond, conflict and breakdown in a relationship or larger structure are distinct possibilities. If not managed effectively, breaches of reciprocity can lead to a cycle of cumulative instability, as actors seek to restore balance and redress what they understand to be injustices.

Destructive Entitlement Reciprocity in the sense of redressing grievances is a traditional source of social conflict, especially between ethnic groups. The psychiatrist Ivan Boszormenyi-Nagy (1993) has coined the succinct phrase *destructive entitlement* to describe the process. At various points in their lives, individuals and groups experience what they believe to be a failure of another to reciprocate appropriately. They may then choose to define the experience as an injustice that needs to be rectified. Because the values underlying the norm of reciprocity are so deeply felt, the actors believe themselves to be *entitled* to restore the balance, to make the episode whole (Jory, Anderson, and Greer 1997).

To the extent that actors believe they were harmed by the breach (in physical or other ways), restoring the balance (by the equality principle) means doing harm to the other (Ducommun-Nagy 2002; Kollock 1993). Thus, actors define themselves as entitled to undertake destructive acts that would otherwise be considered deviant. In this way, destructive entitlement justifies doing injury to another person or group. Such justification is required for two reasons. First, it is an assertion that the actor was wronged, contrary to the assertion of the other that the response was appropriate. Second, such acts contradict the universal standard of doing unto others as we would have them do unto us (*not* as we believe they have done). In such cases, reciprocity has taken precedence even over the Golden Rule in the individual's or group's value system.

When a group, such an ethnic subpopulation, shares the belief that its members are collectively entitled to harm members of another group, reciprocal conflict can take on a life of its own. The belief becomes part of a cultural heritage transmitted within generations and passed to future ones in close association with the strong norm of reciprocity. Thus, children may at a very early age internalize an emotionally charged understanding that they are justified in taking revenge against members of a specific ethnic group. This transmission and collective sharing increase the chances that destructive acts will take place. Such acts, in turn, promote the sense of destructive entitlement in the other group, and thus the chances for further, harmful reciprocity (see Astill and Chevallot 2003).

In pursuit of their own personal aims, political leaders and others who seek power (including religious officials) can benefit considerably by tapping into this belief and appealing to the feelings surrounding the norm of reciprocity. Recalling unrectified injuries done to "our" group by the "other" can make one a cultural hero, especially in the case of charismatic individuals. Identified by their constituents with a just cause, it is to the leader's and group's advantage to perpetuate such definitions of the situation. This occurs instead of seeking other resolutions: determining whether or not an unjust act actually did occur, taking a relativistic view and acknowledging the possibility of different interpretations, or simply forgiving (Kaplan 1993, chap. 1).

As human relations continue to expand and accelerate, destructive entitlement stands as a major obstacle to peace. International and intercultural understanding require a very high degree of cooperation because globalization can mean global domination by the few who do work together. Without such cooperation, potentially vast improvements in humanity's ability to survive and prosper will not be realized. In this post–Cold War world and with the powerful assistance of electronic information technology, a considerable amount of time and energy can be wasted in redressing old grievances through destructive means. Yet, for many religious and ethnic groups in our emerging global village, revenge based on destructive entitlement appears to be a higher priority than cooperation for the sake of mutual well-being.

The United Nations, private human rights organizations, and national governments are currently considering this dilemma (Drinan 1993; *UN Chronicle* 1993). Even at this early stage in the effort to resolve ethnic disputes at a world level, it is clear that the belief in destructive entitlement is deeply lodged in many cultures. It will demand attention and management for many years to come, for with every passing day, contact between people of different ethnic backgrounds increases through interpersonal, organizational, and electronic media. Thus new opportunities are created, not only for cooperation but also for injustices—real and imagined—that seem to demand rectification (Hargrave and Sells 1997).

International Stratification

Some of the most important social research since the 1960s has been conducted on inequality at a world level. This section outlines four major approaches in this field:

Box 10.3 THE RAVAGES OF DESTRUCTIVE ENTITLEMENT

The aftermath of the September 11, 2001, attack on the New York World Trade Center. As this aerial photograph, taken by the National Oceanic and Atmospheric Administration (NOAA), indicates, much of downtown Manhattan was destroyed by the planes crashing into the Twin Towers (center and center right). Approximately 3,500 people were killed and thousands injured. The perpetrators firmly believed that their destructive behavior was justified because of their suffering from the allegedly evil deeds of the United States and the West.

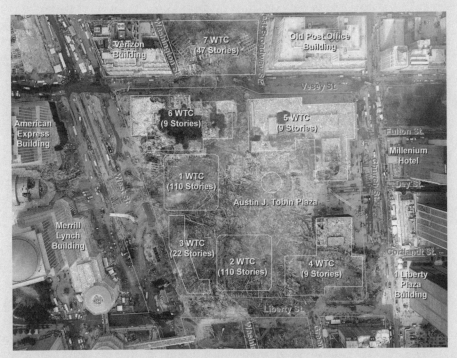

Source: NOAA, National Institute of Standards and Technology, September 23, 2001, http://wtc .nist.gov/. Image in the public domain.

(1) the quantitative measurement of socioeconomic development, (2) the three worlds perspective, (3) dependency theory, and (4) world system theory. Although there are differences in emphasis among the four, they all agree on one crucial point: the process of globalization has been and will continue to be deeply affected by vast inequalities among the world's peoples in wealth, political power, and other resources.

The study of international stratification began with the comparative research on human populations pioneered by Herbert Spencer (Turner 1993, chap. 3). The anthropologist George P. Murdock, in creating the Human Relations Area Files (HRAF), later expanded his efforts (Murdock 1940, 1967). More recently, work by the United Nations, nongovernmental organizations (NGOs) such as the World Bank, national government organizations, and several university and private researchers has greatly increased our stock of knowledge about the variety of human types.

Complexity and Development

The passage of time (thus, the opportunity for more variation to occur), revisions in evolutionary theory such as those discussed in chapter 2, and improvements in the technologies of research have revealed a far more diverse and complicated picture of international stratification than could have been imagined in the nineteenth century. Nevertheless, there are some very clear and interesting patterns in all of these observations, especially regarding structural differentiation, that support some of the earliest theories. First and foremost, among all existing national populations, there is a clear gradation in level of social complexity. This has been associated with several additional demographic, social, and cultural characteristics.[6]

For example, today the most highly differentiated, most complex societies are also the most industrialized, most urbanized, most secularized, most dominated by bureaucratic (and increasingly flexible) organizations, most dependent on tertiary relationships, and wealthiest; and, contrary to nineteenth-century expectations, they have the slowest growing populations.[7]

Since the early 1960s, considerable effort has been devoted to the quantitative measurement of these sociocultural differences. The object is to capture the strongest correlations, especially the close association between social complexity and industrial wealth, in a single index. The most comprehensive index of this type was created by the United Nations Research Institute for Social Development (UNRISD; 1972; see box 10.4). Also in wide use by development researchers is the World Bank "development diamond." This indicator combines information about education, health, wealth, and access to water resources (see www.worldbank.org/data/countrydata/countrydata.html).

The UNRISD index consists of industrialization and urbanization measures, along with more than eighty other demographic, social, and cultural variables. Table 10.1 lists fifty national populations along with information on literacy, infant mortality, income, and the corresponding UNRISD index score. The disparities between the industrialized and formerly colonized countries are obvious.[8] In numerous studies using this type of index, three specific variables have been found to be the most closely and positively correlated with overall score. These are infant survival rates (the reciprocal of infant mortality), per capita gross domestic product (GDP), and literacy rate. The disparities between the industrialized and formerly colonized countries are obvious from the information in the table. With this in mind, it would not be too far-fetched to say that the index measures the three things that Benjamin Franklin, for one, believed to be everyone's desired goals: health, wealth, and wisdom.[9]

Using more contemporary terms, the UNRISD concluded that a country's score on the index reflects its level of socioeconomic development. Countries with high scores (the more complex) are "developed," and those with low scores (the structurally simpler ones) are "underdeveloped."

Box 10.4 UNITED NATIONS RESEARCH INSTITUTE FOR SOCIAL DEVELOPMENT (UNRISD)

The United Nations Research Institute for Social Development (UNRISD) is an autonomous UN agency engaging in multidisciplinary research on the social dimensions of contemporary problems affecting development. Through its research, UNRISD stimulates dialogue and contributes to policy debates on key issues of social development within and outside the United Nations system.

UNRISD was created in 1963 as part of the first United Nations Development Decade. The decade emphasized a "new approach to development," in which "purely economic indicators of progress were seen to provide only limited insight and might conceal as much as they indicate." UNRISD thus became a pioneer in developing social indicators and broadened the development debate. Since then, the institute has sought to promote a holistic and multidisciplinary approach to social development by focusing on decision-making processes, often conflicting social forces, and the question of who wins and who loses as economies grow or contract and societies change.

Over the years, UNRISD research has been guided by two core values: that every human being has a right to a decent livelihood and that all people should be allowed to participate on equal terms in decisions that affect their lives. The challenge for research is to not only reinforce and help operationalize these values but also expose the extent to which they are ignored.

Source: www.unrisd.org/.

Despite the cautions of project director Donald McGranahan (1973), many researchers took this one step further, interpreting the index as a measure of evolutionary advance. In particular, they assumed the following:

1. A single development continuum exists, as represented as a curved line in figure 10.1.
2. National populations occupy different ("more" and "less") positions along it, as represented by their index score.
3. There is a natural process, or "track," along which populations normally progress over time from lower to higher levels.

To be more developed, according to these assumptions, means to be more like the United States, Japan, and Western Europe.

TABLE 10.1 Fifty Nations: UNRISD Index, World Type, and Development Variables

	Literacy rate	Infant mortality rate	Per capita gross national income	World type	UNRISD index
Norway	100	3.4	36390	First	100
United States	98	6.7	36110	First	97
Switzerland	100	4.4	31840	First	96
Denmark	99	4.4	30600	First	94
Austria	100	4.5	28910	First	94
Belgium	100	4.4	28130	First	93
Japan	100	3	27380	First	93
Canada	99	5.2	28930	First	93
Australia	100	4.7	27440	First	93
Sweden	100	2.8	25820	First	92
France	99	4.1	27040	First	92
United Kingdom	100	5.3	26580	First	92
Finland	99	3.2	26160	First	91
Greece	98.5	5.9	18770	First	84
Czech Republic	97	3.9	14920	Second	81
Hungary	99.5	7.3	13070	Second	80
Slovak Republic	99	7.6	12590	Second	79
Latvia	99.8	9	9190	Second	77
Chile	96	6.3	9420	Third	75
Argentina	96.8	16.8	12460	Third	75
Belarus	99.7	8	5500	Second	74
Bulgaria	99	12.3	7030	Second	74
Ukraine	99.7	10	4800	Second	73
Romania	100	16.7	6940	Second	73
Malaysia	91.4	11	8500	Third	70
Albania	92.1	11	4960	Second	68
Mexico	93.4	25	8800	Third	67
Georgia	99	24	2270	Second	66
Jordan	95.1	22	4180	Third	66
Vietnam	95.5	21	2300	Third	65
Colombia	91.7	26	6150	Third	64
Armenia	99.2	36	3230	Second	63
Saudi Arabia	83.1	25	9760	Third	61
Ecuador	93.3	30	3340	Third	61
China	91.6	32	4520	Third	60
Brazil	85.1	33	7450	Third	58
Jamaica	82.9	24	3680	Third	57
El Salvador	81.6	25	4790	Third	56
Iran	83.2	32	5630	Third	56
Indonesia	91.8	46	3070	Third	55
Egypt	66.6	36	3810	Third	42
Kenya	88.9	78	1010	Third	41
Ghana	80.3	64	2080	Third	41

	Literacy rate	Infant mortality rate	Per capita gross national income	World type	UNRISD index
India	68.4	64	2650	Third	34
Cambodia	79.8	95	1970	Third	30
Nigeria	72.4	100	800	Third	23
Bangladesh	52.3	66	1770	Third	22
Rwanda	73.6	107	1260	Third	22
Bhutan	34	61	797	Third	11
Mali	48.1	123	860	Third	1

Source: United Nations Research Institute for Social Development (UNRISD), *Contents and Measurement of Socioeconomic Development* (New York: Praeger, 1972); Population Research Bureau World Population Data Set 2008; World Bank Indicators, www.worldbank.org/data/wdi2003/tables/table1-6.pdf.

However, as Myrdal (1970) first pointed out, variations between dates cannot be inferred directly from the differences between index scores of countries at a particular date. Rather, as he put it, the economic and demographic changes that a country experiences over time are "qualitative":

> The usual view that difference in levels of development have only a "dimensional" not a qualitative character, and more specifically, that there is only a "time lag" between developed and underdeveloped countries—which, like much else in the post-war approach goes back to Marx—is mistaken. As these thoughts have developed in the so-called theory of the "stages of growth" they are based on metaphysical preconceptions of the teleological variety. (Myrdal 1970, 58)

Differences between countries on the UNRISD index are partly the outcome of interactions with other countries, not simply the progressive movement from point to point as suggested by the development continuum. Thus, no single-period quantitative measures, single variables, or even eighty-item indexes faithfully reproduce the actual sources of international stratification.

Such criticism by leading specialists in the field helped cast doubt on the practice of equating level of societal complexity with evolutionary development. On the other hand, neither evolutionists nor their critics can deny that a strong correlation does exist between complexity and the underlying property that the UNRISD index measures. The world of nations is surely divided, although it is unlikely it came to be that way through a progressive, "dimensional" process.

The "Three Worlds" Concept

Debate over the origins of this global stratification system continued through the early 1960s. At that time, an alternative to the developed/underdeveloped concept, with its suggestion of progressive evolution, was first adopted by social scientists in France,

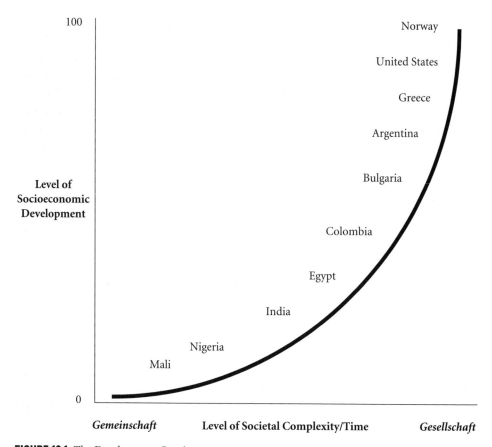

FIGURE 10.1 The Development Continuum

England, and the United States. This is the now-familiar three worlds classification (Horowitz 1966; Worsley 1964, 1980, 1984; see figure 20.1).

In table 10.1, each of the fifty countries in the sample is also identified by the world type category in which it is ordinarily placed. These categories correspond quite closely, although not perfectly, to UNRISD score. The fit is not exact because the three worlds classification is not directly based on the kinds of quantitative variables that make up indices such as the UNRISD. Rather, it refers to historical, geographical, and political (specifically Cold War–related) factors.

The First World consists of the highly industrialized countries that had democratic political systems and market-oriented economies for all or most of the twentieth century. They are located in Western Europe and North America (plus Australia and New Zealand). Japan, although it established democracy later, fits this category in all other respects.

The Second World consists of the former Communist nations of Central and Eastern Europe. These are largely industrialized, and they recently had autocratic governments and command economies. They and the First World nations, respectively, were the principal adversaries during the Cold War that lasted from 1945 to 1989, though the principal battles were fought in the Third World.

The Third World is, in this respect, a residual or "leftover" category: neither industrial capitalist nor industrial Communist as of the 1960s. It includes all of Latin America, by virtue of this region's lack of industrialization and less substantial experience with democracy. It also includes a large number of countries that did not exist as such until after World War II. These are the areas that were formerly under the colonial administrations of England and other European nations and were granted independence and recognition through UN auspices. In addition, the Asian republics of the former Soviet Union, such as Armenia, Uzbekistan, and Turkmenistan, are in most respects Third World nations. Finally, there is a group of countries that are older sovereignties or local empires, such as Egypt, Turkey, Iran, and China, that remained partly independent and were partly colonized during the age of European imperialism.

In grappling with this diversity within the Third World, social scientists sought a common denominator, something that would help explain why all of these countries, despite their diversity and geographical spread, are relatively less complex and have such low levels of infant survival, wealth, and literacy. In the years following independence, such a common denominator of sorts emerged spontaneously, as these nations, through their revolutionary intellectuals, declared themselves a group with common interests.

These interests were first officially articulated by Pandit Nehru, the first prime minister of newly independent India, and Marshal Tito (Josip Broz), who engineered the first breaking of ranks with the Soviet Union by a Central European autocracy. Under their leadership, seventy-seven of the Third World countries formed an alliance of the nonaligned (nonaligned with either the First or Second Worlds). At that point, Third World identity became a group for itself and a motivating force in social movements for

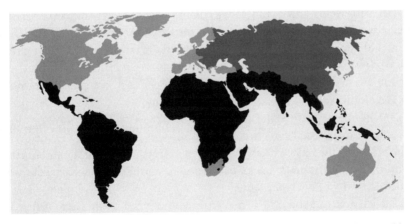

FIGURE 10.2 The Three Worlds of Development. Light shading indicates First World, medium shading indicates Second World, and dark shading indicates Third World. Photo credit: Roke, used under a Creative Commons Attribution ShareAlike 3.0 License; http://commons.wikimedia.org/wiki/File:Third_world_countries_map_world_2.PNG.

national independence and socioeconomic development on three continents. The labels *Third World* and *Group of Seventy-Seven* came to symbolize postcolonial liberation.

The new identity was not accepted unanimously or unequivocally. In some countries, such as Ghana and Kenya, it was embraced with enthusiasm; in others, such as South Korea and Taiwan, there was reluctance to take on the "Third Worlder" persona.

Yet, throughout the newly independent nations and the other less industrialized countries, there emerged the understanding that their billions of inhabitants somehow shared a collective fate and collective goals.

Dependency Theory

The coming to consciousness of the Third World nations directed social scientists to seek out the two factors that cause a group *in itself* to become a group *for itself*. As you will recall from chapter 5, these are (1) common conditions, particularly conditions of exploitation by a common source against which the group can identify, and (2) individuals authorized to define the situation, or a vanguard party.

Both factors were suggested in the words and deeds of Third World intellectuals who had been charismatic movement leaders: India's Gandhi, Ghana's Kwame Nkrumah, Kenya's Jomo Kenyatta, Chile's Salvador Allende, Algeria's Frantz Fanon (born in Martinique), China's Mao Zedong, and Cuba's Fidel Castro. The two factors can be summarized as follows:

1. The formative condition was colonial and neocolonial dependency. The Third World nations were alike because they were all subject to the economic and political will of the First and Second World superpowers. Their common conditions of poverty, poor health, and low levels of education were the product of these relations, not of evolutionary "backwardness."
2. The vanguard was these people, themselves, and their charismatic parties. Kenyatta and the rest were granted authority to define postcolonial reality in these neocolonial terms. They would continue to lead the independence movement, beyond the formal political level to economic and cultural liberation as well.

Among the first to introduce the concept of dependency into social scientific circles were the economists Raúl Prebisch (1964) and Andre G. Frank (1967). With their studies, dependency theory turned the anticolonial ideologies of Third World revolutionary intellectuals into a revised classification system. This consisted of (1) the dependent (Third World), (2) the independent, imperialist powers (First World), and (3) the (Second World) Communist nations of Central and Eastern Europe, which were perceived as neither dependent nor imperialist.[10]

Social scientists of the mid-nineteenth century, the golden age of the colonial empires, attributed observed differences in social complexity, wealth, and military prowess to "race." In a meaningful shift of perspective, social scientists of the mid-twentieth century, the era that saw the end of the empires, came to attribute these differences (and their correlates) to the colonial system itself (Surin 1998).

Dependency Theory developed in the late 1950s under the guidance of the Director of the United Nations Economic Commission for Latin America, Raúl Prebisch. Prebisch and his colleagues were troubled by the fact that economic growth in the advanced industrialized countries did not necessarily lead to growth in the poorer countries. Indeed, their studies suggested that economic activity in the richer countries often led to serious economic problems in the poorer countries. . . . At this point dependency theory was viewed as a possible way of explaining the persistent poverty of the poorer countries. (Ferraro 1996)

The Modern World System

The dependency theories of the 1960s gave way to the world system approach of the 1970s, largely though the work of the historians Fernand Braudel (1966, 1973) and Carlo Cipolla (1965), and the sociologist Immanuel Wallerstein (1966, 1974).

A new body of thought, called the world systems approach, argued that poverty was a direct consequence of the evolution of the international political economy into a fairly rigid division of labor which favored the rich and penalized the poor. . . . The debates among the liberal reformers (Prebisch), the Marxists (Andre Gunder Frank), and the world systems theorists (Wallerstein) was vigorous and intellectually quite challenging. There are still points of serious disagreements among the various strains of dependency theorists and it is a mistake to think that there is only one unified theory of dependency. Nonetheless, there are some core propositions which seem to underlie the analyses of most dependency theorists. (Ferraro 1996).

Their main contribution was deceptively modest, that is, they simply pointed out that the dependency relationships that had been established during the colonial era were mutual. Not only were the peoples of the Third World profoundly affected by the colonial experience, but England and the other colonial powers were significantly affected by their contacts abroad as well.

In fact, as these commentators argued, Europe's Industrial Revolution depended on the contacts and could not have occurred without such well-functioning colonial empires. In the process, an extensive structure of interdependencies was created that endures to this day (Evans, Rueschemeyer, and Stephens 1985; O'Hearn 1994).

This new system was based on the international division of labor. Raw materials and the human labor power to extract the wealth were exported from the colonized areas into Europe and the Americas. But the capital and management necessary to sustain the enterprise were supplied by the colonial powers. The exchanges were coordinated in European ports, such as Lisbon, Cadiz, Amsterdam, and London, and in the harbor towns created abroad by the Europeans at New Amsterdam, Bombay, Rio de Janeiro, and Cape Town. These cities became the "nodes," or switching points, in the system. They were, and remain, distinctively cosmopolitan and externally oriented ("heterogenetic"), and their foreign origins continue to be a major factor in Third World urban growth and industrialization (Bollen and Appold 1993). These are the premature metropolises discussed in chapter 9. Through these nodes, the framework for a world-level society was created.[11]

Global Inequality   The world system is thus a rudimentary global social structure, but it is not a society of equals, for its colonial origins have left an enduring mark. It is a stratified system in which the former imperial powers retain a central, *core* position. The former colonial areas form the *periphery*. And the areas that were neither entirely colonial nor entirely colonized (such as Turkey and Iran) occupy a middle position as the *semiperiphery*.[12] With the national boundaries of today, the core consists of the First and Second World countries, and the periphery and semiperiphery make up today's Third World.

This theory establishes a historical connection between a population's level of social complexity and its position on the international core-semiperiphery-periphery hierarchy. So, for example, the more prosperous core countries, which were the later participants in the colonial enterprise (e.g., England compared to Portugal), also have the most complex societies; conversely, the least prosperous peripheral countries (e.g., Somalia as opposed to India) have the simplest.

In fact, this correlation stands up regardless of which set of categories one employs. The UNRISD index, the three worlds classification, dependency theory, and the world system strata all reaffirm the close association between social complexity, on one hand, and prosperity and geopolitical characteristics on the other.

However, because of its emphasis on historical factors, world system theory does more than simply classify societies into categories, types, or quantitative index values. Rather, it offers the beginning of a deeper explanation of how present-day societies became more or less wealthy and industrialized (see Smith 2005; Wallerstein 2005). As noted in chapter 2, it is a modified evolutionary explanation because it assumes that, at the dawn of the colonial era, relatively isolated populations throughout the world had evolved a diverse set of societies at different levels of complexity. Since then, their evolutionary courses have been joined at a world level. Everywhere, the values and organizations that had traditionally sustained local systems were augmented by sociocultural traits entering through diffusion from Europe, and later from North America and Japan.

Thus, in addition to responding to local conditions, today's regional populations are also affected by changes occurring abroad. Port cities still serve as nodes for the essential interpersonal contacts and organizations that sustain the system, such as multinational corporations and UN agencies. But electronic media have now transcended these spatial nodes, so that direct social contact is possible from village to village (as it is in India's innovative satellite education program; Agrawal 1986; Kumar 1999). As a result, human events occurring anywhere on Earth now reverberate everywhere, authoritatively and instantaneously.

The Roots of Cultural Leveling   The principal result of this globalization process is that populations at the periphery, regardless of the stage of complexity they had reached by

1600 or so, now contain elements of the most complex societies, such as modern industries and large cities. Myrdal (1968) was one of the first to bring this "dual societies" thesis to the attention of researchers and policy makers. As he noted in his major study on *The Challenge of World Poverty* (1970), the colonial experience had certainly made Third World society complex in a new and unprecedented manner.

This became evident in the wake of Third World independence and nonaligned movements. When leaders began to affirm their new, native identity, previously latent competition between two different sets of norms and relationships became manifest. Two systems vied for legitimacy under the new regimes: one cosmopolitan (the core norms and relationships) and the other local (indigenous traditions and values—recall Fanon's telling phrase "black skins, white masks").

This phenomenon was further complicated by the fact that, in Asia and Africa especially, there was not just one local society. By virtue of administrative definitions of colonial territory, the political units that later became nations and provinces often included several populations that had previously been in limited contact. For example, prior to colonization, the Indian subcontinent was made up of hundreds of sovereign states speaking dozens of languages. In other cases, the new boundaries now artificially divided a previously unified population into parts. This occurred, for instance, in the 1947 partition of Palestine and in the former Belgian Congo.

Dualism (or even "multiplicity") continues to dominate Third World society. People in all walks of life are faced daily with choices between alternative styles (European versus traditional dress, and so on), dual school systems, two or more languages, and competing opportunity structures. As mentioned in earlier chapters, this ambiguity in the Third World is also a source of intra- and international ethnic conflict, in the Middle East, the Congo and Zaire, and especially during the 1990s in Somalia and Rwanda and in the early twenty-first century in Indonesia.

The world system has brought this new form of complexity to the industrialized nations as well. Beginning in the colonial era, but accelerating dramatically since World War II, elements of local societies and cultures from Asia, Africa, and Latin America have become part of life in Europe and North America. Some of these foreign ways have come from mediated sources such as books, TV programs, and imported goods. But most are the result of the massive migrations from the less to the more industrialized countries that have occurred since colonial days, especially in the past fifty years.

For millions of Third World migrants, the motivation has been largely economic. The industrialized countries have been able to absorb labor far more effectively than has been possible in the former colonies. For others, the main "pull" factor is refuge. Prior to independence, migration was forced through slavery and the other colonial labor practices discussed, but by the 1990s, much of it was also politically motivated, as Third World people sought the democratic rights and stability of the First World.

This periphery-to-core migration is the major source of the increasing sociocultural diversity that now exists in Europe and North America (whereas Japan's homogeneity reflects both the country's isolation from the European colonial network and present immigration policies). The movement's main legacy is this: just as a part of Europe remains deeply lodged in the populations, societies, and cultures of the old empires, there is now a substantial part of the old colonies in Europe (Castro 1999; Levine 1987).

These conditions have led to a new kind of sociocultural change, one that operates independently of whatever evolutionary processes may have occurred before the sixteenth century. It is true that something like dual societies and sociocultural diversity has always existed, whenever previously isolated peoples have come into prolonged contact with one another. But since the colonial era, these have become the rule: at the core, the semiperiphery, and the periphery.

Dualism and diversity are local reflections of a global system. Periphery-to-core migration has pushed population contact to a world scale, with people mixing freely (and reproducing) with others of very different backgrounds. This demographic change has, in turn, brought about an unprecedented shift in social scale: the creation of a functioning, partly self-conscious intersocietal system. I reiterate that this is not just a system of differences, diversities, and dualities. It also is a system of *unequals*: like all large-scale structures, the emerging world society is stratified—significantly and deeply so.

As social scientists look to the future, the gaps between core and peripheral nations in their respective levels of health, wealth, and education are evident. Most have wondered whether these gaps will ever be closed, whether they will remain as they are, or whether cumulative advantage will lead them to widen for some time to come. Part of the answer to this question lies in the fate of world capitalism, to which we turn in the following chapter.

Summary

Cultural diversity, international stratification, and the creation of the world system have emerged as the main forces that countervail the process of globalization. Because they underlie today's most dramatic episodes of intergroup conflict at home and abroad, including rounds of seemingly justified violence, they are common themes in media reports and social research. Indeed, it is difficult even to think about contemporary social relations without considering the effects of ethnic rivalry within countries or the politically charged North-South dimension now defining international affairs. For these reasons, a strong consensus exists among experts representing a wide range of disciplines and ideologies that the prospect of peaceful coexistence among humans may be as dim at the beginning of the third millennium as it was at the beginning of the second.

Although one cannot deny that these forces are prominent and formative in today's dynamic world, two points discussed in this chapter can provide some perspective as we look ahead. First, these forces, in their present forms, are themselves the products of globalization. Today's clashes between cultures, inequalities between the more developed and less developed countries, and exclusivist nationalist movements are possible only because demographic assimilation, cultural diffusion, and the creation of a world economy have set the stage. The resolution of these conflicts, where resolution is forthcoming, will thus represent a significant movement toward universal peace. Second, people have never been better prepared, morally and technologically, to manage such sources of conflict so effectively.

Armed with a vast inventory of technological solutions and a renewed ethical sensitivity in the wake of the Holocaust, the Third World liberation, the U.S. Civil Rights movement, and European anti-Communist movements, humanity can now attempt to repair misunderstandings and rectify injustices in a rational, mutually beneficial manner. The "truth and reconciliation" tribunals that originated in postapartheid South Africa under the leadership of Bishop Desmond Tutu and movement leader Nelson Mandela represent an extremely important step in this direction (Wilson 2001).

Social scientists teach cultural relativism because we are aware that ethnocentrism exists. But we also teach it because we believe (or at least hope) that, through our efforts, people will become more tolerant and understanding. As noted, this is fortunately no longer just our "secret."

With this in mind, our discussion of macrolevel change continues in chapter 11, with a close examination of the rise and development of the economic institution. Economic conditions and trends have been decisive in the globalization process, especially the conditions and trends that converged to create the modern world system, and they have also been the major source of the intergroup and international conflicts that characterize our divided world.

Relevant Websites

www.c-c-c.org/chineseculture/minority/minority.html
This site is on Chinese minority groups.

www.indians.org/welker/faithful.htm
Here is a compelling Native American account of genocide during colonization.

www.cultural-relativism.com/
As noted in the text, the doctrine of cultural relativism is the subject of criticism on moralistic grounds. Here is a Christian fundamentalist attack on the doctrine.

www.frosina.org/about/infobits.asp?id=198
www.csmonitor.com/1997/0807/080797.intl.intl.5.html
These two sites are about the *Kanun of Leke Dukajinit*, the so-called Albanian Code of the Mountains. The first is the complete *Kanun*, as provided by the leading U.S.-Albanian organization, the Frosina Foundation. The second is a discussion of *Kanun* from the *Christian Science Monitor*.

www.unrisd.org/
This is the home page of the United Nations Research Institute on Social Development (UNRISD). This is the UN affiliate that specializes in the measurement of development and its (more than eighty) components.

www.worldbank.org/data/countrydata/countrydata.html
The World Bank uses this link to explain its key measure of development, the "Development Diamond."

www.indianembassy.org/indusrel/India_US_treaties/satellite_september_18_1969.html
At this site, you will find the historic document establishing the India village satellite program with cooperation from NASA.

www.pbs.org/newshour/bb/asia/east_timor
This is the online version of the *PBS Newshour Special* on East Timor independence, May 20, 2002.

www.tv.cbc.ca/newsinreview/apr99/nunavut/indep.html
www.gov.nu.ca/
Here are two websites from Canada on the newly autonomous territory of Nunavut. The first is the Canadian Broadcasting Corporation site on Nunavut independence, April 1, 1999. The other is the official Nunavut government website.

www.wsu.edu/~dee/DIASPORA/REBEL.HTM
http://search.eb.com/blackhistory/micro/551/34.html
Two sites with information on slave rebellions in the United States.

http://epe.lac-bac.gc.ca/100/205/301/ic/cdc/underground/default.htm
The Canadian Underground Railroad story (posted by the government of Canada).

www.thestudentroom.co.uk/wiki/Revision:Development_versus_Dependency_theory
Here are online notes on dependency theory versus development theory.

www.doj.gov.za/trc
Here is a relevant site on how destructive entitlement might be countered. It is the official website of the South African Truth and Reconciliation Commission.

CHAPTER

11

The Market, Capitalism, and Socialism

E
VERY HUMAN population must devise ways of extracting food and other resources from its environment, transforming these into a useable form (as commodities), and distributing them among its members. These are referred to as economic functions, from the Greek word *oikos* meaning "household." As noted in chapter 2, it has the same root as the word *ecology*.

The Elements of Capitalist Economies

Although there have been many different types of economic systems throughout history, when we think of the economy today, we are almost certain to be thinking about capitalism. Capitalism, in the most general sense, is a type of economic system in which wealth is generated from the sale of the output from an industrial process and is reinvested in the process itself. Wealth used in this manner is capital, which is a constant and defining characteristic of all such economies. On the other hand, how capital is generated, what mechanism is used to sell the products, and who is entitled to reinvest are all variable features of the system. These have differed from place to place and have changed substantially over time.

During the mid-eighteenth century, the new economic system was institutionalized in an environment in which three major innovations occurred more or less simultaneously: markets, corporations, and private ownership.[1]

Observers did not originally distinguish between the three specific innovations and capitalism, as such. Instead, for many years, economists and participants in the economy understood them all to be necessary features of a single system. More than two hundred years of growth, experimentation, criticism, reform, and revolution have revealed that, although the innovations are closely related, each does operate today according to different principles. In fact, at times markets, corporations, and ownership are in conflict. Based on this experience and on the collapse of all of the world's major noncapitalist economies around 1990, they are now increasingly being viewed as separate elements, that is, they are seen as variables that can (and, some believe, should) be adjusted to make an economy function more effectively, according to local and, ultimately, world standards.

The Generation of Capital

Capital can be generated only if the costs of production are less than the revenue from sales. The system thus depends on the efficient use of resources (i.e., frugality pays). Karl Marx was one of the first to observe that this amounted to an imperative under which capitalists operate: workers must be paid less than the full value of what they produce. The difference, called *surplus value*, is used by capitalists to pay other costs of production, to support themselves, and to be reinvested as capital (Marx [1891] 1969). The greater the surplus, the more that is available for reinvestment.

During the years following the Industrial Revolution, the economies of England and other countries were generating a surplus of unprecedented size. In the hands of skillful capitalists (and with immeasurable assistance from the flow of wealth from the colonies via the modern world system), this stock of surplus was reinvested to an extent that it not only became very large but also went beyond anyone's wildest expectations for rate of growth.

This reinvestment was achieved by purchasing additional labor time and other inputs such as machinery and raw materials and putting them to work. The greater the productive output, the more revenues that can be generated, provided that the capitalist can sell the output at a profitable price. At this point, with the buying and selling of inputs and outputs, the market comes into play.

The Market

A market is a highly specialized type of social organization: a system of relationships governed by norms (some of which are informal). The nature of the rules of the market, along with the means by which they are created and amended, make the system distinctive in comparison to any other part of society (McMillan 2002).

Market relationships involve two basic statuses and their associated roles, the buyer and the seller. The relationship itself consists of an exchange of commodities, with each commodity having its own distinct market. A specific commodity is assigned a cultural value in relation to all others: one commodity is defined as having greater intrinsic worth than some, the same as others, and less than others. One key innovation of the emerging markets of eighteenth-century Europe was the definition of labor, specifically labor time (e.g., an hour of work), as a commodity (Marx [1865] 1969; Ricardo [1821] 1971; see also Dinerstein and Neary 2002).[2]

This added a dimension to the modern concept of the individual then emerging: as a free worker with the right to place labor time on the market for purchasers to use as they see fit. The purchasers of such labor time are the investors of wealth, that is, capitalists.

Markets range from perfect to highly imperfect (Robinson 1960, 1968). The ideal-typical perfect market is based on pure competition: each of an infinite number of sellers possesses an infinitesimally small portion of a commodity on the market, and each of an infinitely large number of buyers can purchase only an infinitesimally small portion of it. The ideal-typical imperfect market is a monopoly or monopsony (labor monopoly) in which there is only one buyer and one seller for the entire amount of particular commodity. All existing markets have lain somewhere between these two extremes, depending on time, place, and sociocultural conditions.

One of the great ideological debates of our time has centered on identifying the point between these abstract extremes that (1) accurately indicates the current situation in specific local or world markets and (2) is the best or optimal point, whether or not it is actually being achieved. Some defenders of capitalism in industrialized countries argue that markets are largely perfect and that this is the preferred state. In contrast, conservative critics on the political right and socialist critics on the left tend to concur that the actual markets for all or most important commodities are much closer to being monopolies and monopsonies. The critics differ in their preferences: conservatives argue for less regulation, and socialists argue for more.

The debate over market realities and ideals also involves the issue of autonomy. Markets exist in environments that include other markets, noneconomic institutions, and locational factors (depending on the extent of territory over which commodities are exchanged). Therefore, they can never operate in complete autonomy, wherein exchange takes place solely on the basis of supply, demand, and price, uninfluenced by other factors. The effect of other institutions is of special interest because these include the outcomes of conscious planning and decision making by people who are neither buyers nor sellers (this is the line of research pursued by 2009 Nobel Laureate in Economics Elinor Ostrom [1990]).

Again, there is an ideological split between defenders of contemporary capitalism and its right- and left-wing critics over how much autonomy markets (1) do have and (2) ought to have, especially in relation to government. Defenders and right-wing critics share the ideal of autonomous markets, and both believe that the government has too much control, although defenders tend to be accepting of some types of intervention. Most socialists believe that government exerts either the wrong kind of control or that it fails to control aspects of the market that it should.

From the point of view of social science, all of these positions are of considerable interest because they have functioned as ideologies in support of institutional change and utopias for social movements. What people believe about the reality and desirability of competitive markets, operating independently from political decisions and other noneconomic influences, determines the kinds of economic norms and policies, even the type of government, they are willing to support. When groups with competing ideologies on these matters interact, they are likely to come into conflict.

The findings of economic research reveal a far more complex reality than that depicted by any of the economic ideologies and utopias referred to here. Existing markets actually vary considerably in the degree to which they are competitive and autonomous, in keeping with cultural differences, political factors, and location (Freeman 1989). Many important commodities today are exchanged in oligopolistic markets

Box 11.1 DEREGULATION RECONSIDERED

As chairman of the U.S. Federal Reserve for eighteen years, from 1988 to 2006, Alan Greenspan had enormous power over world economic institutions. "Lawmakers doted on him as an economic sage. Markets jumped up or down depending on what he said. Politicians in both parties wanted the maestro on their side." Through the entire period, he was a strong and outspoken opponent of any type of government regulation and a staunch proponent of the self-adjusting nature of the capitalist system.

In the summer of 2008, a series of crises occurred in the U.S. financial industry. The especially deep troubles in mortgage banking and hedge funds (1) revealed that Greenspan's philosophy and policies contributed significantly to the problem and (2) world capitalism had entered the worst period of long-term recession since the Great Depression of the 1930s.

Critics, including many economists, now blame the former Fed chairman for the financial crisis that is tipping the economy into a potentially deep recession. Mr. Greenspan's critics say that he encouraged the bubble in housing prices by keeping interest rates too low for too long and that he failed to rein in the explosive growth of risky and often fraudulent mortgage lending.

Greenspan had been a dedicated disciple of the philosophy of objectivism. This creed, which novelist Ayn Rand[1] developed with Greenspan's assistance, strongly endorses self-interested behavior and the elimination of any government intrusion into economic activity. As the magnitude of the crisis became apparent, Greenspan admitted that these intensely antiregulatory views had led him astray. "Those of us who have looked to the self-interest of lending institutions to protect shareholders'

dominated by a few multinational corporations. Such markets are not, nor do they operate as, monopolies. However, they are subject to a far greater degree of control by small minorities than is possible in a more competitive type of market. Moreover, local markets are increasingly influenced by international conditions. Geographical isolation is becoming a relatively insignificant factor in determining supply, demand, and price. And everywhere, government controls, regulation, and taxation play a major role in markets, a role that has expanded substantially since the eighteenth century.

Corporate Power

The development of oligopolistic markets, increasingly influenced by external institutional and geographical conditions, has made it possible for a few individuals to occupy key positions in economic and noneconomic organizations. From these, they control the flow of vast amounts of resources (Mannheim 1950, chap. 1). The most important such positions today are in private corporations.

equity, myself included, are in a state of shocked disbelief," he told the House Committee on Oversight and Government Reform.

"You had the authority to prevent irresponsible lending practices that led to the subprime mortgage crisis. You were advised to do so by many others," said Representative Henry A. Waxman of California, chairman of the committee. "Do you feel that your ideology pushed you to make decisions that you wish you had not made?"

Mr. Greenspan conceded, "Yes, I've found a flaw. I don't know how significant or permanent it is. But I've been very distressed by that fact. . . . This modern risk-management paradigm held sway for decades," he said. "The whole intellectual edifice, however, collapsed in the summer of last year."

Mr. Waxman noted that the Fed chairman had been one of the nation's leading voices for deregulation, displaying past statements in which Mr. Greenspan had argued that government regulators were no better than markets at imposing discipline.

"Were you wrong?" Mr. Waxman asked. "Partially," the former Fed chairman reluctantly answered, before trying to parse his concession as thinly as possible.

Source: Edmund Andrews, "Greenspan Concedes Error on Regulation," *New York Times*, October 24, 2008, B1.

1. One of Rand's most famous devotees is Alan Greenspan, the former chairman of the Federal Reserve. . . . Mr. Greenspan met Rand when he was 25 and working as an economic forecaster. She was already renowned as the author of "The Fountainhead," a novel about an architect true to his principles. Mr. Greenspan had married a member of Rand's inner circle, known as the Collective, that met every Saturday night in her New York apartment. Rand did not pay much attention to Mr. Greenspan until he began praising drafts of "Atlas," which she read aloud to her disciples, according to Jeff Britting, the archivist of Ayn Rand's papers. He was attracted, Mr. Britting said, to "her moral defense of capitalism." (From Harriet Rubin, "Ayn Rand's Literature of Capitalism," *New York Times*, September 15, 2007, www.nytimes .com/2007/09/15/business/15atlas.html.)

Two aspects of corporate power are of special concern. The first is the origin and development of corporations as cultural artifacts, from the early laws that first allowed private individuals to incorporate as "firms" to the contemporary, massive multinational corporation (MNC; Heinberg 2002). Second are the shifts in the concentration of power within corporations, from the single, all-powerful factory owner to a micropolitical system in which a multitude of owners, directors, managers, and labor unions come to collective decisions.

Firms and Multinational Corporations

The corporation has turned out to be one of the most remarkable social technologies ever invented. It is based on the feudal practice of chartering, in which the Crown gave the right to a group of individuals to conduct business on its behalf.

In the United Kingdom a royal charter is a charter granted by the sovereign on the advice of the Privy Council, which creates or gives special status to an incorporated body. It is an exercise of the Royal Prerogative. At one time a royal charter was the only way in which an incorporated body could be formed, but other means such as the registration of a limited company are now available. Among the historic bodies formed by royal charter were the British East India Company and the American colonies (Heinberg 2002).

This became especially important around the turn of the eighteenth century, when Holland, England, and other European empires were establishing regular trade channels abroad. The first corporations were, thus, major trading companies, such as the British and Dutch East India Companies. The former was founded in 1600, by order of Elizabeth I; the latter was chartered in 1621 (see box 11.2).

When the monarchies lost power to parliaments or, as in France and the United States, were entirely overthrown, royal charters were replaced by articles of incorporation that granted the right to do business in the name of "the nation" or "the people."

In the United States and other countries, corporations are recognized as persons by law, in accord with the concept of group *persona* introduced in chapter 5 (Ranken 2004; Stites 2003). A decision rendered on May 10, 1886, by the Santa Clara, California, court, in the case *Santa Clara County v. Southern Pacific R. Co.*, set the precedent with this simple statement: "The defendant Corporations are persons within the intent of the clause in section 1 of the Fourteenth Amendment to the Constitution of the United States" (U.S. Supreme Court 1886).

This is, in essence, an extension of the legal fiction that the king can transmit his personal powers to others. As such, corporations have a social existence that is independent of the people who own or participate in them. They can borrow, loan, or

Box 11.2 THE FIRST CORPORATIONS

The corporation was invented early in the colonial era as a grant of privilege extended by the Crown to a group of investors, usually to finance a trade expedition. The corporation limited the liability of investors to the amount of their investment—a right not held by ordinary citizens. Corporate charters set out the specific rights and obligations of the individual corporation, including the amount to be paid to the Crown in return for the privilege granted.

Thus were born the East India Company, which led the British colonization of India, and Hudson's Bay Company, which accomplished the same purpose in Canada. Almost from the beginning, Britain deployed state military power to further corporate interests—a practice that has continued to the present. Also from the outset, corporations began pressuring government to expand corporate rights and to limit corporate responsibilities. The corporation was a legal invention—a socioeconomic mechanism for concentrating and deploying human and economic power. The purpose of the corporation was and is to generate profits for its investors. As an entity, it has no other purpose; it acknowledges no higher value.

Source: Richard Heinberg, "A History of Corporate Rule and Popular Protest," *Nexus Magazine* 9 (October–November 2002), www.nexusmagazine.com/articles/corporations.html; and http://batavia.rug.ac.be/.

spend money, they can incur debt, and they can realize profits and losses on their investments.

Because of this measure of independence, capitalists can minimize their personal risks by investing only part of their resources in a corporation. In exchange, investment is open to other owners, with whom benefits must also be shared. This is in contrast to the situation of the unincorporated capitalist, who must finance an enterprise directly with personal funds. The fact that a corporation has a persona also makes it possible for it to have a true life of its own. It can outlive any particular individual or group and can act in ways that differ from the intentions of any particular actors. A corporation can even take over control of markets without anybody necessarily planning it.

According to Adam Smith and other eighteenth-century commentators, most of the earliest companies to take advantage of incorporation were small family operations, although partnerships and single proprietor (unincorporated) business remained the norm for many years (Carney 1995; Jackson 1990). With this in mind, it appears that the earliest theories of capitalism focused on the activities of the *petit bourgeois* class: small shop owners, attorneys, financiers, and the like. In this model, there is not much of a difference in the scale of operation between a corporation and an individual or small group. They all behave as "firms," producing and consuming commodities to be distributed among one another.

Large corporations, the heirs of charters, were already doing business in Adam Smith's Europe. Some private financial organizations, such as Lloyds Ltd., were attracting thousands of investors by the end of the eighteenth century (Flower and Wynn-Jones 1987), and stock markets were established throughout the capitalist world at that time (Verdier 1999). As industrialization spread in England and beyond, the wealthy families who owned the factories took the formal step of incorporating (usually with public offerings of stock).

Each of these types of ventures expanded the limits of size and complexity of corporate individuals, far beyond the small firms that crowded the City of London in 1776. The international trading companies prospered as well, as their wealth fed the general economy and the corporate climate as a whole. This growth created another class of capitalists, the *grande bourgeoisie*, smaller in numbers of members but far wealthier and more powerful than the class of independent shop owners of the classic market model.

In a distinct stratum beneath the grande bourgeoisie, one finds the vast majority of corporations even today—local, small enterprises—and much business continues to be conducted by nonincorporated individuals and groups. In every capitalist country (especially the less industrialized ones), there exists an informal economy, which operates in relative independence of the corporate world (Ferman, Henry, and Hoyman 1987; Henry 1981). Here, unofficial and largely unrecorded exchanges of commodities, some of them illegal, take place daily, such as clothes, food, autos and auto parts, drugs, foreign currency (Wiegland 1994), and guns. Untaxed profits and unreported incomes are earned in these exchanges and in "fencing" stolen goods, unauthorized "moonlighting," fraudulent billing, and similar practices (Baker and Faulkner 1993). Some researchers have estimated the volume of the informal economy to be as high as one-tenth of a country's gross national product (GNP). In the United States, this would amount to approximately two trillion dollars annually. In these marginal sectors, and in a few specialized markets such as stocks and agricultural commodities, we still find the vestiges of the small-scale, entrepreneurial capitalism that existed in late-eighteenth-century London, Paris, and New York.[3]

Despite this diversity, in most important markets today, a few large corporations can readily dominate as buyers or sellers. For the past several years, this pattern has even been on the rise in stock and commodity exchanges, a situation that some observers view as a structural cause of the world economic crisis of 2008 (Gjelten 2009). These corporations do not behave like classic firms. Rather, their size creates distortions in prices. Market values and use values of commodities become unbalanced, with the difference typically favoring the larger actor. Moreover, when corporations can operate multinationally, they create further distortions (to their benefit) by seeking low prices for labor and other inputs in external markets, so that local supply and demand only partly determine local prices (Korten 2001). In these instances, the corporation has made it possible for capitalism to grow beyond its original limits, and beyond the point at which it was once believed to operate most effectively (Charkham 1994).

Nevertheless, because contemporary economies are so huge and include a complex combination of small and large corporations, unincorporated enterprises, and an active informal sector, even wealthy multinational companies must operate in a competitive environment. Even where there is little competition, the "Big Three" or "Leading Four" corporations in various industries play the roles of buyers and sellers, each against all. But this kind of competition is so remote from the conditions of the perfect market that it is possible for a small amount of collusion to lead to virtual total control ("cornering the market") of the production and distribution of automobiles, petroleum, steel, wheat, coal, and many other critical commodities.

Through licensing, trade and tariff laws, and various other mechanisms, national governments and multinational regulatory bodies (including several agencies of the United Nations, the General Agreement on Trade and Tariffs [GATT], and regional alliances such as North American Free Trade Agreement [NAFTA]) can and do affect the prices and availability of commodities. This exerts further limitations on how far corporate collusion and market control can be taken. Rather than restoring the conditions for free exchange, however, this regulatory activity merely adds to the amount of noneconomic influence to which markets are subject.

So, in addition to the distortions of a perfect market introduced by large (especially multinational) corporations, external authorities provide further incentives and disincentives that are bound to affect the decisions of buyers and sellers. Current capitalist markets everywhere are thus, to one degree or another, oligopolistic, open to foreign markets, and controlled by noneconomic norms and sanctions (see Derber 2000).

Capitalists and Corporate Directorships

The contrast between this situation and that envisioned by the early theorists of capitalism is striking. The new system was to free economic relations from political authority, in which no individual actor was to be allowed to have more than a minimal effect. Yet it evolved in such a way that some corporate actors are now able to exercise more control than was humanly possible when the system was established. (Here is another instance in which a revolutionary ideal becomes obsolete when the revolution is won.) The recognition of how much things have changed has led social scientists to consider the logical question: who controls the corporate actors?

Here, too, the situation is very different today from what it was during the early days of capitalism. Most of the original companies, as is true of most companies even today, were directly controlled by their owners. A person, family, or small group would invest their resources (and in small family businesses, this usually meant the owners' personal labor time) in a company that ran a store, ran a factory, or engaged in trade. They also made the important decisions concerning production and reinvestment. In this manner, the firm became the main organization within which contemporary microlevel planning was initiated.

This is an important part of the story of the transition to a planned society because, as more and more people participated in these simple business activities, the future was being determined in advance and with forethought, in unprecedented ways and at an unprecedented scale. It is also significant that, in a perfect market, macrolevel outcomes are of no concern to actors; the macrolevel is, or should be, outside of their control.

The outcome of all of the microlevel planning would result instead from the operation of the invisible hand, to the benefit of the general economy. It would also work to the advantage of the successful firms that could remain profitable under such conditions.

As some corporations grew to enormous, multinational proportions, personal and family resources, even of the super rich, proved inadequate to support necessary investments. Thus, public ownership became the only way for large companies to raise capital. By the end of the nineteenth century, even the most conservative capitalist families, such as the Carnegies, the Rockefellers, the Mellons, and the DuPonts in the United States (Myers 1936), were forced to make public offerings.

It is now virtually a universal practice for a corporation to distribute shares when it reaches a certain size. These ventures have benefited many companies and have allowed the system as a whole to prosper. But they have proved to be something of a Trojan horse from the point of view of the traditional owner-entrepreneurs. With the sale of stock, the power of ownership became diluted.

It became apparent to Marx during his later years that joint stock ownership was the wave of the future. He also recognized that it made capitalism a very different system from the image earlier depicted by him and his colleague Frederick Engels (himself a wealthy capitalist), that is, a group of companies dominated by patriarchs who owned, controlled, and operated their businesses with the single-minded goal of maximizing personal profits. With joint stock, Marx even envisioned the possibility of a peaceful transition to socialism, in which the working class would *purchase* capitalist enterprises. Although he did not anticipate the possible differences, even antagonism, that can develop between ownership and control (in fact, Marxist theory depends on the two being identical), his vision is in some ways being realized today.

An especially important innovation along these lines is the employee-owned corporation. There are several variations of this system, including cooperative ownership, profit-sharing trusts, and stock purchase plans. The most common type of employee-owned company is administered under an employee stock ownership plan (ESOP; Thompson 1929; see table 11.1). This has been instituted in several industries, including the once-bankrupt United Airlines, Publix and Hy-Vee supermarkets, the *Chicago Tribune*, and McLouth Steel Corporations (Kerwin 1987; Norman 1988). There are approximately ten thousand of these companies in the United States, all of which are owned by the workers: a seeming oxymoron in the classic Marxist vocabulary (McWhirter 1993). Although still a rare type of company, ESOPs reflect a more general, significant shift in the concept of ownership of capital. According to the national ESOP Association,

> An Employee Stock Ownership Plan (ESOP) is an employee benefit plan which makes the employees of a company owners of stock in that company. Several features make ESOPs unique as compared to other employee benefit plans. First, only an ESOP is required by law to invest primarily in the securities of the sponsoring employer. Second, an ESOP is unique among qualified employee benefit plans in its ability to borrow money. As a result, "leveraged ESOPs" may be used as a technique of corporate finance. (National Center for Employee Ownership [NCEO] 2009)

Through many cycles of organization and reorganization within large corporations, owners have largely settled on a system in which major decisions are made collectively, typically through an elected board. Owners are accorded influence in such decisions in proportion to the percentage of shares they hold, but few individuals have anything near majority ownership. Even in many conservative companies today, labor unions are also entitled to membership or representation on corporate boards.

This pattern of minority holdings and indirect representation has led to practices such as coalition formation, block voting, and other mechanisms intended to preserve the link between ownership and control, as the gap between the two gradually increases. Today, "institutional" owners also play a major role. These are funds, such as pension funds and mutuals, that buy and sell stock on behalf of many people. Through these arrangements, the actual owners, such as employees of a company that has a stock-based pension fund, remain two or three steps removed from the decision-making process.

Size and complexity also make it increasingly difficult for owners or directors to manage the routine operations of their companies (Davis, Diekmann, and Tinsley 1994). Thus, as corporations grow, it becomes necessary to hire professional managers who themselves have some independent influence on production, investment, and other critical matters—more or less influence depending on personal and organizational factors.

This group of professionals has become so large and so powerful that, in all of the industrialized countries, it now constitutes a new managerial class *in* itself or even, according to some commentators, *for* itself (Burnham 1941; Mills 1951, 1963). To this extent, it represents a third force in the competition for control over the corporations. These managers are likely to own stock (DeAngelo and DeAngelo 1985), but they have far greater access to information and procedures than do other owners (Ehrenreich and Ehrenreich 1977) . They must report to the board of directors, and thus to their coinvestors and bosses, but the board has only limited ability to monitor their day-to-day activities (Prechel 1994).

A recent series of reforms in the automobile industry, which have now spread to many other manufacturing and commercial enterprises, has served to dilute corporate

TABLE 11.1 The Thirty Largest U.S. Employee-Owned Companies

Company	City	State	Plan	Industry	Employees
Publix Super Markets	Lakeland	FL	ESOP, SP	supermarkets	142,000
Hy-Vee	W. Des Moines	IA	PS	supermarkets	55,000
CH2M Hill Inc.	Denver	CO	SP	engineering/construction	24,800
Golub Corporation	Schenectady	NY	PS	supermarkets	24,000
Lifetouch	Minneapolis	MN	ESOP	photography studios	20,000
Nypro	Clinton	MA	ESOP	plastics manufacturer	18,000
The Tribune Company	Chicago	IL	ESOP	media	16,000
Houchens Industries	Bowling Green	KY	ESOP	supermarkets & other services	16,000
Daymon Worldwide	Stamford	CT	ESOP	private label broker	15,000
WinCo Foods	Boise	ID	ESOP	supermarkets	12,200
Parsons	Pasadena	CA	ESOP	engineering/construction	11,500
Black & Veatch	Kansas City	MO	ESOP	engineering	9,600
Amsted Industries	Chicago	IL	ESOP	manufacturing	9,200
Graybar	St Louis	MO	SP	electrical wholesale	8,600
W.L. Gore & Associates	Newark	DE	ESOP	manufacturing	8,000
HDR, Inc.	Omaha	NE	ESOP	engineering/architecture	7,700
Davey Tree Expert	Kent	OH	ESOP	tree service	7,000
MWH Americas	Broomfield	CO	ESOP	engineering/consulting	6,100
Brookshire Brothers	Lufkin	TX	ESOP	supermarkets	6,100
Austin Industries	Dallas	TX	ESOP	construction	6,000
Coborns	St. Cloud	MN	ESOP	supermarkets	6,000
Schreiber Foods	Green Bay	WI	ESOP	cheese producer	5,100
Piggly Wiggly Carolina	Charleston	SC	ESOP	supermarkets	5,000
McCarthy Building	St. Louis	MO	ESOP	construction	4,800

(Continued)

TABLE 11.1 The Thirty Largest U.S. Employee-Owned Companies (Continued)

Company	City	State	Plan	Industry	Employees
Stanley	Arlington	VA	ESOP	systems integration	4,700
Tharaldson Lodging	Fargo	ND	ESOP	motel management	4,600
Herff Jones	Indianapolis	IN	ESOP	awards & gifts	4,000
Evergreen Healthcare Management	Vancouver	WA	ESOP	healthcare staffing	4,000
HNTB	Kansas City	MO	ESOP	architecture/engineering	3,800
Alion Science And Technology	McLean	VA	ESOP	technology services	3,400

ESOP: Employee Stock Ownership Plan
PS: Profit Sharing Trust
SP: Stock Purchase Plan

Source: National Center for Employee Ownership (NCEO), "The Employee Ownership 100: America's Largest Majority Employee-Owned Companies," May 2009, www.nceo.org/.

Box 11.3 MICHIGAN'S STATE LAW ENCOURAGING THE ESTABLISHMENT OF EMPLOYEE-OWNED CORPORATIONS

THE EMPLOYEE-OWNED CORPORATION ACT

Act 152 of 1985

AN ACT to prescribe the powers and duties of the department of labor and the department of commerce relative to the formation of employee-owned corporations.

The People of the State of Michigan enact:

450.733 Program to assist in developing employee-owned corporations; establishment; operation; duty of department.

Sec. 3. The department, in cooperation with the department of commerce, shall establish a program to assist in developing employee-owned corporations. The program may operate when an establishment is closing or transferring operations resulting in a loss of jobs and when a request for assistance is made by an affected individual or group of individuals. When such a request is made, it shall be held in confidence by the department. The program also shall operate when workers of an existing or new establishment wish to develop an employee-owned corporation and request assistance. The department shall inform local government, business organizations, labor organizations, and others in the state of the availability of this program and services authorized by this act.

Source: Courtesy of www.legislature.mi.gov/.

power further. These center on the inclusion of worker input in the management of the company's routine operations. The idea is the direct descendant of recommendations made in the Hawthorne Western Electric plant study (see chapter 5), and it is a well-founded one.

During the late 1960s, some companies, especially the major automakers of Germany and Japan, rediscovered that productivity could be improved if the gap was narrowed between formal (company) and informal (employee) work norms. This led to the creation of management teams that included line workers, especially in decisions regarding aspects of the operation with which they were intimately familiar. A U.S. statistician and businessman who was well acquainted with the industrial relations research that the Hawthorne study spawned, W. Edwards Deming, was especially influential in having the Japanese companies experiment with the "new" approach (Deming 1982, 1992).

Such phrases as *quality circles* (a group of people, manual laborers and administrators alike, who work in a particular area of production) and *humanization of industry* have been used to refer to these innovations. These suggest that, in the past, management was mistaken in assuming that workers (1) lacked the ability to participate effectively in the control of corporations and (2) were not already exercising considerable control, informally, by making up and obeying their own norms of productivity.

By including workers in the decision-making process, the company can institutionalize their norms, and the company's norms become legitimated by the workers ("representative bureaucracy," as Alvin Gouldner called it). As a result, it is argued, a better product is made—and made more efficiently—than under the old system. The Saturn Corporation, a former subsidiary of what was for decades the world's largest multinational company, General Motors, issued the following five-point "Memorandum of Agreement" in the late 1980s:

1. Recognition of stakes and equity of everyone in the organization being represented
2. Use of consensus decision-making processes
3. Placement of authority and decision making in the appropriate parts of the organization, with emphasis on work groups [quality circles]
4. Free flow of information
5. Clear definition of decision-making processes (Saturn Corporation 1990)

Critics of this type of reform have observed that much of the work of quality circles and management teams is oriented toward routine operations and that it does not really affect the important decisions still made by upper-level executives (Hodson et al. 1993). In fact, it is argued, there is a somewhat manipulative quality to these reforms. As corporate downsizing and technological innovations have diminished the size of the industrial labor force, workers are being exploited in new ways, to the point that they now identify with the company and make personal sacrifices for it (Moore 1996). But they still lack the power, wealth, and prestige of the managers and large shareholders who benefit most from quality circles. In brief, according to observers more skeptical than the late Deming, these reforms are hollow for they fail to rectify serious structural inequities in the capitalist system itself.

Although this view is worth considering, it is also important to see these reforms in perspective. They alone cannot drastically "humanize" capitalism. But we know that worker participation in management is just one of several trends now occurring (including the growth of ESOPs) in which the old, clear distinctions between worker, owner, and manager no longer hold. As a result of these new sources of complexity, a balance of powers among owners, directors, managers, and labor rules many corporations today. Each company has a distinctive orientation, some toward management control, others toward a strong board, and so on. These orientations change with time and with fluctuating economic conditions (Kanter 1983).

Permanent, absolute rule by an individual or family, therefore, is quite rare today, especially in the largest corporations. Nevertheless, some owners, directors, and managers have accumulated considerable power, have held on to it for years, and can even pass it on to their heirs. If the same few individuals who exert influence on the operation of major corporations can extend their power to government regulatory agencies, as critics of lobbying contend, then they will have achieved a historically unprecedented degree of control over human and other resources.

As the direct result of the system of exchanges created by European colonial empires, world capitalism today reaches far into the interiors of all of the continents. With the fall of Communism in Central and Eastern Europe, it has extended its influence, its organizations, and its norms even where it was once considered an illegal and immoral system. Capitalism has dramatically transformed economic and social relations wherever it has penetrated, and there is every reason to believe that it will continue to do so.

Yet, as capitalism reaches new geographical and cultural frontiers, it comes in contact with traditional economic practices, still-rural populations, and local norms. They, too, diffuse back to the core of the system, to corporate headquarters, where they must be accommodated and managed with highly imperfect knowledge and control. These, and other conditions related to the global expanse of capitalism, make it very difficult to carry out an effective conspiracy—difficult, but perhaps not unthinkable.

A far more common distortion in corporate practices, a sort of miniconspiracy, came to the attention of the public in 2000–2001 and, with even more disastrous consequences, in 2008: fraud at the highest executive levels, including the falsification of financial reports, insider trading, collusion, pyramid schemes, and more. To say "mini" is not to deny that billions of dollars are at stake, for the amounts of money and the numbers of victims involved are staggering. But this is not the kind of conspiracy of control that concerns some elite rule theorists. Rather, it is more or less the "natural" outcome of a system that places nearly irresistible temptation in the career path of people for whom greed and self-promotion are positive values and who are rewarded throughout their careers for the aggressive pursuit of personal advantage.

When these conditions are combined with a lack of accountability, as they often are in today's corporate world, the results can be disastrous for the employees, stockholders, and consumers who have come to depend upon big business and its alleged integrity. This is perhaps one reason outrage is often directed as much against regulators and auditing firms, who turned out to be coconspirators, as against the extremely highly paid executives with whom they were conspiring, as in the case of JPMorgan Chase and Goldman Sachs (listed as among the world's largest corporations in table 11.2). With the regulators serving the interests of the corporations they are supposed to regulate, we have a classic case of the fox guarding the henhouse (see Silone 1961).

One would be naive to believe that the kinds of fraudulent activities that were revealed in 2000 and 2008 are unprecedented or that they will never happen again. Regulatory agencies such as the U.S. Securities and Exchange Commission (SEC) and legislation such as the antitrust laws were established in response to similar corporate malpractice in the past. What is unprecedented about the current situation are the number of revelations, the rapidity with which they came, and—as is true of much else about capitalism today—the huge scale of the white-collar criminal activity.[4]

Tables 11.2 and 11.3 indicate this scope and the degree of oligopoly at which today's multinational corporations operate. The annual sales of each of the world's ten largest companies (2008 base year) average more than $100 billion, with Wal-Mart leading the

FIGURE 11.1 Reykjavik, the Capital of Iceland. The economy of this small nation (population approximately 250,000) was destroyed by the 2008 U.S. mortgage loan crisis because of the dependence of its banking system on international capitalism. Author photo.

group at just under $379 billion. Each of these exceeds by far the *total annual* national incomes of several large poorer countries such as Egypt and Bangladesh. In fact, the revenues of ExxonMobil and Wal-Mart exceed the national income of Vietnam by a factor of six and seven, respectively. Note, too, that five of the ten largest MNCs are in banking and finance and four are in the oil or automobile business. Similarly, the oil and automobile industries dominate the U.S. top ten, which also includes Wal-Mart, General Electric, AT&T, and Hewlett Packard.

Yet capitalism remains at root a system of economic competition. But it is obvious that the scale at which this competition now takes place could not have been anticipated a short two centuries ago. It is a competition

- within enterprises for access to positions of influence;
- between large and small enterprises;
- among large enterprises;
- between, as well as within, markets; and
- involving a seemingly unending stream of commodities, each competing for the trillions of consumer dollars spent each year.

As a multinational system, capitalism incorporates competing values and religious traditions, and it must manage competition between societies at various stages of technological development. There may still be an invisible hand that sorts out all this, but it has an enormous job to accomplish. Moreover, the "hand" must now negotiate around an ever-more effective campaign on the part of corporations and governments to seize control from it. The lack of autonomy that has come to characterize capitalism today has led many economists to conclude that the idea of "rational market" has become a "myth" (Fox 2009). It was once believed that "stock and bond markets are nearly perfect . . . and that prices on the exchanges instantly and accurately reflect the available information about publicly traded securities. After the market crash of 1987, Yale University

TABLE 11.2 The Twenty-five Largest Multinational Corporations

Rank	Company	Country	Industry	Sales	Profits	Assets
1	HSBC Holdings	UK	Banking	146.50	19.13	2,348.98
2	General Electric	US	Conglomerates	172.74	22.21	795.34
3	Bank of America	US	Banking	119.19	14.98	1,715.75
4	JPMorgan Chase	US	Banking	116.35	15.37	1,562.15
5	ExxonMobil	US	Oil & Gas Operations	358.60	40.61	242.08
6	Royal Dutch Shell	Netherlands	Oil & Gas Operations	355.78	31.33	266.22
7	BP	UK	Oil & Gas Operations	281.03	20.60	236.08
8	Toyota Motor	Japan	Consumer Durables	203.80	13.99	276.38
9	ING Group	Netherlands	Insurance	197.93	12.65	1,932.15
10	Berkshire Hathaway	US	Diversified Financials	118.25	13.21	273.16
11	Royal Bank of Scotland	UK	Banking	108.45	14.62	3,807.51
12	AT&T	US	Telecommunications	118.93	11.95	275.64
13	BNP Paribas	France	Banking	116.16	10.71	2,494.41
14	Allianz	Germany	Insurance	139.12	10.90	1,547.48
15	Total	France	Oil & Gas Operations	199.74	19.24	165.75
16	Wal-Mart Stores	US	Retailing	378.80	12.73	163.38
17	Chevron	US	Oil & Gas Operations	203.97	18.69	148.79
18	American Intl Group	US	Insurance	110.06	6.20	1,060.51
19	Gazprom	Russia	Oil & Gas Operations	81.76	23.30	201.72
20	AXA Group	France	Insurance	151.70	7.75	1,064.67
21	Banco Santander	Spain	Banking	72.26	10.02	1,332.72
22	ConocoPhillips	US	Oil & Gas Operations	171.50	11.89	177.76
23	Goldman Sachs Group	US	Diversified Financials	87.97	11.60	1,119.80
24	Citigroup	US	Banking	159.23	3.62	2,187.63
25	Barclays	UK	Banking	79.70	8.76	2,432.34

Note: All figures in $US billion.

Source: Forbes, "The Global 2000," April 2, 2008, www.forbes.com/lists/2008/18/biz_2000global08_The-Global-2000_Rank.html.

TABLE 11.3 The Twenty-five Largest U.S.-Based Multinational Corporations

Rank	Company	Revenues	Profits
1	Exxon Mobil	442,851.0	45,220.0
2	Wal-Mart Stores	405,607.0	13,400.0
3	Chevron	263,159.0	23,931.0
4	ConocoPhillips	230,764.0	*16,998.0*
5	General Electric	183,207.0	17,410.0
6	General Motors	148,979.0	*30,860.0*
7	Ford Motor	146,277.0	*14,672.0*
8	AT&T	124,028.0	12,867.0
9	Hewlett-Packard	118,364.0	8,329.0
10	Valero Energy	118,298.0	*1,131.0*
11	Bank of America Corp.	113,106.0	4,008.0
12	Citigroup	112,372.0	*27,684.0*
13	Berkshire Hathaway	107,786.0	4,994.0
14	IBM	103,630.0	12,334.0
15	McKesson	101,703.0	990.0
16	JPMorgan Chase	101,491.0	5,605.0
17	Verizon Communications	97,354.0	6,428.0
18	Cardinal Health	91,091.4	1,300.6
19	CVS Caremark	87,471.9	3,212.1
20	Procter & Gamble	83,503.0	12,075.0
21	UnitedHealth Group	81,186.0	2,977.0
22	Kroger	76,000.0	1,249.4
23	Marathon Oil	73,504.0	3,528.0
24	Costco Wholesale	72,483.0	1,282.7
25	Home Depot	71,288.0	2,260.0

Note: All figures in $US billion. Figures in *italics* indicate net loss.

Source: CNNMoney.com, "Fortune 1000," May 4, 2009, http://money.cnn.com/magazines/fortune/fortune500/2009/full_list/.

economist Robert Shiller called that belief 'the most remarkable error in the history of economic theory'" (Lowenstein 2009).

Capitalism in Transition

Capitalism has changed in many ways during the past two hundred years or so. In part, this is because there are, in fact, many different capital*isms*, each operating according to local norms and changing in response to local conditions. Taxation and labor laws, tariffs, and geographical factors vary considerably between capitalist societies. So, for example, the business climate in some places has become highly conducive to investment, as it is in the United States and Japan, whereas elsewhere markets have been getting less and less profitable (for example, in Scandinavian countries).

Over and above these local variations, however, capitalism is and always was an international system. As such, it has undergone several basic, general changes that are reflected in specific corporations wherever they operate.

In the first place, the degree to which the system is international has increased manifold. Since the early days of enterprises such as the British East India Company, corporations have steadily expanded their ability to coordinate production, investment, and growth on a worldwide basis. The system continues to operate according to the well-worn diffusion channels and international division of labor first established during the colonial era, but it now does so far more rapidly and efficiently. Raw material and human labor from the less developed, less industrialized peripheries (today's Third World) are extracted, transformed, marketed, and reinvested according to decisions made instantaneously at the highly industrialized core (Western Europe, North America, and, most recently, Japan).

These corporate decisions, however they are arrived at, can and often do affect the lives of many millions of people, and they do so in asymmetric ways. They can bring prosperity to some places, and they can drive some populations to the brink of extinction. This certainly is a major source of their power, of the unprecedented control that can be exercised from their positions of influence, and at a more general level of the new and remarkable ability that people now have to create social and cultural change with purpose.

Along with this dominant trend of international expansion, in markets and in the scope of corporate operations, several other changes have helped to shape contemporary capitalism. Some of these have been discussed in this section, and others will be considered in later chapters. The following list of ten items identifies those that have contributed most to creating today's highly planned societies and institutions (Hodgson, Itoh, and Yokokowa 2001; Kitschelt et al. 1999):

1. growth in the size and scale of corporations;
2. concentration of wealth in several industries into the hands of a few multinational corporations;
3. development of technologies of information creation, storage, and communication and the growing dependence of business on these;
4. rise to political power of capitalists and the middle class in general;
5. modifications of the system in the direction of socialism: labor unions, welfare, and public ownership of capital;
6. increases in the level of wealth generated and consequent changes in the quantity and types of social inequality in capitalist societies and throughout the world;
7. institutionalization of corporate (and government) research and development (R&D) programs: programmed innovation (as discussed in chapter 8);
8. dominant role of the United States and Japan and the declining status of European capitalism;

9. creation of international organizations to establish and monitor trade and commerce such as NAFTA, the GATT, and the United Nations Conference on Trade and Development (UNCTAD); and

10. the emergence of new, dynamic markets in southern and eastern Asia: Korea, Singapore, India, and Taiwan.

The now-familiar connection between expanding scale, diversification, and globalization is abundantly clear in these trends. The following section focuses specifically on the fifth item, the challenge of socialism. According to many social scientists, this factor has been as important in transforming capitalism as the development of MNCs (if not more so), altering it to the point at which Adam Smith would probably not know what to call the system.

The Socialist Alternative

Capitalism was institutionalized in eighteenth-century Europe as the outcome of gradual changes in economic conditions: the expansion of colonial rule, the accumulation of finance capital in European port cities, and increases in agricultural productivity. This combination of factors led to the revolutionary rise of the bourgeoisie, the class that most benefited from the changes. By 1776, when the theory of capitalism was first formalized, capitalist practices as such had existed for decades, first as a set of deviant (but increasingly successful) ideas and activities, then as the culturally approved mode of doing business. The theory was thus based on observations of an ongoing system: some extremely perceptive and insightful, others less so.

Socialism, on the other hand, began as an ideal long before there were institutions or classes that corresponded with its abstract principles, indeed, long before the word itself was coined. Speculation about socialism had been well developed, debated, revised, and differentiated into various schools of thought for centuries before it was actually put into practice.

Because of this heritage of speculative thinking, socialist economies are and always have been the product of premeditated planning (along with other causes, of course). They all require some measure of overt, conscious control of markets. Indeed, socialism is premised on the belief that planned social change is both possible and desirable. If economic relations are allowed to follow their "natural" course, socialists argue, negative unintended consequences will occur.

Socialism before Marx

Contemporary socialist thought is usually traced back to the work of Sir Thomas More, whose book *Utopia* was first published in 1519 (More [1519] 1961). This book "may have also been intended as a counterblast to Machiavelli's *The Prince*" (Hyams 1973, 8). It describes in great and still-interesting detail a fictitious society that happens to be perfect (by More's standards). The people refer to their island nation as *Utopia*, which is a play on the Greek words *topos* for "place" and *u* for "no" or *eu* for "good": it is no place, and it is perfect.

Ideal societies had been created by authors before More (since biblical times and probably much earlier), but they had always been placed *somewhere* (Turner 1973), that is, they were tales of a past Golden Age or a Garden of Eden. (It was widely believed before the modern era that things had progressively deteriorated from this perfect state.) When attempts were made to put these older ideals into practice through social reforms, as Plato did in Syracuse more than two thousand years ago, they were hailed as *restorations*. *Restoration* also has the same root as the word *revolution*: to come around again. In the approach established by More, however, the better world began to be viewed as something for which to strive in the future.

More's ideal society is characterized by justice and harmony among all groups and by peace with members of all other nations. Utopian culture emphasizes altruism, pacifism, and antimaterialism: "The inhabitants of the island despise gold" (Hyams 1973, 9). And there is no private property. Everything is held in common, as within a large, but close-knit, family.

During the turbulent mid-eighteenth century in England and France, several books appeared by writers who were influenced by More. These include Jean Meslier (Morehouse 1973), Thomas Spence, William Ogilvie, Robert Owen, and William Godwin. You will recall (from chapter 3) that Godwin was the object of Malthus's criticism and inspired Malthus to develop his principles of population. These works mark the beginning of an intellectual movement that continues to this day.

As products of their time, these authors associated the evils of contemporary society, disharmony, war, and injustice, with the emerging capitalist system. They sought to put their ideas into practice by establishing experimental communities, such as Owen did at New Lanark (Donnachie and Hewitt 1993; see also Clayes 1987; Smith 2002), or by promoting changes in cultural norms and social institutions.

Their works were a major source of inspiration for the invention and institutionalization of social science in France at the turn of the nineteenth century. Antoine Destutt de Tracy, Claude Helvetius, and especially Henri Saint-Simon and his disciples had considerable influence in and beyond academic circles in this movement (Durkheim [1895] 1962). They believed that science and technology had made it possible to create a society that would be reasonably close to More's ideal, which they were first to label "socialism."

There were differences in detail between the strategies proposed by the various people involved in the movement, including differences between Saint-Simon and his student Auguste Comte. But there was general agreement that socialism would be institutionalized through planned cultural change—that is, its principles would be taught to people so they could behave accordingly, and these principles would guide the making of rules and decisions in government, the economy, and all institutions.

In order to create—and the emphasis is on consciously and collaboratively creating—a socialist society, people would require a much more scientific and rationalistic outlook on their organizations, institutions, values, and norms. They would have to learn to see them as subject to human control and improvement, in contrast to the fatalistic orientation that was still widespread, though waning, during the days of Saint-Simon and Comte. The new science of *sociology*, which these writers were developing, would be the doctrine of knowledge to guide socialist planning:

> The French Revolution thus established a new view of social realities. History was no longer written in terms of dynastic empires, individual genius, or self-proclaimed spiritual leaders, but in terms of the flow and thrust of mass man. By conceiving of development as a secular process, historians like Michelet and, earlier, Condorcet, fashioned a theory of change that was simultaneously scientific and moral. (Horowitz 1972, 43)

Throughout the nineteenth century, attempts were made in France, England, the United States, and elsewhere to establish utopian communities, separated physically from the rest of society and governed according to the ideals of More, Saint-Simon, Owen, and the others. Indeed, a communitarian movement has been part of Western culture for some time, and it has experienced several revivals in the twentieth century (Etzioni 1995; Foster 1981; Kanter 1968, 1972). Today, the socialist community is an established, though minority, institution in the State of Israel. However, rather than seeking to create self-contained communities, the mainstream of socialist thought has tended to promote changing society at large: cities, industries, and all relevant organizations and institutions. This comes in part from the French movement's emphasis on general education and reform of society's laws, but even more so from Marx's emphasis on industrial relations.

Marxist Socialism

Marx (along with his associate Engels) is the defining personality in socialist thought after the middle of the nineteenth century. He was well acquainted with the works of More, Godwin, Owen, and the French sociologists. He was the first, however, to reflect on this tradition as it might apply to the cultural changes then occurring in Prussia (now eastern Germany), especially the philosophical movement that began with Immanuel Kant and was continued by Kant's student and Marx's teacher, G. W. F. Hegel. This merging of cultures helped to shape the socialist movement for the following century and beyond.

As a doctrine, Marxist socialism has three distinctive characteristics:

1. It takes More's observation that the ideal society does not have private property as a statement of cause and effect—that is, the elimination of private property becomes a necessary condition for the achievement of the ideal, which Marx called "communism" in reference to the ethic of sharing for the common good. This is quite different from Saint-Simon's belief (which was closer to what More meant) that people's attitude toward "gold" could be reeducated so that they would no longer see any benefit in private property.
2. Marxism therefore views socialism as an economic means to achieve a more general social transformation: socialism leads to communism. In this sense, *socialism* is

used to refer to one institution rather than to the society as a whole. It is an alternative to capitalism (whereas, for Saint-Simon, the term describes all institutions in concert).

3. Marx believed that socialism would replace capitalism when the latter had developed to such an advanced point that it was no longer a rational system and that this replacement would take place through a revolutionary social movement of workers and intellectuals (like himself). He directly compared this movement with that of the bourgeoisie when they overthrew feudalism and replaced its economic institution with capitalism.

In 1848, Marxism was adopted by the Communist Party in Paris, of which Marx was a founder, in a conscious attempt to turn socialist theory into political practice. Marx and the party sought out the newly forming labor movement in Europe, in the United States, and throughout the world as their natural allies. This alliance served to diffuse the ideals of Communism, along with the strategy of seizing the capitalist means of production, among people who were paying the price at home (along with the colonized people abroad) for industrial prosperity.

Working conditions during the early days of capitalism were miserable by any standards, as more and more people were being submitted to what Marx called "the discipline of the machine": long hours, subsistence wages, child labor, dangerous and often deadly work environments, and no concept of retirement or benefit packages. And, as Engels famously documented, the living conditions of the working class in industrial cities like Manchester (where his own father owned a factory) were appalling: "One penetrates into this chaos of small one-storied, one-roomed, hovels, in most of which there is no artificial floor; kitchen, living, and sleeping rooms all in one. . . . Everywhere before the doors refuse and offal" (Engels [1844] 2006).

"Perks" such as benefits or decent housing came as the result of the labor movement and, at least in part, because of the appeal and the threat of Marx's ideas. Marxism was embraced by labor to varying degrees in different countries and among the various groups and personalities associated with the general socialist movement (probably least in the United States among the major nations). Through these connections, it helped achieve many of the reforms that improved the quality of life and the social status of members of the working class throughout the capitalist world.

The Rise and Fall of Bolshevik Socialism

In November 1917, in the midst of general strikes and street demonstrations in Moscow and other major cities, the Communist Party, led by its secretary, V. I. Lenin (born Vladimir Ilyich Ulyanov), formed a successful opposition coalition in Russia's Duma. This coalition declared the first socialist, workers' government (Hyams 1973, 175–84; Skocpol 1979; Trotsky 1932). Because the party was able to gain a majority in critical votes against the ruling Social Democrats between 1905 and 1917, its coalition was referred to as the *Bolsheviks* from the Russian word *bolshoi*, meaning "the larger part," and the provisional government was termed the *Mensheviks*, or "the smaller part."

In winning control of the Russian government, the party declared its sovereignty over the vast territory that had made up the old Czarist Empire, including the European patrimonies of Ukraine, Byelorussia, and Georgia, along with the Asian regions that had been part of the Muslim world. Following two years of bloody civil war, these holdings were solidified into the new nation of the Soviet Union. It became the physically largest country the world has ever known, with more than 150 million people in over five million square miles. (Canada and the United States were the largest nations up to that point, and they are once more, with approximately 4.5 and 3.5 million square miles, respectively.)

The significance of the Bolshevik victory to economic history lay in the fact that, for the first time, socialist principles were actually *applied* to the operation of an existing system. With the Russian Revolution came the first opportunity to develop real socialist theory: not just ideas about how the economy ought to run but also a body of knowledge based on the observation of how such a system actually works (Nove 1982).

Socialism after the Fall The collapse of Communist rule in the Soviet Union and in the other countries of Central and Eastern Europe after 1989 represents another significant chapter in the history of socialism. But it would be premature to consider it the last chapter (Michnik 2009). Just as the Communist regimes began to crumble in Europe, China began a massive reform program (Byrd 1991). As a result, during the 1990s and much of the first decade of the twenty-first century, it experienced the highest economic growth rates in the world (BBC News 2009; Holman 1994; Munfson 1993).

Socialist parties and ideals continue to influence government, business, and labor organizations in post-Communist Europe, where they regained control of several national

FIGURE 11.2 Shanghai: China's largest city and the center of the country's economic explosion. The synthesis of a market-driven economic system and a Communist political system that defies both capitalist and socialist theory. Author photo.

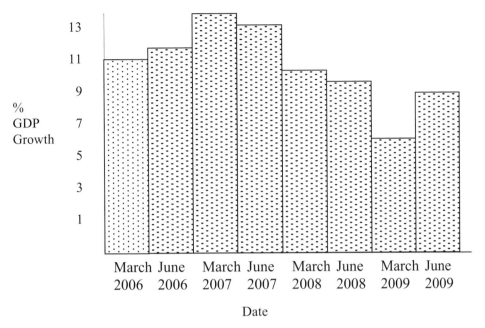

FIGURE 11.3 China's Economic Growth. Gross domestic product 2006–2009. *Source*: Trading Economics Global Economics Research, "China GDP Growth Rate," October 23, 2009, www.tradingeconomics.com/Economics/GDP-Growth.aspx?Symbol=CNY#.

parliaments in the 1993–1994 round of elections (Szelenyi 1994). Marxist-inspired labor parties are now in either the majority or the main opposition party in nearly every parliamentary government in the world. Even in the United States, socialist ideals and programs are routinely incorporated into the platforms of the Democratic Party.

In view of these remarkable changes, many social scientists have attempted to characterize the status of the theory of socialism today, after two centuries of experimentation, success, and failure. It would be difficult to locate a single statement that summarizes everything we have learned, but in the years immediately following the collapse, several researchers tried to put events into such perspective.[5] In the following section, some of the major findings of this work are reviewed.

The Elements of (Actual) Socialist Economies

We now understand socialism to be a system in which markets are intentionally modified and controlled in order to achieve what is claimed to be a more equitable distribution of resources. It is premised on the observation that capitalism, if left to its own accord, does not ensure just prices and the optimal use of labor, capital, and raw materials. Rather, it leads to oligopolistic and monopolistic markets dominated by huge corporations, and conspicuous consumption by those who can benefit from the distorted markets. It also involves the distribution of wealth to the working class and other members of society only to the extent that it does not detract from the enrichment of the bourgeoisie.

Yet, despite these several points of conscious opposition between the two systems, socialism has not turned out to be the very antithesis of capitalism, as, for example, capitalism was to feudalism. Instead, we now realize that it requires the same essential conditions:

- markets in which producers and consumers exchange commodities;
- capital that must be reinvested in production and carefully managed;
- rules governing who owns the capital and who is entitled to decide how it is to be invested; and
- a division of labor in which the labor time of some people (workers) is allocated by others (managers) in exchange for wages and benefits.

In this respect, socialism has proved to be a *modification* of capitalism, not an outright alternative to it. Indeed, some observers of the Soviet approach concluded that the party itself had taken on the role of the owning class in a system of "state capitalism" (James 1969).

The Fallacy of Economic Determinism   What, then, is the source of the substantial differences between the social structure, culture, and everyday life in the former Communist countries of Europe and their capitalist neighbors (or the United States)? As social scientists now understand it, the real antithesis is to be found between the two types of political systems within which the respective economies operated (Berger 1992; Miliband 1992). This is an important observation, especially in relation to Marxist theory, because it indicates that *politics can shape economics.*

As noted above, Marx interpreted More's correlation between the absence of private property and the ideal society as a cause-and-effect relationship. Based on this, he concluded that economic relations, especially the norms and practices governing who owns the means of production, determine other relations: the type of political system a society has is the effect of the type of economy it has.

This doctrine of economic determinism remained a key element of the ruling ideology of Communism, in which the belief was fostered that politics as a whole was just a temporary expedient that would "wither away" as socialism expanded. But the party leaders knew better than anyone else that their decisions were the driving force behind economic relations and that changes in the economy occurred when they were viewed as politically necessary. Political factors—that is, who did and did not have governmental authority—thus determined (although, of course, never perfectly so) economic ones, relatively unaffected even by market fluctuations, for, barring dramatic environmental changes, the party, in principle, controlled all supply and demand.

It is now clear that a socialist economy does not inevitably produce a better society and that (like capitalism) in practice there are many social*isms*. These vary principally in (1) the extent to which markets are controlled and (2) by what institutional mechanism they are controlled. The Marxist-Leninist model employs a political mechanism: the only legitimate political party, which rules ("temporarily") in what are defined as the interests of the working class.

But socialist markets can be controlled by other noneconomic organizations, such as the religious bodies in contemporary Islamic republics. There, market activity must conform to the principles of the Qu'ran, including crucial restrictions on debt financing. And, in one of the boldest ever socialist experiments, the Communist Party of China is currently opening its national markets to control by worldwide corporate interests and yet retaining a planned economy (McKinnon 1994).

Social Planning in Capitalist Countries During the economic depression of the 1930s, knowledge about and respect for central planning spread widely, as every country in Europe, and the United States under President Franklin D. Roosevelt, sought new means to reform their ineffective economies. As a result, legislation and programs were created to promote new techniques of centralized economic control. In this way, scientific management was adopted as routine government activity in capitalist societies. It was certainly not orthodox Stalinism, but it was also far different from a laissez-faire market system.

This emphasis on economic management allowed political authorities to set standards and quotas on production, to limit or encourage growth where deemed most appropriate, and to make labor time a highly protected and subsidized commodity. University research was directed to solving national economic and environmental problems, led by the agricultural experiment stations of the country's land grant universities (as discussed in chapter 6; see also Mills 1969). The Depression thus provided the context and the incentive for the creation of what people now think of as normal, big government.

When World War II came, the new economic powers of government in capitalist societies were quickly and effectively directed to creating and sustaining a war economy (Hooks 1993). In fascist and democratic countries alike, production priorities, prices, and wages were centrally manipulated to achieve the strategic military and diplomatic goals of the state, just as earlier experiments had manipulated these for the sake of economic reconstruction. Resources for the support of scientific and technological research were invested in military projects, of which the Manhattan Project that developed the atomic bomb was the largest and best remembered (Spiegel-Rosing and Price 1977, chap. 1). In the fascist countries, Germany in particular, the coordination (*Gleichschaltung*) was very complete. In the United States, in contrast, many markets remained essentially under corporate control, and informal markets for all manner of commodities developed during the war as a direct reflection of the fact that real supply and demand were not being served by the official system.

Centralized planning remained a part of capitalism after the war. Depression and wartime programs had strengthened the hold of government on markets, and they had increased the cultural acceptability, or at least the legitimacy, of government activities and laws that "interfered" with the "natural" processes of supply and demand. In adjusting their economies to postwar conditions or in reconstructing them in the case of the defeated fascist powers, governments in capitalist countries all retained some degree of central control over markets and some degree of permanent war readiness in major industries (such as aircraft and electronics).

In the United States, the end of the world war brought the immediate beginning of the Cold War against Stalin and the Soviet Union, so that the military-industrial complex remained largely outside of normal markets (Eisenhower 1961). Most of Roosevelt's more massive civilian programs were scaled down or eliminated during the Truman and Eisenhower administrations (the Tennessee Valley Authority [TVA] is an important exception; Selznick 1949), but the potential for big government intervention in all industries and the universities remains to the present (for a partly contrasting view, see Derber 2000).

Varieties of Socialism Socialist command economies were modified in several ways between 1930 and 1990. By 1948, centralized planning had become law in seven sovereign European nations, China, and elsewhere. This diversity made it evident there was no one correct way to plan an economy. The Soviet Union was obviously unique, and its planning principles would need to be adapted and changed to fit local conditions.

The result is that, between countries and over time, there was considerable variation in the amount of latitude allowed for free market forces. In particular, substantial differences existed among the Communist states in terms of which commodities and what proportion of them had their supply, demand, prices, and production determined not by the plan but rather outside of formal political channels.

Throughout Central and Eastern Europe, the command economy was under the control of the local party, which was ruled to varying degrees by party headquarters in Moscow. Party rule was officially unchallengeable, although dissident movements developed everywhere. Generally speaking, the countries with the closest ties between the local party and Moscow, such as East Germany, had the greatest monopolies of domestic power. In contrast, relations between Soviet officials and local leaders in Yugoslavia, Hungary, and Czechoslovakia were seriously strained where control from Moscow was seriously challenged; and these countries did experiment with more flexible and open systems.

This connection did not always hold. Conditions changed significantly in the USSR, especially after Stalin's death in 1953 and during the Khrushchev era, which began in 1956. Moreover, Albania took the exceptional position of opposing Moscow on the grounds that the latter was not closed and rigid *enough*. But overall, the more autocratic regimes (Stalin's and Stalinistic ones after his death) allowed the least latitude for free markets.

Oceania of George Orwell's *Nineteen Eighty-Four* ([1949] 1984) is an extreme version of this command-economy–total-autocracy connection, as everything essential in that society must be in accord with the plans of INGSOC. In reality, Albania probably came as close as any country ever has to realizing the INGSOC ideal, with East Germany a close second. The USSR, where centralized planning and party autocracy changed together over the course of sixty years, was clearly the most extensive system, and Hungary was, toward the end of the era, the most permissive in allowing independent markets to operate.

Capitalism and Socialism Today

In all contemporary capitalist societies, some form of socialism and some degree of centralized planning are now part of everyday economic life (Amenta 1993). As in the command economies prior to 1989, these variations are the result of how much external control is exerted on markets. The difference is that, in a Stalinist system, these variations are viewed as permissive norms within a restrictive environment that allow people to do things otherwise prohibited. In a more open system, they are viewed as restrictions within a permissive environment: they prohibit actors (corporate and individual) from doing what they otherwise would prefer (Sartori 1987, chap. 11).

All capitalist countries have welfare programs that redistribute resources in order to distort the real costs, supply, and demand of health care, housing, food, education, and possibly other services or commodities (Hicks and Misra 1993). It is important to remember that these everyday practices are the result of working-class, socialist (and often Marxist) ideals and movements outside of the Communist world.

At the same time, multinational corporations continue to expand in size, complexity, and "global reach" (Barnet and Muller 1974; Derber 2000). Nearly all of these are headquartered in the United States and a few other capitalist nations, where they operate in permissive environments, although (generally) within the laws and norms of the land. Thus, they represent the unrestrained side of contemporary economic institutions. With the help of electronic communications media and other techniques of minority control, corporations now have the ability to formulate plans (separately or in concert with other corporations) that rival the greatest achievements of the Stalinist era.

In times of depression, military war, or international economic war (as many have characterized the current competition between U.S. and Japanese multinationals for world markets), corporate planning is expressly coordinated with government goals and interests. In these circumstances, the power of big government can be directed to achieving corporate objectives.

In the United States, such a coalition has often been viewed as natural and normal, as summarized in Charles Wilson's often-quoted remark, "What is good for General Motors is good for the United States" (Wilson was the president of General Motors and U.S. secretary of defense during the Khrushchev era). When a corporate-government coalition can also draw on the results of the latest, prohibitively expensive scientific and technical research, it can far surpass any known variety of socialism in controlling markets—and at a truly global level—to achieve premeditated goals.

Summary

No purely capitalist or purely socialist economy exists anywhere in the world. Classic, laissez-faire markets are nearly impossible to maintain under conditions of population growth and increasing social complexity (that is, the conditions under which capitalism actually has developed). The pure command economy has been repudiated root and branch by the now-failed Soviet experiment, and market-oriented alternatives are being tested throughout the region (Amsden, Kochanowicz, and Taylor 1994; Winiecki 1993). Surviving it all, however, is a residue of collective control in the form of the big institutions, business, labor, and government that affects all economies throughout the world, regardless of their specific mix.

The chapters in the next and final section examine the capacity for unprecedented control that now exists in human affairs—and that almost certainly will be used. The problem that all societies now face is how to ensure it is used for the better.

Relevant Websites

www.kalama.com/~zimba/indrev.html
This site includes a short summary of the Industrial Revolution and references to numerous other sources.

www.absoluteastronomy.com/topics/Luddite
Here is the story of Luddism, the Luddites, and the mysterious Ned Lud. Of special interest is the connection between the spread of industrial "progress" and rebellion against industrialization and machines.

www.silk-road.com/toc/index.html
www.ess.uci.edu/~oliver/silk.html
These are two informative sites on the Silk Road and its role in history and geopolitics. The first is an online noncredit course on the Silk Road, and the second, posted by Oliver Wild, has many links and pictures.

www.esopassociation.org/
The U.S. National Association for Employee Stock Ownership Plans (ESOPs) maintains this page. It may surprise some readers that there are literally thousands of such companies in the United States and that the movement has experienced considerable growth in recent years.

http://entoen.nu/voc/en
This is the home page for the Dutch East India Company (yes, it still exists).

www.wikipedia.org/wiki/British_East_India_Company
Here you will find the history of the British East India Company.

http://aleph.mcgill.ca/F/?find_code=WHD&func=find-b&request=underground+
economy&local_base=catalogue
The McGill University Redpath Library provides this guide to resources on the underground economy.

http://reclaimdemocracy.org/pdf/primers/hidden_corporate_history.pdf
http://hbr.harvardbusiness.org/search/Corporate%2BGovernance/4294934738/HBRO?
Here are two sites on corporations. The first is a history that is critical of their growth and global reach. The other is a corporate governance search page on the online *Harvard Business Review*.

www.counterpunch.org/landau02142003.html
Here is a satirical but serious discussion of who's to blame for the corporate fraud of 2000 by Saul Landau, California Polytechnic Institute filmmaker and professor.

http://money.cnn.com/news/specials/enron
This is the online version of the *CNN News Special* on corporate fraud, posted May 20, 2003.

www.time.com/time/international/1995/950911/publishing.html
www.fas.harvard.edu/~hpcws/resources.htm
Here are two sources on the secret files of the Stalin Era in the USSR. The first is an article, "Fountain of Truth," posted by *Time* magazine. The second is the Harvard University online archives of the files.

Planned Change:
Making Tomorrow's Society

T HE PRECEDING three chapters featured several macrolevel trends: urban growth, intergroup and international conflict, and the seemingly irresistible expansion of economic institutions. For the past two centuries, these trends have contributed significantly to creating today's dynamic and puzzlingly complex social world. In the following three chapters that make up this final part, we turn to the future, to the plans and programs that will lead humanity into the next millennium and beyond.

The principles, theories, and case studies considered thus far all point to the unprecedented degree of control that people have managed to attain over natural forces and over their own behavior. The benefits are substantial and obvious. Governments, multinational corporations, and other large-scale bureaucratic organizations have accumulated enormous wealth. The middle-class majority in today's industrialized societies enjoys a standard of living that would have been the envy of royalty not long ago. Democratic government has been achieved, or looms on the near horizon, in most of the world's nations. Instantaneous communication between people in the most remote corners of the Earth is a daily reality. Age-old inequalities between women and men are being systematically eroded everywhere. Medical breakthroughs have prolonged life and reduced suffering far beyond the most utopian scenarios of the past. Schools now exist in regions where just a few decades ago illiteracy reigned. And we have crossed the frontiers of interplanetary space. For these and similar reasons, there is much to make one optimistic about the human prospect.

Nevertheless, ours is an anxious and dangerous world. As modern institutions have accumulated power, the average person has been increasingly relegated to the role of a cog in giant machine. With the decline in the importance of family and primary relationships, we find ourselves members of the "lonely crowd" (Riesman, Denny, and Glazer 1950) surrounded physically by others but morally and spiritually isolated from them. For every individual born into comfortable material circumstances in the cities and suburbs of the United States, Japan, and Western Europe today, two are born into a life of poverty and want in the rural areas of the Third World and in urban slums everywhere.

Thomas More's dream of a stateless, scarcity-free society has been largely abandoned with the collapse of Communist regimes that, in the end, proved incapable of providing their citizens with even the most basic human rights and material security. In their wake, new forms of autocracy have emerged, and old conflicts among nations, ethnic groups, and political ideologies have resurfaced in new, post–Cold War form. Terrorism, actual and alleged, appears to loom in every corner of the world. Even industrial progress, a once-uncontroversial goal of social planners and idealists alike, has produced apparently irreversible environmental degradation on a global scale. Is it any wonder that grave doubts have been expressed about not only the future prosperity of *Homo sapiens* but also its very survival? What is next?

Of course, there are no sure and certain answers to this question. But it is not because we are entirely ignorant about human relations on such a large scale, although in some ways we are just beginning to learn how to live together. Rather, we do not know what will happen next because, in principle, we cannot. The future of the world system is indeterminate (Stehr 2004).

Some trends are practically inevitable, such as increasing bureaucratization, more urban growth, and the globalization of economic and political relations. However, the social world of the future is to a significant extent being spontaneously planned and created along the way, right now. Even the powerful momentum toward greater scale and complexity that these trends represent can be mitigated and redirected. This, at least, is the message of movements for more responsive democratically controlled bureaucracy, deindustrialization (Hill and Indegaard 1988), rediscovery of the countryside, and thinking small. This means that, in principle, the future is up to you, and me, and our fellow inhabitants of Spaceship Earth.

Therefore, instead of asking, "What next?" a more pertinent question is "What can *I* do about it?" In providing at least a partial answer to this question, these final chapters explore the process of planned social change once again. The focus, here, is the ordinary individuals' prospects of participating meaningfully, as citizens, clients, and consumers, in the decisions that will affect their and their children's futures.

I conclude on a cautiously optimistic note, for I believe that the social scientific perspective has given us a very useful set of tools for delving into "human nature and social circumstance" (as Adam Smith phrased it). Usually, we can do more, much more, about controlling our lives and futures than we have been led to believe. In *this* age of democratic revolution, it is our right and duty to take an active role in the planning of tomorrow's society. This is an empowering insight, and I hope that these concluding chapters convey it effectively.

CHAPTER

12

The Paradoxes of Development

THIS AND the following chapter look at two major contemporary undertakings that are bound to affect the future of human society: (1) Third World socioeconomic development programs and (2) the professions of planning and applied sociology. These are large-scale projects that consciously seek to incorporate rational coordination and technological innovations into the process of sociocultural change, based on neither Bolshevist nor fascist models but rather democratic means. In the first case, the aim is specifically to raise living standards of large, poor rural masses in the less industrialized parts of the world. In the second, the goal is to maximize the involvement of citizens everywhere in the political processes through which conscious social planning is pursued in modern society, from the grass roots of community organizing to the national level of party and interest group politics.

The Development Project

Socioeconomic development is the partly official post–World War II reconstruction project financed and directed by several donor organizations: the U.S. Agency for International Development (USAID), similar governmental agencies in other First World countries, the United Nations Development Programme (UNDP), and numerous private foundations, led by the Ford Foundation (Berman 1983). The project emerged from the highly successful Marshall Plan (see box 12.1), originally targeted at the economies of war-torn Western Europe (Gimbel 1976; Hogan 1987). In the Soviet Union, the government also promoted an alternative development model, first in the reconstruction of East Germany and other Warsaw Pact allies, then, beginning in the

Box 12.1 USAID'S HISTORY AND MISSION

From the USAID website:

This Is USAID

The United States has a long history of extending a helping hand to those people over-seas struggling to make a better life, recover from a disaster or striving to live in a free and democratic country. It is this caring that stands as a hallmark of the United States around the world—and shows the world our true character as a nation. U.S. foreign assistance has always had the twofold purpose of furthering America's foreign policy interests in expanding democracy and free markets while improving the lives of the citizens of the developing world. Spending less than one-half of 1 percent of the fed-eral budget, USAID works around the world to achieve these goals. USAID's history goes back to the Marshall Plan reconstruction of Europe after World War Two and the Truman Administration's Point Four Program. In 1961, the Foreign Assistance Act was signed into law and USAID was created by executive order. Since that time, USAID has been the principal U.S. agency to extend assistance to countries recovering from disaster, trying to escape poverty, and engaging in democratic reforms. USAID is an independent federal government agency that receives overall foreign policy guid-ance from the Secretary of State. Our work supports long-term and equitable eco-nomic growth and advances U.S. foreign policy objectives by supporting:

economic growth, agriculture and trade;
global health; and,
democracy, conflict prevention and humanitarian assistance.

We provide assistance in five regions of the world:

Sub-Saharan Africa;
Asia;
Latin America and the Caribbean;
Europe and Eurasia; and
The Middle East.

With headquarters in Washington, D.C., USAID's strength is its field offices around the world. We work in close partnership with private voluntary orga-nizations, indigenous organizations, universities, American businesses, Interna-tional agencies, other governments, and other U.S. government agencies. USAID has working relationships with more than 3,500 American companies and over 300 U.S.-based private voluntary organizations. For more information on our business and procurement opportunities, please visit our Business section. If you would like to know more about employment opportunities with USAID, please visit our Careers section of our web site.

Source: www.usaid.gov/about_usaid.

Khrushchev era, in cooperation with Third World Communist and socialist regimes. By whatever means it is now to be achieved, with the Cold War factor all but eliminated from the picture and the capabilities of USAID greatly curtailed, development remains the highest priority goal in the Third World today.

Ideals and Realities

I emphasize the project's political, organization-driven character, but development also has a less formal side that stems back to its origins in revolutionary eighteenth-century Europe. Then, for the first time ever, conscious efforts were undertaken to raise the standard of living for not just the privileged few but also the common person. This was what the Industrial Revolution promised, and, to a greater extent than could have been imagined before, the promise was realized. Prosperity became possible where survival had been imperative. And, as we saw in chapter 10, it all came down to some fairly straightforward changes. Development in the unofficial sense meant, and still means, improvement in the health, wealth, and wisdom of everyone.

> What people want and need is enough food to eat and water to drink. A roof over their heads, a job, a school for their children, and medicine and care when they are sick; the chance to live in peace without fear of violence or war; and the opportunity to realize the potential in each and every one of us. That is what development at its best has always been about. (Benn 2006, iii)

These are the development ideals that are now sweeping the Third World: elites, middle classes, and masses alike. They have been so attractive because they refer to universally desirable ends. Every culture welcomes improvements in health, for example, especially when the first concrete evidence comes in the form of offspring who for the first time can be reasonably expected to live beyond their first year.[1]

Since the 1960s, these ideals of development have often come into conflict with its organizational realities. This is most readily observed in the frequent clashes that have occurred between the official programs of international development bureaucracies such as USAID and the development movement. This is the movement led by groups such as the International Labor Organization (ILO), United Nations Children's Fund (UNICEF), Oxford Committee for Famine Relief (OXFAM), Society for International Development, and many individual dissidents within the system. At issue are the goals, strategies, and tactics of the official agencies.

Much research in the field has focused on this conflict, in part because it also relates closely to Cold War politics and dependency theory (Lewis and Kallab 1986; Morss and Morss 1986). The most basic issue has been whether or not development, as USAID defines it or as realized in a specific Ford-Rockefeller–sponsored family-planning program, is authentic (Krauss 1983): Do official programs actually raise the standard of living of all? Or do they merely help some groups at the expense of others because Cold War priorities or similar political considerations are defined as more urgent? Have technological failures and higher-order impacts actually worsened the plight of the average Third Worlder (Firebaugh and Beck 1994)?

These questions have led to some significant reforms in "the development game" over the years. The 1970s were an especially active period, when, in response to pressures from ILO and others, USAID began to promote appropriate technology. Reform is in the air today as well, as tying development aid to a global struggle against Communism no longer makes sense, even within the U.S. Department of State, where USAID resides.

The post–World War II era has seen the institutionalization of development, as trillions of dollars have been spent in the Third World by the U.S. government and others to improve agricultural productivity, promote industrialization, expand educational systems, and control population growth. At the same time, thousands of articles and books have been written, and countless hours have been spent in debate and discussion in college classrooms, congressional and UN hearings, and the media, evaluating the work and assessing its impact. The results have been mixed.

It is clear that many dramatic successes have been achieved, as evidenced by the elimination of smallpox and other public health breakthroughs, most of them eventuating in rapid declines in infant mortality (a key variable in the United Nations Research Institute for Social Development [UNRISD] development index introduced in chapter

FIGURE 12.1 Small Plot in China. For decades, official development programs have favored direct transfers to government agencies abroad and have encouraged large-scale industrialization. From the point of view of the family that works this small plot in China, this strategy seriously fails to address their day-to-day needs. Author photo.

10). Primary education, a special program of the U.S. Peace Corps volunteers, is now available for the first time in tens of thousands of villages, with literacy rates in South Asia and parts of Africa having increased by a factor of four or five since the 1950s.

Many Third World people are materially much better off than their parents because of development aid, from the farmers of Punjab who benefited from the Green Revolution to the growing South Korean middle classes who have seen their country rapidly industrialized under USAID guidance. Substantial improvements in the health, wealth, and wisdom of millions can be justly credited to official development efforts.

Nevertheless, few, if any, institutionalized programs escaped the scrutiny of critics during the Cold War era. These include influential movement leaders and intellectuals such as ILO's Hans Singer (1977) and professors Kusum Nair (1969), Mahmood Mamdani (1972), and Andre G. Frank (1967, 1969). These and more recent observers have taken pains to underscore the clear record established by both First World and Second World aid donors of giving only to their friends, often in open conflict situations, in order to gain advantage over their enemies (Cassidy and Bischak 1995; Payne 1995).

During the entire period, Israel, South Korea, Turkey, and Taiwan received a lion's share of U.S. development assistance, obviously in large measure because of their strategic locations. Why, we might ask, is North Korea so underdeveloped compared to its neighbor to the south? Are they not one population, society, and culture? The answer, in part, is that since the 1950s, the most effective aid donor and the government of North Korea have viewed each other as implacable enemies. Is this, critics asked, a legitimate reason to deprive the North Korean people of an equal chance at improving their living standards? The answer, according to Cold War logic, was, unfortunately, "Yes."

Institutionalized development has also been criticized because of the many negative impacts associated with its programs (Hammond and McGowan 1993). Some of these "disappointments" undoubtedly have been exaggerated because of the ideological stakes involved (Goulet 1989). From a Communist point of view, the failure of a USAID program was tantamount to a failure of the capitalist system itself. From the perspective of the U.S. Department of State, success in one was proof of success in the other.

Ideology aside, there have been some real and very serious shortcomings in both First World and Second World attempts to improve the lot of the masses of the Third World—serious, in the first place, because these people make up a large and rapidly growing majority of humankind. The confrontation between development ideals and realities in this post–Cold War era has brought into bold relief more basic, practical issues such as where the food to feed us all will come from.

> Since their creation at the Bretton Woods Conference in 1944, the primary international development organizations have played a leading role in coordinating and implementing international development policies. However, these policies, rooted in Western standards of democratic capitalism, have done little to improve the poor economic and political conditions in less developed nations around the world. Contemporary approaches encourage large-scale development through international organizational cooperation and global market structures. (Current "macro" approaches miss the mark by calling for broad-based policies that do

not recognize, much less build on, the cultural and social "ground-level" realities within underdeveloped nations. Modern development, although grounded in the best of intentions, attempts to replicate the characteristics of a Western democracy within the developing nation. (Patterson 2009)

Development and Evolution

Development (like *modernization*) has a history of being a loaded, value-laden term. One fortunate outcome of the long debate between the development establishment and its critics is that many of the former connotations have been eliminated. Until a few years ago, the process was widely understood to be self-regulating and automatic: a society develops from lesser to greater degrees of prosperity much as an acorn develops into an oak. Given the appropriate resources and strategies, and under favorable diplomatic conditions, people in less developed regions could, it was believed, take control of their destinies and "catch up" with the more developed countries.

This position is deeply rooted in nineteenth-century evolutionism, and its hold in intellectual circles and beyond was all the more tenacious because it was supported by both Marxists *and* modernization theorists (Higgott 1983, 99–103). Today, most social scientists agree with Gunnar Myrdal that development, that is, sustained improvement in the standard of living of the masses, is not guaranteed to anyone. It is not a single, inevitable path on which some parts of the world simply happen to be further along than others (see chapter 10).

Marxist theories in particular assume that human history has been following a grand design, namely, that it is evolving (in a dialectical fashion) toward the global, stateless, nonexploitative society and culture of world Communism. With this in view, all past, present, and possible future development efforts can be understood in relation to this final goal. Marxists are especially concerned with social inequality, alienation, and class struggle, which have motivated important reforms and revolution (as well as reaction) in the past. These lessons of conflict and struggle have been widely applied in analyzing and managing change in the Third World, by Soviet foreign aid specialists and by Marxist critics and movement activists everywhere.

Myrdal (1968, 1970) and others have taken issue with this approach because it confuses ends with means. So long as "development" is defined in relation to how far along a society is on the road to Communism, it is always possible that improvement in standards of living must be postponed or temporarily sacrificed in order to promote the cause. Because Marxist-inspired development programs were (or are) directed by parties with clear political agendas, development resources could be justifiably diverted to support the party or government in conflict with domestic and foreign enemies in the name of The Revolution.

The people of Oceania in George Orwell's *Nineteen Eighty-Four* ([1949] 1984) lead miserable lives, although their leaders assure them it is only a temporary inconvenience. Development is always is just around the corner, but, above all, INGSOC must prevail. In fiction and in fact, when development is viewed as inevitable, provided that people follow the proper orthodoxy, then the orthodoxy becomes a higher good than development itself. As Orwell warned, this may be okay for Big Brother and The Party but not for the bureaucrats and proletarians.

A similar bias can be seen in modernization theory. This approach focuses on the evolution of society and culture toward increasing complexity and the dominance of impersonal relations, especially in the form of bureaucratic organizations, urban growth, and industrialization. At the very apex of this evolutionary scheme, we find the modern societies of North America, Western Europe, and Japan. At the other extreme are the tribally organized, subsistence economy–based societies of antiquity and the least developed regions of the contemporary world. From this perspective, development is measured according to how effectively and quickly the transition to *Gesellschaft* occurs (White 1987).

Modernizers view this type of change as cumulative advance, driven by technological innovation and characterized by increasing mastery of human beings over natural forces. The approach relies heavily on structural-functionalist principles and language to express the evolutionary metaphor: whereby social and cultural systems are seen to "adjust" and readjust in response to an equilibrium-seeking imperative in the face of internally caused "strains."

As with Marxism, modernization theory reduces complex and ambiguous events to a single, integrated, and convincing general framework. It has been employed extensively to both explain the historical development of today's industrialized societies, such as that of the contemporary United States, and assess the future course of change in Third World nations. In practice, it treats development as a process susceptible to the principles of effective management:

> Applying management concepts to economic and social development programs in the Third World is a complex and multifaceted task, for the manager must deal with elusive goals, changing environments, and uncertain means. In addition, optimal directions for organizing donor programs to assist the management of Third World programs have been ambiguous. The comparatively new field of economic and social development management is challenged to create more useful intellectual resources for both developing country management and donor cooperators. (White 1987, xi)

Because the Third World remains rural, poor, and poorly educated, but its populations continue to explode, modernizers are increasingly faced with a choice between long-range institution building and immediate improvement in general standards of living. Most have opted for the first, arguing that any temporary dislocations caused by modernization will be compensated by richer payoffs later. The economics of modernization theory, based largely on the work of W. W. Rostow, encourage saving over consumption, the investment of resources in capital projects over welfare spending, and rapid industrialization.[2] (If these sound to you like the spirit of capitalism, you are right. That is exactly what this development strategy promotes.)

When put into practice, the idea that capitalist development is inevitable if pursued "by the book" (e.g., Rostow's "Non-Communist Manifesto"; Rostow 1960) has often led to goal displacement. The modernization imperative means support for certain kinds of programs and aid targets at the expense of others. So, for instance, development grants are awarded to university professors, engineers, and farm owners, but not to landless peasants, because the model indicates that these are the wiser investments.

Most development specialists now accept some aspects of both Marxism and modernization theory but are also critical of each. Much remains valuable in these once-dominant approaches, but recent events and analysis have significantly challenged them. A considerable body of literature has already been created seeking to describe and explain the fall of Communism in Central and Eastern Europe. At the very least, this dramatic upheaval (and commentary on it) has called into question some of the most fundamental assumptions and laws of Marxist development. Similarly, the substantial critiques by dependency and world system theorists have convinced most observers that the main premises of the modernizers are also partial truths.

Researchers are now well aware of the complex costs and benefits of widespread industrialization, urban growth, and bureaucratization. And it is now commonly acknowledged that these did not occur in Europe, or anywhere else, as a purely internal, "equilibrium-seeking" process.

In brief, the differences in the levels of socioeconomic development that exist between nations and regions today cannot simply be the result of differences in the rates at which these nations and regions have "evolved." To treat them as such can, we now know, lead to the waste of scarce resources on partisan causes.

The Costs of Development: Lessons Learned

Despite the many significant achievements of official development organizations, much remained to be accomplished at the end of the Cold War. This is true whether we judge the situation by the organizations' own standards or in comparison to the less formal Enlightenment ideals of movement critics.

Five specific sources of failure have been identified in one or more programs, as follows (for a discussion of how development programs are evaluated, see Earl et al. 2001).

1. They have been insensitive to cultural differences.
2. They have favored the rich and powerful.
3. They have created a new international elite: "the development set."
4. They have had serious negative higher-order impacts.
5. They have created an unbearable debt burden on those who can least afford it. (Myrdal 1970; Patterson 2009; Stewart 1985, 1–13)

Cultural Differences   Development assistance is often irrelevant to the real needs of the recipients. Initiatives that appeared to be rational strategies when worked out on paper in Washington, New York, or Moscow were not understood or employed effectively in Third World villages. The Green Revolution gave millions of farm owners access to new Ford Escort tractors, an important factor in the geometric increases in wheat and soybean production experienced in many areas. But for the average South Asian farmer who worked less than one acre of land, the tractor was of no value, except as a status symbol parked conspicuously in the landlord's front yard.

Family-planning clinics dispensed uncounted millions of contraceptive pills and other fertility control devices, along with lessons on their proper use. But traditional villagers often failed to see the apparent connection between having fewer children and being better off. In fact, they considered children to be their major source of support and security. As a result, they "used" the pills but in highly innovative ways. During a visit to the home of a household that had participated in the local family-planning program, one sociologist "saw small rectangular boxes and bottles piled one on top of the other, all arranged as a tiny sculpture in the corner of the room. . . . Asa Singh said, 'Most of us threw the tablets away. But my brother, here, he makes use of everything'" (Mamdani 1972, 33).

Help to Dominant Groups Official development has assisted some people but not others, often reinforcing the position of dominant groups in local stratification systems (Cochrane 1986; Singer 1977, chaps. 1 and 8). Because the vast majority of development aid flowed from one government to another, the elite of the Third World benefited far more than the masses. Rural development programs were routinely administered from capital cities, where interest groups and partisan politics often determined which regions would be targeted and how much would be spent. Local educated people, especially those who could speak English, had special advantages in filling administrative posts, but the majority of illiterate farmers were left out of the loop. Under still-effective systems of patronage in the Third World countryside, absentee landowners who received development aid had newfound means to increase the debt load of their dependents (*employees* is too modern a term for the relationship), for instance, by selling them fertilizer they had been given free by USAID.

Creation of a New International Elite A related consequence of more than thirty years of Big Development is that a new elite has been created in Third World countries, made up of local officials and their foreign advisors. These are the people who work with the missions (as local USAID and other development agency offices are called) and enjoy the advantages of First World technologies and salaries.

This group, known in international aid circles as "the development set," is privileged by any standards, although its U.S. and European members typically receive *hardship* pay from home.[3] Through their auspices, a large portion of development resources inadvertently never reaches target populations. Rather, the aid has formed a thin film of dollars circulating on the top of local society, far above the masses.

This phenomenon was vividly demonstrated to me during a recent visit to Bangladesh, a very poor, highly rural, rice-growing country that has subsisted on development aid since it won its independence from Pakistan in 1971. I was staying in the capital, Dacca, and I woke very early one morning to walk around the city center. Turning a corner, I was struck by a neat, new, three-story brick building jammed between shanties and bamboo huts. There was a powerful generator in the back (public utilities are unreliable at best) and a new Jeep parked in front (most people either walk or pull others in human-powered rickshaws). "Was this the urban villa of some hereditary prince?" I wondered. The answer was on a small plaque at the entrance: CARE. This was the local mission of an agency that delivers the most basic kinds of development aid: rice rations, simple tools, and medicine, with much well-deserved acclaim. But whereas we in the United States view it as a desperate last hope, in Bangladesh, it is a wealthy, powerful, even "posh," organization.

This conveys some idea of the discrepancy in First World and Third World standards of living, and what a twenty-to-one exchange rate for the dollar can mean. A donation of seventy-five cents a day, as CARE and other private aid agencies urge from us in their public service announcements, can certainly feed a hungry child. Indeed, when it translates to 150 rupees, it can also feed a few hungry aid workers.

Negative Higher-Order Impacts   The large scale of most official development programs has caused significant environmental degradation, labor force dislocations, and technological dependency. One of the most commonly cited shortcomings of Cold War development aid is that it was insensitive to the fragile balance between population and environment that exists in Third World rural areas. Nearly all of the intended aid beneficiaries live at the margins of subsistence. For many, the situation became precarious to the point of extinction during the active spread of colonialism. We have noted that change was traditionally something people have feared and valued negatively because of the good chance that doing anything differently might threaten survival. For many millions of Third World villagers and tribal people, Big Development has realized these fears.

When official Third World development programs began in earnest in the late 1950s, they were strongly influenced by the Marshall Plan and Stalinist aid activities in postwar Europe. Although these were often ideologically polar opposites, they shared the crucial emphasis on prosperity through industrialization. The success of the Marshall Plan in England, France, West Germany, and other countries seemed to verify that the best way to raise general standards of living rapidly was to invest in high-capital, high-technology manufacturing (which also was Stalin's position). However, the strategy proved increasingly inapplicable—or at least more costly than expected—when it was applied in areas that had never been industrialized before.

Through the late 1970s and beyond, the Third World lacked the social and technological infrastructure assumed by official, industrialized country–sponsored development programs (and by many UN agencies as well). To raise living standards to anything near European levels would require much more than stimulating a once-well-functioning system that had been wrecked by war and autocracy. It would require the virtual undoing of decades of colonial inequities. Thus, these programs undertook some very basic changes in largely uncharted waters because most were unnecessary in Europe's reconstruction: massive swamp drainage projects, hydroelectric projects on rivers that had never been dammed, public immunizations, mass distribution of fertilizers, high-yield seeds, and high-tech farm equipment.

With each innovation, geophysical and human environments were altered beyond recognition. Rivers were diverted, deserts were expanded, waters became polluted, for-

TABLE 12.1 Development Aid Donors and Recipients

a. Leading Development Aid Donors, 2008

Country	Aid in $US billion	Rank	Aid as a percent of GDP	Rank
US	19.00	1	0.16	9
Japan	8.86	2	0.19	8
France	8.47	3	0.42	5
UK	7.84	4	0.37	6
Germany	7.50	5	0.28	7
Netherlands	4.23	6	0.74	4
Sweden	2.70	7	0.77	3
Italy	2.48	8	0.15	10
Norway	2.20	9	0.87	1
Denmark	2.03	10	0.84	2

Note: The largest donors in 2008, by volume, were the United States, Germany, the United Kingdom, France, and Japan. The largest volume increases came from the United States, the United Kingdom, Spain, Germany, Japan, and Canada. In real terms, net official development aid (ODA) rose in fourteen countries as follows: Belgium (+13.4 percent), Denmark (+0.3 percent), Finland (+6.7 percent), France (+2.9 percent), Germany (+5.7 percent), Greece (+26.9 percent), Ireland (+6.4 percent), Italy (+2.2 percent), Luxembourg (+1.8 percent), Netherlands (+4.8 percent), Portugal (+ 21.1 percent), Spain (+19.4 percent), Sweden (+3.9 percent), and United Kingdom (+24.1 percent).

b. Leading Development Aid Recipients, 2008

Region	Country	Aid in $US billion
Latin America	—	6.1
Asia	—	20.1
Eastern Europe	—	3.4
Africa	—	26.3
	Egypt	1.58
	Tanzania	1.00
	Mozambique	0.80
	Morocco	0.68

Note: The total amount of international development aid as of 2008 was more than one hundred billion dollars a year, its highest level ever.

Source: Organisation for Economic Co-operation and Development (OECD), www.oecd.org/dac.

ests were cut down, the air in Mexico City and other Third World capitals could no longer be breathed because of industrial smog, farmers were flooded out of traditional land, and millions more were squeezed out by labor-saving technology.

In the eye of the demographic cyclone now blowing through the Third World are the cities, especially the colonial ports, growing twice as fast as the already rapidly booming general population (Bilsborrow 1998; Gilbert and Gugler 1992). Millions have come to these cities, many with no job and no place to live—only hope. They come like Ram, whom we met in chapter 9, in the belief that, because opportunities are diminishing at home, their fortunes must lie in the capital. After all, it is the source of the "progress" that changed their lives on the farm or fishery. So far, the urban economies have been unable to absorb this exploding labor force, and rural areas need fewer hands to run industrialized agricultural estates and ranches or to tend the continually marginalized (and degraded) holdings of subsistence farmers (Geyer 2002).

The Debt Burden   Even for the fortunate few who have benefited from large-scale development programs, progress has come at a price. Dam building, mass immunizations, and Green Revolutions are expensive undertakings. Big Development required enormous initial investments, much of which was secured in the form of loans by private banks and a UN Agency, the World Bank (the International Bank for Reconstruction and Development, or IBRD).

More significant in the long run, the dams, clinics, and machinery all need to be maintained. Petroleum and other expensive, nonrenewable resources are required to fuel development. These costs have proved to be especially high in the poorer Third World nations that must pay for their oil imports at world prices and in hard currency. When the bill for the first three decades of development came in the 1980s, the world economy received a shock from which it has still not recovered (Beenstock 1984, chap. 10). And the amount increases as the fifth decade begins.

By the early 2000s, Third World countries had accumulated a debt of approximately two trillion dollars, borrowed to initiate and maintain agricultural and industrial development programs (Roodman 2001). Many of these loans also carry compound interest, although there have been two rounds of debt forgiveness and interest reduction. (Principal owed at the relatively low annual rate of 8 percent doubles in less than nine years.) Some countries, China for example, weathered the experience better than others. Brazil and Mexico, at the other extreme, owe more than three hundred billion dollars each, even after the cancellation of a substantial portion of their principal (see table 12.2).

The remarkable development successes achieved in India, Brazil, and Korea since World War II have been difficult and costly. The smaller, poorer countries such as Somalia, Rwanda, and Bangladesh have achieved rapid gains in infant survival and literacy. But their entire economies have been financed almost exclusively through loans and transfers by the United States and UN. As a new millennium begins, the burden of development has been made more difficult for large and small nations alike, for the world's most needful people are starting not at ground zero but rather already in the hole and getting deeper at continuously compounding rates.

TABLE 12.2 Total External Debt, 1997 and 2002 (millions US$)

Region/Category	Total debt		Total debt as % of GNP		Long-term debt as % of total	
	1997	2002	1997	2002	1997	2002
All developing countries	2,122,611	2,338,848	36	39	79	82
East Asia & Pacific	526,312	497,354	35	28	73	78
Europe & Central Asia	387,545	545,842	36	49	80	80
Latin America & Caribbean	665,833	727,944	34	45	79	84
Middle East & North Africa	172,634	189,010	35	33	80	79
South Asia	149,611	168,349	28	26	93	94
Sub-Saharan Africa	220,677	210,350	67	70	78	83
Low income	520,179	523,464	53	49	83	86
Middle income	1,602,432	1,815,384	33	37	77	81
Heavily indebted poor countries	204,992	188,582	109	86	83	84

Source: World Bank, *Global Development Finance, 2004* (Washington, DC: Author, 2004), table 3, "External Debt."

The Demographic Component

Even the dramatic progress that has been made by public health and other development programs cannot sustain populations that continue to grow more than twice as fast as England's did during its Industrial Revolution. In addition to having to bear the burdens of underdevelopment and debt, efforts to improve the standard of living of Third World people have for some time been haunted by the Malthusian specter. Many have wondered whether population growth due to declining death rates will surpass carrying capacity. This situation is an especially ironic concern because the classic "geometric" population increase currently underway in the Third World (while growth rates in Europe are nearly all below zero) is the direct result of development aid.

As discussed in chapter 3, the dreaded Malthusian crash has not come yet, despite the many prophecies to that effect. This is not to deny that bouts of war, pestilence, famine, vice, and misery have happened in the Third World. For example, in September 1994 an outbreak of bubonic plague was reported in Gandhi's birthplace of Western Gujarat. In 2003 a runaway epidemic of the flulike SARS (severe acute respiratory syndrome) was—belatedly—reported in Hong Kong and quickly spread around the world. In 2009, an outbreak of a relatively unknown influenza strain (H1N1) spread from southern Asia with such rapidity and to such a degree of severity that the World Health Organization quickly declared it a pandemic (Saunders 2009).

According to the UN Food and Agricultural Organization, more than twenty million people in Africa and other parts of the Third World are facing imminent famine. Hardest hit are Ethiopia, the Sudan, Angola, Kenya, Zambia, and Mozambique. Outside of Africa, the countries affected include Afghanistan, Lebanon, Laos and Sri Lanka,

Haiti, Nicaragua, and Peru. "The crisis has pushed prices to an all-time high and could lead to further hikes in the price of bread, beer, biscuits, and other basic foods. It could also exacerbate serious food shortages in developing countries, especially in Africa (Leake 2008). Despite such emergencies, with the essential support of development programs (and credit), most of the Third World has been able to feed itself. India began to be a net exporter of rice in the 1980s, and all of the major famines in Asia and Africa since the 1950s have been the result of not absolute scarcity but rather political conflict over food supplies. Most Third World people continue to subsist on traditional, low-calorie, low-fat (largely vegetarian) diets. But, so far, they have also been able to support the extra children who now survive infancy at astoundingly high rates.

The third UN World Population Conference, held in Cairo in August 1994, issued a plan of action after much controversy between a minority of pronatalist delegates and the neo-Malthusian majority (Moffett 1994). Like the first two plans issued in Bucharest in 1974 and Mexico City in 1984, it is explicitly focused on the relationship between population growth and socioeconomic development. Although it stresses the importance of limiting family size in the Third World so the fruits of progress can be enjoyed by all, it also recognizes that the cause-and-effect relationship can work the other way—that is, development can lead to declining population growth.

If the rural masses who continue to bear children at rates that were once necessary for survival could be provided with the amenities of a middle-class lifestyle, they, too, would see the wisdom in family planning (and they might even take the pills rather than make sculptures with them). Of course, this is no simple undertaking.

Despite conflict over major issues, the 1994 conference unanimously agreed that one absolutely crucial social component was to be unambiguously linked to family planning: the status of women. Until and unless women improve their standing in the family and the community, delegates concurred, population control efforts will be seriously hampered. Thus, the relationship between high fertility and gender inequality, which had been demonstrated by researchers since the 1960s, was at last institutionalized as a principle of international planning.

This is significant for many reasons, some of which may be obvious from earlier discussions. The current plan, like its predecessors, will guide population research and policy until well into the twenty-first century. It is bound to affect international development, in official and unofficial channels, because it links the definitive issue of population control to the most important social movement of our time, the struggle for the equality of women.

Regardless of the outcome, official development programs will continue to stress family planning for many years. At the same time, it has never been more evident that the success of family planning depends, as it always has, on the changing sociocultural environment in which small families become necessary for survival and prosperity. Third World people still have little but their families on which to rely. And as long as the worth of a woman depends on the number of sons she bears, it will always be a difficult choice to use the Pill, get a patch, have the operation, or simply "accept" family-planning services.

Technology plus Altruism: Cutting the Gordian Knot

You may be familiar with the metaphor of the Gordian knot (after Gordius, mythological founder of the Greek city-state of Phrygia). This refers to a problem so complex that no ordinary mortal can solve it. The dilemmas of socioeconomic development have been characterized by this metaphor several times since the 1960s. How, observers have wondered, can Third World countries raise their standards of living when programs designed to do expressly that cost so much? How can they industrialize without creating massive rural unemployment? Where will the resources come from as environments are increasingly used up or degraded by "progress"? How can poor, rural societies develop without family-planning programs that, ironically, are most effective when people have achieved a fairly high standard of living?

Although there are many reasons to despair at the tenacity of this Gordian knot, not all social scientists are equally pessimistic about the fifth decade of development. This section concludes with a brief look at two of the more hopeful trends worth following. The first consists of breakthroughs in technology that have allowed people to achieve what was once considered impossible. Second is the spread of an altruistic, global awareness that acknowledges a set of human interests that transcend local and national priorities.

The Technological Fix: North-South Dimension and Appropriate Technology

Electronic communication technology has all but obliterated the special advantages that once accrued to central places, especially cities. The first educational television programming in India was in the countryside (Agrawal 1986), and farmers all over the world now routinely watch videos produced by UNDP, USAID, and other donors. Innovations ranging from oral polio vaccine to Internet-linked classrooms have diffused to the remote corners of Earth in their most sophisticated forms, without the necessity for local people to invest resources (which they seriously lack) in costly research and development. This has allowed the rural poor to reap "the benefits of being second" far more completely and rapidly than was possible when Thorstein Veblen first observed the phenomenon in late-nineteenth-century Germany.

Most of these technologies are still concentrated in modern countries or in the modern sectors of Third World societies, and their present use and future improvements remain under the control of multinational corporations and national governments. But they represent a potential tool for development that was undreamed of when the Marshall Plan was formulated: a way to overcome the limitations of time and distance. As post–Cold War development planning continues, electronic technologies and other significant innovations will add a new, largely untried, and promising dimension to the project.

When development activists and theorists began to observe the negative impacts of large-scale programs, two concepts emerged that are now part of established wisdom in the field: the *North-South dimension* in international relations and *appropriate technology* for development. The first refers to a new understanding about the similarities between the "North's" (First and Second World) development models and the contrasts between these models and actual conditions in the "South" (the Third World; Jones

1983). This concept points to the fact that the real interest blocs in world politics today, especially resource politics, are no longer divided along East-West lines.

As industrialized nations, the East and West have similar needs and goals. Therefore, the greatest opportunities for conflict and the greatest challenges to cooperation lie in the relations between the United States, Japan, Australia, New Zealand, and all of Europe (West, Central, and East) in one camp and, in the other, the people of Asia, Africa, and Latin America. With the end of the Cold War, this characterization has become increasingly credible (Gaonkar 2001).

The appropriate technology movement was initiated in direct response to the obvious discrepancies between the scale and sophistication of northern development technologies and the immediate needs and capabilities of indigenous southern peoples (McIntyre and Papp 1986). It is based on the understanding that the most effective means of raising standards of living in the Third World is with local tools and materials used in novel and environmentally friendly ways (Singer 1977). In this manner, productivity can be increased, health improved, and education promoted—perhaps not as rapidly as might occur with high-tech solutions but with fewer costs in human and environmental terms and less dependency on foreign debt (Loxley 1986; Willoughby 1990).

The call for appropriate technology began as a movement, a protest against Big Development. Although the main trend in development continues to be toward high-tech solutions, experts and policy makers are now well aware that there are alternatives. In this respect, appropriate technology is like flexible bureaucracy, employee ownership programs, and quality circles: an innovation meant to moderate modernization. These humanizing ideals seek the benefits of applying science in human affairs at a more reasonable cost (for a critique of the approach, see Hazeltine and Bull 1999).

The Future of Altruism

The environmental movement has increased awareness of resource issues everywhere (Klinkenborg 1992; Taylor 1995). At this very moment, local, national, and international policies are being revised to account for our new appreciation of the delicate

FIGURE 12.2 The Centre for Appropriate Rural Technology (CART) is a community-driven sustainable development project located in the Eastern Cape of South Africa. It functions as a life skills center in the heart of Sicambeni Village, a rural village near Port St. Johns. *Source*: http://en.wikipedia.org/wiki/File: AllofCART.jpg. Photo credit: Kyle Butler. Image in the public domain.

balance between development and habitat loss, reflecting a change in the very assumptions under which planned social change is conducted. Since the publication of the pioneering studies by the ecologists Barry Commoner (1966) and Rachel Carson (1962), most scientists have come to view the more and less industrialized regions of the world as interdependent parts of a single natural system. We now also understand that it is a system that happens to be under considerable stress because of development. With this in mind, it makes little sense in the long run to expect some areas to prosper at the expense of others.[4]

The idea that the geophysical world constitutes one gigantic ecosystem originated with Ernst Haeckel's research in the 1890s, and it is a logical outcome of the Darwinian revolution that had begun some decades earlier. It has been expressed in many ways in recent years, most memorably, perhaps, in R. Buckminster Fuller's (1983) appealing phrase "Spaceship Earth." The power of modern technology, the new methods for monitoring its impacts, and the speed with which information about these impacts can be communicated have all contributed to a new sense of urgency. As a result, we are all now genuinely concerned when we learn about holes in the ozone layer over Antarctica, cutting of rain forests in Brazil, massive pollution of the Danube river system, oil spills in Alaska, and nuclear reactor meltdowns in Ukraine.

Why, one might wonder, should such dangers concern a person living in suburban Detroit; Dacca, Bangladesh; or Tirana, Albania? Not long ago, this would have been a reasonable question with a seemingly obvious answer: there is no good reason. Detroiters, Bangladeshi, and Albanians have enough to worry about without getting involved with events in distant and unheard-of places. Today, another answer is even more obvious to any schoolchild: we must be concerned because these things are bound to affect us all. No passenger on Spaceship Earth is secure if any part of the vessel has a problem. That is how interdependently things have come to be viewed.

This realization is changing the modern concept of the relationship between humanity and nature. Conquest and exploitation were once positively valued as a measure of how well a society is developed. Now we speak of cooperation and conservation. This shift is the outcome of decades of research showing that the actions we take in transforming our environments always have higher-order impacts and that these impacts accumulate until they eventually make their presence known, often in the form of disaster. Nature does not get conquered, but she sometimes gets even. This is something that traditional people have known all along.

This experience of technology shock has made people more aware of the costs of northern-oriented development programs. Social scientists and political activists throughout the world, modernizers and Marxists alike, are now seriously questioning the old orthodoxy that to be more developed is equated with being more effective in exploiting nature. Visionaries such as Fuller and Marshall McLuhan have even suggested that the Third World might be better off skipping the Industrial Revolution altogether and getting right to the more environmentally friendly Information Age.

The development establishment has been more reluctant than movement intellectuals to embrace this anti-industrial sentiment, and in some countries, such as Brazil, officials have argued that as the First and Second Worlds abused their natural resources along the path to development, the Third World is entitled to do the same. Nevertheless, official development policy has never been so explicitly concerned about balancing economic growth with environmental conservation (while hundreds of thousands of acres of rain forest continue go up in smoke every hour). The implications of this global awareness go beyond the geophysical level, to the ever-expanding sociocultural interdependencies between more and less developed regions.

For a very long time (Marxists would say almost forever), human relations from the interpersonal to the international levels have been guided by the same values of conquest and exploitation that have shaped our treatment of the environment. The colonial system, which played a decisive role in creating today's underdeveloped conditions, was explicitly designed to conquer and exploit the people and resources at the peripheries. Whatever benefits local people derived were a by-product, not a goal, of the system. These predatory roots were institutionalized during the imperial and neo-colonial eras and are reflected today in the relationship between the Third Word masses and dominant northern corporations and government "missions."

Armed with the understanding that the ultimate costs of exploiting nature are often higher than we expected, social scientists are now in a position to suggest that the developed countries consider ending their conquest of the Third World. One of the earliest, and still most profound, statements on the price that must now be paid for colonialism is that of Franz Fanon in his book *The Wretched of the Earth* (1963; the title is from the second line of "The International," the anthem of socialism).[5] Trained as a psychiatrist, Fanon was especially aware of a common personality disorder that he was the first to label *colonial mentality*, a condition in which people come to believe they are inferior to others because others have enculturated them to that belief over years and generations. This view is so contrary to human nature, Fanon argued, that it can only be enforced with a tremendous expenditure of violence: military rule, terror, torture, slavery, and execution, all of which were indeed inflicted during the colonial and imperial eras.

People in the Third World were, to use a common metaphor of the time, "whipped into shape," coerced to accept what is an absurd conclusion, that another group is inherently superior to their own. When liberation came, there was a reservoir of repressed hostility against this self-hatred waiting to be expressed. For Freudians, such as Fanon, these kinds of psychological traumas do not dissipate; they are stored deep in the soul. Fanon thus argued that violent rebellion was a natural response to the inevitable discovery that the colonial mentality is a disease, not just the normal state of mind for a "properly Europeanized" native (Fanon explored this issue in his *Black Skins, White Masks* [1967]).

This phenomenon is something of which Gandhi was also well aware. Unlike Fanon, however, he taught with considerable success how to resist the lure of destructive entitlement. Recognizing the evident, high personal costs of colonial rule, his Quit India movement pursued the moral high ground of forgiving and the highly effective weapon of strategic retreat.

In contrast, the Algerian independence movement of the 1950s, in which Fanon himself participated, was especially bloody, and it sent a strong shock wave through the French intellectual world. It was then that Jean-Paul Sartre's aptly named journal

Modern Times (*Les Temps Moderne*) became a forum for anticolonial sentiment, often in debate with the Algerian-born writer Albert Camus. Through the work of Fanon, Sartre, Camus, and others, social scientists and the general public came to understand that the rules of international relations would simply have to change. Violence once directed at colonial authorities was now being enacted in ethnic and national conflict.

Other types of resistance, active in the form of anti-Western protest and passive in the form of dual societies and multiple personalities, became institutionalized. They all bear a strong, common message to the developed countries that Third World people no longer care to be exploited in order to enrich their "masters." Continued conquest is bound to be expensive, if not in blood, then in other ways.

Of course, not everything about our recent discovery of colonialism's human costs is so permeated with echoes of hostility and revenge. As with other elements of modern culture, the idea that the conquest of others is a justifiable means to increase our own prosperity, the "zero-sum" theory of development, is under attack from within. As noted in earlier chapters, the bureaucracies and corporations that play a perhaps unjustly large role in the destinies of Third World people are not the rigid, closed organizations that first established colonial ties. An increasingly viable world government exists, with a universal doctrine of human rights pledged, formally at least, to intervene in matters such as corporate activities and international development programs when local group or individual interests are threatened (Engberg-Pederson 1982).

A new sensitivity to cultural diversity and relativism in our educational curricula and the abundant information and pictures that continually race around the global information highway have made northerners sympathetic to Third World interests. People in the industrialized countries are learning something that Gandhi, Fanon, and the anticolonial avant-garde knew firsthand. We who live in the world's few developed nations can no longer prosper at the expense of the majority because we will surely pay for their underdevelopment. Just as it is in the interests of everyone who lives in South Asia that "local" oil spills in Alaska be prevented, it is in the interests of everyone who lives in Detroit, Montreal, Tokyo, or London that standards of living in Rwanda and Bangladesh be raised.

The creative altruism movement discussed in chapters 2 and 7 is another small, but sociologically significant, example of the trend toward cooperative development. You will recall that Pitirim Sorokin explicitly formulated this idea at Harvard University during the late 1940s as an antidote to the main trend of late sensate culture: egoism. In this respect he was harking back to the founding ideals of Henri Saint-Simon and Auguste Comte, to the effect that science and technology would make it possible, for the first time in history, for people to actually live by the Golden Rule (Johnston 1995; Matter 1974; Sorokin 1954b).[6]

Control of people and nature is an inherently sensate concept, as Sorokin frequently pointed out. In its early, active stages, it leads to discovery and progress, at least in material terms. But by the time it ripens to its late, cynical form (as it has today), it becomes an end in itself. Individuals, groups, and organizations fight each other for control of resources that would be more effectively used if they were to cooperate. Ultimately, they know no other way; in our competitive economies and states, we are not socialized for cooperation or for authentic democracy. This generalization clearly applies to Big Development during the Cold War era, when every major donor was willing to raise living standards in Asia or Africa, provided that it did not (1) cost them anything or (2) give comfort to the enemy.

Sorokin's view that the doctrine of unbridled self-interest has reached the limits of its effectiveness is increasingly shared within and outside of academe, as in the Saturn memorandum (Saturn Corporation 1990) quoted in chapter 11. The principle of cooperation has been incorporated in formal industrial relations, in appropriate technology, and in every realm of social life. In each case, we are being reoriented away from egoism and toward altruism, not "inevitably" or because we wish to be saints or angels, but rather because conquest and exploitation have proved to be too expensive.[7]

In the fall of 1994, several notorious Los Angeles youth gangs that had been at war for years (at the cost of many lives) declared a universal alliance (Emshwiller 1994). Graffiti appeared throughout the city: "We are all in the same gang." And so we are.

Imagine this development scenario for the twenty-first century. Cooperative First and Second World programs are designed to promote the interests of the rural and urban poor of the Third World, without regard for political or economic advantage. These use the latest technology and research and development systems once earmarked for military purposes: a worldwide "Star Wars" to shield against ignorance and poverty, so to speak (Cassidy and Bischak 1995). Improbable? Impossible? So were near-zero infant mortality, satellite rural education, and informational websites maintained by the Aboriginal people of Australia until just a few years ago.

Political instability, civil wars, guerilla movements, and lack of political will to better the lot of the majority continue to plague the Third World. Under the circumstances, this is an improbable scenario. But it is closer to being realized than we could ever have forecast before the fall of Second World Communism, close enough to argue that despite the failures and dilemmas, the Third World actually can continue to develop and prosper—to the benefit of all. Much depends on the speed with which international economics catches up with ecological awareness in incorporating one of the great discoveries of our time: there really is no such thing as comparative advantage if we are all in the same gang (Wuthnow 1995).

Summary

This chapter has focused on the paradoxes of development. As an ideal and as a self-conscious project, development has been a major force driving all of humanity toward a "Westernized" world. Decades of practical experience and research have revealed that Europe's Industrial Revolution and colonial expansion caused a significant shift in the trajectory of social and cultural change everywhere. By the end of World War I, no region or continent had been left unaffected by bureaucratization, materialism, and the several other elements of Western culture.

By virtue of centuries of political, economic, and cultural domination, the costs and benefits of Westernization have been very unevenly distributed, creating a global stratification system between core northern and peripheral and semiperipheral southern regions. While the North developed, the South became underdeveloped.

The diffusion of modern culture throughout the world always had a missionary aspect. So it is not entirely coincidental that the Anglican faith spread alongside the British East and West India Companies and the English army, and Roman Catholicism came with Italian and French colonization. International assistance branch offices are called "missions" for much the same reason, that is, the world has become so highly Westernized, in large part, because Westerners have meant to make it that way.

These efforts were reinvigorated following World War II, when Third World nations won independence. During the 1950s, the reconstruction of their local societies became institutionalized in large-scale development programs. Most of these, sponsored by USAID, the World Bank, and other national and international organizations, incorporated modernization models based on the assumption that development equals industrialization. Marxist (or Maoist) and other, less formal experiments and movements were also promoted as alternatives to Big Development. Although ideologically opposed, all, however, sought to not just change Third World society but also raise standards of living for hundreds of millions of poor rural people to a level closer to that enjoyed in industrialized countries. As seen, this approach has resulted in a complex combination of miraculous achievements and miserable failures—a Gordian knot of development.

One can find many prophets of doom in academic circles today, from neo-Malthusian population specialists to environmentally concerned anthropologists. They warn that the world is on a disastrous course in which resources are being used up, habitats are being destroyed, and species are being driven to extinction at unprecedented rates, including *Homo sapiens* if we are not very careful. Many point to Cold War development programs as major culprits.

We have also seen that there are more hopeful voices that suggest that a cooperative, democratic world system is possible, despite the continuing need to create a more just distribution of diminishing resources. For these optimists, a key to twenty-first-century development may lie with technology. Innovations have, on countless occasions, let people do things that had once been impossible. Current discoveries in electronics, nuclear technology, and related industries can help us do the same in Third World development.

By the time of Thomas Malthus's death in the early nineteenth century, food resources in Europe and North America were increasing geometrically and population growth rates were turning toward zero (and they have fallen beneath it today), in flat contradiction to his forecasts. Malthus was wrong, not because he lacked wisdom, but rather because he stuck closely to the facts of history and had dismissed William Godwin's "utopian" speculations about prolonging life for everyone beyond eighty years, eliminating infant mortality, controlling fertility with chemicals, and increasing agricultural productivity as needed. Today, these formerly "utopian" goals have very nearly been achieved—for some people in some parts of the world.

Sorokin and other idealists have argued that Western civilization is not well equipped to undertake the heavy responsibilities it first assumed under colonialism.

We have deeply internalized the values of late sensate culture, but the times demand a more altruistic worldview in which materialism and conquest are deemphasized. These sentiments are not common, but they do constitute a voice in the development debate that will continue to be heard. In the following chapter, we consider various attempts to put these more idealistic views into practice according to programs of democratic planning.

Relevant Websites

www.care.org/
This is the home page for CARE, the private international aid organization. This organization invented the CARE package.

www.usaid.gov/
This is the USAID home page. This site is filled with interesting information, data, policy statements, and even job opportunities.

www.american.edu/ted/chipko.htm
This site is about Chipko. Posted by American University, it tells the story of Chipko and Gaura Devi.

www.jubilee2000uk.org/
This sites focus on Third World debt. It is from Jubilee Research and is dedicated to debt forgiveness. According to the Old Testament, every seventh cycle of seven years is known as a "Jubilee" and is celebrated with creditors canceling the principal and interested owed by their debtors.

www.nsi-ins.ca/
Here is another Canadian site, this one focusing on North/South issues.

www.cdc.gov/ncidod/sars
This is the U.S. Centers for Disease Control 2003 alert on SARS.

Democratic Planning and Applied Sociology

F OR THE PAST several decades, the modern profession of planning has served as an especially clear illustration of how people have taken the matter of social and cultural change into their own hands (Caves 2005; Christensen and Levinson 2003). The field of sociology has developed along a similar track since its origins in nineteenth-century Europe. Auguste Comte, Karl Marx, Max Weber, Emile Durkheim, and the other founders viewed themselves as not only scientists but also social *engineers* whose aim was to apply the knowledge of their discipline to solving social problems and improving the human condition.[1] In fact, on several occasions, individual professionals and organizations have consciously merged the two approaches. The Scottish sociologist/planner Patrick Geddes—who worked extensively in India—made especially important contributions to this endeavor in the early 1900s (Meller 1990). Geddes program for merging planning and sociology was based on the principles of applied science that remain relevant today.

> The department of sociological studies should evidently be, as far as possible, concrete in treatment. . . . Thus there is emerging more clearly for sociological studies in general, for their concrete fields of application in city after city, the conception of a scientific centre of observation and record on the one hand and of a corresponding centre of experimental endeavor on the other—in short of Sociological Observatory and Sociological Laboratory, and of these as increasingly coordinated. (Geddes [1904] 2007, 7)

At about the same time, the renowned Chicago School, so named because most of its members were at the University of Chicago and because the neighborhoods of the city were the focus of their work, was establishing its decades-long program of planned social change (Bulmer 1984; Deegan 1988; Shils 1991). At Atlanta University, sociologist and social activist W. E. B. Du Bois created the first "Sociological Laboratory" in 1897 to serve the large, poor African American community of that city (Williams 2002). In a later generation, Herbert Gans, William J. Wilson, and William Whyte combined sociology and planning in their research and action programs.[2] More recently, Jammie Price, Roger Straus, and Jeffrey Breese, in collaboration with several other members of the Association for Applied and Clinical Sociology, have published a set of case studies that illustrate and define the boundaries of the field in its current form (Price, Straus, and Breese 2009).

Sociology was born in the midst of industrial and political revolution and civil unrest, in the period extending from the late eighteenth to the mid-nineteenth centuries. Since that time, it has experienced recurring cycles in which its applied side has been emphasized and then downplayed or even denied. The beginning of the twenty-

Box 13.1 ASSOCIATION FOR APPLIED AND CLINICAL SOCIOLOGY

Mission Statement

The mission of the Association is to accomplish the following five purposes:

1. Provide a common meeting ground for individuals interested in the application of sociological knowledge.
2. Promote the application of sociological knowledge for beneficial social change through scholarly, educational, programmatic, community, and policy activities.
3. Enhance the understanding of the interrelationship between sociological knowledge and sociological practice.
4. Advance theory, research, methods, and training that promotes the use of sociological knowledge for beneficial social change.
5. Promote the use of applied and clinical sociology in local, regional, state, national, and international settings.

What Is Applied and Clinical Sociology?

Sociological practice is a more general term for both Applied and Clinical Sociology. Sociological practice is defined as "any use (often client-centered) of the sociological perspective and/or its tools in the understanding of, intervention in, and/or enhancement of human social life." The American Sociological Association notes that applied and clinical sociologies are complementary approaches.

first century is an era of renewed emphasis on application, in which more interest is being generated in sociological practice than in the preceding fifty years (see Weinstein [1982], especially chap. 1; Weinstein 1997).

Lester Frank Ward, the first president of the American Sociological Society (later renamed the American Sociological Association), and the first to use "applied sociology" in the title of a book, traced the action orientation of the field to its founder, Comte. "Sociology was founded on this broad basis, and Comte, notwithstanding the twelve years devoted to writing the Positive Philosophy, which forms its scientific basis, never for a moment lost sight of his purpose. Science with him was only a means to action. Indeed it was a secondary means, viz a means to prevision, which is the direct means to action" (Ward 1906, 289).

In practically every country in the world today, including some unlikely places such as the Kingdom of Bhutan,[3] social planners and applied sociologists are engaged daily in formulating goals for the allocation of resources to change social relationships and organizations, environments, and even our beliefs and values. As discussed in chapter 3,

Clinical sociology is often a role, and applied sociology is a method. Both stress the application of sociology.

Examples of Clinical Sociologist roles include

- Counselor
- Mediator
- Group Facilitator
- Mitigation Expert
- Organizational Consultant

Examples of Applied Sociology include

- Evaluating the effectiveness of various educational policies/programs
- Investigating the social norms promoting or inhibiting the spread of AIDS
- Evaluating and assessing the effectiveness of various criminal justice programs
- Analyzing employment records for evidence of discrimination
- Planning medical services and facilities for a target population
- Bringing together knowledge of our social, political, and economic world to better understand the world around us: Where we are, how we got here, and where we are going. A solid understanding of the world is the first step for improving living conditions of all people throughout the world.
- Using the above understanding to improve society by addressing and preventing problems, thereby developing an optimal society

Source: www.aacsnet.org/

the modern idea of social planning emerged in part from the family-planning movement in the early nineteenth century (to which William Godwin and Benjamin Franklin belonged). It also has roots in agrarianism and in the Public Health, Garden City, and City Beautiful movements of the mid- to late 1800s (American Planning Association [APA] 1990, 83).

Many applied sociologists and most professional planners now work in government organizations. In the United States, Canada, and to lesser degrees in other capitalist countries, this work also occurs in private corporations and consulting organizations. In fact, there are several different models or approaches to planning, some of which are currently in open competition in professional and government circles (Alexander 1992, chap. 5; Pack and Pack 1975).

Planning Models

At one extreme is the Bolshevist model, in which all planning is centralized, all is conducted within the government, and the plans themselves (1) are comprehensive, that is, meant to encompass all aspects of social change, and (2) carry the authority of law. At the other extreme is the U.S. urban and regional model, which was developed largely by architects and civil engineers during the mid-1800s (Krueckeberg 1983). This model allows considerable scope for the private sector. Rather than being comprehensive and centralized, it focuses on specific, limited problems at local sites.

Because of its intellectual roots, U.S.-type planning has traditionally been physically oriented: emphasizing land use regulation, transportation, and environmental management (Willhelm 1962). Through the years, however, its approaches to problem formulation, theory, and method have been shaped by the social sciences, especially in the area of community organization and management. In this way, it has developed as an independent discipline, distinct from architecture and engineering, that includes a definite social improvement program (APA 1990, chap. 2; Dentler 2002).

In the United States, professional social planners (that is, those with graduate degrees in sociology, planning, and related fields or AICP [American Institute of Certified Planners] certification)[4] generally work for state and local governments. In addition, during the Depression era, several federal planning agencies were created. Although many have long since been closed down, they established a precedent for national-level planning.[5] Even during the height of the New Deal, however, federal- and local-level plans always have been subject to approval through normal legislative processes. They have never had the force of law in themselves as in the Bolshevist model.

A decisive amount of economic planning in the United States occurs in private corporations, usually by people who carry administrative and managerial titles other than *planner* or *applied sociologist*. This activity is technically separate from public sector planning, in accord with the ideals of a free market. Although it is often a complex and time-consuming procedure, especially in organizations as large as contemporary multinational companies, it has a very simple goal, at least in principle: the maximization of surplus value (the profit motive).

Corporate planning, therefore, centers on the creation of projected budgets that specify in advance how resources are to be allocated and capital accumulated. This makes accountancy one of the most important types of planning in the United States today (and one of the most embattled following the revelations of 2001–2003; see chapter 11). With literally trillions of dollars at stake each year in these budgetary decisions, corporate plans are "the law" within companies, in the economic sense of being virtually inviolable operating procedures. Those who control the budgeting process thus occupy key positions of minority influence, especially if the same individual or few individuals have access to the budgets of several related companies, as in the case of interlocking directorates.

Over the years, public and private sector planning in the United States have become mutually dependent. Since the Great Depression, government has increasingly regulated corporate activity so that companies must now balance planning for profit with consideration of public relations, the existing laws, tax codes, ordinances, and the ever-present possibility of changes in regulations. At the same time, because the public sector is financed through the taxes of private citizens and corporations, public plans to accumulate and invest resources (for example, to build new highways) depend on the will of the private sector, as voters and as economic actors.

Much current political debate in the United States centers on the competition between public and private organizations over resources to implement their respective plans. Regardless of which side may be on the ascent at any given moment, it is an element of competition that was eliminated from the Bolshevist system. It has ensured that planning in the United States has a procapitalist orientation and that it is not centrally coordinated (although, as in other areas, the influence of special interest groups can distort the process).

In England, where many of the early concepts of social planning originated, and elsewhere in Europe and the Third World, societies are now routinely governed according to a mixed system lying somewhere between the command state and the U.S. model (Amenta 1993; Firebaugh and Beck 1994). Figure 13.1 divides planning models into four groups, with socialist regulation or welfare capitalism and "strongly welfarist" as intermediate categories.

As you can see, the United States is in the minority of countries with limited formal planning, yet even it is hardly a laissez-faire system. In fact, throughout the world, at the international, national, and regional levels, professionals today are deliberately shaping our collective futures. It is highly likely that this activity will not only continue but also increase and be extended to new frontiers as the years go by. The age of the planned society has arrived. What remains to be resolved is which model will prevail.

Many social scientists and practitioners, including members of the planning profession, have reflected seriously on this question. The choice of models today has both technological and political implications because it means attempting to reconcile the reality of planned society with the ideals of democratic government.

With the collapse of European Communism, it is clear that the Bolshevist model is essentially one of elite, oligarchic control. It is fundamentally at odds with the principle of self-rule, despite the fact that the leaders termed their system a *workers' democracy*.

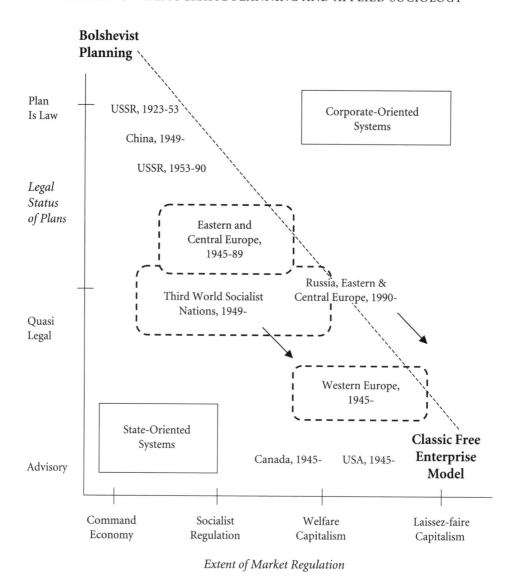

FIGURE 13.1 Planning Models

In fact, "even before the demise of the Soviet Union, its communist rulers had acknowledged the failure of centralized planning and adopted the goal of moving toward a market economy" (Plattner and Diamond 1992, 3). With the growth of the multinational corporation and its positions of minority influence, however, the market economy alone is no longer capable of protecting citizens from another form of elite control, that of economic rulers. In response, democratic governments have acknowledged the failure of markets and adopted the goal of moving toward centralized planning. Markets have, in fact, been regulated by government for decades, even in the highly private sector–oriented countries such as the United States. World trade and commerce are now being conducted daily in the explicit terms of new multinational communities, pacts, treaties, and agreements, all of which represent the intentional, external manipulation of markets.

The Concept of Democratic Planning

Most sociologists interested in the prospects of social planning have concluded that the older market and Bolshevist models are now rapidly converging on one another. This observation is also shared among professional planners, including Sherry Arnstein (APA 1990, 161) and other observers (Form 1979; Kerr 1983). In the process, a new approach has been developed: *democratic planning* (Alexander 1992; Ben Asher 1977; Moulaert and Cabaret 2006). Like democracy itself, this concept is best understood as an ideal, a goal that can never be perfectly achieved but that can be used to measure progress.

Democratic planning is based on the assumption that planning does occur and will continue to occur in all complex societies and, increasingly, at the world level (Gans 1968; Mannheim 1950). It also acknowledges that capitalism as such remains a dynamic and effective economic system, emphasizing that proponents neither accept pure market solutions nor reject capitalism. Rather, they endorse some type of government participation in market decisions. The issue, then, is how best to use representative political systems, especially in relation to corporate activities, so that the results of planning truly serve the interests of citizens. The U.S. sociologist Philip Selznick, who—along with Karl Mannheim in England—introduced the concept of *democratic planning* to sociologists as early as 1949, posed the issue this way:

> Whatever the ultimate outcome, it is evident that modern society has already moved rather far into the age of control. It is an age marked by widening efforts to master a refractory industrial system. That a technique for control will emerge, that there is and will be planning, is hardly in question. . . . It is therefore especially important to examine those organizations which are proposed as contributors to the technique of democratic planning. (Selznick 1949, 3)

In 2007, Virginia Polytechnic Institute and State University (Virginia Tech) established a pioneering center for democratic planning within its policy studies institute. Designated as the Center for Democratic Planning and Participatory Research (CDPPR), its principal goals underscore the basic features of the approach as Selznick and Mannheim envisioned it:

- To provide civic education to undergraduate and graduate students in order to cultivate new generations of civic professionals, citizen/scholars with real-life experience, skills, values and emotional commitment to work at the intersection of policy, research and civic participation.
- To apply social theory to concrete, community-based problem-solving, including questions relating to the constitution of democratic public space, civic deliberation and communication, identity politics, ecological and political imagination.

- To organize appropriate interdisciplinary teams of scholars and students to support communities, grassroots networks (GRNs, NCOs) and civil society organizations (CSO's) to inventory community assets or solve community problems.
- To catalyze and coordinate international, interdisciplinary research collaborations with GRNs, NCOs, CSO's and local government in selected global regions—oriented towards comparative, holistic, place-based, long-term, asset-based audits of local and regional well-being in the context of economic globalization. (www.aspect.vt.edu/?q=node/80)

Because of its sociological roots, the concept of democratic planning always includes awareness of unintended outcomes. In both public and private sector contexts, planners are routinely confronted with shortfalls and unmet goals. These are as much part of the profession as are successes (Seidman 1979). Just as often, planners are faced with the higher-order impacts of their work, as, for example, when a dam to provide water for people upstream inadvertently destroys the fishing industry downstream. All of this serves as a reminder that sociocultural change is a superorganic process and cannot be controlled in the same sense that nonhuman systems can. Those who forget or deny this essential property of collective life are in serious danger of dehumanizing the people for whom they presumably plan (Du Bois and Wright 2001).

Harking back to Comte's notion of the *positive polity*, scientific planning in the post–Cold War era is returning to its base in social science. In large part, this means it acknowledges the role of human will, human error, and the unexpected in the planning process. This attitude is in marked contrast to the Bolshevist ideal of physics-based planning, which sought the "engineering" of everything nonorganic, organic, and human according to simple principles of cause and effect. This element of Bolshevism was captured by the novelist Alexsander Solzhenitsyn in noting the typical response of planning officials to criticism of their system: "*We* never make mistakes" (Solzhenitsyn 1993).[6] Democratic planning, on the contrary, acknowledges that "we" make mistakes all of the time. With this in mind, it is a cautious and circumspect, as opposed to utopian, strategy of intentional change.

Two Approaches to Democratic Planning

Unlike the Bolshevist and other bureaucracy-dominated models, democratic planning does not focus on what "experts" believe to be the desired goals for society, nor does it strive specifically to centralize (or, for that matter, to decentralize) the political and economic resources necessary to achieve them. Rather, it seeks to maximize citizen participation in the planning process, beginning with the articulation of what society's desired goals actually are, which may or may not agree with expert opinions.

As a nonutopian approach, democratic planning lacks a predetermined image of the ideal future, except that it should be arrived at through the maximum degree of conscious, rational control by the electorate over goal setting and how the goals are to be pursued (see Oakeshott 1962). As a social science–based program, it is

TABLE 13.1 Features of Expert-Driven and Democratic Planning Approaches

Planning model	Expert-driven	Democratic
1. Funding Sources	Public sector, taxes; private sector, corporate income	Mass-based canvassing, membership dues, special events, government and foundation grants
2. Organizational context	Established, centralized, bureaucratic institution	"Grassroots," decentralized, nonhierarchical association
3. Ideological origins	Planning profession, politicians, and vested interests	Social community
4. Public good definition	Definition of needs	Articulation of demands
5. Ongoing priority	Generating rational policy choices, incremental decisions	Maximizing citizen engagement in political decision making
6. Action style	Analytical, consensus building	Competition, conflict, negotiation, cooperation
7. Efficiency definition	Decision-making speed and accuracy	Scope of citizen engagement in exercise of public power
8. Planner's relation to citizens	Citizens provide advisory input to planners	Planners provide advisory input to citizens
9. Planner's relation to politicians	Planners are on the output side of political decision making	Planners are on the input side of political decision making
10. Outcome orientation	Policy change without affecting relations of power	Institutional change in relations of power and reallocation of resources

Note: The two types of planning differ substantially along the ten dimensions listed in the first column, from funding sources to outcome orientation.

Source: Moshe Ben Asher, "Democratic Planning," SW 253A UC Berkeley School of Social Welfare (winter 1977), www.gatherthepeople.org/ (accessed October 27, 2009): 6.

obliged to maintain public awareness of the role of error and unintended outcomes in a planned society. Nothing can ever be perfectly planned, so beware of planners.

The emphasis on maximizing citizen access to planning has developed in two complementary but separate directions. One is the community organizing (CO) approach, with which Saul Alinsky's work in Chicago and several other U.S. cities is closely associated (Alinsky 1972; Orenstein 1998). The other is the political movement approach that originated in the Progressive Era around World War I, especially in the writings of Upton Sinclair, founder of the League for Industrial Democracy (LID).

In both cases, organizations have been created to promote the extension of democratic ideals and procedures beyond the limits of formal government. Their aim is to increase the participation of the legitimate, sovereign rulers (the people acting in their own interests) in positions of influence, where elites and large organizations have distorted the functioning of the democratic political economy.

Community Organizing   Community organizers work at the local level, in cities, towns, and neighborhoods (Fisher and Romanofsky 1981). Although, in principle, theirs is a day-to-day job, they often enter a situation during an impending episode of violent social conflict or in the wake of one. They participate in meetings of local organizations and interact individually with members of the community. In the process, they act as teachers and advocates, helping the citizens understand better what their rights are and how to achieve access to positions of political and economic influence. U.S. president Barack Obama, who was an active community organizer and instructor before he pursued a political career, describes the approach as follows.

> In theory, community organizing provides a way to merge various strategies for neighborhood empowerment. Organizing begins with the premise that (1) the problems facing inner-city communities do not result from a lack of effective solutions, but from a lack of power to implement these solutions; (2) that the only way for communities to build long-term power is by organizing people and money around a common vision; and (3) that a viable organization can only be achieved if a broadly based indigenous leadership—and not one or two charismatic leaders—can knit together the diverse interests of their local institutions. (Obama 1990, 37)

To the extent they are successful, the activities set in motion by community organizers help create more democratic local societies, in which the rulers, their representatives, and their economic organizations have achieved a more equitable balance of interests (which, of course, can always be improved). The potential for conflict is often reduced, and more important, the conflicts that inevitably occur can be managed more peacefully.

Since its inception in the late 1950s, the CO approach has had its share of both successes and failures. By the early 1980s, it had become fairly well institutionalized as a nonpartisan, "parapolitical" activity. Most local governments recognize its value today, and many routinely pay for such services. The work is also supported by private foundations, universities, wealthy individuals, and even local membership dues.[7]

At times, organizers have made mistakes, usually the mistake of acting and thinking like elites rather than as servants of the citizens (Delgado 1993). Some have been viewed as intruders, at which point the best, such as Alinsky himself, defer to the will of the people and consider not organizing as the best strategy. In other instances, in most of the major cities and smaller towns throughout the world, CO has been credited with

FIGURE 13.2 Barack Obama as a Community Organizer. Prior to serving as an Illinois state senator, Barack Obama worked as a community organizer on the Developing Communities Project in Chicago. He also served as an instructor with the Gamaliel Foundation, a faith-based "network of grassroots, interfaith, interracial, multi-issue organizations working together to create a more just and more democratic society" (www.gamaliel.org/default.htm). Based on this experience, he published a memoir, *After Alinsky: Community Organizing in Illinois* (1990). Photograph by the U.S. Congress.

significant improvements in social relations. It will certainly continue to be a part of our social lives, especially urban life, well into the twenty-first century.

Participatory Democracy Of course, our social lives are not entirely encompassed by participation in local community affairs. In recognition of this, proponents of democratic planning have supplemented the CO approach with a more general, political program that was promoted by Sinclair and the LID.[8] It is based on the principle of industrial democracy (Sartori 1987, 9–10, 422), according to which all large-scale organizations in a democratic society should be run as democracies from the local to the world level.

The argument in favor of industrial democracy is based on the understanding that highly consequential planning is carried on within and between large organizations, yet most of them retain essentially oligarchic structures. This means that, in effect, citizens have access to only a small subset of the decisions that influence their lives and futures through the formal political system. To the extent that corporate elites and organized interests have unfair influence on the electoral and legislative processes (which is always variable and difficult to discern), even this small share of the power that actually resides with the citizens is compromised.

In 1962, the student branch of the LID at the University of Michigan broke with the parent organization over the issue of extending membership privileges to members of the Communist Party (Cohen and Hale 1967; Unger 1974). The students character-ized themselves as not only non-Communist but also non-anti-Communist, in reaction to the Cold War hysteria known as McCarthyism (see chapter 7). This backlash move-ment, with the help of the U.S. Congress, had done great injury to the lives and reputa-tions of many distinguished citizens by labeling them "subversive," typically without good reason. The students sought to openly avoid this association, whereas the parent organization was still wary of the atmosphere of red baiting that prevailed. The group was renamed the Students for a Democratic Society (SDS), and members expressed their doctrine in one of the major documents of the U.S. New Left Movement, *The Port Huron Statement* (SDS 1964).

As reformulated by SDS, industrial democracy became "participatory democracy" (Sartori 1987, 112–15, 158–59, 315–16) to stress that the local communities, schools (including the University of Michigan), and other organizations were as much in need of democratic reforms as industry per se. *The Port Huron Statement* became a move-ment manifesto during the early 1960s, inspiring Civil Rights workers, pacifists, and student movement activists throughout the United States and well beyond. *The Port Huron Statement* defines participatory democracy as follows:

> In a participatory democracy, the political life would be based in several root prin-ciples: that decision-making of basic social consequence be carried on by public groupings; that politics be seen positively, as the art of collectively creating an acceptable pattern of social relations; that politics has the function of bringing people out of isolation and into community, thus being a necessary, though not sufficient, means of finding meaning in personal life; that the political order should serve to clarify problems in a way instrumental to their solution; it should provide outlets for the expression of personal grievance and aspiration; opposing views should be organized so as to illuminate choices and facilitate the attainment of goals. (http://history.hanover.edu/courses/excerpts/111hur.html)

As the turbulent 1960s and 1970s progressed, SDS experienced organizational cri-ses and was eventually dissolved, which was in part a reflection of general political crisis in the Civil Rights movement.

During the 1980s and 1990s the concept of participatory democracy was debated at length, and often criticized, in academic circles. At the same time, its practice increased substantially. Nearly every type of large-scale organization, from Big Three automobile manufacturers to colleges and state universities, has in fact become internally more democratic. Moreover, many of the former New Left students and others who shared their views, including those who authored *The Port Huron Statement*, are themselves in positions of social influence today (for example, as congressional representatives and professors of sociology at leading universities; Gitlin 1985; Hayden 1988).

During the early 1990s, two trends converged to significantly increase interest in the movement. One is the development and spread of Internet-based communication tech-nologies, especially social-networking sites that facilitate tertiary relations (see chapter 5) such as Facebook and Twitter (Rheingold 1993). The other is the integration of these technologies into fund-raising, recruitment, and other aspects of citizen-oriented political activity, especially as achieved by Obama into his senatorial and presidential campaigns.

The potential for employing the Internet to strengthen democratic practices and institutions was envisioned well before the technology was widely accessible. Now that cyber-communication is a routine part of everyone's daily activities in the highly industrialized countries—and, increasingly, throughout the world—this potential is being rapidly realized. In an article published in a journal whose title is clearly a sign of the times, the *International Journal of Electronic Democracy*, Professor Gregory Kersten (2008) states the case succinctly:

> *Participatory democracy*, like the Athenian democracy, requires that the citizens be involved in all phases of decision-making rather than solely in the acceptance of an alternative through, for example, a vote. . . . A truly participatory democracy in which people are engaged in every decision process at each level of government may not be feasible. However, information and communication technologies (ICTs) provide opportunities to augment and complement the existing democratic mechanisms. (52)

Most observers of Obama's rapid rise to political prominence acknowledge that a considerable share of his success was the result of his use of the Internet, cell phones, and other electronic communication technologies to create a "virtual community" of supporters (Wellman and Haythornthweait 2002). "Obama won because he and his staff built an incredible grassroots organization where everyone was encouraged to join in. From signing up to get an early text message as to his V.P. pick (and be part of the 'inner circle') to going online during idle moments to get lists of phone numbers" (Kelly 2008). Obama himself explicitly noted the connection between his support of participatory democracy and his use of electronic media.

> We need to connect citizens with each other to engage them more fully and directly in solving the problems that face us. We must use all available technologies and methods to open up the federal government, creating a new level of transparency to change the way business is conducted in Washington and giving Americans the chance to participate in government deliberations and decision-making in ways that were not possible only a few years ago. (Obama 2007)

Thus, with the integration of electoral politics with the Internet, participatory democracy has now become part of modern culture. Although still perhaps a minority trend, it is hardly the "fringe" or "radical" project it was in the 1960s.

Democratic Planning and the Paradox of Control

From the late-eighteenth-century ideal of an entirely unplanned political economy to the late-twentieth-century program of democratic planning, the paradox of control has plagued and fascinated contemporary society. Every problem in reconciling self-rule with representation has elicited a variety of solutions, and every solution has presented new problems. There is little reason to believe that this process will not, or should not, continue into the foreseeable future.

Summary

In chapter 12, we examined large-scale attempts to apply technology to solve or at least mitigate problems of global stratification. We also observed that, unfortunately, technology does not invent and diffuse itself. Here in chapter 13, we have focused on the point at which people and conscientious planning play crucial roles. If the Gordian knot of social injustice is to be cut, it will not occur with technology alone. Such a major undertaking will require a concerted and cooperative effort to ensure that the right technologies are created and targeted at the right places in the most effective ways. This in turn will involve democratic planning at local and global levels, and at the scale of the arms and space races.

We still live in the shadow of an era in which paternalism and so-called laissez-faire models dominated the process of social planning. But we are also beginning to see children from every possible social, economic, and ethnic background joining their peers throughout the nation and the world in instantaneous global classrooms. Such an image clearly represents a much more sophisticated understanding of how we can, and indeed must, plan our common futures.

Relevant Websites

www.sociosite.net/topics/city.php
http://urpl.wisc.edu/academics/phd.php#
Here are home pages of the University of Amsterdam and the University of Wisconsin joint programs in sociology and urban planning. These are two of several such programs throughout the world that bring the two disciplines together.

www.sociologycommission.org/
www.aacsnet.org/
www.techsociety.com/asa
These three applied sociology websites relate to the use of sociology in planned social change, from the level of small organizations to global issues. The first is the Commission on Applied and Clinical Sociology, which accredits university-level programs. The second is the professional society the Association for Applied and Clinical Sociology. The third is the American Sociological Association Section on Sociological Practice and Public Sociology.

www.hud.gov/progdesc/copc.cfm
Information and current reports about the Community Outreach Partnership Centers (COPCs) that are sponsored by the U.S. Department of Housing and Urban Development can be found at this address.

www2.iath.virginia.edu/sixties/HTML_docs/Resources/Primary/Manifestos/SDS_Port_
Huron.html
This site contains the entire text of the *Port Huron Statement*.

www.nfg.org/cotb
This site is dedicated to CO and is maintained by the National Funders Group. It provides information about grants and other resources to support CO work.

The Political Economy of Globalization

A T THE HEIGHT of the Cold War in the late 1950s and early 1960s, sociologists wrote of the awesome power concentrated in the hands of a few highly placed individuals (Horowitz 1963; Mills 1958). It had become possible for the President of the United States, the Premier of the Soviet Union, and perhaps one or two others to press a button that would set off a nuclear juggernaut.

Although conflict and war have always been part of social relations, never before had people been capable of obliterating at will all of human civilization, if not the entire species—and most other species along the way. As Sigmund Freud (1961) observed in his last writings, "Men have gained control over the forces of nature to such an extent that with their help they would have no difficulty in exterminating one another to the last man" (92). How, we wondered, could this have happened? Were things meant to turn out this way? As often occurs in social science, the best answer we have come up with is a definite "yes and no."

The ability to destroy purposely what had taken billions of people millennia to create is a remarkable, although frightening, achievement. Some even characterized it as "playing God," in reference to the belief that the once-exclusive domain of overarching divine authority, as in the Old Testament story of Noah, had now been arrogated by mere mortals (Ellul 1964).

Such fears and moral evaluations aside, the nuclear showdown represented the latest stage in a cumulative quest to control sociocultural change in accord with what is believed to be necessary, just, or in society's best interests. In this respect, it was the ultimate outcome of the scheming and meddling of politicians that Bernard Mandeville had warned against at the dawn of the Industrial Revolution (Schneider 1987).

FIGURE 14.1 The Uros People, who live on floating reed islands in Lake Titicaca, high in the Peruvian Andes. Will globalization ever affect the lives of such remote societies? Photo by Catherine Collins; used with permission.

The Cold War ended in 1990. With the uneasy peace that has followed, the threat of the juggernaut has receded (although it has certainly not been entirely eliminated). In its wake has come the realization that our newly gained power to control human destiny can be turned to cooperative ends (Ekins 1992). On February, 12, 1994, the space shuttle *Discovery* landed in California after a two-week mission in which, for the first time, U.S. and Russian citizens together planned and executed an exploration of outer space (*New York Times* 1994). The Russian cosmonaut in the crew Sergei Kirkalev will always be remembered as the person who, two years before the *Discovery* mission, was launched in a rocket from the Cold War Soviet Union. He had been left to orbit indefinitely while the Soviet state was overthrown and landed weeks behind schedule in post-Soviet and post–Cold War Russia (*Wall Street Journal* 1992). Could Kirkalev possibly have imagined that his next ride would be on a U.S. vessel?

There is much that is merely symbolic in all of this, but there is more that reflects a real, profoundly consequential change as well. By the first decade of the twenty-first century, cooperative space missions between the United States, Russia, and even unlikely countries such as Israel and India had become routine.[1] To seek to establish human life on worlds where it has not existed before also is to "play God." The difference between this and the old way, however, is monumental. Now, formerly mortal (in the strongest possible sense of the word) enemies are cooperating to create rather than to destroy.

Achievements such as nuclear weaponry and space exploration are the products of institutionalized planning (Richter 1982). They are the intended outcomes of activities coordinated and conducted at the highest levels of social complexity yet attained. This complexity is characterized by worldwide networks of large-scale bureaucratic organizations, linked through elaborate tertiary relationships, at the cost of uncountable billions of dollars, decades of human labor time, and many (but, in some respects, surprisingly few) human lives. Moreover, the projects were undertaken in an atmosphere of social conflict, also at the largest scale yet achieved, with most of the world's nations divided into two warring camps struggling to dominate each other.

In these ways, the arms and space races have helped push the age-old dialectic of social conflict and cooperation to its global limits. Their higher-order impacts have significantly accelerated the momentum that has been gathering since the Industrial Revolution toward a universal society and culture. Like socioeconomic development and modernization programs, these projects are landmarks in the quest for control, bringing us to the brink of both world destruction and world creation.

This final chapter is about global conflict and cooperation: yesterday, today, and tomorrow. The main point is that urban growth, bureaucracy, economic planning, and representative government have led to a dramatic increase in the ability of people to direct sociocultural change. These institutions have provided the means to accumulate unprecedented economic resources and political power, to establish elaborate communication networks, and to use them to achieve practically whatever goals one can imagine. Drawing on this premise, our conclusion considers the future implications of these trends and the fact that they have given humanity godlike capacities.

For one last time, we underscore the superorganic nature of change in human systems. Tomorrow's global society will be the product of institutional planning, legislation, social movements, development and modernization projects, and the programmed invention and diffusion of new technologies. All of these involve conscious purpose and the formulation and pursuit of premeditated, collective goals.[2] Human individuals and groups surely change in accord with the laws of physics, chemistry, and biology. But, unlike any other object of scientific study, they are also quite capable of altering those laws for their presumed benefit and of devising their own, which they then proceed to obey (and disobey).

Globalization and Localism

As we proceed through the new millennium, a single human society is no longer a dream or a remote potentiality. Rather, social scientists now take it for granted that the several trends that together are referred to as globalization will continue and will continue to accelerate as they have since the Industrial Revolution (Bird et al. 1994). Multinational corporations, borderless telecommunications, world government, scientific research in all fields, and air and space travel, along with international human rights, environmental, and other issue-oriented organizations, have all assumed unprecedented levels of sophistication and geographical reach.

FIGURE 14.2 Localism or Globalization? Local and traditional institutions continue to thrive in the era of globalization. This photograph shows a donkey carrying empty coke bottles. Does this situation represent a contradiction that must be quickly resolved or a synthesis between the local and the global that will continue long into the future? Photo by Catherine Collins; used by permission.

Philosophers and dreamers have spoken of One World for centuries. It has been known for some time that, contrary to the arguments of some racial doctrines, humanity is a single species. Demographers have been pointing out for many years that a world population exists that has its own unique dynamic reflecting its relationship to the environment—the planet Earth—and the complex interplay of the thousands of local populations and subpopulations of which it consists.

In a similar vein, the planner Buckminster Fuller (1983, 1992) coined the phrase "Spaceship Earth" to emphasize the common lot of humanity as we hurtle through interplanetary space sharing the limited resources of the "vehicle" on which we are the "passengers." In October 1982, the Epcot Disney Theme Park opened a "Spaceship Earth display, featuring Fuller's best known innovation, the geodesic dome. And it has been three decades since the sociologist Harold Innes and his student Marshall McLuhan first spoke of the 'global village'" (McLuhan and Fiore 1968). They were referring to the fact that technology has made it possible for any person on the planet to communicate directly and instantaneously with any other person, as was once common (minus the electronic connections) only in small villages.

Amidst such observations, it is important to remember that the single world-level society and culture inherent in these trends is still far from being a *fait accompli*, a finished thing. The editors of a publication on globalization by the International Sociological Association described the situation in this way:

> If we already lived in a single world society then all the talk about globalisation would be in the past tense. Instead, globalisation is the present process of becoming global: globality itself lies in the future, but the very near future. Each major aspect of social reality (the structure, culture and personality of traditional terminology) is simultaneously undergoing globalisation, as witnessed by the emergence of the world economy, a cosmopolitan culture, and international social movements. (Albrow and King 1990, 1)

With so much at stake, the attention of most researchers and theorists of social and cultural change has now turned to these issues, with the result that many hundreds of books and articles have appeared on the subject since the mid-1980s. In them, one can find an impressive range of scenarios of the future, from the credible to the not so credible. In fact, the phenomenon referred to as *globalization* is one of the most intensively studied, as well as one of the most controversial, topics in contemporary social science. It has captured the interest of specialists and nonspecialists alike. It is difficult to surf the Internet, watch TV, or read a newspaper without encountering discussion and debate about it.

For many people, concern about globalization has been stimulated by one or more popular books on the subject, including the best-selling *The World Is Flat* by the *New York Times* journalist Thomas Friedman (2005). Among the many scholarly works on the subject, *Sociology of Globalization* (Sassen 2007) by one of the acknowledged leading experts in the field, Saskia Sassen, covers the topic especially well. The genre of science fiction, an enormously important literary movement in itself, specializes in constructing imaginative world systems.[3] It has been a rich source of sociological insights about globalization since the pioneering works of Jules Verne, H. G. Wells, Yvgenii Zamiatin, and, of course, George Orwell.

Among all the potentially relevant themes that have emerged from this extensive thinking about tomorrow, some have special bearing on our interest in the paradox of control. First and foremost is a question that concerns everyone: to what extent is the structure of future world society already determined, and to what extent do people still have a role in shaping it? In addressing this question, this book has explored such areas as world government, the state of international stratification today, the origins of the modern world system, the role of communication and information technologies, and the general problem of cultural lag. The following sections summarize some of the main points in these areas.

The Roots of the Global System

By the end of World War II, especially with the rise of the Third World nations, it had become clear to most observers that the ideal of one world was close to being realized. Karl Mannheim (1950) was among the first sociologists to record his views on the matter: "Imperialism, the cause of recurrent international friction and economic upheaval, seems to have reached a point of saturation. The world is divided; there are no more open spaces with free homelands for immigrants, and the backward peoples have been awakened through communication with and education by their rulers or trading partners" (9).

The reference to imperialism is crucial because the social structures and diffusion channels that form the world system today were first established during the ages of European exploration and colonialism. These roots have left a definite stamp on the emerging world society, the divided character of which Mannheim spoke. Not only did the vast empires organize markets in every type of essential commodity, including human labor, into an international system, but also they ensured that control was centralized in London and other capitals of the industrializing powers. Political domination by European governments of hundreds of millions of people throughout the peripheral, Third World areas served to authorize the domination of world economic relations by European companies. Thus, the system, as it had developed up to the World War II era, was truly a stratified political economy of control: divided between Europe at the core, the colonies at the periphery, and semiperipheral societies.

Through the first decades of the twentieth century, big corporations and big representative governments in industrialized countries assumed prominent roles as the major actors in the world system. The Soviet command state, which combined the powers of corporations and representative government, introduced a new level of control into human affairs, and it provided a serious source of competition in international relations for the democratic-capitalist models. With each step in this seemingly irreversible process of expansion, the Enlightenment ideals of self-rule and free markets became ever-more difficult to sustain.

In the midst of economic depression and disillusionment with democracy, fascist ideology was created with a strong appeal to the average person's feelings of impotence. When fascist parties came to power in Italy, Spain, Portugal, and Germany, they institutionalized their non-Bolshevist versions of the command state (in which both self-rule and free markets were subordinated to national priorities). Thus, competition for control of the world system intensified. With Germany's invasion of Poland in 1939, the competition turned to war, a war of the big powers: capitalist democracies, versus fascist autocracies, versus the Soviet Union.

The world system inherited by the post–World War II generation was in severe crisis. Europe had experienced physical and social devastation as serious among the winners, such as England and the USSR, as it was for the losing fascist powers. Europe's Jews, Gypsies, and several other "degenerate" civilian populations were very nearly annihilated by the German authorities and under the orders of government officials in approximately twenty other European countries. Russia and the Ukraine alone lost approximately twenty million people to the Nazi armies. Indeed, there will never be a way to calculate how much Europe paid for that war.

It had been a costly war for the United States and Canada as well (Bothwell, Drummond, and English 1987; Li 1996). But the fact that very little of it was fought on their own territories permitted them to emerge as the healthiest and the wealthiest of the capitalist democracies.[4] In the East, Stalin had gained considerable territorial concessions following his liberation of Europe (Harbutt 1986; Kanet 1987). Under occupation by the Red Army, between 1944 and 1948, Bolshevist command states were established in eight countries. These were Albania, Bulgaria, Czechoslovakia, East Germany (one piece of the country that was created by dividing it between the victorious armies), Hungary, Poland, Romania, and Yugoslavia; Latvia, Estonia, and Lithuania had been absorbed into the Soviet Union earlier.

In the colonial peripheries, independence movements that had been temporarily suspended during the war were resumed with renewed dedication. Leaders such as Mohandas K. Gandhi, Chaim Weitzman, and Kwame Nkrumah used a very powerful argument for ending colonial rule. Because the colonial masters had just fought a war for democracy, it was natural for Gandhi and the other independence leaders to want to extend it to their own people. These movements had been routinely met with military resistance for decades before the war and, briefly, afterward. But England, France, and the other imperialist nations proved incapable or unwilling to continue the resistance. Postwar reconstruction at home, greatly aided by Marshall Plan resources from the United States, presented more pressing priorities.

As independence was granted and colonial authority, including military authority, was withdrawn in the Third World, local political and ethnic-national conflict broke out. In China, resolution came in 1949 with the victory of Mao Zedong's Communist forces over the Nationalists, and the subsequent establishment of a command state over the largest national population in the world. In some places, resolution is yet to be achieved into the twenty-first century.

Thus, it appeared to observers of Mannheim's generation that the world society was not only divided but also shattered (Steiner 1970). It should be recalled that the war broke out when the first attempt at world government, the League of Nations, failed to contain the spread of antidemocratic movements (Cooper 2001; Walters 1952). In place of the lofty rhetoric of the Versailles Treaty that established the League, the realities of war and reconstruction proved disheartening in the extreme. Mannheim's (1954) pessimism reflected the genuine fear that a similar round of disappointments lay ahead: "Philosophers and sociologists once thought that there was a tendency toward rational and moral progress inherent in the human mind. That this is untrue is clear to everyone who knows what is happening in the contemporary world. For it can be asserted with confidence that in the past decades, we have receded rather than advanced as far as moral and rational progress is concerned" (51).

The World System Today

As it has turned out, the end of the war was the beginning of a new era, in which the world system has experienced rational and moral progress *and* regress. On the positive side, the war and the Holocaust taught humanity some important negative lessons that are incorporated in the structure of world government today.

World government made it possible for over one billion people in the former European colonies to gain sovereignty as citizens of independent nations: the Age of Imperialism had at last ended. Liberation movements in the Third World, and the wartime experiences of the African American community, helped spark the U.S. Civil Rights movement, in which the concept of self-rule was extended significantly in the first democracy. The U.S. Civil Rights movement was, in turn, an important source of inspiration for the women's and gay rights causes and the revolutionary movements in the Soviet Union and the satellite states in which Communism was overthrown. In each case, the gap between the ideal of self-rule and its reality has been narrowed, as moral and rational progress have, in this respect, surely begun to advance once more.

As with other major social trends, the resurgence of democracy after World War II has occurred in a conflict-filled and uneven manner. Immediately following the war, Bolshevist autocracies were established throughout Central and Eastern Europe. Although these regimes had considerable success in dismantling fascist institutions, they managed to dismantle the vestiges of democracy as well. Nationalism and movements for ethnic sovereignty, especially in the Third World and former Communist countries, have also complicated the process of democratization. Despite significant progress on diplomatic fronts, territorial and ethnic tensions in the Middle East appear to be as recalcitrant as ever. Moreover, the power of multinational corporations, a chief cause of concern to Mannheim and his contemporaries, has not diminished since the war. On the contrary, it has increased enormously.

World War II did not destroy the world economy, although it was severely damaged and at times it appeared that such a cataclysm was imminent. Rather, the result was a fundamental reorganization that left the United States in a position of virtually unchallenged dominance among the capitalist countries and the Soviet Union as the main political power of Europe. Through the late 1980s, control of a staggering amount of resources was centralized in the positions of minority influence in corporations and in democratic and autocratic governments, much of it directed to a multitrillion-dollar arms race. In this respect, moral and rational progress did recede.

As a result of government efforts to limit the power of corporations, labor unions, and other large-scale organizations, some type of market control is the norm in every capitalist economy today. Similarly, the pure Bolshevist model of state domination of markets has been all but abandoned everywhere, even in China (Cardoso and Yusuf 1994; McKinnon 1994). A planned, but only partly planned, society is now the rule.

Meanwhile, the largest and fastest growing segment of the world's population remains poor and dependent. In Third World countries, neocolonialism has left imperial economic relations essentially intact, within a framework of fragile national sovereignty. There, multinational corporations continue the pattern of core (European, and now U.S. and Japanese) domination of local markets while bringing industrialization and creating jobs (Biersteker 1978).[5]

Self-rule, which has a critical economic dimension in the Third World, is today intimately tied to policies for control of multinational corporate interests. Social movements are regularly organized for and against U.S. and European corporations.

FIGURE 14.3 Gun over Golan. This gun from a deserted Israeli tank is aimed at the Syrian border, over the disputed Golan Heights. It is a vivid symbol of the continuing animosity between Israel and her Arab neighbors. The future of the emerging global society depends in large part on the resolution of this conflict. Author photo.

Foreign investment is alternately encouraged and discouraged. Industries are nationalized and denationalized. And leading companies such as IBM and Coca-Cola are routinely invited into (and dismissed from) countries throughout Asia, Africa, and Latin America (Dixon, Drakakis-Smith, and Watts 1986; Sharma, Vridenburg, and Westley 1994).

These relations are also crucial at the level of national planning. Multinational corporate investment and disinvestment, loans from international banks, and aid from foreign governments are essential, if not at times the only, ingredients in local programs of resource allocation and investment. For these reasons, democratic government in the Third World today depends on democratic participation in complex and highly technical corporate decision-making processes (Amba-Rao 1993).

The amount of communication, knowledge, and education that effective participation requires is formidable, especially in places where between 20 and 60 percent of the population is still illiterate. In the poorer countries of the world, democratic government has a strong competitor, for the ideals of Communist autocracy are not dead, even though in China and Cuba capitalist enterprises are legal and are increasing in number and importance (Betancourt 1995; Fewsmith 2001; Travieso-Díaz 1997). The road to democracy in the Third World is thus bound to be long and difficult, and much the same applies to the post-Communist countries of Europe.

Information and Globalization

The modern technologies of information creation, storage, and communication have played a significant role in the development of the world system, and they will undoubtedly continue to do so for the next several generations (Benedikt 1991; Gore 1991). The central feature of these technologies is the increased potential for control they provide to positions of minority influence: they favor and reinforce elite rule.

This phenomenon is the outcome of two trends (introduced in chapter 4) that were accelerated greatly with the invention of the printing press, although they have roots in the invention of writing itself. First is the capacity of the technologies to overcome the limits of space and time in long-distance communications. Second is the emergence of a new social institution, the communications system, from organizations that were formerly parts of other institutions.

This combination of technological and institutional developments has served to coordinate previously discrete realms of people's lives. Homes become offices and commuting became "telecommuting" (Conroy 1995; Niles 1994, chap. 1). Books, video and audio recordings, telephones, and computers are integrated into a single unit. Factories become classrooms. At the same time, the activities of previously unrelated individuals are being increasingly linked. Wherever multinational corporations operate, whether in the First, Second, or Third World, people all experience the coordination of the information side of their lives. The link will be completed very soon, as people everywhere get access to an e-mail address that will connect their individual book-video-audio-telephone unit to everyone else's (Calem 1992; Cerf 1991). The entire human species is quickly becoming involved in a single and instantaneous network of tertiary relationships (Gilster 1993; McNichol 1994).

Information and its flow are essential to the functioning of representative government, as well as in corporations and other large-scale organizations. With this in view, social scientists have recently raised several questions about the politics of the information superhighway and the potential for its democratic governance in the future (Drucker 1986; Roszak 1994). This is obviously a highly consequential matter because such control truly has come to mean control over a great part of the destiny of humanity. So we ask the following.

Who Controls the System?

Orwell provides the clearest negative prototype of a pure information autocracy.[6] The world of *Nineteen Eighty-Four* is divided into three interacting alliances. Oceania, the alliance in which the novel's action takes place, is at constant war with one or both of the others, thus necessitating Big Brother's (permanent) emergency takeover of the Ministry of Truth (Minitrue). This includes the decision that only the Inner Party can receive information from the other two alliances.

In Minitrue, one finds the master units that control all individual communication systems on the information superhighway, the monitors for the feared, ubiquitous telescreens. From Minitrue, all government-authorized interpretations of events (which are the only ones allowed on the superhighway) are transmitted. As The Party constantly reminds the citizens, "He who controls information controls society."

Considerable debate exists among contemporary scholars about how close the world is, or parts of the world are, to the Oceania ideal. Some, ranging from moralists such as Jacques Ellul to sociologists such as Ralf Dahrendorf, believe that Orwell underestimated the degree to which even the powerful—the Big Brothers and Inner Parties of the world today—are subject to the workings of the technological imperative.

From this perspective, the level of coordination that Minitrue attained in Oceania is impossible in the real world because knowledge from outside, along with the secret of how to turn off the unit, is bound to infiltrate and circulate in the cracks and leaks typical of real organizational structures. This certainly proved to be true in Europe's former Communist regimes, whose leaders themselves participated in introducing the "polluting" bourgeois culture through recordings and televisions purchased during trips abroad (see chapter 1; see also Weinstein 1993). And similar leaks were evident in the Tiananmen Square uprising in Beijing, when dissident students used imported fax machines to coordinate their antiregime tactics.

Others, including Mannheim (1954) and Theodore Roszak (1994), believe that the centralization of information technologies is an inherent threat to democratic process, characterized as not the conspiratorial scheming of an all-powerful inner party but rather the result of how power accumulates in the positions of influence within government and corporations. To the extent that a few individuals can determine what information will be created, who has possession of it at any given moment, and how and to whom it will be communicated, they are free to behave according to their interests. They can be especially effective today because of the powerful technologies at their disposal.

As the influence of organized interest groups in democratic government has increased, so specifically has the influence of the organizations and corporations that dominate the new information system: government regulating agencies, telecommunications companies, research universities, computer manufacturers, and professional scientific associations. Those concerned by the antidemocratic implications of this trend have wondered about the extent to which such organized interests coincide with the collective will. Are the decisions made in these positions of influence compatible with the ideal of self-rule? By the very nature of the technologies involved, self-rule in this case includes international relationships—that is, it is now quite meaningful to wonder whether a particular decision or procedure related to information management is compatible with democracy at a *world* level.

Communication Technology and Cultural Lag

Such academic and political debate over control of the new information institution reveals a significant cultural lag. On one hand is the rapid and accelerating rate of change of the information technologies and organizations. On the other are the slower rates of change in norms whereby society governs their application and functioning. As in the operation of contemporary political and economic institutions, neither a pure Bolshevist nor a pure free market model is viewed as appropriate to the management of the communication system. But this means that an alternative remains to be developed.

Since the early 1990s, courts all over the world have been asked to decide perplexing questions in the absence of specific legislation or precedent: to whom does electronic material "belong" (Boldrin and Levine 2002; Maskus 2002)? What constitutes a "monopoly" over something invisible, such as airwaves? Should government business be conducted on live television? Who can legislate which electronic signals enter a private home? Can an employer or government electronically monitor, via telescreen or other means, the activities (and thoughts) of an employee or citizen, as in Oceania (Garon 2002; Minow 2002)?

Box 14.1 CHINA POSTPONES INTERNET FILTER SOFTWARE PLAN

China's state media says the government has postponed a rule mandating all computers be sold with internet filtering software. The order, which requires manufacturers to pre-install or supply the Green Dam Youth Escort software with PCs made for sale in China, was to take effect Wednesday. The Xinhua news agency said in a brief report late Tuesday that the Ministry of Industry and Information Technology decided to delay the plan, though no new deadline or reason for the delay was given. U.S trade officials, industry and free speech groups have all made direct appeals to China to scrap the order, citing security and privacy concerns. "The Green Dam mandate raises significant questions of security, privacy, system reliability, the free flow of information and user choice," said a letter delivered to Chinese Premier Wen Jiabao from 22 chambers of commerce and trade groups representing the world's major technology suppliers. U.S. trade officials in Washington said the order, which was abruptly introduced in May, might violate China's World Trade Organization free-trade obligations. China already has the most extensive system for monitoring communications and blocking content on the internet, but Green Dam is its most intrusive tool yet, as it brings the censorship directly onto the individual's computer. China said the system is needed to block access to violent and obscene material found online. Yet independent researchers who have tested the software found it also blocks key words deemed politically sensitive in China, such as Falun Gong. Researchers at the University of Michigan who studied the program said it also makes computers more vulnerable to security risks. A California company, Solid Oak Software, also claims parts of its software were used in Green Dam, raising the possibility of an intellectual property rights dispute.

Source: CBC Online Technology and Science, "China Postpones Internet Filter Software Plan," June 30, 2009, www.cbc.ca/technology/story/2009/06/30/china-postponed-filter-deadline-green-dam.html.

These lags have helped bring society to even higher levels of complexity than was anticipated just one generation ago. New government departments and ministries of information or communication have recently been created in the United States and other countries and are, officially, charged with coordinating and regulating the information superhighway (Markoff 1993; National Coordinating Office for Information Technology Research and Development [NCITRD] 1999).[7] Schools and businesses, too, have had to revise their rules and operating procedures to accommodate the new technologies. And, in a self-reinforcing process, the information revolution itself is increasingly featured as the subject matter of communication on the superhighway. Books, movies, television series, CD-ROM packages, and e-mail network bulletin boards all diffuse information about the diffusion of information. The medium most certainly is the message here. Taken together, this activity constitutes an astounding episode of cultural change. Norms and even deeply held values are in the process of being altered (partly intentionally) in response to lags, as society attempts once more to catch up with its inventions.

Similar episodes have occurred before, generally as signals of technological revolution: agrarian, agricultural, and industrial. Indeed, many social scientists believe we are in the midst of an authentic postindustrial revolution, the coming of the Information

TABLE 14.1 Globalization Indices

A. *Economic globalization*

Trade (percent of GDP)
Foreign direct investment, flows (percent of GDP)
Foreign direct investment, stocks (percent of GDP)
Portfolio investment (percent of GDP)
Income payments to foreign nationals (percent of GDP)

B. *Information globalization*

Internet users (per 1,000 people)
Cable television (per 1,000 people)
Trade in newspapers (percent of GDP)
Radios (per 1,000 people)

C. Cultural globalization

Number of McDonald's restaurants (per capita)
Number of IKEA (per capita)
Trade in books (percent of GDP)

Note: The globalization variables used in table 14.2 (see box 14.2) are based upon the three measures, A, B, and C, developed by the KOF Research Center, Berne, Switzerland.

Source: Axel Dreher, "Does Globalization Affect Growth? Empirical Evidence from a New Index," *Applied Economics* 38 (10) (2006): 1091–1110.

Age (Bell 1973, 1989). Previous technological changes of this magnitude have transformed social life in the past, so there is every reason to believe that the current one will also have profound consequences. This time, however, major events are occurring at the speed of light, and they surely will affect humanity as a whole.

Globalization: Geopolitical Dimensions

With our courts, legislatures, companies, schools, and families seeking to comprehend and benefit from the new information technologies, two other major sources of contemporary international conflict continue to demand attention. In the political realm, we face the perennial contradictions between democratic access and elite rule, now on a global scale. In geographical affairs, we find people everywhere struggling to reconcile local and cosmopolitan interests, as expressed in emerging nationalist and fundamentalist movements.

These tensions are likely to be among the most consequential forces in shaping future social relations. The information institution has transcended international boundaries from its inception because of the nature of the technologies themselves and because the corporations in which they were developed had already achieved multinational reach. The result is that government (whether autocratic or democratic) and business (whether capitalist or socialist) in one part of the world must now consider people and their interests everywhere else, to a far greater degree than ever in human experience. With continued globalization, world society will be increasingly dependent on the communication system that develops. Under these conditions, the kind of society that emerges will very much depend on how these geopolitical conflicts are managed (Wallerstein 1991).

Box 14.2 GLOBALIZATION AND DEVELOPMENT VARIABLES FOR SELECTED COUNTRIES (RANKING IN PARENTHESES)

Variables:
- Globalization 2005—combined economic, information, and cultural index for the year 2005
- Globalization 2000—combined economic, information, and cultural index for the year 2000
- Globalization change—(Globalization 2005 – Globalization 2000)
- Dev't index—level of socioeconomic development, maximum 100 (see chapter 12)
- GNI change—change in per capita gross national income between 2000 and 2005

(Continued)

Box 14.2 GLOBALIZATION AND DEVELOPMENT VARIABLES FOR SELECTED COUNTRIES (RANKING IN PARENTHESES) (Continued)

Table 14.2 Index of Globalization

Country	Globalization 2005	Globalization 2000	Globalization change	Dev't index	GNI change
Estonia	89.52 (1)	85.16 (3)	5.12 (13)	63 (10)	139.05 (3)
Denmark	88.00 (2)	87.97 (1)	0.03 (18)	92 (3)	53.38 (10)
Sweden	87.49 (3)	86.54 (2)	1.10 (15)	90 (4)	142.65 (1)
Iceland	83.99 (4)	74.73 (7)	12.39 (2)	93 (2)	0.07 (24)
Latvia	80.99 (5)	74.46 (8)	8.75 (7)	63 (10)	130.27 (5)
United Kingdom	80.83 (6)	80.62 (4)	0.26 (17)	87 (5)	49.64 (11)
Israel	78.09 (7)	78.32 (5)	-0.29 (19)	85 (7)	9.16 (21)
Slovenia	77.59 (8)	70.65 (10)	9.82 (5)	66 (8)	70.14 (8)
Lithuania	73.31 (9)	67.02 (13)	9.38 (6)	64 (9)	131.83 (4)
Australia	71.02 (10)	77.74 (6)	-8.64 (26)	86 (6)	64.94 (9)
Panama	69.93 (11)	71.12 (9)	-1.67 (21)	60 (13)	18.11 (18)
Costa Rica	66.91 (12)	67.48 (12)	-0.82 (20)	60 (13)	23.03 (16)
Malaysia	66.77 (13)	68.15 (11)	-2.01 (22)	63 (10)	46.60 (12)
El Salvador	58.77 (14)	51.44 (19)	14.25 (1)	52 (19)	19.80 (17)
Zimbabwe	56.70 (15)	52.78 (16)	7.43 (9)	26 (25)	-20.45 (26)
Dom. Republic	56.65 (16)	58.89 (15)	-3.80 (24)	55 (18)	14.95 (19)
Fiji	56.59 (17)	60.20 (14)	-5.99 (25)	51 (21)	160.0 (2)

Country	Globalization 2005	Globalization 2000	Globalization change	Dev't index	GNI change
Thailand	55.41 (18)	52.07 (17)	6.41 (11)	50 (22)	35.32 (14)
Tunisia	52.03 (19)	51.89 (18)	0.27 (16)	56 (17)	38.46 (13)
Bolivia	49.92 (20)	46.44 (22)	7.49 (8)	43 (24)	3.06 (23)
Albania	48.51 (21)	46.53 (21)	4.27 (14)	52 (19)	110.65 (6)
Peru	48.37 (22)	43.92 (24)	10.13 (4)	58 (16)	29.27 (15)
Japan	47.45 (23)	44.72 (23)	6.10 (12)	100 (1)	10.03 (20)
Brazil	45.25 (24)	46.85 (20)	-3.4 (23)	60 (13)	-2.74 (25)
China	43.00 (25)	40.12 (25)	7.17 (10)	48 (23)	107.14 (7)
Uganda	39.92 (26)	36.12 (26)	10.49 (3)	16 (26)	3.70 (22)

(Continued)

Box 14.2 GLOBALIZATION AND DEVELOPMENT VARIABLES FOR SELECTED COUNTRIES (RANKING IN PARENTHESES) (Continued)

The countries in this sample that are the most "globalized" are not necessarily globalizing rapidly. And the countries that are globalizing the most rapidly are not necessarily experiencing the most rapid economic growth. Unfortunately, the actual effects of globalization on ordinary people are difficult to discern. The source of this difficulty may be an actual lack of impact on the general population—although this does not mean that some (relatively privileged) groups are not benefiting. Globalization is occurring, no doubt. But it is not penetrating beyond the elites who, after all, are setting the terms for globalization. In this respect, globalization is reminiscent of the official socioeconomic development programs of the 1960s and 1970s, as discussed in chapter 12. A large portion of development resources never reached target populations. Rather, the aid formed a thin film of dollars circulating on the top of local society, far above the masses. So it may be with globalization, at least as defined in terms of foreign direct investment, portfolio investment, Internet, cable TV, radios, newspapers, McDonalds, and IKEAs.

Source: Axel Dreher, "Does Globalization Affect Growth? Empirical Evidence from a New Index," *Applied Economics* 38 (10) (2006): 1091–1110: table B1 "2008 KOF Index of Globalization."

World Government

The growth of the communication system and other aspects of globalization have transformed world government from a utopian dream (or nightmare) to a necessity of daily life (Commission on Global Government 1995). At the center of numerous, still largely uncoordinated activities and organizations seeking control over global change today is the United Nations, founded October 24, 1945. The UN has had a difficult adolescence, but by 2009 it had lasted nearly three times as long as any other previous attempt. Although it is a highly imperfect confederation of organizations, it may well be humanity's best hope for solving the issues of cultural lag brought on by our latest political and technological revolutions. The UN Charter establishes a sovereign body that in principle has authority over all of the common affairs of humanity (Vandenbosch and Hogan 1970). This body is a collectivity that is itself made up of collectivities. The primary unit is the nation-state. The UN reserves for itself the right to recognize new nations and to create them when deemed appropriate, which it has now done more than one hundred times.

The body is made up of all nation-states in the world, with a few currently holding a pending membership status based on sovereignty issues. Within this body, the rules are strictly democratic, based largely on the U.S. model (see chapter 12). Real elections are held, due process is observed, and an amendable constitution with a doctrine of basic rights has final legislative authority, as interpreted by a supreme court, the International Criminal Court.

The body meets in assemblies, with each nation represented by a duly selected delegation, headed by an ambassador. It is a presidential system, with the secretary general elected by the constituent body and presiding over a bicameral legislature. This consists of the General Assembly, in which all members of the body meet, and a Security Council that includes a smaller set of members. Security Council members vary over time, with permanent seats held by the larger nations victorious in World War II (the United States, the United Kingdom, France, China, and Russia—originally the USSR). The assumption of the charter is that ambassadors and other representatives are themselves democratically elected or appointed by democratically elected officials and confirmed according to due process. (The system diverges from the principle of self-rule when this assumption is violated, as it frequently has been.)

The UN maintains a multinational military force and scores of specialized educational, humanitarian, and technical agencies. It is financially supported by the contributions of its member nation-states in an assessment based on national wealth. The effectiveness of the UN has been severely limited by the fact that its authority is essentially symbolic. Nations have been reluctant to forfeit their sovereignty to the General Assembly or the Security Council when they have disagreed with its decisions.[8] Democratic governments have shown concern over "universal" proclamations and rules promoted by representatives of dictatorial regimes, and dictators have challenged UN authority over what they have considered to be interference in their own internal affairs.

It is difficult to enforce the dues-paying system, and many countries (led by the United States) are collectively several billions of dollars in arrears. As national political and economic leaders have often correctly perceived, the UN is a potential threat to local and corporate interests (see Chavez 2003). Nevertheless, slowly but surely, the UN's authority has become a reality.

Nearly all of the world's national governments now recognize it as a legitimate budget item—notwithstanding partisan resistance in the United States and elsewhere. The selection of representatives is official business in all sovereign states. Through its agencies such as the Conference on Trade and Development (UNCTAD); Educational, Scientific, and Cultural Organization (UNESCO); World Bank; and International Monetary Fund (IMF), world government has made tentative but critical inroads into the control of multinational corporate activities and democratic access to the information superhighway.

At the same time, concerned corporations and governments have come to show increasing respect for UN authority. Since the end of the Cold War, the UN military forces have taken on a far more active and respected role, although they have been severely discredited in several confrontations, perhaps most significantly with the Bosnian Serbs in 1995. In several encounters in the 1990s and early 2000s, the UN army has been able to seize at least partial, temporary command of antidemocratic regimes in Asia, Africa, Latin America, and Europe.

The criticism that has been leveled against the General Assembly for its many political decisions is often well deserved. But no longer needing to face the issue of taking sides between the U.S. and Soviet blocs, the UN can now act as the independent force of authority that was conceived by the founders (who included Stalin, along with presidents Roosevelt and Truman, and Prime Minister Churchill). And even more important than the force of arms, the UN has its Charter of Human Rights.

A set of universal standards that include due process, self-rule, and sanctity of life and liberty has now been ratified by members. This, along with establishment of the International Criminal Court in 2002 and the ever-increasing authority of the UN in support of these principles, has provided people everywhere a measure of protection from tyranny once reserved only for tyrants themselves (Human Rights Watch 1995; Stephens 1993; Zuijdwijk 1982)[9]—that is, beyond its role as world government, the UN has served as a humanizing force, promoting and promising to protect the rights of individuals over and above the claims of nationalists and dictators. Despite its troubles, the UN today is closer to realizing its broader ideals than ever:

> This psychological or educational effect may be the United Nation's most valuable feature. A world federation presupposes a new kind of loyalty on the part of people, a sense of responsibility that does not stop short at the national boundaries. To be truly effective, such loyalty must embrace more than purely political issues. Understanding among different cultural groups, mutual economic and cultural aids, are the necessary conditions. (Einstein 1954, 164)

The Future of the World System

Advanced communication technologies have made it easier than ever for elites and autocrats to intrude into the lives of ordinary people. But they have also made it more difficult for them to keep their true nature secret from those they rule or from the outside world, at least for long. Telecommunications have opened the world to the scrutiny of organizations such as the Human Rights Watch and Amnesty International, which have dedicated themselves to ensuring that the Charter of Human Rights is respected. Their task, of realizing the Enlightenment ideal of one world at peace, is a notoriously difficult one. But, for the first time ever, it is not entirely impossible.

Humanity has now developed the organizational and technological capabilities of traveling to other worlds (with crews made up of former mortal enemies), of colonizing them, and adding unknown quantities of resources into the carrying-capacity equation. With world government, we now also have the social and moral capabilities to allow the human species as a whole to act in such endeavors as a group for itself. The story of social and cultural change, especially those parts of the story that concern the political economy of control, suggests that these two developments may not be coincidental. If we can truly act in our own best interests, then we will have achieved an ultimate level of cooperation and altruism, a level that might actually bring about a solution to the eternal problem of scarcity of space and riches on our single, finite planet.

According to the ancient Brahmin tale of Panspermia, God originally created millions and millions of planets populated by human beings, spread throughout the universe. This myth-history is also found in numerous other cultures.

The panspermia theory has antecedents which go back to the Old Kingdom in Egypt, and which are also found in early Hinduism, the philosophy of the Greek pre-Socratic philosopher Anaxagoras, and amongst the Jewish and Christian Gnostics. It is remarkable how explicit some of these early sources are in suggesting that the entire cosmos is full of seeds, and that life on earth originated from them. (Temple 2007, 169)

These many planets were, however, placed vast distances apart, so that the inhabitants of one could not pollute the others as they took their independent evolutionary paths toward godhood. When, it is said, the entire group of human inhabitants of a world resolve their moral differences, so that all can truly live as one, they will then achieve the technological capacity to meet with their fellow humans elsewhere in the universe

Box 14.3 432 PLANETS

As of March 18, 2010, 432 extrasolar planets had been discovered. The *Extrasolar Planets Encyclopedia* classifies these according to how they were detected (some have been detected by more than one method).

All Candidates Detected   **432 planets**

Method of Detection

Radial velocity or astrometry   341 planetary systems including
(observation of changes in a star's velocity)   402 planets
                                                    41 multiple planet systems

Transiting planets   71 planetary systems including
(interaction with nearby bodies)   71 planets
                                                    3 multiple planet systems

Microlensing   9 planetary systems including
(observation of gravitational effect)   10 planets
                                                    1 multiple planet system

Imaging   9 planetary systems including
(observation with telescope)   11 planets
                                                    1 multiple planet system

Timing   6 planetary systems
(observation of variation in pulsar timing)   9 planets
                                                    2 multiple planet systems

Source: Jean Schneider, "The Extrasolar Planets Encyclopaedia," http://exoplanet.eu/ (accessed March 18, 2010).

(Internet Encyclopedia of Science 2009; Zimmer 2008; see also Hoyle and Wickrama-singhe 1981).

In Vienna, during October 1993, the UN members voted overwhelmingly in favor of a "sweeping Human Rights Declaration" (World Commission on Human Rights [WCHR] 1993). Six months later, on April 21, 1994, the existence of potentially life-supporting planets orbiting a far-off star was at last confirmed (Wilfred 1994). As of October 2009, 373 extrasolar planets had been discovered (Berman 2007; Borenstein 2009; Schneider 2009). Perhaps we are about to take that next step in the evolution of *Homo sapiens*.

Relevant Websites

www.yourata.com/ata-adv.html
This is the home page of the American Telecommuting Association. This organization provides information and a forum for exchange for the millions of people who work in virtual offices via the Internet, telephone, and fax.

www.nitrd.gov/
The U.S. National Coordinating Office for Information Technology Research and Development (NCITRD), which maintains this site, is a federal agency that deals with innovation and impact of electronic communication technology.

www.un.org/
The official website of the United Nations has a predictably simple URL and links to all associated organizations and publications.

www.stentorian.com/politics/un
Here is a strongly anti-UN website with a libertarian approach.

http://fusionanomaly.net/panspermia.html
This site has a discussion of the Panspermia myth.

Notes

Part I: The Study of Change

1. An interesting and informative collection of alternative futures can be found in sociologist Arthur Shostak's *Viable Utopian Ideas* (Shostak 2003).

2. One theme that is briefly introduced here, although not directly addressed until later sections, is socioeconomic development and the contemporary reality of the developing world. Because of the complexity of these matters, their connection to sociocultural evolution, and the value premises used in their study, I have chosen to postpone discussion until chapter 9, on urban growth and the increasing complexity of human societies; chapter 10, in connection with international stratification; and chapter 12, on development and planned social change.

Chapter 1: The Social Scientific Perspective

1. Ritzer's study, originally published in 1993, has given rise to numerous books and shorter works on the subject of McDonaldization, including the popular collection by Mark Alfino, John Caputo, and Robin Wynyard (1998). Of special interested is the frequently updated McDonaldization website (see www.mcdonaldization.com/). In a related incident, supporters surrounded French antiglobalization activist Jose Bove after his release from prison on August 1, 2002. One thousand people turned up to greet Bove, who entered jail six weeks earlier after receiving a three-month sentence for the 1999 anti-U.S. protest in which he trashed a McDonald's restaurant (Bartoli 2002). See www.commondreams.org/headlines02/0801-03.htm. The related case of the "invasion" by rock 'n' roll in Russia, specifically, has been carefully documented by sociologist Tom Cushman (1995).

2. The argument that today's rapid changes terrify people was popularized by Alvin Toffler with the vivid term "future shock" (Toffler 1970). This may be a generational phenomenon, as

contemporary youth culture places a premium on novelty and is quick to condemn styles, technologies, and tastes as obsolete (Johnasson 1992).

3. This was the topic of an important symposium that appeared in the *American Journal of Sociology* in 1995 (Hechter 1995). Contributors included the leading sociologists of change: James Coleman, Randall Collins, Edgar Kiser, Timur Kuran, Alejandro Portes, and Charles Tilly (all cited with 1995 dates in the references). We refer to individual papers in later chapters.

4. David A. Smith (1996) published an early overview of college and university courses in the field under the auspices of the American Sociological Association (ASA). This material is continually updated on the website of ASA's Section on Comparative Historical Sociology: www2.asanet.org/sectionchs/teaching.html#mixed.

5. Many historians believe that it was Saint-Simon's disciple, Saint-Armand Bazard (1791–1832) who first coined this paired concept. See Flint (1874, 164).

6. Herbert Spencer first coined the term *superorganic*. With it, he sought to draw attention to the fact that the human sciences require laws that cannot be derived from purely physical or organic principles, that these are "super-organic" fields. This concept (with the term spelled without the hyphen) was later extended by the anthropologist Alfred L. Kroeber (1917), the evolutionary theorist Theodore Dobzhansky (1963), and the sociologist Pitirim A. Sorokin (1966). Sorokin wrote, "Explicitly or implicitly, all currents of sociological thought now accept the meaningful, normative, value-laden superorganic character of sociological phenomena as a realm of reality different from inorganic and organic realities. They also agree that so far this meaningful form of reality is found in its fully developed form only in the world of 'mindful' and symbolically interacting human beings" (635). The superorganic perspective was developed in opposition to mechanistic and "biologistic" theories that attempt to reduce sociocultural reality to inorganic or organic processes. These latter theories "either completely miss it in their verbal reductionism or acknowledge the specific character of this reality as a sui generis [self-generated] combination of biophysical realities different from all the other physical and biological phenomena" (635).

7. The *Teaching and Learning Guide* distributed by the American Sociological Association (Porter and Hoffman 1999) contains thorough bibliographies of published works on the Holocaust and syllabi from courses taught at colleges and universities throughout the world. Included are major general references from Chartock and Spender (1978), Engleman (1987), Gilbert (1981), Shirer (1978), and Winkler (1979). For further bibliographical information, see Goldenberg (1992). *Dimensions: A Journal of Holocaust Studies* is the leading periodical in the field. Accounts of survivors are increasingly available, including the very well-written accounts of Primo Levi (1986, 1995, 1996).

8. This is not to say that Hitler and his accomplices never made mistakes in their planning and execution of the race war. The record is filled with instances of botched campaigns, unclear or contradictory orders, and elaborate files filled with errors and just plain nonsense. For example, Heinz Höhne (1969) demonstrates this convincingly in the case of the SS. Historians are divided between the "intentionalist" and "functionalist" schools of thought concerning just how purposeful the Holocaust was. The intentionalists see the whole affair as meticulously planned and executed with clear design. Steven T. Katz (1994) is a widely read proponent of this position. One of the most effective cases in favor of the functionalist position, which argues that no grand design was in play but that event led to event largely haphazardly, is Christopher R. Browning (1992). According to the position taken here, mistakes and confusion occurred, but they did so as deviations from a strictly organized program.

9. On July 1, 2002, the first-ever International Criminal Court (ICC) began operation in The Hague, Netherlands. Its purpose, according to the Treaty of Rome that authorized its estab-

lishment, is to prosecute cases of genocide and crimes against humanity when national courts or tribunals fail to do so. Thus, following some fifty-seven years of planning, a core ideal of the Nuremberg judgment was at last realized. See www.iccnow.org/.

10. In addition to numerous books, articles, and chapters on the subject, several journals are exclusively or predominantly devoted to Third World studies, including *Economic Development and Cultural Change, Third World Review, Third World Planning Review,* and *Studies in Comparative International Development.*

11. One of the most comprehensive and compelling presentations of the history and personalities of the Civil Rights movement is the multipart documentary *Eyes on the Prize* (part 1, 1986; part 2, 1989), produced for the U.S. Corporation for Public Broadcasting. In 2006, PBS issued the series on seven DVDs (ISBN 0-7936-9262-8), but initially only educational institutions had access. A critical moment in the Civil Rights movement came on April 15, 1947, although it has received relatively little attention by social scientists. On that day, Brooklyn Dodgers' first basemen Jack Roosevelt "Jackie" Robinson took to the field as the first African American to play baseball in the Major Leagues. David Falkner (1995) is one writer who has made this important connection between Robinson and the *Brown* decision.

12. Among the first set of general references on the fall of Communism are Brzezinski (1989), Chirot (1991), Kraljic (1988), Plattner and Diamond (1992), Stokes (1991), and Szamtka, Mach, and Mucha (1993). Also, see Tarifa and Weinstein (1995–1996). A leading "second-generation" review is by Richard Pipes (2001). A more recent update has been offered by a key participant in Poland's Solidarity movement, Adam Michnik (2009).

Chapter 2: Social and Cultural Evolution

1. A documentary biography of Ishi, *Ishi: The Last of His Tribe,* was shown on the History Channel and later distributed as a video recording and DVD (A&E Home Video, 1990, ASIN: 0767018001). The HBO network produced a fictionalized account in 1992, *The Last of His Tribe* (produced by John Levoff and Robert Lovenheim, and directed by Harry Hook, Yahi Productions, April 2). The popular notion that Ishi was the last of his kind (tribe) appears to have been partly mythical. According to the organization that repatriated him, the notion that Ishi was the "last of his people" comes from the fact that Ishi was the last-known Yana to live a life essentially outside of direct contact with whites. There were always many of his tribe still alive, but they had become enmeshed in the larger "American" society, as had other natives. One might say that Kroeber and the early anthropologists thought of him as the last "real Indian"—a notion that is largely defunct today (see www.nmnh.si.edu/anthro/ishitop.htm).

2. Some people may be unaware that Freud wrote a set of books on social and cultural change in his later years (including *Moses and Monotheism* [1967], *The Future of an Illusion* [1975], and *Civilization and Its Discontents* [1961], and his dialogue with Albert Einstein on *Why War?* [Nathan and Norden 1960, 186–203]). In this work, he applied his psychoanalytic theories specifically to the problem of sociocultural evolution and to the question of whether or not humanity can be said to have "advanced" since the Stone Age and the Industrial Revolution. As he makes abundantly clear, his conclusion is that, despite periods of great "progress," the broad sweep of sociocultural evolution has brought us to the brink of our darkest hour. Thus, overall, he was a "regressive" evolutionist.

3. The following is Linneaus's 1735 classification scheme, verbatim.

- *Americanus*: reddish, choleric, and erect; hair black, straight, thick; wide nostrils, scanty beard; obstinate, merry, free; paints himself with fine red lines; regulated by customs.
- *Asiaticus*: sallow, melancholy, stiff; hair black; dark eyes; severe, haughty, avaricious; covered with loose garments; ruled by opinions.
- *Africanus*: black, phlegmatic, relaxed; hair black, frizzled; skin silky; nose flat; lips tumid; women without shame, they lactate profusely; crafty, indolent, negligent; anoints himself with grease; governed by caprice.
- *Europeaeus*: white, sanguine, muscular; hair long, flowing; eyes blue; gentle, acute, inventive; covers himself with close vestments; governed by laws. (www-personal.umich.edu/~jonmorro/race.html)

4. The works of anthropologist Franz Boas (1934), geneticist Theodore Dobzhansky (1951, 1962), and especially anthropologist Ashley Montagu (1964, 1975) mark a turning point in the scientific treatment of race. Montagu, in particular, "led a lifelong campaign to rid science of the term 'race'" (Andreasen 1998, 200). This research clearly established that human racial categories are arbitrary. They are abstractions, based on observed geographical distributions of gene pools at a specific moment in human development. So-called racial boundaries are routinely crossed today, even if the practice was uncommon in the past, creating so many "sub-" and "hybrid" races that the "system" now defies classification.

5. References to "race" and to the association between it and sociocultural traits are found throughout the writings of the classic evolutionists. Essentially, it is an unscientific term that can easily be replaced by more useful terms. *Local population* or, in ethnically diverse general populations, *ethnic subpopulation* expresses the very same factual distinctions between people without conveying the false notion that they are natural or permanent.

6. As you are well aware, the problem with "race" goes far beyond how useful the term may or may not be to social scientists. When it is associated with "higher," "more advanced," or "superior/inferior," it becomes a dangerous word. It was dangerous during the Holocaust, and it is today in urban neighborhoods everywhere. As the philosopher Bertrand Russell (1951) observed, "The most bitter struggles between different groups of mankind have been caused by one or more of three differences: of economic interest, of race or of creed" (179). We can now look back on the twentieth century as a century of Holocaust, ethnic cleansing, discrimination, and genocide. Many members of the social science community believe that the time is right to state very clearly that there is no inherent, biological basis underlying such struggles. The "differences of race" to which Russell refers are and always were socially constructed and exploited by those who could benefit from belief in them. Sociologist James McKee of Michigan State University has written a thorough, highly critical study of the way in which some have treated the concept of which he characterizes as the "failure of a perspective" (McKee 1994; see also the volume in honor of Ashley Montagu by Reynolds and Lieberman 1996). For the official statement on the concept of race adopted by the American Sociological Association, go to www2.asanet.org/media/asa_race_statement.pdf.

7. World system theory has attracted many proponents, and critics as well, since it was first created in the 1970s (for information on world system archives, sources, and journals, see http://fbc.binghamton.edu/ and www.fordham.edu/halsall/mod/wallerstein.html). One major critique is that it has Eurocentric bias. Wallerstein did acknowledge, even in his earliest work on the subject (Wallerstein 1974), that as of the late fifteenth century Europe had competition from two other potential world empires, the Chinese and the Ottomans. Yet, he and most other world system theorists afford these two powers only a subordinate, "semiperipheral" role in the history of

globalization. More recent studies have shown that the influence of China and the Muslim world was far more significant, both in their effects on the core, colonizer cultures and on the colonized areas as well. The Great Silk Road that connected all three world systems is both a symbolic and an actual element of this "reorientation" (see Frank 1998).

8. Some sociologists consider dialectical and cyclical approaches to be two essentially different types of theories or "models" that are then contrasted with a third, linear type (e.g., Harper 1993, 84–87). Although this matter is somewhat technical, it would be more accurate to say there are at least three broad groups of dialectical theories, one of which is cyclical (the Pareto, Sorokin, or Spengler type; see Jay 1979 for a discussion of the Frankfurt Institute's broad-ranging applications of dialectical principles; see also Schneider 1971, [1975b] 1985; and Machalek 1979).

9. "Comte considered altruism and egoism to be two distinct motives within the individual. He did not deny the existence of self-serving motives, even for helping; the impulse to seek self-benefit and self-gratification he called *egoism*. But Comte believed that some social behavior was an expression of an unselfish desire to 'live for others.' It was this second type of motivation to benefit others that he called *altruism*" (Comte [1851] 1875, quoted in Batson 1991, 5). Recent studies that explore this theme include works from Ozinga (1999), Krebs and Van Hesteren (1994), and—in brief summary form—Krebs (2002).

10. Mannheim was one of the first to use the term *third way*. Such labels, including *creative altruism* itself, have never captured the imagination of social scientists in the United States, although most theorists are quite familiar with the underlying concepts. As the current self-analysis among students of social and cultural change continues, the contributions of Mannheim and Sorokin are being reassessed. In particular, their concern with diagnosing the major "crises of our age" (a phrase used by both) and their interest in developing an applied social science that would go beyond Marxist and bourgeois conceptions of change are as relevant today as they were three or four decades ago, if not more so.

Chapter 3: Population Growth and Demographic Transition

1. This phrase is from "The Master Song" (1965).

2. In stressing that populations are the proper units of observation in the study of social and cultural change, I am not saying that demographic attributes and their changes are necessarily the most important or most basic types. This view, demographic determinism, has been defended from time to time, but we now know that it expresses only a partial truth. Sometimes demographic changes are very important, as is true of the incredible increase in the mortality rates of several ethnic populations during the Holocaust. At other times, they may be relatively minor causes and effects, such as the small decline that occurred in the birth rates of the African American population in the 1950s and 1960s. In still other instances, such as the language law changes in Quebec, they appear to be on an equal footing with the social and cultural components.

To repeat, the principle at work here is that, in differing degrees of importance, all three always occur together. Rather than endorsing demographic determinism, I am pointing out that social and cultural, as well as demographic, change is easier to understand if we study it as it occurs in historical (or even prehistoric) populations. From a scientific perspective, this is preferable to relying too heavily on unobservable phenomena or on individual actors in understanding Quebec's language law changes, the fall of Communism, or other actual episodes of change, great and small.

3. Place's writings (e.g., Place [1822] 1930) clearly indicate that he accepted Malthus's basic argument but felt that something other than natural disasters could dampen population growth, that is, the conscientious application of birth control. It is in this respect that he was also the first neo-Malthusian. It has also been noted that twenty years before Place's first writings, Benjamin Franklin had preached (but apparently did not practice) the use of contraceptive techniques (Petersen 1975, 516).

4. According to the UN Population Division, approximately four out of five Third World countries officially support some type of family-planning policy (United Nations Population Division 2009).

Chapter 4: The Heritage and Dynamics of Culture

1. Lewis Coser's widely cited article on Weber's theory includes the following summary.

Weber's discussion of authority relations—why men claim authority, and feel they have a legitimate right to expect willing obedience to their command—illustrates his use of the ideal type as an analytical tool and his classification of types of social action. Weber distinguished three main modes of claiming legitimacy. Authority may be based on rational grounds and anchored in impersonal rules that have been legally enacted or contractually established. This type is *rational-legal authority*, which has increasingly come to characterize hierarchical relations in modern society. *Traditional authority*, on the other hand, which predominates in pre-modern societies, is based on belief in the sanctity of tradition, of "the eternal yesterday." It is not codified in impersonal rules but inheres in particular persons who may either inherit it or be invested with it by a higher authority. *Charismatic authority*, finally, rests on the appeal of leaders who claim allegiance because of their extraordinary virtuosity, whether ethical, heroic, or religious. (Coser 1977, 226–27)

2. This is the definition by Professor Robert Sherrill as quoted in Bruce Murray, "With 'God on Our Side'? How American 'Civil Religion' Permeates Society and Manifests Itself in Public Life," FacsNet, www.facsnet.org/ (accessed March 30, 2005). See also the "Civil religion" entry at www.translationdirectory.com/glossaries/glossary007_c.htm.

3. This is vividly portrayed in the film *Triumph of the Will*, available on You Tube at www.youtube.com/watch?v=GcFuHGHfYwE.

4. Much debate has gone on among scholars in several fields about the extent to which Cardinal Pacelli, later Pope Pius XII, cooperated with Hitler's racial program. What we do know is that Hitler had little respect for the Church and its doctrine, and that many Catholics felt exactly the same way about him, but that to the day he died he officially remained a member in good standing (see Cornwell 1999; Lewy 1964).

5. As Beeman (2002) indicates,

The movement took its name from a compendium of twelve volumes published between 1910 and 1915 by a group of Protestant laymen entitled: *The Fundamentals: A Testimony of the Truth*. These volumes were circulated in the millions and served as the concretization of a cross-denominational set of traditions with roots in previous centuries. It owes its existence particularly to the same evangelical revivalist tradition that inspired the Great Awakening of the early 19th Century and a variety of early millenarian movements. Spurred on by reactions to Darwin's theory of evolution, the original Fundamentalist Movement was seen as a religious revival. It came to embody both principles of absolute religious orthodoxy and evangelical practice which called for believers to extended action beyond religion into political and social life. (129)

6. Benjamin Barber's (1995) widely read account of this confrontation has helped many scholars and journalists to understand the rise of fundamentalism as a response to the spread of secularism.

7. Javid Iqbal (2003) has characterized this struggle between religious and secular (and military) factions as an "identity crisis":

> His thesis is that the state in Islam has always been in the process of "becoming" and that the state was never considered a finished political product. In his view there was a complete departure from the implementation of Islam in Pakistan as visualized by the founding fathers as well as a complete departure from their aspiration of constructing permanent democratic political structures in the country. Pakistan is not a "failed state"; it is in the hands of a "failed generation." (www.dukandar.com/islampakidentity.html [accessed November 3, 2009])

8. The people who drew these conclusions (e.g., Veblen) used the term *Aryan* in a neutral (e.g., linguistic) sense, without necessarily tying it in with some "racial purity" notions. However, as you may know, these conclusions were made part of Nazi doctrine during the 1920s. Hitler concluded that the Nordic-Germanic race was directly descended from the *Urvolk*. The Nazis adopted the name Aryan, the swastika, and other symbols from Indology.

9. Several new academic disciplines that focus on language have been established since the 1960s. These include linguistics, semiotics, and the specialized branch of anthropology that deals with the development of both nonwritten and written languages, glottochronology. For founding statements, see Swadesh (1972) and Smith (1966).

10. Local variants derived from Latin include French, Spanish, Italian, and Romanian; some of the languages with Dravidian roots are Tamil, Telegu, Kanada, and Malayalam.

11. Esperanto has a completely uniform grammar: its rules have no exceptions, and there are no irregular verbs. These have been viewed as special advantages that make it the most appropriate universal tongue. Numerous books have been written in Esperanto, and at least two movies feature Esperanto dialog, including the 1965 horror film *Incubus* starring William Shatner. Ironically, English, the obvious actual choice as the world's language, is among the least regular ever invented.

Chapter 5: Social Structures, Systems, and Processes

1. Georg Simmel, George Herbert Mead, and Charles Horton Cooley established the foundations of microsociology in the late nineteenth and early twentieth centuries. Their influence continues in the contemporary fields of social psychology, symbolic interactionism, and ethnomethodology.

2. Consider the case of the Sunday evening bridge club. Four people (Pat, Bruce, Marilyn, and Jay) created this informal association in order to meet weekly and play a game of cards. After some time, Pat learns that she must take care of her sister on Sunday nights and drops out. However, Karen takes her place. Now the club consists of Karen, Bruce, Marilyn, and Jay. At one point, Bruce takes a job in another town, so he can no longer participate. But before leaving, Bruce recruits Ron. Finally, Marilyn and Jay get tired of bridge and drop out. Soon after, Ron recruits another couple, Sue and Charles, to take their place. Thus, the Sunday evening bridge

club now consists of Karen, Ron, Sue, and Charles. None of the original members belongs, but the club endures.

3. However, the ancient bureaucracies did not dominate in day-to-day affairs because family was still the major institution in these largely rural societies (Weber 1951, 1958).

4. George Orwell's ([1949] 1984) INGSOC presents the pure case of bureaucracy in support of antidemocratic rulers in a completely closed, rigid system.

5. Corporate law depends heavily on the concept of persona. An aggregate corporation is an ideal body, created by law and composed of individuals united under a common name. Its members succeed each other so that the body continues the same, notwithstanding the changes of the individuals who compose it; for certain purposes, it is considered as a natural person (Browne's Civ. Law 99; Civ. Code of Lo. art. 418; 2 Kent's Com. 215). Mr. Kyd (Corpor. vol. 1, p. 13) defines a corporation as follows:

> A corporation, or body politic, or body incorporate, is a collection of many; individuals united in one body, under a special denomination, having perpetual succession under an artificial form, and vested by the policy of the law, with a capacity of acting in several respects as an individual, particularly of taking and granting property, contracting obligations, and of suing and being sued; of enjoying privileges and immunities in common, and of exercising a variety of political rights, more or less extensive, according to the design of its institution, or the powers conferred upon it, either at the time of its creation, or at any subsequent period of its existence. (*Bouvier's Law Dictionary*, rev. 6th ed., 1856, www.wordiq.com/definition/corporation; emphasis added.)

6. The early representative democracies were still incomplete in serious ways. Traditional and rational-legal norms often commingled. Such was the case in the first decades of U.S. history, when slaves, natives, and women were designated nonmembers by a democratic constitution. In France, the movement for representative government eventually brought about a restoration of imperial rule under Napoleon Bonaparte, again within a "democratic" framework.

Part III: The Engines of Change

1. The contrast between public issues and private problems (or "troubles") is a key aspect of C. Wright Mills's sociological imagination (Mills 1959, 3–4). For a more recent examination of this contrast, see Dandaneau (2001).

Chapter 6: Social Movements: Concepts and Principles

1. In the context of collective behavior, social and/or political revolutions can be understood as large-scale social formations that encompass several movements: a movement of movements so to speak. For example, the French Revolution of 1789 brought together antimonarchist, anticlerical, nationalist, land reform, and other movements of the era. On the American Revolution, see Jameson (1968).

2. Tilly and Wood (2009) reserve use of the term to refer to specifically political movements. Under these conditions many of the events referred to as movements in these chapters would

not qualify, on two grounds. (1) They are not strictly political in the sense employed by Tilly and Wood: "Analysts and activists often extend the term loosely to all protest activity" (Tilly and Wood 2009, 6). 2. In the sense employed by them, no social movements occurred outside of Europe or before the middle of the eighteenth century: "As it developed in the West after 1750, the social movement emerged from an innovative consequential synthesis of three elements" (Tilly and Wood 2009, 3). In some respects, this is a useful way to think about movements. But its narrowness obscures the fact that there are many ways in which organized activity intended to change the status quo is expressed.

3. You may recall that The Party invents a phony movement, The Brotherhood, to entice potential dissidents. Winston Smith is lured into the movement and trapped. During his subsequent imprisonment and torture, he learns that he had been constantly watched and that BB had recorded every disloyal word he uttered during movement encounters.

4. A recent summary of various theories of violence by Gregg Barak (2003) distinguishes between interpersonal, institutional, and structural forms from an interdisciplinary perspective. Of special interest is the section on "Pathways to Nonviolence."

5. For Freud, in particular, aggression is not a basic instinct but rather a differentiated form of the more general contents of the id, referred to in *Civilization and Its Discontents* (Freud 1961) and other sources as "libidinal energy." Eros, or the sex drive, stems from the same source and is in this way intimately related to aggression.

6. Classic Marxism argues that the most consequential, and ultimately the only truly effective, changes emanate from not the state but rather the economy. It is significant that Lenin placed seizure of the state prior in time, and in principle, to the establishment of worker control of industry. But the classic theory stresses attacking capitalism (that is, the economic system): first comes seizure of the factories; then the overthrow of the state by the worker's party (the Communists) follows.

7. The word *ideology* has French roots and was originally used in the late eighteenth century by Antoine Louis Claude Destutt de Tracy ([1817] 1970; Head 1985) and Claude Adrien Helvétius ([1810] 1969; Horowitz 1954), to refer to any system of ideas. With Marx and Engels's *The German Ideology* ([1864] 1970), the concept was given its current connotation as an interest-serving distortion. Marx and, in his subsequent critical work, Mannheim were the first to draw a sharp contrast between ideology and science, although we now understand the difference between the two to be quite subtle, if not at least partly arbitrary. For extended comments on the relationship between ideology and science, see Bendix (1971) and Zeitlin (1968).

8. In a strict sense, all highly elaborated descriptive reports about reality, even scientific ones, must be distorted to some extent, for we are always bound to draw conclusions before the last possible piece of evidence is unearthed (Rudner 1953). Moreover, we act on our imperfect diagnoses in ways that we more or less strongly feel, but never know for certain, are in our interests. So we make mistakes. In this respect, scientific accounts differ from ideologies in the understanding that no particular party's interest is to be served by their depiction of reality and that no particular therapy is endorsed (a difficult ideal to achieve, as noted). This promotes science's stubborn quest for exceptions and disconfirming evidence, which is something ideologues seek to avoid. In this light, the difference between science and ideology is technically quite narrow, resting on a leap of faith that the scientist will remain faithful to the principle of truth before "cause," no matter how just it may be. The ideologue, on the other hand, must promote the cause, even if literal truths must be bent. This, it seems to many sociologists of science, is a very important but rather fragile distinction.

Chapter 7: Movements and Revolutions in Context

1. The following is from the glossary at Marxists.org:

Narodniks: Originally the name for Russian revolutionaries of the 1860s and 1870s, *narodniki* meaning "going to the people." . . . The Narodniks believed the peasantry was the revolutionary class that would overthrow the monarchy, regarding the village commune as the embryo of Socialism. The Narodniks, however, did not believe that the peasantry would be able to achieve revolution on their own accord, but instead that history could only be made by heroes, outstanding personalities, who would lead an otherwise passive peasantry to revolution. (www .marxists.org/glossary/orgs/n/a.htm)

2. The leading expert on genocide, Steven Katz (1994, 96, 96n), indicates that, despite published estimates ranging to the tens of millions and as much as 80 percent of the population destroyed, "exact demographic evidence is difficult to acquire," and "it is impossible to be certain" about such numbers and associated proportions.

3. Leo Robert Klein, web coordinator and digital resources developer at the William and Anita Newman Library, Baruch College, CUNY, has created an image database on the Red scare that immediately followed the Bolshevik victory in Russia: http://newman.baruch.cuny .edu/digital/redscare.

4. This is one reason the movement for democracy itself is never completed. See Lappe and Du Bois (1994) and Somers (1993) on the unending process of democratic transition.

5. The McCain-Feingold Act of 2002 was intended to eliminate a key tool of interest groups by seriously limiting the amount and type of funds that can be contributed to political campaigns (see Charles 2003). Yet, soon after Congress passed the bill with overwhelming majorities in both houses, interest groups filed legal challenges to prohibit its implementation. One key argument of the opponents of the bill is that, by limiting the ability of donors to do what they please with their money, their First Amendment rights of free speech would be abridged.

6. See Hedstrom (1994) for a study of the movement's diffusion in Sweden.

7. This section is based on several sources, especially Sartori (1987, vol. 2). His bibliography is very comprehensive and fairly up to date. For more recent comments, see also Lipset (1994) and Plattner and Diamond (1992).

8. The human rights organization, Freedom House, published a report in 2009 in which it described the nations with "the worst human rights conditions." These are as follows: Burma, Equatorial Guinea, Libya, North Korea, Somalia, Sudan, Turkmenistan, Uzbekistan, Belarus, Chad, China, Cuba, Eritrea, Laos, Saudi Arabia, and Syria. In these countries, "state control over daily life is pervasive, independent organizations and political opposition are banned or suppressed, and fear of retribution for independent thought and action is ubiquitous" (Freedom House 2009).

9. On October 1–3, 1999, an important conference was held in Cambridge, Massachusetts, entitled "Empathy, Altruism and Agape: Perspectives on Love in Science and Religion"; its proceedings, excerpted below, are available at www.altruisticlove.org/:

The goal of the conference is to initiate creative thinking toward stimulating and promoting excellence in research into the phenomenon and interpretation of altruistic love. The approach is highly integrative, linking the biological and social sciences with philosophical, ethical, and religious themes. Love includes a variety of concepts, and in particular the John Templeton

Foundation and the Fetzer Institute are interested in genuine generosity and self-giving love. Many religious perspectives affirm in various and diverse ways that love is at the "heart of being" and that the ultimate reality or ultimate purpose of things is related to love. To explore this topic fully, there needs to be an inclusion in the discussion and research of a broad range of concepts, including altruism, attachment, bonding, empathy, and others.

The sponsors, the John Templeton Foundation and the Fetzer Institute, are leading movement organizations. Their addresses are John Templeton Foundation, c/o www.altruisticlove.org, Five Radnor Corporate Center, Suite 100, 100 Matsonford Road, Radnor, PA 19087, altruism@templeton.org; and Fetzer Institute, 9292 West KL Avenue, Kalamazoo, MI 49009, www.fetzer.org/. A private group interested in altruism maintains a website, www.altruism.org/, that serves as a communication and information resource for people interested in the movement.

Chapter 8: The Process of Technological Innovation

1. The Science, Technology, and Society website has links to numerous resources related to this field. www.personal.u-net.com/~nchadd/home.htm.

2. The journal *Social Impact Assessment* has been published monthly since the 1970s by the Social Impact Center in New York City.

3. On February 16, 1996, a Liberian-registered ship went aground off the coast of Milford, Wales, spilling seventy thousand tons of oil into the water and onto the beaches of one of Europe's most important wildlife reserves. This was comparable to the one hundred thousand tons spilled into the English Channel in 1967 off the coast of Brittany, France, by the *Torrey Canyon* (then one of the world's largest ships). Included in the carnage immediately evident after the Milford disaster were "7,000 birds [including] a colony of puffins. Grey seals . . . found covered in oil and dolphins . . . spotted ploughing through the slicks" (*New York Times* 1996). Oil spills constitute a kind of hallmark disaster of our era because they pose such a stark choice: we may have either living oceans or industrial prosperity but apparently not both. The frequency and scope of such accidents have underscored the urgency to develop affordable fusion power and other alternative energy sources.

4. For a more recent, satirical account of this process, see Moore (1996).

5. Funding for the OTA was withdrawn in 1995.

6. Work on applying the concept of iatrogenesis in policy contexts has been underway for several years at the University of Oslo, according to former Sociology Department head, Ragnvald Kalleberg.

7. There is no better way to appreciate the abundance and the complexity of contemporary innovations than to scan the pages of "The Best of What's New," published by *Popular Science* magazine. See, for example, *Popular Science* (2009).

Chapter 9: From Gemeinschaft to Gesellschaft: The Urbanization of the Human Population

1. The subtitle of this chapter is borrowed from Davis (1974). As he stresses, the invention of cities in the Bronze Age and the rise of urban society during the Industrial Revolution mark two monumental increases in societal complexity.

2. The foundation work in urban sociology is Weber's *The City* ([1900] 1958). Also, the collection by Abu-Lughod and Hay (1977) contains several classic essays on the city and urban life, including one by the Arabic-speaking founder of social science Ibn Khaldun of Tunis.

3. This account is based on the "multiple culture-hearth" theory, as opposed to the "single culture-hearth" theory. According to the latter, the first cities occurred in the Middle East and then "the urban form diffused from this region to the great riverine depressions of the Nile Valley, Indus Valley, Yellow River Valley, and the hinterlands of Mesoamerica. The single culture-hearth theory argues that the construction of similar spatial designs is too distinct and too specific to have developed accidentally" and independently. "The multiple culture-hearth theory, on the other hand, contends that cities in these various regions developed independently (Padilla 2006, 5).

4. In February 2002, China's Xinhua news agency announced that "six ancient cities, the oldest dating back 2000 years, have been found" in Henan Province. "Each was built on top of the previous one and all except the oldest have now been fully excavated. . . . Officials made the announcement in the city of Kaifeng." The director of Kaifeng's heritage bureau said, "The findings confirm the centuries-old suspicion among Kaifeng residents that here, underground, lies a pile of lost cities—one built atop another." The findings are the result of a search that began in 1981, "after workers found a Ming Dynasty mansion, once the home of a prince, while dredging a lake. Cities from the Qing Dynasty, the Jin period, the Northern Song Dynasty and the Tang Dynasty have all been uncovered." This area is also the ancestral home of one of China's most improbable minority groups, the Jews of Kaifeng. (Ananova News Agency, February 8, 2002, www.ananova.com/news/story/sm_516420.html?menu=AnanovaNewsService).

5. Central place theory has been referred to as one of the "geographic ideas that changed the world," and it has been widely celebrated among geographers and others (e.g., Berry and Harris 1970; Preston 1985). Much research has been guided by the theory, and perhaps even more theoretical work has been dedicated to exploring its implications (Berry 1965). It has also been subject to critical scrutiny on several grounds. For example, it appears not to distinguish carefully between a territory's geographic center and its population center (or centers), the latter of which is the valid central point in terms of the theory's basic principle. Also, Christaller himself and the theory as a potential tool for territorial domination have been questioned for their ties to the Nazi regime in Germany (Roessler 1989).

6. This and the following section are based on Davis (1974), Massey (2002), Petersen (1975), and Sjoberg (1960).

7. Steven Kreis (2000) recounts the Athenian origins as follows:

In 508 B.C., Cleisthenes instituted a new political organization whereby the citizens would take a more forceful and more direct role in running the city-state. He called this new political organization *demokratia*, or democracy—rule by the entire body of citizens. He created a Council of Five Hundred which planned the business of the public assemblies. All male citizens over the age of thirty could serve for a term of one year on the Council and no one could serve more than two terms in a lifetime. Such an organization was necessary, thought Cleisthenes, so that every citizen would learn from direct political experience. With such a personal interest in his democracy, Cleisthenes believed that there would be no citizens to conspire and attempt to abolish the system.

8. Immanuel Wallerstein (1974) introduced this term to sociologists. It indicates that, although Turkey was the seat of the empire during much of the latter portion of the period (through the Ottoman Dynasty of the early twentieth century), the founding of Islam and a

Muslim Empire preceded Turkish rule. In the seventh century CE, Mecca and Medina became independent centers of influence, as did Iberia later under the Muslim Moors. Thus it was a Turco *and* Muslim world empire.

9. Joseph Ben-David's reference to these scholars as *amateurs* is not meant to imply that they were unskilled or less than professional. Rather, they worked in an environment that had not yet become professionalized. In this sense, an amateur is someone whose first motivation is love of the job (from the Latin *amare*, "to love").

10. The other 100 percent urban countries are Anguilla, Bahrain, Bermuda, Cayman Islands, Gibraltar, Guadeloupe, Monaco, Nauru, and Qatar.

11. This is the Spanish word for a shantytown. Other Third World terms include *bustee* (Hindi), *bidonville* (French), *favela* (Portuguese), *slum* (English), and *cherri* (Bengali).

Chapter 10: A World Divided

1. Contemporary national boundaries coincide to varying degrees with culturally and subculturally distinct populations. Some nations, even very large ones such as Japan, do not have significant ethnic subcultures; others, even quite small ones such as Luxembourg, are highly diverse. The correspondence between ethnic and national boundaries has been and remains subject to change. In fact, it is a serious political issue in many parts of the contemporary world (Shafir 1995).

2. The impression that China is entirely ethnically homogenous is based on the fact that well over 90 percent of its population is of Han background. However, dozens of minority groups live at the geographical peripheries of the country: "China serves as home to 56 official ethnic groups. The largest group, the Han, make up over 92% of China's vast population, and it is the elements of Han civilization that world considers 'Chinese culture.'" Yet the fifty-five ethnic minorities nestled away on China's vast frontiers maintain their own rich traditions and customs, and all are part of Chinese culture (see www.c-c-c.org/chineseculture/minority/minority .html; estimates provided by this site are from the 1990 Census of China).

3. The court's references to the social science literature appear verbatim as footnote 11, pages 494–95, of the opinion, as follows:

> K.B. Clark, "Effect of Prejudice and Discrimination on Personality Development" (Midcentury White House Conference on Children and Youth, 1950); Witmer and Kotinsky, "Personality in the Making" (1952), c. VI; Deutscher and Chein, "The Psychological Effects of Enforced Segregation: A Survey of Social Science Opinion," 26 j. Psychol 259 (1948); Chein, "What are the Psychological Effects of Segregation Under Conditions of Equal Facilities?", 3 *Int J. Opinion and Attitude Res.* 229 (1949); Brameld, "Educational Costs," in *Discrimination and National Welfare* (MacIver, ed., 1949), 44–48; Frazier, *The Negro in the United States* (1949) 674–681. **And see generally Myrdal, *An American Dilemma*, 1944.** (my emphasis in bold; Brown v. Board of Education 1954)

4. Kant did not refer to this as a cultural universal. Rather, the term he used was a *categorical imperative*, or a self-justifying principle. His definition is as follows: "An imperative is Categorical [when] it concerns not the matter of action, or its intended result, but its form and the principle of which it is itself a result; and what is essentially good in it consists in the mental disposition, let the consequence be what it may. This imperative may be called that of Morality" (Kant 1961, 581–82).

5. This quotation is from the website of the Frosina Foundation at www.frosina.org and www.csmonitor.com/1997/0807/080797.intl.intl.5.html).

6. I stress national-level populations because nearly all of the measurement and theory focus on the nation as a unit of observation. This assumes, incorrectly, that the nation-state is always a natural aggregate and that there are no major intranational differences in social complexity, wealth, or other important characteristics. It also ignores the fact that people who live near borders are as much, if not more, like the foreigners who are their neighbors than their fellow citizens in the interior (Teune 1990).

7. There is no particular association between complexity and sheer numbers. When using national populations as the unit of analysis, size is not very closely correlated with industrialization or any of the other variables. Some of the most and the least differentiated societies occur in both large and small populations: for example, agricultural India has a larger population than the industrialized United States, and urban Singapore and rural Albania have about the same size, small populations.

8. The index numbers listed in table 10.1 are based on factor scores for the year 2008, weighted to make one hundred the maximum. The original UNRISD Index employed factor scores based on eighty variables.

9. Moreover, many classical theorists, including Spencer and Max Weber, did agree with Franklin that the type of prosperity reflected by a high score on the index was the result of one's capacity for a certain kind of industriousness, like going to bed and rising early. These are the "Protestant" virtues that support capitalism.

10. Most of these movement intellectuals were Marxists. They tended to overlook Russian cultural and economic imperialism in Europe and Asia, partly because many of the dependent societies there, such as Chechnya, Latvia, and Ukraine, had been absorbed into the Soviet Union.

11. As discussed in chapter 2, it is now acknowledged by world system theorists (including Wallerstein) that the account originally had a Eurocentric tone. More than thirty years of research since the publication of Wallerstein's first book on the subject has shown that China and the Muslim (especially Ottoman) world played an active role in the creation of a multicentric world system (see Frank 1998; Khaldoun and Al-Zo'by 2008).

12. This is the worst defined category of the three, and there is considerable disagreement about the areas that should be counted in it. See, for example, the discussion by Eva Etzioni-Halevy (1981, chap. 3).

Chapter 11: The Market, Capitalism, and Socialism

1. Because of its trade primacy in the seventeenth century, Holland was able to innovate with a capitalist-like system based on investment financing. Economic historians generally categorize this system as a form of mercantilism and thus credit England in the eighteenth century as the founders of the modern capitalist economic institution. This entire interpretation has recently been called into question by Roger Krohn (1999), among others.

2. This "labor theory of value" is closely associated with Marxist economics, although Marx borrowed it from David Ricardo. Because of this association and for other reasons, most liberal economists consider it a discredited theory. Nevertheless, in every new generation it is rediscovered. See, for example, Chao (1991), Gordon (1990), Horvat (1995), and Meek (1976).

3. I don't mean to suggest that all illegal business is governed by free markets. Obviously, drug trafficking, prostitution, and gunrunning are oligopolistic industries, just as their legitimate counterparts. The point is that the less seriously criminal, and more common, types of informal-sector activity are relatively free of multinational corporate control. Compare, for instance, unreported babysitting earnings by U.S. teenagers with legitimate retail automobile sales.

4. Those who followed the seemingly unending series of revelations during the crises of 2000 and 2008 are well aware that this was hardly a case of the corner butcher putting his thumb on the scale to increase the weight of your order. Those involved are at the very pinnacle of the corporate elite. Research and commentary continue as we write, and it is anticipated that it will take years, if not decades, to sort everything out. The following four sources provide a good start: A *CNN News Special* (May 20, 2003) provided the following inventory:

Convicted: Arthur Andersen. Settled: Merrill Lynch, Citigroup, CSFB, Xerox, and Piper Jaffray. Under Investigation: Enron, WorldCom, Qwest, Tyco, ImClone, Global Crossing Dynegy, CMS Energy, El Paso Corp., Halliburton, Williams Cos., AOL Time Warner, Goldman Sachs, Salomon Smith Barney, Citigroup, J.P. Morgan, Chase, Schering Plough, Bristol-Myers Squibb, Kmart, Johnson & Johnson, Adelphia, Merrill Lynch, and Rite Aid.

5. These include Amenta (1993); Hicks and Misra (1993); Huber, Ragin, and Stephens (1993); Plattner and Diamond (1992); Rigby (1990); Rona-Tas (1994); and Smith (1990).

Chapter 12: The Paradoxes of Development

1. The popularity of development ideals does not carry over to the related, but far more controversial, program of modernization. Modernizers speak of means, whereas development focuses on results. Modern values and structures may have been instrumental in bringing about development in Europe, but they do not necessarily have the same effects in non-Western cultures. This is one reason birth control has been much more difficult to institutionalize than death control, since the former contradicts traditional values. In Europe, modernization led somewhat automatically to development. In Third World cultures, they are not always linked. (Must one literally be Protestant to be a good capitalist? Not literally. For more on the answer, see Bellah 1957.)

2. Unfortunately, if industrialization were rapid and extensive enough, it would place two billion people on the world's unemployment rolls.

3. In 1976, a satirical poem by Ross Coggins entitled "The Development Set" circulated at international aid agencies. A few lines should suffice to indicate what this group was up to:

The Development Set is bright and noble,
Our thoughts are deep and our vision global;
Although we move with the better classes,
Our thoughts are always with the masses.
In Sheraton hotels in scattered nations,
We damn multinational corporations;
Injustice seems so easy to protest,
In such seething hotbeds of social rest.

For the entire poem, go to www.owen.org/blog/116.

4. This really is a radically new understanding. In fact, it contradicts the still-prevalent economic theories that continue to be based on the principles of comparative advantage, for instance, that the economy of one country grows to the extent that it can establish a trade surplus over others.

5. Fanon was born in Martinique and practiced medicine in Algeria. He died there during the Algerian war of independence against France.

6. In stressing that the Communist ideal embodied a highly cooperative society, Marx was making the same basic point.

7. Of course, many people believe that a more altruistic world society is an unpleasant prospect, and perhaps many more believe that it is simply impossible—given what they understand to be "human nature." But, as Comte showed long ago, both altruism and egoism are part of our nature, and it is social circumstance that causes us to emphasize one or the other. For Sorokin, the popular arguments against the desirability or the very possibility of altruism are to be expected as value judgments of an egoistic era. However, that does not make them valid arguments. I, for one, agree with Comte and Sorokin (see Weinstein 2003).

Chapter 13: Democratic Planning and Applied Sociology

1. The evolution of the planning profession is encapsulated on two online timelines sponsored by the American Planning Association (APA): http://myapa.planning.org/pathways/history.htm; and http://faculty.wwu.edu/zaferan/index%20-%20timeline_us_planning_history%5B2%5D.pdf.

2. Most applied sociologists do not refer to themselves as *social planners*, although that is one of the several labels used. Others include *clinical sociologist* and *sociological practitioner*. The website maintained by The Association for Applied and Clinical Sociology defines these terms and discusses how they are employed at www.aacsnet.org/wp/?page_id=59. For general overviews of the field, see Straus (2002) and Steele, Scarisbrick-Hauser, and Hauser (1999).

3. I have personally visited a training program for planners from Thimphu, Bhutan's capital, organized annually in Pune, India, by Chris Benninger, a U.S.-born development expert. See Benninger's web site at www.ccba.in.

4. The AICP is an organization that certifies professionals with degrees in planning and closely associated fields. The Commission on Applied and Clinical Sociology accredits applied sociology programs, and the Association for Applied and Clinical Sociology certifies individual practicing sociologists. (See www.aacsnet.org.)

5. Sociologists worked in research and planning roles in several federal agencies between World Wars I and II. Of special interest are their activities within the U.S. Department of Agriculture, often in connection with the Agricultural Experiment Stations. See Larson, Zimmerman, and Moe (2003, especially 61, 90–91).

6. "We" is the name of the party in the book with that title by Yvgenii Zamiatin ([1924] 1993) that was the prototype for Orwell's *Nineteen Eighty-Four*.

7. In the United States, the approach was institutionalized at the federal level in the early 1990s by the Department of Housing Development's Community Outreach Partnership Center (COPC) program. This program supports the work of academic sociologists, planners, and other professionals in cooperative projects in their local communities. The centers, of which there are approximately a hundred in all parts of the country, focus on participatory action on economic, social, political, and housing issues. (See www.oup.org/programs/aboutCOPC.asp.)

8. Native ("Indian") people of North America may well have been the first to practice participatory democracy, as we understand the term today.

> The people of the Six Nations, also known by the French term, Iroquois Confederacy, call themselves the Hau de no sau nee (ho dee noe sho nee) or People of the Longhouse. . . . Together these peoples comprise the oldest living *participatory* democracy on earth. Their story, and governance truly based on the consent of the governed, contains a great deal of life-promoting intelligence for those of us not familiar with this area of American history. The original United States *representative* democracy, fashioned by such central authors as Benjamin Franklin and Thomas Jefferson, drew much inspiration from this confederacy of nations. (www.ratical.org/many_worlds/6Nations)

Chapter 14: The Political Economy of Globalization

1. As most of the world will long remember, an Indian and an Israeli astronaut were among the crew of seven who died in February 2003 when the shuttle *Columbia* exploded shortly after reentry. See "World Grieves Loss of Shuttle," CNN Special, February 2, 2003, www.cnn.com/2003/TECH/space/02/01/shuttle.columbia.reax.

2. The study by Burstein, Bricher, and Einwohner (1995) describes how social reform in the economy, family relations, and other institutional realms gets on legislative agendas.

3. The analysis of Sassen's work by Robinson (2009) and Sassen's (2009) rejoinder examine several issues in the sociology of globalization, especially the role of what Sassen (2000; 2001) calls "global cities."

4. According to many observers, the war in fact played a major role in bringing an end to the Great Depression in the United States, although Canada did not benefit nearly as much. Huge investments in military industry under conditions of geographical isolation from the battlefronts proved that a healthy economy can generate both "guns" and "butter."

5. As in the colonial system, these benefits accrue to the local economy within the limits of corporate profitability. For more on multinational impact, see chapter 11 of this book; see also Bollen and Appold (1993); Dixon, Drakakis-Smith, and Watts (1986); Moaddel (1994); Weinstein and McIntyre (1986); Williams (1985); and Yang and Stone (1985).

6. The question used for this section's title is the twenty-first-century version of the one posed by Pitirim Sorokin and Walter Lunden (1959) at the height of the Cold War: "Who shall guard the guardians?"

7. The National Library of Australia maintains a site dedicated to communication developments and regulation at www.nla.gov.au/lis/govnii.html. Included in their statement of purpose is the observation that "governments worldwide are responding to the challenges and opportunities presented by developments in national and global networking. The move towards establishing national and global information infrastructure policies is reflected in a number of significant government reports and documents."

8. For a summary of the dispute between the United States and the other Security Council members over the invasion of Iraq in 2003, see Berke (2003).

9. A government is judged, in part, by those who oppose it. An inventory of the characteristics of leading resistors to UN authority today is revealing. For one thing, they are almost without exception autocrats who place racial or national integrity above democratic values.

References

A&E Home Video. 1990. *Ishi: The Last of His Tribe*. The History Channel, ASIN: 0767018001.

Abizadeh, Arash. 2001. "Ethnicity, Race, and a Possible Humanity." *World Order* 33 (1): 23–34.

Abu-Lughod, Janet. 1966. "The City Is Dead, Long Live the City: Some Thoughts on Urbanity." *American Behavioral Scientist* 10 (1): 3–5.

Abu-Lughod, Janet, and Richard Hay. 1977. *Third World Urbanization*. New York: Methuen.

Adams, Richard E. W. 1997. *Ancient Civilizations of the New World*. Boulder, CO: Westview Press.

Adelman, Jonathan R., ed. 1986. *Superpowers and Revolution*. Westport, CT: Praeger.

Agrawal, Binod C. 1986. "Television Studies in India: The State of the Art." Paper presented at the International Television Studies Conference, London, England, July 10–12.

Ahlberg, Dennis A. 1998. "Julian Simon and the Population Growth Debate." *Population and Development Review* 24 (2): 317–27.

Albrow, Martin, and Elizabeth King, eds. 1990. *Globalization, Knowledge, and Society*. London: Sage.

Alemán, José. 2004. "Mass Political Conflict: Evidence from Three Regimes." Paper presented at the 2004 Annual Meeting of the American Political Science Association, Chicago, September 2–5.

Alexander, Ernest R. 1992. *Approaches to Planning: Introducing Current Planning Theories, Concepts, and Issues*. Luxembourg: Gordon and Breach Science Publishers.

Alexander, Jeffrey. 2002. "On the Social Construction of Moral Universals: The Holocaust from War Crime to Trauma Drama." *European Journal of Social Theory* 5 (1): 5–85.

Alexander, Ken, and Avis Glaze. 1996. *Towards Freedom: The African-Canadian Experience*. Toronto: Umbrella Press.

Alfino, Mark, John S. Caputo, and Robin Wynyard, eds. 1998. *McDonaldization Revisited: Critical Essays on Consumer Culture*. Westport, CT: Greenwood.

Alinsky, Saul. 1972. *Rules for Radicals: A Practical Primer for Realistic Radicals*. New York: Vintage Books.

Allen, Philip J., ed. 1963. *Pitirim A. Sorokin in Review*. Durham, NC: Duke University Press.

Amba-Rao, Sita C. 1993. "Multinational Corporate Social Responsibility, Ethics, Interactions, and Third World Governments: An Agenda for the 1990s." *Journal of Business Ethics* 12 (July): 553–72.

Amenta, Edwin. 1993. "The State of the Art in Welfare State Research on Social Spending Efforts in Capitalist Democracies since 1960." *American Journal of Sociology* 99 (3): 750–63.

American Planning Association (APA). 1990. *A Study Manual for the AICP Comprehensive Planning Examination*. Memphis, TN: Graduate Program in City and Regional Planning, Memphis State University.

Amsden, Alice, Jack Kochanowicz, and Lance Taylor. 1994. *The Market Meets Its Match: Restructuring the Economies of Eastern Europe*. Cambridge, MA: Harvard University Press.

Andreasen, Robin. 1998. "A New Perspective on the Race Debate." *British Journal of the Philosophy of Science* 49:199–225.

Andrews, Edmund. 2008. "Greenspan Concedes Error on Regulation." *New York Times*, October 24, B1.

an-Naim, Abdullah Ahmed. 2008. *Islam and the Secular State: Negotiating the Future of Sharia*. Cambridge, MA: Harvard University Press.

Anti-Defamation League (ADL). 1993. *Hitler's Apologists: The Anti-Semitic Propaganda of Holocaust "Revisionism."* New York: Author.

Antohi, Sorin, and Vladimir Tismaneanu. 2000. *Between Past and Future: The Revolutions of 1989 and Their Aftermath*. New York: Central European University Press.

Arendt, Hannah. 1958. *The Origins of Totalitarianism*. Cleveland, OH: World Publishers.

———. 1964. *Eichmann in Jerusalem: A Report on the Banality of Evil*. New York: Viking Press.

Aron, Raymond. 1967. *The Industrial Society: Three Essays on the Ideology of Development*. New York: Simon & Schuster.

Ashford, Douglas E. 1967. *National Development and Local Reform: Political Participation in Morocco, Tunisia, and Pakistan*. Princeton, NJ: Princeton University Press.

Ashford, Lori. 1995. *New Perspectives on Population: Lessons from Cairo*. Washington, DC: Population Reference Bureau.

Astill, James, and Isabelle Chevallot. 2003. "Conflict in Congo Has Killed 4. 7m, Charity Says: Starvation and Disease Multiply Toll from Fighting." *The Guardian*, April 8.

Ausubel, Nathan. 1960. *A Pictorial History of the Jewish People*. New York: Crown Publishers.

Baali, Fuad. 1988. *Society, State, and Urbanism: Ibn Khaldun's Sociological Thought*. Albany: State University of New York Press.

Baker, Wayne E., and Robert R. Faulkner. 1993. "The Social Organization of Conspiracy: Illegal Networks in the Heavy Equipment Industry." *American Sociological Review* 58 (6): 837–60.

Balow, John. 1978. *Understanding Violence*. National Commission on the Causes and Prevention of Violence. Wellington, New Zealand: Victoria University of Wellington, Institute of Criminology.

Banks, J. A. 1954. *Prosperity and Parenthood: A Study of Family Planning among the Victorian Middle Classes*. London: Routledge & Kegan Paul.

———. 1968. "Population Change and the Victorian City." *Victorian Studies* 11:277–89.

Barak, Gregg, ed. 1991. *Crimes by the Capitalist State: An Introduction to State Criminality*. Albany: State University of New York Press.

———. 2003. *Violence and Nonviolence: Pathways to Understanding*. Thousand Oaks, CA: Sage.

Barber, Benjamin R. 1995. *Jihad vs. McWorld*. New York: Times Books.

Barkan, E. 1992. *The Retreat of Scientific Racism: Changing Concepts of Race in Britain and the United States between the World Wars*. Cambridge: Cambridge University Press.

Barnet, R. J., and R. E. Muller. 1974. *Global Reach: The Power of the Multinational Corporations*. New York: Simon & Schuster.

Barras, Collin. 2009. "Neutron Tracks Revive Hopes for Cold Fusion." *New Scientist*, March 23. www .newscientist.com/article/dn16820-neutron-tracks-revive-hopes-for-cold-fusion.html#.

Bartoli, Georges. 2002. "French Anti-Globalization Activist Jose Bove Released from Prison." Common Dreams News Center, August 1. www.commondreams.org/headlines02/0801-03.htm.

Barzun, Jacques. 1981. *Darwin, Marx, and Wagner: A Critique of a Heritage*. Chicago: University of Chicago Press.

Basu, Amrita, and Elizabeth C. McGrory. 1995. *The Challenge of Local Feminisms: Women's Movements in Global Perspective*. Boulder, CO: Westview Press.

Bateson, Gregory. 1939. "Culture Contact and Schismogenesis." *Man* 35 (article 199): 178–83.

Batson, C. Daniel. 1991. *The Altruism Question: Toward a Social Psychological Answer*. Hillsdale, NJ: Lawrence Erlbaum.

Bauer, Raymond A. 1966. *Social Indicators*. Cambridge, MA: MIT Press.

Bauer, Raymond A., Richard S. Rosenbloom, and Laure Sharp. 1969. *Second-Order Consequences: A Methodological Essay on the Impact of Technology*. Cambridge, MA: MIT Press.

Bauman, Zygmunt. 1989. "Sociological Responses to Post Modernity." *Thesis Eleven* 23:35–63.

Bausum, Ann. 2004. *With Courage and Cloth: Winning the Fight for a Woman's Right to Vote*. Washington, DC: National Geographic.

BBC News. 2009. "China Economic Growth Accelerates." October 22. http://news.bbc.co.uk/2/hi/business/8319706.stm.

Beard, Mary. 1993. "Classic Woman?" *History Today* 43 (7): 29–35.

Beaver, Steven E. 1975. *Demographic Transition Theory Reinterpreted*. New York: Longman.

Beck, Sanderson. 2007. *China, Korea and Japan to 1800*. Goleta, CA: World Peace Communications.

Becker, Gary S. 1985. "Human Capital, Effort, and the Sexual Division of Labor." *Journal of Labor Economics* 3 (1, part 2): S33–S58.

Beeman, William O. 2002. "Fighting the Good Fight: Fundamentalism and Religious Revival." In *Exotic No More: Anthropology on the Front Lines*, edited by J. MacClancy. Chicago: University of Chicago Press.

Beenstock, Michael. 1984. *The Transformation of the World Economy*. London: George, Allen & Unwin.

Bell, Daniel, ed. 1963. *The Radical Right*. Garden City, NY: Doubleday.

———. 1973. *The Coming of Post-Industrial Society: A Venture in Social Forecasting*. New York: Basic Books.

———. 1989. "The Third Technological Revolution and Its Possible Socioeconomic Consequences." *Dissent* (spring): 164–76.

Bellah, Robert N. 1957. *The Tokugawa Religion: Values of Pre-Industrial Japan*. Glencoe, IL: Free Press.

———. 1987. *Uncivil Religion: Interreligious Hostility in America*. New York: Crossroads Press.

———. 1992. *The Broken Covenant: American Civil Religion in Time of Trial*. New York: Seabury Press.

Bellah, Robert N., and Philip E. Hammond. 1980. *Varieties of Civil Religion*. New York: Harper & Row.

Ben Asher, Moshe. 1977. "Democratic Planning." SW 253A UC Berkeley School of Social Welfare (winter). www.gatherthepeople.org/ (accessed October 27, 2009).

Benda, Julien. 1955. *The Treason of the Intellectuals*. Boston: Beacon Press.

Ben-David, Joseph. 1971. *The Scientist's Role in Society: A Comparative Study*. Englewood Cliffs, NJ: Prentice Hall.

Bendix, Reinhard. 1971. "Sociology and Ideology." In *The Phenomenon of Sociology*, edited by E. A. Tiryakian. New York: Appleton-Century-Crofts.

Benedikt, Michael A., ed. 1991. *Cyberspace: First Steps*. Cambridge, MA: MIT Press.

Benjamin, Daniel. 1994. "Preserving the Printed Word." *Time* reprint. New York: National Yiddish Book Center.

Benn, Hillary. 2006. "The Challenge for Our Generation." Preface to *Eliminating World Poverty: Making Governance Work for the Poor*, Department of International Development. London: Secretary's Office.

Berger, Peter L. 1969. *A Rumor of Angels: Modern Society and the Rediscovery of the Supernatural*. Garden City, NY: Doubleday.

———. 1992. "The Uncertain Triumph of Democratic Capitalism." *Journal of Democracy* 3 (3): 7–16.

Bergman, Peter M. 1969. *The Chronological History of the Negro in America*. New York: Harper & Row.

Berke, Ronnie. 2003. "Blix: Iraq's Actions 'Very Limited. '" CNN Online, February 27. www.cnn .com/2003/WORLD/meast/02/27/sprj.irq.main.

Berman, Edward. 1983. *The Influence of the Carnegie, Ford, and Rockefeller Foundations on American Foreign Policy: The Ideology of Philanthropy*. Albany: State University of New York Press.

Berman, Jessica. 2007. "Astronomers Discover Earth-like Planet outside Solar System." Voice of America, Washington, DC, April 25.

Berry, Brian J. L. 1965. *Central Place Studies: A Bibliography of Theory and Applications*. Philadelphia: Regional Science Research Institute.

———. 1975. *The Human Consequences of Urbanization*. New York: St. Martin's Press.

Berry, Brian J. L., and Chauncy D. Harris. 1970. "Walter Christaller: An Appreciation." *Geographical Review* 60 (1): 116–19.

Berry, John W. 2008. "Immigration, Acculturation, and Adaptation." *Applied Psychology* 46 (1): 5–34.

Betancourt, Roger R. 1995. *Markets, the State and Corruption in a PCPC Reform Process: Why China and Vietnam Grow While Cuba Stagnates*. College Park: Center for Institutional Reform and the Informal Sector, University of Maryland at College Park.

Biddes, M. D. 1970. *Father of Racist Ideology: The Social and Political Thought of Count Gobineau*. New York: Weyblight and Talley.

Biersteker, Thomas J. 1978. *Distortion or Development? Contending Perspectives on the Multinational Corporation*. Cambridge, MA: MIT Press.

Bilsborrow, Richard E., ed. 1998. *Migration, Urbanization, and Development: New Directions and Issues: Symposium on Internal Migration and Urbanization in Developing Countries (1996: New York, N.Y.)*. Norwell, MA: United Nations Population Fund, Kluwer Academic Publishers.

Bird, Jon, Barry Curtis, Tom Putnam, George Robertson, and Lisa Tickner. 1994. *Mapping the Futures: Local Cultures, Global Change*. New York: Routledge.

Blühdorn, Ingolfur. 2009. "The Participatory Revolution: New Social Movements and Civil Society." In A *Companion to Europe since 1945*, edited by K. Larres. London: Blackwell.

Blum, Harold F. 1963. "On the Origin and Evolution of Human Culture." *American Scientist* 51:32–47.

Blumer, Herbert. 1951. "Collective Behavior." In *New Outline of the Principles of Sociology*, edited by A. M. Lee. New York: Barnes and Noble.

———. 1962. "Society as Symbolic Interaction." In *Human Behavior and Social Process: An Interactionist Approach*, edited by A. Rose. Boston: Houghton Mifflin.

Boas, Franz. 1934. *Aryans and Non-Aryans*. New York: Information and Service Associates.

Boldrin, Michelle, and David Levine. 2002. "The Case against Intellectual Property." *American Economic Review* 92 (2): 209–12.

Bollen, Kenneth A., and Stephen J. Appold. 1993. "National Industrial Structure and the Global System." *American Sociological Review* 58 (2): 283–303.

Bonner, John Tyler. 1980. *The Evolution of Culture in Animals*. Princeton, NJ: Princeton University Press.

Borenstein, Seth. 2009. "Found: Firm Place to Stand outside Solar System." Associated Press, September 16.

Borrell, John. 1989. "No Longer If but When." *Time*, November 13, 42–44.

Bose, Nirimal K. 1965. "Calcutta: A Premature Metropolis." *Scientific American* 213:91–102.

Boston Globe. 2009. "The Big Picture." June 15. www.boston.com/bigpicture.

Boszormenyi-Nagy, Ivan. 1993. "Destructive Entitlement: From Here to Eternity (Interview)." *Psychology Today* (March–April): 12–13.

Bothwell, Robert, Ian M. Drummond, and John English. 1987. *Canada, 1900–1945*. Toronto: University of Toronto Press.

REFERENCES

Bourdeaux, Michael. 1984. *Religious Minorities in the Soviet Union: A Report*. London: Minority Rights Group.

———. 1995. *The Politics of Religion in Russia and the New States of Eurasia*. Armonk, NY: M. E. Sharpe.

Bouvier's Law Dictionary. 1856. Rev. 6th ed. www.wordiq.com/definition/corporation.

Boyer, Mark A., series ed. 2008. *Global Democracy and the World Social Forums*. Boulder, CO: Paradigm Publishers.

Bracey, John H., Jr. 1971. *Conflict and Competition: Studies in Recent Black Protest Movements*. Belmont, CA: Wadsworth.

Bradby, Hannah, ed. 2000. "Defining Violence: Understanding the Causes and Effects of Violence." *Peace Research Abstracts* 37 (5): 607–18.

Branch, Taylor. 2006. *At Canaan's Edge: America in the King Years, 1965–68*. New York: Simon & Schuster.

Braudel, Fernand. 1966. "European Expansion and Capitalism: 1450–1650." In *Chapters in Western Civilization*. New York: Columbia University Press.

———. 1973. *The Mediterranean*. New York: Harper & Row.

Breo, Dennis L. 1993. "Kicking Butts: AMA, Joe Camel, and the 'Black Flag' War on Tobacco." *Journal of the American Medical Association* 270 (October 27): 1978–84.

Bright, Michael. 1994. *Intelligence in Animals*. London: Reader's Digest Association.

Brinton, Crane. 1938. *The Anatomy of Revolution*. Englewood Cliffs, NJ: Prentice Hall.

Brody, David. 1993. *In Labor's Cause: Main Themes on the History of the American Worker*. New York: Oxford University Press.

Brown, Donald E. 1991. *Human Universals*. Philadelphia: Temple University Press.

Brown, Norman O. 1959. *Life against Death: The Psychoanalytic Meaning of History*. Middletown, CT: Wesleyan University Press.

Brown v. Board of Education. 347 U.S. 483 (1954). www.brownvboard.org/.

Browning, Christopher R. 1992. *The Path to Genocide*. Cambridge: Cambridge University Press.

———. 1993. *Ordinary Men: Police Battalion 101 and the Final Solution in Poland*. New York: HarperCollins.

Brunvand, Jan H. 1999. *Too Good to Be True: The Colossal Book of Urban Legends*. New York: Norton.

———. 2001. *Encyclopedia of Urban Legends*. Santa Barbara, CA: ABC-CLIO.

Bryan, Elizabeth, and Jessica Varat, eds. 2007. *Strategies for Promoting Gender Equity in Developing Countries: Lessons, Challenges, and Opportunities*. Washington, DC: Woodrow Wilson International Center for Scholars.

Brzezinski, Zbigniew. 1989. *The Grand Failure: The Birth and Death of Communism in the Twentieth Century*. New York: Charles Scribner.

Buber, Martin. 1960. *The Origin and Meaning of Hasidism*. New York: Horizon Press.

Buckingham, Peter. 1988. *America Sees Red: Anti-Communism in America, 1870s to 1980s*. Claremont, CA: Regina Press.

Bulatao, Rodolfo, and John B. Casterline. 2001. *Global Fertility Transition*. New York: Population Council.

Bulbeck, Chilla. 1998. *Re-Orienting Western Feminisms: Women's Diversity in a Postcolonial World*. New York: Cambridge University Press.

Bulmer, Martin. 1984. *The Chicago School of Sociology: Institutionalization, Diversity, and the Rise of Sociological Research*. Chicago: University of Chicago Press.

Burchfield, R. W. 1988. *The Oxford English Dictionary and the State of the Language*. Washington, DC: U.S. Library of Congress.

Burckhardt, Jacob, and Oswyn Murray. 1998. *The Greeks and Greek Civilization*. New York: St. Martin's Press.

Burnham, James. 1941. *The Managerial Revolution*. New York: John Day.

REFERENCES

Burstein, Paul, R. Marie Bricher, and Rachel L. Einwohner. 1995. "Policy Alternatives and Political Change: Work, Family, and Gender on the Congressional Agenda, 1945–1990." *American Sociological Review* 60 (1): 67–83.

Byrd, William A. 1991. *The Market Mechanism and Economic Reforms in China.* Armonk, NY: M. E. Sharpe.

Calem, Robert E. 1992. "The Network of All Networks." *New York Times,* December 6, F12.

Calhoun, Craig, Donald Light, and Susan Keller. 1994. *Sociology.* New York: McGraw-Hill.

Campbell, Colin. 2007. *The Easternization of the West: A Thematic Account of Cultural Change in the Modern Era.* Boulder, CO: Paradigm Publishers.

Campbell, Robert W. 1992. *The Failure of Soviet Economic Planning: System, Performance, Reform.* Bloomington: Indiana University Press.

Candelaria, Michael R. 1990. *Popular Religion and Liberation Theology.* Albany: State University of New York Press.

Cardoso, Eliana, and Shahid Yusuf. 1994. "Red Capitalism: Growth and Inflation in China." *Challenge* 37 (May–June): 49–56.

Carey, John. 1970. *U.N. Protection of Civil and Political Rights.* Syracuse, NY: Syracuse University Press.

Carlson, Peter. 1983. *Roughneck: The Life and Times of Big Bill Haywood.* New York: Norton.

Carney, W. J., ed. 1995. "Limited Liability Companies: Origins and Antecedents." Symposium on Limited Liability Companies and the Evolving Corporate Form. *University of Colorado Law Review* 66: 855–1103.

Carrow, David J. 2002. "The FBI and Martin Luther King: New Documents Explain the Notorious Wiretaps." *Atlantic Monthly* 80 (July): 27–34.

Carson, Rachel. 1962. *Silent Spring.* Boston: Houghton Mifflin.

Cassidy, Kevin S., and Gregory A. Bischak, eds. 1995. *Real Security: Converting the Defense Economy and Building Peace.* Albany: State University of New York Press.

Castro, Max. 1999. *Free Markets, Open Societies, Closed Borders? Trends in International Migration and Immigration Policy in the Americas.* Coral Gables, FL: North-South Center Press.

Caves, Roger W., ed. 2005. *Encyclopedia of the City.* New York: Routledge.

CBC Online Technology and Science. 2009. "China Postpones Internet Filter Software Plan." June 30. www.cbc.ca/technology/story/2009/06/30/china-postponed-filter-deadline-green-dam.html.

Census Commissioner, India. 1921. *Census of India.* Calcutta: Superintendent Government Printing.

————. 1971. *Census of India.* Series 1. Delhi: Manager of Publications, Office of the Registrar General.

Cerf, Vinton G. 1991. "Networks." *Scientific American* 265: 71–81.

Cerroni-Long, E. L. 1994. "Evolution and Human Choices." *World Futures* 40: 215–25.

C. F. Net. 1995. *C. F. Net: Cold Fusion/New Energy Technology News Update* (Concord, NH) 1 (1).

Chadwick, Owen. 1990. *The Secularization of the European Mind in the Nineteenth Century.* New York: Cambridge University Press.

Chamberlain, M. E. 1985. *Decolonization: The Fall of the European Empires.* New York: Blackwell.

Chan, Sewell. 2007. "A Yiddish Revival, with New York Leading the Way." *New York Times* City Room. http://cityroom.blogs.nytimes.com/2007/10/17/a-yiddish-revival-with-new-york-leading-the-way.

Chang, Kwang-chih. 1986. *The Archaeology of Ancient China.* New Haven, CT: Yale University Press.

Chao, Tzu-yuan. 1991. *New Labour Theory of Value: The Basic Theory of Economics and Guide to the Development of Human Society.* Ammersbek bei Hamburg, Germany: Verlag an der Lottbek Peter Jensen.

Charkham, Jonathan P. 1994. *Keeping Good Company: A Study of Corporate Governance in Five Countries.* New York: Oxford University Press.

Charles, Guy-Uriel. 2003. "Mixing Metaphors: Voting, Dollars, and Campaign Finance Reform." *Election Law Journal* 2 (2): 271–83.

Chartock, Roselle, and Jack Spender, eds. 1978. *The Holocaust Years: Society on Trial*. New York: Bantam Books.

Chatters, Linda M., Robert J. Taylor, and Joseph Jayakody. 1994. "Fictive Kinship Relations in Black Extended Families." *Journal of Comparative Family Studies* 25 (3): 297–312.

Chavez, Linda. 2003. "Commentary: Should U.S. Quit the U.N.?" *Reporter*, March 25, 3–4.

Childe, V. Gordon. 1950. "The Urban Revolution." *Town Planning Review* 21:3–9, 11–17.

Ching, Kwan Lee and Guobin Yang, eds. 2007. *Re-envisioning the Chinese Revolution: The Politics and Poetics of Collective Memories in Reform China*. Stanford, CA: Stanford University Press.

Chirot, Daniel. 1989. *The Origins of Backwardness in Eastern Europe*. Berkeley: University of California Press.

———. 1991. *The Crisis of Leninism and the Decline of the Left: The Revolutions of 1989*. Seattle: University of Washington Press.

———. 1994a. *How Societies Change*. Newbury Park, CA: Pine Forge Press.

———. 1994b. *Modern Tyrants: The Power and Prevalence of Evil in Our Age*. New York: Free Press.

Chon, Bum Soo Chon, Junho H. Choi, George A. Barnett, James A. Danowski, and Sung-Hee Joo. 2003. "A Structural Analysis of Media Convergence: Cross-Industry Mergers and Acquisitions in the Information Industries." *Journal of Media Economics* 16 (3): 141–57.

Chong, Dennis, and Ruel Rogers. 2002. "Reviving Group Consciousness." Paper presented at the Notre Dame University Conference on the Politics of Democratic Inclusion, South Bend, Indiana, October 18–19.

Christaller, Walter. 1972. "How I Discovered the Theory of Central Places: A Report about the Origin of Central Places." In *Man, Space, and Environment*, edited by P. W. English and R. C. Mayfield. Oxford: Oxford University Press.

Christensen, Karen, and David Levinson, eds. 2003. *Encyclopedia of Community: From the Village to the Virtual World*. Thousand Oaks, CA: Sage.

Cipolla, Carlo. 1965. *Guns and Sails in the Early Phase of European Expansion*. Cleveland, OH: Collins.

Clarkson, Frederick. 1997. *Eternal Hostility: The Struggle between Theocracy and Democracy*. Monroe, ME: Common Courage Press.

Clayes, Gregory. 1987. *Machinery, Money, and the Millennium: From Moral Economy to Socialism, 1815–1860*. Princeton, NJ: Princeton University Press.

CNNMoney.com. 2009. "Fortune 1000." May 4. http://money.cnn.com/magazines/fortune/fortune500/2009/full_list/.

Coale, Ansley. 1964. "How a Population Ages or Grows Younger." In *Population: The Vital Revolution*, edited by R. Freedman. New York: Doubleday.

Cochrane, Glynn. 1986. *Reforming National Institutions for Economic Development*. Boulder, CO: Westview Press.

Codrescu, Andrei. 1991. *The Hole in the Flag: A Romanian Exile's Story of Return and Revolution*. New York: W. Morrow.

———. 2000. *The Devil Never Sleeps and Other Essays*. New York: St. Martin's Press.

Cohen, I. Bernard. 1994. *Interactions: Some Contacts between the Natural Sciences and the Social Sciences*. Cambridge, MA: MIT Press.

Cohen, Joel E. 1995. "Population Growth and Earth's Human Carrying Capacity." *Science* 269 (July 21): 340–46.

———. 1997. *How Many People Can the Earth Support?* New York: Norton.

Cohen, Mark. 1978. *The Food Crisis in Prehistory: Overpopulation and the Origins of Agriculture*. New Haven, CT: Yale University Press.

Cohen, Michael, and Dennis Hale, eds. 1967. *The New Student Left: An Anthology*. Boston: Beacon Press.

REFERENCES

Cold Fusion Times. 2009. "Old Spawar Recurring Resurrections of 'Cold Fusion.'" August 2. http://world.std.com/~mica/cft.html.

Coleman, James S. 1995. "Comment on Kuran and Collins." *American Journal of Sociology* 100 (6): 1616–19.

Collins, Randall. 1995. "Prediction in Macrosociology: The Case of the Soviet Collapse." *American Journal of Sociology* 100 (6): 1552–93.

Commission on Global Government. 1995. *Our Global Neighborhood: The Report of the Commission on Global Government.* New York: Oxford University Press.

Commoner, Barry W. 1966. *Science and Survival.* New York: Viking Press.

Comte, I. Auguste. [1851] 1875. *System of Positive Philosophy.* Vol. 1. London: Longmans, Green.

Conroy, Cathryn. 1995. "Working Your Way in the Alternative Office." *CompuServe Magazine* 14 (February): 10–17.

Conway, John S. 1968. *The Nazi Persecution of the Churches 1933–1945.* New York: Basic Books.

Cooper, John Milton. 2001. *Breaking the Heart of the World: Woodrow Wilson and the Fight for the League of Nations.* New York: Cambridge University Press.

Coria, Jessica. 2009. "Unintended Impacts of Multiple Instruments on Technology Adoption." *Working Papers in Economics* 344. Göteborg, Sweden: Göteborg University, Department of Economics.

Cornwell, John. 1999. *Hitler's Pope: The Secret History of Pius XII.* New York: Viking Books.

Coser, Lewis. 1977. *Masters of Sociological Thought.* New York: Harcourt Brace Jovanovich.

Cottrol, Robert J., Raymond T. Diamond, and Leland Ware. 2003. *Brown v. Board of Education: Caste, Culture, and the Constitution.* Lawrence: University Press of Kansas.

Cristi, Marcela. 2001. *From Civil to Political Religion: The Intersection of Culture, Religion and Politics.* Waterloo, Ontario: Wilfrid Laurier University Press.

Cushman, Thomas. 1995. *Notes from the Underground.* Albany: State University of New York Press.

Cviic, C. 1991. *Remaking the Balkans.* London: Pinter.

da Costa, Emilla. 1994. *Crowns of Glory, Tears of Blood: The Demerara Slave Rebellion of 1823.* Oxford: Oxford University Press.

Dahrendorf, Ralf. 1967. *Society and Democracy in Germany.* New York: Norton.

———. 1968. "Out of Utopia." In *Essays on Social Theory,* edited by R. Dahrendorf. Stanford, CA: Stanford University Press.

Dahrendorf, Ralf, and George Soros. 2000. *The Paradoxes of Unintended Consequences.* Budapest: Central European University Press.

Dandaneau, Steven P. 2001. *Taking It Big: Developing Sociological Consciousness in Postmodern Times.* Thousand Oaks, CA: Pine Forge Press.

Dandekar, Hemalata C. 1986. *Men to Bombay, Women at Home: Urban Influence on Sugao Village, Deccan, Maharashtra, India, 1942–1982.* Ann Arbor: Center for South and Southeast Asian Studies, the University of Michigan.

Darwin, Charles. [1859] 2008. *On the Origin of Species.* New York: Sterling Publishers.

Daswisha, Karen. 1988. *Eastern Europe.* London: Cambridge University Press.

Davis, Gerald F., Kristina Diekmann, and Catherine H. Tinsley. 1994. "The Decline and Fall of the Conglomerate Firm in the 1980s: The Deinstitutionalization of an Organizational Form." *American Sociological Review* 59 (4): 547–71.

Davis, Kingsley. 1963. "The Theory of Change and Response in Demographic History." *Population Index* 29:145–66.

———. 1974. "The Urbanization of the Human Population." In *An Urban World,* edited by C. Tilly. Boston: Little, Brown.

———. 1984. "Wives and Work: The Sex Role Revolution and Its Consequences." *Population and Development Review* 10:397–418.

Davis, Kingsley, and J. Blake. 1956. "Social Structure and Fertility: An Analytic Framework." *Economic Development and Cultural Change* 4:211–35.

REFERENCES

Dawidowicz, Lucy S. 1975. *The War against the Jews 1933–45*. New York: Holt, Rinehart, and Winston.

Dawood, Janmohammed. 1994. *The Role of Superior Judiciary in the Politics of Pakistan*. Karachi, Pakistan: Royal Book Co.

DeAngelo, Harry, and Linda DeAngelo. 1985. "Managerial Ownership of Voting Rights: A Study of Public Corporations with Dual Classes of Common Stock." *Journal of Financial Economics* 14 (1): 33–69.

Deegan, Mary Jo. 1988. *Jane Addams and the Men of the Chicago School 1892–1918*. New Brunswick, NJ: Transaction Books.

Deevey, E. S. 1960. "The Human Crop." *Scientific American* 203: 194–204.

de Huszar, George B., ed. 1960. *The Intellectuals: A Controversial Portrait*. New York: Free Press.

De Jong, Gordon F., Richard, G. Abad, Fred Arnold, Benjamin V. Cariño, James T. Fawcett, and Robert W. Gardiner. 1983. "International and Internal Migration Decision-Making: A Value-Expectancy Based Analytical Framework of Intentions to Move from a Rural Philippine Province." *International Migration Review* 17 (3): 470–84.

Delgado, Gary. 1993. *From the Ground Up: Problems and Prospects for Community Organizing*. Oakland, CA: Ford Foundation Applied Research Center.

Della Porta, Donatella. 2006. *Social Movements, Political Violence, and the State: A Comparative Analysis of Italy and Germany*. Cambridge: Cambridge University Press.

Delzell, C. 1974. *The Papacy and Totalitarianism*. New York: Wiley.

Deming, W. Edwards. 1982. *Quality, Productivity, and Competitive Position*. Cambridge, MA: MIT Center for Advanced Engineering Study.

———. 1992. *Out of the Crisis*. Cambridge, MA: MIT Center for Advanced Engineering Study.

Dentler, Robert A. 2002. *Practicing Sociology: Selected Fields*. Westport, CT: Praeger.

Department of International Development (UK). 2006. *Eliminating World Poverty: Making Governance Work for the Poor*. London: Secretary's Office.

Derber, Charles. 2000. *Corporation Nation: How Corporations Are Taking Over Our Lives and What We Can Do about It*. New York: St. Martin's Griffin.

Derksen, Linda, and John Gartrell. 1993. "The Social Context of Recycling." *American Sociological Review* 58 (3): 434–50.

Destutt de Tracy, Antoine Louis Claude. [1817] 1970. *A Treatise on Political Economy*. New York: A. M. Kelley.

Devereux, W. 1955. *A Study of Abortion in Primitive Societies*. New York: Julian Press.

Dinerstein, Ana C., and Mike Neary. 2002. *The Labour Debate: An Investigation into the Theory and Reality of Capitalist Work*. Burlington, VT: Ashgate.

DiPrete, Thomas A. 1993. "Industrial Restructuring and the Mobility Response of American Workers in the 1980s." *American Sociological Review* 58 (1): 74–96.

Dixon, C. J., D. Drakakis-Smith, and H. D. Watts, eds. 1986: *Multinational Corporations and the Third World*. Boulder, CO: Westview Press.

Dobzhansky, Theodore. 1951. *Genetics and the Origin of Species*. New York: Columbia University Press.

———. 1962. *Mankind Evolving: The Evolution of the Human Species*. New Haven, CT: Yale University Press.

———. 1963. "Evolution: Organic and Superorganic." *Rockefeller Institute Review* 1:1–9.

Domhoff, G. William. 1970. *The Higher Circles: The Governing Class in America*. New York: Vintage Books.

———. 1983. *Who Rules America Now? A View for the Eighties*. Englewood Cliffs, NJ: Prentice Hall.

———. 1990. *The Power Elite and the State: How Policy Is Made in America*. New York: A. de Gruyter.

Donaldson, Peter J., and Amy Ong Tsui. 1990. "The International Family Planning Movement." *Population Bulletin* 45 (8): 1–46.

Doner, V. 1998. *The Late Great GOP and the Coming Realignment.* Vallecito, CA: Chalcedon Foundation.

Donnachie, Ian L., and George Hewitt. 1993. *Historic New Lanark: The Dale and Owen Industrial Community since 1785.* Edinburgh: Edinburgh University Press.

Donnelly, Jack. 1984. "Cultural Relativism and Universal Human Rights." Human Rights Quarterly 6 (4): 400–419.

Doyle, Michael. 1986. *Empires.* Ithaca, NY: Cornell University Press.

Dreher, Axel. 2006. "Does Globalization Affect Growth? Empirical Evidence from a New Index." *Applied Economics* 38 (10): 1091–1110.

Drinan, Robert F. 1993. "The ABA in Vienna: At the U.N. World Conference on Human Rights." *Human Rights* 20: 22–23.

Drucker, Peter. 1986. "New Technology: Predicting Its Impact." In *Technology and the Future*, edited by A. Teich. New York: St Martin's Press.

D'Souza, Placido P. 2003. "Commemorating Martin Luther King, Jr.: Gandhi's Influence on King." *San Francisco Chronicle* (January 20): B7.

Dubofsky, Melvyn. 1969. *We Shall Be All: A History of the Industrial Workers of the World.* Chicago: Quadrangle Books.

Du Bois, William, and R. Dean Wright. 2001. *Applying Sociology: Making a Better World.* Boston: Allyn & Bacon.

Ducommun-Nagy, Catherine. 2002. "Contextual Therapy." In *Comprehensive Handbook of Psychotherapy*, edited by F. Kaslow. Vol. 3. New York: Wiley.

Durand, John. 1973. "A Long-Range View of World Population Growth." In *Population, Environment, and Social Organization*, edited by M. Micklin. Boston: Dryden.

Durkheim, Emile. [1893] 1933. *The Division of Labor in Society.* New York: Free Press.

———. [1895] 1962. *Socialism.* New York: Macmillan (Collier).

———. [1912] 1965. *Elementary Forms of the Religious Life.* New York: Free Press.

Earl, Sarah, F. Carden, Michael Quinn Patton, and Terry Smutylo. 2001. *Outcome Mapping: Building Learning and Reflection into Development Programs.* Ottawa: International Development Research Centre.

Easterlin, Robert. 1968. *Population, Labor Force, and Long Swings in Economic Growth.* New York: National Bureau of Economic Research.

Ehrenreich, Barbara. 1990. *Fear of Falling.* New York: Praeger.

Ehrenreich, Barbara, and John Ehrenreich. 1977. "The Professional-Managerial Class." *Radical America* 1 (11) (March–April): 7–31; 2 (11) (May–June): 7–22.

Ehrlich, Paul. 1968. *The Population Bomb.* New York: Ballantine Books.

Einstein, Albert. 1954. *Ideas and Opinions.* New York: Crown Publishers.

Eisenhower, Dwight D. 1961. *Peace with Justice: Selected Addresses.* New York: Columbia University Press.

Eisenstadt, S. N., ed. 1978. *Revolutions and the Transformation of Societies: A Comparative Study of Civilizations.* New York: Free Press.

Ekins, Paul. 1992. *A New World Order: Grassroots Movements for Global Change.* New York: Routledge.

Elkins, Stanley M. 1959. *Slavery: A Problem in American Institutional and Intellectual Life.* Chicago: University of Chicago Press.

Ellul, Jacques. 1964. *The Technological Society.* New York: Knopf.

"Empathy, Altruism and Agape: Perspectives on Love in Science and Religion." 1999. Conference sponsored by John Templeton Foundation and the Fetzer Institute. MIT, Cambridge, MA, October 1–3.

Emshwiller, John R. 1994. "The Rise and Fall of Hope in L.A." *Wall Street Journal*, April 21, A1.

Engberg-Pederson, Poul. 1982. *The United Nations and Intervention in International Economic Processes*. Copenhagen: Center for Development Research.

Engels, Frederick. [1844] 2006. "The Great Towns" (extract from *The Conditions of the Working Class in England*). In *Perspectives on Urban Society: From Preindustrial to Postindustrial*, edited by E. Padilla. Boston: Allyn & Bacon.

———. [1870] 1969. "Preface to *The Peasant War in Germany*." In *Selected Works*, by K. Marx and F. Engels, 158–65. Vol. 2. Moscow: Progress Publishers.

———. [1871] 1969. "Apropos of Working Class Political Action." In *Selected Works*, by K. Marx and F. Engels, 245–46. Vol. 2. Moscow: Progress Publishers.

———. [1884] 1969. "The Origins of the Family, Private Property, and the State." In *Selected Works*, by K. Marx and F. Engels, 204–334. Vol. 3. Moscow: Progress Publishers.

Engleman, Bernt. 1987. *In Hitler's Germany: Everyday Life in the Third Reich*. New York: Schocken Books.

Ericson, Erik H. 1969. *Gandhi's Truth: On the Origins of Militant Non-Violence*. New York: Norton.

Erlich, Reese. 1995. "Suu Kyi's Release Won't Spur Investments in Burma." *Christian Science Monitor*, July 21, 8.

Esposito, John L. 2002. *Unholy War: Terror in the Name of Islam*. New York: Oxford University Press.

Ethnologue. "Languages of the World." www.ethnologue.com/.

Etzioni, Amitai. 1991. *A Responsive Society: Collected Essays on Guiding Deliberate Social Change*. San Francisco: Jossey-Bass.

———. 1995. *New Communitarian Theory: Persons, Virtues, Interests, and Communities*. Charlottesville: University of Virginia Press.

Etzioni-Halevy, Eva. 1981. *Social Change: The Advent and Maturation of Modern Society*. London: Routledge & Kegan Paul.

Evans, Peter, Dietrich Rueschemeyer, and Evelyne Huber Stephens, eds. 1985. *States versus Markets in the World-System*. Beverly Hills, CA: Sage.

Falkner, David. 1995. *Great Time Coming: The Life of Jackie Robinson, from Baseball to Birmingham*. New York: Simon & Schuster.

Faludi, Susan. 1991. *Backlash: The Undeclared War against American Women*. New York: Crown Press.

Fanon, Frantz. 1963. *The Wretched of the Earth*. New York: Grove Press.

———. 1967. *Black Skins, White Masks*. New York: Grove Press.

Ferman, Louis, Stuart Henry, and M. Hoyman, eds. 1987. "The Informal Economy." In *The Annals of the American Academy of Political and Social Science* 492 (September): 154–72.

Ferraro, Geraldine A. 1995. "Women's Rights, Human Rights." *New York Times*, August 22, A11, A15.

Ferraro, Vincent. 1996. "Dependency Theory: An Introduction." Mount Holyoke College, South Hadley, MA, July. www.mtholyoke.edu/acad/intrel/feros-pg.htm.

Fewsmith, Joseph. 2001. *China since Tiananmen: The Politics of Transition*. New York: Cambridge University Press.

"Fiftieth Anniversaries of 1995." 1995. Editorial. *Tikkun* 10 (3): 8–10.

Firebaugh, Glen, and Frank D. Beck. 1994. "Does Economic Growth Benefit the Masses? Growth, Dependence, and Welfare in the Third World." *American Sociological Review* 59 (5): 631–53.

Fisher, Robert, and Peter Romanofsky, eds. 1981. *Community Organization for Social Change*. Westport, CT: Greenwood.

Flexible Automation and Integrated Manufacturing Conference (FAIMC). 1993. *Flexible Automation and Integrated Manufacturing: Proceedings of the Third Conference on Flexible Automation and Integrated Manufacturing* (University of Limerick, Ireland). Boca Raton, FL: CRC Press.

Flint, Robert. 1874. *The Philosophy of History in France and Germany*. Edinburgh: W. Blackwood.

Flower, Raymond, and Michael Wynn-Jones. 1987. *Lloyd's of London: An Illustrated History*. Colchester, UK: Lloyd's of London.

Flynn, John F. 1994. "Questioning Technology and Progress." *Academe* 80 (6): 42–45.

Fogelman, Eva. 1994. *Conscience and Courage*. New York: Anchor Books.

Forbes. 2008. "The Global 2000." April 2. www.forbes.com/lists/2008/18/biz_2000global08_The-Global-2000_Rank.html.

Form, William. 1979. "Comparative Industrial Sociology and the Convergence Hypothesis." *Annual Review of Sociology* 5:1–25.

Fortune. 2007. "Fortune 500 2007." April 30.

Foster, Lawrence. 1981. *Religion and Sexuality: The American Communal Experiments of the Nineteenth Century*. New York: Oxford University Press.

Fox, Justin. 2009. *The Myth of the Rational Market: History of Risk, Reward, and Delusion on Wall Street*. New York: Harper Business.

Fox, Leonard, ed. and trans. 1990. *Kanuni I Leke Dukagjini (The Code of Leke Dukagjini)*. New York: Gjonlekaj Publishing.

Frank, Andre G. 1967. *Capitalism or Underdevelopment in Latin America*. New York: Monthly Review Press.

———. 1969. "The Development of Underdevelopment." In *Latin America: Underdevelopment or Revolution*. New York: Monthly Review Press.

———. 1998. *ReOrient: Global Economy in the Asian Age*. Berkeley: University of California Press.

Frank, Thomas. 2004. *What's the Matter with Kansas? How Conservatives Won the Heart of America*. New York: Henry Holt.

Frankfurt Institute for Social Research. 1972. *Aspects of Sociology*. Boston: Beacon Press.

Freedman, Ina N. 1990. *The Other Victims: First-Person Accounts of Non-Jews Persecuted by the Nazis*. Boston: Houghton Mifflin.

Freedom House. 2009. "Worst of the Worst: The World's Most Repressive Societies." Selected data from "Freedom in the World: Freedom House's Annual Global Survey of Political Rights and Civil Liberties." www.freedomhouse.org/.

Freeman, John R. 1989. *Democracy and Markets: The Politics of Mixed Economies*. Ithaca, NY: Cornell University Press.

Freud, Sigmund. 1947. *Freud: On War, Sex, and Neurosis*. New York: Arts and Science Press.

———. 1961. *Civilization and Its Discontents*. New York: Norton.

———. 1967. *Moses and Monotheism*. New York: Vintage Books.

———. 1975. *The Future of an Illusion*. New York: Norton.

Friedman, Philip. 1978. *Their Brother's Keeper: The Christian Heroes and Heroines Who Helped the Oppressed Escape the Nazi Terror*. New York: Holocaust Library.

Friedman, Thomas. 2005. *The World Is Flat*. New York: Farrar, Straus and Giroux.

Frisbie, W. Parker. 1977. "The Scale and Growth of World Urbanization." In *Cities in Change: Studies on the Urban Condition*, edited by J. Walton and D. E. Carns. Boston: Allyn & Bacon.

Fromm, Erich. 1961. "Afterword." In *1984*, by G. Orwell. New York: New American Library.

———. 1968. *The Revolution of Hope: Toward a Humanized Technology*. New York: Harper & Row.

Fubini, Riccardo. 2003. *Humanism and Secularization: From Petrarch to Valla*. Durham, NC: Duke University Press.

Fuller, R. Buckminster. 1983. *Humans in Universe*. New York: Mouton.

———. 1992. *Cosmography: A Posthumous Scenario of the Future of Humanity*. New York: Macmillan.

Furet, François. 1989. *Unanswered Questions: Nazi Germany and the Genocide of the Jews*. New York: Schocken Books.

Gamson, William A. 1995. "Hiroshima, the Holocaust, and the Politics of Exclusion." *American Sociological Review* 60 (1): 1–20.

Gans, Herbert. 1962. *The Urban Villagers*. New York: Free Press.

———. 1968. *People and Plans: Essays on Urban Problems and Solutions*. New York: Basic Books.

Gaonkar, Dilip P. 2001. *Alternative Modernities*. Durham, NC: Duke University Press.

Garland, Robert. 1986. "Mother and Child in the Greek World." *History Today* 36 (3): 40–46.

Garon, Jon M. 2002. "Information and Technology Law: Privacy and Anonymity in an Age of Patriotism." *Interface Tech News* (March). www.interfacenow.com/.

Gastil, Raymond D. 1986. *Freedom in the World: Political Rights and Civil Liberties*. Westport, CT: Greenwood.

Geddes, Patrick. [1904] 2007. *Civics as Applied Sociology*. Eastbourne, UK: Gardners Books.

Geyer, H. S., ed. 2002. *International Handbook of Urban Systems: Studies of Urbanization and Migration in Advanced and Developing Countries*. Northampton, MA: E. Elgar.

Ghai, Dharam, and Samir Radwan. 1983. *Agrarian Policies and Rural Poverty in Africa*. Geneva: International Labour Office.

Gibbon, Edward. [1776] 1921. *The History of the Decline and Fall of the Roman Empire*. London: Methuen.

Gibbons, Michael. 1994. *The New Production of Knowledge: The Dynamics of Science and Research in Contemporary Societies*. Thousand Oaks, CA: Sage.

Gibson-Robinson, Jo Ann. 1987. *The Montgomery Bus Boycott and the Woman Who Started It*. Knoxville: University of Tennessee Press.

Giddens, Anthony. 1981. *A Contemporary Critique of Historical Materialism*. Berkeley: University of California Press.

———. 1990. *The Consequences of Modernity*. Stanford, CA: Stanford University Press.

———. 1997. *Sociology*. Cambridge, UK: Polity Press.

Gilbert, Alan, and Josef Gugler. 1992. *Cities, Poverty, and Development: Urbanization in the Third World*. New York: Oxford University Press.

Gilbert, Martin. 1981. *Auschwitz and the Allies: A Devastating Account of How the Allies Responded to the News of Hitler's Mass Murder*. New York: Holt.

Gilster, Paul. 1993. *The Internet Navigator*. New York: Wiley.

Gimbel, John. 1976. *The Origins of the Marshall Plan*. Stanford, CA: Stanford University Press.

Ginger, Ray. 1949. *The Bending Cross*. New Brunswick, NJ: Rutgers University Press.

Gitlin, Todd. 1985. *Inside Prime Time*. New York: Pantheon.

Gjelten, Tom. 2009. "Economic Crisis Stirs Free-Market Debate." NPR, June 23. www.npr.org/templates/story/story.php?storyId=105783108.

Glanville, Jennifer. 2003. "Voluntary Associations and Social Network Structure: The Importance of Organization Type." Paper presented at the annual meeting of the American Sociological Association, Atlanta, GA, August 16.

Glassner, Barry. 1999. *The Culture of Fear: Why Americans Are Afraid of the Wrong Things*. New York: Basic Books.

Glendon, Mary Ann. 2001. *A World Made New: Eleanor Roosevelt and the Universal Declaration of Human Rights*. New York: Random House.

Glickfeld, Madelyn, Tom Whitney, and J. Eugene Grigsby. 1978. *A Selective Analytical Bibliography for Social Impact Assessment*. Monticello, IL: Council of Planning Librarians.

Gloede, William F. 1985. "AMA Urges Total Tobacco Ad Ban." *Advertising Age* 56 (December 9): 3–4.

Godwin, William. [1820] 1964. *Of Population*. New York: Augustus Kelly.

Goffman, Erving. 1961. *Asylums: Essays on the Social Situation of Mental Patients and Other Inmates*. Chicago: Aldine.

Goldenberg, Myrna. 1992. "Literature of the Holocaust." In *The Sociology of Genocide/The Holocaust*, edited by J. N. Porter. Washington, DC: American Sociological Association.

Goldhagen, Daniel Jonah. 1996. *Hitler's Willing Executioners: Ordinary Germans and the Holocaust*. New York: Knopf.

Goldstone, Jack A., ed. 1986. "Introduction." In *Revolutions: Theoretical, Comparative, and Historical Studies*, edited by J. Goldstone. San Diego, CA: Harcourt Brace Jovanovich.

———. 1989. "Revolution." In *The Social Science Encyclopedia*, edited by A. Kruper and J. Kruper. London: Routledge.

Goodman, Ellen. 1993. "Breaking the Silence." *Wall Street Journal*, June 19, A21.

Goodwin, Jeff, and James M. Jasper. 2009. *The Social Movement Reader*. Malden, MA: Blackwell.

Gordon, David. 1990. *Resurrecting Marx: The Analytical Marxists on Freedom, Exploitation, and Justice*. New Brunswick, NJ: Transaction Books.

Gore, Albert. 1991. "Infrastructure for the Global Village." *Scientific American* 265: 150–53.

Gouldner, Alvin W. 1954. *Patterns of Industrial Bureaucracy*. New York: Free Press.

———. 1960. "The Norm of Reciprocity: A Preliminary Statement." *American Sociological Review* 25 (2): 16161–78.

———. 1975–1976. "Prologue to a Theory of Revolutionary Intellectuals." *Telos* 26 (1): 2–36.

Goulet, Dennis. 1977. *The Cruel Choice*. New York: Atheneum.

———. 1989. *Incentives for Development: The Key to Equity*. New York: New Horizons.

Green, James. 1958. *The United Nations and Human Rights*. Menasha, WI: George Banta.

———. 2009. *Democracy at Work: The Union Movement in U.S. History*. Boston: University of Massachusetts Boston Labor Resource Center.

Gross, Michael L. 1994. "Jewish Rescue in Holland and France during the Second World War: Moral Cognition and Collective Action." *Social Forces* 73 (2): 463–96.

Guha, Ranajit. 2009. *Small Voice of History: Collected Essays*. Delhi: Permanent Black Publishers.

Guha, Ranajit, and Gayatri Chakravorty Spivak, eds. 1988. *Selected Subaltern Studies*. New York: Oxford University Press.

Guha, Sudeshna. 2007. "The Indus Civilization." *History Today* 57 (10): 50–57.

Gunaratna, Rohan. 2002. *Inside Al Qaeda: Global Network of Terror*. New York: Columbia University Press.

Guobin Yang. 2009. *The Power of the Internet in China: Citizen Activism Online*. New York: Columbia University Press.

Gurr, Ted. 1970. *Why Men Rebel*. Princeton, NJ: Princeton University Press.

Habermas, Jurgen, and Adam Michnik. 1994. "Overcoming the Past." *New Left Review* 203 (January–February): 3–16.

Hackett, Edward J., Olga Amsterdamska, Michael Lynch, and Judy Wajcman, eds. 2007. *The Handbook of Science & Technology Studies*, 3rd ed. Cambridge, MA: MIT Press.

Hadaway, C. Kirk, Penny Long Marler, and Mark Chaves. 1993. "What the Polls Don't Show: A Closer Look at U.S. Church Attendance." *American Sociological Review* 58 (6): 741–52.

Haëckel, Ernst W. 1917. *Evolution in Modern Thought*. New York: Boni & Liverwright.

Hafter, Daryl M. 1995. *European Women and Preindustrial Craft*. Bloomington: Indiana University Press.

Hall, Edward T. 1966. *The Hidden Dimension*. New York: Doubleday.

Hamilton, Daniel. 1989. "Dateline East Germany: The Wall behind the Wall." *Foreign Policy* 76 (fall): 176–97.

Hamm, Mark S. 1997. *Apocalypse in Oklahoma: Waco and Ruby Ridge Revenged*. Boston: Northeastern University Press.

Hammond, Ross, and Lisa A. McGowan. 1993. *The Other Side of the Story: The Real Impact of World Bank and IMF Structural Adjustment Programs*. Washington, DC: Development GAP.

Handlin, Oscar. 1953a. *The New Comers: Negroes and Puerto Ricans in a Changing Metropolis*. London: Oxford University Press.

———. 1953b. *Uprooted: From the Old World to the New*. London: Oxford University Press.

Harbutt, Fraser J. 1986. *The Iron Curtain: Churchill, America, and the Origins of the Cold War*. New York: Oxford University Press.

Harcourt, Wendy. 2009. *Body Politics in Development: Critical Debates in Gender and Development*. London: Zed Books.

Hardin, Garrett. 1973. "The Tragedy of the Commons." In *Toward a Steady-State Economy*, edited by H. Daly. San Francisco: W. H. Freeman.

————. 1980. "The Life Boat Ethic." In *Energy and the Way We Live*, edited by M. Kranzberg, T. Hall, and J. Scheiber. San Francisco: Boyd & Fraser.

Hardin, Garrett, and J. Baden, eds. 1977. *Managing the Commons*. San Francisco: W. H. Freeman.

Hargrave, Terry D., and James N. Sells. 1997. "The Development of a Forgiveness Scale." *Journal of Marital and Family Therapy* 23 (1): 41–62.

Harper, Charles L. 1993. *Exploring Social Change*. Englewood Cliffs, NJ: Prentice Hall.

Harrington, Michael. 1963. *The Other America: Poverty in the United States*. Boston: Penguin.

————. 1986. *The Next Left: The History of a Future*. New York: Henry Holt.

Hauerwas, Stanley. 1977. "The Moral Limits of Population Control." In *Truthfulness and Tragedy: Further Investigations in Christian Ethics*, edited by S. Hauerwas and R. Bondi. Notre Dame, IN: University of Notre Dame Press.

Hawley, Amos. 1968. "Human Ecology." *International Encyclopedia of Social Sciences* 4: 328–37.

Hayden, Tom. 1988. *Reunion: A Memoir*. New York: Random House.

Hazeltine, Barrett, and Christopher Bull. 1999. *Appropriate Technology: Tools, Choices and Implications*. San Diego: Academic Press.

Head, Brian. 1985. *Destutt de Tracy and French Liberalism*. Boston: Kluwer Academic.

Healy, Tim. 2008. "The Unanticipated Consequences of Technology." Markkula Center for Applied Ethics, Santa Clara University, Santa Clara, CA. www.scu.edu/ethics/publications/submitted/healy/consequences.html.

Hechter, Michael. 1995. "Introduction to Symposium on Prediction in the Social Sciences: Reflections on Historical Prophecy in the Social Sciences." *American Journal of Sociology* 100 (6): 1520–27.

Hedstrom, Peter. 1994. "Contagion and Collectivism: On the Spatial Distribution of Swedish Trade Unions." *American Journal of Sociology* 99 (3): 1157–79.

Heinberg, Richard. 2002. "A History of Corporate Rule and Popular Protest." *Nexus Magazine* 9 (October–November). www.nexusmagazine.com/articles/corporations.html.

Helvétius, Claude Adrien. [1810] 1969. *A Treatise on Man: His Intellectual Faculties and His Education*. London: Albion Press.

Henry, Stuart, ed. 1981. *Informal Institutions: Alternative Networks in the Corporate State*. New York: St. Martin's Press.

————, ed. 1990. *Degrees of Deviance: Student Accounts of their Deviant Behavior*. Salem, WI: Sheffield.

Henslin, James M. 1998. *Essentials of Sociology: A Down-to-Earth Approach*. Boston: Allyn & Bacon.

Herskovits, M. J. 1972. *Cultural Relativism: Perspectives in Cultural Pluralism*. New York: Random House.

Hicks, Alexander, and Joya Misra. 1993. "Political Resources and the Growth of Welfare in Affluent Capitalist Democracies, 1960–82." *American Journal of Sociology* 99 (3): 668–710.

Higgott, Richard A. 1983. *Political Development Theory*. New York: St. Martin's Press.

Hilberg, Raul. 1971. *Documents of Destruction: Germany and Jewry, 1933–1945*. Chicago: University of Chicago Press.

————. 1985. *The Destruction of the European Jews*. New York: Holmes and Meir.

Hill, Richard C., and Michael Indegaard. 1988. "Downriver: Deindustrialization in Suburban Detroit." In *Business Elites and Urban Development: Case Studies and Critical Perspectives*, edited by S. Cummings. Albany: State University of New York Press.

Hiller, Harry H. 2000. *Canadian Society: A Macro-Analysis*. Scarborough, Ontario: Prentice Hall.

Himes, N. E. 1936. *Medical History of Contraception*. London: Williams & Williams.

Hintz, Robert A., and Carl J. Couch. 1978. "Mediated Messages and Social Coordination." *Journal of Communication* 28 (1): 117–23.

Hippel, Eric von. 1998. *The Sources of Innovation*. New York: Oxford University Press.

399

REFERENCES

Hitler, Adolf. [1925] 1948. *Mein Kampf*. Boston: Houghton Mifflin.

Hodgson, Geoffrey, Makoto Itoh, and Nobuharu Yokokowa. 2001. *Capitalism in Evolution: Global Connections—East and West*. Northampton, MA: E. Elgar.

Hodson, Randy, Sandy Welsh, Sabine Rieble, Cheryl Sorenson Jamison, and Sean Creighton. 1993. "Is Worker Solidarity Undermined by Autonomy and Participation? Patterns from the Ethnographic Literature." *American Sociological Review* 58 (3): 398–416.

Hoebel, E. Adamson. 1966. *Anthropology: The Study of Man*. New York: McGraw-Hill.

Hoffer, Eric. 1951. *The True Believer*. New York: Mentor Books.

Hogan, Michael. 1987. *The Marshall Plan: America, Britain, and the Reconstruction of Western Europe*. New York: Cambridge University Press.

Höhne, Heinz. 1969. *The Order of the Death's Head: The Story of Hitler's SS*. Harmondsworth, UK: Penguin.

Holman, Richard L. 1994. "China Cranks Up Propaganda Arm: Communist Party Orders Media to Support Market Reforms." *Wall Street Journal*, January 26, A10.

Hooks, Gregory. 1993. "The Weakness of Strong Theories: The U.S. State's Dominance of the World War II Investment Process." *American Sociological Review* 58 (1): 746–72.

Horowitz, Irving Louis. 1954. *Claude Helvetius: Philosopher of Democracy and Enlightenment*. New York: Paine-Whitman.

———. 1963. *The War Game: The New Civilian Militarists*. New York: Ballantine Books.

———. 1966. *Three Worlds of Development*. New York: Oxford University Press.

———. 1972. *Three Worlds of Development*, 2nd ed. New York: Oxford University Press.

———. 1980. *Taking Lives: Genocide and State Power*. New Brunswick, NJ: Transaction Books.

———. 1982. *Beyond Empire and Revolution: Militarization and Consolidation in the Third World*. New York: Oxford University Press.

———. 1983. *C. Wright Mills: An American Utopian*. New York: Free Press.

———. 1993. *The Decomposition of Sociology*. New York: Oxford University Press.

Horowitz, Irving Louis, Claude E. Welch Jr., and Augustus Richard Norton. 1984. "Beyond Empire and Revolution: Militarization and Consolidation in the Third World." Review Symposium. *Studies in Comparative International Development* 19 (2): 59–77.

Horvat, Branko. 1995. *The Theory of Value, Capital, and Interest: A New Approach*. Brookfield, VT: E. Elgar.

Hourani, Benjamin T. 1987. "Toward the 21st Century: The Organization of Power in Post-Industrial Society." *Public Policy* 14: 217–29.

———. 1994. "Some Thought on Global Ethics and Cultures of Peace." *Future Bulletin* (October): 13–14.

House Committee on Energy and Commerce. 1983. *Love Canal Study and Habitability Statement*. Washington, DC: U.S. Government Printing Office.

Hoyle, Fred, and N. C. Wickramasinghe. 1981. *Lifecloud: The Origin of Life in the Universe*. New York: Harper & Row.

Htwe, Ko. 2009. "Suu Kyi Meets Junta's Liaison Minister Again." *Irrawaddy* (October 7). www .irrawaddy.org/article.php?art_id=16948.

Huber, Evelyne, Charles Ragin, and John D. Stephens. 1993. "Social Democracy, Christian Democracy, Constitutional Structure and the Welfare State." *American Journal of Sociology* 99 (3): 711–49.

Hughes, James, and Gwendolyn Sasse. 2002. *Ethnicity and Territory in the Former Soviet Union: Regions in Conflict*. London: Frank Cass Publishers.

Hull, D. S. 1969. *Film in the Third Reich: A Study of the German Cinema 1933–45*. Berkeley: University of California Press.

Human Rights Watch. 1995. *Human Rights Watch World Report, 1995*. New York: HRW Publications.

Huttenbach, Robert A. 1971. *Gandhi in South Africa: British Imperialism and the Indian Question, 1860–1914*. Ithaca, NY: Cornell University Press.

Huxley, Julian. 1953. *Evolution in Action*. New York: Harper & Row.

Hyams, Edward. 1973. *The Millennium Postponed: Socialism from Sir Thomas More to Mao Tse-tung*. New York: New American Library.

Ibn Khaldun of Tunis. 1958. *The Muqaddimah: An Introduction to History*. New York: Pantheon Books.

————. 1987. *An Arab Philosophy of History: Selections from the Prolegomena of Ibn Khaldun of Tunis (1332–1406)*. Princeton, NJ: Darwin Press.

Ibsen, Charles A., and Patricia Klobus. 1972. "Fictive Kin Term Use and Social Relationships: Alternative Interpretations." *Journal of Marriage and the Family* 34 (4): 615–20.

Illich, Ivan. 1974. *Medical Nemesis*. London: Calder & Boyars.

Inder Singh, Anita. 1987. *The Origins of the Partition of India, 1936–1947*. Delhi: Oxford University Press.

Industrial Workers of the World (IWW). 1984. *IWW Songs: To Fan the Flames of Discontent*. Chicago: Author.

Innes, Harold. 1971. *The Bias of Communication*. Toronto: University of Toronto Press.

International Association for Impact Assessment (IAIA). 2009. *Impact Assessment and Project Appraisal* (pamphlet). Surrey, UK: Beech Tree Publishers.

International Conference on Collective Phenomena (ICCP). 1985. *International Conference on Collective Phenomena: Report from the Moscow Refusnik Seminar*. New York: New York Academy of Science.

Internet Encyclopedia of Science. 2009. "Cosmic Ancestry." www.daviddarling.info/encyclopedia/P/panspermia.html (accessed October 13, 2009).

Iqbal, Javid. 2003. *Islam and Pakistan's Identity*. New York: Vanguard.

Ishtiaq, Ahmed. 1991. *The Concept of the Islamic State in Pakistan: An Analysis of Ideological Controversies*. Lahore, Pakistan: Vanguard Press.

Jackson, Christopher. 1990. *A Cambridge Bicentenary: The History of a Legal Practice, 1789–1989*. Bungay, UK: Morrow.

James, C. L. R. 1969. *State Capitalism and World Revolution*. Detroit: Facing Reality Publishing.

Jameson, John Franklin. 1968. *The American Revolution Considered as a Social Movement*. Princeton, NJ: Princeton University Press.

Janton, Pierre. 1993. *Esperanto: Language, Literature, and Community*. Albany: State University of New York Press.

Jasanoff, Sheila. 1995. *Handbook of Science and Technology Studies*. Thousand Oaks, CA: Sage.

Jay, Martin. 1979. *The Dialectical Imagination*. Boston: Little, Brown.

Jeffries, Vincent, Barry V. Johnston, Lawrence T. Nichols, Samuel P. Oliner, Edward Tiryakian, and Jay Weinstein. 2007. "Altruism and Social Solidarity: Envisioning a Field of Specialization." *American Sociologist* 37 (3): 67–83.

Jéquier, Nicholas. 1979. *Appropriate Technology Directory*. Paris: Development Centre of the Organisation for Economic Co-operation and Development.

————. 1981. "Appropriate Technology Needs Political 'Push.'" *World Health Forum* 2 (4): 541–43.

Johnasson, Thomas. 1992. *Lifestyle and Identity in Contemporary Youth Culture*. Stockholm: Almquist and Winsell.

Johnson, Donald B. 1978. *National Party Platforms*. Urbana: University of Illinois Press.

Johnston, Barry V. 1987. "Pitirim A. Sorokin and the American Sociological Association: The Politics of a Professional Society." *Journal of the History of the Behavioral Sciences* 23: 103–22.

————. 1995. *Pitirim A. Sorokin: An Intellectual Biography*. Lawrence: University Press of Kansas.

————, ed. 1998. *Pitirim A. Sorokin: On the Practice of Sociology*. Chicago: University of Chicago Press.

Jonas, Gerald, and Sarah Wheaton. 2009. "Norman Borlaug, Plant Scientist Who Fought Famine, Dies at 95." *New York Times*, September 14, A1.

Jones, Charles A. 1983. *The North-South Dialogue: A Brief History*. New York: St. Martin's Press.

Jones, Gavin W., ed. 1997. *The Continuing Demographic Transition*. New York: Oxford University Press.

REFERENCES

Jones-Jackson, Patricia. 1976. "The Status of Gullah: An Investigation of Convergent Processes." Ph.D. diss., University of Michigan, Ann Arbor.

Jory, B., D. Anderson, and C. Greer. 1997. "Intimate Justice: Confronting Issues of Accountability, Respect, and Freedom in Treatment for Abuse and Violence." *Journal of Marital and Family Therapy* 23:399–420.

Kabagarama, Daisy. 1993. *Breaking the Ice: Understanding People from Other Cultures.* Boston: Allyn & Bacon.

Kafka, Franz. [1956] 1968. *The Trial.* New York: Schocken Books.

Kalache, A. 1997. "Demographic Transition Poses a Challenge to Societies Worldwide." *Tropical Medicine and International Health* 2 (10): 925–26.

Kale, Madhavi. 1998. *Fragments of Empire: Capital, Slavery, and Indian Indentured Labor Migration in the British Caribbean.* Philadelphia: University of Pennsylvania Press.

Kaminer, Wendy. 1992. *I'm Dysfunctional, You're Dysfunctional: The Recovery Movement and Other Self-Help Programs.* Reading, MA: Addison-Wesley.

Kanet, Roger E. 1987. *The Soviet Union, Eastern Europe, and the Third World.* New York: Cambridge University Press.

Kant, Immanuel. 1961. "Foundations for the Metaphysics of Morals." In *Philosophical Classics: Bacon to Kant,* edited by W. Kaufman. Englewood Cliffs, NJ: Prentice Hall.

Kanter, Rosabeth Moss. 1968. "Commitment and Social Organization: A Study of Commitment Mechanisms in Utopian Communities." *American Sociological Review* 33 (3): 499–517.

———. 1972. *Commitment and Community: Communes and Utopias in Sociological Perspective.* Cambridge, MA: Harvard University Press.

———. 1977. *Men and Women of the Corporation.* New York: Basic Books.

———. 1983. *The Change Masters: Innovation and Entrepreneurship in the American Corporation.* New York: Simon & Schuster.

Kaplan, Robert D. 1993. *Balkan Ghosts.* New York: St. Martin's Press.

Karim, M. Bazlul. 1986. *The Green Revolution: An International Bibliography.* Westport, CT: Greenwood.

Katz, Steven T. 1994. *The Holocaust and Mass Death before the Modern Age.* Vol. 1 of *The Holocaust in Historical Context.* New York: Oxford University Press.

Kecskemeti, Paul. 1991. *The Unexpected Revolution.* Stanford, CA: Stanford University Press.

Kelly, Kate. 2008. "Moving Forward: A Participatory Democracy." *Huffington Post,* November 10, 2008. www.huffingtonpost.com/kate-kelly/moving-forward-a-particip_b_142579.html.

Kepel, Gilles. 1994. *The Revenge of God: The Resurgence of Islam, Christianity, and Judaism in the Modern World.* University Park: Pennsylvania State University Press.

Kerr, Clark. 1983. *The Future of Industrialized Societies.* Cambridge, MA: Harvard University Press.

Kersten, Gregory E. 2008. "e-Democracy and Participatory Decision Processes: Lessons from e-Negotiation Experiments." *International Journal of Electronic Democracy* 1 (1): 51–84.

Kerwin, Kathleen. 1987. "Proving Its Mettle: An Ex-Bankrupt Company Is Back." *Barron's* 67:14.

Keyfitz, Nathan. 1966. "How Many People Have Ever Lived on the Earth?" *Demography* 3 (3): 581–82.

Khaldoun, Samman, and Mazhar Al-Zo'by. 2008. *Islam and the Orientalist World-System.* Boulder, CO: Paradigm Publishers.

Khan, Yasmin. 2007. *The Great Partition: The Making of India and Pakistan.* New Haven, CT: Yale University Press.

Kilborn, Peter T. 1995. "Three Unions Agree to Merge into One." *New York Times,* July 30, E2.

King, Mary. 1999. *Mahatma Gandhi and Martin Luther King Jr.: The Power of Nonviolent Action.* Paris: UNESCO.

Kiser, Edgar. 1995. "What Can Sociological Theories Predict? Comment on Collins, Kuran, and Tilly." *American Journal of Sociology* 100 (6): 1611–15.

Kitschelt, Herbert, Peter Lang, Gary Marks, and John D. Stephens, eds. 1999. *Continuity and Change in Contemporary Capitalism*. Cambridge: Cambridge University Press.

Klass, Morton. 1978. *From Field to Factory*. Philadelphia: ISHI Press.

Klinkenborg, Verlyn. 1992. "Biopolitics: An Idea Whose Time Has Come?" *Audubon* 94 (1): 90–93.

Knoke, David, and Arne L. Kalleberg. 1994. "Job Training in U.S. Organizations." *American Sociological Review* 59 (4): 537–46.

Knox, Robert. 1862. *The Races of Men: A Philosophical Inquiry into the Influence of Race in the Destinies of Nations*. London: H. Rennhaw.

Kolakowski, L. 1990. "Uncertainties of a Democratic Age." *Journal of Democracy* 1 (1): 47–50.

Kollock, Peter. 1993. "'An Eye for an Eye Leaves Everyone Blind': Cooperation and Accounting Systems." *American Sociological Review* 58 (6): 768–86.

Koopmans, Ruud. 1993. "The Dynamics of Protest Waves: West Germany, 1965 to 1989." *American Sociological Review* 58 (5): 637–58.

Korten, David C. 2001. *When Corporations Rule the World*. Bloomfield, CT: Kumarian Press.

Kovel, Joel. 1994. *Red Hunting in the Promised Land*. New York: Basic Books.

Kposowa, Augustine J., and J. Craig Jenkins. 1993. "The Structural Sources of Military Coups in Postcolonial Africa." *American Journal of Sociology* 99 (1): 126–63.

Kraljic, Matthew A. 1988. *The Breakup of Communism: The Soviet Union and Eastern Europe*. New York: H. W. Wilson.

Kramer, Samuel Noah. 1963. *The Sumerians: Their History, Culture, and Character*. Chicago: University of Chicago Press.

Krauss, Melvyn B. 1983. *Development without Aid: Growth, Poverty, and Government*. Lanham, MD: University Press of America.

Krebs, Dennis L. 2002. "Adaptive Altruistic Strategies." *Behavioral and Brain Sciences* 25 (2): 265–66.

Krebs, Dennis L., and Frank Van Hesteren. 1994. "The Development of Altruism: Toward an Integrative Model." *Developmental Review* 14 (2): 103–58.

Kreis, Steven. 2000. "The Athenian Origins of Direct Democracy: Lecture 6." www.historyguide.org/ancient/lecture6b.html (accessed May 15, 2003).

Krinsky, Fred. 1968. *Democracy and Complexity: Who Governs the Governors?* Beverly Hills, CA: Glencoe.

Kroeber, Alfred L. 1917. "The Superorganic." *American Anthropologist* 19:162–213.

Kroeber, Alfred L., and Talcott Parsons. 1958. "The Concepts of Culture and of Social Systems." *American Sociological Review* 23 (2): 582–83.

Kroeber, Theodora. 1961. *Ishi in Two Worlds: A Biography of the Last Wild Indian in North America*. Berkeley: University of California Press.

Krohn, Roger G. 1999. "Dutch 17th-Century World Trade Primacy and 'Unthinking' English Economics." Paper presented at the annual meeting of the American Sociological Association, Chicago, August.

Krueckeberg, Donald A. 1983. *Introduction to Planning History in the United States*. New Brunswick, NJ: Center for Urban Policy Research, Rutgers University.

Krugman, Paul. 2002. "Plutocracy and Politics." *New York Times*, June 14, A37.

Kumar, Ashish. 1999. "Localizing the Global in India: New Imperatives for International Communication Scholarship in the Satellite Era." *TBS Archives* 2 (spring). www.tbsjournal.com/Archives/review_index.html.

Kuran, Timur. 1995. "The Inevitability of Future Revolutionary Surprises." *American Journal of Sociology* 100 (6): 1528–51.

Kurtz, Fred. 2000. "The New American Plutocracy." *Free Inquiry* 20 (4). www.secularhumanism.org/library/fi/kurtz_20_4.html.

Landes, David S. 1969. *The Unbound Prometheus: Technological Change and Industrial Development in Europe, 1750 to the Present*. Cambridge: Cambridge University Press.

Lappe, Frances Moore, and Paul Du Bois. 1994. *The Quickening of America: Rebuilding Our Nation, Remaking Our Lives*. San Francisco: Jossey-Bass.

Laqueur, Walter. 1980. *The Terrible Secret*. Boston: Little, Brown.

Laqueur, Walter, and George L. Mosse, eds. 1978. "Conservative Movements." Special issue of *Journal of Contemporary History* 13 (4).

Larson, Olaf F., Julie N. Zimmerman, and Edward O. Moe. 2003. *Sociology in Government: The Galpin-Taylor Years in the U.S. Department of Agriculture, 1919–1953*. University Park: Pennsylvania State University Press.

Lasch, Christopher. 1973. *The World of Nations*. New York: Knopf.

———. 1991. *The True and Only Heaven: Progress and Its Critics*. New York: Norton.

Lawless, Edward. 1977. *Technology and Social Shock*. New Brunswick, NJ: Rutgers University Press.

Leake, Jonathan. 2008. "Food Shortages Loom as Wheat Crop Shrinks and Prices Rise." *Sunday Times*, February 24. http://business.timesonline.co.uk/tol/business/industry_sectors/natural_resources/article3423734.ece.

Le Bon, Gustave. [1895] 1960. *The Mind of the Crowd*. New York: Viking.

Leiser, Edward. 1974. *Nazi Cinema*. New York: Macmillan.

Lenski, Gerhard, and Jean Lenski. 1987. *Human Societies: An Introduction to Macrosociology*. New York: McGraw-Hill.

Léonard, Émile G. 1968. *A History of Protestantism*. Indianapolis, IN: Bobbs-Merrill.

Lerner, Daniel. 1958. *The Passing of Traditional Society*. New York: Free Press.

Levi, Primo. 1986. *Moments of Truth*. New York: Summit Books.

———. 1988. *The Damned and the Saved*. New York: Summit Books.

———. 1995. *The Reawakening*. New York: Simon & Schuster.

———. 1996. *Survival in Auschwitz: The Nazi Assault on Humanity*. New York: Simon & Schuster.

Levine, Barry B. 1987. *The Caribbean Exodus*. New York: Praeger.

Levinson, David. 1998. *Ethnic Groups Worldwide: A Ready Reference Handbook*. Santa Barbara, CA: Greenwood.

Levy, Daniel, and Natan Sznaider. 2006. *The Holocaust and Memory in the Global Age*. Philadelphia: Temple University Press.

Lewin, Roger. 1984. *Human Evolution: An Illustrated Introduction*. New York: W. H. Freeman.

Lewis, Anthony. 1994. "South Africa's Miracle: Election Is the Result of Careful Crafting." *Detroit Free Press*, May 1, 3.

Lewis, David C. 2000. *After Atheism: Religion and Ethnicity in Russia and Central Asia*. New York: St. Martin's Press.

Lewis, Jerry M. 1973. "McLuhan: A Sociological Interpretation." In *The Humanities as Sociology*, edited by M. Truzzi. Columbus, OH: Charles Merrill.

Lewis, John P., and Vallerina Kallab, eds. 1986. *Development Strategies Reconsidered*. New Brunswick, NJ: Transaction Books.

Lewy, Guenter. 1964. *The Catholic Church and Nazi Germany*. New York: McGraw-Hill.

———. 2000. *The Nazi Persecution of the Gypsies*. New York: Oxford University Press.

Li, Peter S. 1996. *The Making of Post-War Canada*. Toronto: Oxford University Press.

Lidz, Victor. 1979. "Secular Life, Ethical Life, and Religion in Modern Societies." In *Religious Change and Continuity*, edited by H. Johnson. San Francisco: W. H. Freeman.

———. 1989. "Secularization." In *The Social Science Encyclopedia*, edited by A. Kruper and J. Kruper. London: Routledge.

Lindqvist, Sven. 1996. *Exterminate All the Brutes*. New York: New Press.

Linz, Juan. 1988. *Democracy in Developing Countries*. Boulder, CO: Lynne Rienner.

Linz, Juan, and Alfred Stepan. 1978. *The Breakdown of Democratic Regimes*. Baltimore: Johns Hopkins University Press.

Lipset, Seymour M. 1963. *The First New Nation: The United States in Comparative and Historical Perspective*. New York: Basic Books.

———. 1971. *Agrarian Socialism: The Cooperative Commonwealth Federation in Saskatchewan*. Berkeley: University of California Press.

———. 1990. *Continental Divide: The Values and Institutions of the United States and Canada*. New York: Routledge.

———. 1994. "The Social Requisites of Democracy Revisited." *American Sociological Review* 59 (1): 1–22.

Lipset, Seymour M., Martin Trow, and James Coleman. 1956. *Union Democracy: Politics of the International Typographical Union*. New York: Free Press.

Lipstadt, Deborah E. 1993. *Holocaust Denial: The Growing Assault on Truth and Memory*. New York: Plume Press.

Lloyd, Emma. 2009. "A Human Evolution Timeline." Bright Hub Inc., July 2. www.brighthub.com/science/medical/articles/6040.aspx.

Lockwood, Lee. 1970. *Conversation with Eldridge Cleaver*. New York: McGraw-Hill.

Lomax, Louis E. 1962. *The Negro Revolt*. New York: New American Library.

London, Jack. [1910] 1980. *The Iron Heel*. Westport, CT: L. Hill.

Lorenz, Konrad. 1966. *On Aggression*. New York: Harcourt Brace Jovanovich.

Lowenstein, Roger. 2009. "On Wall Street, the Price Isn't Right." *Washington Post*, June 7. www.washingtonpost.com/wp-dyn/content/article/2009/06/05/AR2009060502053.html.

Lowi, Theodore, Jr. 1981. "The Political Impact of Information Technology." In *The Microelectronic Revolution*, edited by T. Forester. Cambridge, MA: MIT Press.

Loxley, John. 1986. *Debt and Disorder: External Financing for Development*. Boulder, CO: Westview Press.

Ludden, David. 2001. "Introduction: A Brief History of Subalternity." In *Subaltern Studies Critical History, Contested Meaning, and the Globalisation of South Asia*, edited by D. Ludden. New Delhi: Permanent Black.

Lynch, Colum. 2002. "Islamic Bloc, Christian Right Team Up to Lobby U.N." *Washington Post*, June 17, A1.

Machalek, Richard. 1979. "Thorstein Veblen, Louis Schneider, and the Ironic Imagination." *Social Science Quarterly* 60 (3): 460–64.

Malis, L. 1992. "Battling the Balkan Disease." *U.S. News and World Report* 45 (June 8): 29.

Malthus, Thomas R. [1798] 1960. *On Population*. New York: Random House.

Mamdani, Mahmood. 1972. *The Myth of Population Control*. New York: Monthly Review Press.

Mannheim, Karl. 1950. *Freedom, Power, and Democratic Planning*. New York: Oxford University Press.

———. 1954. *Man and Society in an Age of Reconstruction*. New York: Harcourt Brace Jovanovich.

———. 1968. *Ideology and Utopia*. New York: Harcourt, Brace & World.

Markoff, John. 1993. "Building the Electronic Superhighway." *New York Times*, January 24, C1.

Marsh, R. M. 1991. "Authoritarian and Democratic Transitions in National Political Systems." *International Journal of Comparative Sociology* 32 (3–4): 219–32.

Marshall, Andrew. 2009. "Putting Myanmar's Junta on Trial." Daw Aung San Suu Kyi's Pages, August 7. http://dassk.org/index.php?PHPSESSID=169efda7738669dd9900b1a3decab033&/topic,11111484.0.html.

Marshall, Gordon. 1998. "Iatrogenesis." In *A Dictionary of Sociology*, Encyclopedia. com, October 15, 2009. www.encyclopedia.com/doc/1O88-iatrogenesis.html.

Martens, Willem H. J. 2001. "Effects of Antisocial or Social Attitudes on Neurobiological Functions." *Medical Hypotheses* 56 (6): 664–71.

Martindale, Don. 1962. *Social Life and Cultural Change*. Princeton, NJ: D. Van Nostrand.

Marx, Karl. [1859] 1969. "Preface to *A Contribution to the Critique of the Political Economy*." In *Selected Works*, by K. Marx and F. Engels, 502–6. Vol. 1. Moscow: Progress Publishers.

———. [1865] 1969. "Wages, Price, and Profit." In *Selected Works*, by K. Marx and F. Engels, 31–76. Vol. 2. Moscow: Progress Publishers.

———. 1867 [1967]. *Capital: A Critique of Political Economy*. New York: International Publishers.

———. [1869] 1969. *The Eighteenth Brumaire of Louis Bonaparte*. In *Selected Works*, by K. Marx and F. Engels, 394–487. Vol. 1. Moscow: Progress Publishers.

———. [1891] 1969. "Wage Labour and Capital." In *Selected Works*, by K. Marx and F. Engels, 142–74. Vol. 1. Moscow: Progress Publishers.

Marx, Karl, and Frederick Engels. [1848] 1969. *Manifesto of the Communist Party*. In *Selected Works*, by K. Marx and F. Engels, 108–37. Vol. 1. Moscow: Progress Publishers.

———. [1864] 1970. *The German Ideology*. New York: International Publishers.

Maskus, Keith Eugene. 2002. *Intellectual Property Rights in the Global Economy*. Washington, DC: Institute for International Economics.

Massey, Douglas S. 2002. "A Brief History of Human Society: The Role of Emotion in Social Life." *American Sociological Review* 67 (1): 1–27.

Massey, Douglas S., Luin Goldring, and Jorge Durand. 1994. "Continuities in Transnational Migration: An Analysis of Nineteen Mexican Communities." *American Journal of Sociology* 99 (6): 1492–1533.

Massey, Douglas S., Andrew B. Gross, and Kumiko Shibuya. 1994. "Migration, Segregation, and the Geographic Concentration of Poverty." *American Sociological Review* 59 (3): 425–45.

Massin, B. 1996. "From Virchhow to Fischer: Physical Anthropology and Modern Race Theories in Wilhelmine Germany." In *Volksgeist as Method and Ethic: Essays on Boasian Ethnography and the German Anthropological Tradition*, edited by G. W. Stocking, 79–154. Vol. 8 of *History of Anthropology*. Madison: University of Wisconsin Press.

Matras, Judah. 1975. *Populations and Societies*. Englewood Cliffs, NJ: Prentice Hall.

Matter, Joseph Allen. 1974. *Love, Altruism, and World Crisis: The Challenge of Pitirim Sorokin*. Totowa, NJ: Littlefield, Adams.

McAdam, Doug, and Ronnelle Paulsen. 1993. "Specifying the Relationship between Social Ties and Activism." *American Journal of Sociology* 99 (3): 640–67.

McCarthy, John D., and Mayer Zald. 1973. *The Trends of Social Movements in America: Professionalization and Resource Mobilization*. Morristown, NJ: General Learning Press.

McChesney, Fred S. 2003. "'Pay to Play' Politics Examined, with Lessons for Campaign-Finance Reform." *Peace Research Abstracts* 40 (2): 123–261.

McGranahan, Donald V. 1973. *Methods of Estimation and Prediction in Socioeconomic Development*. Geneva: United Nations Research Institute for Socioeconomic Development.

McIntyre, John R., and Daniel S. Papp, eds. 1986. *The Political Economy of International Technology Transfer*. New York: Quorum Books.

McKee, James. 1994. *Sociology and the Race Problem: The Failure of a Perspective*. Urbana: University of Illinois Press.

McKinlay, R. D., and A. Mughan. 1984. *Aid and Arms to the Third World: An Analysis of the Distribution and Impact of Official Transfers*. New York: St. Martin's Press.

McKinnon, Ronald I. 1994. "Financial Growth and Macroeconomic Stability in China, 1978–1992: Implications for Russia and Other Transitional Economies." *Journal of Comparative Economics* 18 (June): 438–69.

McKnight, Gerald D. 1998. *The Last Crusade: Martin Luther King, Jr., the FBI, and the Poor People's Campaign*. Boulder, CO: Westview Press.

McLuhan, Marshall. 1964. *Understanding Media: Extensions of Man*. New York: McGraw-Hill.

McLuhan, Marshall, and Quentin Fiore. 1968. *War and Peace in the Global Village*. New York: Bertram Books.

McMillan, John. 2002. *Reinventing the Bazaar: A Natural History of Markets*. New York: Norton.

McNichol, Tom. 1994. "Fellow Travelers on the Info Highway." *USA Weekend*, January 21–23, 4–6.

McPhail, Clark. 1989. "Blumer's Theory of Collective Behavior: The Development of a Non-Symbolic Interaction Explanation." *Sociological Quarterly* 30 (3): 401–23.

———. 1991. *The Myth of the Maddening Crowd*. New York: Aldine de Gruyter.

———. 1994. "The Dark Side of Purpose: Individual and Collective Violence in Riots." *Sociological Quarterly* 35 (1): 1–32.

McPhail, Clark, and Charles W. Tucker. 1990. "Purposive Collective Action." *American Behavioral Scientist* 34 (1): 81–94.

McWhirter, Doreen A. 1993. *Sharing Ownership: One Manager's Guide to ESOPs and Other Productivity Incentive Plans*. New York: Wiley.

Meadows, D. H., D. L. Meadows, J. Randers, and W. Behrens. 1972. *The Limits to Growth*. New York: New American Library.

Mechanic, David. 1985. "Physicians and Patients in Transition." *Hastings Center Report* (December): 9–12.

Meek, Ronald. 1976. *Studies in the Labor Theory of Value*. New York: Monthly Review Press.

Meller, Helen E. 1990. *Patrick Geddes: Social Evolutionist and City Planner*. London: Routledge.

Menard, Scott, and Elizabeth Moen. 1987. *Perspectives on Population*. New York: Oxford University Press.

Mencken, H. L. 1921. *The American Language: An Inquiry into the Development of English in the United States*. New York: Knopf.

Merton, Robert K. 1968. *Social Theory and Social Structure*. New York: Free Press.

———. 1970. *Science, Technology and Society in Seventeenth Century England*. New York: H. Fertig.

Michels, Roberto. 1959. *Political Parties*. New York: Dover Books.

Michnik, Adam. 2009. "Amnesia and Amnesty in Postcommunist Societies." Paper presented at the International Conference on Politics and History, Tirana, Albania, May 15.

Miliband, Ralph. 1992. "The Socialist Alternative." *Journal of Democracy* 3 (3): 118–24.

Miller, Arthur. "McCarthyism." PBS *American Masters*, August 23, 2006, www.pbs.org/wnet/americanmasters/episodes/arthur-miller/mccarthyism/484.

Mills, C. Wright. 1951. *White Collar*. London: Oxford University Press.

———. 1956. *The Power Elite*. New York: Oxford University Press.

———. 1958. *The Causes of World War Three*. New York: Simon & Schuster.

———. 1959. *The Sociological Imagination*. New York: Oxford University Press.

———. 1963. "A Marx for Managers." In *Power, Politics, and People*, edited by I. L. Horowitz. New York: Oxford University Press.

———. 1968. "Three Types of Rationality." In *De hombres sociales y movimentos politicos*. Mexico City: Siglo Vientiuno Editores.

———. 1969. *Sociology and Pragmatism: The Higher Learning in America*. London: Oxford University Press.

Milton, Sybil. 1988. *In Fitting Memory: Holocaust Memorials and the Political Culture*. Detroit: Wayne State University Press.

Minow, Mary. 2002. "The USA PATRIOT Act and Patron Privacy on Library Internet Terminals." *Library Law Resource Exchange*, February 15. www.llrx.com/features/usapatriotact.htm.

Mizruchi, Ephraim H. 1983. *Regulating Society: Marginality and Social Control in Historical Perspective*. New York: Free Press.

Moaddel, Mansoor. 1993. *Class, Politics and Ideology in the Iranian Revolution*. New York: Columbia University Press.

———. 1994. "Political Conflict in the World Economy: A Cross-National Analysis of Modernization and World-System Theories." *American Sociological Review* 59 (3): 276–303.

Moffett, George D. 1994. "The Population Clock Keeps Ticking after Cairo." *Christian Science Monitor*, November 9, 7.

Mohanty, Chandra T., and Ann Russo. 1991. *Third World Women and the Politics of Feminism*. Bloomington: Indiana University Press.

Monroe, Kristen Renwick. 1996. *The Heart of Altruism: Perceptions of a Common Humanity*. Princeton, NJ: Princeton University Press.

———. 2001. "Morality and a Sense of Self: The Importance of Identity and Categorization for Moral Action." *American Journal of Political Science* 45 (3): 491–507.

Monroe, Kristen Renwick, M. C. Barton, and U. Klingermann, eds. 1990. "Altruism and the Theory of Rational Action: Rescuers of Jews in Nazi Europe." *Ethics* (October): 103–22.

Montagu, Ashley. 1964. *The Concept of Race*. New York: Free Press.

———. 1975. *Practice of Love*. Englewood Cliffs, NJ: Prentice Hall.

———, ed. 1980. *Sociobiology Examined*. New York: Oxford University Press.

Montas, Michele. 1975. *Haiti*. Papeete, Tahiti: Les Editions du Pacifique.

Moore, Barrington, Jr. 1979. *Injustice: The Social Bases of Obedience and Revolt*. New York: Putnam.

Moore, Geoff. Aboriginal Art Online. http://aboriginalart.com.au/.

Moore, Jesse Thomas. 1981. *The Search for Equality: The National Urban League 1910–1961*. University Park: Pennsylvania State University Press.

Moore, Michael. 1996. *Downsize This*. New York: Crown Publishers.

More, Thomas. [1519] 1961. *Utopia*. In *The Yale Edition of the Works of Sir Thomas More*, edited by Frank Manley. New Haven, CT: Yale University Press.

Morehouse, Andrew. 1973. *Voltaire and Jean Meslier*. New York: AMS Press.

Morley, John E. 1980. *Vatican Diplomacy and the Jews during the Holocaust 1949–1943*. New York: Ktav Publishers.

Morris, Aldon D. 1981. "Black Southern Student Sit-In Movement: An Analysis of Internal Organization." *American Sociological Review* 46 (6): 744–67.

———. 1984. *The Origins of the Civil Rights Movement: Black Communities Organizing for Change*. New York: Free Press.

———. 1993. "Birmingham Confrontation Reconsidered: An Analysis of the Dynamics and Tactics of Mobilization." *American Sociological Review* 58 (5): 621–36.

———. 1999. "A Retrospective on the Civil Rights Movement: Political and Intellectual Landmarks." *Annual Review of Sociology* 25:517–39.

Morss, Elliott R., and Victoria A. Morss. 1986. *The Future of Western Development Assistance*. Boulder, CO: Westview Press.

Mother Jones. 2007. "And Then There Were Eight: 25 Years of Media Mergers from GE-NBC to Google-You Tube.'" March. www.motherjones.com/files/legacy/news/feature/2007/03/and_then_there_were_eight.pdf.

Moulaert, Frank, and Katy Cabaret. 2006. "Planning, Networks and Power Relations: Is Democratic Planning under Capitalism Possible?" *Planning Theory* 5 (1): 51–70.

Mu, Ch'ien. 1982. *Traditional Government in Imperial China*. Translated by Chün-tu Hsüeh and G. O. Totten. Hong Kong: Chinese University Press.

Mumford, Lewis. 1963. *Technics and Civilization*. New York: Harcourt, Brace & World.

———. 1967. *Technics and Human Development: The Myth of the Machine*. New York: Harcourt Brace Jovanovich.

Munfson, Steven. 1993. "China Ends Two-Track Currencies: Move Seen as Sign Reforms Will Go On." *Washington Post*, December 30, A17.

Murdock, George P. 1940. "Cross-Cultural Survey." *American Sociological Review* 5 (1): 361–70.

———. 1967. *Ethnographic Atlas*. Pittsburgh: University of Pittsburgh Press.

Murray, Bruce. 2005. "With 'God on Our Side'? How American 'Civil Religion' Permeates Society and Manifests Itself in Public Life." FacsNet. www.facsnet.org/ (accessed March 30, 2005).

Myers, Allan R. 1987. "Lumping It: The Hidden Denominator of the Medical Malpractice Crisis." *American Journal of Public Health* 7 (December): 1544–48.

Myers, Gustavus. 1936. *History of the Great American Fortunes*. New York: Random House.

REFERENCES

Myrdal, Gunnar. 1944. *An American Dilemma*. New York: Harper & Row.

———. 1968. *Asian Drama: An Inquiry into the Poverty of Nations*. Harmondsworth, UK: Penguin.

———. 1970. *The Challenge of World Poverty: A World Anti-Poverty Program in Outline*. Harmondsworth, UK: Penguin.

Nair, Kusum. 1969. *In Defense of the Irrational Peasant*. Chicago: University of Chicago Press.

Nathan, Otto, and Heinz Norden, eds. 1960. *Einstein on Peace*. New York: Schocken Books.

National Center for Employee Ownership (NCEO). 2009. "The Employee Ownership 100: America's Largest Majority Employee-Owned Companies." May. www.nceo.org/.

National Cold Fusion Institute. 1990. *Proceedings of the First Annual Conference on Cold Fusion* (March 28–31). Salt Lake City, Utah: Author.

National Coordinating Office for Information Technology Research and Development (NCITRD). 1999. *President's Information Technology Advisory Committee Report* (February). Alexandria, VA: Author.

National Environmental Justice Advisory Council (NEJAC). 2006. *Unintended Impacts of Redevelopment and Revitalization Efforts in Five Environmental Justice Communities* (August). Washington, DC: U.S. Environmental Protection Agency.

Nelan, Bruce W. 1995. "The Balkans World's Wrath." *Time International*, November 6. www.time.com/time/international/1995/951106/thebalkans.warcrimes.html.

Nelson, Jack. 1993. *Terror in the Night: The Klan's Campaign against the Jews*. New York: Simon & Schuster.

News Asia Pacific. 2009. "Uighur Exiles Deny China Riot Claim." Aljazeera.net, July 6. http://english.aljazeera.net/.

New York Times. 1994. "5 Americans and Russian End Historic Shuttle Trip." February 12, A7.

———. 1996. "Britain Faulted on Oil-Spill Damage." February 16, A3.

Niles, John S. 1994. *Beyond Telecommuting: A New Paradigm for the Effect of Telecommunications on Travel*. Washington, DC: Global Telematics. www.globaltelematics.com/.

Nisbet, Robert A. 1967. "The Irreducibility of Social Change: A Comment on Professor Stebbins' Paper." In *Readings on Social Change*, edited by W. E. Moore and R. M. Cook. Englewood Cliffs, NJ: Prentice Hall.

———. 1969. *Social Change and History*. New York: Oxford University Press.

Nkrumah, Kwame. 1965. *Neocolonialism: The Last Stage of Imperialism*. London: Nelson.

Norman, James R. 1988. "A Hardheaded Takeover by McLouth's Hardhats." *Business Week*, June 6, 90–93.

Nove, Alex. 1982. *An Economic History of the U.S.S.R.* Harmondsworth, UK: Penguin.

Oakeshott, Michael J. 1962. *Rationalism in Politics, and Other Essays*. New York: Basic Books.

Obama, Barack. 1990. *After Alinsky: Community Organizing in Illinois*. Springfield: University of Illinois at Springfield Press.

———. 2007. Presidential announcement speech. Springfield, IL, February 10. www.slideshare.net/timoreilly/gtec-government-as-a-platform (accessed October 29, 2009).

Ober, Josiah. 1998. *The Athenian Revolution: Essays on Ancient Greek Democracy and Political Theory*. Princeton, NJ: Princeton University Press.

Oberschall, Anthony. 1973. *Social Conflict and Social Movements*. Englewood Cliffs, NJ: Prentice Hall.

Ogburn, William F. 1922. *Social Change*. New York: W. B. Heubsch.

———. 1934. *You and Machines*. Chicago: University of Chicago Press.

———. 1957. "The Meaning of Technology." In *Technology and Social Change*, edited by F. Allen. New York: Appleton-Century-Crofts.

O'Hearn, Denis. 1994. "Innovation and the World-System Hierarchy: British Subjugation of the Irish Cotton Industry, 1780–1830." *American Journal of Sociology* 100 (3): 587–621.

Oldfield, Duane. 1996. *The Right and the Righteous: The Christian Right Confronts the Republican Party*. Lanham, MD: Rowman & Littlefield.

Oliner, Samuel P. 2000. *Narrow Escapes: A Boy's Holocaust Memories and Their Legacy*. St. Paul, MN: Paragon House.

Oliner, Samuel P., and Pearl M. Oliner. 1992. *The Altruistic Personality: Rescuers of Jews in Nazi Europe*. New York: Free Press.

Olzak, Susan, Suzanne Shanahan, and Elizabeth West. 1994. "School Desegregation, Interracial Exposure, and Antibusing Activity in Contemporary Urban America." *American Journal of Sociology* 100 (1): 196–241.

Omara-Otunnu, Amii. 2004. "The Trouble with the USA PATRIOT Act." CREC Summer Institute for International Studies. Saint Joseph College, West Hartford, CT, July 16.

Opp, Karl-Dieter. 2001. "Social Networks and the Emergence of Protest Norms." In *Social Norms*, edited by M. Hechter and K.-D. Opp. New York: Russell Sage Foundation.

Opp, Karl-Dieter, and Christiane Gern. 1993. "Dissident Groups, Personal Networks, and Spontaneous Cooperation: The East German Revolution of 1989." *American Sociological Review* 58 (5): 659–80.

O'Reilly, Kenneth. 1983. *Hoover and the Un-Americans: The F.B.I., H.U.A.C., and the Red Menace*. Philadelphia: Temple University Press.

———. 1994. *Black Americans: The F.B.I. Files*. New York: Carroll & Graff.

Orenstein, Bruce. 1998. *The Democratic Promise: Saul Alinsky and His Legacy*. Video produced by Bob Hercules. Chicago: Media Process Group.

Orloff, Ann S. 1993. "Gender and the Social Rights of Citizenship: The Comparative Analysis of State Policies and Gender Relations." *American Sociological Review* 58 (3): 303–28.

Orwell, George [1933] 1950. *Down and Out in Paris and London*. New York: Harcourt Brace.

———. 1935. *Burmese Days*. London: V. Gollancz.

———. 1946. *Animal Farm*. New York: New American Library.

———. [1949] 1984. *Nineteen Eighty-Four*, facsimile ed. Weston, MA: M&S Press.

———. 1958. *The Road to Wigan Pier*. New York: Harcourt Brace.

———. 1988. *The Lost Writings*. New York: Avon.

Orwell, Sonia, and Ian Angus, eds. 1978. *Collected Essays, Journalism and Letters of George Orwell*. 4 vols. Harmondsworth, UK: Penguin.

Ostrom, Elinor. 1990. *Governing the Commons: The Evolution of Institutions for Collective Action*. Cambridge: Cambridge University Press.

Ostwald, Martin. 1986. *From Popular Sovereignty to the Sovereignty of Law: Law, Society, and Politics in Fifth-Century Athens*. Berkeley: University of California Press.

The Oxford English Dictionary, 2nd ed. 1989. Prepared by J. A. Simpson and E. S. C. Werner. Oxford: Oxford University Press.

Ozinga, James R. 1999. *Altruism*. Westport, CT: Praeger.

Pack, Howard, and Janet R. Pack. 1975. *The Adoption and Use of Urban Development Models*. Berkeley: Institute of Urban and Regional Development, University of California.

Padilla, Effren, ed. 2006. *Perspectives on Urban Society: From Preindustrial to Postindustrial*. Boston: Allyn & Bacon.

Paik, H. 1999. "Prosocial Television Programs and Altruistic Behavior: A Meta-Analysis." *Communication Abstracts* 22 (4).

Pampel, Fred C. 1993. "Relative Cohort Size and Fertility: The Socio-Political Context of the Easterlin Effect." *American Sociological Review* 58 (4): 496–514.

Parekh, Bhiku C. 2000. *Rethinking Multiculturalism: Cultural Diversity and Political Theory*. London: Macmillan.

Pareto, Vilfredo. [1901] 1968. *The Rise and Fall of Elites: An Application of Theoretical Sociology*. Towota, NJ: Bedminster Press.

REFERENCES

Parsons, Talcott. 1937. *The Structure of Social Action*. New York: McGraw-Hill.

——. 1951. *The Social System*. Glencoe, IL: Free Press.

——. 1964. "Evolutionary Universals in Society." *American Sociological Review* 29 (1): 339–57.

——. 1975. "The Sick Role and the Role of the Physician Reconsidered." *Health and Society* (summer): 257–78.

Patterson, Zachary J. 2009. "A Critique of the Current International Development Policies." Paper presented at the Indiana University International Public Affairs Association Conference, Indianapolis, October 20.

Payne, Richard J. 1995. *The Clash with Distant Cultures: Values, Interests, and Force in American Foreign Policy*. Albany: State University of New York Press.

Penner, Paul S. 1995. *Altruistic Behavior: An Inquiry into Motivation*. Amsterdam: Ropi B. V.

Perelman, Michael. 1987. *Marx's Crises Theory: Scarcity, Labor, and Finance*. New York: Praeger.

Perkins, John H. 1997. *Geopolitics and the Green Revolution: Wheat, Genes, and the Cold War*. New York: Oxford University Press.

Pestoff, Victor. 1983. "Mediating between Individuals, Interest Groups, and the State-Neocorporatism." In *The Future of Politics*, edited by W. Page. New York: St. Martin's Press.

Petersen, William. 1975. *Population*. New York: Macmillan.

Philipsen, Dirk. 1993. *We Were the People*. Durham, NC: Duke University Press.

Picou, J. Steven. 2009. "Katrina as a Natech Disaster: Toxic Contamination and Long-Term Risks for Residents of New Orleans." *Journal of Applied Social Science* 3 (2): 36–55.

Pipes, Richard. 2001. *Communism: A History*. New York: Modern Library.

Pirenne, Henri. 1939. *Medieval Cities*. Translated by F. D. Halsey. Princeton, NJ: Princeton University Press.

Place, Francis. [1822] 1930. *Illustration and Proofs of the Principle of Population*. Boston: Houghton Mifflin.

Plant, Richard. 1986. *The Pink Triangle: The Nazi War against Homosexuals*. New York: Holt.

Plattner, Marc F., and Larry Diamond, eds. 1992. "Capitalism, Socialism, and Democracy." *Journal of Democracy* 3 (3): 3–6.

Pollack, Fredrich. 1957. *The Economic and Social Consequences of Automation*. London: Oxford University Press.

Popper, Karl. 1952. *The Open Society and Its Enemies*. London: Routledge & Kegan Paul.

Popular Science. 2009. "Best of What's New 2009." www.popsci.com/bown/2009.

Population Reference Bureau (PRB). 1995. *World Population Data Sheet*. Washington, DC: Author.

Porter, Alan, Frederick A. Rossini, Stanley R. Carpenter, and A. L. Roper. 1980. *A Guidebook for Technology Assessment and Impact Analysis*. New York: North Holland.

Porter, Jack Nusan, ed. 1992. *The Sociology of Genocide/The Holocaust*. Washington, DC: American Sociological Association.

Porter, Jack Nusan, and Steve Hoffman, eds. 1999. *The Sociology of the Holocaust and Genocide: A Teaching and Learning Guide*. Washington, DC: American Sociological Association.

Portes, Alejandro. 1995. "On Grand Surprises and Modest Certainties: Comment on Kuran, Collins, and Tilly." *American Journal of Sociology* 100 (6): 1620–26.

Possehl, Gregory L. 1999. *Indus Age: The Beginnings*. Philadelphia: University of Pennsylvania Press.

Postman, Neil. 1993. *Technopoly: The Surrender of Culture to Technology*. New York: Vintage Books.

Powledge, Fred. 1991. *Free at Last: The Civil Rights Movement and the People Who Made It*. Boston: Little, Brown.

Prebisch, Raúl. 1964. *Towards a New Trade Policy for Development*. New York: United Nations.

Prechel, Harland. 1994. "Economic Crisis and the Centralization of Control over the Managerial Process: Corporate Restructuring and Neo-Fordist Decision Making." *American Sociological Review* 59 (5): 723–45.

Preston, R. E. 1985. "Christaller's Neglected Contributions to the Study of the Evolution of Central Places." *Progress in Human Geography* 9:177–93.

REFERENCES

Price, Don K. 1965. *The Scientific Estate*. Cambridge, MA: Harvard University Press.

Price, Jammie, Roger Straus, and Jeffrey Breese, eds. 2009. *Doing Sociology: Case Studies in Sociological Practice*. Lanham, MD: Rowman & Littlefield.

Przewowski, Adam. 1991. "The 'East' Becomes the 'South'? The 'Autumn of the People' and the Future of Eastern Europe." *Political Science and Politics* 24 (1): 20–24.

Ramati, Alexander. 1986. *And the Violins Stopped Playing: A Story of the Gypsy Holocaust*. New York: Franklin Watts.

Ranken, Nani L. 2004. "Corporations as Persons: Objections to Goodpaster's Principle of Moral Projection." *Journal of Business Ethics* 6 (8): 633–37.

Ravetz, Jerome R. 1978. "Technology as Master." *Science* 200 (May 12): 642–43.

Rawls, John. 1971. *A Theory of Justice*. Cambridge, MA: Harvard University Press.

Reich, Charles A. 1995. *Opposing the System*. New York: Crown Press.

Rendell, Jane. 1984. *The Origins of Modern Feminism: Women in Britain, France and the U.S., 1780–1860*. London: Macmillan.

Reynolds, Larry T. and Leonard Lieberman, eds. 1996. *Race and Other Misadventures: Essays in Honor Of Ashley Montagu In His Ninetieth Year*. Dix Hills, NY: General Hall Publishing.

Rheingold, Howard. 1993. The *Virtual Community: Homesteading on the Electronic Frontier*. Reading, MA: Addison-Wesley.

Ricardo, David. [1821] 1971. *On the Principles of Political Economy and Taxation*. Harmondsworth, UK: Penguin.

Ricci, R. A., F. DeMarco, and E. Sindoni. 1990. *Understanding Cold Fusion Phenomena*. Bologna: Italian Physical Society.

Richter, Maurice. 1982. *Technology and Social Complexity*. Albany: State University of New York Press.

Riesman, David, Ruel Denny, and Nathan Glazer. 1950. *The Lonely Crowd*. New Haven, CT: Yale University Press.

Rigby, T. H. 1990. *The Changing Soviet System*. Brookfield, VT: E. Elgar.

Rittner, Carol, and Sondra Meyers. 1986. *The Courage to Care: Rescuers of Jews during the Holocaust*. New York: New York University Press.

Ritzer, George. 1998. *The McDonaldization Thesis: Explorations and Extensions*. Thousand Oaks, CA: Sage.

———. 2002. *McDonaldization: The Reader*. Thousand Oaks, CA: Pine Forge Press.

———. 2008. *The McDonaldization of Society 5*. Los Angles: Pine Forge Press.

Robertson, Ian. 1987. *Sociology*. New York: Worth.

Robinson, Joan. 1960. *Collected Economic Papers*. Oxford: Blackwell.

———. 1968. *Economic Philosophy*. Harmondsworth, UK: Penguin.

Robinson, William I. 2009. "Saskia Sassen and the Sociology of Globalization: A Critical Appraisal." *Sociological Analysis* 3 (1) (Spring): 5–30.

Roessler, M. 1989. "Applied Geography and Area Research in Nazi Society." *Environment and Planning D* 7: 419–31.

Roethlisberger, F. J., and W. J. Dickinson. 1939. *Management and the Worker*. Cambridge, MA: Harvard University Press.

Rogers, Daniel E. 2009. "The Nazi Takeover: The Reichstag Fire Decree." University of South Alabama Department of History, October 13. www.southalabama.edu/history/faculty/rogers/348/reichstagfiredecree.html.

Rona-Tas, Akos. 1994. "The First Shall Be Last? Entrepreneurship and Communist Cadres in the Transition from Socialism." *American Journal of Sociology* 100: 40–69.

Roniger, Emil, ed. 1925. *Gandhi in Sudafrika*. Zurich: Rotapfel Verlag.

Roodman, David M. 2001. "The Third World Debt Crisis: Facts and Myths." In *Still Waiting for the Jubilee: Pragmatic Solutions for the Third World Debt Crisis*, Worldwatch Paper no. 155. Washington, DC: Worldwatch Institute.

REFERENCES

Roof, Wade Clark. 1991. *World Order and Religion*. Albany: State University of New York Press.

Rose, H. 1993. "From Command to Free Polities." *Political Quarterly* 64 (2): 156–71.

Rostow, W. W. 1960. *The Stages of Economic Growth: A Non-Communist Manifesto*. New York: Cambridge University Press.

Roszak, Theodore. 1969. *The Making of a Counterculture*. New York: Doubleday.

———. 1994. *The Cult of Information*. Berkeley: University of California Press.

Roth, John K., and Michael Berenbaum. 1989. *Holocaust: Religious and Philosophical Implications*. New York: Paragon.

Rouner, Leroy S. 1986. *Civil Religion and Political Theology*. Notre Dame, IN: University of Notre Dame Press.

Roy, Ramashray. 1984. *Self and Society: A Study in Gandhian Thought*. New Delhi: Sage.

Rubin, Harriet. 2007. "Ayn Rand's Literature of Capitalism." *New York Times*, September 15. www.nytimes.com/2007/09/15/business/15atlas.html.

Rucker, Walter. 2001. "Conjure, Magic, and Power: The Influence of Afro-Atlantic Religious Practices on Slave Resistance and Rebellion." *Journal of Black Studies* 32 (1): 84–103.

Rudner, Richard S. 1953. "The Scientist qua Scientist Makes Value Judgments." *Philosophy of Science* 20: 1–6.

Russell, Bertrand. 1951. "Creeds and Ideologies." In *New Hopes for a Changing World*. New York: Simon & Schuster.

Sanderson, Stephen K. 1990. *Social Evolutionism: A Critical History*. London: Blackwell.

———. 2007. *Evolutionism and Its Critics: Deconstructing and Reconstructing an Evolutionary Interpretation of Human Society*. Boulder, CO: Paradigm Publishers.

Sapir, Edward. 1958. *Selected Writings*. Berkeley: University of California Press.

Sapolsky, Robert M. 2006. "Culture in Animals: The Case of a Non-Human Primate Culture of Low Aggression and High Affiliation." *Social Forces* 85 (1): 217–33.

Sartori, Giovanni. 1987. *The Theory of Democracy Revisited*. Chatham, NJ: Chatham House.

Sartre, Jean-Paul. 1963. "Preface." In *Wretched of the Earth*, by F. Fanon. New York: Grove.

Sassen, Saskia. 1996. *Losing Control? Sovereignty in an Age of Globalization*. New York: Columbia University Press.

———, ed. 1998. *Globalization and Its Discontents: Essays on the New Mobility of People and Money*. New York: New Press.

———. 2000. *Cities in a World Economy*. Thousand Oaks, CA: Pine Forge Press.

———. 2001. *The Global City: New York, London, Tokyo*. Princeton, NJ: Princeton.

———. 2007. *Sociology of Globalization*. New York: Norton.

———. 2009. "On Robinson's Appraisal of Sassen's Work on the Sociology of Globalization." *Sociological Analysis* 3 (1): 105–8.

Saturn Corporation. 1990. "Memorandum of Agreement." Spring Hill, TN.

Saunders, Laura. 2009. "Origins of the Swine Flu Virus Researchers Use Evolutionary History to Trace the Early Days of the Pandemic." *Science News*, June 11. www.sciencenews.org/view/generic/id/44643/title/Origins_of_the_swine_flu_virus.

Savigny, Karl F. 1829. *The History of the Roman Law during the Middle Ages*. Edinburgh: A. Black.

Schaeffer, Robert. 2009 *Understanding Globalization*. Lanham, MD: Rowman & Littlefield.

Schlesinger, Stephen C. 2003. *Act of Creation: The Founding of the United Nations*. Boulder, CO: Westview Press.

Schmookler, Andrew B. 1995. *The Parable of the Tribes: The Problem of Power in Social Evolution*. Albany: State University of New York Press.

Schneider, Jean. 2009. "The Extrasolar Planets Encyclopaedia." http://exoplanet.eu/ (accessed October 9, 2009).

Schneider, Louis. 1964. "Toward Assessment of Sorokin's View of Change." In *Explorations in Social Change*, edited by G. Zollschan and W. Hirsch. Boston: Houghton Mifflin.

———. 1971. "Dialectic in Sociology." *American Sociological Review* 35 (4): 667–77.

———. 1975a. *The Sociological Way of Looking at the World.* New York: McGraw-Hill.

———. [1975b] 1985. "Ironic Perspective and Sociological Thought." In *The Grammar of Social Relations,* edited by J. Weinstein. New Brunswick, NJ: Transaction Books.

———. 1987. *Paradox and Society: The Social Thought of Bernard Mandeville.* New Brunswick, NJ: Transaction Books.

Schrecker, Ellen. 1998. *Many Are the Crimes: McCarthyism in America.* Boston: Little, Brown.

Schuler, Monica. 1970. "Ethnic Slave Rebellions in the Caribbean and the Guineas." *Journal of Social History* 3 (4): 373–85.

Schwartz, Michael. 1976. *Radical Protest and Social Structure.* New York: Academic Press.

Scott, Mel. 1969. *American City Planning since 1890: A History Commemorating the Fiftieth Anniversary of the American Institute of Planners.* Berkeley: University of California Press.

Seidman, Robert B. 1979. "Development Planning and Legal Order in Black Anglophonic Africa." *Studies in Comparative International Development* 14 (1): 3–27.

Selznick, Philip. 1949. *TVA and the Grass Roots.* Berkeley: University of California Press.

Shafir, Gershon. 1995. *Immigrants and Nationalists.* Albany: State University of New York Press.

Shah, Anup. 2009. "Media Conglomerates, Mergers, Concentration of Ownership." *Global Issues,* January 2. www.globalissues.org/article/159/media-conglomerates-mergers-concentration-of-ownership.

Sharma, Sanjay, Harriet Vridenburg, and Frances Westley. 1994. "Strategic Bridging: A Role for the Multinational Corporation in Third World Development." *Journal of Applied Behavioral Science* 30 (December): 458–76.

Shils, Edward, ed. 1991. *Remembering the University of Chicago: Teachers, Scientists, and Scholars.* Chicago: University of Chicago Press.

Shinnie, Peter Lewis. 1965. *New Light on Medieval Nubia.* Cambridge: Cambridge University Press.

Shirer, William. 1978. *The Rise and Fall of the Third Reich.* New York: Fawcett.

Shostak, Arthur, ed. 2003. *Viable Utopian Ideas: Shaping a Better World.* Armonk, NY: M. E. Sharpe.

Shryock, Henry S., and Jacob Siegel. 1976. *Methods and Materials of Demography.* Washington, DC: U.S. Bureau of the Census.

Silone, Ignazio. 1961. *The Fox and the Camellias.* New York: Harper.

Simmel, Georg. 1955. *Conflict.* Glencoe, IL: Free Press.

———. 1978. *The Philosophy of Money.* Boston: Routledge & Kegan Paul.

Simon, Julian. 1981. *The Ultimate Resource.* Princeton, NJ: Princeton University Press.

———. 1989. "On Aggregate Empirical Studies Relating Population Variables to Economic Development." *Population and Development Review* 15: 323–32.

Simon, Phil. 2009. "Kranzberg's Six Laws of Technology." http://www.philsimonsystems.com/blog/technology/enterprise-2-0/kranzberg_six/ posted September 30, 2009.

Simpson, George Gaylord. 1951. *The Meaning of Evolution.* New Haven, CT: Yale University Press.

Singer, Dorothy G., and Jerome Singer. 2005. *Imagination and Play in the Electronic Age.* Cambridge, MA: Harvard University Press.

Singer, Hans. 1977. *Technologies for Basic Needs.* Geneva: International Labour Office.

Singer, Milton. 1968. *Structure and Change in Indian Society.* Chicago: Aldine Press.

———. 1972. *When a Great Tradition Modernizes.* New York: Praeger.

Sjoberg, Gideon. 1960. *The Preindustrial City.* New York: Free Press.

Skocpol, Theda. 1976. "France, Russia, and China: A Structural Analysis of Social Revolutions." *Comparative Studies in Society and History* 18:175–209.

———. 1979. *States and Revolutions.* New York: Cambridge University Press.

———. 1994. *Social Revolutions in the Modern World.* New York: Cambridge University Press.

Sloan, Alan. 1995. "With the Sales of ABC and CBS Three Old Guys Cash In and Bail Out." *Washington Post,* August 8, D3.

REFERENCES

Smelser, Neil J. 1963. *Theory of Collective Behavior*. Glencoe, IL: Free Press.

Smith, Alfred G. 1966. *Communication and Culture*. New York: Holt, Rinehart and Winston.

Smith, Anthony D. 1987. *The Ethnic Origins of Nations*. London: Blackwell.

Smith, Brian K. 1994. *Classifying the Universe: The Ancient Indian* Varna *System and the Origins of Caste*. New York: Oxford University Press.

Smith, David A. 1996. *ASA Curriculum Guide for Comparative Historical Sociology*. Washington, DC: American Sociological Association.

Smith, Hedrick. 1990. *The New Russians*. New York: Random House.

Smith, Jackie. 2005. "Response to Wallerstein: The Struggle for Global Society in a World System." *Social Forces* 83 (3): 1279–85.

Smith, William L. 2002. "Intentional Communities 1990–2000: A Portrait." *Michigan Sociological Review* 16 (fall): 107–31.

Snow, David, Louis Zurcher Jr., and Sheldon Ekland-Olson. 1980. "Social Networks and Social Movements: A Microstructural Approach to Differential Recruitment." *American Sociological Review* 45: 787–801.

Solzhenitsyn, Alexsander. 1993. *We Never Make Mistakes*. Columbia: University of South Carolina Press.

Somers, Margaret R. 1993. "Citizenship and the Place of the Public Sphere: Law, Community, and Political Culture in the Transition to Democracy." *American Sociological Review* 58 (5): 587–620.

Sorel, Georges. [1905] 1950. *Reflections on Violence*. Glencoe, IL: Free Press.

Sorokin, Pitirim A. 1925. *The Sociology of Revolution*. Philadelphia: J. B. Lippincott.

———. 1947. *Society, Culture, and Personality*. New York: Harper & Row.

———. 1948. *The Reconstruction of Humanity*. Boston: Beacon Press.

———. 1950. *Altruistic Love*. Boston: Beacon Press.

———. 1951. *SOS: The Meaning of Our Crisis*. Boston: Beacon Press.

———. 1954a. *The Ways and Power of Love*. Boston: Beacon Press.

———. 1954b. *Forms and Techniques of Altruistic and Spiritual Growth*. Boston: Beacon Press.

———. 1962. *Social and Cultural Dynamics*. New York: Bedminster Press.

———. 1964. "Reply to Professor Schneider." In *Explorations in Social Change*, edited by G. Zollschan and W. Hirsch. Boston: Houghton Mifflin.

———. 1966. *Sociological Theories of Today*. New York: Harper & Row.

Sorokin, Pitirim A., and Walter Lunden. 1959. *Power and Morality: Who Shall Guard the Guardians?* Boston: Porter Sargent.

Spencer, Herbert. 1862. *First Principles*. New York: Appleton.

———. 1898. *The Principles of Sociology*. New York: Appleton.

Spengler, Oswald. 1926–1928. *The Decline of the West*. New York: Knopf.

Spiegel-Rosing, Ina, and Derek S. Price, eds. 1977. *Science, Technology, and Society*. Beverly Hills, CA: Sage.

Spiro, Melford E. 1986. "Cultural Relativism and the Future of Anthropology." *Cultural Anthropology* 1 (3): 259–86.

Springer, Philip B., and Marcello Truzzi, eds. 1973. *Revolutionaries on Revolution*. Pacific Palisades, CA: Goodyear.

Stavis, Ben. 1999. Home page, course material. Temple University Political Science Department, Philadelphia, September. http://astro.temple.edu/~bstavis/courses/442patrimonial-system.htm.

Stebbins, G. Ledyard. 1965. "Pitfalls and Guideposts in Comparing Organic and Social Evolution." *Pacific Sociological Review* 8: 220–33.

Steele, Stephen F., AnneMarie Scarisbrick-Hauser, and William Hauser. 1999. *Solution Centered Sociology: Addressing Problems through Applied Sociology*. Thousand Oaks, CA: Sage.

Stehr, Nico. 2004. "Nothing Has Been Decided: The Chances and Risks of Feasible Globalization." Paper presented at the annual meeting of the American Sociological Association, San Francisco, August 14.

Stein, Stephen J. 1992. *The Shaker Experience in America: A History of the United Society of Believers*. New Haven, CT: Yale University Press.

Steiner, George. 1970. *Language and Silence*. New York: Atheneum.

Stephens, Beth. 1993. "Hypocrisy on Rights: Who Decides What Constitutes a Human Right?" *New York Times*, June 24, A15, A23.

Sterngold, James. 1995. "Disney's Rival Studios Face Longer Competitive Odds: ABC Deal Provides Best of Network Access." *New York Times*, August 7, C9, D6.

Stewart, Frances. 1985. *Basic Needs in Developing Countries*. Baltimore: Johns Hopkins University Press.

Stinchcombe, Arthur L. 1994. "Freedom and Oppression of Slaves in the Eighteenth-Century Caribbean." *American Sociological Review* 59 (6): 911–29.

Stites, Tom. 2003. "How Corporations Became 'Persons.'" *UU World: The Magazine of the Unitarian Universalist Association* 17 (3) (May/June).

Stokes, Gale, ed. 1991. *From Stalinism to Pluralism*. New York: Oxford University Press.

Straus, Roger A., ed. 2002. *Using Sociology: An Introduction from the Applied and Clinical Perspective*. Lanham, MD: Rowman & Littlefield.

Students for a Democratic Society (SDS). 1964. *The Port Huron Statement*. New York: Author.

Studer, Kenneth E., and Daryl E. Chubin. 1980. *The Cancer Mission: Social Contexts of Biomedical Research*. Beverly Hills, CA: Sage.

Surin, Kenneth. 1998. "Dependency Theory's Reanimation in the Era of Finance Capital." *Cultural Logic* 1 (2). http://eserver.org/clogic/1-2/surin.html.

Sutton, John R., F. Dobbin, J. W. Meter, and W. R. Scott. 1994. "The Legalization of the Workplace." *American Journal of Sociology* 99 (4): 944–71.

Swadesh, Morris. 1972. *The Origin and Diversification of Language*. London: Routledge & Kegan Paul.

Swatos, William H., Jr., and Kevin J. Christiano. 1999. "Secularization Theory: The Course of a Concept." *Sociology of Religion* 60 (3): 209–28.

Szamtka, J., Z. Mach, and J. Mucha, eds. 1993. *Eastern European Societies on the Threshold of Change*. Lewiston, ME: Edwin Mellen.

Szelenyi, Ivan. 1994. *After the Cold War: Autobiographic Notes*. Ann Arbor: University of Michigan, Advanced Study Center, International Institute.

Sztompka, Piotr. 1991. *Society in Action: The Theory of Social Becoming*. Chicago: University of Chicago Press.

Talbot, Strobe. 1992. "End of Empire for Good." *Time* 139 (June 29): 60.

Tarifa, Fatos. 2008. *Vengeance Is Mine: Justice Albanian Style*. Chapel Hill, NC: Globic Press.

Tarifa, Fatos, and Jay Weinstein. 1995–1996. "Overcoming the Past: Decommunization and the Reconstruction of Post-Communist Society in Europe." *Studies in Comparative International Development* 29 (4): 63–78.

Taubes, Gary. 1993. *Bad Science: The Short Life and Weird Times of Cold Fusion*. New York: Random House.

Tavalage, Joseph. 1988. *Flexible Manufacturing Systems in Practice*. New York: M. Dekker.

Taylor, Keith, and Henri Saint-Simon. 1975. *Henri Saint-Simon (1760–1825)*. London: Croon Helm.

Taylor, Raymond. 1995. *Ecological Resistance Movements: The Global Emergence of Radical and Popular Environmentalism*. Albany: State University of New York Press.

Taylor, Telford. 1992. *The Anatomy of the Nuremberg Trials: A Personal Memoir*. New York: Knopf.

Teilhard de Chardin, Pierre. 1969. *The Future of Man*. New York: Harper & Row.

Telles, Edward E. 1994. "Industrialization and Racial Inequality in Employment: A Brazilian Example." *American Sociological Review* 59 (1): 46–63.

Temple, Robert. 2007. "The Prehistory of Panspermia: Astrophysical or Metaphysical?" *International Journal of Astrobiology* 6: 169–80.

REFERENCES

Teune, Henry. 1990. "Comparing Countries: Lessons Learned." In *Comparative Methodology: Theory and Practice in International Research*, edited by E. Oyen. London: Sage.

Thomas, Joseph. 2001. *Social Movements and Violence*. New Delhi: Mittal Publications.

Thomas, W. I. 1923. *The Unadjusted Girl*. Boston: Little, Brown.

Thompson, Warren S. 1929. "Population." *American Journal of Sociology* 34 (6): 959–75.

Tilly, Charles. 1984. *Big Structures, Large Processes, and Huge Comparisons*. New York: Russell Sage Foundation.

———. 1989. *Strikes, Wars, and Rebellions in an International Perspective*. New York: Cambridge University Press.

———. 1990. *Coercion, Capital, and the Rise of European States, A. D. 990–1990*. Cambridge, MA: Blackwell.

———. 1995. "To Explain Political Processes." *American Journal of Sociology* 100 (6): 1594–1610.

Tilly, Charles, and Lesley Wood. 2009. *Social Movements, 1768–2008*. Boulder, CO: Paradigm Publishers.

Tocqueville, Alexis de. [1835] 1969. *Democracy in America*. Garden City, NY: Doubleday.

Toffler, Alvin. 1970. *Future Shock*. New York: Random House.

Tönnies, Ferdinand. [1887] 1957. *Community and Society*. East Lansing: Michigan State University Press.

"Top Twelve Earth Languages by Number of Speakers." 1999. http://personal.bgsu.edu/~swellsj/languages.html.

Totten, George O. 1982. "Introduction." In *Traditional Government in Imperial China*, by Mu Ch'ien. Translated by Chün-tu Hsüeh and George O. Totten. Hong Kong: Chinese University Press.

Touraine, Alain. 1989. "Is Sociology Still the Study of Society?" *Thesis Eleven* 23: 5–34.

Trading Economics Global Economics Research. 2009. "China GDP Growth Rate." October 23. www.tradingeconomics.com/Economics/GDP-Growth.aspx?Symbol=CNY#.

Travieso-Díaz, Matías. 1997. *The Laws and Legal System of a Free-Market Cuba: A Prospectus for Business*. Westport, CT: Quorum Books.

Troeltsch, Ernst. 1958. *Protestantism and Progress: A Historical Study of the Relation of Protestantism to the Modern World*. Boston: Beacon Press.

Trotsky, Leon. 1932. *The History of the Russian Revolution*. New York: Simon & Schuster.

———. 1963. *The Essential Trotsky*. London: Unwin Books.

Tsoukalas, Ioannis. 2007. "Exploring the Microfoundations of Group Consciousness." *Culture and Psychology* 13 (1): 39–81.

Turner, Jonathan H. 1973. "From Utopia to Where: A Critique of the Dahrendorf Conflict Model." *Social Forces* 52 (1): 236–44.

———. 1993. *Classical Sociological Theory: A Positivist's Perspective*. Chicago: Nelson Hall.

Turner, Ralph, and Lewis Killian. 1972. *Collective Behavior*. Englewood Cliffs, NJ: Prentice Hall.

Tushingham, A. Douglas. 1953. "Excavations at Old Testament Jericho." *Biblical Archaeologist* 16 (3): 46–67.

Tushnet, Mark V. 1987. *The NAACP's Legal Strategy against Segregated Education*. Chapel Hill: University of North Carolina Press.

Tuttle, Lisa. 1986. *Encyclopedia of Feminism*. New York: Facts on File Press.

Uehara, Edwina S. 1995. "Reciprocity Reconsidered: Gouldner's 'Moral Norm of Reciprocity' and Social Support." *Journal of Social and Personal Relationships* 12 (4): 483–502.

UN Chronicle. 1993. "Vienna Declaration and Programme of Action Set Goals for 21st Century." September. www.findarticles.com/p/articles/mi_m1309/is_n3_v30/ai_14667503.

Unger, Irwin. 1974. *The Movement: A History of the American New Left 1959–1972*. New York: Dodd, Mead.

United Nations. 2001. *World Urbanization Prospects, the 1999 Revision*. New York: Author.

United Nations Population Division. 2009. *World Population Prospects: The 2006 Revision and World Urbanization Prospects: The 2007 Revision*. New York: Population Division of the Department of Economic and Social Affairs of the United Nations Secretariat, http://esa.un.org/unup.

United Nations Population Fund (UNFPA). 2004. "ICPD Plan of Action." http://149.120.32.2/wpd/2004/index.htm.

United Nations Research Institute for Social Development (UNRISD). 1972. *Contents and Measurement of Socioeconomic Development*. New York: Praeger.

U.S. Census Bureau. 2009. "International Data Base." December. www.census.gov/ipc/www/idb.

U.S. Congress. 2006. *A Failure of Initiative: Final Report of the Select Bipartisan Committee to Investigate the Preparation for and Response to Hurricane Katrina*. Washington, DC: Government Printing Office. www.gpoaccess.gov/katrinareport/fullreport.pdf.

U.S. Department of Labor, Bureau of Labor Statistics. 2008. "Union Affiliation Data from the Current Population Survey." series numbers LUU0204466800 and LUU0204899600.

Useem, Michael. 1975. *Protest Movements in America*. Indianapolis, IN: Bobbs-Merrill.

U.S. National Oceanic and Atmospheric Administration (NOAA). 1994. "Guidelines and Principles for Social Impact Assessment." May. www.nmfs.noaa.gov/sfa/social_impact_guide.htm.

U.S. Supreme Court. 1886. *Santa Clara County v. Southern Pacific R. Co.* 118 U.S. 394. http://supreme.justia.com/us/118/394/case.html.

Vandenbosch, Amy, and Willard Hogan. 1970. *The United Nations: Background, Organization, Functions, Activities*. Westport, CT: Greenwood.

van der Valk, A. C. 1997. "Cloning as a Test-Case of Autonomous Technology." *Techné: Journal of the Society for Philosophy and Technology* 3 (1): 1–10.

Veblen, Thorstein. [1913] 1969. "The Mutation Theory and the Blond Race." In *The Place of Science in Modern Civilization and Other Essays*. New York: Capricorn Books.

———. [1915] 1969. "The Blond Race and the Aryan Culture." In *The Place of Science in Modern Civilization and Other Essays*. New York: Capricorn Books.

———. 1939. *Imperial Germany*. New York: Viking.

Verdier, Daniel. 1999. *Financial Capital Mobility and the Origins of Stock Markets*. San Domenico, Italy: FI Publications.

Vincent, Andrew. 1989. "Can Groups Be Persons?" *Review of Metaphysics* 42 (4): 687–715.

Visser, Jelle. 2006. "Union Membership Statistics in 24 Countries." *Monthly Labor Review* 129 (1) (January): 38–49.

Voss, David. 1999. "Whatever Happened to Cold Fusion?" *Physics World*, March 1. http://physicsworld.com/cws/article/print/1258.

Wachter, R. M. 2006. "Expected and Unanticipated Consequences of the Quality and Information Technology Revolutions." *Journal of the American Medical Association* 295 (23) (June 21): 2780–83.

Wagner, Richard A. 1995. "Fictive Kinship." http://family.jrank.org/pages/630/Fictive-Kinship.html#ixzz0SbF6GEVm.

Wallechinsky, David. 2006. "*Parade*'s Annual List of the World's Ten Worst Dictators." January 2. www.parade.com/articles/editions/2006/edition_01-22-2006/Dictators.

Wallerstein, Immanuel. 1961. *Africa: The Politics of Independence*. New York: Vintage.

———, ed. 1966. *Social Change: The Colonial Situation*. New York: Wiley.

———. 1974. *The Modern World-System*. New York: Academic Press.

———. 1991. *Geopolitics and Geoculture: Essays on the Changing World-System*. Cambridge: Cambridge University Press.

———. 2005. "After Developmentalism and Globalization, What?" *Social Forces* 83 (3): 1263–78.

Wall Street Journal. 1992. "Stranded Cosmonaut Is Set to Return to Changed Land." March 17, A10.

Walters, F. P. 1952. *A History of the League of Nations*. London: Oxford University Press.

Ward, Geoffrey C., Martha Saxton, Ann D. Gordon, and Ellen Carol DuBois. 1999. *Not for Ourselves Alone: The Story of Elizabeth Cady Stanton and Susan B. Anthony*. New York: Knopf.

Ward, Lester Frank. 1906. *Applied Sociology: A Treatise on the Conscious Improvement of Society by Society*. New York: Ginn.

REFERENCES

Warner, Oswald, and Teresa Swezey. 1994. "The Indian Diaspora in a Comparative Context: A Comparative Historical Analysis of Trinidad and Uganda." Paper presented at the Annual Meetings of the Michigan Academy of Science, Arts, and Letters, East Lansing, March 11.

Warwick, Donald. 1974. *Ethics and Population Control: The Case of the Developing Countries*. Hastings-on-Hudson, NY: Institute of Society, Ethics, and the Life Sciences.

———. 1975. "Contraception in the Third World." *Hastings Center Report* 5: 9–12.

Warwick, Donald, T. W. Merrick, and A. Caplan. 1977. "Population Programs: Should They Change Local Values?" *Hastings Center Report* 3: 17–18.

Waterman, Robert H., Jr. 1987. *The Renewal Factor*. New York: Bantam Books.

Weakliem, David. 1993. "Class Consciousness and Political Change: Voting and Political Attitudes in the British Working Class, 1964–1970." *American Sociological Review* 58 (3): 382–97.

Weber, Max. [1900] 1958. *The City*. New York: Free Press.

———. [1922] 1968. *Economy and Society*, edited by G. Roth and C. Wittich. New York: Bedminster Press.

———. 1951. *The Religion of China*. New York: Free Press.

———. 1958. *The Religions of India*. New York: Free Press.

———. 1976. *The Agrarian Sociology of Ancient Civilizations*. London: Humanities Press.

Weeks, John R. 1992. *Population: An Introduction to Concepts and Issues*. Belmont, CA: Wadsworth.

Weinstein, Jay. 1976. *Demographic Transition and Social Change*. Morristown, NJ: General Learning Press.

———. 1978a. "Fertility Decline and Social Service Access: Reconciling Behavioral and Medical Models." *Studies in Comparative International Development* 13 (1): 71–99.

———. 1978b. "Political and Economic Equilibrium in a Society of Immigrants." *Indian Journal of Comparative Sociology* 4: 10–21.

———. 1981. "Do We Need a Theory of Demographic Transition?" *Humboldt Journal of Social Relations* 8 (1): 71–97.

———. 1982. *Sociology/Technology: Foundations of Postacademic Social Science*. New Brunswick, NJ: Transaction Books.

———. 1987. "The Third World and Developmentalism." In *The Mythmakers*, edited by R. Mohan. Westport, CT: Greenwood.

———. 1991. "Iatrogenesis, Vulnerability, and Client Participation in Planned Social Change." *Michigan Sociological Review* 5: 17–25.

———. 1991–1992. "Urban Growth in India: Demographic and Sociocultural Prospects." *Studies in Comparative International Development* 26 (4): 29–44.

———. 1993. "Advertising the Transition in Central and Eastern Europe." Paper presented at the Annual Meeting of the Society for Applied Sociology, St. Louis, October 10.

———. 1997. "Applied Sociology Is the Answer, but What Was the Question?" *Michigan Sociological Review* 11 (fall): 18–44.

———. 2001. "Using Orwell's *Nineteen Eighty-Four* in a Course on Social and Cultural Change." In *Utopian Thinking in Sociology: Creating the Good Society*, edited by A. B. Shostak. Washington, DC: American Sociological Association.

———. 2003. "Why Altruism Is Considered Deviant Behavior: Obstacles on the Path to a Viable Utopia." In *Viable Utopian Ideas: Shaping a Better World*, edited by A. B. Shostak. Armonk, NY: M. E. Sharpe.

Weinstein, Jay, and John R. McIntyre. 1986. "Multinational Corporations and the Diffusion of World Standards: A Theoretical Exploration." *Studies in Comparative International Development* 21 (3): 51–84.

Weinstein, Jay, and Vijayan K. Pillai. 2001. *Demography: The Science of Population*. Boston: Allyn & Bacon.

Weinstein, Jay, and Nico Stehr. 1999. "The Power of Knowledge: Race Science, Race Policy, and the Holocaust." *Social Epistemology* 13: 1.

Wellman, Barry, and Caroline Haythornthweait, eds. 2002. *The Internet in Everyday Life* Oxford: Blackwell.

Wenk, E., Jr., and T. J. Kuehn. 1977. "Interinstitutional Networks in Technological Delivery Systems." In *Science and Technology Policy*, edited by J. Haberer. Lexington, MA: Lexington Books.

Western, Bruce. 1993. "Postwar Unionization in Eighteen Advanced Capitalist Countries." *American Sociological Review* 58 (2): 266–90.

———. 1994. "Unionization and Labor Market Institutions in Advanced Capitalism." *American Journal of Sociology* 99 (5): 1314–41.

Wheaton, Bernard. 1992. *Velvet Revolution*. Boulder, CO: Westview Press.

White, Leslie. 1949. *The Science of Culture*. New York: Farrar and Strauss.

White, Louise G. 1987. *Creating Opportunities for Change: Approaches to Managing Development Programs*. Boulder, CO: Lynne Rienner.

White, Robert W. 1993. "On Measuring Political Violence: Northern Ireland, 1969 to 1980." *American Sociological Review* 58 (4): 575–85.

Whitfield, Harvey. 2007. "Black Loyalists and Black Slaves in Maritime Canada." *History Compass* 5 (6): 1980–97.

Whorf, Benjamin L. 1940. *Language, Thought, and Reality*. New York: Wiley.

Whoriskey, Peter. 2009. "American Union Ranks Grow after 'Bottoming Out': First Significant Increase in 25 Years." *Washington Post*, January 29. www.washingtonpost.com/wp-dyn/content/article/2009/01/28/AR2009012801621.html.

Whyte, William. 1988. *The City: Rediscovering the Center*. New York: Doubleday.

Wiebe, Paul D. 1976. *Indian Malaysians: The View from the Plantation*. New Delhi: Manohar Press.

Wiegland, Bruce. 1994. "Black Money in Belize: The Ethnicity and Social Structure of Black-Market Crime." *Social Forces* 73 (1): 135–54.

Wilfred, John Nobel. 1994. "Yes, Earth, There Are Other Planet Systems." *New York Times*, April 24, A4, E2.

Willhelm, Sidney. 1962. *Urban Zoning and Land Use Theory*. New York: Free Press.

Williams, Horace R. 2002. *WEB DuBois: A Scholar's Courageous Life*. Montgomery, AL: Junebug Books.

Williams, Juan, producer. 1986. *Eyes on the Prize*, part 1 (television documentary). U.S. Corporation for Public Broadcasting.

———. 1989. *Eyes on the Prize*, part 2 (television documentary). U.S. Corporation for Public Broadcasting.

Williams, Kristen. 1985. "Is 'Unequal Exchange' a Mechanism for Perpetuating Inequality in the Modern World-System?" *Studies in Comparative International Development* 20 (3): 4–23.

Willoughby, Kelvin W. 1990. *Technology Choice: A Critique of the Appropriate Technology Movement*. Boulder, CO: Westview Press, Intermediate Technology Publications.

Wilson, Richard. 2001. *The Politics of Truth and Reconciliation in South Africa: Legitimizing the Post-Apartheid State*. Cambridge: Cambridge University Press.

Winiecki, Jan. 1993. *Post-Soviet-Type Economies in Transition*. Brookfield, VT: Ashgate.

Winkler, Heinrich August. 1979. "German Society, Hitler, and the Illusion of Restoration 1930–33." In *International Fascism: New Thoughts and Approaches*, edited by G. L. Grosse. Beverly Hills, CA: Sage.

Winner, Langdon. 1977. *Autonomous Technology: Technics-out-of-Control as a Theme in Political Thought*. Cambridge, MA: MIT Press.

Wistrich, Robert. 1985. *Hitler's Apocalypse*. New York: St. Martin's Press.

Woetzel, Robert K. 1962. *The Nuremberg Trials in International Law*. New York: Praeger.

Wood, James L., and Maurice Jackson. 1982. *Social Movements: Development, Participation, and Dynamics*. Belmont, CA: Wadsworth.

World Bank. 2004. *Global Development Finance, 2004*. Washington, DC: Author.

World Commission on Human Rights (WCHR). 1993. "Vienna Declaration and Programme of Action Set Goals for 21st Century." *United Nations Chronicle* 30 (September): 54–61.

"World Grieves Loss of Shuttle." 2003. CNN Special. February 2. www.cnn.com/2003/TECH/space/02/01/shuttle.columbia.reax.

Worsley, Peter. 1964. *The Third World: A Vital New Force in International Affairs*. London: Weidenfeld and Nicholson.

———. 1980. "One World or Three? A Critique of the World-System Theory of Immanuel Wallerstein." In *Socialist Register*, edited by R. Miliband and J. Savile. London: Merlin Press.

———. 1984. *The Three Worlds: Culture and World Development*. Chicago: University of Chicago Press.

Wright, Rosemary, and Jerry A. Jacobs. 1994. "Male Flight from Computer Work: A New Look at Occupational Segregation and Ghettoization." *American Sociological Review* 59 (4): 511–36.

Wrigley, Edward A. 1969. *Population and History*. New York: McGraw-Hill.

Wuthnow, Robert. 1983. *The New Christian Right: Mobilization and Legitimation*. Hawthorne, NY: Aldine.

———. 1992. *Rediscovering the Sacred: Perspectives on Religion in Contemporary Society*. Grand Rapids, MI: W. B. Eerdmans.

———. 1995. *Rethinking Materialism: Perspectives on the Spiritual Dimension of Economic Relations*. Grand Rapids, MI: W. B. Eerdmans.

Wysocki, Diane K. 1996. "Somewhere over the Modem: Self-Disclosure in Interpersonal Relationships and Computer Bulletin Boards." *Dissertation Abstracts International, A: The Humanities and Social Sciences* 57 (9): 4157.

Yahi Productions. 1992. *The Last of His Tribe*. Produced by John Levoff and Robert Lovenheim, and directed by Harry Hook. HBO, April 2.

Yang, Jonghoe, and Russell A. Stone. 1985. "Investment, Dependence, Economic Growth, and Status in the World-System: A Test of 'Dependent Development.'" *Studies in Comparative International Development* 20 (1): 98–120.

Yinger, J. Milton. 1994. *Ethnicity: Source of Strength? Source of Conflict?* Albany: State University of New York Press.

Young, Marguerite, and Charles Ruas. 1999. *Harp Song for a Radical: The Life and Times of Eugene Victor Debs*. New York: Knopf.

Zald, Mayer N., and John D. McCarthy. 1979. *The Dynamics of Social Movements*. Cambridge, MA: Winthrop.

Zamiatin, E. I. [1924] 1993. *We*. New York: Penguin.

Zeitlin, Irving M. 1968. *Ideology and the Development of Sociological Theory*. Englewood Cliffs, NJ: Prentice Hall.

Zetka, James R., Jr. 1995. "Union Homogenization and Organizational Foundations of Plantwide Militancy in the U.S. Automobile Industry, 1959–1979." *Social Forces* 73 (3): 789–810.

Zhou, Xueguang. 1993. "Unorganized Interests and Collective Action in China." *American Sociological Review* 58 (1): 54–73.

Zimmer, Carl. 2008. *Microcosm: E. Coli and the New Science of Life*. New York: Vintage.

Zuckerman, Harriet. 1977. *The Scientific Elite: Nobel Laureates in the U.S.* New York: Free Press.

———. 1991. *The Outer Circle: Women in the Scientific Community*. New York: Norton.

Zuijdwijk, Ton J. M. 1982. *Petitioning the United Nations: A Study in Human Rights*. New York: St. Martin's Press.

Index

Africa, 3, 17–18, 34, 41–42, 51, 59, 62, 71, 75–76, 78, 80, 92, 96, 103, 163, 228, 234, 237, 239–40, 244, 250–54, 271, 273, 310, 313, 319, 321–22, 324, 328, 354, 363. *See also* South Africa

African Americans, 20, 166; diaspora, 251

African Canadians, 251

agricultural experiment station (Ag. Station), 209, 301

Albania, 23, 25, 259, 264, 273, 302, 325, 352, 361

altruism, 49–50, 112, 187, 192, 295, 323–25, 327–28, 364; creative, 48–50, 52–53, 187, 192, 327

anti-Communism, 141

apartheid, 252–53

Asia, 3, 17–18, 21, 34, 42, 59, 62, 71, 75–76, 78, 88, 92, 105, 163, 197, 232–34, 237, 239–40, 249–50, 252, 271, 294, 310, 313, 319, 321–22, 324, 327–28, 354, 363

authority(ies), 17, 19, 21, 24, 48, 64, 85–87, 92–95, 97, 112, 119, 121–26, 128, 134, 139, 143, 145, 147, 150–51, 153, 154, 156, 159–68, 172, 185, 191, 197, 201–03, 207–08, 210, 212, 217, 225, 228–30, 236–07, 259, 268, 278, 282, 288, 300–02, 327, 334, 346, 351–52, 362–64; charismatic, 87, 123–24, 126; rational-legal, 86–87, 119,123–25,

128, 143; traditional, 87, 123–26, 143, 153, 217, 225

autocracy, 25–27, 50, 98, 124–28, 168, 185, 189, 214, 225, 229, 267, 302, 308, 318, 354–55; classic-direct, 124, 225; and mass control, 128; representative-indirect, 125–26, 128; social movements in, 168

birth, 35, 59–62, 65, 71–72, 74, 76–77, 80, 82, 113, 152–53, 230–31; control, 72–74, 80, 152–53; crude rates (CBR), 60, 76

Bolshevism, 126, 182, 189, 203, 309, 334–38, 351–53, 357

bourgeoisie, 38, 40, 49, 74–75, 122, 281, 294, 297, 299, 356

Buddhism, 51, 92, 187, 233, 246

bureaucracy, 100, 111, 112, 116, 118–21, 124, 126–27, 129–30, 288, 308, 324, 338, 348

Canada, 18, 59, 64, 75, 104, 130, 179, 182, 189, 250–51, 264, 274, 280, 298, 319, 334, 352, 383

capitalism, 47–48, 93–94, 184, 218, 272, 275, 277, 278, 281–83, 288–90, 292–94, 297, 299–303, 313, 315, 335, 337; origin and elements of, 275–77, 280–84; state, 300

caste, 49, 231–33, 235, 240, 254, 258–62

China, 5, 18, 76, 80, 88, 92, 121, 142, 151, 161, 163, 177, 184, 185, 221, 224, 234–35,

241–42, 248–49, 264, 267–68, 298–99, 301–02, 312, 320, 352–54, 357, 361, 363

Christianity, 51, 92, 234, 259

Cold War, 19, 23–25, 128, 182, 260, 266–67, 302, 308, 311, 313, 316, 318, 323–24, 328–29, 338, 342, 346–47, 363

collective behavior, 126, 137–39, 148, 158–59, 169, 189–91

colonialism, 19–20, 41, 85, 163, 247, 318, 326–27, 329, 351, 353

communication, 4–7, 12, 48, 87, 93, 103, 106, 110, 127, 152, 154, 167, 203, 210–11, 222, 234, 238, 240, 244, 256, 291–93, 303, 307, 323, 337, 342–43, 348, 350–51, 354–59, 362, 364, 366; electronic, 4, 87, 103, 127, 240, 303, 323, 343, 366; telecommunication, 4, 203, 291, 348, 356, 364

Communism, 9, 21, 24, 25, 26, 29, 59, 141–42, 144, 146, 177, 188, 212, 289, 296, 297, 300, 312, 314, 316, 328, 335, 353, 369

Communist Party, 23, 25, 123, 141, 178, 193, 297, 301, 342

complexity, sociocultural, 41, 44–45, 52, 89, 100, 107, 112, 191, 219–21, 224, 226–28, 235–36, 238–39, 244, 262, 265, 268, 270–71, 303, 308, 315, 348; and modernization, 39, 46–47, 87

corporations, 4–5, 7, 9, 74, 86, 129, 134, 148, 160, 169, 185, 209, 213, 257, 270, 275–76, 278–84, 287–93, 303–04, 307, 323, 326–27, 334–35, 348, 351, 353, 355–56, 359, 363; and democratic process, 356; multinational (MNC), 4, 86, 129, 134, 185, 213, 257, 270, 279, 282, 288–89, 291–94, 303, 307, 323, 334, 336, 348, 353–55

critical periods, 9, 115, 123, 138, 192. *See also* episodes

cultural: authority, 85, 123, 237; diversity, 33, 86, 217, 247–49, 256–57, 271–72, 327; imperialism, 96–97; leveling, 217, 247, 270; priorities, 196; relativism, 255–57, 273; revolution, 3, 78, 162; universal(s), 51, 88, 90, 174, 257

culture, 4, 8–10, 13, 20–21, 26–27, 32–37, 40–42, 44–48, 56, 58–59, 70, 73, 81, 84–93, 98–100, 102–05, 108, 115, 124, 126, 128, 130, 133, 139, 144, 174, 184, 187, 191–92, 196, 200, 209, 217, 221, 224, 226, 231, 234–36, 239, 245, 248–52, 254–57, 260, 271–73, 295–96, 300, 311, 314–15, 327–30,

350; sacred and secular aspects, 87, 89, 92; sensate, 45–49, 187, 196, 327, 330

death, 21, 25, 27, 33, 35, 40, 50, 60, 62, 64–65, 67, 69–71, 76–77, 79, 82, 89, 103, 113, 115, 120, 123, 150, 167, 199, 231, 233, 237, 255, 321, 329; age-specific rates, 62; control, 77, 237; crude rates (CDR), 62, 64, 67, 76–77; rates, 58, 62, 64–65, 67, 70, 71, 73, 77, 79, 321. *See also* mortality

democracy, 19, 26–27, 50, 57, 94, 112, 121, 124–25, 127–28, 160–61, 163–64, 166, 168–69, 171–73, 183–84, 228–29, 245, 266–67, 304, 310, 314, 328, 335, 337, 340, 341–43, 351–54, 356; classic-direct, 24, 229; participatory, 169, 341–43; representative, 126, 130, 161, 163, 175, 184, 337

demography/demographic, 8, 17, 35, 55, 57–60, 62–64, 68–70, 72–73, 75–83, 88, 100, 106, 113, 122, 145, 191, 199, 206, 228, 245, 262, 265, 272, 320, 321; collapse, 199; component of change, 57; processes, 35, 55, 58. 113, 191; transition, 8, 55, 57–58, 60, 62, 64, 66, 68–82

dependency theory, 261, 268–70, 274, 311

destructive entitlement, 247, 259, 260, 274, 326

dialectic(al), 38–39, 44, 87–88, 138, 140, 217, 314, 348

diffusion, 36, 47, 75, 84, 86, 126, 134, 159, 196, 203–04, 211–12, 215, 234, 236, 239, 270, 272, 293, 329, 348, 351, 358

division of labor, 129–30, 174–75, 177, 221–22, 224, 230–31, 240, 249, 269, 293, 300; gender-specific, 177; international, 249, 269, 293; spatial, 222; world, 240

economic: crisis, 74, 282; determinism, 300; functions, 231, 275; surplus, 124, 221, 223, 237

economy(ies), 48, 67, 93–94, 96, 179, 229, 237, 238, 242, 254, 269, 272, 275, 278, 281, 283, 290, 295, 298, 300, 301–04, 315, 320, 336, 340, 343, 346, 350–51, 353, 364; capitalist, 94, 353; and ecology, 275; informal, 281; socialist, 300, 303; urban, 237

egoism, 48–49, 52, 187, 327–28, 371

electronic media, 14, 36, 44, 110, 159, 260, 270, 343

elites, 23, 44, 138, 155, 162, 164, 169, 311, 340, 341, 362, 364; political, 188 empire, 17–18, 23, 26, 70, 92, 97, 104, 107, 162, 189, 226–28, 231, 234–37, 239, 248, 250, 254, 267–69, 272, 279, 289, 296, 298, 351

England, 17, 21, 42, 67, 69–71, 74, 77, 126–27, 152, 168, 179, 238–39, 266–67, 269–70, 276, 279, 281, 295–96, 318, 335, 337, 351–52

episodes, 8–10, 14, 26, 106, 189, 257, 272, 358; critical, 9, 13–28, 59, 174, 212

ethnic: conflict, 19, 249, 271; dialects, 102; diversity, 248, 250, 254–55; divisiveness, 217; groups, 15, 19, 183, 248–49, 254, 259–60, 308

ethnocentrism, 8, 256–57, 273

Europe, 4, 10, 17–19, 24–26, 34, 42–44, 62, 69–78, 86–88, 92–93, 96–97, 99, 115, 122–24, 126–27, 141, 146, 157, 168, 175, 178, 189, 223, 235–40, 250, 254–5, 269–72, 276, 281, 294, 297–98, 300–01, 310–11, 316, 318, 321, 324, 329, 331, 335, 351–54, 363; capitalism in, 93–94, 281, 293–94; Central, 3, 9, 15, 23, 25, 27, 59, 75, 97, 103, 184, 266, 268, 289, 298, 302, 316, 353; Eastern, 3, 9, 23–25, 27, 59, 75, 97, 103, 142, 162, 184, 266, 268, 289, 298, 302, 316, 319, 353; feudal era in, 38; Western, 3, 23, 75, 151, 177, 184, 263, 266, 293, 308–09, 315

European Americans, 59

evolution, 8–9, 29, 31–43, 50, 52, 68, 85, 87, 99, 103, 188, 211, 265, 269, 315, 366; defined, 32; and language, 99–104; and modernization, 315; organic, 32, 35–36, 43, 52, 55; sociocultural, 1, 3, 8, 13–14, 34, 37, 40, 42, 47, 49–50, 52. *See also* superorganic

evolutionary theory, 8, 32–33, 46–47, 50, 108, 227, 262; of language, 99

family, 35, 40, 45, 64–65, 74, 86, 93, 104, 108–10, 112–14, 124, 146, 162, 207, 217, 221, 224, 229, 240, 242–43, 245, 281, 283, 288, 295, 308, 312, 322; planning, 69, 74–75, 79–82, 152, 157, 175, 186, 311, 317, 322–23, 334; rule, 225–26; values, 112. *See also* kinship

fascism, 174; Italian, 126

fertility, 60–62, 65, 69–71, 73–75, 80, 322; age-specific, 61–62; control, 1, 35, 69, 71–75, 79–80, 152, 317, 329; decline, 73–75, 80;

general rates (GFR), 60–61. *See also* birth; reproduction

feudalism, 4, 50, 235, 300; defeat of Russia and Eastern Europe, 162; fall of, 93, 123, 157, 162, 175, 195, 297

first world, 19, 266–68, 271, 309, 313, 317–18

France, 16, 18, 21, 71, 76, 126, 163, 175, 188–89, 241–42, 264–65, 280, 291, 295–96, 318–19, 352, 363; representative democracy in, 163

fundamentalism, religious, 94, 160, 177, 186

Gemeinschaft, 112, 124, 219–20, 244; defined, 112

gender, 3, 8, 58, 61, 65, 81, 114–15, 144, 221, 322; and division of labor, 177; equality movement, 140, 151, 164, 174–75, 177, 186, 191–92; stratification, 174; structure of population, 61

genocide, 33, 103, 112, 120, 128, 256–57; in ancient China, 163; under colonialism, 250, 273

Gesellschaft, 219, 224, 244, 247, 315; defined, 112

global: bureaucracy, 100; level, 184, 212, 219, 244, 303, 344; networks, 203; revolution, 4, 7, 85, 107–08; society, 52, 106, 244, 348, 354; system, 86, 185, 244, 272, 351; village, 216, 218, 260, 350

globalization, 4, 6, 43–44, 50, 58, 107, 185, 187, 192, 215, 217, 247, 260–61, 270, 272–73, 294, 308, 338, 346–48, 355, 358–62; geopolitical dimensions of, 359; and localism, 348–50

goal displacement, 119–21, 316

The Golden Rule, 49–51, 187, 257, 259, 327

government(s), 3, 5, 10–11, 15, 17, 19, 23–24, 49–50, 74–75, 79–80, 88, 93, 96–97, 102, 104, 121, 126–28, 134, 137, 140–43, 150–51, 159, 161, 164, 167–72, 183–84, 186, 198, 200, 202–04, 207–10, 212–13, 215, 229, 235, 239, 245, 260, 262, 274, 277–80, 282, 287–88, 290, 293, 295, 297–303, 307, 309–10, 312–14, 317, 323, 326, 334–40, 343, 351, 353–59, 363; autocratic, 50, 129, 266, 353; organizations, 148, 262, 334; representative, 40, 94, 130, 170–71, 348, 351, 355; workers, 182; world, 17, 107, 185, 187, 327, 348, 350, 352–53, 362–64. *See also* autocracy; democracy; political systems

Great Depression, 175, 209, 278, 335
Great Man thesis, 151
Green Revolution, 19, 197, 313, 316, 320
group(s), 20, 22, 25, 27, 42, 48, 50, 66, 91–93, 104, 113–16, 118–19, 121–26, 129, 131, 146, 163–64, 179, 183–86, 207, 214, 224–26, 229, 247, 256, 259–60, 267–68, 279–81, 283–84, 287, 290, 309, 317, 326–27, 342, 365; closed, 115, 228–29; dynamics, 10; interests, 122, 124; for itself, 122–23, 155, 247, 267–68, 364; in itself, 122–23, 268; membership, 93, 112–13; open, 115; as persons, 121–128 (*see also* persona); secondary, 113, 124

Hawthorne Western Electric study, 130
Holocaust, 9,13, 15–17, 23, 27–29, 40, 49, 53, 59, 95, 120, 126, 168, 193, 212, 273, 353, 368, 370–71; and civil religion, 94–95; defined,15; demographic aspects of, 59; and events in Bosnia, compared, 128; impact of, 15; museums and memorials, 15; references on, 30
human rights, 17, 20, 40, 128, 151, 172, 185, 247, 257, 260, 308, 327, 348, 364–65
hyperurbanization, 243, 245

iatrogenesis, 206, 208–09, 211–12
imperialism, 41, 162, 185, 267, 351, 353; cultural, 96–97
India, 17–19, 36, 65, 76–77, 80, 97, 102–03, 123, 145, 151, 162, 198, 206, 224, 231, 234–35, 239, 241–43, 252–54, 265, 267–68, 270–71, 273–74, 280, 294, 320, 322–23, 326, 331, 347; ancient civilizations of, 121, 224; British, 100, 123, 162, 279, 293, 304, 329; ethnic diversity in, 249–50, 271; urban growth in, 240–41
industrial: change, 9, 225, 228; estate, 202, 211; growth, 71, 94, 175, 196; revolution, 76–77, 238; wealth, 52, 262
industrialization, 31, 44, 69, 75, 79, 88, 240, 244, 262, 281, 304, 308, 312, 315–16, 318, 329, 353; and the premature metropolis, 240–41; in the Third World, 267, 270
Industrial Revolution, 70, 77, 88, 115, 124–25, 238–39, 244, 251, 269, 276, 304, 311, 321, 325, 328, 346, 348
informal structure, 116

information, 4–5, 18, 25, 50, 57, 127, 139, 146, 152, 154, 160, 172, 182–83, 187, 189, 196, 202, 214, 260, 262, 288, 290, 293, 325, 327, 328, 343, 350, 355–59, 366; and democracy, 183; and globalization, 355; institution, 146, 356, 359; organizations, 160; revolution, 50, 358; super-highway, 87, 215, 355, 358, 363; two-way flow of, 211
Information Age, 196, 325
innovation diffusion process, 211, 215
institutionalization, 99, 107, 118, 121, 124, 206, 293, 295, 312
institutions, 1, 4–6, 9–10, 14, 17, 28, 35, 41, 50, 53, 57–58, 74, 85, 87–88, 92–94, 102, 107, 113, 118–19, 129, 133, 138, 140, 143, 146–47, 151, 157, 159–60, 162, 164, 172, 186–88, 191–92, 207–09, 217–19, 229, 239, 244–45, 255, 277, 293–97, 308, 315, 339, 340, 343, 348–49, 353, 355–56, 359; economic, 96, 129, 234, 237, 273, 277–78, 303, 307; information, 146, 356, 359; political, 95, 138, 191, 224, 234; religious, 87, 89, 94–96
intellectuals, 141, 146, 149, 151, 154–55, 157, 160, 162, 164, 166, 168, 178, 187, 190–192, 240, 267–68, 297, 313
intentional change, 13–14, 88, 244, 338
interest(s), 8–10, 15, 28, 30, 46, 49, 58, 86, 88, 93–94, 99, 108, 119, 122–29, 134, 139, 143, 150, 155–57, 159, 164, 169–70, 174, 182–83, 187, 192, 197, 202–04, 211–14, 225, 267, 277–78, 280, 289, 300–01, 303, 343; groups, 169, 179, 184, 207, 309, 317, 335, 356; human, 321
Islam, 51, 92, 97, 259, 301; birth of, 234–35
Israel, 15–17, 19, 36, 97, 103, 224, 296, 313, 347, 354, 360
Italy, 34, 76, 126, 168, 236, 242, 319, 351; fascism established in, 126, 351

Japan, 3, 19, 75–76, 86, 99, 182, 240–42, 249, 263–64, 266, 270, 271, 287, 291, 293, 303, 308, 315, 319, 324, 361; capitalism in, 291, 293, 303
Jews, 15–17, 51, 59, 96, 103, 161, 166–167, 315, 351, 365; and the Holocaust, 15–16, 49, 167
justice, 16, 20, 22, 39, 45, 49–50, 121, 134, 147, 157, 160, 174, 180, 209, 253–54, 258–60, 273, 295, 333, 344

kinship, 86, 89, 109, 112, 115, 122–24, 126, 131, 218, 220–23, 225, 229–31; fictive, 108–9; traditional, 109, 124
kinship-based production, 223
kinship-oriented communities,126

labor movement, 158, 275; international, 166; U.S., 179–81, 183
language(s), 36, 55, 59, 84–87, 98–105, 115, 170, 177, 189, 195, 234, 251, 271, 315; acquisition, 102; artificial, 101; change in and of, 102–04; Chinese, 99; European, 86, 100, 102–03, 239, 254; and evolution, 99; natural, 103, 96; North American tribal, 100; official, 103; policy, 17, 116; regulation of, 55, 85, 98–99, 102, 104
Latin America, 3, 18–19, 59, 62, 71, 75–76, 88, 184, 197, 239, 267, 269, 271, 310, 319, 321, 324, 354, 363
leadership, 9, 77, 117–18, 122–23, 141, 148, 151, 154, 162, 175, 228–29, 267, 273, 340; charismatic, 15, 18, 123–24, 139, 143, 151, 153, 156, 168, 268, 340; of social movements, 139, 147, 150–51, 154–55
League of Nations, 17, 352
lobbyists, 169–71, 213

Malthusian "laws", 67, 69, 79
Malthusian responses to Third World population explosion, 79–80
Marshall Plan, 309–10, 318, 323, 352
Marxism, 26, 44, 46–47, 50, 52, 94, 146, 178, 296–97, 315–16; and the labor movement, 297; theories of revolution of, 146
Marxist-Leninist, 25, 94, 182, 300
materialism, 44, 49, 187, 295, 328, 330
media, 6–7, 14, 27, 36, 44, 86, 110, 159, 203, 260, 270, 272, 285, 303, 312, 343, 357; impact of, 197. See also electronic media
mediating structures, 129, 230
Mediterranean, 42, 234; Eastern, 228
membership, 66, 93, 111–16, 179, 181–83, 224, 228, 284, 339–41, 362; as a right, 263, 284
microchip, 6
microlevel, 9–11, 106, 283
Middle Ages, 92, 248
middle class, 74–75, 141, 256. See also bourgeoisie

migration, 3, 11, 35, 59, 60, 62, 65–66, 83, 113, 249–51, 254, 271–72; and ethnic diversity, 250, 254; rates, 35, 76
militant change, 9, 87, 192
minority group(s), 2, 21–22, 207–08, 273; rights of 21–22. See also ethnic, groups
modernity/modernism, 4, 6, 34, 55, 87, 94
mortality, 60, 62, 64, 65, 67, 69, 71, 73, 76–77, 79, 200; control of, 35, 69–71, 76–77, 199; decline, 64, 71, 79, 241; infant, 64, 70, 73–74, 76, 199, 241, 262, 312, 328–29. See also death
MTV, 104
Muslim(s), 17, 20–21, 92–93, 97–98, 123, 161, 234–36, 248–49, 298

nationalism, 13–14, 96, 186, 217–18, 353
nation-state, 146, 189, 224, 244, 249, 284, 351, 362–63
natural increase, 35, 60, 62 , 67, 78; rates of, 65, 70, 78
Nazism, 16, 26, 95, 126; and civil religion, 95–96; and nationalism, 13, 96
neo-Malthusianism, 68, 80
New World, 71, 92, 218, 234, 249–51; slavery in, 251–52
nonviolence, 255
norms, 20, 35–36, 48, 84, 89, 92, 107, 111–12, 114, 118, 120, 122, 124–26, 129, 133, 137–38, 144–46, 150, 155, 163, 172, 177, 186–87, 191, 230, 231, 247–48, 257–58, 271, 276–77, 282, 287–99, 292, 295, 300, 303, 333, 356, 358; feudal, 175; formal, 116; of gender relations, 175; informal, 118–19; official, 116, 128; of reciprocity, 257–60; religious, 89, 231
North America, 3, 10–11, 19, 33, 65, 71, 73, 76–77, 86–88, 100, 103, 114–15, 168, 177–78, 189, 240, 252, 266, 270–71, 282, 293, 315, 329
Nuremberg Laws, 15
Nuremberg Tribunal, 17, 120

order of impact, 10, 11; first, 11; second, 11, 14
organic periods, 9
organic solidarity, 112, 129
organizations, 4–6, 9–10, 13–15, 19–20, 48, 74, 82, 87, 89, 94–95, 102, 106–07, 111–12, 114–16, 118–21, 123–27, 129, 134, 137,

140–41, 148, 159–60, 163, 166, 169, 178–80, 185, 187, 190, 204, 213, 216, 224–25, 237, 239, 244, 256–57, 259–60, 262, 270, 279, 281, 287, 289, 294–96, 298, 301, 307, 309–10, 313, 315–16, 327, 329, 331, 333–35, 337–38, 340–42, 344, 348, 353, 355–56, 362, 364, 366; complex, 14, 111–12; democratic planning, 331–33, 337–39, 341, 343–44; information related, 160; secondary, 74, 111, 116; in social movements, 160, 164, 166, 169–70, 178–80, 185, 187, 190; and technological innovation, 204, 213, 216; voluntary, 112, 310

Pacific region, 17
Pakistan, 20, 76, 97, 100, 123, 221, 224, 241, 252, 317; early civilizations in, 17, 19; as a theocracy, 88, 97
penalty of leadership, 77, 228
persona, 112, 121–24, 268, 280
planned change, 49, 171, 307
planning, 10–11, 14–15, 23, 47, 74, 102, 186, 203, 207–08, 212, 244, 277, 281, 283, 294, 296, 301–03, 308–09, 322–23, 331–32, 334–39, 341, 344, 347–48, 354; Bolshevist, 203; democratic, 49, 169, 203, 211, 330–33, 337–39, 341, 343–44; models, 334–37
Poland, 15, 18, 23–24, 96–97, 351–52
political institutions, 95, 138, 191, 224, 234
political parties, 95, 126, 164, 300
political systems, 5, 23, 93, 97, 124, 126, 146, 160, 184, 225, 266, 279, 298, 300, 337, 341
political violence, 143, 145
population(s), 10–11, 13–15, 17, 19, 33, 35–37, 40–43, 45, 47, 50, 55–71, 73–88, 90, 92, 96, 100, 102–03, 107, 112–13, 122, 124, 126–27, 130, 133, 159, 181, 183–84, 194, 196, 199–200, 206–07, 211, 214, 219–22, 224, 226, 228–31, 234–45, 248–52, 254–56, 260–63, 265, 270–72, 275, 289–90, 293, 295, 303, 312–13, 315, 317–18, 320–22, 329, 333, 349, 351–54, 362; growth and decline of, 13, 36–38, 40, 45, 57–70, 72, 74, 76, 78–82, 196, 199–200, 226, 234, 237, 240, 242, 303, 312, 321, 322, 329; pyramids, 62–64, 78; structural aspects of, 65; as units of observation, 58–59; world, 59, 62, 70, 79, 81–82, 220, 241–42, 265, 322, 349. See also demography

precipitating events, 157, 160, 162, 168, 175, 184, 190
premature metropolises, 239–41, 270
primary bond, 108–09, 122
primary relationships, 107–08, 110–12, 217, 221, 308
primary sector, 222, 229
pronatalism, 73–75
propaganda, 190, 203
prophecy, 20, 47, 154
Protestantism, 93; as a reform movement, 143

Quebec, 59, 102, 104

race, 17, 22, 41–43, 45, 47, 49, 53, 58, 66, 82, 95, 224, 254, 256, 268, 344, 348, 353
rationality, 119, 121, 127
reform(s), 21, 24–25, 88, 93–94, 96, 118, 140, 143, 146–47, 152, 161, 168–71, 178, 181, 189, 191, 200, 205, 211, 278, 284, 288, 295, 297–98, 310, 312, 314, 342; and the U.S. labor movement, 179–81, 183
relationships, 9, 33, 41, 44, 55, 57–58, 86, 89, 91, 106–13, 115, 118–19, 122, 129, 143, 177, 197, 217, 221–23, 239, 248, 256–58, 262, 269, 271, 276, 308, 310, 333, 348, 355–56
relative deprivation, 74, 157, 164, 175
religion(s), 51, 55, 66, 75, 87–90, 93–98, 146, 154, 160, 186, 233, 259; as an institution, 87, 89, 93–96; traditional, 89, 95–98
reproduction, 32, 60, 68–69, 75, 91, 135, 152, 177; net rates, 60–61; technologies of, 177
research and development (R&D), 134, 196, 202, 204, 209–10, 212–14, 293, 323, 328, 358, 366
revolution(s), 1, 3–4, 10, 14, 19, 24–26, 69, 73, 75, 78, 97–98, 121, 123, 126, 134, 137, 139–40, 145–47, 157, 159–60, 162–64, 166–68, 170, 172, 174, 177–78, 180, 182–84, 186, 188–92, 197, 229, 233, 235, 237, 239–40, 276, 282, 295, 308, 313–14, 316, 320, 325, 358, 362; agricultural, 31, 41, 124, 175, 220, 224, 228–29, 234–36; French, 155, 251, 296; global, 4, 7, 85, 107–08; industrial, 70, 76–77, 88, 115, 124–25, 238–39, 244, 251, 269; information, 50, 358; Iranian, 96–97, 184; nonpolitical, 146; permanent, 134, 189; political, 8, 122,

130, 133, 139, 146, 159–60, 175, 187–88, 190–92, 240, 332; Russian, 46, 94, 298

roles, 109, 111, 113–15, 120; of membership, 114; obligations of, 109

Roman Catholic, 252, 329; Church, 93, 95, 143; countries, 96; cultures, 93

Roman Empire, 70; rise and fall of, 70

Rome, 92, 121, 130, 223, 229, 234–36, 239, 248

Russia, 18, 25, 46, 62, 76, 86, 94, 126, 141, 162, 168, 178, 188, 189, 193, 229, 235, 241, 297–98, 347, 351, 363

Sanskritization, 103, 254

scale of change, 9

secondary groups, 113, 124

secondary organizations, 74, 111, 116

secondary relationships, 41, 108–11, 122, 221

secondary sector, 229

second world, 3, 313, 323, 328; nations, 19–20, 75, 266–68, 270

secularization, 85, 88, 92–94, 96–98, 104

slavery, 49–50, 135, 221, 248, 251–52, 256–57, 271, 326; and agricultural revolutions, 177; and the status of women, 174

social Darwinism, 32, 49, 52, 80

social engineering, 50

social facts, 133, 256

social impact analysis, 192, 197, 204, 206

social inequality, 174–75, 217, 233, 243, 245, 293, 314

socialism, 27, 44, 47, 283, 293–94, 298–300, 302–03, 326; Bolshevik, 297–98; before Marx, 294–96; Marxist, 296–97

social movements, 10–11, 14, 17, 23–24, 26–27, 43, 47–48, 88, 115, 130, 133–34, 137–39, 143–47, 149–50, 156, 158–59, 164, 166, 170–71, 174, 184, 190–92, 228, 231, 240, 267, 277, 297, 322, 348, 350, 353; antilob-bying, 170; civil rights, 9, 20–21, 26, 28–29, 59, 98, 139–40, 145, 151, 161, 164–66, 177, 254, 273, 342, 353; for creative altrusim, 187, 192, 327; democratic rights, 174, 183; family planning, 69, 74–75, 80, 82, 152, 157, 334; labor, 164, 177–81, 183, 297; per-manent, 174; political, 10, 145, 160, 168, 188, 191, 339; protest, 9, 123, 145, 150, 154–55, 157; radical, 143, 151, 153–54, 166, 168; and violence, 145

social science, 1, 6, 8, 13, 26, 29, 31–32, 37, 45–46, 49, 57, 87, 119, 189, 192, 205, 209, 255–56, 277, 346, 350; for democracy, 334, 338; founding of, 32, 67, 129; Institution-alization of in Europe, 99, 295; reinvention of, 8

social stratification, 162, 174–75, 222, 226, 231, 235, 255, 317, 329, 344; caste system of, 231–32; core-periphery system of, 223; ethnic, 250; international, 130, 247, 260–62, 265, 272, 350; origins of, 217; the Platonic model of, 227

social technologies, 279

social theory, 32, 337

socioeconomic development, 61, 261–62, 265, 268, 309, 316, 322–23, 348, 359, 362; con-tinuum, 263, 265–66; costs of, 316

South Africa, 18, 250, 252–54, 273, 324

South America, 103, 124, 250; African dias-pora in, 251

Soviet Union, 19, 21, 24–25, 103, 161, 191, 267, 298, 302, 309, 336, 346–47, 351–53; fall of Communism in, 298

state, 17, 25, 88, 95–97, 123, 128, 145–47, 150, 153, 160, 162–64, 166–68, 172, 184, 185, 188, 190–91, 212, 224–30, 234–35, 237, 280, 300–01, 323, 347, 353, 357; command, 25, 335, 351–52. See also nation-state

superorganic, 35, 41, 43, 47, 49, 52, 85, 102; change, 36, 58, 338, 348; defined, 13.

technological: delivery system (TDS), 209–11; fix, 201, 323; imperative, 201, 203, 356; innovation, 11, 47, 69, 130, 133, 192, 194–96, 204, 211–14, 240, 244, 315; revolution, 245, 358

technology, 4, 11, 23, 44, 48, 81, 129, 192, 194–98, 200–06, 211, 215, 247, 260, 295, 318, 320, 323, 325, 327–29, 343–44, 350, 356–57, 366; appropriate, 204, 216, 312, 323–24, 328; assessment, 196–97, 201, 204–06, 210–11; autonomous, 196, 200–01, 203; conquest-oriented, 45, 196; electronic communication, 4, 87, 103, 127, 240, 303, 323, 343, 366; of elite rule, 355; fertility control, 35, 71, 73, 75, 80, 153; mortality (death) control, 35, 69–71, 76–77, 199; of sanitation, 35, 70, 77, 237;

of social control, 121; and Third World development, 198, 316, 326

television, 11, 103, 356–58; educational, 323; invention of, 11; in *Nineteen Eighty-Four*, 26–27; public, 11

tertiary relationships, 86, 107, 110–11, 217, 223, 262, 348, 355

tertiary sector, 229

theocracy, 88; representative, 97

Third World, 3, 9, 17, 19–21, 25, 29, 58–59, 61, 64–65, 68, 86, 162, 168, 197, 199, 239–40, 242–43, 245, 247, 254, 267–71, 273, 293, 308–09, 311–18, 320, 321, 322–29, 330, 335, 351–355; debt burden, 320–21, 330; demographic transition in, 75, 77–81; European imperialism in, 267; family-planning programs, 80; independence movement, 21, 96, 247, 268, 271; modernization, 204; nationalist movements, 14, 96; population explosion, 78–82; urban growth in, 239–41, 243, 270

tradition, 4, 8, 47–48, 51, 55, 85–87, 108, 119, 123, 126, 134, 139, 151, 153–54, 163, 203, 218, 225, 233, 296, 372; great and little, 124, 224, 234

unintended consequences, 12, 27, 140, 209, 294; of technology, 244

United Nations, 3, 66–67, 80, 81–82, 257, 260, 262, 269, 282, 294, 309, 311, 362, 366; Charter of, 128; Commission on Human Rights, 128, 185, 365; creation of, 17; Population Division, 62; Research Institute for Social Development (UNRISD), 262–63, 273, 312; structure and functioning of, 362

United States, 3, 15–16, 18–23, 25, 28, 30, 46–48, 61, 64, 66, 75–76, 81–83, 86, 88, 94–96, 104, 108, 135, 137, 140–42, 152–53, 161, 163, 166, 168–71, 175–84, 189, 195, 197, 204–05, 210, 215, 240, 249–52, 254–55, 261, 263–64, 266, 174, 280–81, 283, 293, 296–304, 308, 310, 315, 318–20, 324, 334–63, 342, 346–47, 352–53, 358, 363; capitalism in, 280–81, 283, 289–90;

as the "First New Nation", 19; representative democracy in, 126–27, 163; slavery in, 135, 252

urban growth, 31, 69, 75, 130, 219, 236–37, 239–40, 243–45, 248, 270, 307–08, 315–16, 348

urbanization, 10, 82, 88, 103, 175, 218–19, 224, 238–40, 244–45, 262

urban middle class, 74

urban neighborhood, 157

urban populations, 92, 226, 230, 237

urban society, 11, 224, 230, 236–37, 245

U.S. Agency for International Development (USAID), 80, 309–13, 317, 323, 329–30

U.S. Civil Rights Movement, 9, 20–21, 28, 59, 98, 140, 145, 151, 165, 177, 254, 273, 342, 353

U.S. Civil War, 251

U.S. Congress, 21, 114, 137, 141, 152, 170–71, 193, 198, 342

U.S. Constitution, 20, 88, 137, 254, 280

U.S. Holocaust Memorial Museum, 53

U.S. League for Industrial Democracy (LID), 169, 340

values, 1, 10, 13, 20, 28, 36, 45, 48, 50, 52, 55, 57, 73–75, 81, 84–86, 91, 94, 96, 108, 112, 121, 128, 133, 138, 144–46, 163, 175, 177, 186–87, 191, 196–97, 200, 205, 212, 229, 239, 247–48, 255–57, 259, 263, 270–71, 282, 289–90, 295, 326, 330, 333, 337, 358

Varna system, 231–32

violence, 23, 81, 108, 134, 143–45, 150, 160, 163–67, 178, 190, 225, 247–48, 255, 272, 311, 326–27

working class, 122–23, 178, 183, 256, 283, 297, 299–300, 303

world system, 4, 27, 46, 50, 87, 104, 187, 217, 219, 237, 239–40, 245, 248, 269–73, 276, 308, 316, 329, 350–52, 355, 364; theory, 43, 53, 223, 247, 261, 270, 316

Yugoslavia, 25, 172–73, 302, 352

About the Author

JAY WEINSTEIN is professor and former head of the Department of Sociology, Anthropology, and Criminology at Eastern Michigan University (EMU). He received his B.A. and Ph.D. degrees from the University of Illinois and his M.A. from Washington University, St. Louis. He has taught and conducted research in the fields of demography, social change, and urban sociology at EMU, Georgia Institute of Technology, and the University of Iowa, and was twice Fulbright Professor in India. He has served as president of the North Central Sociological Association, the Society for Applied Sociology, and the Michigan Sociological Association and as chair of the American Sociological Association Council on Sociological Practice. He is the recipient of the John F. Schnabel Award for lifetime Achievements in Teaching Sociology, two EMU Excellence in Teaching Awards, the Charles Horton Cooley Award for Outstanding Contributions to Sociology in Michigan, the Alex Boros Award for contributions to the field of applied sociology, and the Marvin Olsen Award for Service to the Profession.